THE
EXPANDING
WORLD

THE EXPANDING WORLD

WORLD

GENERAL EDITOR : ESMOND WRIGHT

HAMLYN
London · New York
Sydney · Toronto

List of contributors
Alan Smith
Gerald S. Graham
F. C. Jones
J. J. Tumelty
David Buisseret
R. R. Palmer
George Metcalf
Frank Thistlethwaite
G. R. Elton
Nathaniel Harris
Esmond Wright
Geoffrey Barraclough
R. Horsman
J. A. Hawgood

Published by
The Hamlyn Publishing Group Limited
London · New York · Sydney · Toronto
Astronaut House, Hounslow Road, Feltham,
Middlesex, England

Original text
© The Hamlyn Publishing Group Limited 1969
Revised and updated 1979
This edition
© The Hamlyn Publishing Group Limited 1979

ISBN 0 600 39433 6

Filmset in the United Kingdom by Tradespools Ltd.,
Frome, Somerset
Printed and bound in Spain
by Graficromo, S.A. – Córdoba

Part II
THE NEW EUROPE
Page 68

Introduction

Manière de brûler ceux qui ont été condamnez par l'INQUISITION.

Part I

THE WARS OF RELIGION

Introduction

Among the deplorable ages in the sad history of Europe, the near-century which followed upon the Religious Peace of Augsburg in 1555 stands high for horror and unpleasantness. War dominated it: war against the Turks, wars among the powers, civil wars in France, the Netherlands and England, war over principle, ideology and profit. And war got ever more frightful, ending in the destruction of Central Europe, as the brutalized armies of the Thirty Years' War swept across once prosperous realms. In the wake of war came plague, typhus and dysentery, killing far more than even the improved firearms of the day could kill—both weapons and disease being assisted by the incompetent medicine of the time. Assassination grew common, intolerance and inhumanity (encouraged by the fanaticisms of faiths that claimed a monopoly of the Christian message of redemption) ever more dominant. The men and women who ruled that world rarely evoke feelings of admiration; some of the best of them fell to the axe, the bullet or the knife. Small-minded intriguers and incompetent meddlers for the most part sat on the thrones of Spain, France, the Holy Roman Empire and Rome; the men of political vision were few. It is little wonder that not only the English came to look with admiration to the relatively prosperous reign of Elizabeth I, whose greatest achievement, in retrospect, turned out to be her survival on the throne for forty-five years, in spite of all that enemies, plotters and doctors could do.

The age was not unaware of its horrors, and some men set about the tasks of reconciliation and peace. There were those who wished to put an end to the quarrels among Christians: philosophers like Richard Hooker who thought to preserve the peaceful traditions of a moderate Christianity among the assertive arrogances of the sects, mystics like St John of the Cross who wished to bring peace to this world by turning its thoughts exclusively to the next, sceptics like Montaigne who pointed out that the causes for which men wished to kill and die did not exist. Hugo Grotius laid the foundations of international law and order among the ruins created by the collapse of common causes. Both James I of England and Henry IV of France devised and promoted idealistic schemes of universal peace on the basis of solemn treaties and settlements among the nations. But of practical effects there were none; indeed, each year seemed to make the situation worse.

What was wrong with Europe? In the first place, it does appear that at this time its political structure was exceptionally unstable, exceptionally devoid of balance and control. The prolonged decline of France in her civil wars left Spain supremely powerful, but there was always something unreal about the Spanish dominance. The redistribution of Charles V's empire had left that ancient trouble centre, the Rhineland and Burgundy, under the distant control of an alien power in Madrid: the result was the Dutch rebellion which effectively destroyed Philip II's chance of bringing peace by force. In the feeble hands of Maximilian II and Rudolph II, the eastern Habsburg power, in any case confronted with a continuous threat from the Ottoman Turks, allowed the splintering of Germany to become permanent. The jockeying for position among those princelings kept the pot on the boil, embroiled every European country from Sweden to Hungary and led directly to the disasters of the seventeenth century. Such chance as Spain might have had to impose herself on this ceaseless turmoil was lost by the miserable government of Philip III in the days of Lerma and in consequence of the restlessly aggressive revival of France. As everyone battled for himself, the devil came in the end to take the foremost, too.

The conflicts of interests were to some extent polarized and altogether intensified by the religious split. It is customary today to deny that this was an age when religion determined policy; and it is perfectly true that most princes were ready, under pressure, to adapt their faith to their interest. The loyalties of religion grew ever less urgent, till in the end a cardinal of the Church of Rome, in alliance with the Swedish and German defenders of Protestantism, resolved the situation by demolishing the champions of the Counter-Reformation. Nevertheless, the battle between the Catholics and Protestants was real, and the wars would have been both less continuous and less violent if the combatants had not been led by men whose banners carried the conflicting messages of a conquering God. In particular, the seemingly remorseless and irresistible reconquest of so much territory by the Papacy drove the Protestants to put their fate in the hands of extremists. The Calvinists and the Catholic Church after the Council of Trent (1545–63) did not command everyone's allegiance; much happened that conflicted with the claims of the militant faiths; but militancy and the bitter will to fight nonetheless grew out of those faiths.

Besides, the Europe engaged in these murderous activities suffered the strains and uncertainties which go with economic crisis and social transformation. Perhaps it would be best to see the age as one in which a new (or partly new) aristocracy, borne up by landed possession and dependent on the king's favour, built up its hold on society and politics. It is true that bourgeois societies throwing off aristocratic dependence did come into being in the Netherlands and Switzerland and that manifestations of the old anti-monarchial policies of the European nobility continued to occur and in the east continued to be effective. But what happened in the main was not so much a social upheaval or the replacement of one class by another, as rather the transformation of a ruling class pulling in fresh elements, absorbing the cultural achievements of the Renaissance, and accommodating itself to the service of princes with absolute power.

The great inflation and population increase of the sixteenth century swelled the coffers of the landowners upon whom in the end the mass production and distribution of food depended; the new technology of war gave overwhelming power to centralized control; resistance was generally less possible, and the frequent outbursts of social discontent were ever less able to win success. It was an age in which the possessors tightened their hold till fears of the people and limitations on the exercise of power that had existed time out of mind could at long last be safely ignored. Even in England and the Netherlands, the ruling classes maintained their command in the midst of rebellions which they prevented from expanding into social revolution.

Of course, this was also the age of Shakespeare, Montaigne and Cervantes; of Veronese, Tintoretto, Velasquez and Rubens; of Kepler and Galileo. There were many who faced their dreadful time with steadfast sense and good humour. Yet, when all is done, one looks upon that century and sees the three horrible Philips who ruled and ruined Spain; the silly Stuarts who drove an obedient realm into civil war; the cynical Henry IV and the savage Richelieu, both men of vast ability who sought power for power's sake and little else; the asinine Rudolph II, in his castle at Prague, neglecting the problems of empire for the fascinations of alchemy. One sees Drake, confusing enterprise with piracy, and Wallenstein, squeezing great wealth from war and then committing his fortunes to the planets. And on all sides there stand embattled ranks convinced that their faith entitles—nay, compels—them to kill.

Chapter 1

France during the Sixteenth Century

The reigns of Francis I and of Henry II saw a continuation of the trend towards absolute monarchy, which had already been strong in the time of Louis XI (1461–83). Slowly a central administration was emerging, which imposed its laws and taxes on an increasingly wide area of the country and eroded the power of the great territorial lords. However, this process was brutally interrupted in 1559, when the death of Henry II plunged France into a period of civil war which lasted until 1598.

Louis XII died on New Year's Day 1515, shortly after his first wife Anne. He was remembered as a good king, who in spite of the expenses of the Italian wars had levied only moderate taxes on his people; for many he recalled the memory of Louis XI, the most economical and even parsimonious of princes. His personal appearance was not impressive, for he was thin and bony with a slight stoop, and enjoyed poor health.

What a contrast with his brilliant cousin and successor, Francis I! Here was a king who looked like one: tall, strong and full of martial ardour. In his early years he seemed to deserve the title of 'the Magnificent' which had been awarded to certain Italian princes, and it is precisely one of his claims to fame that he looked to Italy for those architects, painters, musicians and men of letters who revitalized French culture at this period.

In 1514 he married Claude of France, daughter of Louis XII and Anne of Britanny; they had seven children before her death in 1524 at the age of twenty-five. The reign started well, with the remarkable victory over the forces of the Holy Roman Empire at Marignano (1515), but as the years went by the inevitable military reverses put more and more strain both on the king and on his country. Not that the French under Francis I were able to show many signs of discontent, for all that time they were known as the most repressed people of western Europe, taxed as the saying went 'like beasts'.

Perhaps Louis XII was not far wrong when he asserted, nodding his head at the future Francis I, that 'this fine fellow will spoil everything'. Like Henry VIII of England, this young, vigorous, attractive king ended his reign in difficulties, his

Above, the Massacre of St Bartholomew, on 24 August 1572, in which the Catholics murdered several thousand Huguenots in Paris and the provinces; the event led to the outbreak of the fourth civil war.

Left, Francis I of France (reigned 1515–47); he was a typical Renaissance prince, eager for glory in war and not above allying himself with the Turks against the Holy Roman emperor to win it. Galleria degli Uffizi, Florence.

On page 8, a French engraving of the burning of heretics by the Inquisition. The Roman Inquisition was less notorious than the Spanish for its pursuit of heresy, but the activities of the Jesuits in opposing Protestantism made it feared to a similar extent

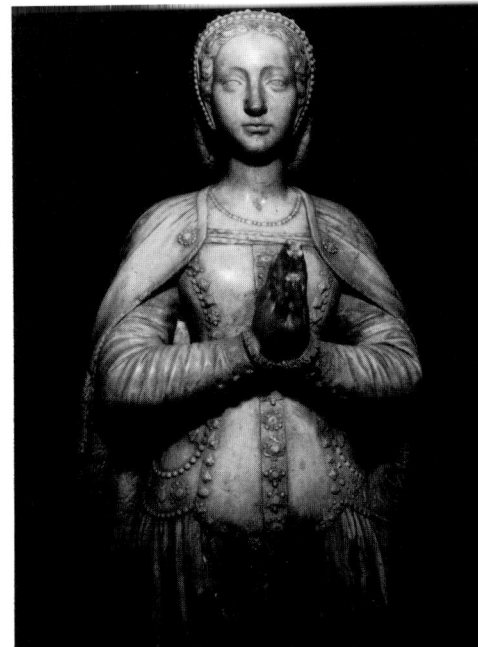

Left, Claude of France, the wife of Francis I and the daughter of Louis XIII, who was the cousin of Francis. Cathedral of Saint-Denis.

policy of grandeur having been based on an inadequate economic and administrative basis. Francis and Henry, so similar in their persons and in their policies, both died in 1547.

Francis I was succeeded by his son Henry II, a muscular Christian if ever there was one. Tall and powerfully built, Henry II excelled at all violent sports and exercises. He was a great huntsman and powerful skater. He loved to have military men about him and at the beginning of his reign had even permitted at his court a duel to the death between two young nobles. However, if some were attracted by his martial qualities, others found him morose and unapproachable; it is certain that he did not share the cultural interests of his father, whom he had very much disliked.

The manner of Henry II's death was curiously appropriate.

In June 1559 there was to be a pair of royal weddings at Paris. Since the Treaty of Cateau-Cambrésis had been signed by the French, Spanish and English in April of that year bringing the Italian wars to a close, relations between Spain and France had been more cordial, and representatives of the King of Spain were to attend the celebrations. What better way to celebrate, than by a great tournament?

Of course the king was among the leading contestants. On 30 June he successfully broke two lances, one on the Duke of Savoy and the other on the Duke of Guise. At the third tilt, with a strong young man called Montgomery, the king was nearly unhorsed. Stubborn as usual, he insisted on tilting again, in spite of Montgomery's protests and the fact that horses and riders were getting tired. During this fourth tilt the king received injuries to his eye from which he died ten days later.

Francis I had a zestful taste not only for society life, with its balls and masquerades, but also for the life of a man of culture; he liked to think of himself, in the Italian style, as the great patron of arts and letters. His mother was a witty and cultured woman, and so was his sister Marguerite d'Angoulême. So all three came to reign over the 'court', which came to be regarded in a new, Italian light, as the centre for all social and cultural life within the realm.

Court life was organized around the great officers: the chamberlain, the four gentlemen of the bedchamber, the royal chaplain, the royal confessor, the master of the stables and so forth. Women had a special place at court, where elegant dress and refined conduct was essential. Eventually each of the queens and each of the great princes came to have his own court, less elaborately organized than that of the king but forming all the same in its own area the magnet of all social and cultural aspirations.

It was in this brilliant setting that the ambitions of the great nobles were worked out. During the reign of Henry II the most powerful magnate was the constable Anne de Montmorency. He was a man after the king's heart, strong, intelligent and sometimes brutal. After him came Francis, Duke of Guise, member of that Lorraine family which had been making such an extraordinary name for itself in the France of Francis I. The Duke of Guise was a remarkable soldier whose energy matched his intelligence; probably his most famous feat of arms was the recapture of Calais from the English in 1558. Within his house there were plenty of other able men, of whom the most outstanding was his brother Charles, the Cardinal of Lorraine.

In France, and for that matter in the other countries of Europe at this time, the system of patronage was widespread. Nobles, while acknowledging a general loyalty to the king, felt themselves more directly the supporters of one or another of these great noble houses. The existence of this network of loyalties meant that apparently trivial quarrels over affairs of honour could have very serious results, if the persons involved were of high rank, for there was always the danger that their respective supporters would band together, and that civil war would follow.

The administration

The very idea of 'administration' was foreign to sixteenth-century France, in which the king's function was considered to be the dispensation of *justice* and the ensuring of *police*, meaning roughly the maintenance of civil order. However, to carry on these activities the kings needed to raise money, and so *finance* gradually joined *justice* and *police* as the three functions came to form the task of the emergent 'administration'.

The heart of the government was the king's small private council, which eventually became known as the council of state (*conseil d' État*). Theoretically, the princes of the blood, peers and great officers—constable, marshal, admiral and chancellor—could all attend meetings of this council. But in practice the kings often called only half a dozen or so of those eligible.

The chancellor was always included, since he was in fact the head of what was eventually to become the civil service. Dispatches were actually written and sent off by the four secretaries of state. These had at first been minor clerks in the royal service, each responsible for one of the four quarters of the world as seen from Paris. But about the middle of the sixteenth century they changed their geographical responsibility for a more purely functional one, each then being responsible for a special department like the army, foreign affairs, the Protestants and so on. In spite of their eclipse in 1588, the sixteenth century saw a remarkable development in the powers of the secretaries of state.

As the king's affairs grew more complex, so he tended to delegate particular functions to special councils. There thus emerged, for instance, the *conseil des parties* (a court of law) and the *conseil des finances*. The *parlement* itself, with its main body in Paris and its offshoots in the greater provinces, was in its origins a section of the royal council specializing in judicial affairs. By the sixteenth century, however, the *parlement* had become totally independent. It was not only the chief court but also enjoyed the right to record all royal decrees; without its agreement no such legislation was valid.

By 1500 there were seven provincial *parlements*, at Toulouse, Grenoble, Bordeaux, Dijon, Rouen, Aix and Rennes. Like the *parlement de Paris*, these courts were responsible for recording and so approving royal decrees. They were bodies of jurists in more or less constant session, in contrast the provincial estates, which represented roughly the same territories and, composed of the three orders, met only once a year and then only for about a fortnight. Whereas the provincial *parlements* confined themselves to legal affairs, the provincial estates claimed to control a wide variety of royal activities within their province, including the raising of taxes. In fact kings were often able to lessen their power, which was vulnerable because of the long intervals between their meetings.

The direct representatives of royal power in the provinces were the twelve or so governors, each of whom was in command of one of the great border provinces. The governors were helped by the ubiquitous *baillis* and *sénéchaux*, survivors of an earlier period of royal growth. Needless to say, the governors often quarrelled with the provincial estates, which in turn often quarrelled with the provincial *parlements*, which in turn were often at loggerheads not only with the governors and estates but also with the great towns.

After about the middle of the sixteenth century the kings made increasing use of itinerant masters of requests (*maîtres des requêtes*, legal officers usually drawn from the Paris *parlement*), who received commissions to go into the provinces in order to do the king's work. Sometimes this involved reporting back on the condition of the province; sometimes it meant putting a decree into effect; sometimes it involved directing the finances of an army or of a town, and so on. During the sixteenth century these commissions were normally for specific purposes and for short periods of time. However, as the years went by the tendency was for the *maîtres des requêtes* to receive broader powers for longer periods, and eventually they emerged as those *intendants* who were so important in the administration of France during the seventeenth and eighteenth centuries.

The art of war

When a master of requests was attached to an army, it was normally directly under the commander, who was nearly always a great territorial lord and often a provincial governor. At the beginning of the century armies still relied to some extent on each lord calling up his serfs, and in fact right up to the French Revolution in 1789 troops continued to be enrolled primarily by local lords, appealing to local loyalties. But as time went on, paid as they were by the royal treasury, these troops came increasingly to attach their allegiance to the Crown rather than to their immediate chief or 'colonel', as he was often called.

This tendency, inevitable with the development of the royal power, was accentuated by the technical developments in the art of war. Improvements in gunnery meant that more and more skilled men were required for the artillery. Although many of the great artillery-chiefs were in fact nobles of ancient lineage, it was not necessary to be a noble in order to excel in the exploitation of his new arm.

Better guns had to be countered by a whole new system of fortifications. This also

Opposite left, Anne, Duke of Montmorency (c. 1493–1567); he was not popular with Francis I but had greater influence under Henry II, during whose reign he opposed the Guise faction. He later joined them in the wars of religion. Musée du Louvre, Paris.

Opposite right, Francis, the second Duke of Guise (1519–63), a notable soldier who dominated the court of Francis II and led the Catholic party after the accession of Charles IX in 1560.

provided opportunities for lowborn men and foreigners, who might have mastered the mathematical techniques required by this new art. In France the cavalry was always much more effective than the infantry. This resulted in the recruitment of hired foreign foot-soldiers (mercenaries) in time of war. Many of them came from Switzerland, though there were also regiments of Germans. The art of fighting on foot had been revolutionized in the late fifteenth century by the Swiss, who taught the other peoples of Europe how to resist a cavalry charge by forming a disciplined square of pikemen. This of course required uniform equipment and good drill, neither easy to obtain until armies ceased to be mixed collections of local levies. Finally, improvements in small-arms meant that armies required increased numbers of foot-soldiers armed with costly arquebusses (an early type of portable gun, supported by a forked rest).

This so-called 'military revolution' on land was not accompanied by any profound changes in naval warfare. There were in principle three provincial admirals in France, those of Brittany, of Guyenne and of Provence. But in practice the only one who counted was the one in Provence, the *amiral de la mer du Levant*. He commanded the Mediterranean galley-fleet, which during the reigns of Francis I and Henry II sometimes counted as many as fifty large vessels. On the Atlantic, however, the 'round boats' (*vaisseaux ronds*, as compared with galleys) of the Crown were very few in number. By 1550 the *amiral de Bretagne* had none left under his command.

The fiscal structure

The long phases of military activity in the first half of the sixteenth century imposed a heavy burden on the royal purse. The time was long past when the king could 'live of his own', by staying with and living off his richer subjects and using merely the produce of his kingdom. Steadily taxes of all kinds had come to supplement this income from the land which by the mid-sixteenth century formed a very small proportion of the total revenue. By then the chief direct tax was the *taille,* supplemented by various indirect taxes such as the *aides* and the *gabelles* (the latter on salt).

To gather these taxes the kings had developed an increasingly complex fiscal structure, consisting of a great number of specialized *trésories*. In 1523 Francis I created the office of *trésorier de l'Épargne* (roughly speaking, chancellor of the exchequer), thereby establishing one official in whose hands were concentrated all receipts and payments. This was a major step towards a more efficient fiscal structure, and was followed in 1532 by another significant regulation, that in future the *trésorier de l'Épargne* would have permanent quarters at the Louvre.

Money raised by direct and indirect taxation was not, however, sufficient for the Crown's requirements. Hence the increase in sales of office, a practice which had been established in the fifteenth century and which would reach its peak in the time of Richelieu. In some ways his venality, which tended to make offices hereditary, strengthened the Crown by establishing a large class interested in the survival of the monarchy. But in other ways it weakened royal power, by installing a mass of immovable officials opposed to any kind of change or reform, by diverting capital from constructive enterprises and by increasing the number of those exempt from direct taxes.

Another way in which the Crown raised money was by loans from bankers. The merchant houses of Lyons made very large advances to Francis I and Henry II, and the latter repaid them in 1557 by declaring his bankruptcy. The failure of this *grand parti* of Lyons had a very harmful effect not only on the town itself but also on the many French commercial centres which enjoyed close relations with the great city.

The towns and the countryside

Urban life was well developed in sixteenth-century France. Towns were thickest in the south, in those regions which had already been intensively settled in the days of the Romans. But there were also great towns all over the northern regions and on the Atlantic seaboard. With the slow decay of the Mediterranean area, the balance of commercial power slowly shifted during the sixteenth century away from the historic centres in the south, towards those regions of the north and west which would come into their own in the later seventeenth century.

Most of the towns of France had a mayor and corporation (*prévôt des marchands* and *échevins*), who did their best to protect local interests. Thus in a great city like Toulouse there would be the competing authority not only of the governor, the *parlement* and the estates, as we have already described, but also of the municipality. The royal agents were therefore faced with very complex problems in their attempts to enforce the king's will, and dissident groups could often hold their own by playing one set of interests off against another.

In the end, the whole elaborate structure of the state rested on the backs of the peasants. France, then as now, was a country of marvellous fertility, with a wide variety of regions each producing some speciality or other. However, the peasants of the sixteenth century lived all the time on the edge of famine. Too often they confined themselves to one corn crop, grown according to those inflexible rules inherited from remotest times. Consequently, in time of drought or of flood the crop might fail altogether, and whole regions would be prey to famine and then to disease. Sometimes scarcity in one region might be relieved by shipments from another, but communications were slow and precarious, and provincial sentiment remained so strong that the people who lived in Burgundy, for instance, were largely indifferent to the plight of the people of Provence.

The church

The only sentiment of unity felt by most of the inhabitants of France was their attachment to the church. However, this loyalty was beginning to be tested. True, there was little trace of earlier heresies, and the healing of the Great Schism (1378–1449) had removed the migrant pope from Avignon. Corruption was extensive among the higher clergy, and among the lower there was widespread ignorance. After the agreement of 1516, the pope in effect permitted Francis I to nominate whom he wished to all the French bishoprics, suppressing the former system of election. This was to open the door to appalling abuses, as the king did not fail to elect noblemen who were not only ignorant of church affairs but were also entirely uninterested in the areas they ruled over. Thus it was that by the 1540s whole regions of France were lacking any kind of effective ecclesiastical structure.

Alongside discontent with the abuses of the clergy went increasing doubts about the soundness of the doctrines of the church. As in the other countries of northern Europe, there were in early sixteenth-century France many learned ecclesiastics who had been captivated by the learning and literature of the Italian renaissance and who in applying what they had learned to the old doctrines found them inaccurate or defective. One of the most outstanding of these critics was Lefèvre d'Étaples. Like many of his contemporaries, he had made the voyage to Italy and had there discovered a new interpretation of the Scriptures, particularly of the Epistles of St Paul. From these he developed a Lutheran-like theory of justification by faith; he had many friends and colleagues who at this period sympathized with this approach.

Thus once Lutheranism had taken root in Germany in the 1520s, its disciples evoked a ready response in France. From the start the *parlement* of Paris and the faculty of theology at the Sorbonne were against Lutherans, of whom the first was burnt in 1523. But the king still held aloof. He was thought to favour some heretical notions and was no doubt influenced by his sister Marguerite d'Angoulême, who openly encouraged the dissidents.

All that changed in 1534, the year in which Francis I concluded an alliance with the pope against Charles V, ruler of the Holy Roman Empire, and the year in which with remarkable rashness the Protestants circulated broadsheets fiercely attacking

Opposite, Henry II of France (reigned 1547–59), the muscular king whose main contribution to the history of his country was to marry Catherine de' Medici. However, she did not win any great importance until the reigns of his sons. Musée du Louvre, Paris.

15

the institution of the Eucharist. One of these broadsheets was nailed to the very door of the king's chamber at Amboise. The king was furious, and encouraged a great wave of persecution and execution by fire. This policy of violent repression was continued and even stepped up after the accession of Henry II in 1547.

Still the Protestant movement grew. At first its adherents had been largely small men in the towns: weavers, dyers, printers and so on. But in the 1550s the new religion began to win converts among the upper classes. Many members of the ancient nobility, particularly in the south and south-west, joined the new churches, and so did increasing numbers of merchants, lesser magistrates and even members of the *parlements*.

Henry II reacted to this development with savage desperation, stepping up the rate of prosecutions and burnings. However, by the late 1550s the Protestants in France were beginning to receive help from the Swiss town of Geneva, rallying point of Protestantism, and in spite of royal attacks the Genevan pastors succeeded in establishing churches in town after town. In the countryside, too, Protestantism was spreading, for once a noble was converted to the new faith his tenants automatically followed his lead. This was all the easier because the old church scarcely existed as an administrative structure in many regions of rural France.

Until the spring of 1559, Henry II had not been able to bring his full attention to bear on the Protestants, because he was distracted by the war with Spain. After the peace treaty of Cateau-Cambrésis in April 1559, however, he was able to turn his mind to internal affairs and was in fact planning a bloody offensive against the Protestants for the following August. In July, however, he ran that fatal fourth tilt and was succeeded by Francis II.

The new king was a sickly youth of fifteen, and for a short while after his accession the Protestants enjoyed a breathing-space. Soon, however, the two Guises, the Duke Francis and the Cardinal Charles, succeeded in taking over the government, as the uncles of the king's wife Mary Stuart (who was also queen of Scotland). The dead king's widow, Catherine de Medici, was for the time being stunned by grief and shock. So a new wave of persecution was mounted by the Guises late in 1559, and the victims included Anne Du Bourg, counsellor the *parlement* of Paris.

The reign of Francis II (July 1559–December 1560) witnessed the first armed Protestant insurrection, when a Huguenot (the name given to the Calvinist Protestants of France) gentleman of Périgord called La Renaudie tried to capture the royal court at Amboise. His plan was a hopeless failure, for the Guises got wind of it and cut the conspirators down as they began assembling in the royal woods.

The reign was important in another way as well; it seems to have been at this time that the infant churches concluded a kind of alliance with the dissident nobility. The nobles had been unwilling to enter conspiracies in the days of Henry II, but now, under the 'tyranny' of the Guises, they saw no reason to hold back. They needed the money and moral support which the churches could provide, and the churches needed the armed protection which the nobility could afford them. So all over France in the summer of 1560 the two elements came together, and what had been a peaceful and primarily religious movement developed into a dynamic and politically aggressive force.

Catherine de' Medici

When Francis II died in December 1560, things seemed ripe for an armed confrontation between the old church and its supporters and this powerful new combination. That war did not break out at once was probably because of the skill of the queen-mother, Catherine de' Medici. The new king, Charles IX, was only nine, and so there had to be a regency. The Guises were shouldered out of the way, and the nearest prince of royal blood, Antoine of Navarre, was a weak fellow easily cowed by Catherine de Medici. In collaboration with her chancellor Michel de l'Hôpital, she began to pursue a policy of conciliation.

This meant in effect provisional toleration. L'Hôpital was a man of his century in that he could not envisage the possibility of more than one religion existing in the same realm. As he said, 'it is foolishness to expect peace and love between persons of different religions, for do we not see today that a Frenchman and an Englishman of the same religion have more in common than two citizens of the same town, and subject to the same lord, but of different religion?' For him the old tag 'one faith, one law, one king' was eminently sound. In fact, L'Hôpital differed from the Guises only on the way in which this unity was to be secured. For him the only appropriate and effective arms were brotherly love and good example, 'laying aside those diabolical words . . . Lutheran, Huguenot and Papist, and keeping only the word "Christian" '.

In practice this attitude resulted in a series of edicts or proclamations making various minor concessions to the new church. At court Catherine de' Medici was sympathetic towards Protestants and was even suspected—entirely without justification—of theological leanings in that direction. Consequently during 1561 there was a formidable growth of Protestantism, that emphasized that very gulf in French society which the policy of conciliation was intended to bridge. In town after town, particularly in the south, the Protestants were openly taking over churches and driving out the Catholics. It seemed only a question of time before general violence broke out.

In this desperate situation Catherine de' Medici now hit on the ingenious idea of calling together the representatives of the old and the new churches, so that they could debate their differences and, she hoped, come to an agreement. So the Catholic prelates were called to Poissy for August 1561, and to Poissy also came among the Protestant delegates Theodore Beza himself, second man of the Genevan reformation after Calvin, and rector of the Genevan Academy.

The so-called 'colloquy of Poissy' opened on 9 September 1561 in the refectory of the Dominican nuns. The Protestant representatives stood in a kind of 'dock', facing the royal family, with the 'bishops and doctors' of the ancient church grouped to the left and right of them. In Beza's opening speech there was an unfortunate incident when, forgetting the susceptibilities of his hearers, he remarked that since the Lord was in Heaven and the Eucharist celebrated on earth, therefore the body of Our Lord might itself be considered as far removed from the bread and wine as Heaven is from earth. However, the theological problems were not insoluble. Even the problem of the Eucharist, for instance, was referred to a mixed subcommittee which in fact produced a definition of the nature of consecration satisfactory to both parties. What was insoluble were the problems of the personal antagonisms aroused and of the emotional commitments already made. In the end the colloquy came to an end without having achieved anything, but it had been a brave try.

Its immediate political effect was unfortunate, for the sight of the despised heretics openly exchanging arguments with the leaders of the ancient church greatly encouraged the Protestant cause. By the autumn of 1561 the Huguenots were too strong to be content with their former passive role, and they began increasingly to look for leaders like Louis de Bourbon, Prince of Condé, to deliver them by force of arms. Condé was not averse to this role. He had been the 'silent captain' of the conspiracy of Amboise and throughout 1561 was sending emissaries to the German

Protestant princes and to Elizabeth of England, asking for their help in the coming struggle.

By the beginning of 1561, then, the Protestants were largely armed and ready. It became only a question of time before some incident involved them in warfare with the numerically superior Catholics. That incident occurred at Vassy, in Lorraine, on 1 March 1562. Returning to Paris from Joinville, the Duke of Guise halted for a time at Vassy. Contrary to the law, the Protestants were holding a service there, and in spite of the duke's efforts his followers were persuaded to assault the terrified congregation. When the bloodshed stopped there were twenty-three Protestant dead and more than a hundred wounded. The 'religious' wars had begun.

The Protestant leader, the Prince of Condé was still in Paris, and Guise soon arrived there. For a time it looked as though the capital might fall prey to furious street-fighting, but on 23 March Condé left Paris and fell back on Orléans. No doubt he foresaw that if it came to battles in the streets his Protestant lords, splendid cavalrymen, would be taken at a disadvantage by the Catholic masses. But his decision to leave the capital was strategically unsound, since it meant that during the years to come the Catholic side could always fall back on the human and financial resources of by far the greatest city in France.

The Catholics, headed by Guise and Montmorency, showed a truer sense of strategy when they marched on Fontainebleau and 'invited' Catherine de' Medici and the young Charles IX to join them. Catherine had a few months earlier been sounding the Protestants out concerning the possibility of their sending her forces; now she had no choice but to join the Guises and Montmorency, and henceforward the Catholic cause was the royal cause. By securing both the capital city and the person of the sovereign, the Catholic leaders had at the start of the hostilities placed themselves in a very advantageous position.

Late in 1562 the first battle of the wars took place, when the rival armies met at Dreux. The conflict ended in a marginal victory for the Catholics, but if they captured Condé the Protestants took Montmorency. With these leaders temporarily out of the way, the struggle was between Guise and Condé's successor Coligny. Eager to press home his advantage, Guise hurried down to Orléans and besieged the city. For a while it looked as if he might win a decisive victory. Then, however, he was assassinated, and the balance swung aback to the Protestants.

Catherine de' Medici took advantage of the death of Guise to proclaim the edict of Amboise (March 1563); freedom of worship was accorded to most nobles within their territories, but denied to the common people except in certain limited cases. When Calvin heard of the terms of the edict he remarked in disgust that the imprisoned Condé had 'betrayed God by his vanity' and his eagerness to be free. Certainly Condé's agreement to this edict did nothing to bind together the noble and popular wings of the Huguenot party.

With the country temporarily at peace, Catherine resolved to go on a great progress, in which she could both show his realm to the young king and show the young king to his subjects. Setting out from Fontainebleau in March 1564, her cortège covered a great circle through southern France, passing through Dijons, Lyons, Marseilles, Montpellier and Toulouse to arrive at Bayonne in May 1565. There she met the representatives of the King of Spain in the famous 'Bayonne interview', at which she and Alva were long supposed to have plotted the massacre of Saint Bartholomew, which took place in 1572. In fact it is certain that they reached no such agreement, but what mattered was what the Protestants thought had been agreed, since this increased their mistrust of the Crown.

In September 1567 their suspicions reached such a pitch that they decided to seize the queen mother and the young king, rather as the Catholic leaders had done in May 1562. With the court at Meaux, about thirty miles east of Paris, Huguenots began to converge on it from all quarters. Catherine

did not hesitate; calling up an escort of 6,000 Swiss pikemen, she made for the safety of Paris. A party of 600 cavalry led by Condé soon caught her up, but on their approach the Swiss surrounding the royal party took off their knapsacks, kissed the ground and lowered their redoubtable pikes. Condé was unwilling to try conclusions with this formidable troop, and so the royal party reached Paris in safety, the Protestant horsemen milling round them up to the very gates of the city.

There ensued a brief siege of the capital by Condé, broken by the battle at Saint-Denis (December 1567) in which Montmorency was killed. Thereafter both sides were so exhausted that they willingly agreed to the Treaty of Longjumeau (February 1568), which brought the so-called 'second war' to a close.

In fact, by 1568 it no longer makes much sense to speak of separate 'wars', since much of France was in a more or less constant state of civil war. It was at this time that the Catholics, realizing their danger, began all over the country to form local leagues, thus foreshadowing the 'Holy League' of 1576. Until 1568 the numerically superior Catholic mass had been largely disorganized; after that year they became increasingly effective as a political and military force.

This Catholic mobilization led directly to a Protestant recoil, when late in 1568 Condé and Coligny went with their families to establish themselves at La Rochelle. This proved to be a very strong base, but it was after all on the very edge of French territory, and its adoption as the Protestant centre was virtually an admission that the high hopes of 1561 were not to be fulfilled.

However, if after the late 1560s it was clear that the Protestants could no longer hope to take over the realm, the campaigns of 1569–70 made it equally plain that the Catholics could not hope to wipe out their enemies by military means. At first there seemed to be a good chance of this happening, when the king's younger brother Henri of Anjou, at the head of royal forces in the southwest, defeated the Protestants at Jarnac (March 1569). Condé was killed there, and the royal army seemed poised for an assault on La Rochelle.

But then Coligny assumed command of the Huguenot forces and with the help of a German contingent pressed the royal armies back up north. Things seemed to be going well for the Protestant cause, when in October 1569 their combined army was routed at Moncontour following a tactical blunder. Again the Catholic forces pushed down into the Protestant region, but again they were forced to a halt before even reaching La Rochelle. Clearly, this see-saw type of campaign was not giving a decisive advantage to either side; both were running short of men and of money, and so in August 1570 they concluded the Peace of

Above, the Peace of Orléans, shown here, and the Edict of Amboise brought the first civil war of 1562–63 to an end by granting the nobility freedom of worship within their territories; but Protestant fears of the government's intentions were barely allayed by these measures.

Opposite left, Catherine de' Medici (1519–89), the wife of Henry II of France and the real power behind the throne during the reigns of his sons Charles IX and Henry III. Her primary concern was to preserve the power of the monarchy, and in the main she tried to prevent outright hostility with the Huguenots. Musée Condé, Chantilly.

Opposite top right, the murder of a number of Protestants at Cahors in central France in November 1561; tensions between the two factions were most strongly felt in the south, and at court.

Opposite bottom right, the massacre of the Huguenots at Tours in July 1562, shortly after the first bloodshed of the wars of religion.

Marguerite de Valoy
Royne de Nauarr

Saint-Germain. This made considerable concessions to the Protestants, who were accorded freedom of worship throughout the whole realm except in specified areas and who received four cautionary towns (*villes de sûreté*). Catherine was in effect returning to that policy of moderation which she had tried to follow up to the time of the Meaux incident in September 1567.

As part of the conciliatory line, she now decided to marry her daughter Marguerite de Valois to Henri de Bourbon, son of the fiercely Protestant Jeanne d'Albret. When Jeanne and her young son came to the court at Bois in September 1571, they were accompanied by Coligny, and the noble, austere Protestant warrior soon began to exercise a kind of fascination over the young king. At this time the rebellion against Spanish rule in the Low Countries was five years old, and Coligny tried to show the young king how this would be the occasion for winning back the northeastern provinces of Artois and Flanders, in collaboration with the rebels. From the Protestant gentlemen of the south could be recruited an army of nearly 8,000 horse and 30,000 foot; why, added Coligny, not take advantage of this opportunity to strike a conclusive blow at Spain and so reverse that clause of the Treaty of Cateau-Cambrésis which had recognized Spanish possession of the northeastern provinces?

Needless to say, the Guises and their supporters did not find talk of this kind at all to their liking. Were the victors of Jarnac and Moncontour to serve in the campaign, then, under the command of the leader of the vanquished Protestants and against fellow-Catholics? Coligny's plans were hotly opposed in the royal council and in the countless discussions among the nobility, many of whom had assembled in Paris for the wedding of Henri and Marguerite. Coligny was a rather dour, insensitive man, and it was now that he is said to have made his famous remark to the queen mother:

Madame, the king does not wish to enter into this war. May God spare him, then, from another, which no doubt it will be harder for him to avoid.

The massacre of St Bartholomew

Catherine began to see where her policy of reconciliation was leading. She found that by being all things to all men she had led Coligny on to a situation in which he was almost bound to clash with the Catholics. If she had now come out strongly against the planned campaign, perhaps catastrophe might have been avoided. As it was, set in her ways of temporization and duplicity, she failed to intervene and simply allowed events to take their course.

But events forced her into the corner ever more tightly. It was almost intolerable for the Guises that Coligny, who had approved the assassination of Duke Francis in 1562, should not ten years later be welcome at court. It was also becoming intolerable for Catherine that he should exercise such an influence over her son. Perhaps it is not too strong to say that she feared the alienation of the young king's affections. So she resolved to act. At her encouragement the Guises hired an assassin, who on 22 August 1572 fired at Coligny as he was going to the Louvre.

If Coligny had been killed outright, there is no knowing what would have happened next. The Protestants would probably have run amok, but there might not have been a cold-blooded massacre. As it was, Coligny was only wounded and was taken back to

his house. The aspiring assassin escaped, but it became known that he had fired from a house belonging to the Guises. So the Protestants became increasingly excited: some came to defend Coligny from further attacks, and others went to shout threats below the windows of the Guises' town-house.

Catherine now found herself in a terrible position, but putting a bold face on things she came with the young king to visit Coligny and to assure him that the assassin would be tracked down. Coligny had been wounded on a Friday morning. Tension grew in Paris throughout that night and on the following day. On the Saturday evening Catherine held a conference at the Louvre to decide what should be done to avert the impending clash between the angry Protestants and the townsfolk with their Catholic allies. Into this council there came a messenger, to say that the Huguenots had decided to mount an attack on the Louvre the next day.

Whether this news was true or false, it terrified the queen, who had not forgotten her narrow escape at Meaux in 1567. The young Duke of Anjou and others suggested that it would be as well to strike before the Huguenots. Catherine eventually accepted this idea and succeeded in persuading Charles IX to agree to it. The mayor of Paris was called and instructed to close the town-gates and to arm the militia. The Guises and other Catholic nobles came and received their instructions.

Early on the morning of Sunday 24 August 1572 the first bell sounded; it was the signal for the massacre. The major Protestant nobles had each been assigned to a group of killers. The Guises themselves looked after Coligny; he was killed as he lay in bed and his body was thrown out of the window. All over the city road-blocks were set up, and passers-by were stopped. Those who could not establish their Catholicism were butchered. The walls were strong and well-guarded, so that few escaped. Once the mania for killing and looting had set in, it was impossible to restrain the mob. Many humble Protestants perished with the lords, and some old scores which had nothing to do with religion were no doubt settled. By the time order could be restored, at day-light on the Tuesday, at least 2,000 people had perished and many houses had been looted.

Clearly, the massacre at Paris had not been premeditated; if it had been, this was a singularly clumsy way to go about it. What made people think in terms of large-scale conspiracy was the fact that in many other French cities, once the news from Paris reached them, similar blood-baths followed. This was especially true of towns like Lyons and Orléans, where Protestantism had been strong.

But these subsequent outbursts of violence were not in fact the outcome of a diabolical plan; they merely reflected the long-standing ambition of the provincial mobs to set on the heretics. What is truly notable about them is that here and there valiant and resolute governors were able to restrain the mob.

The news of the massacre was greeted differently in different places. The pope and Philip II of Spain were both delighted and felt that Charles IX had come to his senses. At Vienna, however, the imperial court was shocked, as were the rulers of Protestant regions. Catherine was on the whole pleased with her work, and to the mass of French Catholics the massacre did not seem altogether unjustifiable, in order to preserve the monarchy. Certainly Coligny had behaved with astonishing rashness in not only coming to his enemies' stronghold but then trying to force them to adopt impossible policies.

It was probably to the young king that the effect was most lamentable. He had only consented to the massacre on the persuasions of his mother, but that did not prevent popular opinion from holding him responsible for it. His character, which had always been severe, now became cruel, and during the two years of life which remained to him he often seemed half-mad, crazed in his dreams by visions of bloody corpses.

The surviving Huguenots were for a short time stunned by the catastrophe which had befallen their party. With the heads of the nobility out of the way, the movement depended at this crucial juncture on the town-congregations of the south. These quickly recovered from their fright, and the leading towns of Montpellier, Nimes, La Rochelle and Sancerre strengthened their fortifications.

La Rochelle went so far as to refuse to admit its royal governor. It was consequently besieged in November 1572. The royal army was led by the king's younger brother, the Duke of Anjou, and as it was large and well-equipped it hardly seemed at first as if the people of La Rochelle could hope to hold out. However, the royalists were divided among themselves, for their ranks contained every range of political and religious allegiance, from the diehard Catholic killers to the loyalist Protestants.

In these circumstances, it is not surprising that the army's operations were lacking both zest and coordination. Indeed, the chief result of the siege, which had to be raised in June 1573, was a political one. It was while a wide variety of leading men were thus assembled together that some among them began developing the thought later known as *politique*, whose chief idea was that religious differences should be minimized in order to draw Frenchmen together again.

The chief supporter of this policy was Damville, governor of Languedoc. Ordered to proceed against the Protestant strong-

hold of Montauban, he found all kinds of reasons for not pressing the campaign with energy and then in May 1574 actually concluded a separate truce with the Huguenots. This was increasingly the pattern throughout Languedoc: alliance between the moderate Catholics and the Protestants. There is no doubt that it spared wide regions of the country from further plunder.

Late in May 1574 Charles IX died and was succeeded by his brother Henry III. At this stage a policy of conciliation was probably the only sensible possibility for the Crown, so as to draw to itself the growing party of *politiques* and to avoid a dangerous dependence on the extreme Catholic groups. However, Catherine was now in an aggressive mood, and it seems to have been largely on her persuasion that the young king resolved to attack the Huguenots.

Royal armies pressed down into the south —and were everywhere brought to a halt. Following their reconciliation with the moderate Catholics, the Protestants had been able greatly to extend their power in the southern provinces, and the Crown was unable to make any headway against them. So the king was obliged to meet almost all the Protestants' demands by the Edict of Beaulieu in May 1576.

The Holy League

This edict severely shook the Catholics of the north, for it now seemed to them, with some reason, that the Crown was incapable of imposing religious unity on the country. So they resolved to do it themselves, and all over the Catholic regions of the north and east there sprang up 'leagues' or armed brotherhoods linked together as the so-called 'Holy League'.

In many areas of France the inspiration behind the Holy League was the Guise family. But the king, fearing its potential, hurried to declare himself its leader. Even

so, when the states-general met in December 1576 they were unwilling to provide him with money to continue the war against the Huguenots. It seems that the constant manoeuvrings of Catherine had finally deprived the Crown of any credibility in the eyes of its subjects. Consequently the king was unable to mount a major campaign and signed a peace with the Huguenots at Bergerac in September 1577.

For the next nine years France enjoyed a kind of peace. The government of Henry III was not idle. An assembly of notables was called and consulted in September 1583, the system of central councils was overhauled, many good laws were passed, and while the arts continued to thrive around the Court the king and his young queen saw to the foundation of several charitable institutions.

It is all the sadder, then, that in this breathing-space the Crown failed to consolidate its power. In marked contrast with Henry IV of France, or for that matter his contemporary Elizabeth of England, Henry III seemed to lack any practical political sense. He did not know how to make himself accessible to, and affable with, those great lords upon whom he had to depend. His laws were readily disregarded in the absence of effective penalties, and even his expenditure on charitable works came to be cricitized as extravagant.

Consequently, when the political situation took a turn for the worse the Crown found itself isolated. That happened in 1584, for in that year the king's younger brother died, and the heretic Henry of Navarre became the heir to the throne. The Catholic party resumed its activity more intensely than before, and in December 1584 the Guises went so far as to sign a formal treaty with the king of Spain, receiving money in return for a promise to destroy heresy when the moment was ripe.

Henry III was the natural defender of legitimacy and sent emissaries to Henry of

Navarre, begging him to turn Catholic. The king of Navarre, however, was by no means ready to take this perilous step, by which he risked alienating his Protestants without convincing the Catholics of his sincerity. Henry III now found himself in an increasingly dangerous situation. He was being urged to make war on the Protestants not only by the Guises, but also by the democratic, revolutionary element of the League, which was increasingly active in the great towns of the north.

He seems to have considered allying himself with the Protestants and *politiques* of the south. But in the end, whatever the danger, it appeared less perilous to join the Leaguers. In July 1585 he therefore concluded the treaty of Nemours with them, by which the League leaders received certain key provinces to govern, in return for which they agreed to support the king in an all-out war on the Protestants.

The war went badly for Henry III. Not only was his beloved friend Joyeuse routed and killed by the Protestants at Coutras in October 1587, but the prestige of the Duke of Guise (Henry, son of Francis who had been assassinated in 1563) was greatly enhanced by his bloody defeat of a band of Germans at Auneau, November 1587.

Following this exploit, the revolutionary government of Paris invited Guise to join them there. The king forbade Guise to come, but he came all the same and was rapturously welcomed by his partisans. The idea of deposing the king had been increasingly widely suggested for some time past, and it was now even more vigorously put forward. To contain the growing number of adherents of the League, flocking to join the idol in Paris, Henry III now ordered up the French and Swiss guards.

The royal troops arrived early on the morning of 12 May 1588 and stationed themselves in the city so as to secure the approaches to the Louvre. No sooner were they in position, however, than the Parisians began erecting barricades at strategic points so as to cut off each group of soldiers. Behind these barricades were arquebusiers, and on the roof-tops were volunteers armed with stones to shower down on the soldiers. The latter had no experience of this kind of fighting, and after they had lost some men they were allowed to fall back on the Louvre.

There the king might eventually have been cornered by the hostile populace, like his successor Louis XVI, who was to die on the guillotine in 1793. But Henry III recognized the danger and on Friday 13 August 1588 hastily galloped off for Saint-Cloud, followed by such members of the court as were also able to escape. The parallel with events in 1791 is striking, but it must not be pushed too hard; Guise realized that the principle of legitimacy remained very strong and had no real wish to get rid of the king. His aim was not so much to depose Henry III as to reduce him to complete dependence on the League.

The murder of the Guises

After the 'day of barricades' Guise's hope was fulfilled, for the king was obliged to sign the so-called 'edict of union', by which Guise became commander-in-chief of the armed forces and the Cardinal de Bourbon was recognized as heir-presumptive. The king was also obliged to call a meeting of the States-General at Blois, where, under the influence of the Guises, the deputies began to put forward the ideas that their decisions should have the force of law and that they should appoint a permanent council or representative.

Henry III was no fool and he saw that these demands, if accepted, would mean a constitutional revolution. At the same time, he was personally mortified by the success of Henri of Guise in getting himself appointed commander-in-chief. He had no means of legal redress, for no Catholic jury would be mad enough to convict the leader of the League, whatever outrages he inflicted on the king. So Henry III was driven to violence. A few years earlier he had appointed a personal bodyguard, the 'forty-five'; on his instructions, a group of these bravos fell on Guise as he left the council-chamber and murdered him. The next day, to make a clean sweep, his brother the cardinal was also cut down.

When the news of the double murder reached Paris there was a general determination to have no more to do with a tyrannical king. The capital had already been building up a kind of league with the other main Catholic cities, and after 1588 this network was systematically extended. Soon only Blois, Bordeaux, Saumur and Tours remained loyal to the king; all the other major towns acknowledged either the League or the Huguenots. It was plainly impossible for the king to rejoin the Catholic camp, and he now threw in his lot with Henry of Navarre.

The combined forces of the two kings now advanced on Paris and early in August 1589 were about to assault the city when Henry III was assassinated by Jacques Clément, a Dominican monk, who was an adherent of the League. Catherine de' Medici had died the previous January, and so the Valois were extinct. Before he died Henry III had recognized Henry of Navarre as his rightful successor and had begged those loyal to the Crown to join the new Henry IV.

Henry of Navarre

However, the new king was far from master in his kingdom. The forces of the League had a cunning leader in the Duke of Mayenne, brother of the murdered Guises, and they could depend on most of the great towns. On the other hand, Henry IV from the start enjoyed the support not only of the Protestants but also of the royal guards and of the nobility of a large part of northern France. Time would show that the greatest royal asset was in fact the king himself and not the outside support he could muster.

From the start he showed himself determined to assert his authority. Some of his councillors advised him to fall back on the area south of the Loire, in the face of Mayenne's greatly superior army. But the king would have none of this and in September 1589 succeeded in defeating Mayenne's army when it imprudently assaulted him at Arques, just south of Dieppe. Henry then made a lightning attempt on Paris, but his forces were too small to carry the city and they were soon menaced by the return of Mayenne.

So the royal forces withdrew and spent the winter capturing key towns around the capital. Mayenne saw that the king meant to starve him out and so in March 1590 came out to give battle. In spite of being outnumbered by about two to one, the royalists again carried the day at Ivry and again laid siege to Paris. This time the siege lasted six months and was raised only when the Duke of Parma led a Spanish army down from the Netherlands to relieve the Catholics.

Foiled in his attempt to take Paris, Henry IV now tried to capture Rouen, which alone of the great towns of Normandy was still holding out for the League. From November 1591 to February 1592 he furiously battered the town, which was eventually relieved by another of Parma's expeditions. By the summer of 1592 things had reached a stalemate. Clearly, the League forces could no longer hope to crush the king in open battle.

Au mois de Iuillet de l'an 1593. Ce Prince fit la Ceremonie de son Abjuration dans L'Eglise de St Denis a deux lieües de Paris entre les mains de l'arche= véque de Bourges et 7. ou 8. Evéques assistans et tous les grands de sa Cour, Gabriel d'Etrée même qui avoit beaucoup Contribué a sa Conversion.

Left, Henry IV accepting the Catholic faith in 1593; Henry, a worldly man, considered that 'Paris is worth a mass' and that this ceremony would reconcile the various factions, most of whom recognized his qualities as a king and a leader.

Opposite top, the assassination of Henry, Duke of Guise (1550–88), instigated by Henry III. This coup against the highly popular and powerful Guise family led to the reconciliation of the king and the Protestant Henry of Navarre.

Opposite bottom, Henry IV (reigned 1589–1610): although he was able to bring the civil wars to a close by leading the growing party of politiques, who preferred peace to religious conviction, he could not secure his throne until he renounced Protestantism in 1593. Musée du Louvre, Paris.

On the other hand, the splendid royal cavalry could not be exploited when it came to besieging towns.

At this stage Mayenne made a blunder. He had brought together a states-general in Paris, in order to select a Catholic prince as League pretender. However, to this League assembly he now called certain Catholic royalists, in the hope that they would desert the king. In fact, the eventual effect was the opposite; coming into contact with the royal representatives, the moderate party among the Leaguers insisted on opening talks with them.

The king's conversion

Once negotiations had begun, the coming of peace could not long be delayed. In May 1593 the king renounced Protestantism, and this removed the last scruple of most of the moderates, so that by February 1594 he was able to enter his capital in triumph. The provincial leaders were readily coming over to the royal side, often in return for handsome payments. By the beginning of 1595 the remaining resistance was concentrated in the territories controlled by the dukes of Mayenne, Mercoeur and Épernon.

Behind these powerful magnates lay the might of Spain, and in January 1595 Henry IV declared war on Philip II. The war did not go particularly well for the French, who were at that time no match for the Spaniards in operations combining infantry and siege-work. However, with the progressive exhaustion of the Spanish economy, Philip II was glad to make peace in 1598, the year of his death.

Meanwhile the rebellious dukes were coming into line. Mayenne was reconciled early in 1596, and Épernon also came to terms that spring. This left only Mercoeur. He was expelled from his duchy of Brittany in 1598 and went off to fight the Turks on

the Danube valley for the Holy Roman emperor.

The year 1598 saw not only the submission of the last of the great League leaders and the conclusion of peace with Spain but also the establishment of a truce in the internal religious conflict. While he was at Nantes, on the expedition against the Duke of Mercoeur, Henry IV signed the edict named after that town, which for nearly a hundred years gave the French Protestants some kind of toleration. In one sense it was not very original; after all, most of its provisions could be found in one or another of the truces which had punctuated the wars of the previous forty years. Protestants were allowed full liberty of conscience and were permitted to hold their services in a large number of specified areas. They were to have special mixed law-courts to ensure them justice when involved with a Catholic, they were permitted to assemble periodically, and they were allocated about one hundred cautionary towns (*places de sûreté*) as refuges in time of danger.

What made this edict different was the king's determination to enforce it.

As long as he still lived its provisions were scrupulously followed, so that the Protestants were able to survive if not to flourish. At the same time, Henry IV showed himself to be sincerely interested in the progress of his new church—the ancient church which had bound France together for so long and which still provided a unifying social force. By 1598 the way was clear for a decade of constructive achievement, after the ravages of the previous forty years.

Above, a dance at the court of Henry IV of France; Henry won the support of most of the French nobility through his policies of compromise and planning for the future. Musée du Louvre, Paris.

Opposite top, Henry IV of France (reigned 1589–1610) defeating the Catholic League at the Battle of Arques in 1589. Henry was unable to complete the victory over the League, which received assistance from Philip II of Spain, but he was able to conciliate the Catholics instead by renouncing his Protestantism. Château de Versailles.

Opposite bottom, the Edict of Nantes of 1598, at which Henry IV promised freedom of conscience to the Protestants, assured their military security, and promised to contribute to the upkeep of the Protestant strongholds.

Chapter 2

The Counter-Reformation

In the face of the mounting Protestant menace, the Roman Catholic Church began setting her house in order. The most effective agents of this reform were the Council of Trent and the new Order of Jesus. thanks to their efforts much formerly Catholic territory was recovered, and many pagan peoples were Christianized.

Long before the great renewal of the years 1540 to 1570, there had been stirrings of reform within the Catholic church. In Spain, for instance, in the later fifteenth century, Cardinal Ximenes had entirely revitalized the old structure, correcting monastic abuses, appointing zealous bishops, founding schools and so on. In France too there were reforming prelates like bishop Briçonnet of Meaux. In Italy itself there was the Oratory of Divine Love, an association of pious laymen and clerics which met for the first time in 1517. However, all these movements were fated to remain local as long as the papacy remained unreformed. In the first part of the century the popes continued to be primarily interested in Italian politics and personal pleasure. They thus failed to see the force behind the movement and to make those moves which might early have contained it.

It was under Clement VII (1523–34) that the papacy suffered its worst humiliation, when Rome itself was taken and sacked by troops of the Holy Roman Empire in 1527. To much of Europe this seemed symbolic of the collapse of the ancient church, while the Protestant Lutheran movement was daily gaining fresh adherents in Germany and elsewhere.

Clement VII's successor was a man no less worldly than he but one who was able to appreciate the nature of the crisis. Paul III saw that the time was past for sterile Italian bickerings, and that the papacy's task was now to unite the Catholic world against the Turks and the Protestants. Not that he accepted the divisions within Christianity as final. In his early years, at any rate, he knew and appreciated the works of the Christian humanist Erasmus and hoped for a reconciliation with the Protestants.

Paul was responsible for organizing or approving the weapons used by the old church in its new offensive: the council, the Jesuits, the Capuchins, the Inquisition and the Index. He intervened actively in European politics, excommunicating the King of England, encouraging the Holy Roman emperor to unite with the King of France against the Turk, and censuring the King of France for his immoral conduct. He also set his own house straight. If there were still few saints at Rome, at any rate after his passing there were fewer incompetent and uninterested prelates than there had been.

Ignatius Loyola

This reform of the central organization was greatly assisted by the growth of the Jesuits. It all began in 1521 when a young Spanish soldier, Ignatius Loyola, was severely injured while attempting to hold Pamplona against the French forces. Deprived at the age of thirty of the possibility of pursuing his chosen career of arms, Loyola took up reading during his convalescence and soon began to experience the same kind of spiritual anguish as that suffered by Luther.

Like the great German reformer, Loyola started from a deeply-felt realization of the sinfulness of man and of his helplessness if deprived of God's grace. Going on from there, Loyola found great comfort in the redeeming message of Christ and in the conviction that salvation was possible through apostolic action. Hence the development of his determination to consecrate his life *ad majorem Dei gloriam*: to the greater glory of God, the future motto of the Jesuits.

Like a good soldier, he converted these personal reflections into a practical manual, which he called the *Spiritual Exercises*, much as one might speak of exercises with the sword, pike or musket. This little manual, which became the devotional guide of the Jesuits, is not a catechism, concerned with faith and doctrine, but is essentially what its title promises: a course of spiritual exercises designed to train the future soldier of Christ.

Loyola realized that he could accomplish nothing without further study, and so, his enthusiasm having become suspect in Spain, he came to France, to work on theology, philosophy, the natural sciences and languages at the Sorbonne. There his capacity for hard work and his unfailing geniality

Above, a Jesuit missionary, painted by Jusepe de Ribera. Such missionaries were highly educated and disciplined; their main policy in the sixteenth century was to gain positions of power within the royal households and to establish schools. The most successful Jesuit campaign was staged in Poland in the 1580s. Museo Poldi, Pezzoli, Milan.

Left, Ignatius Loyola (1491–1556), the founder of the Society of Jesus. He intended at first to concentrate on preaching to the Muslims, but Paul III encouraged him to work for the Catholic Church against the Protestants.

Opposite, Pope Paul III (reigned 1534–49) with his two grandsons, painted in a revealing portrait by Titian in about 1545. Earlier the Pope had summoned the Council of Trent to counter the drive of Protestantism and had supported the foundation of the Jesuit Order. Palazzo di Capodimonte, Naples.

greatly impressed his young fellow-students, several of whom began to fall under his spell as a leader of men. Six of them became particularly attached to him: François de Jassu from Navarre (the future Saint Francis Xavier), the Spaniard Diego Lainez, Pierre Lefèvre from Savoy, the Spaniards Nicolas Bobadilla and Alonso Salmeron and Simon Rodriguez, member of a great Portuguese family.

On 15 August 1534 these seven went up to Montmartre, and there took together three vows, of poverty, chastity and of a pilgrimage to the Holy Land. Then they set out for Venice, whence they planned to set sail for the Middle East. Along the way they gathered companions for the adventure and gave themselves the name of the 'Company of Jesus'.

However, when the time came to leave, Loyola had doubts. Not only was he short of funds, but friends suggested that things had changed so radically over the past few years that there was now as much to be done in Europe as in the Holy Land. Loyola thought for a while of entering the new Theatine order but in the end resolved to

found his own, whose basis would be obedience to the pope. Perhaps it was rather a military concept, this idea of creating around the head of the church an impregnable citadel. Anyway, Paul III rapidly saw what great use the Order could be to the papacy, and on 27 September 1540 he granted it official recognition in the Bull 'on the government of the church militant'.

It took ten years or so for the Company to settle down and work out its organization. Loyola borrowed here and there such features of the other orders as seemed appropriate but never lost sight of the primary function of the Jesuits—support of, and obedience to, the pope. New members were chosen not only for their moral but also for their physical qualities: they had to be sturdy to work effectively.

Within the Company, fasting and contemplation were minimized so as to allow the maximum possible time 'in the world'. The Jesuit training lasted for fifteen years, beginning with the mastery of the *Spiritual Exercises* and going on to study the classics, philosophy and theology. After that the young aspirant might well teach in one of the

many colleges the Jesuits set up, before finally being ordained a priest. After that, he could still advance in rank within the Company, perhaps eventually to become its 'general'. The use of this title for the head of the Jesuits was very characteristic, as was the idea that within the Company advancement came through merit, efficiency and excellence. Of the virtues, humility seemed less important than strength of mind.

This organization was marvellously well calculated to serve the papacy's ends. 'Provinces' were set up all over the world, and in them missionary activity went on apace. Very soon the Jesuits won a name for their schools, which flourished not only in Europe—and especially in France and Germany—but also in all the regions penetrated by Catholic Europeans. Within Europe virtually the whole of the Catholic governing classes came to send their children to Jesuit schools, and in countries of mixed religion like France they often received Protestants as well. So they came to wield a remarkable influence over the ways of thought of the people who counted in every country. They also proved adept at penetrating the highest social circles, often as confessors to kings and noblemen.

But the activities of the Jesuits were not confined to elegant salons. All over the world they were to be found, from the snowy wastes of Canada to the jungles of India, preaching, instructing, converting. Some entered even too wholeheartedly into the customs of their regions and had to be repudiated by their provincial superiors. Many were martyred by the savage peoples

among whom they lived. All were a testimony to the dynamism of Loyola's vision and the effectiveness of his organization.

The Council of Trent

Meanwhile, following great difficulties overcome largely by the insistence of Paul III, a general council of the church had been called at the little town of Trent, on the borders of what are now Italy and Austria. the opening sessions were bedevilled by the oroblem of what should be done about the Protestants and by the unwillingness of the French and Spanish sovereigns to let their 'national' prelates commit themselves to any greater degree of papal control.

However, as the sessions went on the council began to get to grips with the most pressing problems in organization and doctrine. The reform of abuses was perhaps the easiest and certainly the most effective aspect of the council's work. Henceforward the popes were men of irreproachable moral character. The cardinals were elected according to less worldly standards. The bishops were chosen for their evangelical zeal and for their learning. Above all, the council reformed the whole position of priests. Henceforward they had to undergo severe training in special seminaries, and their celibate status was confirmed.

The doctrinal aspect of the council's work was in some ways less satisfactory. But it had at any rate the great advantage of letting Catholics clearly know what they had to believe, rather as the *Institutes of the Christian Religion* gave clear instructions to

Calvinists in what they must hold to be true.

The council reaffirmed the theological importance of tradition, which might be just as directly inspired as the Bible. A definitive edition of the scriptures was prepared and published in 1592. Against Luther, the fathers took care to redefine the place of faith in its traditional terms, in no sense to be isolated from works. Against Calvin, they were at pains to emphasize both the freewill of man and the infinite mercy of God, which made predestination unthinkable. Finally, they reaffirmed the validity of all seven sacraments, insisting particularly on the real presence of Christ in the sacrament of the Eucharist.

After the announcement of the council's decisions after 1563, Catholics knew how to think. The doctrinal messages of Trent were successfully spread throughout Catholic Europe not only in catechisms but also by paintings, sculpture and music. Architecture itself was pressed into the service of the renewed church with the adoption of the baroque, the so-called 'Jesuit style'.

Alongside these positive aspects of the ancient church's revival went two repressive measures, the Inquisition and the Index. First used against medieval heretics, the Inquisition had already been revived in Spain in 1478 and in 1542 was extended to all the Catholic countries under the name of the 'Holy Office'. There is no doubt that it succeeded in stamping out Protestantism in Spain and Italy, but at a cost to the freedom and spontaneity of society there that only late became evident.

Much the same reflections come to mind

in considering the work of the Index devised in 1557. Although it doubtless ensured the destruction of many worthless books, it also encouraged the kind of censorship fatal to the growth and development of social and cultural institutions.

Philip II

Given the political and religious divisions of Europe in the second half of the sixteenth century, it was inconceivable that the Counter-Reformation could remain a purely spiritual affair. So it was that the cause of Trent came to be taken up by Philip II of Spain, who in extremely uneasy alliance with Rome became the champion of the ancient church's revival.

Against the pagan Turks, Philip was remarkably successful. In 1571, with the aid of the Venetian fleet and papal diplomacy, he inflicted such a defeat on the sultan's fleet at Lepanto that the western Mediterranean was henceforward free from large forces of Turkish warships.

He was less successful in his campaigns against the heretical Europeans. Elizabeth of England long held him in suspense with her enigmatic religious policy, and when he finally decided to invade in 1588 the Invincible Armada came to grief.

In the Netherlands the revolt of 1566 eventually led to the establishment of the autonomous United Provinces in the north of the country, even though during four decades Philip II had tried to impose Spanish rule and Catholicism on the whole of the Low Countries. However, if the

Above, the Battle of Lepanto in 1571, at which an alliance of the Papacy, the Spaniards and the Venetians defeated the Ottoman fleet. The victory gave the Catholics a greater confidence in dealing with opposition inside Europe as well. National Maritime Museum, London.

Left, an interrogation by the Inquisition; faced with the spread of independent thinking through widespread education and the popularity of printing, the Inquisition fell back on a belief in authority and tradition to test an individual's adherence to Catholicism.

Opposite, the Council of Trent, painted by Titian in 1586. Despite its interruptions and delays (the Council was convened in 1545–47, 1551–52 and 1562–63), it managed to arrive at a firm restatement of Catholic doctrine, as the original intention of a reconciliation with the Protestants was abandoned. Musée du Louvre, Paris.

seven provinces of the north escaped him, the ten of the south did not, and in the so-called 'Spanish Netherlands' there developed a thriving culture epitomized early in the next century by the work of Rubens.

In France, too, the Spanish intervention was not altogether unsuccessful. The two expeditions led from the Low Countries by the Spanish general Parma retrieved the situation for the Catholic forces before Paris (1590) and Rouen (1592), and even if Henry of Navarre did eventually become King of France it was not without having to abjure Protestantism. Philip II played his part in this abjuration, which opened the way to a great flowering of Catholicism in early seventeenth-century France.

This spiritual revival owed a good deal to the work of the Jesuits, who from the mid-sixteenth century onwards had been establishing schools and colleges in the areas particularly affected by Protestantism. However, it owed much as well to other orders, some of which reflected very faithfully the new spiritual zeal of the period.

Typical of these orders was the Congregation of the Mission, founded in 1624 by St Vincent de Paul. Its members were to evangelize the French countryside in total obedience to the diocesan bishop. St Vincent de Paul, in collaboration with Louis de Marillac, also founded in 1633 the Company of Daughters of Charity, to work among the poor. He was a very dynamo of a man,

founding seminaries, reforming older orders and organizing charitable work for all the needy: foundlings, beggars, prisoners, galley-slaves, old soldiers and so on.

Another remarkable figure in French Catholicism of the early seventeenth century was Pierre de Bérulle. Founder of the Oratorian order in France (1611), he also encouraged Madame de Sainte-Beuve to found the order of Ursulines, which by the mid-seventeenth century had over 250 schools in France. The Ursuline schools did not aim to turn out well-educated women but young women of strong moral character, resolved to run their families, and to reform society, in accordance with Catholic principles. The educational principles of the Ursulines owed much to the advice of St François de Sales, whose combination of mysticism and dynamic charitable activity is very typical of this phase of the Catholic renewal.

Both the Oratorian and the Ursuline orders derived from Italy, where again the influence of the decisions taken at Trent was strongly felt. There the outstanding bishop was St Charles Borromeo (1538–84). Nephew of Pius IV, Borromeo had attended the closing sessions of the Council of Trent and then returned to Rome. There, in 1562, he went through the *Spiritual Exercises* and emerged a changed man.

Taking priest's orders, he reduced his life to one of ascetic simplicity and besought

the pope to let him return to his See of Milan. Permission was finally granted on the accession of the saintly Pius V (1566–72), and Borromeo at once set about reforming the archdiocese.

Provincial and diocesan councils were regularly held. Three seminaries were established, and when they could not easily be staffed by Jesuits Borromeo founded his own order, the oblates of St Ambrose, to fill the posts. He encouraged the order of Barnabites to preach their spectacular missions within his diocese. He founded a congregation of Ursulines. He encouraged and commissioned the work of ecclesiastical musicians, including Palestrina. He established a whole series of elementary schools within his See. In short, he was actively and energetically concerned with anything which could revive Christian life in the archdiocese of Milan. It is easy to comprehend the great effect of the Counter-Reformation when we reflect that Borromeo was only one of many prelates who were taking similar action all over Catholic Europe.

In Spain the Catholic reformation took a rather different form. The church had been largely reformed in the days of Cardinal Ximenes and had been 'purified' since then by the ferocious activity of the Inquisition. Consequently, the great Counter-Reformation figures of St Teresa of Avila and St John of the Cross, while not negligible from the point of view of reform, especially

MISERICORDIAS DOMINI · INETERNVM CANTABO

Left, St Teresa of Avila (1515–82), a Spanish nun who founded several convents and encouraged the rebirth of spirituality and mysticism in Spain. Her religion combined a personal awareness of God with a strong common sense and poetry. Convento de Santa Teresa, Seville.

Opposite, St Charles Borromeo (1538–84), an ardent advocate of the Counter-Reformation who inspired the work of the last session of the Council of Trent. As Bishop of Milan from 1563 he aroused much opposition in his vigorous pursuit of reform. Santa Maria della Passione, Milan.

in the monasteries, are chiefly remarkable for their mystical writings. Some indeed have affirmed that, with the Inquisition raging as it was, mysticism was the final refuge for personal religion.

The political Counter-Reformation was not very successful in England or the United Provinces. It also failed to affect Scandinavia and the north German provinces. However, a combination of political and cultural penetration was very successful for the Catholic cause in southern and central Germany during the later sixteenth century. This advance was led by the Jesuits and Capuchins, who skilfully won the friendship of secular rulers and then, by establishing their remarkable colleges and universities, won back whole regions for the ancient church.

The great name associated with this movement is that of St Peter Canisius, provincial of the Jesuits in Germany, Austria and Bohemia after 1556. Not content with founding colleges, he produced a masterly catechism in 1556 and conducted successful preaching tours all over his province. Steadily Catholic influence and Jesuit colleges penetrated central and even northern Germany, until by 1600 the disunited Protestants were everywhere in retreat. Alas, this peaceful reconquest was destined to come to a violent end, for the Catholic revival was sowing the seeds for the 'thirty years' war'.

IVLIVS TERTIVS PONTIFEX MAXI

Left, Giovanni Palestrina offering his book, of masses to Pope Julius III in 1554. His work represented one of the great artistic achievements of the Counter-Reformation.

33

Chapter 3

France from Henry IV to Mazarin

In the first half of the seventeenth century France was the prey of conflicting constitutional tendencies. After the strong government of Henry IV (1589–1610) came the minority of Louis XIII (1610–24), and after the strong government of Richelieu (1624–42) came the minority of Louis XIV (1643–61). During each minority elements hostile to the extension of royal power once again emerged, chiefly among the nobility and the members of the *parlements*. Thus when Louis XIV took over in 1661, he was obliged from the start to come to grips with a general constitutional disorder.

Henry IV

Once he was firmly established on his throne, in 1598, Henry IV was able to turn to the problem of the succession. His ill-fated Saint Bartholomew marriage with Marguerite de Valois had borne him plenty of quarrels but no children. It is true that he had conceived numerous offspring as a result of irregular liaisons, but these were not normally eligible for the crown of the Most Christian King—unless, Henry IV thought, he perhaps married one of the mothers. The lucky woman he chose was Gabrielle d'Estrées; Marguerite refused to divorce him, but he planned to marry Gabrielle in 1599 anyway.

Most of the king's advisers were against the move, but in the end it was death which stepped in, taking poor Gabrielle as she was about to bear another royal bastard. Henry IV therefore had to choose again, and this time he chose more wisely, marrying the daughter of the Duke of Tuscany—one of his greatest creditors—Marie de' Medici. This was a more regular union, Marguerite having consented to the divorce, and if Marie was rather fat she was at any rate energetic, faithful, cultivated and, best of all, prolific.

So with his private affairs settled the king turned to the renewal of his realm. It is an extraordinary experience to read the correspondence during the next ten years of Henry IV, who in his origins after all was merely a Pyrenean rustic. He seems to have thought of everything which could make France great, whether in the realm of government, economics, war, culture or

social welfare. He kept the great nobles quiet by his affability and by drastic action when it was necessary. Thus the Duke of Biron lost his head in 1602 for conspiring with the Spaniards, and in 1606 the Duke of Bouillon was forcibly cornered in his duchy and obliged to give up Sedan.

In economic matters he relied chiefly on the Duke of Sully, who had served him faithfully in all his campaigns since the 1570s. For once the budget showed a steady surplus, bogus creditors were sent packing, taxes were levied a little less unfairly, marshes were drained and roads and canals built. In the last four hundred years France has always been quick to recover from the effects of war, and this time, helped by the Crown's efforts, the recovery was dramatic.

Foreign relations were largely the business of another minister, Villeroy. Unlike Sully, he had only come over to Henry IV relatively lately, but the king was never one to let past grudges stand in the way of possible future services. France came once again to play a part in European diplomacy, supporting the United Provinces in their increasingly successful revolt against the Spaniards, settling a dispute between Venice and the papacy, establishing a Francophile party among the cardinals, and even regaining friendly contact with the Turks.

To back up this diplomatic effort, the king and Sully saw to the preparation of a great war-machine. Large numbers of guns and great supplies of powder and equipment were stored up in the arsenals at Paris and in the frontier provinces. The payment of troops were regularized and their number reduced to a small but well-trained elite. On the Mediterranean, the galley-fleet was built up and Toulon now came into prominence as a naval base.

Sometimes the king would visit Sully at the Paris arsenal, where as grand master of

the artillery the latter had apartments, and together they would gloat over the store of weapons. Together too they would plan fresh improvements to the city of Paris. At this time the Louvre was greatly extended, the place des Vosges ('place Royale') and the Saint Louis hospital built, and the plan was drawn up for a great 'place de France', a semi-circular 'square' into which a dozen or so streets would lead, each one named after one of the great French provinces.

Architecture was not the only art to be encouraged. A tapestry-works was established at Paris, using skilled workers from the Netherlands, and a factory was also set up for the manufacture of fine glass. At the Louvre a whole wing was set aside for the lodging and maintenance of artists and craftsmen, many of whom worked on the royal buildings. Overseas ventures were also encouraged, and it was at this time that Samuel Champlain, under the patronage of the king, explored the Saint Lawrence and founded Quebec (1603).

However, all this constructive activity rested on a fragile basis—the life of the king. Henry IV had followed the traditional policy of the French kings in opposing the Habsburgs by his support of their enemies, not only in the United Provinces but also among the German princes. In 1610 he was actually preparing to go to war over the Cleves-Jülich succession, in alliance with certain German Protestant princes, so as to avoid control of the duchy passing to the Habsburgs. The tension within France was very great, since it seemed that the king was in some sense bent on frustrating the progress of the Counter-Reformation. So it was not very surprising that on 14 May 1610 Henry IV was fatally stabbed as he was on his way to see Sully at the Arsenal. The murderer was at once apprehended and even under torture insisted that he had acted

Left, the Place Royal in Paris, built in the early seventeenth century and centred on a statue of Louis XIII.

Opposite, Henry IV of France (reigned 1589–1610) with his wife Marie de' Medici and their children. Equally happy with his family and with his army, Henry became one of the best-loved kings of France and restored prosperity and unity after the ravages of the wars of religion.

Left, the map of New France drawn by the explorer Samuel de Champlain (1567–1635) in 1632. Henry IV encouraged the exploration of the New World and founded several colonies to which he tried (unlike the English) to attract the best craftsmen and farmers.

Left, the assassination of Henry IV in 1610 by François Ravaillac. The murderer can be seen undergoing torture in the background. The king's death led to the revival of the aspirations of the Catholic nobility.

on his own initiative. However, many of the extreme Catholics were no doubt glad of the king's death, and as always in such cases there was the suspicion that he was the victim of a general plot.

Louis XIII

If the king's death was the result of a Spanish conspiracy, then it was a singularly successful one. The kingdom was plunged into disarray overnight, and France's entry into the German struggle was delayed for a quarter of a century. The young king was only nine, and so his mother Marie de' Medici became regent. She at once reversed the anti-Spanish policy, marrying two of her children to the children of Philip III of Spain. Needless to say, this about-turn was very disquieting to the Protestants, who drew even closer together throughout the south and began rebuilding their military forces.

Even for some Catholic nobles the assassination was welcome, since now they felt free from royal control. Many of them began to grow rebellious, and the regent was able to keep their allegiance only by handing out high offices and pensions with a free hand. When even this began to fail she called a meeting of the States-General (1614), but the different orders merely fell to quarrelling in a way which revealed the profound disunity within French society. What did emerge from the meeting was that all the money stored up by Henry IV in the Bastille had been spent. His policies now lay in ruins.

Meanwhile the discontent of the Protestants had translated itself into open warfare, with the revolt in 1614 of Henry II, prince of Condé (grandson of the Condé killed at Jarnac). He found a ready following among the Huguenots of the south, who encouraged his dreams of the French crown and pushed him into another revolt in 1616. This time, following the advice of a young bishop of Luçon called Richelieu. Marie de' Medici laid hands on Condé and shut him up in the Bastille.

Unfortunately it was not to Richelieu that she generally turned for advice. Her chief councillor seems to have been the sinister Leonora Galigaï, one of her ladies-in-waiting, and her husband Concini. These two Florentines enriched themselves in a remarkable way during the regency, and even after Louis XIII reached his nominal majority in 1614 (when he was thirteen) they continued to treat him as a small child.

So the young king began to listen to the advice of his falconer, Albert de Luynes, who thought it best to get rid of the Concinis. One day in 1617, as he was arriving at the Louvre, Concini himself was shot down by Vitry, the captain of the guard, and some of the royal gentlemen; his wife was accused of sorcery and beheaded. Thereafter falconer Luynes became a duke and directed affairs. Marie de' Medici was exiled to Blois and her admirer Richelieu retired to Luçon.

The next few years saw various campaigns in which Luynes fought Marie de'

Medici's forces and the Protestants, while whole regions of the countryside slowly reverted to anarchy. In the end Luynes died directing the siege of Montauban in 1621, and Marie de' Medici, having been reconciled with her son, arranged the entry of Richelieu to the council of state in 1624.

Richelieu

By then Richelieu was thirty-nine and had been a cardinal for two years. Originally intending to pursue a military career, he had been obliged to enter the church for family reasons. But his real genius was political; within that frail body there dwelt an intellect of astonishing political subtlety and a willpower which conquered both enemies and disease. Richelieu was also capable of affection, and the mutual liking which he and the king had for each other was to prove crucial in establishing his power.

From the start he began organizing a European resistance to the Habsburgs. The subsidies paid to the Dutch in the time of Henry IV were renewed, and Christian IV of Denmark was promised yearly aid in support of his proposed war against the Holy Roman Empire. A marriage was also arranged between Henrietta Maria, the king's sister, and charles, Prince of Wales, and late in 1624 the strategic valley of the Valtelline was seized, thereby cutting the Spanish link between Italy and Flanders. The seizure of the Valtelline, which aroused

great resentment at Rome and at Madrid, made it clear that a decisive break between France and Spain would be imminent if Richelieu continued in power.

If he was hostile to the pretensions of the Catholic powers abroad, that did not mean that Richelieu was friendly towards the Protestants at home. Quite the contrary; with his exalted notion of the king's power, he was scandalized by the existence of a Huguenot state within the French monarchy. In fact, the Huguenots played into his hands by revolting again in 1624. By then the only major towns they held were Montpellier, Montauban and the great fortress of La Rochelle, the latter almost an independent republic. In the summer of 1627 the English Duke of Buckingham, favourite of both James I and Charles I, arrived off La Rochelle with an army and fleet destined to strengthen the Protestant capital. But Buckingham found the town hesitant to receive him, and so he concentrated his efforts on trying to capture the island of Ré, which commands the approaches of La Rochelle.

However, the royalist fort on the island was stubbornly defended, and early in the winter of 1627 Buckingham had to sail home without having accomplished anything. By that time Richelieu had strengthened the forces investing La Rochelle and had come in person with the king to direct the siege. The royal navy was still very weak, and so Richelieu decided to cut the Rochelais off from the sea by building an immense dyke. He was entirely successful in this, and by the early winter of 1628 the town was obliged to surrender, its inhabitants reduced in number from 25,000 to 5,000. The survivors were spared and permitted to exercise their religion freely, in keeping with Richelieu's policy of 'moderation and graciousness'. But the town's defences were razed and the republic

was at an end. There were further Protestant revolts in the south in 1629–30, but these too were crushed. With the loss of its capital at La Rochelle Protestantism was effectively stifled as a major political force.

A certain French nobleman is said to have observed to one of his friends at the time: 'you will see, we shall be stupid enough to capture La Rochelle'. His point was a good one, for once Richelieu had brought the Protestants to heel he turned on the rest of the nobility. Aristocratic plots tended to centre around Gaston d'Orléans, the king's brother and heir to the throne, since Louis XIII had not at that time had any children. In 1626, for instance, the Count of Chalais was caught conspiring with Gaston and some others. He lost his head. A year later it was the turn of Montmorency-Bouteville, who in spite of the cardinal's prohibition tried to take part in a duel on what is now the place des Vosges at midday. He too lost his head. Meanwhile numerous other magnates were perturbed at the way in which royal power was again threatening their privileges.

All this discontent came to a head on the 'Day of Dupes' in November 1630. Marie de' Medici had never been contented with Richelieu's anti-Habsburg policy, and when her son fell gravely ill that September she took advantage of her increased contact with him to press for the cardinal's dismissal. She was supported not only by Gaston d'Orléans but also by the king's wife Anne of Austria, who had political ambitions of her own. In his weakened state the king seemed ready to listen to the conspirators. Popular opinion held the cardinal to be as good as dismissed, but then Richelieu was able to secure a decisive interview with the king. Marie de' Medici fled to Cologne, Gaston d'Orléans exiled himself in Lorraine, and one or two lesser conspirators were executed. Henceforth, secure in the king's favour, Richelieu was impregnable.

That is not to say that the nobility had come to heel: the next few years were full of aristocratic conspiracies, which of course flourished again at the middle of the century. In 1632 Gaston d'Orléans succeeded in persuading Henry of Montmorency, godson of Henry IV and governor of Languedoc, to revolt. Henry was caught and executed in the town hall of Toulouse, an extraordinary measure for the times. In 1641 the Count of Soissons led a conspiracy, and the next year it was the turn of young Cinq-Mars, who plotted with the Spaniards and lost his head for it at Lyons in 1642. The nobility remained decidedly turbulent.

The growth of royal power

All the same, the royal power continued to develop. At Paris the tendency already perceptible in the early sixteenth century grew more marked. In particular, the power of the four secretaries of state yearly increased. In the provinces the intendants (officials with wide judicial powers, directly responsible to the Crown) were more and more active, directing armies, administering towns and checking on governors. There still was no general network of intendants, but the way was being prepared for this development under Louis XIV.

In the time of Henry IV and earlier, the Atlantic fleet had been neglected. Richelieu, who was himself the equivalent of the English lord high admiral, saw to the creation of a fleet of 'round ships' capable of sailing the Atlantic and other oceans, a fleet eventually capable of challenging those of Spain, England and the United Provinces. This went hand-in-hand with his policy of developing overseas commerce, which he entrusted to ten companies operating all over the world. It was at this time that Guadeloupe and Martinique were occupied (1635) and that merchants from Dieppe and

Above, the Marquis de Cinq-Mars (1620–42), a protégé of Cardinal Richelieu who plotted with Gaston d'Orléans against Richelieu and signed a secret treaty with Spain. He was executed after the discovery of the plot. Musée d'art et céramique, Narbonne.

Opposite, the Duke of Richelieu (1585–1642), who sought to promote the monarchy inside France and France within Europe, even if that meant allying with Protestants against the Habsburgs. He also encouraged the development of the French colonies in the New World. Musée du Louvre, Paris.

Rouen founded houses in Senegal, Madagascar and Guyana.

During the sixteenth century it had been rare for an army to muster 30,000 men. By 1640, however, Richelieu had raised the French army to the incredible total of 160,000 men, in anticipation of the still more demanding efforts of Louis XIV. The strain that these military and naval forces put on France's resources is easy to imagine. Richelieu seems to have had very little idea of the relationship between economic resources and political power and recklessly sold offices in order to sustain the war-effort. Needless to say, this sale of offices contributed greatly to the troubles during the minority of Louis XIV.

With these great armies, Richelieu aimed, as he wrote, to 'return to Gaul the frontiers destined to her by nature'; that is, the Rhine, the Alps and the Pyrenees. It was on the north-east frontier that France's 'natural frontier' was most sadly shrunken, and it was here that Richelieu concentrated his efforts. Between 1631 and 1634, while the Swedes diverted the imperial forces in Germany, the French succeeded in bringing under their control a whole series of bishoprics and principalities stretching from Switzerland to the Rhineland.

When open war with Spain began in 1635, Richelieu had to defend these newly-acquired territories. At first things went badly for the French, and in 1636 a Spanish invasion from Flanders gained rapid successes and for a time menaced Paris. But the merchants of the capital rallied strongly to Richelieu, offering him large sums of money. The French nobility was slowly mobilized, and when the Dutch were persuaded to take the imperial forces from the rear the danger was over. France was never again as badly threatened during this war, and its eventual upshot was that she acquired Artois, Alsace

and also the bishoprics of Metz, Toul and Verdun. Richelieu died in 1642, but it was already clear by then that the immense efforts that he had demanded of France had not been fruitless in terms of the expansion of her territory.

The social structure

Whether they had been worthwhile from the point of view of French society as a whole is more debatable. By far the greatest number of Frenchmen were peasants, and for them Richelieu's wars meant cruel taxation and occasional invasions by Spaniards or Germans, not to mention billeting-officers seeking to quarter French troops. The result was the peasant revolts which were so frequent during the reign. The early seventeenth century does not seem to have been a time of rapid economic development, but it is all the same true that many merchants were greatly prospering, often by fulfilling lucrative war-contracts.

It is often said that in the face of this 'rising bourgeoisie' the ancient nobility was in retreat. Such an idea is absurd for seventeenth-century France. If all merchants and lawyers, however successful, had pleased the sociologists by remaining in their 'class', then no doubt the bourgeoisie would rapidly have become the most important element in the state. But in the France of Richelieu, the one ambition of most successful members of the third estate—composed of those who were neither clerics (first estate) nor nobles (second estate)—was to acquire a patent of nobility. Thus for generation after generation the most successful merchants, lawyers and so forth escaped from the class into which they were born and went to strengthen the second estate. So throughout the seventeenth century the nobility remained the group which mattered.

The classical culture

With the acquisition of a title often went the purchase of a country seat. There the noble, new or old, was likely at this time to be contemplating the erection of a mansion, designed to demonstrate his wealth and taste. In the time of Henry IV this building was normally in a traditional French style, using brick for the body of the work and stone to strengthen it at the corners and around the windows. Under Louis XIII, however, this native style increasingly gave way before a fresh wave of Italian influence. Now the château was more likely to be built entirely of stone and to incorporate such Italian features as colonnades and cupolas.

What was true of country houses was also true of urban architecture. Even the greatest squares erected in Paris by Henry IV have a certain homely touch, with their warm brick and stone and their intimate proportions. In the time of Louis XIII this native style was ousted by a return to elaborate façades, with columns and domes, of which the Luxembourg palace is typical. In ecclesiastical architecture too the Italian influence was strong, inspiring churches like the chapels of the Val-de-Grâce and of the Sorbonne.

This struggle between native and Italian influences is also found in the painting of the period. The le Nain brothers, whose subject-matter was found mostly at rural inns and on farms, were the representatives of the rustic native school. In the same way, the robust and shockingly realistic engravings of Jacques Callot owe nothing to Italy, while the work of Philippe de Champaigne derives from a general European tradition in portraiture. With Claude Lorrain, however, we reach a painter heavily influenced by the Italians; indeed, he lived most of his life in Italy. The great Nicolas Poussin, too, was an 'Italian', not only in his style but also in his subject-matter, often derived from the legends of antiquity.

It seems to be true that in the visual arts—and there is proof in this from the 'minor arts' as well—the reign of Henry IV saw the shortlived emergence of a national French school, rapidly crushed out after 1610 by the fresh Italian wave. It is tempting to link this cultural phenomenon with contemporary political events, and to suggest that the essentially national political compromise worked out by Henry IV reflected itself in a fresh national art, whereas the reversion to the Spanish alliance in politics and to ultramontanism (literally, what is 'south of the Alps', i.e. by derivation excessively 'Roman') in religion resulted necessarily in a turning-away from these native sources in favour of the devices of Counter-Reformation Italy. Be that as it may, it is certain that in the visual arts the period is one of striking contrast in styles.

The same is true of literature, where on the one hand we have the tortured, elaborate and very long-winded novels of writers like

Left, Hagar and the Angel *(1668) by Claude* *Lorraine (1600–82), the French landscape painter* *who worked closely within the Italian tradition.* *National Gallery, London.*

Opposite, the Luxembourg Palace in Paris, built *between 1615 and 1620 for Marie de' Medici and* *decorated by Rubens. In style it is heavily reliant* *on Italian models.*

Left, Landscape with a Snake *by Nicholas* *Poussin (1594–1665), whose ordered, balanced* *compositions expressed the intellectual aims of* *contemporary French classicism. National* *Gallery, London.*

Honoré d'Urfé (1567–1625), while on the other there is the move towards a sparer, more precise use of language advocated by François de Malherbe (1555–1628). The cause of the purists gradually gained ground, with the publication of the grammar of Claude de Vaugelas (1585–1650) and still more with Richelieu's foundation in 1634 of the *Académie française*, one of whose aims was precisely to purify the French language and to free it from 'baroque' new words and phrases.

Absolutism

It was characteristic of the direction that France took in the time of Richelieu that its Academy should have been founded and sustained by the government, whereas in countries like England and Holland such societies remained distinct from the machinery of the state. Under the great cardinal the state had to have its finger in every pie. Trading companies were organized by the state. The *parlements* had to toe the state's line. Architects were commissioned to glorify the state. Factories were founded and controlled by the state. Painters were required to exalt the power and majesty of the king and his ministers. In a word, the state sought to control all activities within its boundaries.

As we have seen, in so doing it roused fierce practical opposition from many different groups, peasants, nobles, lawyers and so on. There was also a 'philosophical' opposition, which grew stronger as the century advanced. Many thinkers in France and elsewhere, from the time of St Thomas More onwards, found it disquieting that Europe seemed to be slipping into the system of collective selfishness which is nationalism.

Some based their protests on the Christian idea of brotherhood of peoples. Others merely pointed out the fact that sovereign units, each acknowledging no good above itself, were bound to come into conflict. The church had not in fact been as universal as it had claimed, but it had after all provided some general framework over and above the rivalries of the medieval 'nations'; now for half Europe there was no such general arbiter.

The idea of common brotherhood expressed itself in economic terms by opposition to commercial policies. It seemed to men like Jean Bodin (1530–96) that the Creator had made the different geographical regions so that each should excel in producing certain goods. It was therefore foolish—worse, impious—for countries to attempt to become self-sufficient, since this was not only economically inefficient but disruptive of the divine plan.

Bodin was a thinker whose works are full of paradoxes, and it is easy to represent him also as the apologist for the absolute state. But in another way too he was its opponent, in his insistence that the king should if possible 'live of his own'. Like many of his contemporaries, he viewed with dismay the growth of the fiscal machinery of the Crown, with all that it would eventually bring in the way of government by officialdom.

The whole process of bureaucratization was of course greatly accelerated, and indeed perhaps initiated, byt the demands of war. In the France of Henry IV and of Richelieu we see the embryonic emergence of the military state, with its uniformed men and their uniform minds geared to a system of mass production for the conflicts. It is all the more ironic that this anti-humanitarian and 'irreligious' development was presided over by a great prince of the ancient church.

Above, The Farm Waggon *(1641) painted by Louis Le Nain. The realism, the lack of drama and stylization, and the clearly observed, everyday subject mark the work of this artist as highly unusual in an age dominated by the styles of Italy. Musée du Louvre, Paris.*

Chapter 4

Spain under Philip III and Philip IV

At the beginning of the seventeenth century, the power of the Spanish kings still seemed invincible. Philip III (1598–1621) ruled not only extensive and wealthy regions of Europe but also immense territories in the New World, from which he drew great supplies of silver. It would not have been easy to predict in 1600 that in fifty years' time this great empire would have been generally defeated in Europe. Yet so it was: the Dutch formally gained their independence in 1648, and the French ate into Spanish possessions all along the Rhine. In 1640 the Portuguese broke away, and only in Italy did the Spaniards remain in control of their territories for a little longer.

The latter years of Philip II's reign saw a series of poor harvests in Castile (by 'Castile' is meant the whole group of central provinces) and this time of famine was followed, as so often happened, by a great plague during the years 1599 and 1600. However, these spectacular catastrophes were in a sense not unexpected, for Castilian agriculture had been showing signs of weakness for at least fifty years previously. Whereas at the start of the century central Spain had been a great corn producing region, by 1570 it was heavily dependent on imports of grain from northern and eastern Europe. Many peasants fled from their holdings, driven to despair by the harshness of nature and the demands of the tax-gatherers.

If agriculture was in full decline, industry and commerce were also faltering. By the end of the century the Spanish colonies in the New World had become largely self-sufficient in those commodities which the Spaniards had formerly exported to them. Any attempt by the Spaniards to switch to new products was hampered by the fact that English and Dutch interlopers increasingly tended to encroach on the former Spanish preserve and to satisfy the colonists' fresh requirements with their own products. The Spaniards, like most imperial peoples, were loth to change the attitudes and methods which had won them such remarkable successes.

That is not to say that they were unwilling to think about their predicament. The later sixteenth century saw the publication of many works by the so-called *arbitristas*

('projectors', or formulators of policy), and their advice was always the same: reduce government expenditure, revise the tax-structure so that it was more equitably shared among classes and provinces, encourage immigration and offer new incentives to farmers and manufacturers.

Philip III and Lerma

1598 saw not only the death of Philip II but also the Treaty of Vervins, marking the end of the war with France. Philip's successor therefore had an interval of peace in which to put his house in order. Philip III, however, was not the man to take this chance. He soon allowed himself to fall into the hands of a favourite, the Duke of Lerma, and together they adopted a policy of masterly inertia, hoping in Micawberish fashion that something would turn up to remedy the monarchy's deep-rooted ills. Needless to say, nothing did turn up, and during the reign of Philip III (1598–1621) Spain's economic and social discontents went from bad to worse.

The royal bankruptcy of 1607 forced upon Lerma the one constructive act of his period of power: the conclusion of a truce with the United Provinces in 1609. That year also saw the expulsion of the Moriscos, an act which has for generations been seized on by historians eager to perpetuate the Black Legend of Spanish ignorance and bigotry. The Moriscos were in fact Moors who had been forcibly 'converted' to Christianity

Above, Philip III of Spain (reigned 1598–1621); he sought peace with his father's many enemies, but was able to do little positive to restore Spain's prosperity, and in 1620 he was dragged into the Thirty Years' War. Hampton Court Palace.

Top, the European possessions of Philip III of Spain in the early seventeenth century. Protecting the vital overland route from Spain to the Low Countries was the main aim of Spanish policy in the Thirty Years' War.

after the reconquest of 1492. Needless to say, the loyalty of these 'New Christians' was suspect, and it is certain that in the early seventeenth century they were intriguing not only with the Muslim Turks in north Africa but also with the French Protestants in Béarn.

To these good political reasons for their expulsion were added less reputable economic ones. Many Valencian lords whose tenants were Old Christians were envious of the prosperity apparently brought to their neighbours by Morisco tenants, and many small men among the Old Christians were frankly hungry for the Moriscos' land. So in 1609 the expulsion was carried through, and of a total Morisco population of about 300,000 perhaps 275,000 were obliged to take ship for the inhospitable shores of north Africa.

In the Black Legend this act has been made to look like an economic catastrophe. But in fact its effects are very difficult to assess, for most of the Moriscos, although hard-working, were not great proprietors or businessmen, and it is possible that many of the jobs and plots of land which they vacated were filled quickly enough. All the same, what might have been a politically acceptable act in a prosperous country was one of grave imprudence in a kingdom whose economy was declining as rapidly as Spain's was; if the expulsion was not a political crime, it was certainly an economic blunder of the first order.

Philip IV and Olivares

Philip III died in 1621 and was succeeded by his son Philip IV. That year too the truce of 1609 with the Dutch expired, so that the young king was at once faced with the need to confront his enemies. Philip IV was more intelligent than his father but had the same lack of drive. Therefore it was fortunate that he chose as his chief minister the dynamic Duke of Olivares, who had been a gentleman of his household.

Throughout his ministry Olivares was torn between two conflicting aims. He appreciated the arguments of the *arbitristas*, and realized that economic, fiscal and administrative reforms were essential if the Spanish monarchy were to retain its power.

At the same time, he inherited the Castilian ambitions for European and indeed worldwide leadership. In fact, it was impossible to pursue these two goals simultaneously, as time would show.

From the start Olivares was obliged to face up to the Dutch and to order a considerable increase in expenditure on the Atlantic fleet. Simultaneously, he authorized a great expansion in the army of Flanders, so that for 1622 projected expenditure was about double projected income. To meet this deficit, he cut royal pensions drastically and pushed through some of the minor reforms called for by the *arbitristas*.

What was needed, however, was to persuade the other provinces, and particularly

Catalonia and Portugal, to help Castile to shoulder the increasingly heavy military burden. Thus during 1624 Olivares worked out the details of the so-called 'Union of Arms', which was to be achieved by all the different components of the monarchy combining to support an army 140,000 strong. Early in 1626 he and the king attended meetings of the *cortes* or parliaments of Aragon, Valencia and Catalonia and succeeded in extracting from them, if not full assent to the Union of Arms, at least substantial contributions for the common military effort.

Meanwhile some of Olivares' other projects were going ahead well. In 1625 Spanish troops captured Breda from the Dutch, and that same year there was founded at Madrid the *colegia imperial*. This was a Jesuit academy for the sons of nobles, designed to provide not only a humanistic education but also a training in the military arts. Olivares hoped that this college would remedy what he sometimes called a 'lack of leadership' among the Spanish people. By 1627 he could boast of considerable reforms achieved at home and of significant victories won abroad.

The year 1628, however, proved to be the turning-point in his administration. In that year it looked as if he could at last concentrate seriously on domestic reform, for the English were disunited, the Habsburgs were victorious in Germany and Richelieu was fully occupied by the Huguenots in France.

This great and final chance for a drastic reorganization of domestic policy was however lost, because Olivares could not resist intervening in the war which broke out over the succession to Mantua (1628–31). Thereafter Spain became increasingly involved in the German aspects of the Thirty Years' War and was obliged to squander what remained of her resources in the struggle against the French and their allies.

At first this struggle did not go badly, and in 1636, as we have seen, a Spanish force seriously threatened Paris. However, by the late 1630s it was clear that Spain's enemies were getting the upper hand, as each year brought a fresh disaster. In 1637 came the loss of Breda, recaptured by the Dutch, 1638 the fall of Breisach, and with it the loss of Spanish control over the route between Italy and the Netherlands, 1639 the defeat of a great Spanish fleet in the Downs and the end of any hope of sending relief to Spanish troops in the Netherlands.

But it was 1640 which was the really disastrous year. Castilian troops had been sent into Catalonia to repel the French attack from the north. As no money was available, they had been billeted on the Catalans, and in the early spring of 1640 many clashes took place between these troops and their unwilling hosts. At first Olivares reacted with severity, but as this only aggravated the populace he eventually ordered the viceroy to attempt to appease

Above, the Spanish flagship in action in the Battle of the Downs in 1639, at which the Dutch demonstrated their control of the Channel and ended Spanish hopes of prolonging their resistance to Dutch independence. Nederlandsch Historisch Scheepvaart Museum, Amsterdam.

Opposite top left, the expulsion of the Moriscos, or converted Moors, from Spain in 1609; Philip was unwilling to be king of a country peopled by converts of dubious faith. For the most part the Moriscos had inhabited the southern regions of Spain, especially Granada. Museo del Prado, Madrid.

Opposite bottom left, the Duke of Olivares (1587–1645), painted by Velasquez. Olivares was chief minister of Spain from 1620 to 1641, and his need to promote Spain's interests in the Thirty Years' War resulted in widespread opposition to his rule, especially in the non-Castilian parts of Spain. Hispanic Society of America, New York.

Opposite bottom right, The Relief of Cadiz in 1625, painted by Francisco de Zurbaran in 1634. Museo del Prado, Madrid.

45

the Catalans by concessions. Too late; the viceroy was himself hunted down and killed, while the rebels proclaimed Louis XIII Count of Barcelona, which now formed part of the republic of Catalonia.

Richelieu had encouraged and organized the revolt of the Catalans; he seems also to have subsidized the Portuguese rebellion, which broke out in December 1640 and resulted in the establishment of John IV as an independent king. With his resources already strained to the limit. Olivares could do little about this secession; he struggled on for a couple of years but then resigned in 1643 and died half-mad in 1645. So ended his valiant attempt to bring order into the chaotic peninsula under a unified central government.

Rocroi and after

The year of his resignation saw the defeat of the hitherto invincible Spanish infantry at Rocroi; thereafter it was just a question of how soon Spain could make peace and how humiliating would be the price she would have to pay. The successor of Olivares was his nephew, Don Luis de Haro, and this discreet, self-effacing courtier was well-suited to retrieve what could be recovered from the general wreck.

In spite of another bankruptcy in 1647, in the following year he succeeded in persuading the Dutch, who by now were beginning to fear the rising power of France, to make a peace. It was at Münster in October 1648 that the seventy-year long struggle was formally ended, when Spain at last recognized the independence and sovereignty of the United Provinces.

Meanwhile there was for a time doubt whether Madrid could recover Catalonia, let alone Portugal. Throughout the mid-1640s the eastern provinces, Aragon and Valencia as well as Catalonia, seemed to be tottering off into independence. However, Olivares' very failure to establish a unified central government was now, paradoxically enough, the saving of the monarchy. In the eastern provinces the

nobility had retained a considerable degree of independence, and the aristocracy there now saw that a loose confederation with Madrid was preferable to a perilous autonomy, in which revolutionary elements might begin to have more influence.

So the Valencians and Aragonese came once more to acknowledge a loose dependence on the government of Haro. Meanwhile the Catalans had lost much of their French support when Mazarin's government became preoccupied with its own internal troubles, and after a slow and painful campaign the Castilian troops were able to recapture Barcelona late in 1652. Thus the possibility of the peninsula reverting to a political structure of three or more sovereign units was averted, the provinces not only fearing to encourage their own revolutionary element but also realizing that dependence on a powerful French monarchy would in the long run be more harmful to them than a loose attachment to the feeble crown at Madrid.

During the 1650s, indeed, the French government was so weakened by internal problems that the Castilian armies were even able to push Mazarin's forces back here and there. By 1659 it was possible for Haro to conclude a relatively favourable peace with France. This so-called 'Treaty of the Pyrenees' recognized that Spain had lost Artois as well as Roussillon and parts of Cerdagne, but this settlement seems moderate bearing in mind Spain's desperate position in 1640.

Her main loss was, of course, the kingdom of Portugal, which remained independent under the Duke of Braganza, John IV. Castile had only acquired Portugal in 1580, and sixty years had not been long enough to reconcile the traditional hostility between the peoples. Moreover, Portugal was independent in a way that Catalonia could never hope to be; she not only had a ready-made dynasty in the Braganza family but could also look to her Atlantic connections for a sound economic basis to her power. In fact, during the 1650s the Portuguese succeeded in reversing the trend of the previous decades when they expelled the Dutch from Brazil; after that they were well set on the way to real independence and a moderate prosperity.

The Spaniards did not recognize Portuguese independence until 1668. By then Philip IV had been dead for three years, having been succeeded by his son Charles II, an apparently sickly individual whose death would be daily awaited by European diplomats for the next thirty-five years. The infanta Maria Teresa had in 1660 married Louis XIV of France, thereby encouraging those French pretensions to the Spanish throne which would only be shattered by the long and costly war of the Spanish succession early in the next century.

All that, however, is another sad tale. No historian who has described the sequence of Spanish decline can resist trying to understand why it came about. For most eighteenth-century 'enlightened' writers, it was the inevitable result of superstitious religion, allied to 'Spanish sloth'. Clearly this explanation is inadequate to explain the transition from the triumphant Spain of the mid-sixteenth century to the wreck of the mid-seventeenth century. However, it does bring out two features of Spanish society which crucially influenced the development of the peninsula: its peoples were devoted to the old church, and they did prize the military virtues above commercial techniques.

Nor was this surprising, given their history: that of a small Christian kingdom, at first penned into the northwestern corner, gradually recovering land from the Moors until the triumphant reconquest of Granada in 1492. During this process, lasting for many centuries, Spanish Christianity acquired a zeal and a militancy which were not found in the more settled regions of western Europe like France or Italy. In a sense, it was this long formation in the struggle against the Moors which made the Spanish conquest of the New World so successful. The conquistadores and their followers were clearly the product of a Catholic and military society such as existed at that time.

However, what had been virtues in 1300 or 1500 were beginning to become vices by 1600. By then the need was for a society which could adapt itself to changing circumstances in order to strengthen its empire in Europe and overseas; more specifically, for a society which could strengthen its economic framework by adopting new techniques in agriculture and industry as well as commerce. It is not surprising that Spanish society, founded in response to quite different challenges, could not rapidly make this transition. Its failure is characteristic of the inability of imperial peoples to adjust to the new realities of power.

So while Dutch and English interlopers drove an ever more thriving trade with the Spanish colonies, industry and trade in the peninsula declined, and political problems became more and more pressing. For the sake of convenience we have used the terms 'Spain' and 'Spaniard', but in fact the political structure of the peninsula was such that these terms do not mean much during the sixteenth and seventeenth centuries. The fifteenth-century union of Castile and Aragon was a dynastic marriage, never consummated on an economic and political level. For all intents and purposes, 'Spain' really meant 'Castile'; the Aragonese continued throughout the period to be excluded from both the burdens and the fruits of empire.

Eventually, of course, the burden of colonizing the New World and subjecting the Old became too much even for the Castilians, and they tried—most notably in the time of Olivares—to draw the rest of the peninsula more fully into their plans. By then though it was too late; defeat in war, economic decline and the inevitable tensions of a mixed society combined to bring on the collapse of the 1640s. It has been well said that 'Castile has made Spain, and Castile has destroyed it'.

The end of the golden age

The sixteenth century saw remarkable achievements in almost every aspect of human activity. There were great mystics like St John of the Cross and St Teresa of Avila, great political theorists like Francisco de Vitoria and Bartolomé de Las Casas, great architects like Juan de Herrera; the list seems endless and extends as well into the natural sciences. The reigns of Philip III and Philip IV witnessed a less varied cultural activity and were chiefly

Above, The Surrender of Breda *(1634), painted by Diego Velasquez (1599–1660). Museo del Prado, Madrid.*

Opposite left, Philip IV of Spain (reigned 1621–65), portrayed by Velasquez. During his reign Spain had to acknowledge the independence of both the United Provinces and Portugal, which had rebelled in 1640, but he was able to avoid permanent French control of Catalonia. Museo del Prado, Madrid.

Opposite right, The Burial of the Count of Orgaz *(1586) by El Greco (1545–1614). Portraits of the notables of Toledo are here juxtaposed with a grand vision of heaven. Santo Tome, Toledo.*

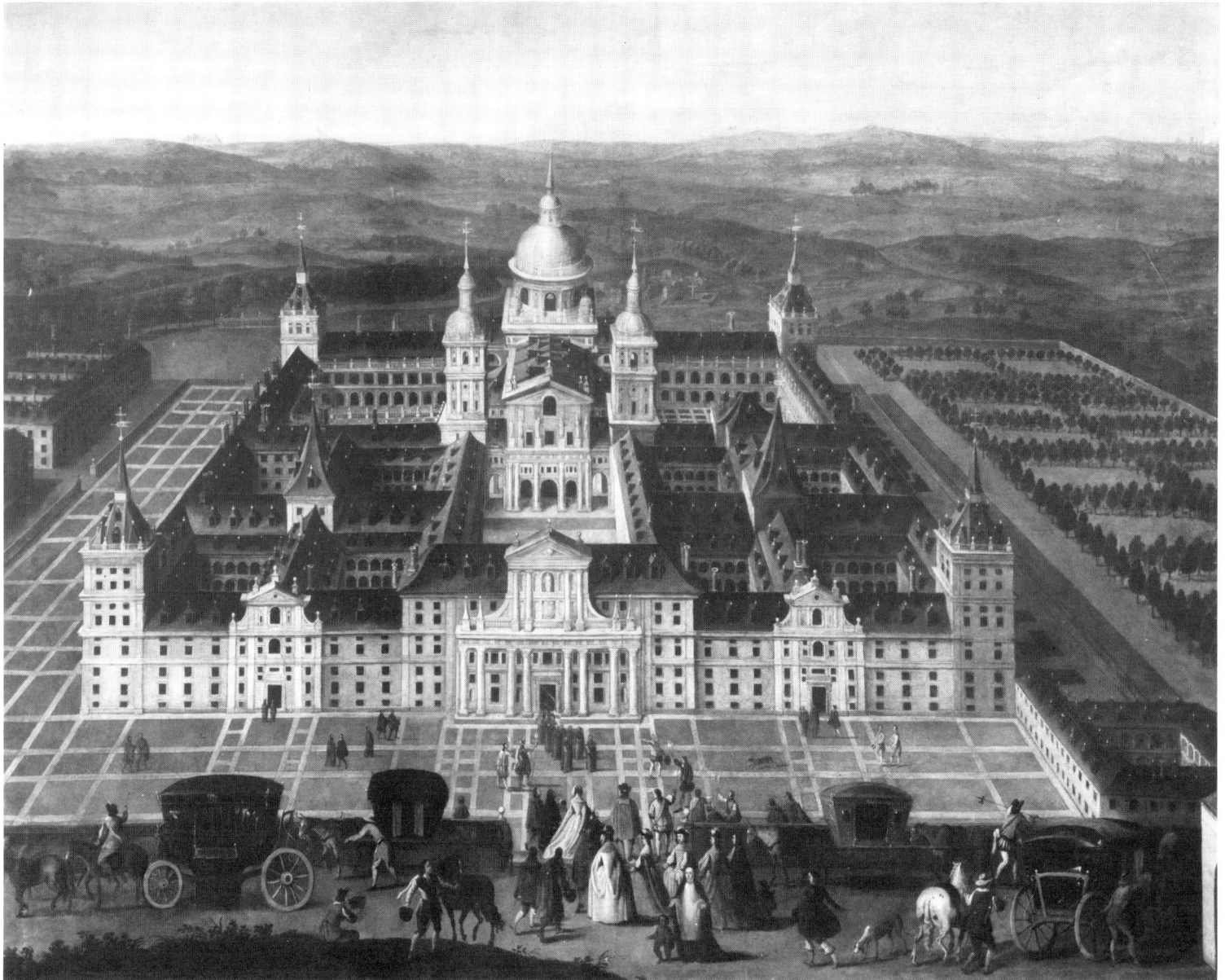

remarkable for their literature and their painting. No doubt this had something to do with the economic situation. The fact, for instance, that the Plaza Mayor of Madrid (1617–19) was the one major new enterprise undertaken at this time probably reflects Spain's increasing impoverishment.

Literature, however, does not demand investment on a large scale, and the wealth of writers in early seventeenth-century Spain is extraordinary. Miguel de Cervantes lived until 1616, producing his works not only during the heroic decades but also during those of disillusionment. *Don Quixote* he created an immortal figure, humanely mocking knightly ideals. This baroque sense of 'illusionism' pervades the work of Cervantes' successors, writers like Lope de Vega Carpio (1562–1635), Francisco Quevedo (1580–1645) and Pedro Calderon de la Barca (1600–81). All were obsessed by the contrast between fact and fancy, between the ideal and the real, between the world as it was and the world as it might have been. So Calderon could write his celebrated and symptomatic *Life Is a Dream*, and Quevedo

could typically exclaim that 'our life is but a comedy, and the whole world a comic theatre'.

It is, perhaps, not too farfetched to suggest that seventeenth-century Spanish writers took refuge in fantasy because the realities of the Spanish situation were too harsh to be faced. It is certainly true that they remained impregnated with the idea that all human activities are vain in comparison with the transcendent reality of God, and some of them carried this conviction over into their lives. Calderon, for instance, entered holy orders in middle age after serving in the royal armies. So one may assume that what was psychologically true for some of the leading writers was also true for the many Spaniards who shared with them these polarizing loyalties.

The concepts of honour and faith underlying much of the literature of the period also inspired seventeenth-century Spanish painters. El Greco (1545–1614), near-contemporary of Cervantes, showed the way in his mystically realistic canvasses, one of the most characteristic of which is the *Burial of*

the Count of Orgaz. Later in the century the works of Bartolome Murillo (1617–82) provided powerful propaganda for the Roman Church of the Counter-Reformation. Murillo is especially remarkable for the skill and feeling with which he painted the Virgin Mary. The subjects of Francisco de Zurburan (1598–1664), too, were usually religious; either tranquil, determined female saints, or monkish ascetics whose intense devotion is most realistically portrayed.

The greatest of them all, of course, was Diego Velasquez (1599–1660). Velasquez drew his inspiration from the Crown rather than from the church and showed an unparalleled virtuosity in his paintings of the Spanish royal family. One of his most famous canvasses shows *The Surrender of Breda* and is unforgettable for the way in which the lances of the victorious Spanish army dominate the right background. In much of his work, however, there is a strain of disillusionment—look, for instance, at many of his royal portraits—which seems to echo the same strain in the great dramatists. The Spaniards of the seventeenth century had lost the easy self-confidence of their fathers, but in literature and art they were technically supreme in expressing this mood of disenchantment.

The Spanish possessions in Europe

Curiously enough, one of the great master-painters of the age, Peter Paul Rubens (1577–1640), was produced by the small and battered Spanish Netherlands. Deprived by the Dutch of access to the sea, the southern Netherlands were about to enter a period of political effacement which would last until the re-opening of the Scheldt in the early nineteenth century restored to Antwerp access to the high seas.

In Italy the Spaniards still held much territory and were particularly concerned to retain their route to the Low Countries, which passed through Genoa and Milan before continuing through Switzerland, Franche-Comté and Luxembourg. Energetic Spanish proconsuls like the Count of Fuentes ensured that even in the days of Philip III Spanish rule was uncontested in Genoa and the Milanese.

To the northwest of this central bloc lay the duchy of Savoy, whose rulers would tread a delicate line for the next century between France and Spain—a policy of masterly vacillation rewarded at Utrecht in 1713, when the reigning duke received the crown of Sicily and so set his house on the way to becoming Italy's first royal line. To the northeast of the Spanish bloc were the possessions of Venice. During the seventeenth century the proud republic fell into an irreversible decline, as the economic foundations of her power were sapped. Yet she retained her political independence and a degree of agricultural prosperity right down to the nineteenth century.

In central Italy the chief princes were the dukes of Tuscany, Spanish clients, and the popes. After the triumphant years of the Counter-Reformation the papacy too declined, as was exemplified by its exclusion from the peace treaties of the middle of the seventeenth century. All the same, Rome continued to be the centre of a now world-wide network of bishops and religions, exercising a steady if unspectacular influence on all the regions colonized by Catholic Europeans. The great city was also at this period being architecturally transformed, most notably by the genius of Bernini (1598–1680).

In southern Italy the Spaniards controlled the kingdom of Naples and the island of Sicily, and, as in the north, they retained their power through the action of vigorous viceroys like the Duke of Osuna. Naples and Sicily were very heavily taxed during the first half of the seventeenth century, and in 1647 the Neopolitan populace, led by a young fishmonger called Masaniello, broke into spontaneous revolt.

At first the Spanish viceroy, the Duke of Arcos, was disconcerted and indeed narrowly escaped with his life. But then, as it became clear to the Neapolitan nobility that they would not profit by the establishment of the republic, the revolt lost momentum, and in 1648 the Spaniards were able to reassert their power. The repression was horribly thorough, and in Naples as in the rest of Italy the Spaniards experienced little more trouble until their Italian possessions passed to the house of Austria by the treaty of Rastadt (1714).

In the long run, this repressive rule had disastrous consequences for Italy. Her central political and economic position was already being challenged by the development of the Atlantic world, and the stifling influence of the Spanish rule meant that the peoples of the peninsula had no chance of adapting themselves to the new economic, political and cultural patterns. Italy, which in the sixteenth century and earlier had been the mistress of Europe in economic and cultural affairs, had by the end of the seventeenth century become one of Europe's stagnant backwaters.

Above, the piazza of St Peter's Cathedral, in Rome, designed by Bernini and one of the greatest expressions of the Baroque in town planning.

Opposite, the Escorial, a combination of palace, monastery and mausoleum, built by Philip II in 1563–84, shown here in a painting of the seventeenth century. Musée du Louvre, Paris.

Chapter 5

The Thirty Years' War

The title of this chapter, drawn from the conventions of historiography, is misleading. We are concerned here not merely with a 'German' conflict originating in 1618 and ending in 1648 but with a European convulsion which, first making itself felt in 1609, was not settled until 1659. This fifty years' war is incomprehensible without a knowledge of those non-German conflicts which helped to determine its development, chiefly of course the abiding rivalry between the Bourbons (of whom the first was Henry IV) and the Spanish, as well as the Austrian Habsburgs. By the time the dust had begun to settle, in 1660, the political shape of Europe for the next two centuries was beginning to emerge.

The conflict known as the Thirty Years' War arose directly out of the religious and administrative settlement of the mid-sixteenth century known as the Peace of Ausburg. For religious affairs, this treaty aimed at freezing the positions achieved by the Catholics and Lutherans—the Calvinists were excluded—in 1555. Evidently, it was severely strained in the decades which followed by the continuing progress of Lutheranism and even more by the development of Calvinism. Moreover, once the tide began to turn in Germany against the reformed churches, the champions of the ancient church could find many infringements of the treaty on which to base their claims to repossess formerly Catholic territories.

The Augsburg settlement was not merely a religious truce but also included provisions for keeping peace within the ten 'circles' of the Holy Roman Empire. In principle each of these was controlled by a presiding prince dependent on the emperor, but in practice the territorial princes—of whom the most outstanding were the seven imperial electors—enjoyed a large degree of freedom. One of the issues at stake in the struggle was precisely this: how close a control could the emperor exercise over his crumbling feudal pyramid?

Within Germany, then, the interests at stake were complex enough. What further complicated the long struggle was the fact that these internal conflicts were overlaid by other rivalries among the European powers. The Swedes and the Danes, for instance, were crucially interested in the control of the shores of the Baltic. The Dutch could not look on unconcerned while territories in the Rhineland changed hands. The French saw in the German struggle an occasion to prosecute their ancient campaign against the Habsburgs. Even the King of England at one stage intervened in the struggle, singularly ineffectively it is true.

The international nature of the conflict was clear from the start. When in 1608 the Protestant princes and cities formed a defensive pact, the Union, it was to Henry IV of France that they looked for support. Similarly, the Catholic league founded a few months later relied from the start on subsidies from Philip III of Spain.

France and Spain also intervened quite openly in the first dispute to test the strength of these two hostile camps. This dispute broke out over the succession to the Rhineland duchy of Jülich-Cleves, whose duke died without heir in 1609. There were both Protestant and Catholic claimants. At first Jülich was occupied by the imperial emissary, but then he was expelled by Dutch troops, aided by a French contingent.

In the early months of 1610 Henry IV of France was mobilizing a large army, with a view to consolidating the Protestant position in the Rhineland and elsewhere. This projected campaign would no doubt have led to a general conflict, but the French king was assassinated before it could get under way. The imperial side was unable to take advantage of his disappearance, since these were the uncertain last months of the unstable emperor, Rudolf II (1576–1612). Moreover, the new rulers, Marie de Medici in Paris and Mathias at Vienna were moderates for the time being. The spectre of a general war thus disappeared.

The Bohemian War (1618–27)

The next major dispute arose over the throne of Bohemia. This predominantly Protestant kingdom, with proud memories both of independence and of the days of the fifteenth-century reformer John Hus, was governed from Prague by a group of Catholic nobles. The Habsburgs claimed that the crown of Bohemia fell by heredity to the Holy Roman emperor, and the Bohemians had in fact accepted both Rudolf II (1576–1612) and Mathias (1612–19) as their king.

Before the death of Mathias in 1619, they had also agreed that his successor should be Ferdinand of Styria, a prince noted for the ruthlessness with which he had crushed Protestantism out of his Austrian territories. Encouraged by the acceptance of Ferdinand, the Catholic group at Prague stepped up their attempts to reconvert the kingdom, and by 1618 their actions had so exasperated the Protestant majority that the latter resolved to break from the Habsburgs. The symbolic occasion of this break was the famous 'defenestration of Prague', when two of the Catholic governors and their secretary were thrown out of the window of the castle in which the Protestant nobles were assembled.

The consequences of this act of rebellion had been weighed by the Bohemian nobles, who in the inevitable struggle with the Habsburgs expected to get help from the Protestant powers of Europe—notably Holland, England and Sweden. Thus when Mathias died in 1619 they proceeded with the election of Frederick, the elector palatine of the Rhine, as his successor, declaring the claims of Ferdinand to be rejected. Almost as soon as Frederick had been elected King

of Bohemia, however, Ferdinand was elected emperor; clearly the latter's first act would be to move against his rebellious Bohemian subjects.

At this stage the behaviour of the Bohemian rebels was foolish and vague in the extreme. Having elected the ineffectual Frederick as their king, they did little to help him. Had they attempted to win over the middle and lower classes in Bohemia to his cause, they might have been able to present a united front to the imperial armies. As it was, rather like the noble rebels of Catalonia or Naples a little later, they refused to abandon their feudal privileges in favour of the common cause. Moreover, they failed to gain that help from abroad on which they were counting. The kings of England and of Sweden were unwilling to involve themselves, and the Dutch were at this period distracted by a constitutional crisis which ended in the execution of the Dutch statesman Oldenbarneveldt after a highly irregular trial for treason.

So in 1620 the imperial armies entered Bohemia virtually unopposed. They brushed Frederick's army aside before Prague at the battle of the White Hill and entered the capital in triumph. The royal family fled to the Netherlands, and the subjection of Bohemia was set in hand. By 1627 it had become a hereditary Habsburg possession, administered by royal officials, with towns and nobles curbed, German the official language and Catholicism the only permitted religion.

The Danish War (1625–29)

The subjection of Bohemia was in a sense a sideshow, since none of the major Protestant powers had cared to come to its help. In the early 1620s the true focus of the conflict was the Rhineland, where hostilities had broken out following the termination in 1621 of the Dutch-Spanish truce of 1609. The Spanish general Spinola undertook campaigns which enjoyed a steady success; he recovered Jülich in 1622 and in 1625 Breda itself fell to Spanish arms.

Meanwhile Olivares had planned a great shipping and trading alliance to break the power of the Dutch. The members of this alliance were to be Spain, the Spanish Netherlands, the Hansa towns and Poland; with this combination Olivares hoped to carry to war into the Dutch preserves in the Baltic and so to ease the pressure on the Spanish colonies in the New World. The Dutch were thoroughly alarmed by this plan, for which Spinola's successes seemed to be laying sound foundations, and so in 1625 by the treaty of The Hague they formed an offensive alliance with England and Denmark.

The chief captain of the anti-imperial forces was Ernest of Mansfeld, and their campaign opened in 1626. They were opposed, however, by the remarkable imperial General Wallenstein, whose colleague Tilly in August inflicted a severe defeat on the Danes at Lutter. Meanwhile the allies' other thrusts at the Habsburg perimeter were not very successful, largely because they could not manage to co-ordinate their efforts. The chief feature of the later 1620s was Wallenstein's steady extension and consolidation of his power in north Germany, in accordance with Olivares' plans for an economic and military offensive against the Dutch. Wismar fell to him in 1627 and Rostock in 1628; only Stralsund held out, thanks to the fleets of Denmark and Sweden. By 1629 the anti-imperial league was defeated; the English were willing enough to withdraw, and the Danes accepted the peace of Lübeck, agreeing to interfere no more in German affairs.

The Emperor Ferdinand now took advantage of his excellent position to issue an imperial decree known as the 'edict of restitution'. This document is often represented as primarily religious, enforcing the restoration to the old church of all property seized since 1552 and so re-establishing the power of Catholicism throughout northern and northwestern Germany. However, it also had great constitutional significance, for in recognizing Habsburg rule over that region it seemed to give to the emperor those absolute powers which the German princes had for centuries sought to deny him. Hence the edict stirred up great resentment among the princes, Catholic as well as Protestant, and at Regensburg in 1630 the electors succeeded in forcing Ferdinand to dismiss Wallenstein, whom they rightly saw as the chief instrument of the emperor's forward policy. In the long run, by making plain Ferdinand's religious and constitutional ambitions, the edict of restitution was a great blunder. Ferdinand did not know how to hasten slowly, and consequently lost his great general just when he needed him most.

The Swedish phase (1630–34)

After the withdrawal of the Danes, a new and more formidable antagonist appeared in the north: Gustavus Adolphus, after some months of deliberation, resolved to pit his armies against those of the Habsburgs. The Swedish king had since his accession in 1611 effected a remarkable reorganization of his kingdom. Whereas in countries like France the offices of the ancient nobility—constable, marshal and so on—were being crushed out by the emergence of new bureaucratic forms, in Sweden Gustavus Adolphus contrived to bring off a happy marriage between them and the councils which he set up for the army, for finances, for justice and so on.

This efficient administrative structure was backed by an economy which thrived on Dutch business enterprise and particularly on the lucrative export of Swedish copper. Many of the new industries were based on military products, and Gustavus Adolphus proved adept at reorganizing his army so as to profit by the ideas of Maurice of Nassau, the late Prince of Orange, who had virtually established Dutch independence; the artillery was made relatively light and mobile, the cavalry and infantry were trained to fight in smaller units, and the three arms were brought under more effective battlefield control.

The soldiers of Sweden also enjoyed exceptionally high morale. By his victories over the Poles and Russians the king had rapidly become a great hero-figure, and in their German campaigns the Swedes were

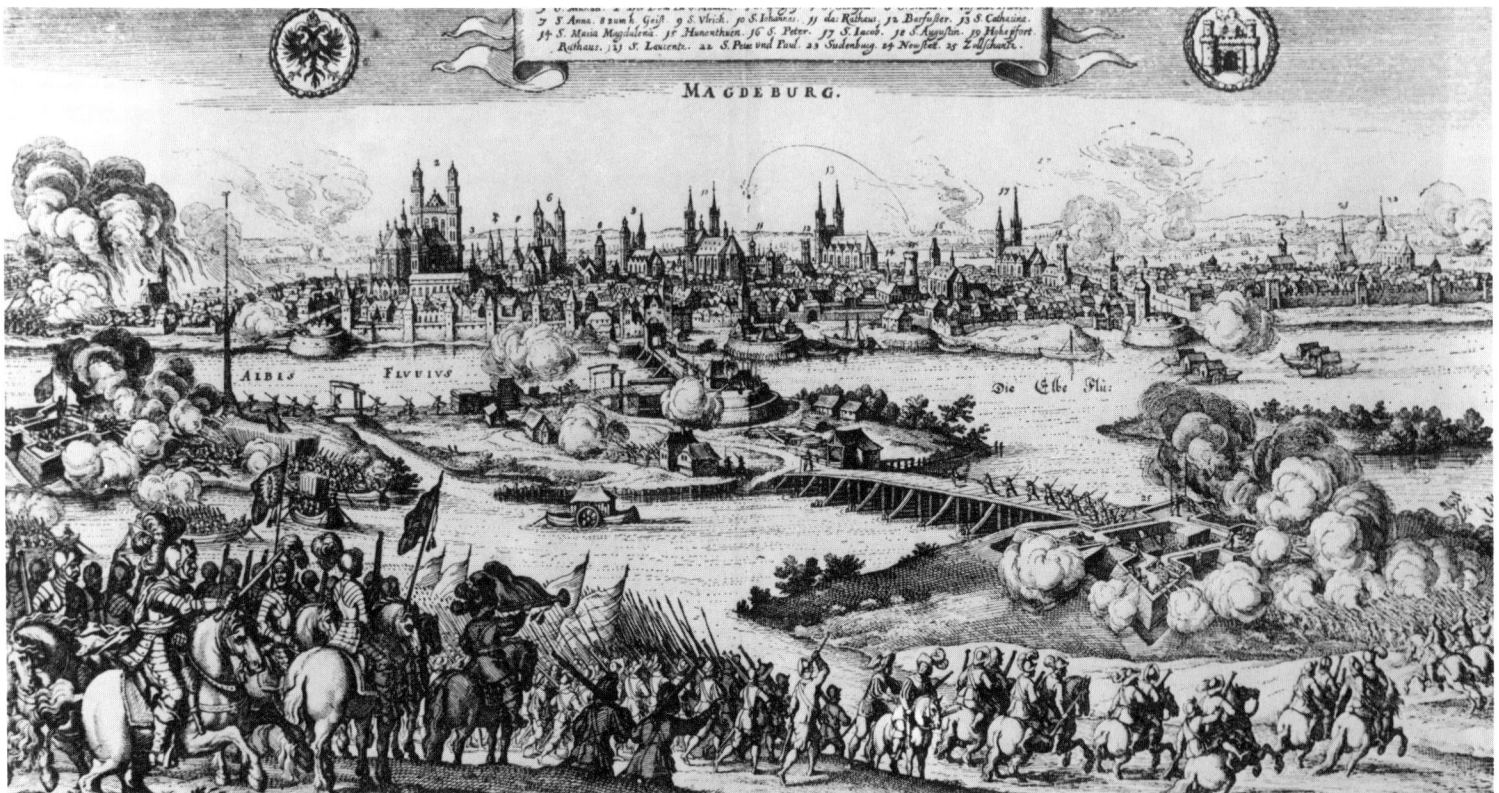

MAGDEBURG.

Left, Axel Oxenstierna (1583–1654), the Swedish chancellor who controlled the administration of his country from 1612 to his death. His financial and commercial efficiency provided the backing required for Gustavus Adolphus' spectacular campaigns. Vitterhetsakademien, Stockholm.

Below, Gustavus Adolphus in action in the Battle of Dirschau. Kungl. Husgeradskammaren, Stockholm.

Opposite, the capture of the Protestant town of Magdeburg by the imperial troops under Tilly in 1631; some 25,000 people were killed and the city was burned down. The Thirty Years' War caused destruction in central Europe unparalleled until the twentieth century.

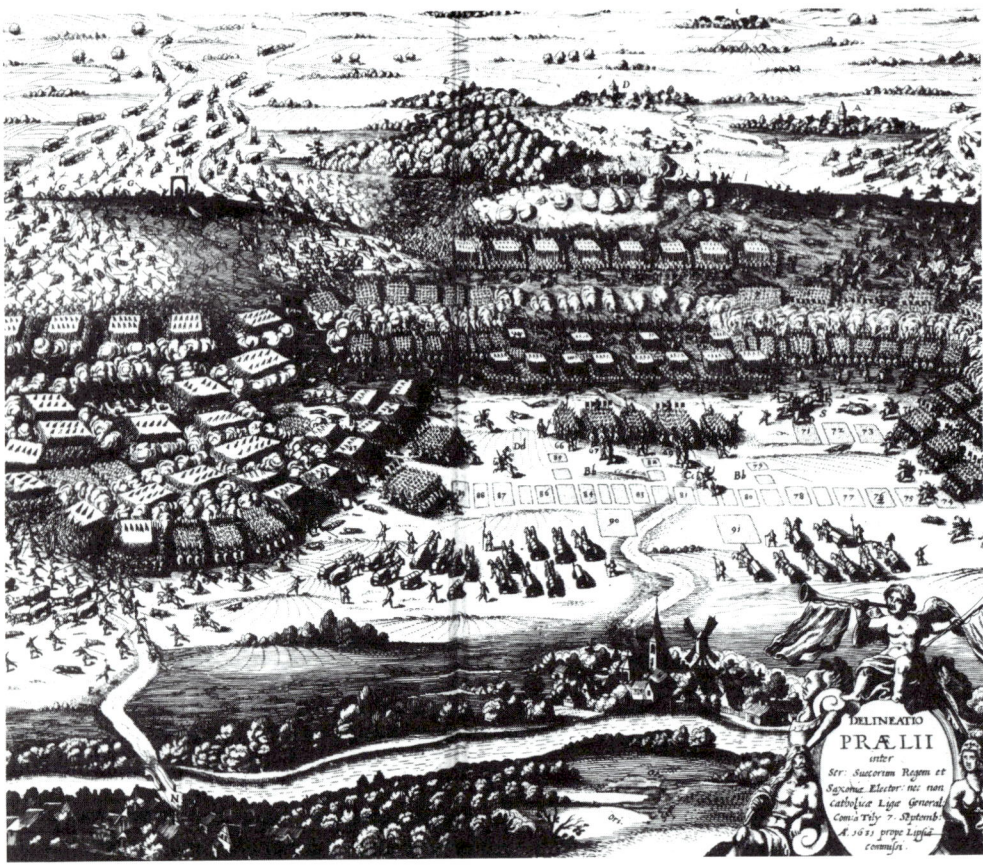

DELINEATIO
PRÆLII

convinced that they came not only to save the provinces from Habsburg tyranny but also to snatch Protestantism from the grips of the Scarlet Woman: the Counter-Reformation. The king and his great minister Oxenstierna were also determined to exclude the Habsburgs from the Baltic and so to foil the grandiose economico-military plan of Olivares.

It was the constitutional and economic aspects of the campaign which were stressed in the preamble to the Treaty of Bärwalde, which was signed in 1631 with the envoys of Richelieu. This treaty was a great triumph for Swedish diplomacy as it secured a large annual subsidy from the French with virtually no strings attached to it. Gustavus Adolphus was therefore well placed for the campaign of 1631. In the spring of that year the imperial troops took and sacked Magdeburg, an event which provided excellent propaganda for the anti-Habsburg cause. In fact it was more of a blunder than a crime on the part of the imperial general Tilly, who had been counting on the city's supplies for his impending campaign and now saw them largely destroyed. Gustavus Adolphus caught up with Tilly just north of Leipzig in September 1631. In the ensuing Battle of Breitenfeld, the new Swedish

Left, Gustavus Adolphus leading the Swedish cavalry against Wallenstein's imperial army in 1632 at Lützen. Although the Swedes won the day, Gustavus was killed and the Swedes never again threatened the Catholics so dangerously. Statens Museum for Kunst, Copenhagen.

Left, Gustavus Adolphus leading the Swedish cavalry against Wallenstein's imperial army in 1632 at Lützen. Although the Swedes won the day, Gustavus was killed and the Swedes never again threatened the Catholics so dangerously. Statens Museum for Kunst, Copenhagen.

Opposite top, Gustavus Adolphus of Sweden (reigned 1611–32), shown at the Battle of Breitenfeld in 1631. This was the first important Protestant victory of the Thirty Years' War and marked the consolidation of Sweden's ambitions in northern Europe. Musée des Beaux Arts, Strasbourg.

Opposite bottom, the plan of the Battle of Breitenfeld in 1631, in which Gustavus Adolphus demonstrated his novel tactics of small mobile brigades of infantry and waves of cavalry charges.

tactics proved greatly superior to the traditional Spanish order of battle. Having successfully resisted the first shock of the imperial cavalry, Gustavus smashed their infantry with his artillery and went on to complete their rout with his highly mobile groups of horse.

Then he advanced into the heart of Germany, taking up his winter-quarters at Mainz. Needless to say, there was despair in the camp of the imperialists, who had seemed on the verge of triumph only two years earlier. In April 1632 Wallenstein was recalled and began to reorganize his forces for the new campaigning season.

It is not clear what Gustavus Adolphus' intentions were, but it seems that he was progressing from his earlier notion of a Swedish protectorate over the German princes to the idea of a frank annexation of certain regions of Germany. In any case, his plans never came to fruition, for in the course of his victorious battle against Wallenstein at Lützen in November 1632 he was killed.

Perhaps it would have been better for Sweden if Oxenstierna had now decided to cut his losses and withdraw his forces. But the chancellor decided to fight on, and in September 1634 his army was decisively defeated at Nördlingen by an imperial army with a strong Spanish contingent.

Thus ended the phase of the war in which Sweden played the major role. After many complicated intrigues, the emperor had had Wallenstein legally but unjustly put to death the previous February, and so when the French declared war on Spain in May 1635 the struggle entered a new phase with new leaders.

The French phase (1635–48)

In this new phase religious and constitutional considerations plainly took second place to the Habsburg-Bourbon power struggle. This was shown not only by the fact that the chief opponent of Catholic Austria was Catholic France led by Cardinal Richelieu but also by the conclusion in May 1635 of the Peace of Prague, which in settling German affairs received the assent of the major princes. Thereafter, in short, the main issues were not the fate of the Counter-Reformation or of princely liberties but the question of whether or not Richelieu could break the power of Olivares.

In 1636 the Spaniards carried the war into France, and one of their armies penetrated almost to Paris, while others operated in Lorraine and Franche-Comté. However, with this lightning offensive the Spaniards had shot their bolt, and the ensuing campaigns saw the increasing predominance of the French and their Dutch and English allies. Throughout 1637 the French were successfully recovering their ancient province of Artois, while the Dutch besieged and took Breda. The following year Bernard of Saxe-Weimar took Breisach, thus cutting the 'Spanish road' between Italy and the Netherlands; it was at this siege that the young Turenne, later to become one of France's most successful commanders, first showed his skill. In 1639 the Spaniards lost the last armada of any size that they were able to equip, when the Dutch won a running battle in the English channel. Then the disastrous year of 1640 was followed in 1643 by the Battle of Rocroi and by the fall of Olivares.

By the early 1640s, in fact, most of the belligerents were ready to begin peace negotiations. Ferdinand II had died in 1637, and his successor Ferdinand III, of a more realistic temperament, was ready to renounce vast imperial ambitions in favour of a policy of consolidation of the inner kernel of Habsburg lands. In France Richelieu had been succeeded in 1642 by Mazarin, while the Battle of Rocroi convinced the Dutch that the threat in future might well lie not in Madrid or Vienna but in Paris. So it was that the negotiations at Münster and Osnabrück, whose outcome would be known as the Treaty of Westphalia (1648), slowly got under way.

The Treaty of Westphalia (1648)

After many complicated deliberations it was agreed that the maxim *cuius regio, eius religio* (literally 'of whom the region, of him the religion' meaning that regions should adopt the religion of their rulers) should be abandoned; henceforward dissident subjects were to be allowed freedom of worship, except in the hereditary Habsburg lands. The struggle between the princes and towns on one side, and the absolutist claims of the emperor on the other, was decided emphatically in favour of the former, as the German 'states' were allowed full sover-

eignty. This abdication of imperial claims was completed by the recognition of the independence not only of the Dutch Republic but also of the Swiss cantons.

Each of the main contestants also gained at the expense of the empire. France acquired Alsace and the imperial cities and bishoprics of Metz, Toul and Verdun, Sweden received a large part of Pomerania, and to Brandenburg fell not only the rest of Pomerania but also various smaller territories which almost linked the duchy of Brandenburg with its Rhineland possessions.

The significance of the settlement was clear: if the Swedes eventually failed to hold their acquisitions on the south shore of the Baltic, the French and the Prussians acquired territories which set them on the road to greater expansion in the ensuing decades. After Westphalia it began to be clear, for instance, that not Saxony but Brandenburg-Prussia would be the power of the future in northern Germany. Equally significant was the eclipsing of the empire and of the papacy. The Habsburg turned to that consolidation of their hereditary lands which was to be so successfully accomplished in the next half-century, and the papacy was forced to realize that it could no longer rely on ecclesiastical sanctions in order to make its voice heard in European politics. In diplomatic history the assemblies at Münster and Osnabrück were important as the

first of a long series of reunions at which, following major wars, European statesmen met to adjust their boundaries in accordance with the new realities of power.

The continuation of the Franco-Spanish struggle (1648–59)

There had been no agreement in the Westphalian negotiations between the representatives of France and of the Spanish Habsburgs, and so their struggle continued. Between 1648 and 1652 the French were crippled by their internal dissensions, but once Mazarin had put an end to the *fronde* he was able to turn French arms against the old enemy. At first the struggle was fairly equal, but then in 1656 Cromwell's England joined the French, and in the 1658 campaign the allies' superiority showed as fortress after fortress fell in the Spanish Netherlands.

So it was that in 1659 Spain was ready to come to terms with France and to put an end to a century and a half of broken warfare. The Treaty of the Pyrenees from the French point of view supplemented the territorial gains already made in 1648. This time it was Roussillon and Cerdagne in the Pyrenees and Artois on the northeastern frontier which passed to the French crown, along with certain fortresses in Lorraine

whose possession meant that sooner or later the whole duchy would also be absorbed. The long nightmare of Habsburg encirclement was over. Time would show that the French were as little capable of using their new power moderately as the Spaniards had been in the previous decades.

The effects of the war

For military historians the period between 1609 and 1659 is full of interest. During the preceding two or three decades most of the new military tactics had been worked out in the United Provinces, under the direction of Maurice of Nassau. After 1617, however, the initiative passed to the Swedes, who under Gustavus Adolphus took up and developed many of the Dutch ideas.

The chief of these was the division of the army into small self-contained units. Whereas the Spanish *tercio* consisted of a solid mass of 3,000 or so men, the basic unit in Gustavus' army numbered only about 500 and fought not in a solid mass, relying on weight, but often in an extended line, in which the power of small firearms could better be brought into action. Instead of the older method of slow 'rolling' fire, Gustavus introduced the 'salvo', delivered at close range and calculated to throw the leading ranks of the enemy into disarray.

This missile blow would be followed by the brute shock of a calvalry charge, for the Swedes gave up the device of the caracole, by which the horsemen wheeled up to deliver pistol-shots at the enemy, and reverted to the more effective device of crushing the enemy foot down by sheer weight. Of course, this cavalry attack could only be successful once the front ranks of the enemy pikemen had been severely mauled, and this was the task either of the

musketeers or of the gunners, using their mobile field-pieces.

The Swedish factories, under the direction of the Dutchman Louis de Geer, were at this time turning out light, quick-firing artillery, which could quickly be brought up to take advantage of the tactical situation. Needless to say, this close collaboration between infantry, cavalry and artillery called for a high degree of skill on the part of all the soldiers and their commanders, and it was to develop this skill that the Swedish troops were endlessly drilled and put through mock manoeuvres.

This tactical revolution, which was to carry the military art to a level of technical perfection scarcely exceeded before the nineteenth century, was not accompanied by any corresponding change in military organization. Supplies continued to be raised in very haphazard fashion, either by taking them from the surrounding countryside or by uncertain private contractors. Moreover, the very chain of command remained ill-defined. Not only Wallenstein, but also French leaders like Condé were closer in their independence to the *condottieri* of Renaissance Italy than they were to the generals of the later seventeenth century.

The very imperfections of the logistical support meant that armies remained relatively small. A general who could muster 30,000 trained men would nearly always outnumber his adversary. Indeed the strongest French army employed in Germany at this period numbered only 14,000 men. When this figure is compared with the 400,000 soldiers whom Louis XIV is said to have had under arms towards the end of the seventeenth century, it is clear that the so-called 'military revolution', as far as scale of operations goes, did not get under way until the latter half of the century.

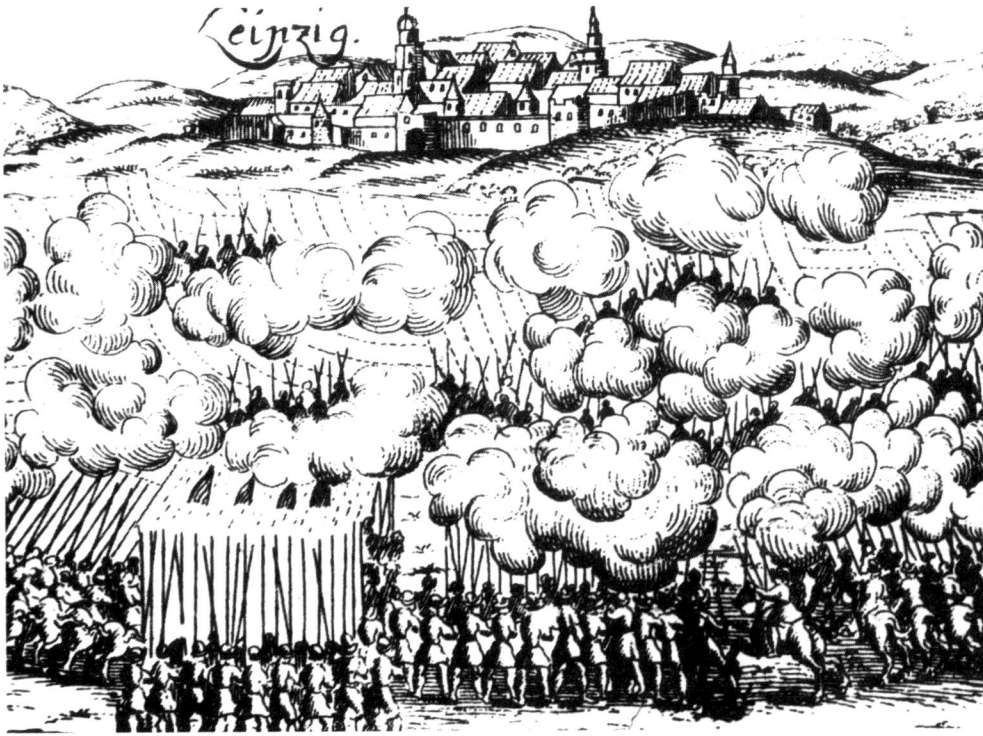

Leipzig.

Moreover, such armies as were raised tended to be disbanded during the winter, and it was regarded as rather 'caddish' of Gustavus of Sweden that he launched many of his offensives almost out of season.

The relatively small size of armies, and their restricted season of operations, bear on another problem, that of the economic effects of the war. These have commonly been described as nothing less than catastrophic and as retarding for generations the regions affected. In fact, things seem to have been much less dramatic. Population, for instance, seems actually to have increased in the Germanic regions from about sixteen million in 1600 to about seventeen million in 1650. Obviously it is possible to cite instances of dramatic decline, particularly in the theatres of war, but very often such reductions in the number of inhabitants were temporary. Once the armies had gone, people returned home.

Sometimes too districts did lose many of their inhabitants, not because they died, but because they emigrated to regions offering a better livelihood. The number of citizens in Cologne, for instance, declined sharply after about 1610; but this was because many of the wealthiest men and their families were moving to Hamburg, whose commercial prospects now seemed brighter. Often these emigrations were rapidly compensated by a high birthrate; for example, Antwerp lost many of her inhabitants to Amsterdam in the late sixteenth century and yet continued to grow in numbers from about 45,000 in 1600 to about 67,000 in 1700. Clearly the temporary depletion of one town or region might be the making of others.

Even towns directly affected by military operations did not necessarily suffer. Danzig, for instance, was often blockaded in the late 1620s, and yet this does not seem to have prevented a steady increase in her trade. Often, indeed, military operations stimulated commercial activity, by temporarily disrupting the trade of rival centres. This was certainly the case with Danzig itself, which profited greatly by the distraction of the Dutch between 1621 and 1625 and also during the Anglo-Dutch war of 1652–3.

Even physical damage does not seem to have had the dire effects imagined by some historians. Leipzig, for instance, saw great battles fought before her gates (Lützen and Breitenfeld) during the 1630s, and both then and during the 1640s suffered several successful assaults both by the imperialists and by the Swedes. All the same, Leipzig throughout this period continued to grow, overtaking her former rivals Nuremberg, Cologne and Frankfurt, and emerging in 1650 as second only to Hamburg. Clearly the legend of catastrophic destruction has been much exaggerated. In fact towns and individuals which knew how to adapt to new circumstances were able not only to survive but also to flourish during this period, and the region in general made marked economic progress between 1600 and 1650.

The myth of the Thirty Years' War

The legend of the widespread devastation was largely the work of writers like Pufendorf, who were hired to improve the 'image' of the rulers of Brandenburg-Prussia. For historians like this the struggle was between Habsburg tyranny and the high-minded Protestant German princes, in the course of which such devastation was wreaked that it could only be repaired by rulers of the calibre of Frederick William of Brandenburg, known as 'the Great Elector'.

So much then for the myth of widespread destruction; what of the idea that the struggle was one for religious freedom? It would be impossible to assign such motives to the Elector of Brandenburg, who, as one historian has recently said, 'sold himself without any scruples successively or almost simultaneously to Sweden, Poland, Denmark, the Netherlands, the emperor and France'. In the case of the Swedes, there is no doubt that the idea of the Lion of the North come to rescue Protestants from the Habsburg menace had much to commend it as propaganda. But Gustavus and Oxenstierna were in fact at least as concerned with establishing themselves on the southern shores of the Baltic as with 'freeing' their co-religionists in Germany. The same is true of the King of Denmark, whose unhappy intervention seems to have been primarily motivated by a desire to seize the declining Hanseatic towns on the North Sea and Baltic.

The notion that the struggle was primarily one for 'German' constitutional liberties can be discarded also. The shifting alliances, which arrayed the princes now on the side of the emperor and now on that of his adversaries, were clearly the result not of a calculation of long-term constitutional interest but of the impulse to profit by short-term political possibilities or perhaps merely to survive. Any attempt to imprison the

EUROPE IN THE SIXTEENTH AND SEVENTEENTH CENTURIES

Date	Rulers	Political events	Culture and religion	Date	Rulers	Political events	Culture and religion
1515	Henry VIII (1509–47)	Battle of Marignano (1515)	Death of Bramante (1444–1514)	1600 (contd)		Truce between Spain and Holland, and founding of the Bank of Amsterdam (1609)	Death of El Greco (1545–1614)
	Francis I (1515–47)	Concordat between the pope and Francis I (1516)	Oratory of Divine Love (1517)		Louis XIII of France (1610–43)	War is averted by the death of Henry IV (1610)	Death of Cervantes (1547–1616) and of Shake-speare (1564–1616)
	Charles I of Spain (1516–56)	Charles I of Spain elected Holy Emperor (Charles V, 1519–56)	Death of Raphael (1483–1520)		Emperor Mathias (1612–19)	Death of the Concinis (1617) Defenestration of Prague (1618)	
			Luther at Worms (1521)			Assassination of Olden-barneveldt (1619)	
	Pope Clement VII (1523–34)	Sack of Rome (1527)			Emperor Ferdinand II (1619–37)	Battle of the White Hill (1620)	
	Pope Paul III (1534–49)	Act of Supremacy (1534)	Recognition of the Jesuits (1540)			Spaniards capture Jülich (1622)	
			Opening sessions of the council of Trent (1545)		Philip IV of Spain (1621–65)	Richelieu becomes chief minister (1624)	
	Henry II of France (1547–59)		Death of Luther (1483–1546)				
1550		Peace of Augsburg (1555)	Saint Peter Canisius pro-vincial in Germany (1556)	1625	Charles I of England (1625–49)	Battle of Lutter (1626)	
		French capture Calais (1558)			Frederick Henry (1625–47)	Siege and capture of La Rochelle (1627–8)	
	Philip II of Spain (1556–98)	Treaty of Cateau-Cambrésis				Wallenstein captures Wismar (1628)	
	Elizabeth of England (1558–1603)	Bankruptcies at Lyons and Antwerp (1559)				Edict of restitution and peace of Lübeck (1629)	
	Francis II of France (1559–60)	Conspiracy of Amboise (1560)	Closing sessions of the council of Trent (1563)			Treaty of Bärwalde, sack of Magdeburg and Battle of Breitenfeld (1631)	Death of John Donne (1573–1631)
	Charles IX of France (1560–74)	Colloquy of Poissy (1561)	Death of Michelangelo (1475–1564) and of Jean Calvin (1509–64)			Battle of Lützen and execution of Montmorency (1632)	
		Edict of Amboise (1563)				Battle of Nördlingen (1634)	
		Catherine de Medici's great tour (1564–5)				Peace of Prague and declaration of war by France on Spain (1635)	Death of Lope de Vega (1562–1635) and of Jacques Callot (1592–1635)
	Pope Pius V (1566–72)	Meaux incident and battle of Saint-Denis (1567)				Spaniards invade France (1636)	Publication of René Descartes' Discourse on Method (1637)
		Treaty of Longjumeau (1568)			Emperor Ferdinand III (1637–57)	Dutch recapture Breda (1637)	
		Treaty of Saint-Germain (1570)				French capture Breisach (1638)	
		Protestants to French court (1571)				Spanish fleet destroyed in the Downs (1639)	
	William the Silent (1572–84)	Massacre of Saint Bartholomew (1572)				Revolt of Portugal and of Catalonia (1640)	Death of Rubens (1577–1640) Death of Van Dyck (1599–1641)
		Siege of La Rochelle (1572–3)				Civil war in England (1642)	
1575	Henry III of France (1574–89)	Edict of Beaulieu (1576)	Death of Titian (1477–1576)		Louis XIV (1643–1715)	Battle of Rocroi and resignation of Olivares (1643)	
	Emperor Rudolf II (1576–1612)	Treaty of Bergerac (1577)	Death of Andrea Palladio (1508–80)			Revolt in Naples (1647)	
	Maurice of Nassau (1584–1625)	Death of the duke of Anjou (1584)	Death of Saint Teresa of Avila (1515–82)			Treaties of Münster and of Osnabrück (1648)	Death of Monteverdi (1567–1643)
		Treaty of Nemours (1585)	Death of Pierre Ronsard (1524–85)		Charles II of England (1649–85)	Execution of Charles I (1649)	Death of Grotius (1583–1645)
	Henry IV of France (1589–1610)	Battles of Coutras and of Auneau (1587)				Fronde parlementaire (1649)	
		Failure of the Armada (1588)		1650		Fronde des princes (1650–2)	Death of Descartes (1596–1650)
		'Day of barricades' at Paris and murder of the Guises (1588)	Death of Michel de Montaigne (1533–92)			Spaniards recapture Barcelona (1652)	
	Pope Clement VIII (1592–1605)	Battle of Arques (1589)				Oliver Cromwell becomes 'Lord Protector' (1653)	
		Battle of Ivry (1590)				English capture Jamaica (1655)	
		States-General of the League at Paris and conversion of Henry IV (1593)	Death of Palestrina (1524–94)			Death of Cromwell (1658)	
		Henry IV enters Paris (1594)				Treaty of the Pyrenees (1659)	
	Philip III of Spain (1598–1621)	Edict of Nantes and treaty of Vervins (1598)			Emperor Leopold I (1657–1705)	Charles II enters London and Louis XIV marries the infanta (1660)	Death of Velasquez (1599–1660)
1600		Charter of the English East India Company (1600)				Death of Mazarin (1661)	Death of Pascal (1598–1662)
		Founding of the Dutch East India Company (1602)					
	James I of England (1603–25)	Gunpowder plot (1605)					
		Philip III repudiates his debts (1607)					
	Pope Paul V (1605–21)	Formation in Germany of the Union and of the League (1608)					
		Expulsion of the Moriscos (1609)					

struggle in some kind of all-explanatory definition is bound to fail, for it was at the same time a religious, political, constitutional and economic struggle, waged not only in Germany but all over Europe and lasting not thirty but something like fifty years.

The career of Wallenstein provides an excellent example of the mixed nature both of the motives and of the fortunes of the participants in the struggle. Wallenstein was born into the minor Bohemian nobility and received a thoroughly Protestant education at school and university. When he was twenty, he was converted by a Jesuit, who introduced him at the imperial court and secured for him an advantageous marriage. Thereafter Wallenstein's prodigious talents as a financier and military organizer carried him to a series of dazzling conquests; Duke of Friedland in 1625, by 1630 he owned enormous areas of north Germany and had arsenals from which he supplied all sides in the struggle. He was equally unselective in his choice of collaborators, who ranged from conventional Catholics to overt Protestants; Wallenstein himself was more interested in astrology than theology.

Wallenstein's fate was as extraordinary as his rise. Having become a sort of co-emperor, thanks rather to his genius than to his alliance with any constitutional or religious movement, he was, as we have seen, dismissed at the demand of the princes, reinstated in the emperor's hour of need and finally murdered when the emperor came to regard him as a dangerous rival. In his extraordinary talents Wallenstein resembles Napoleon, but unlike the great Corsican he lived at a time when the hereditary principle was still too strong for adventurers to clothe their bids for power with a cloak of legality. In its motives and progress his career defies logical analysis; like the so-called 'Thirty Years' War', it cannot be fitted into the neat categories of historiography.

Opposite left, a battle fought within sight of the city of Leipzig, which was then an important cultural centre. The effects of the war, economically and demographically, have been the subject of long dispute among historians.

Opposite top right, Wallenstein (1583–1634), the great imperial general who used his military power for political ends, trying to negotiate with the Swedes on his own account to bring the war to a close.

Opposite bottom right, the assassination of Wallenstein in 1634 in his castle in Bohemia by the agents of the emperor.

Chapter 6

France and Europe in the Time of Mazarin

The 1640s and 1650s mark a period of turmoil in European constitutional history. In France there were the revolts of the *frondeurs* (meaning, literally, urchins with *frondes*, or catapults), in England the 'great revolution', in the United Provinces the palace revolution of 1650, and all over Europe lesser tumults, which have led historians to speak of the 'six (or more) contemporaneous revolutions'.

This constitutional unrest had its effects on economic development, and the two decades in the middle of the century seem to have been a period of consolidation rather than of expansion. After about 1660, however, most of the major countries worked out a settled form of government, and the European economy entered on one of its most dynamic phases, eventually to be slowed down only by persistent wars.

After the death of Richelieu, late in 1642, Louis XIII appointed Mazarin as chief minister. Then in April 1643 the king made preparations for the succession; Anne of Austria would be regent and Gaston d'Orléans lieutenant general. The real power however, would lie with a council of regency, including Mazarin, chancellor Séguier, the financial chief Bouthillier and his son Chavigny, secretary of state, all of whom had been Richelieu's collaborators. This was in theory; in fact, when Louis XIII died in May 1643, Anne of Austria persuaded the *parlement* of Paris to set aside these provisions. Supreme power was vested in her, and she confirmed Mazarin's position as first minister.

Mazarin

Mazarin, whose enemies called him the 'Sicilian trickster', was then forty-one. Born in 1602 of a Sicilian father in the service of the powerful Roman Colonna family, he had been educated by the Jesuits and then at the university of Alcala with one of the Colonna sons. With such powerful patrons he soon came to command a company of papal foot-soldiers and served in the Valtelline campaign.

But it was the affair of the Mantuan succession which determined his future. As papal representative he was required to mediate between France, Savoy and Spain

and succeeded in satisfying Richelieu by maintaining the Duke of Nevers in Mantua and Montferrat, while Savoy became France's ally and ceded to her the fortress of Pinerolo (1630). Thereafter his progress was rapid; by 1634 he was papal legate at Paris and at the same time one of Richelieu's collaborators. Five years later he gave up his legation and was naturalized so as formally to enter French service; Louis XIII made him a cardinal in 1641. If the king found him a trusted servant, the queen found him something more even than that; she seems to have come to love him and naturally turned to him on the death of Louis XIII.

Needless to say, the great nobles were not pleased to see Richelieu succeeded by another man of ability, however diffident and self-effacing he might seem, and in the so-called *cabale des importants* they plotted to kill Mazarin. However, the queen got wind of the conspiracy, and arrested its leaders; her Italian minister was saved and thenceforward lived in the security of a strong guard.

Mazarin was well qualified to carry on Richelieu's successful foreign policy, which was consummated by the treaties of Westphalia. But he also inherited from the great cardinal grave internal problems. Revenues had never been sufficient to pay for the expensive wars, and Mazarin was driven to desperate measures in his search for money. His *surintendant des finances* was an Italian financier called Particelli d'Émery, who was not content with the normal devices such as the sale of redundant offices but thought up fresh taxes like the building-tax which caused riots in Paris in 1644.

Other duties followed thick and fast. The so-called *taxe des aisés* (wealth tax) had to be revoked in the face of widespread protests, but in 1647 d'Émery succeeded in levying a higher rate on various goods entering Paris. These new taxes were stubbornly resisted by the Parisians, whose resentment found expression in the *parlement*.

So when in 1648 Charles I of England was imprisoned by his parliament, the *parlement* of Paris—whose resemblance to the English institution lay chiefly in the similarity of their names—considered that the time was ripe for a move against the monarchy. They put forward a whole programme for legislation bypassing the royal administration but making use of the great.

princes of the blood, and they called a general meeting of the members of the sovereign courts to deliberate on measures of 'reform'. Their example was taken up by the provincial *parlements*, which followed them in revoking the commissions of the intendants, denying the validity of the new taxes, and condemning arbitrary arrests.

The *fronde parlementaire*

Emboldened by the victory over the Spaniards at Lens (August 1648), Mazarin seized the leader of the malcontents, a man named Broussel. However, this set off a popular insurrection reminiscent of the 'day of barricades' of 1588; the royal family was blockaded in the Palais Royal, and Mazarin had eventually to let Broussel go, on the condition that the *parlement* would not meddle with politics for the next few months. Even so the discontent was by no means at an end, and it became clear to Mazarin that nothing short of a military blockade would bring the capital to its senses.

Early in January 1649 he therefore evacuated the royal family from Paris. They went to Saint-Germain-en-Laye, and Louis II, Prince of Condé (son of the Protestant rebel prominent under Louis XIII), began the siege. Within the city the resistance was led by the Prince de Conti, Condé's brother, and Paul de Gondi, the future cardinal of Retz. Gondi did his best to organize the defence, but the royal troops steadily drew the noose tighter around Paris. An envoy from the Spanish king offered the *frondeurs* help, but the *parlement* was not willing to go that far, and with the failure of this mission the Parisians' revolutionary ardour began to cool.

In April 1649 the two sides came to an agreement; the *parlement* would not meet for a year, and the royal family would return to Paris. So the *fronde parlementaire* came to an end. In tactical terms it had not been very dangerous for the monarchy, since the king had always had the largest forces, which was more than he would have during the impending *fronde des princes*. But in the long-term view the *fronde parlementaire* was very significant, as the last concerted revolutionary attempt before 1789 when the French Revolution broke out.

The *fronde des princes*

With the *parlementaires* temporarily silenced, Mazarin now had to turn to the princes. The leader of the malcontents was Condé, and early in 1650 Mazarin arrested not only him but also his brother Conti, thus hoping to stifle the revolt before it could get under way. This hope was illusory, for Condé's friends now fled to their territories: Turenne to Stenay, Bouillon to Limousin, Madame de Longueville to Normandy and so on.

Mazarin quickly sent troops after the turbulent nobles, but as fast as he pacified one area another would rise up. With astonishing irresponsibility, Turenne and Madame de Longueville went so far as to sign an alliance with the Spaniards, which for a time cost the French crown the strategic frontier town of Rethel. Mazarin showed at this time an energy almost worthy of his master Richelieu, travelling all over the country with the royal armies.

For while he seemed to be getting the upper hand, but then Gondi, who had a remarkable grasp of the possibilities of the political situation, succeeded in drawing the members of the former *fronde parlementaire* into an alliance with the noble malcontents. When in January 1651 this united front demanded the freeing of Condé and Conti and the dismissal of Mazarin, the cardinal judged it best to comply with their demands, and retired to Germany.

Thence he kept up a constant stream of advice to Anne of Austria, while what he had

Above, Anne of Austria (1601–66), daughter of Philip III of Spain and wife of Louis XIII of France after 1615. Although she was opposed to Richelieu, she became regent to Louis XIV in 1643 and supported the rule of Mazarin.

Opposite top, the château *of Vaux-le-Vicomte, built in 1657–61 by Louis Le Vau, who was later the architect of Versailles. Unlike Versailles, it is built in a complete block, surrounded by a moat and balustrade.*

Opposite bottom left, Louis II, Prince of Condé (1621–86), the French general who began the fronde *as a supporter of the government but later changed sides and fought for Spain against France. He later served as one of Louis XIV's generals in the Low Countries. Musée Condé, Chantilly.*

Opposite bottom right, the vicomte de Turenne (1611–75), a French general who won several important victories in the Thirty Years' War, began the fronde *as a rebel but later took the government side and served Louis XIV in Spain and the Low Countries.*

foreseen rapidly came about. Liberated, Condé proved so arrogant and violent that he not only split the alliance of the two *frondes* but even induced malcontents like Bouillon, Gondi and Turenne to beg the queen's forgiveness. Having thus alienated all his supporters, Condé was obliged to flee. After some inconclusive skirmishes, the queen was able to return to Paris in October 1652. When Mazarin rejoined her there in February 1653, the *frondes* were over.

Its participants were treated with great clemency, for most were included within a general amnesty, and were permitted to return to their former place in society. Some historians see the *frondes* as part of a general pattern of unrest caused by the economic stagnation which affected many

European countries in the 1640s, as a result of which their inhabitants tended to revolt against the increasingly burdensome apparatus of the state. This interpretation is of only limited use in explaining events in France. The *parlementaires* were certainly exasperated by d'Émery's methods of raising money, but their primary motive was constitutional, but their fearful of, and so opposed to, the extension of royal power.

The same is true of the princes, who do not seem to have been particularly poor; both *frondes* were primarily protests against that centralizing policy which the monarchy had been pushing forward with increasing success. It should hardly be necessary to point out that there was nothing 'democratic' about either movement, even if both made use of misleading phrases in order to rally

malcontents to their cause. The leaders of both *frondes* were uniformly remarkable for the way in which they found it impossible to commit themselves to any programme save that of increasing their own power and wealth.

With the troubles over, Mazarin was able to re-establish royal control through *intendants,* while Fouquet saw to the raising of funds. Mazarin was also concerned with the education of the young king, who until his early twenties seemed rather an unremarkable youth. Mazarin took him to council-meetings, so that he might see how the country was administered, and sent him off with the armies, to learn how campaigns were organized. He also seems to have passed on to the young king some of his own love for books, paintings and *objets d'art.*

France and her neighbours

The *frondes* had done much damage to the French economy, particularly in Picardy and Champagne. Behind the all-devouring armies there normally followed first famine and then plague, so that in the early 1650s many towns of northeastern France lost up to a quarter of their inhabitants, in spite of the remarkable efforts of the new religious orders to feed and care for the starving. The peasantry suffered just as badly; without the protection of town-walls, they were terribly vulnerable if they happened to lie across the paths that the various armies cut across the countryside.

However, French agriculture was still so primitive that its power of recovery was very great. Around the major towns like Paris there had been some consolidation and rationalization of land-tenure as early as the sixteenth century, but this tendency was very slow away from great urban centres, and the bulk of the land continued to be held and tilled by small peasants using antiquated methods. Conditions were very different in Holland and England, where by the mid-seventeenth century the main features of the impending 'agricultural revolution' were beginning to emerge. The Dutch were the leaders in the new husbandry, skilfully developing crops like clover and turnips to remedy the deficiencies of the former crude rotational systems. It was in Holland too that land-drainage began to be most skilfully developed, so that as early as the reign of Henry IV Dutchmen were called to France and set to work on the marshes of Poitou and Saintonge. In England, because of the production of wool, agriculture had long been penetrated by a capitalist, rationalizing mentality, and the seventeenth century saw a continuation of those enclosures which had already aroused so much discontent under Henry VIII and Elizabeth. However, if enclosure was a short-run social misfortune, it was a long-run economic advantage, and by 1650 agriculture in England, based on larger units than its French counterpart and geared to the requirements of the great capital, was notably more efficient.

In industry too the English of the first half of the seventeenth century had been outstripping the French. Their new prosperity was based on the production of coal, which increased from about 200,000 tons in 1540 to about 1,500,000 tons in 1640; by the latter date England produced three times as much coal as the rest of Europe put together. The availability of this fuel meant that new industries like sugar-refining and paper-making could emerge and that old industries like brewing, dyeing, salt-refining and cannon-founding could forge ahead without being hampered by shortage of wood-fuel.

Industrial development in the Low Countries was less spectacular, in part perhaps because political differences cut the thriving northern area off from the abundant coal-supplies of the Liège region. However, the cotton-textile industry thrived on exports to Dutch possessions overseas, and in the shipyards of the United Provinces systems of mass production and standardization of parts were introduced, resulting in a rate and cheapness of production unrivalled elsewhere. The maritime ventures of both the English and the Dutch were backed by a variety of precision industries, like cartography and instrument-making, which were greatly in advance of their French counterparts. The Spaniards had been early leaders in cartography but lost this primacy as the seventeenth century wore on.

The Dutch were also foremost in the development of economic institutions. Whereas the kings of Spain, for instance, were notoriously incapable of mobilizing their economic potential and had to repudiate their debts in 1557, 1575, 1596, 1607, 1627 and 1647, the government of the United Provinces succeeded in funding even the expensive wars of 1621–48 without undue strain.

This was made possible chiefly through the Bank of Amsterdam, founded in 1609 in imitation of various Italian banks. The function of the Bank was to receive surplus money and then to lend it out where most profit was to be made. The Bank thus came to act as a kind of regulator for the country's monetary resources. The root cause of its great success was the fact that creditors could rely on the state to enforce their claims. The situation was thus very different from that in France or England or Spain, where events had shown that impecunious kings showed no mercy to creditors. The relationship between an economic institution and the constitutional situation was

GERARDUS MERCATOR NATUS
RUPELMUNDÆ III NON.MARTII ANNO
CIↃIↃXII:VIXIT ANN.LXXXII.M.VIII.D.
XXVI:DENATUS IV NON.DECEMBRIS
ANNO CIↃIↃXCIV.

IUDOCUS HONDIUS NATUS IN
PAGO FLANDRIÆ DICTQ WACKENE XVI
KALEND.NOVEMBRIS ANNO CIↃIↃLXIII:
VIXIT ANN.XLVII.M.VII.D.XXIX:DENATꞬ
US XIV KAL.MARTII ANNO CIↃIↃCXII.

Above, the Dutch cartographer Gerhard Mercator (1512–94) and the globe-maker Hondius. Dutch commerce had demanded the development of such technical skills which were unknown in France, still surviving on a medieval economy.

Opposite, a late seventeenth-century English tapestry of agricultural labour; by this time the English peasantry were proud that they were far better off than their French counterparts, both more efficient and less heavily taxed. Victoria and Albert Museum, London.

and continued to be orientated towards, non-economic aims primarily those of reconquest. Similarly, in France the merchant community went largely unheard at Paris, partly because of the problem of distance and partly because the French kingdom too had developed out of the stress of war and continued to be preoccupied with the need to defend and expand the eastern frontier of France.

Things were very different in England and Holland, for in both these countries the governmental and economic capitals coincided, in London and Amsterdam respectively. By the early seventeenth century it was becoming very difficult for English kings to avoid taking account of the feelings of the merchants and bankers of London, which was in fact by far the largest town in the country. Similarly in Amsterdam the States-General could not think of ignoring the merchants; indeed, it was largely composed of merchants.

Thus it was that constitutional development in both of these countries diverged widely from the French or Spanish pattern of increasing absolutism. James I of England had great pretensions, it is true, but he was always careful not to put his pretensions to divine right to the test of general practice. Charles I was less prudent; for a time it looked as if he might have found his Richelieu or Olivares in the person of Thomas Strafford, but then the inevitable happened and the true balance of power within the community reasserted itself with the toppling of the monarchy.

The new forces emergent in England felt themselves to be 'national' in a way that was impossible for the feudal or municipal elements in France or Spain. When the nobles of Catalonia revolted, it was not in order to place themselves at the head of a popular movement but in order to reassert their ancient privileges. The same is true of the *frondeurs* in France; whether nobles or *parlementaires,* they were essentially reactionaries swimming against the tide, trying to put the clock back to a period which political and economic developments had already left behind.

In contrast with them, the Dutch ruling classes had skilfully identified themselves with the popular feeling of national revolt against Spain. So it was that the flag and the song of the House of Orange became the leading symbols of the revolutionary new republic. This is not to say that there were no tensions in the United Provinces, but it is to affirm that the general consensus concerning the form and attitude of government were not in dispute.

In the first half of the seventeenth century Holland was in fact the 'mistress of Europe' rather as Italy had been during the sixteenth and earlier. It was not just a matter of Dutch techniques in shipping and trade being superior to those of the rest of Europe; in almost every aspect of human activity there were great men in the United Provinces

neatly illustrated when one of the *stadtholders* (governors) refused to be crowned king, alleging that this step might ruin the republic by shaking confidence in the Bank.

The colonial trade, on which the prosperity not only of Holland but also of England increasingly depended, was organized by great joint-stock companies—associations, that is, in which individuals invested and which paid a yearly dividend on their operations. The greatest of these companies was probably the English East India Company, chartered in 1600; it was followed in 1602 by the founding of the Dutch East India Company. Shortly afterwards Henry IV did his best to found a French East India Company, but the attempt failed in the face of Dutch opposition, and it was only under Richelieu that the French companies got under way. However, throughout the seventeenth century

they were markedly less successful than those of the English and of the Dutch. In part this was a result of the excessive intrusion of the state, and in part because of the apparent absence of a vociferous and influential trading community, able to bring pressure to bear on government. This absence of the merchants' voice from the councils of state was no doubt largely a consequence of the considerable distance which separate Paris from the great commercial centres like Marseilles, Bordeaux and Nantes.

The lack of collaboration between government and the mercantile community goes far to explain the constitutional differences which came to separate countries like France and Spain from countries like Holland and England. In Spain the interest of the merchants went by default, because as we have seen society grew as a result of, at this period. Among the natural scientists, for instance, were Antony van Leeuwenhoek and Christian Huyghens, respectively famous as a pioneer of microscopy and as the inventor of improved telescopes and pendulum clocks. Dutch architects developed a whole new style of town-planning, taking into account the practical needs of their inhabitants and using efficient and homely materials. The Dutch school of painting, headed by great masters like Rembrandt van Rijn (1606–69) and Pieter de Hooch (1629–77), attracted collectors and students of art from all over Europe. Dutch universities, too, were very popular, in part because they welcomed all shades of Protestantism and in part because the dependence of each on one of the great federal provinces made for considerable individuality. A long list could be made of the scholars of European repute who taught at this time in Dutch universities; as an example we may take Hugo Grotius of Leyden (1583–1645), whose attempt to work out a system of international law between sovereign states made him the leading political theorist of his generation.

The period between 1600 and 1660, the so-called 'age of the Baroque', was one which in many countries of Europe saw the emergence of men of genius. It was at this time, for instance, that in the natural sciences the foundations for the scientific revolution were laid and the way made clear for the modern quantitative world. All the same, even if many other countries enjoyed at this time the emergence of great men of science and of letters, it was in Holland that the all-round achievement was most remarkable—and this in a country whose people numbered only about a tenth of those inhabiting France.

Holland began to lose her superiority about the middle of the century, when the English began to outstrip her in economic progress and the French began to promote an aristocratic culture, based on Versailles, which would eventually bedazzle half the world. In other ways too the period after 1660 marks a break. For the relations between the European states, it is a time of lull after great storms. The long Franco-Spanish struggle had been settled in 1659 by the peace of the Pyrenees, and the treaties of Oliva and Copenhagen (both 1660) introduced a period of calm into the affairs of northern and eastern Europe. The coming of peace meant that the decades after 1660 saw a vigorous economic spurt all over Europe, particularly on its western seaboard. It was at this time that the colonial trades began to transform the economies of the Old World.

Even in the internal affairs of the states, the period around 1660 marks a watershed. It is clearest in England, where that very year saw the restoration of Charles II, committed to the development of a system of constitutional monarchy. Two years earlier Leopold I had become Holy Roman

emperor, and during his long reign (1658–1705) the ramshackle empire would be transformed into the compact and powerful Habsburg monarchy, tacitly abandoning its wider pretensions. Philip IV of Spain died in 1665 and was succeeded by Charles II. This marked no new constitutional departure, but the new king's anaemic state fitly symbolized the Castilian monarchy in its declining years.

Finally, 1661 saw a great change in the government of France. In that year Mazarin died, and Louis XIV at the age of twenty-three resolved to rule for the future by himself. For the next fifty years, until the next great political and constitutional divide in about 1715, the history of Europe was largely the story of Louis XIV's ambitions and their eventual failure.

Above, a German port in the late seventeenth century; the ideas of mercantilism, whereby each country tried to control its own trade and become more self-sufficient as far as possible, helped the growth of national economies and hindered international trade within Europe.

Top, a Dutch East Indiaman of 1647; the Dutch and English were now firmly in control of the trade with the East, but Richelieu was to encourage the development of colonies in Canada and the West Indies.

Opposite, Cardinal Mazarin (1602–61), who founded the policy of centralization of royal power that culminated in the rule of Louis XIV. Musée Condé, Chantilly.

Part II

THE
NEW EUROPE

Introduction

From the point of view of world history, the outstanding development of the whole period from 1500 to 1700 was the expansion of Europe. Until 1500 man had lived in regional isolation, and Europe had been hemmed in, isolated and vulnerable, by the civilization of Islam, the great Muslim empires and the conquerors from the steppes of Asia. After 1500 the process was reversed and Europe began to press out on the world with a new momentum, which continued unabated right down to 1947.

Traditionally we date the expansion of Europe from the voyages of Columbus in 1492 and Vasco da Gama in 1497, and it is true that the Spanish conquistadores laid the foundations of a great colonial empire in South and Central America between 1520 and 1550, though they destroyed Aztec civilization in the process. But it was in the seventeenth century that voyages of discovery and trading and sheer exploitation gave way to colonization in the true sense of the word and that the Dutch, French and British empires were established. The foundation of Virginia in 1607 (earlier attempts at colonization had failed) and of Massachusetts in 1620, of Acadia (or Nova Scotia) and Quebec in 1605 and 1608, and of New Amsterdam on Manhatten Island in 1612, marked the beginning of a new stage in European and world history.

Parallel with the colonization of the New World was the great movement of Russian expansion across Siberia. One band of Russians reached the Arctic coast in 1645; two years later another reached the shores of the Pacific; and the first stage of Russian expansion in Asia was formally completed by the Treaty of Nerchinsk between Russia and China in 1689. Taken together, these different waves of expansion, eastwards and westwards, were the most important developments of the seventeenth century in the longer perspective of world history. They are also important in a shorter and more narrowly European perspective. The new knowledge of the world which resulted—of the old world as well as the new—and the widening of horizons consequent upon contact with the ancient civilizations of China and the Indies profoundly affected the seventeenth-century European's view of the world and his attitude to himself and his past. In particular, the irreconcilability of the new knowledge with biblical tradition prepared the way for a new, secular view of world history. This was evident from about 1655, when the French Calvinist Isaac de la Peyrère found it impossible to reconcile Chinese history with the story of Adam and Eve, and the Dutch historian Hornius composed the first truly universal history, which included both China and pre-Columbian America.

This change in men's attitude to history, and the secularization of thought which it illustrates, is only one example of a more far-reaching transformation which is usually described as the 'scientific revolution' of the seventeenth century. This revolution, which extended far beyond the limits of natural science and affected the whole intellectual atmosphere of Europe after about 1680, marks a great turning point in the history of European thought and civilization. The age of Newton saw the emergence of most of the characteristic attitudes of the modern mind. Far more than the Renaissance it marked 'the dividing line between medieval and modern', and that is the reason, above all others, why historians today pick out the seventeenth century as the time of 'the foundation of modern Europe'.

The great transformation of European life and attitudes came relatively late in the century. Thomas Hobbes' *Leviathan* is often acclaimed as the first enunciation of the modern theory of sovereignty, but two of its four books deal specifically with the Christian Commonwealth and with the Kingdom of Darkness. Hobbes, atheist though he is said to have been, was firmly anchored in the old world of religion and demonology. But with a writer like Locke, whose second *Treatise on Government* appeared in 1689, we are in another, firmly secular and pragmatic, environment. The years between 1651, when *Leviathan* was published, and 1689 are the great watershed. Historians have spilt a great deal of ink trying to probe the causes of the change. We shall probably never know exactly the answer. But one thing that is certain is that Europe underwent a great crisis and testing-time in the 1640s and 1650s, and when it emerged its character and temper, as well as its political structure, were different.

Political and military history is the necessary background for understanding the social and intellectual changes this crisis brought about. It is also of importance in its own right. Here also the seventeenth century saw a process of modernization, both in the internal structure of government and in the balance of political forces, which mark a major advance towards the Europe we know.

In part at least, this process of modernization was the consequence of a military revolution, associated with the name of Gustavus Adolphus of Sweden, the significance of which extended far beyond the purely military sphere. This was a period when the demands of finance, recruitment and equipment for ever growing armies forced governments to interfere increasingly in the lives of their subjects. 'Just as the modern state was needed to create the standing army,' one writer has said, 'so the army created the modern state.' The little principality of Brandenburg, for example, increased its military forces from 900 to 80,000 men within a hundred years, and though Brandenburg was in some respects exceptional a similar process was taking place through the length and breadth of continental Europe.

As a result of the exigencies of war, in other words, modern administrations began visibly to take shape. A second result of the wars of the seventeenth century was the re-drawing of the political map of Europe on lines familiar to us all. At the beginning of the seventeenth century that was not the case. Spain was still the dominant power in Europe, Holland its greatest financial and commercial centre, Poland a force to be reckoned with in the east; and in the north it looked as though Sweden was in the process of carving out a mighty empire on the Baltic. How different the map of Europe would have been, how strangely changed its destinies, if the possibilities inherent in this constellation of forces had been realized! By the end of the seventeenth century it was obvious that they would not be. Germany and Italy, it is true, were still 'geographical expressions,' though their future outlines were reasonably clear. But the circle of Great Powers was closing. Brandenburg under the Great Elector (1640–88) had taken the first steps which later—though no one could have foreseen it at the time—were to make it the nucleus of a new German empire. Austria, having driven back the Turks from the very gates of Vienna, assumed the position in southeast Europe which it was destined to retain until 1918. And Russia, emerging from its 'time of troubles', became an integral part of the Concert of Europe.

By the time of the peace of Utrecht in 1713 the European balance of power, the framework of European politics and international relations for the next two centuries, was in existence. The foundations of modern Europe had been laid. It is surprising how firm they remained, withstanding the shocks of the French Revolution and of the Industrial Revolution, until that fateful day in 1914 when the old Europe went into the melting-pot. Today, after the shattering experience of two world wars, we have passed into a new age, a post-European age of global politics, when Europe is faced by a resurgent Asia and Africa and dwarfed by the two great superpowers on its flanks. The old Europe, whose beginnings in the seventeenth century we now trace is no more.

Chapter 7

Seventeenth-century England

In March 1603, on the death of Queen Elizabeth, King James VI of Scotland became James I of England as well. When he travelled southwards the following month he received a rapturous reception from his new subjects. Their enthusiasm was to some extent a commentary on the last years of Elizabeth's reign. As the seventeenth century progressed people looked back on the Elizabethan era as a golden age, but in 1603 there was considerable discontent in England. The last decade of the sixteenth century had brought difficulties for the country. These included the war with Spain—which had begun in 1585—financial problems, the Crown's relations with parliament, increasing corruption in the administration and the social distress which accompanied a series of bad harvests in the mid-1590s. The queen and her chief minister, Lord Burghley, an ageing conservative whose policies had served the country well in the early years of the reign, had no new ideas to offer to meet changing conditions and, as a result, at the time of Elizabeth's death her popularity was perhaps at its lowest level of the entire reign.

James therefore ascended the throne amidst great goodwill. No section of the community had higher expectations of the new monarch than the Catholics, who had been subjected to intermittent persecution during Elizabeth's reign. James at first held out hopes of a relaxation of the severe Elizabethan penal laws, which threatened their property and even their lives, but as a result of the consequent rapid growth in the number of those who openly declared themselves Catholic he took alarm and the policy of persecution was resumed.

Some of the bolder spirits among the Catholics, led by Robert Catesby, a Warwickshire squire, and Guy Fawkes, an Englishman who had served in the Spanish armies, resorted in despair to the Gunpowder Plot, a scheme to blow up King, Lords and Commons at the opening of parliament on 5 November 1605.

The conspirators leased a cellar under the Parliament House and placed in it twenty barrels of gunpowder with a number of iron bars on top to make the blast even more

Below, James I of England (reigned 1603–25) and VI of Scotland (reigned 1567–1625), and his wife Anne of Denmark, both painted by Nicholas Hilliard. James was unable to comprehend many of the political problems facing him as King of England, and his political, religious and financial policies all left his parliaments infuriated with his rule.

On page 68, The Card Players (c. 1665) by Pieter de Hooch. Musée du Louvre, Paris.

destructive. The government got wind of the plot, the cellar was searched, and the ringleaders were killed or executed. In 1606, in the ensuing anti-Catholic hysteria, parliament passed two further penal statutes and Catholics continued to be persecuted throughout the early Stuart period.

James's initial reluctance to persecute his Catholic subjects reflected to a considerable extent, his genuine hatred of violence, an admirable personal quality which extended to an intense dislike of wars. He was determined to bring the conflict with Spain to a speedy end. This was done in August 1604. The terms of the treaty, which was concluded after negotiations in London, reflected the stalemate which prevailed in the war. James gave practically nothing away, standing his ground on all the points at issue between the two countries, in particular England's claims to trading rights in the New World.

The end of the war and the vast expenses which accompanied it, together with the better harvests of the first decade of the seventeenth century and James's initial popularity, augured well for a successful reign. Unfortunately, however, there was another, much less happy side of the picture. Though he did have good points, James had serious defects of character. He was lazy, he was extravagant, and he had exalted ideas of the divine right of kings—their right to rule unquestioned—which led to conflicts with parliament. James's laziness—he much preferred hunting to the hard work of routine government business—was to some

extent redressed in the early years of the reign by the diligence of his principal minister, Robert Cecil, who was created Earl of Salisbury in 1605. As secretary of state and later as lord treasurer as well, Salisbury toiled away endlessly over his papers while the king hunted and feasted.

James's extravagance had more immediately serious effects. Elizabeth had left a debt of perhaps £350,000. James who scattered money lavishly among the Scottish favourites who accompanied him to England and spent far more on the royal household than Elizabeth had ever done, soon increased this. By 1608, the year Salisbury became lord treasurer, it stood at perhaps £600,000. Salisbury managed to reduce this to under £300,000 by 1610, but there was still a large deficit on the annual budget— well over £100,000.

In these circumstances Salisbury supported the Great Contract, a scheme which was discussed in parliament in 1610; it proposed the abolition of certain antiquated royal prerogatives which were burdensome to the king's subjects in return for a fixed annual compensation of £200,000. The scheme was eventually abandoned because of mutual suspicion between Crown and Commons. It has been argued that, if it had gone through, it might have given the Crown virtual financial independence of parliament. This is speculation—we can only guess what James would have done with the money. One thing is certain. The failure of the Contract marked the end of Salisbury's political power. He remained in

office until his death in 1612, but the king had lost confidence in the man who had been the principal protagonist of the failed Contract.

King and Commons

In 1611 James dissolved his first parliament. His bitter words to Salisbury about it reflected his disillusionment both with the House of Commons and with his principal minister. 'Your greatest error', he wrote, 'has been that you ever expected to draw honey out of gall, being a little blinded with the self-love of your own counsel in holding together of this parliament, whereof all men were despaired, as I have often told you, but yourself alone.'

The clashes between Crown and Commons in the parliament of 1604–11—there were many other disputes besides that over the Contract—showed very clearly that already in the first decade of the seventeenth century there were important differences between the Crown and the House of Commons, which mainly comprised representatives of the gentry class. At that time the overwhelming majority of the peers were loyal supporters of the king and the government, but with James I's and Charles I's lavish additions to the peerage between 1615 and 1628, increasing the number of English peers from eighty-one to a hundred and twenty-six, a split developed within the ranks of the aristocracy. Many members of the older peerage despised the new 'upstarts', and in the parliaments of the 1620s there was a significant opposition group to the Crown in the Lords as well as in the Commons.

The peerage and gentry taken together formed the English political community, and the Crown depended on their general cooperation and goodwill for the successful running of the country. There were several reasons why that cooperation was very clearly breaking down in the second and third decades of the century.

One of the most important was the increasing gap between the 'Court', that is, the king and his entourage, and the 'Country', those members of the aristocracy and gentry who had no access to the profits of office or the largesse which James I distributed so freely to his chosen favourites, like the worthless Robert Carr, created Earl of Somerset, on whom the king showered gifts and honours between 1611 and 1615. Somerset was disgraced in 1616 following disclosures of his complicity in a sordid murder, but he was soon replaced by a new favourite, George Villiers, created Duke of Buckingham in 1623, who was the dominant influence in the kingdom from 1618 until 1628. Under the regimes of Carr and Buckingham corruption at court and in the administration became a scandal, offices and honours being openly sold in the interest of the favourites.

Those noblemen and gentlemen outside the charmed circle of the court, and some within it, looked on the situation with growing distaste. By 1628 the position of Buckingham, who was as secure in the friendship of Charles I (1625–49) as he had been in the affections of James I, had become one of the greatest grievances in the kingdom, a leading obstacle to the improvement of relations between the king and his subjects. He was not, however, by any means the only obstacle, as clashes between Crown and Commons in 1629, the year after Buckingham's assassination, were to show very plainly.

Another source of conflict was the continuing financial needs of the Crown, especially after the outbreak of war with Spain in 1624, a conflict which lasted until 1630. The parliaments of 1624 and 1625 voted some money—though not nearly enough—for the prosecution of the war, but in 1626 the Commons refused to consider any supply until their grievances had been redressed. They proceeded with a formal impeachment of the Duke of Buckingham, and Charles had to dissolve parliament to prevent the continuation of attacks on his favourite. As no money had been forthcoming for the war effort he then had recourse to a forced loan, which caused widespread resentment. Some gentlemen refused to pay and were imprisoned. Their appeal to the courts was turned down in 1627 when the King's Bench upheld Charles's view that he had the right to imprison men without showing specific cause. This decision,

together with unparliamentary taxation, was attacked in the Petition of Right, a statement of the liberties of the subject drawn up by the House of Commons in 1628.

Charles grudgingly agreed to the Petition, though he made it quite plain that he interpreted it as merely confirming existing liberties (as he understood them) and not creating new ones. By 1628, therefore, the war and the growing financial problems which attended it had led to serious disputes and great ill-feeling between Crown and Commons.

Charles's religious ideas also provoked trouble with many of his subjects, and that trouble too was reflected in the parliaments of the 1620s. He supported the Arminian party within the Church, a group led by William Laud, who was made Bishop of London in 1628 and Archbishop of Canterbury in 1633. Laud and his followers stressed the freedom of men's wills as opposed to the Anglican Church's traditional emphasis on predestination—the idea that God determined each soul's destiny in advance and that men were powerless to aid their salvation by their own efforts.

Many moderate Anglicans regarded Laud's theology with as much suspicion as the Puritan wing of the Church did, but it was the Puritans who took the lead in opposing not only Laud's theological ideas but also his change in Church services, changes designed to restore some of the dignity and beauty of pre-Reformation ritual. To the Puritans some of his innovations, such as railing off the altar and his insistence on kneeling at communion, suggested the doctrine of the real presence in the sacrament—one of the very foundations of Catholicism. This explains the bitterness of their opposition, both inside and outside parliament. James I had already made life

difficult enough for the Puritans, and in 1620 a large group of them had set sail in the *Mayflower* for America, where they hoped for freedom to practise their religion as they pleased. When in March 1629 parliament was adjourned amid excited scenes in the Commons, it was religious issues which raised the greatest passions in the hearts of members. They acclaimed a resolution asserting that anyone who proposed innovations in religion—a clear reference to Laud and his followers—should be considered 'a betrayer of the liberties of England and an enemy to the same'.

Charles rules alone

The crisis in the relationship between Crown and Commons in 1628–9 made Charles decide to rule without calling parliament, which he did for the next eleven years. The key to the whole situation during this period was the financial position of the Crown. Charles had to obtain sufficient money to administer the country without recourse to parliament. This meant keeping out of wars —peace was made with Spain in 1630—and exploiting the royal prerogative for financial ends. Ship money, the most important of the numerous fiscal devices of the personal rule, was imposed on the whole country from 1636 onwards. There were good precedents, going back to the sixteenth century, for raising this tax in coastal shires in times of national emergency. The money was used to equip fleets to defend these areas against possible attacks from abroad. Charles, however, argued that the whole country benefited, at least indirectly, from the protection this afforded and that all counties should contribute to the tax. He also contended that he alone had the right to decide when an emergency existed. The judges upheld the king's views in Hampden's case (1637), but only by a majority of seven to five. Still, it looked as if Charles had obtained the right to impose a non-parliamentary tax which could easily become a regular levy.

Ship money and all the other financial expedients which were employed improved the royal revenue, which rose from about £600,000 a year at the beginning of the 1630s to about £900,000 a year at the end of the decade. Even this increase was not enough, however, to wipe out the large Crown debts, and Charles had to borrow more money to pay off these previous liabilities. In other words, his continuing solvency depended on his ability to obtain loans, and it was clear that any sudden large demand upon his purse—a war, for example—would necessitate the calling of parliament. Crisis point came for the king in 1638 when his Scottish subjects openly defied his authority.

The trouble in Scotland arose from Charles's and Laud's efforts to impose their religious ideas there. The climax came in 1637 when they tried to introduce a new prayer book, based on that of the Church of England. The Scots refused to accept this and at the beginning of 1638 the National Covenant, a document asserting Scotland's rights to its traditional religious and civil

74

liberties, was drawn up and signed by large numbers of Scotsmen. The king decided to coerce the Scots. It was a fateful decision, as it set in motion the events which led directly to civil war. It soon became clear that Charles did not have sufficient financial resources to impose his will in Scotland. In 1640, therefore, he was forced to call parliament. The first parliament which met that year, the Short Parliament, was dissolved hastily without voting the king any money. Its successor, the famous Long Parliament, which opened in November 1640, was one of the most important in English history.

At the beginning of the Long Parliament the king had little support in the House of Commons, and in 1641 he had to agree to a series of measures which profoundly and, as it turned out, permanently modified the structure of the English state. The institutions of conciliar government created during the Tudor period, notably the courts of Star Chamber and High Commission and the other prerogative courts, upon which James I and Charles I had depended for the enforcement of their policies, were swept away and Parliament embarked on a radical course of restoring its old position vis-à-vis the Crown.

The death of Strafford

The Commons also succeeded in 1641 in disposing of Thomas Wentworth, Earl of Strafford, the king's ablest minister, who was condemned to death by act of attainder and executed in May. Charles never forgave himself for consenting to Strafford's death, and there is no doubt that the earl's abilities would have been of the greatest use to him in the years ahead. The Commons, however, were determined that he should die. They feared that otherwise he might succeed in enforcing the royal will in England with the same ruthlessness he had shown during his rule in Ireland, where he had represented the king as lord deputy during the 1630s.

Events in Ireland contributed to the breakdown of the virtual unanimity which was a striking feature in the House of Commons during the early months of 1641. So did religious differences among MPs. The Commons were united in their desire to do away with Arminian practices—Laud was imprisoned in 1641—but some members wanted to go much further and abolish espiscopacy altogether, 'root and branch', This Puritan policy was abhorrent to many middle of the road Anglicans and it played a large part in the reaction towards the king's side which was apparent by the autumn of 1641. That reaction can be seen very clearly in the voting on the Grand Remonstrance, a summary of parliament's previous grievances against the Crown and a statement of further measures necessary to satisfy their wishes. John Pym, the ablest of the parliamentarian leaders and a supporter of the 'root and branch' policy, obtained a majority of only eleven votes (159 to 148) for the document when it was passed in November. Broadly speaking, those who voted for the Remonstrance wished for further radical changes in church and state, while those who voted against it were convinced that previous measures had been sufficient.

While the Remonstrance was being discussed news of a great Irish Catholic revolt against English authority reached London. Coming at such a time, this rebellion was a very important link in the chain of events leading to the outbreak of civil war in England. It was obvious that an army would have to be raised to crush the revolt, but the Commons as a whole were not prepared to concede control of it to the king. They feared that it might be turned against themselves. The king, on the other hand, was not prepared to surrender his control of the armed forces, the very basis of the royal prerogative.

In January 1642 he tried personally to arrest five of his leading opponents in the House of Commons. They had been warned and had already fled and the king had to withdraw baffled. This attempted coup was very unwise. It lost Charles a good deal of the moderate support which he had gained and left a virtually unbridgeable gulf of fear and suspicion between him and his opponents. Soon afterwards he left London and during the early part of 1642 the country drifted towards civil war. General hostilities began in September.

The civil war

Few historical subjects have provoked more discussion or greater disagreement among historians than the causes of the English Civil War. Only one thing is certain: no one explanation or group of explanations is entirely satisfactory. The best interpretation of the origins of the war is probably one which takes the widest possible view of its causes, and the English revolution should be seen in a European as well as in a local context. Much attention has recently been devoted to the social and economic background of

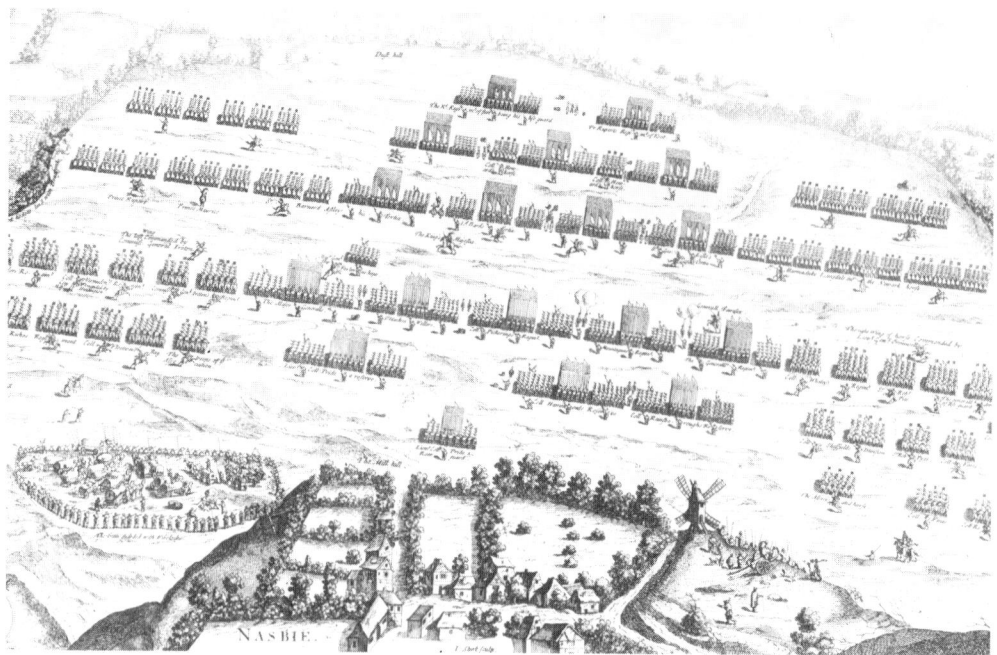

the political conflict. No generally accepted picture has emerged, but many historians see economic and social developments behind the obvious political fact that the leadership in the struggle against the Crown was taken by the gentry and their lawyer allies rather than by the aristocracy. This, it can be argued, reflected a relative increase in the wealth and political maturity of those middling groups in society—principally the landed gentry—which were increasingly resentful of the Crown's exactions. These were the people who looked to the common law to defend their interests and who were finally prepared to risk an open conflict with the king.

Any comprehensive interpretation must also take into account the increasing division between the Laudian and Puritan parties in the Church in the years before the Civil War, the constitutional conflicts of the reigns of James I and Charles I and the significance of the foreign policy of the first two Stuarts. Despite the wars of 1624–30, this was generally friendly towards Spain, still the arch-champion of militant Catholicism and as such anathema to most Englishmen.

The First Civil War lasted from 1642 until 1646. It ended with the defeat of the king, and during its course Oliver Cromwell, who dominated English history in the 1650s, emerged as a significant figure on the political stage. When the struggle began—and now we are speaking in the broadest possible terms—Charles controlled the north and west, the poorer part of the country, while the richer southern and eastern regions of the kingdom supported parliament. The king had an initial superiority in the quality of his troops, notably of his cavalry, but he failed to exploit this effectively, and the parliamentarians, who concluded an alliance with the Scots in 1643, took the initiative from that year onwards. The royal forces in the north were

defeated at Marston Moor in 1644 and in the following year the king's own army in the Midlands was beaten at Naseby. In 1646 Charles realized that further resistance was useless and surrendered to the Scots.

It was during the later stages of the war that Oliver Cromwell really made his mark. Cromwell, who came from East Anglian gentry stock, was an Independent in religion. As such he was one of a growing body of men who believed in the right of the congregation of each church to choose its own minister and worship in its own way. Cromwell's great contribution to parliament's victory in the war was as an organizer and trainer of cavalry. By its end he was second-in-command of the New Model Army, an efficient military force which had been organized in 1645 under the command of Sir Thomas Fairfax. Independency was very strong in the army, but it was much weaker in parliament, where both houses were dominated by Presbyterians who drew strength from their alliance with the Scots.

The king's execution

The two following years, 1646–8, were occupied by a series of tortuous intrigues in which the principal parties were Charles, the army, parliament and the Scots. The outcome was a Second Civil War, fought in 1648 between the Scots, who had allied with Charles, and the army. The Scots were soon defeated and the army leaders decided that they must get rid of Charles, the 'man of blood' whose intrigues had been responsible for the renewal of conflict. This provoked a direct clash with the Presbyterians in parliament, who had maintained an equivocal attitude during the Second Civil War but had eventually reopened negotiations with the king. The army took drastic action. In December 1648, the Presbyterian MPs were excluded from the Commons and only some seventy members, army supporters,

were allowed to remain. The purged parliament, in alliance with the army, set up a special court to try the king, who was executed in January 1649. Immediately afterwards the monarchy and the House of Lords were abolished.

It is easy to condemn Charles I's execution as a crime—there was, of course, no legal process by which a sovereign could be arraigned—but less easy to show what other solution was possible. Charles had many virtues both as a man and as a king. He was a faithful husband and a dutiful father. He was sincerely religious, and he worked hard at the routine business of kingship. Despite these admirable qualities, however, it can be argued that the most notable defect of his character—his total untrustworthiness—made his final execution necessary. Throughout the period between 1642 and 1648 he played his opponents off against one another with a total lack of scruple, which he himself would have justified by arguing that he was entitled to use virtually any means available to preserve the monarchy and the Church of England. In these circumstances he inevitably alienated any goodwill which remained among his enemies.

Although, therefore, the king in some ways brought about his own death, the very fact of his execution was a heavy burden for the regicides to bear. In England itself many people were horrified at his death. An eyewitness records that after the execution 'there was such a groan by the thousands then present, as I never heard before'.

Abroad the reaction was almost universally hostile, and in the United Provinces and Spain envoys of the new government were murdered by the hostile populace.

This new government took the form of a Commonwealth, with the remaining members of the House of Commons, the Rump as it came to be called, as the supreme authority in the state. Between 1649 and 1651 Cromwell reconquered Ireland and once again defeated the Scots who intervened on behalf of Charles I's son, the future Charles II. These victories made Cromwell, now the acknowledged leader of the army, the most powerful man in the state, though on many issues he did not see eye to eye with the Rump. There were clashes over foreign policy—Cromwell was unhappy about the war between England and the United Provinces which broke out in 1652—over the slowness of the Rump in reforming the country's archaic legal system, and, above all, over its determination to perpetuate its own existence. Cromwell and the army wanted a general election for a new parliament, but in April 1653 the Rump decided to have piecemeal by-elections with existing members keeping their seats. Cromwell then dissolved the Rump by force.

Between July and December 1653 he tried what was perhaps the most extraordinary constitutional experiment ever attempted in England, the Nominated Parliament, sometimes called the Barebones Parliament, after Praise-God Barbon, a London tradesman who was one of the MPs for the City. Its members were not elected in the normal

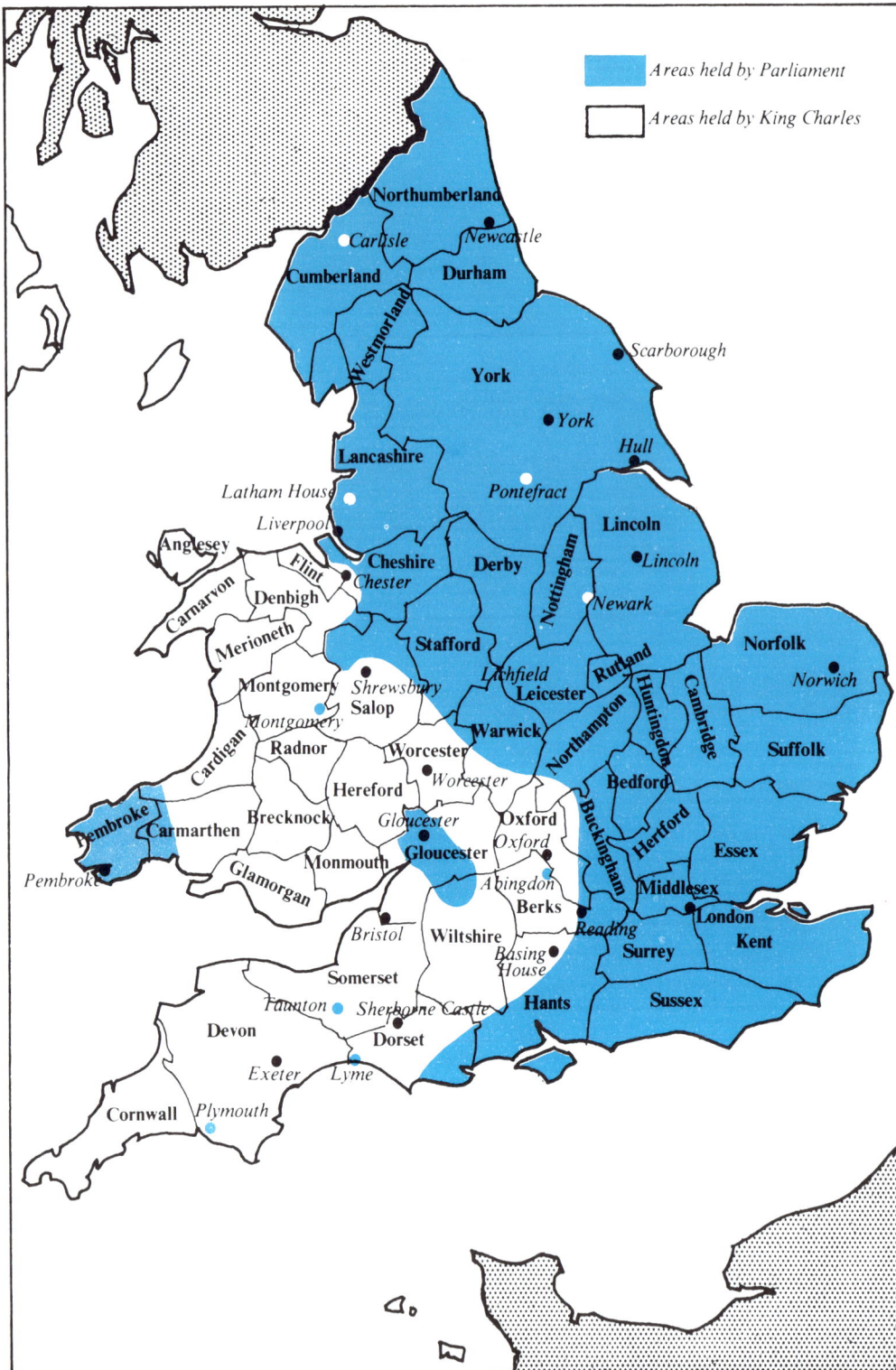

Areas held by Parliament
Areas held by King Charles

Map labels: Northumberland, Carlisle, Newcastle, Cumberland, Durham, Westmorland, Scarborough, York, York, Hull, Lancashire, Latham House, Pontefract, Liverpool, Lincoln, Lincoln, Anglesey, Flint, Cheshire, Derby, Chester, Nottingham, Newark, Carnarvon, Denbigh, Stafford, Norfolk, Merioneth, Lichfield, Rutland, Norwich, Montgomery, Shrewsbury, Leicester, Salop, Montgomery, Warwick, Northampton, Huntingdon, Cambridge, Cardigan, Radnor, Worcester, Suffolk, Hereford, Worcester, Bedford, Pembroke, Brecknock, Gloucester, Oxford, Hertford, Essex, Carmarthen, Gloucester, Oxford, Buckingham, Pembroke, Glamorgan, Monmouth, Abingdon, Middlesex, Berks, London, Bristol, Wiltshire, Reading, Surrey, Kent, Basing House, Somerset, Hants, Sussex, Taunton, Sherborne Castle, Devon, Dorset, Exeter, Lyme, Cornwall, Plymouth

only one chamber. Under the Humble Petition and Advice his powers as protector were increased, and a second chamber, the so-called 'Other House', was instituted. Originally the Humble Petition and Advice proposed to restore the monarchy, with Cromwell as king. He hesitated but in the end, under pressure from the army, refused the Crown. It is clear that Cromwell, who throughout his career was involved in so many constitutional experiments, was not wedded to any particular form of government. Its structure was always a secondary consideration in his eyes. It was, he thought, 'but a mortal thing', merely 'dross and dung compared with Christ'. For Cromwell religious considerations came first.

Cromwell the radical

In his attitude towards religion Cromwell was far in advance of his time. He had a deep and abiding belief in men's right to freedom of conscience and throughout his protectorate, tried to secure as wide a measure of religious toleration as was compatible with the safety of the state. The Cromwellian Church, set up in 1654, covered a wide spectrum of religious beliefs. No agreement on ritual or doctrine was required from its members except for the acceptance of the main principles of Christianity. In the words of a distinguished historian, 'it was not so much a Church as a confederation of Christian sects working together for righteousness under the control of the state.'

Outside this tolerant Establishment dissenters were allowed freedom of worship as long as their conduct did not threaten the integrity of the state. Anglicanism, which did constitute such a threat, was in theory banned but in practice enjoyed a wide degree of toleration. Even Catholics, who were regarded by most Englishmen of the day as idolators, and, like Anglicans, were not officially tolerated, were treated with a good deal of leniency. Cromwell's belief in wide religious toleration was very different from the attitude of the two protectorate parliaments of 1654 and 1656, which were dominated by moderate Presbyterians and conservative Independents who sought a much clearer definition of the doctrine of the state Church and wanted to exclude large sections of English Protestantism from legal recognition and protection.

Cromwell, a radical in religious matters, was profoundly conservative in his social attitudes. He saw secular society as an ordered hierarchy based on private property and regarded democratic or crypto-democratic ideas with abhorrence. He showed this very clearly in his attitude towards the Levellers, a group of men both inside and outside the army who were a power of some importance in England between 1647 and 1649. They advocated, among other reforms, a wide extension of the franchise in parliamentary elections. Cromwell thought

way. They were 'godly' men chosen by the leading army officers. The Nominated Parliament therefore reveals very clearly Cromwell's belief in the efficacy of religion in solving the problems of human society; he thought that if he collected a body of devout men they would soon put the state in order. He was disillusioned. The new parliament soon split into moderate and radical wings, the radicals pressing for the abolition of tithes and for sweeping law reforms. The alarm of the moderates at these proposals led them, with the encouragement of some of the more conservative army officers, especially General

Lambert, to meet unusually early one morning in December and, in the absence of many of their radical colleagues, to surrender their authority to Cromwell.

In December 1653, therefore, Cromwell had to construct another constitutional settlement. The new government which was set up was based on a written constitution produced by Lambert. This 'Instrument of Government' as it was called was the foundation of Cromwell's rule until it was replaced in 1657 by the 'Humble Petition and Advice'. By the Instrument Cromwell, with the title of Lord Protector, shared power with a parliament which consisted of

that this might lead in due course to social as well as political equality. His horror was reflected in his words to the Council of State early in 1649: 'You have no other way to deal with these men but to break them in pieces. . . . If you do not break them they will break you.' He then proceeded himself to suppress the London Levellers and Leveller-led mutinies in the army. The year 1649 brought the end of the Levellers as a serious political force and as a focus for potential social revolution. Throughout the 1650s the traditional social hierarchy remained undisturbed in Cromwell's England.

Cromwell pursued an active foreign policy. England had been a power of secondary importance in European affairs during the reigns of James I and Charles I, but he made the country feared and respected abroad. As at home, religious idealism played an important role in his policies. He hastened to make peace with the Protestant United Provinces in 1654 and in 1656 engaged in a war, waged in both the West Indies and Europe, against Spain, still regarded as the arch-enemy of Protestantism. In 1658 he won a bridgehead on the continent, when, following an Anglo-French victory over Spain at the Battle of the Dunes, the allies captured the town of Dunkirk, which was later handed over to England.

In September of the same year Cromwell died. The protectorate, which depended so much on his personality, did not long survive him. His ineffectual son and successor, Richard Cromwell, who did not have the support of the army leaders, was pushed into private life in 1659 when the Rump of the Long Parliament was restored. This now represented an alliance between the army leaders and anti-protectorate Republicans, but soon army and parliament fell out. The country seemed to be drifting towards anarchy. The situation was saved by George Monck, Cromwell's commander-in-chief in Scotland. He marched his well disciplined army south and restored those members of the House of Commons who had been purged in 1648. It soon voted to dissolve itself, and when elections for a new parliament were held monarchists won a large majority. The way was open for the restoration of Charles II, who arrived in London, amidst scenes of great rejoicing, in May 1660.

The period between 1642 and 1660 was a unique interlude in English history. During these years the Puritans took advantage of their victory over the established rulers of the country to impose a moral code which proved as distasteful to the populace at large as it was satisfactory to the whole range of Puritan opinion from the conservative Presbyterians of the Long Parliament to the radical sectaries of the Commonwealth and Protectorate.

Accepting the Scriptures as an absolute code of behaviour, they exacted Biblical penalties for moral offences: a law of 1650,

for example, imposed the death sentence for adultery.

Other legislation tried to stamp out drunkenness, swearing and gambling and to preserve the sanctity of the Sabbath. Such attempts to interfere with everyday social habits met, however, with little success. They did turn the bulk of the population into active enemies of Puritan morality and paved the way for the hedonistic atmosphere of the reign of Charles II.

On the restoration of 1660, the House of Lords and the Established Church of England returned along with the monarchy. The events of 1640 to 1660 could not,

Above, Oliver Cromwell (1599–1658), who ruled England after 1649 as head of the army and from 1653 as lord protector. Like many of the parliamentary leaders, he was anxious to preserve the social system of the time, to allow religious toleration and to prevent any body such as an established church or the monarchy to have sovereignty over the people. National Portrait Gallery, London.

Opposite, England and Wales during the Civil War, in 1644. Charles' support came mainly from the west country, and his capital was at Oxford. With the resources of London at their disposal, the parliamentarians had overwhelming material superiority.

79

however, be obliterated. The monarchy of Charles II and the restoration Church of Juxon and Sheldon were very different institutions from the pre-civil war kingship and the Laudian Church of England.

As far as the monarchy is concerned Charles II had none of the apparatus for personal rule that all his predecessors in the sixteenth and seventeenth centuries had possessed. The prerogative courts which had been abolished by the Long Parliament in 1641 were not restored and the common law courts reigned supreme. The events of 1640 to 1660 had also reduced the power and prestige of the Crown in a more intangible way. A section of the English political community had waged a successful war against the king and had later executed him in public. The death of Charles I on the scaffold was a permanent reminder to later monarchs that they might be held to account by their people.

In the Church the idea of comprehension —the theory that every English man and woman should belong to the state Church as well as to the state itself—was for all practical purposes abandoned soon after the restoration. This was because the Puritans, who had dominated religious life during the Interregnum, and the restored hierarchy of the Established Church could not settle their differences. Efforts were made to do so at the Savoy Conference of 1661 but no agreement was reached, and when the bishops produced a revised version of the prayer book the Puritan leaders found it quite unacceptable. The book was, however, incorporated in an Act of Uniformity, passed in 1662, and all ministers were required both to use the book and to make public declarations of 'unfeigned assent and consent' to all its contents. By the end of 1662 nearly 2,000 ministers had lost their livings—a much more sweeping change in the personnel of the Church than had occurred at any one time during the 1640s and 1650s.

Many of these ministers set up independent congregations which were subject to persecution under the Clarendon Code, a series of repressive laws against dissenters passed between 1661 and 1665. The intensity of persecution, however, varied a good deal and many congregations survived. Their continuing existence symbolized the end of the Tudor and early Stuart ideal of a united Christian society in which Church and state were one.

The House of Lords, just like the Crown, lost prestige as a result of the Interregnum. Neither the peers nor the Commons ever forgot that between 1649 and 1657 the upper house had been abolished. In the last resort England could do without a house of peers.

The new king

Charles II certainly never forgot that the country had done without a king for eleven

years. He was resolved not to 'go on his travels' again, and that determination explains why he was never prepared to make heroic stands on matters of conscience, except when the exclusion movement attempted to debar his brother James from the throne and thus destroy the very principle to which he (Charles) owed his crown, that of hereditary right. Charles, in fact, wanted to enjoy life, and the country as a whole was sympathetic to a monarchy and court which so openly rejected the rigours of Puritan morality. The king, unassuming and friendly, surrounded by his dogs and his mistresses, was personally popular.

In 1660 Charles took as his chief minister Edward Hyde, Earl of Clarendon, who had been the mainstay of the Royalist party in exile. He fell from power after the Dutch War of 1665–67 had revealed appalling inefficiency in his administration and went into exile abroad, where he wrote his *History of the Rebellion and Civil Wars in England*, still one of the finest pieces of English historical writing.

It was during the Dutch War that two of the most dramatic episodes of Restoration history took place—the Great Plague and the Great Fire of London. The plague, which raged from the spring of 1665 to the end of 1666, was the last, and one of the worst, of a series of outbreaks which had occurred in England in the three centuries following the Black Death in 1348. At its height in London, in autumn 1665, thousands died each week, many of them covered with the huge sores which were the most appalling signs of the plague's visitation.

Then, just as the plague was waning, came the Great Fire, which swept through the City of London for five days in September 1666, destroying more than 13,000 houses and more than eighty churches, including London's historic cathedral, old St Paul's. The tragedy of the fire, though it was a traumatic experience for the citizens of the capital, did, however, provide the opportunity for rebuilding London. This produced not only a city of superior private houses but also Wren's magnificent series of London churches, over fifty in all, including his masterpiece, new St Paul's.

Between 1667 and the early 1670s, while his capital was beginning to recover from the plague and the fire, Charles relied for advice on a group of ministers—themselves holding very different views on many subjects—who came to be known as the Cabal. In 1673, however, Sir Thomas Osborne, who had shown considerable financial ability as Treasurer of the Navy, was appointed Lord Treasurer and soon achieved primacy in the kings counsels. He was created Earl of Danby in 1674 and remained in office until 1679. Danby tried to wean Charles away from a pro-French foreign policy out of tune with the growing fears of most of his subjects about Louis XIV's expansionist ambitions. Charles had signed the treaty of Dover with France in 1670. By this he agreed, in return for a subsidy, to join France in war against the Dutch. By secret clauses he also promised to declare openly, at a time of his own choosing, his loyalty to the Catholic religion.

As a result of this treaty England joined France in attacking the Dutch in 1672, but in the autumn of the following year the Commons, suspicious of the French alliance, refused to vote supplies for the continuance of the war. Charles was forced to make a separate peace with the Dutch in 1674. For most of the rest of the 1670s Danby tried to persuade Charles to adopt an openly Protestant stance in foreign affairs, but the king shrank away from a complete break with France. Then, at the end of 1678, everything else was overshadowed by the Popish Plot.

It was in 1678 that Titus Oates, a liar and a scoundrel of the first order, announced that he had secret information about a plot by the Pope and the Jesuits to kill the king

and place his brother James, Duke of York, an avowed Catholic, on the throne. Protestant Englishmen of the day were prepared to believe almost anything about Catholics and by the time parliament met in October London was in ferment. The plot was the only subject of discussion and when Oates obtained support from the Earl of Shaftesbury, a skilful and unscrupulous politician who believed in strictly limited monarchy, the situation became serious for the government. Shaftesbury took advantage of the anti-Catholic feeling produced by the plot to try to secure James's exclusion from the throne. He won the support of three successive Houses of Commons between 1679 and 1681, but Charles refused to consider depriving his brother of the succession. When he dissolved the parliament of 1681 the Whigs—as those who favoured exclusion had come to be called to distinguish them from the Tory supporters of hereditary right—talked of armed resistance. In the end, however, they dispersed quietly. Charles had won.

He took advantage of the royalist reaction which followed the defeat of the exclusionist movement to remodel the borough corporations, which elected most MPs. Many of these were Whig strongholds, but the new charters which Charles imposed upon them made it probable that in future elections they would select royalist MPs.

A Catholic monarch

James II felt the benefit of these changes immediately after his accession to the throne in 1685. His first parliament was loyal to the point of subservience. Despite this, however, his reign lasted for only three years. The reason was basically James's desire to restore the Catholic faith to an official and respected place in English society at a time when the great majority of Englishmen still feared and detested it. In such a situation there was sure to be serious conflict.

James tried to further the cause of Catholicism by a variety of measures, each of which increased antagonism towards the Crown in the country at large. He appointed Catholics to high office in both the army and civil government, he set up an ecclesiastical commission reminiscent of the old Court of High Commission, he received a papal envoy at Whitehall, he issued declarations of indulgence suspending the penal laws against Catholics and dissenters. He wanted to persuade parliament to repeal the penal laws altogether, but in order to achieve this he had to set about a further remodelling of the municipal corporations. Charles II's reforms, it is true, had handed control of the boroughs over to fervent Tories, but these men were committed Anglicans as well and clearly would not have been prepared to approve of measures harmful to the position of the Church of England. James's reforms meant that in many boroughs the parliamentary franchise and the administration of justice were handed over to Catholics and dissenters. He also instituted a great purge of Anglican county notables.

In 1686 and 1687 most of the established JPs in England and Wales, the effective rulers of the country in the localities, were

Above, James, Duke of York, painted in 1661. James was the brother of Charles II, and as he became overtly Catholic, and as it became clear that Charles would have no legitimate heirs, attempts were made to exclude James from the throne. Nevertheless, he acceded as James II in 1685. Victoria and Albert Museum, London.

Top, the Great Fire of London in September 1666, which practically devastated the whole of the city, and enabled it to be rebuilt on more spacious lines. Half its population lost their homes.

Opposite, an English doctor during the Great Plague of 1665–66; more than 70,000 people died during this last great outbreak of bubonic plague.

81

replaced by men of inferior social rank. These changes caused the most profound resentment among the propertied classes who felt that the country was faced with two major threats, one to the whole established fabric of society, the other to the position of the Church of England. The crowning blow from their point of view was the birth of a son and heir to James in June of 1688. Until then the Crown's opponents could take comfort in the thought that he would be succeeded by one of his Protestant daughters.

In this situation seven prominent Englishmen signed an invitation to William of Orange, ruler of Holland, a grandson of Charles I and husband of James's elder daughter Mary, to come to England and save the country from James's policies. William landed in November and the following month James fled to France. The stage was set for the joint accession of William and Mary to the throne and the settlement of 1689.

Thus the political and constitutional history of seventeenth-century England was dominated by conflicts between the Crown and large numbers of its subjects. Domestic arguments did not, however, prevent the country from expanding abroad or inhibit literary and scientific developments. The century saw the foundation of an English colonial empire in America and a great expansion in both the volume and the content of English trade. These developments set the scene for further advances in the eighteenth century when the country emerged as a great colonial, commercial and financial power. In the field of culture and science Englishmen made unique contributions to the age. The names of Shakespeare, Bacon, Milton, Hobbes, Locke, Dryden and Newton—a roll-call of genius—are sufficient explanation of the fact that, by the end of the century, England was challenging France for the intellectual leadership of Europe.

Chapter 8

The Golden Age of the United Provinces

In 1609 the Spanish government concluded a military truce with the Seven United Provinces of the Netherlands which had been in revolt against its authority since the 1570s. Philip III of Spain was not prepared at that time to recognize formally the complete sovereignty which his rebellious subjects had claimed since the 1580s, but his government had negotiated with them 'as if' they were an independent power. Although Spain was thus forced by military and financial exhaustion to concede what amounted to practical recognition of sovereign authority to the northern Netherlands, the king and his advisers had some consolation. Thanks to the military genius of the Duke of Parma the southern Netherlands, which in the 1570s had also seemed likely to break away, had been recovered for Spain in the early 1580s. The Netherlands were thus divided—permanently as it turned out. The factors which determined the line of division were not linguistic or religious—there were many Dutch speakers in the Spanish Netherlands and very many Catholics in the north—but geographic and military: the position of the Spanish and Dutch forces in the country at the time of the truce determined the frontier.

The seven provinces which had struggled against Spain for some forty years to win their freedom were to enjoy a glorious career in the seventeenth century as the world's greatest commercial power, but in 1609 powerful forces in the country feared that its independence might be short-lived. Those who took this view believed that the truce was a great mistake. The Spanish government, they argued, had concluded it from a position of weakness but with a view to renewing the struggle later, after a period of peace had enabled the still mighty Spanish Empire to mobilize new resources.

The principal protagonist of this view was Prince Maurice of Orange, son of William the Silent. He held the position of *stadtholder* (governor) in five of the seven provinces, an office which gave him considerable influence in the internal affairs of each province and of the country as a whole. He had strong support among the more zealous Calvinists, men who regarded any agreement with the Spaniards, short of complete victory, as a sign of weakness.

On the other side stood the ruling 'regent' families, who dominated the states or governing assemblies of each of the provinces and through them the States-General of the United Provinces. The regents were an oligarchy of wealthy burghers, particularly strong in Holland, the dominant province in the Union, who thought, on the whole, that the advantage of the state would best be served by peace. They believed firmly in the need to subject the Church to the secular power. The Calvinist ministers and the enthusiasts among their flocks, on the other hand, stressed the independent rights of the Church; they criticized not only the eagerness of the regents to negotiate with the Spanish heretics but also their readiness to extend toleration at home to the large number of Catholic and Protestant dissenters. The leader of the regent party and the man who was principally responsible for the successful negotiation of the 1609 truce was Oldenbarnevelt, advocate (that is principal official) of the States of Holland. His disagreement with Prince Maurice over the conclusion of the truce was the beginning of a conflict between the two men which was to end in tragedy in 1619.

Religious divisions

The whole domestic history of the republic in the years before the renewal of war with Spain in 1621 was dominated by disputes in which religion and politics were inextricably intermingled. The religious side of the conflict turned on a theological dispute between two professors at the University of Leyden in Holland. One of these, Arminius, put forward views on free will which stressed man's ability to help to determine the fate of his soul by his own efforts. The other, Gomarus, stressed the traditional Calvinist concept of predestination, the idea that God has decided each soul's fate in advance and that man is powerless to aid his salvation by his own efforts.

These rival ideas became involved with politics in 1610, when the supporters of Arminius, a minority in the ministry, set out their views on the disputed questions in a Remonstrance, which they presented to the States of Holland, together with a request for protection from their opponents. The States, with their firm views on the responsibility of the secular power for ecclesiastical affairs, could hardly refuse an appeal couched in these terms. Under Oldenbarnevelt's leadership they granted the desired protection, an action which infuriated the majority among the ministry who followed Gomarus. In the heated atmosphere thus engendered the States' subsequent efforts at mediation between the two sides did little to help matters, and in 1611 the Gomarists presented a Counter-Remonstrance containing their own views on the points at issue. For the next few years the arguments of Remonstrants and

Above, Johan van Oldenbarnevelt (1547–1619), the Dutch statesman who championed the rule of the merchants, and of the state of Holland, within the United Provinces from the 1580s until his execution.

Opposite left, the arrival of William of Orange in England in November 1688; his invasion, which had probably been planned before he was invited to sail to England, was universally welcomed and the coup was achieved virtually without bloodshed.

Opposite top right, Francis Bacon (1561–1626), the English scientist who argued for the adoption of the scientific method – observation and hypothesis – and who served as lord chancellor after 1618, until he was convicted of accepting bribes in 1621. National Portrait Gallery, London.

Opposite bottom right, John Milton (1608–74), the poet of Paradise Lost, *who was a supporter of the parliamentary cause in the civil war, argued for freedom of speech in his pamphlet* Areopagitica *(1644) and discussed many of the ideas of the religious sects in his poetry. National Portrait Gallery, London.*

Opposite bottom left, an English plate of 1691 celebrating the accession of William and Mary. The Glorious Revolution was supported by almost all sectors of English society, Ashmolean Museum, Oxford.

Counter-Remonstrants resounded throughout the province of Holland and indeed throughout the United Provinces as a whole. Prince Maurice, alienated from Oldenbarnevelt as a result of the truce of 1609 and at odds with him in subsequent years over other issues of foreign policy, openly joined the Counter-Remonstrant side in 1617. The political issue was thus very clearly joined: a struggle between Maurice and Oldenbarnevelt for the dominant position in the state, a conflict no less real because it was waged under the cloak of high religious principles.

Arminianism had comparatively little support outside Holland, and the other states tended to follow the lead of their Counter-Remonstrant ministers. Accordingly the majority in the States-General supported the Gomarists against the States of Holland which, though with loud and important dissenting voices, particularly from Amsterdam, were for the Arminian party. Matters came to a climax in August 1618 when Maurice, acting on a warrant from the states-general, ordered the arrest of Oldenbarnevelt. He followed this up by purging the advocate's supporters from the town councils of Holland and replacing them with Counter-Remonstrants. The States of Holland, thus transformed, authorized the trial of Oldenbarnevelt before an extraordinary court which, in May 1619 sentenced him to death for jeopardizing 'the position of the faith . . . and of the state'. He was executed the following day. It was a poor reward for a man who had probably done more than any other, with the exception of William the Silent himself, to establish the Dutch republic.

Prince Maurice

Even before Oldenbarnevelt's trial and execution a national synod of the Church, from which Remonstrants were excluded, had met at Dort and condemned Arminian doctrines. The leading Remonstrant ministers were banished from the country and their supporters excluded from public office and denied the right to freedom of worship, though freedom of conscience was still allowed: there was no suggestion of enforcing attendance at the State Church. The events of 1618–19 were, of course, a great triumph for Prince Maurice. From then until his death in 1625 he was virtually supreme in the state. In 1621, however, Maurice turned his attention away from the internal affairs of the Republic and focused it on the war with Spain, which broke out again that year on the expiry of the twelve-year truce.

This war, the second stage of the great struggle against Spain, lasted until the Treaty of Münster in 1648, when the Spanish government at last formally recognized the sovereignty of the United Provinces and also their territory in the southern Netherlands—parts of Flanders and Brabant—which had been conquered during the

Above, John de Witt (1625–72), the leader of the opposition to the power of the House of Orange. De Witt's policy of conciliation towards Louis XIV in 1672 led to his overthrow and murder by Orange supporters.

Left, the Grand Assembly of the States of the United Provinces at The Hague in 1651, at which the decision was taken to reduce the authority of the quasi-royal Orange family and extend the authority of the individual states.

Opposite, a street plan of Amsterdam in the seventeenth century showing its harbours, canals and fortifications; at the corners are shown the main civic buildings, the city hall, the bank, the West India Company House and the East India Company House.

war. Indeed, during the 1640s Maurice's successor, his brother Frederick Henry, became more and more committed to a personal foreign policy which took little heed of the real interests of the republic. That policy combined support for the royalists in England—his son William had married Princess Mary, daughter of Charles I, in 1641—with a continuing dependence on and even subservience to the growing power of France, which had been the republic's ally in the war but which might and indeed later did prove as great a threat to the Netherlands' liberties as Spain had ever been. His death, therefore, came at a most opportune time for the peace party, as his son and successor, William II, lacked the influence and experience necessary to prevent the conclusion of the agreements the war against Spain without Dutch aid.

William, however, was not prepared to accept the situation. He was determined to renew the war and also, if possible, to secure the restoration of his brother-in-law Charles Stuart in England. These ambitious plans, which necessitated the maintenance of a large army, led to bitter conflict with the States of Holland and at one time civil war seemed imminent. In November 1650, however, William died. Eight days later his only child, the future William III, was born. There could be no question of appointing the infant prince to his father's dignities and between 1650 and 1672 most of the republic's provinces were without a stadtholder.

This was the 'republican' period, a distinctive phase in Dutch history. It was ushered in by the Grand Assembly, which met at the Hague in 1651. The States of Holland hoped that this body which represented all the provincial estates, would produce a new form of government for the republic. Their hope was disappointed, but the Assembly did take important decisions which greatly strengthened the control of the individual provinces over the army. As a result the armed forces of the country were virtually split into seven. This was a considerable triumph for the centrifugal tendencies within the United Provinces; indeed, after 1651 the country seemed more like a union of independent states than a federal republic.

Power follows wealth

The years 1650–1 thus witnessed a 'revolution' in the United Provinces. William II's attempt to enforce his personal foreign policy, an attempt which would surely have had important constitutional results if it had succeeded, was followed by his early and unexpected death and a reaction in which the views of the ruling regent oligarchy of Holland won the day. Indeed, in the decentralized republic of 1651–72 Holland's position was stronger than ever. This was partly a result of its intrinsic economic strength—it was by far the wealthiest province, contributing some fifty-eight percent of the total taxes of the union—and partly because of the emergence in 1652 of John de Witt, a statesman of note, as grand pensionary of Holland.

De Witt's policy was fundamentally conservative. Essentially, he wanted to preserve the status quo of 1651 both at home

85

Haarlem · Amsterdam · Leyden · The Hague · Delft · Utrecht · Rotterdam · Nijmegen · Breda · Bruges · Antwerp · Ghent · Louvain · Maastricht · Cologne · Brussels · Liège

United Provinces
Generality Land
Principality of Liège

Canton · FORMOSA · MALAYA · SUMATRA · BORNEO · CELEBES · JAVA · TIMOR

and abroad. The great threats to this ambition came from the House of Orange and its partisans at home and from England and France abroad. The Orange family was not resigned to the loss of its great position in the republic; England was jealous of the commercial dominance of the United Provinces; and after 1668 France, under Louis XIV, was determined to humble the country which had opposed her political ambitions in the Spanish Netherlands during the War of Devolution. De Witt's system thus collapsed in ruins in 1672 with the Anglo-French attack on the republic and the restoration of the office of stadtholder to the House of Orange in the person of William III. The people held de Witt responsible for the disasters of the French invasion, and in August 1672 he and his brother were lynched at the Hague. Like Oldenbarnevelt he deserved a better fate. He had served the republic to the best of his very considerable abilities and it is difficult to see what he could have done to prevent the French invasion.

From 1672 until his death thirty years later William III dominated the history of the United Provinces. When he assumed office it seemed that, because of the successes of French arms the republic was on the brink of dissolution. By 1674, however, the French had withdrawn from Dutch soil. This was a result of at least as much of Louis XIV's errors as of William III's energy, but the events of 1672–4 gave the latter a prestige as saviour of his country which stood him in good stead in later years. After the end of the war in 1678 the United Provinces enjoyed a decade of peace, but William's régime in the republic, just like his rule in England after 1689, was dominated by his determination to oppose Louis XIV's ambitions and to reduce the power of France. He had the satisfaction of living to see the first major check to French power in the war of 1688–97 and died in 1702 at the beginning of the long and costly struggle over the Spanish succession. This war put an end to France's hopes of dominating Europe but at the same time imposed a strain on Dutch resources from which the republic never really recovered.

Even before William's death the effects of war in the 1690s had considerably reduced

his popularity. That had been at its height in the 1670s. In 1674 the States of Holland and Zeeland made his title a hereditary office and in 1675 the States-General did the same for his offices of captain-general and admiral-general of the union. By 1700, however, the lower middle classes in particular were suffering severely from the increased burdens of war taxation. The middle class as a whole resented William's failure to curtail the power of the ruling regent oligarchy. They also objected to the growing corruption in appointments to official posts which secured the nomination of his own followers and obtained much needed revenue to further the war effort.

The social system

An outline political and diplomatic history of the United Provinces in the seventeenth century with its ecclesiastical squabbles and recurrent conflicts between the House of Orange and the republican party does little to suggest a 'golden age': quite the

contrary. Yet there is no doubt that the seventeenth century was the greatest period in the history of the Netherlands. It witnessed a commercial and imperial expansion and cultural flowering which were among the wonders of the contemporary world and which should not be obscured by the often sordid details of domestic political rivalries.

The imperial expansion of the United Provinces took place against a social background entirely different from that of any other country in Europe. It is not easy to make generalizations about the social structure of the republic, which varied greatly from province to province. The nobility, for example, was much more important in Guelderland than in Holland, where it was numerically weak and economically insignificant. Holland, of course, dominated the union, and it is not altogether unrealistic to take the social situation there as representative of the ethos of life in the country as a whole during the period of its greatest glory.

Holland was dominated by its urban patriciate, the 'regent' class, which by the middle of the seventeenth century had established itself firmly as a burgher oligarchy in control of the administration and economic life of the province. It is not easy to estimate the number of regent families, but they certainly formed a very small minority of the population—perhaps only one in every thousand belonged to the regent class. Below them in the social hierarchy there was a large middle class with wide variations of income and status but all sharing to some extent in the prosperity which unparalleled economic expansion brought. Even the artisans and other members of the lower classes who thronged the province's cities and towns enjoyed on the whole a standard of life which would have been the envy of their fellows in other European countries. Moreover, the really poor were not neglected. Dutch workhouses, orphanages and other charitable institutions may have been primitive by modern standards, but they were far in advance of anything found in most other countries at the time.

This variegated population belonged to a number of religious groups. Perhaps a

Above, The Shipbuilder and his Wife, *painted by Rembrandt Van Rijn (1606–69), prosperous members of the Dutch middle classes. National Maritime, Museum, London.*

Above left, Michael de Ruyter (1607–91), the Dutch admiral who supported Denmark in 1658–59, and commanded the fleet during the Second Anglo-Dutch War.

Top, the Dutch burning the English fleet at anchor in the River Medway during the Second Anglo-Dutch War in 1667.

Top left, the Battle of the Sound, in 1658, in which the Dutch narrowly defeated a Swedish fleet and managed to end the Swedish domination of Denmark. Rijksmuseum, Amsterdam.

Opposite left, the United Provinces according to the Treaty of Münster, whereby Spain at last recognized their independence. The Generality Land was a part of the southern Netherlands conquered by the United Provinces and ceded to them by Spain; and the Principality of Liège was still technically part of the Holy Roman Empire.

Opposite right, the Dutch empire in the East Indies, won in the early seventeenth century by the Dutch East India Company.

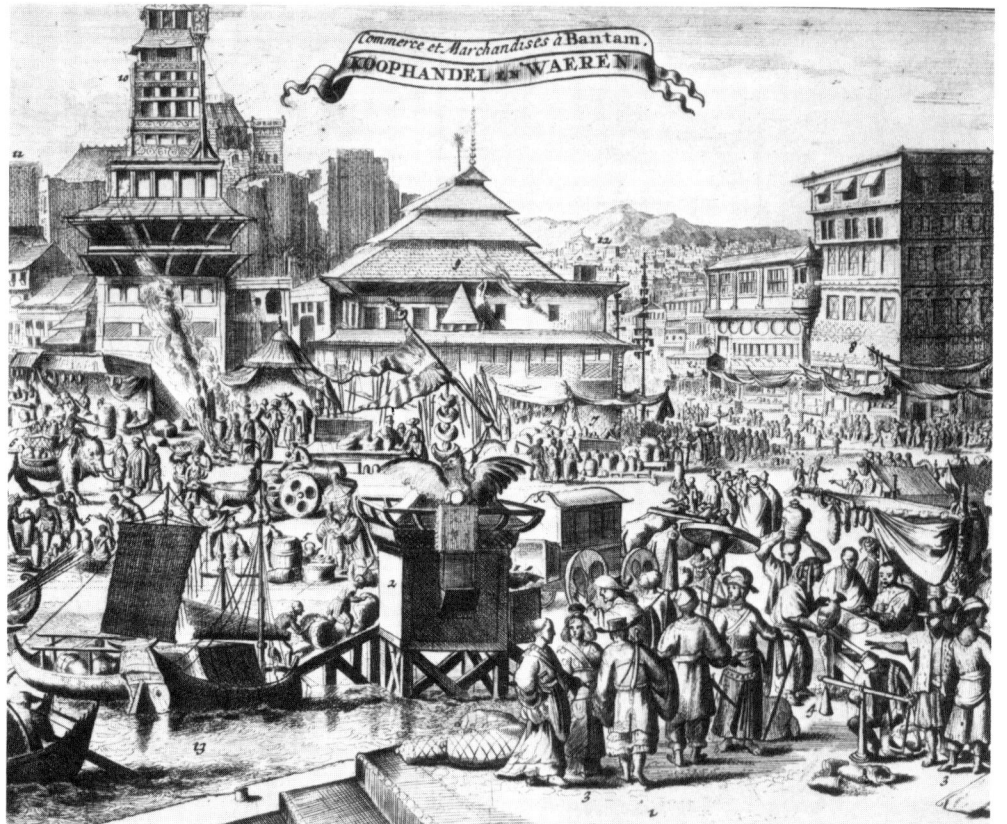

Commerce et Marchandises à Bantam.
KOOPHANDEL EN WAEREN

third of the population—and now we are speaking of the union as a whole—belonged to the official Reformed Church as it emerged at the Synod of Dort. Nearly half may have been Catholics, and the remainder were Remonstrants, Lutherans, Baptists and adherents of numerous small sects. There was freedom of conscience; the state Church made no systematic effort to enforce Calvinism, but freedom of worship was restricted and dissenters often found it difficult to hold administrative posts. All in all, however, the religious policy of the Dutch states was liberal. Certainly, when compared with contemporary France, where the Huguenots were subjected to violent persecution, it was a model of enlightenment.

The population of the United Provinces thus enjoyed a combination of religious freedom and economic prosperity which was unique in Europe. The prosperity was based upon the success of Dutch trade. Although the foundations of Dutch commercial greatness had been laid in the Middle Ages it was only during the period of the revolt against Spain, probably sometime between the 1590s and the 1620s, that the northern Netherlands became unquestionably the leading seafaring and trading nation in the world. Dutch commercial preponderance in the seventeenth century was based upon a combination of factors: the geographical situation of the republic, ideally placed to act as an entrepôt for the trade of northern and central Europe; the long seafaring traditions of the country's maritime provinces; the absence of state interference in economic life; the fact that the States-General had neither the authority nor the desire to introduce economic planning; and the absence, at least for most of the century, of really efficient competitors.

It was a combination of these factors which enabled a group of Amsterdam merchants to tell the States of Holland 'during the truce, through our economic management and exertions we have sailed all nations off the seas, drawn almost all trade from other lands hither and served the whole of Europe with our ships.' This was not an exaggerated boast.

French, English and Mediterranean ports were filled with Dutch vessels carrying raw materials or manufactured goods which they sold or exchanged for other commodities. Grain and naval stores were obtained in the Baltic, cloth in England, linens in Germany, salt and wines in France. oil, fruit and silks in the Mediterranean. From America came sugar, from the East Indies spices and other luxuries.

This great Dutch carrying trade was centred in the ports of Holland, especially in the town of Amsterdam. By the mid-seventeenth century Amsterdam was one of the great cities of Europe, with a population of perhaps 150,000. It was the centre of the Baltic trade, the great source of its prosperity, and of the West and East Indian trades. During the seventeenth century, however, Amsterdam became much more than the world's greatest port. It also became the centre of the international money market, outstripping Venice and Genoa. The accumulation of capital in the United Provinces which made this development possible was based on the country's trading successes and was aided by the policy of the town government of Amsterdam which in 1609 set up a Bank designed to finance international trade. It had considerable success and by the mid-seventeenth century the republic was clearly the leading financial as well as the leading commercial power in the world. This was very plain at the time of Louis XIV's invasion in 1672. In that year, when the rate of interest on the Dutch national debt stood at only $3\frac{3}{4}$ per cent there was a negligible response to a French public loan even when offered at $5\frac{1}{2}$ percent.

Most of the ships which constantly filled the port of Amsterdam were engaged in European trade, but an increasing number sailed to and from other continents, notably the Americas and Asia. In the seventeenth century the republic won two empires, one in America and the other in the East Indies. She soon lost most of her American acquisitions but her great East Indian possessions remained a valuable asset until the twentieth century.

Wealth from the Spice Islands

The republic's possessions in the East Indies were controlled by the Dutch East India Company which became, in the seventeenth century, the most powerful European institution in Asia and the greatest trading corporation in the world. The company had been founded in 1602 to regulate and protect the already considerable trade carried on by the Dutch in the eastern seas. This was necessary because that trade was challenged by the traditional dominance of Portugal in the area, and Portugal, then a possession of the Spanish crown, was inevitably involved in Spain's war against her rebellious Netherlands provinces.

The company was given full authority in the east, with the right to maintain military forces on sea and by land, to make war and peace, coin money and found colonies. Under two great proconsuls, Coen and Van Diemen, whose careers in the East.Indies spanned the period between 1618 and 1645, it made spectacular progress, founding its capital at Batavia on the island of Java, obtaining and then consolidating a hold on the Moluccas, the fabulous 'spice islands', which were, in the eyes of the company's servants, the most valuable part of the whole eastern commercial system, and expelling the Portuguese from Malacca and from part of Sri Lanka. In 1652 the company established a colony at the Cape of Good Hope on the southern tip of Africa and after 1660 consolidated its hold on the East Indies as a whole.

The company's chief imports into Holland were spices and textiles. The latter, principally silks and cotton piece goods, became more and more important as the century advanced and by 1700 were the most valuable part of the eastern trade. Although it was first and foremost a commercial organization the company's conquests and the need to supervise and control the native principalities in the Indies involved it in heavy expenses. In 1669 it possessed forty ships of war and 10,000 soldiers in addition to its 150 trading vessels. Military expenditure as heavy as this soon reduced its profits and in addition it suffered from servants who tended to promote their own private trading interests at the expense of those of the company as a whole. By 1700 therefore the company had begun to decline. This decline was, of course, entirely relative. Although its profits were less than they had been in the great years of the seventeenth century it remained a very important body until nearly 1800.

The East India Company was founded principally as a trading body. The reasons for the inception of the West India Company in 1621 were different. It was formed essentially to fight against Portugal and

Spain in the Americas and was thus an instrument of war rather than a commercial company. It soon captured some islands in the West Indies but its principal efforts were made in Brazil and in New Netherland, a Dutch colony centred on Manhattan island, which it took over in 1623. New Netherland was ceded to England in 1667 after the second Dutch war, and substantial conquests made in northeastern Brazil after 1630 had to be abandoned to the Portuguese by the 1650s. The prospects of a Dutch American empire, which came to the fore only in the early years of the seventeenth century, ahd thus collapsed by the 1660s.

The arts

The Dutch expansion overseas, symbolized by the creation of the West and East India Companies, was paralleled by the expansion of Dutch cultural horizons at home. The seventeenth century was the great age of Dutch art and literature. The growing numbers and wealth of the middle class in the republic led to an increasing demand for aesthetic satisfaction, a demand which produced forms of artistic expression different from those found in the absolutist and Baroque culture which dominated most of the rest of western Europe.

Painting was by far the most important of the Dutch arts. There was little scope for notable architecture or sculpture. These, in the seventeenth century, depended largely on the existence of patrons dedicated to conspicuous consumption, great princes and cardinals, or nobles of the highest rank, the kind of men who were not to be found in the Netherlands. On the other hand, those who enjoyed even modest prosperity could aspire to the ownership of paintings. Thousands of Dutchmen did. The pictures which they bought were characterized by realism and by infinite variety: still-lifes, landscapes, seascapes, individual and group portraits, views of towns, studies of animals, pictures of the interiors of churches—to select just some of the subjects favoured by Dutch artists of the time. There were dozens of good Dutch painters in the seventeenth century, several great ones—like Frans Hals, who painted really splendid portrait groups, and Jan Vermeer of Delft, who produced magnificent scenes of his native towns—and one unquestioned genius, Rembrandt, a man whose work can never be adequately described but which, with its humanity and its inner simplicity, gives the impression that its creator had looked at some of the great secrets of the universe. To prove the point it is only necessary to look at his wonderful series of self-portraits, which depict the physical and spiritual development of a genius.

The greatness of Dutch literature in the seventeenth century has received less general recognition than the greatness of its painting, but in both prose and poetry it was a time of the highest achievement. Cats, Huygens, Hooft and Vondel, to mention only four names, wrote verse and prose of the highest calibre. Vondel, regarded by his fellow countrymen as their greatest poet, on a par with Shakespeare, has never won equal recognition in other countries, but the perennial fascination which he has exercised over the minds of Netherlands through such plays as *Lucifer* (1654) and *Jephta* (1659) makes him the worthy leader of a golden age in literature.

When he died in 1679 that golden age was almost over, in other aspects of Dutch life as well as in literature. Dutch cultural inspiration, as well as the country's economic and political strength, declined in the eighteenth century. The political and economic deterioration must not be exaggerated or antedated. The United Provinces entered the war of the Spanish Succession as a great power, and her commercial and financial predominance in Europe lasted well into the eighteenth century. But already by 1700 there were signs that the rising power of England, with a larger population and superior natural resources, would in a generation or so outstrip her in both trade and finance. The cultural decline came earlier and was more dramatic. By 1680 the great age of Dutch painting and literature was over. The men of genius had died leaving no successors.

Above, A Group Portrait of the Officers of the St Hadrian Militia, *painted in 1633 by Franz Hals; Dutch portraits of civic officials and people carrying out their public duties were common in the seventeen century. Frans Halsmuseum, Haarlem.*

Left, Self-portrait at a Window, *by Rembrandt, done in 1640. Although more poetical than the work of any of his contemporaries, Rembrandt's paintings and etchings reflect the popular taste for self-portraits and subjects of human curiosity.*

Opposite, Interior with Soldiers, *painted by Pieter de Hooch (c. 1629–c. 1677). Such scenes of relaxation and conviviality are said to express the love of life and lack of pretentiousness of the Dutch bourgeoisie. National Gallery, London.*

Chapter 9

The Changing Pattern of Europe

When Louis XIV assumed personal charge of his kingdom in 1661, France was the greatest power in Europe. She had achieved that position as a result of a long struggle with the Austrian and Spanish branches of the Habsburg family, a conflict which, in its most recent phase, had lasted from 1635 to 1659. The Austrian Habsburgs, headed by the Holy Roman emperor, were humiliated at the Treaty of Westphalia in 1648, when France not only gained the three bishoprics of Metz, Toul and Verdun, comprising important territories on her eastern frontier, but the emperor's rights in Alsace as well. In 1659 the Treaty of the Pyrenees, which brought the Spanish phase of the war to an end, gave her the provinces of Roussillon and Cerdagne, Spanish territory lying to the north of the Pyrenees and most of Artois in the Spanish Netherlands as well.

The Treaty of the Pyrenees demonstrated clearly to the world at large that the great days of the Spanish Empire were over. In the sixteenth century Spain had been the dominant power. After her acquisition of Portugal in 1580 she controlled the greatest empire that the world had yet seen, with far flung possessions in Europe, Africa, Asia and the Americas. That empire had largely been created by the Castilian provinces which formed the heartland of the Iberian peninsula, and the strength and stability of Spain as a whole depended on the continuing power of Castile. The years between 1590 and 1620, however, saw a rapid erosion of the three fundamental foundations of Castile's greatness, rising population, productivity and the revenue which she obtained from her American colonies. The decline of Castile's ability to support the burdens of empire led the Count-Duke of Olivares, Philip IV's leading minister from 1621 to 1643, to turn to the kingdoms of Portugal and Aragon for greater contributions. This led to revolts there, and these, in turn, further weakened the empire as a whole. By 1661 Spain was very clearly in decline.

The greatness of France in 1661 was founded at least as much on the weaknesses of the other European states as on her own intrinsic strength. Wherever Louis looked conditions seemed favourable for extending French influence. The newly restored Charles II of England was pre-occupied with the settlement of his kingdom after the upheavals of 1640 to 1660 and was in any case an admirer of Louis. The United Provinces, under John de Witt, were pre-occupied with defending their commercial supremacy and preventing a return to power of the House of Orange. Moreover, they had fought with France against Spain in the 1630s and 1640s and, though very well aware of the potential threat of growing French power, continued their traditional anti-Spanish stance.

Louis, therefore, had nothing to fear from England or the Dutch. He had equally little cause to worry about the Emperor Leopold I. From the 1660s until the 1680s Leopold's main preoccupation was the defence of his own hereditary Austrian and Hungarian dominions against the Ottoman Turks. The Turkish Empire, which had declined sharply in power in the early seventeenth century under a series of incompetent sultans, revived dramatically after 1656 with campaigns against Austria and Hungary, which culminated in the siege of Vienna, the imperial capital, in 1683. Leopold, so strongly threatened in the east, was in a very weak position to resist French ambitions in the west.

Of the other states, the vast Russian Empire was hardly, in the mid-seventeenth century, part of Europe at all. It had a large population and great unexploited natural resources but its army was inefficient by west European standards and its administration primitive. Russian foreign policy centred around its immediate neighbours, the Ottoman Empire, Poland and Sweden. The vast Polish state was in decline, but Sweden, in 1661 the dominant country in the Baltic, was a great European power, a position which she had won under Gustavus Adolphus and in alliance with France during the Thirty Years War. In 1660, however, she lost a notable warrior-king, Charles X, and a regency became essential for the four-year-old Charles XI. The main aim of the regency in foreign policy was to preserve Swedish dominance in the north. This determination led to tactical switches in Sweden's alliances in the 1660s, though the tradition of friendship with France remained strong. She did not have the ability, even if she had had the will, to undertake sustained resistance to French ambitions in the west.

The weaknesses of most of the European states appeared doubly dramatic when contrasted with France's intrinsic strength. France's population was about eighteen million, perhaps three times as large as that of England or Spain and about eight times greater than that of the United Provinces or Sweden. Even the vast Russian Empire had fewer inhabitants. France had other impressive natural resources, notably fertile soil, and in the early years of Louis' personal rule, under Colbert's direction, financial reforms and industrial development added to the country's strength. The army steadily increased in size, from under 100,000 in the early 1660s to nearly 400,000 during the war of the Spanish Succession. In addition, under the direction of two administrators of genius, Michel le Tellier and his son, the Marquis de Louvois, its munitions and supply services were greatly improved and discipline in all ranks was tightened up. Moreover, Louis had at the beginning of his reign, the greatest generals in Europe, Turenne and Condé.

There was no naval tradition in France comparable with her great military reputation, dating back to the Middle Ages. Colbert, however, resolved to make France a great naval power. He built dockyards, ordered French ships to be constructed at home rather than abroad and developed an elaborate bureaucratic machine for the government of the navy. By the time of his death in 1683 France was almost ready to challenge England and Holland for control of the seas. Indeed, at the beginning of the War of the League of Augsburg in 1688 it looked as if France might become the dominant naval power. This possibility was ended in 1692 at the Battle of La Hogue, when the French under Admiral Tourville were decisively defeated by an Anglo-Dutch fleet. The French navy never recovered from this blow and by the end of Louis' reign England had clearly outdistanced France as the country with the most powerful war fleet in the world.

The army and navy were, of course, Louis' ultimate weapons in international affairs, but he had one more subtle instrument. Like his army, Louis' diplomatic service was unrivalled in Europe. When he assumed personal power the foreign office consisted of a few clerks. By the time of his death it had become a large bureau with elaborate archives and a whole host of officials who supplied much of the information upon which royal policy decisions were based. Abroad, Louis kept permanent ambassadors in all the leading European countries except Russia and in addition residents of subordinate rank in the lesser states, such as the German and Italian principalities. These representatives were on the whole capable and conscientious men. No other country equalled France in the number or quality of its agents abroad, and no other country was able to provide its diplomats with the lavish subsidies which Louis distributed freely in order to win friends.

The quest for glory

With these great sources of strength behind him Louis could confidently embark on an ambitious foreign policy. What was his real aim? It has been claimed that the issue of the Spanish succession was the pivot of Louis' whole foreign policy, but this question was all-important only in the later years of the reign. Other interpretations, that Louis' policies were determined by a desire to

extend France to her natural frontiers or by a wish to increase French influence in Germany, are open to even greater objection. It may be more realistic to argue that Louis was, above all, resolved to reduce still further the already waning power of the Habsburgs. Such a view, however, neglects the obsessive determination with which he set out to crush the United Provinces in the early 1670s. It is probable that the primary motive for Louis' actions was a desire for glory: glory for France but, above all, glory for himself.

Louis' quest for glory and the reactions of the other European states to it can be followed in four wars—the War of Devolution (1667–8), the Dutch War (1672–8), the War of the League of Augsburg (1688–97) and the War of the Spanish Succession (1701–13)—and also in the 'reunions' policy of the early 1680s.

In the War of Devolution Louis fought against Spain, in theory to safeguard the rights of his wife, the Spanish princess, Maria Theresa, to territory in the Spanish Netherlands but in practice to win territory for France and military reputation for his armies and himself. He achieved considerable triumphs, first of all by isolating Spain internationally—a fine achievement for his splendid diplomatic service—and then by winning notable victories in the field. These successes, however, alarmed England, Holland and Sweden, and in 1668 these three countries formed a Triple Alliance, designed to force France to make peace. Louis did agree to peace in 1668, though it is not certain how far the Triple Alliance influenced him. One thing is clear, however; he never forgave the Dutch for their intrigues against him. As a result of the War of Devolution he gained a number of important towns in the Spanish Netherlands for France, and after 1668 he planned to extend still further French influence in the north east, this time by an attack on the Dutch.

Territorial gains by France during 1643-1715

REDIIT CONCORDIA FRATRVM.

He worked as hard in the years after 1668 to isolate the United Provinces as he had to isolate Spain in the period before 1667 and with almost equal success—Brandenburg was the republic's only ally in 1672. His and his diplomats' greatest triumph was the break-up of the Triple Alliance. In 1670 by the Secret Treaty of Dover, which reflected Charles II's personal views on foreign policy, England allied with France against the Dutch, and in April 1672 Sweden, in return for a subsidy, agreed to oppose any German prince who supported Holland.

Louis was thus able in 1672 to join England in an attack on the United Provinces in the knowledge that the diplomatic situation was decisively in his favour. With his huge army, some 120,000 strong and led by generals of genius, he won a series of great victories.

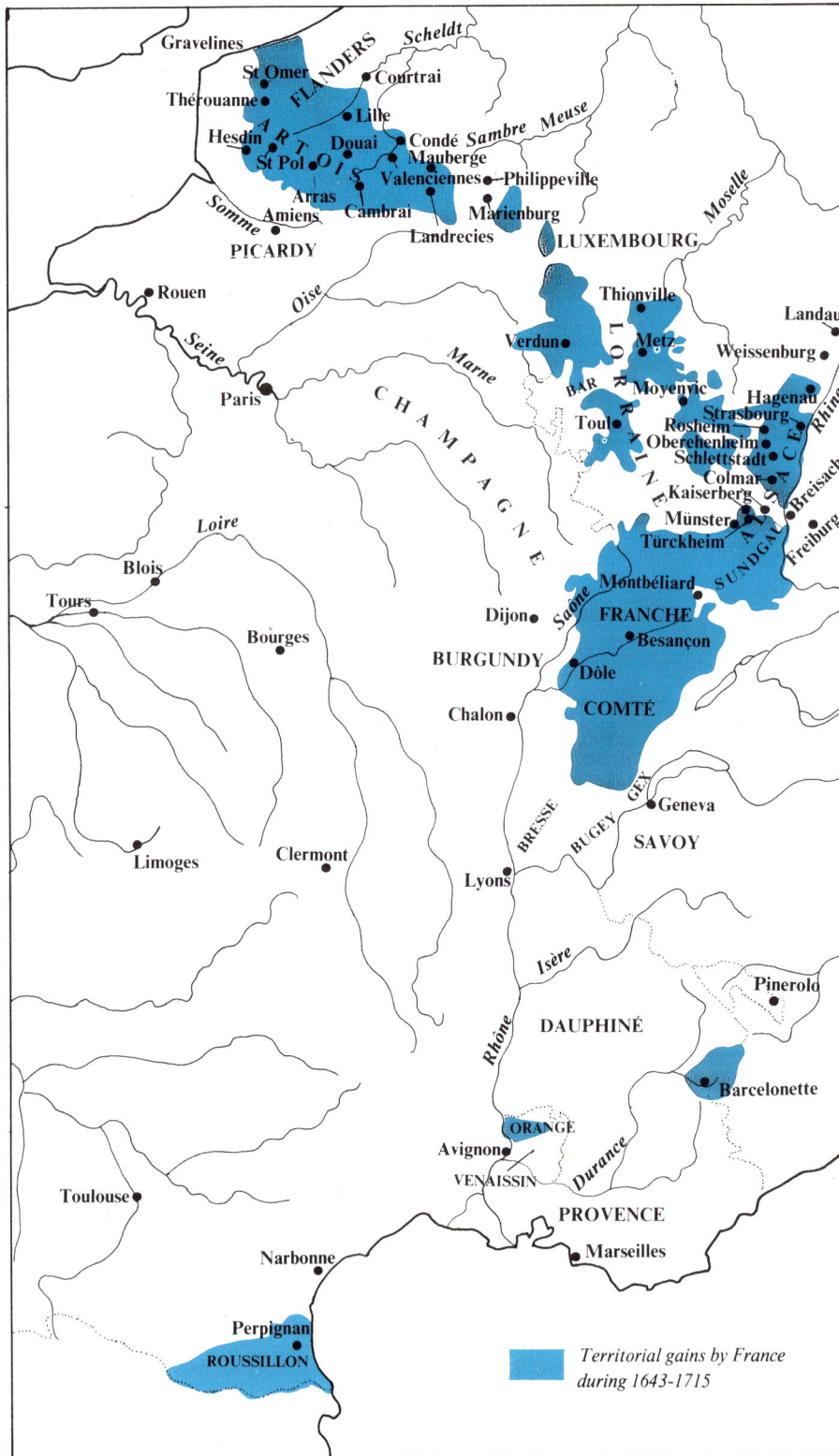

In the summer of 1672 the capture of Amsterdam seemed imminent: the very existence of the United Provinces was in the balance. At this point the republic saved itself by piercing the walls and dykes along the banks of some of its numerous canals and rivers and thus flooding a large area around Amsterdam. This brought a temporary respite to the Dutch and during 1673 and 1674 they obtained much needed allies. There was a virtual diplomatic revolution in these years as the other European powers, terrified by the prospect of a complete French victory, hastened to support the United Provinces. By the end of 1674 Louis was at war with the emperor, Spain and most of the leading German princes. In addition he had lost the support of England, for in 1674 Charles II was forced by parliamentary pressure to make peace with the Dutch. As a result of these changes in the international scene Louis was forced to withdraw from Dutch territory, and after 1674 he waged war chiefly against the Habsburgs.

The war was brought to an end by a series of treaties signed at Nymegen in 1678 and 1679. Louis obtained very favourable terms from Spain. The great territory of Franche Comté was confirmed as a French possession and, although several of the towns in the Spanish Netherlands which France had gained at the Treaty of Aix-la-Chapelle were restored, she obtained in exchange a string of other strongholds including Saint-Omer and Ypres.

The treaty with the Dutch was much less to Louis' liking, as he made no territorial gains at all from the republic. Very clearly, his objective of crushing the Dutch had not been realized. Nevertheless, the Peace of Nymegen probably represents the summit of his power and success in Europe. In the later stages of the war, he had fought against a great coalition, yet his armies had never been beaten.

After Nymegen, Louis' confidence was high and he tried to achieve further triumphs by his 'reunions' policy. His idea was to exploit the vague wording of recent treaties, such as that of Westphalia, which, in ceding lands to France, often failed to make clear the precise limits of the territory granted.

From 1679 onwards he set up a number of 'chambers of reunion', which assigned large stretches of territory in western Germany to France. By 1681 French sovereignty had been proclaimed over the whole of Alsace, including the city of Strasbourg. Louis also won important successes in the Spanish Netherlands, where he captured Luxembourg in 1684.

Spain, infuriated by French attacks on her possessions, had declared war in 1683, but she was much too weak to have any real hope of success. In 1684 she had to agree to a twenty-year truce, by which France was left in possession of Alsace, Strasbourg, Luxembourg and some territory in Spanish Flanders. Spain had been unable to find allies against France because the general diplomatic situation in Europe was still favourable to Louis, though this was the last period when that was true. In 1683, the Austrian Habsburgs were fighting for their lives against the Turks and Charles II of England was a French pensioner. By the end of 1688, when the next great military conflict broke out in western Europe, the emperor was winning notable victories in the east against a retreating Ottoman army. Above all, William of Orange had become King of England.

France's enemies gather

Between 1684 and 1688 Louis took a series of steps which could almost have been designed to unite his enemies against him. In 1685 his revocation of the Edict of Nantes, which had safeguarded the rights of French Protestants, infuriated all the Protestant powers of Europe. In 1687 he quarrelled violently with the pope over the

conduct of the French ambassador in Rome, and in 1688 he tried to intrude his own candidate, Cardinal Furstenburg, into the important Electorate of Cologne against the wishes of both pope and emperor. Moreover, he also invaded and devastated the Palatinate in support of the flimsy claims of his sister-in-law, the Princess Elizabeth Charlotte, to that territory.

This final aggression led to the outbreak of war with the emperor. In 1689–90 a grand coalition was formed against Louis consisting of England, the Dutch, the emperor, Spain, Saxony, Savoy, Hanover, Bavaria and Brandenburg.

The war was fought in Flanders, Germany, Italy and Spain as well as at sea. France won some notable military successes, but the naval defeat at La Hogue in 1692 marked the beginning of a permanent decline in her strength at sea, while the bad harvest of 1693 brought famine and discontent at home. By 1695 it was clear that the strain of waging war against most of Europe was too much even for France and in 1697 peace was concluded at Ryswick. Louis made very great concessions, probably because the long expected death of the ailing Charles II of Spain seemed imminent and he was anxious to obtain part of the inheritance for his son, the Dauphin Louis.

He agreed to give up all his reunions' acquisitions gained since 1679, except for Strasbourg and the town of Landau, and to abandon his candidates for the electorates of Cologne and the Palatinate. He recognized William III as King of England, made considerable concessions to the Dutch, and agreed that they should be allowed to garrison, for their own protection, a series of border fortresses in the Spanish Netherlands.

The issue of the Spanish succession, uppermost in Louis' mind in 1697, dominated the remainder of his reign. Charles II of Spain had no children or brothers, but his two half-sisters—daughters of Philip IV by his first wife—had married into the reigning houses of France and Austria. The elder, Maria Theresa, had married Louis XIV, the younger, Margaret Theresa, the Emperor Leopold I. Louis and Leopold had further dynastic connections with the Spanish Habsburgs through their mothers, who were both daughters of Philip III. The French royal house and the Austrian imperial family thus had the best hereditary claims to the Spanish throne, and as early as 1668 Leopold and Louis had signed a partition treaty providing for the division of the Spanish dominions between them on Charles II's death.

In 1698, however, after much haggling, France, England and the United Provinces reached a settlement by which the greater part of the Spanish dominions was to go to the Electoral Prince of Bavaria. He was a grandson of Leopold I but had little chance of inheriting the Habsburg's hereditary possessions or the imperial crown. In this way it was made clear that Spain was not to be united either with France or with the Empire. Louis did, however, obtain Sicily, Sardinia and the Tuscan ports for the dauphin, a splendid inheritance which would pass in due course to the French crown and make France a dominant power in Italy. It was also agreed that the Archduke Charles, Leopold's second son, should get the Duchy of Milan. Such terms, it need hardly be said, were quite unacceptable to the emperor.

The fate of an empire

Any slight chance which the arrangement of 1698 may have had of success collapsed in February 1699 when the electoral prince died. A few months later France, England and the United Provinces agreed on a second treaty, by which the Archduke Charles was to get Spain, the Spanish

Netherlands and the Spanish Empire overseas and the dauphin was to obtain Milan (which he was then to exchange for the duchy of Lorraine) as well as the territory which he had been promised in 1698. The emperor, however, refused to accept these provisions—he feared the aggrandizement of France in Italy.

In Spain the treaty provoked an outburst of fury: Spaniards were indignant that foreigners should presume to settle the fate of their empire without even consulting them. Charles II himself was determined that the Spanish inheritance should be preserved intact. In October 1700, after much hesitation, he signed a will which made Philip, Duke of Anjou, second son of the dauphin, his sole heir. If Anjou refused, the inheritance was to pass to his younger brother, the Duke of Berry. If he too declined, it was to go to the Archduke Charles. Louis accepted the will on behalf of his grandson, but this decision did not immediately lead to a general war. The hostility of the emperor was certain, but the English and Dutch governments recognized Philip as King of Spain.

It was only a series of unwise actions by Louis—difficult to understand in the delicate diplomatic situation of the time—which led to the War of the Spanish Succession. He took measures to safeguard Philip's rights to the French throne, drove the Dutch from the barrier fortresses in the Spanish Netherlands which they had been allowed to garrison in 1697, obtained commercial advantages for France in Spain's American colonies and, in September 1701, on the death of James II, recognized the Old Pretender as James III, King of England. War was officially declared in May 1702, though the French and Austrians had

already been engaged in hostilities in Italy since the spring of the previous year.

The odds were heavily against Louis in the conflict. His three main opponents, England, the United Provinces and Austria, had support from Brandenburg, Hanover, Denmark and the Palatinate, while he had the support of only Spain, Savoy, Portugal, Bavaria and Cologne. Spain was a liability to be defended against allied attacks rather than an asset, and in 1703 Savoy and Portugal changed sides. The latter's desertion in particular was a bitter blow for Louis. It gave his enemies a convenient land base from which to assault Spain, already vulnerable to attack from the powerful Dutch and English navies, which commanded the seas.

The French army, with fewer troops than the allies, had to conduct operations in Spain and Italy and along the whole eastern boundary of France. With such considerable commitments Louis had to stand on the defensive, an unusual posture for France. Moreover, for the first time in his reign, his opponents' generals were much better than his own. Marlborough and Eugene, the principal allied commanders, demonstrated that they were soldiers of genius, whereas France, though she had distinguished service from Marshal Villars, no longer had officers of the calibre of Turenne and Condé. In 1704, at Blenheim in Germany, Eugene and Marlborough inflicted a crushing defeat on a large French and Bavarian army, the first really serious reverse suffered by France on the battlefield during the entire reign of Louis XIV. It was a portent of things to come. Further defeats in the Netherlands at Ramillies (1706), Oudenarde (1708) and Malplaquet (1709) reduced France to desperate military straits. To make matters worse the winter of 1708–9 was appallingly severe in France and many peasants were faced with the threat of starvation.

In this situation Louis was prepared to make almost any concession to obtain peace, but the allies' demand that he should provide military aid to help in the expulsion of his grandson from Spain was too humiliating for him to accept. The French nation rallied around him in this desperate time, and colossal efforts were made to raise new troops. The allies had overreached themselves: after 1709 prospects improved for France. Spain as a whole showed that it stood behind Philip V and was not prepared to accept an Austrian king. In 1710 a Tory government anxious for peace came to power in England. Above all, in 1711, on the death of the Emperor Joseph I, the Archduke Charles ascended the imperial throne. If he were to be established as king of Spain as well, the whole balance of power in Europe would be seriously affected.

These developments and an important French victory at Denain in the Netherlands in 1712 meant that Louis was able to obtain more favourable treatment in the peace

settlement of 1713–14 than would have seemed possible in 1709. By the treaties of Utrecht (1713) and Rastadt (1714) Philip V was allowed to retain Spain and the Spanish Empire in the New World, although the Spanish possessions in Italy and the Netherlands passed to Austria. The Dutch right to a 'barrier' against France was confirmed. Louis recognized Anne as Queen of England and made considerable commercial and colonial concessions to England in the New World.

When Louis died in 1715, therefore, he had the satisfaction of seeing his grandson established on the throne of Spain and of leaving to his successor Louis XV a larger France that he had inherited in 1643—he did not lose in 1713 the territorial gains made as a result of his triumphs up to the 1680s. It is clear, however, that between about 1685 and 1715 the balance of power had swung strongly against France. In 1683–4, the years of the siege of Vienna and the truce of Ratisbon, France had been by far the most powerful state in Europe and there seemed a real possibility that she might establish complete dominance on the continent. In 1715, because of her large population and great natural resources, she was still the strongest single power, but the reverses of the years between 1688 and 1713 meant that she had ceased to threaten the very existence of her neighbours. Moreover, the treaties of 1713–14, together with

the treaty of Nystadt, which brought the Great Northern War of 1700–21 to an end, marked the rise of England, Austria and Russia to the status of great powers, a position which none of them had really enjoyed in 1683.

The rise of England

In the early 1680s England, under Charles II, had been little more than a French tributary state. Between 1688 and 1713, however, under William III and Queen Anne, she had built up her strength at an astonishing rate and had been the paymaster of the coalitions which humbled Louis XIV. In 1715 she was certainly a power of the very first rank and by far the greatest naval power in the world.

In 1680 Austria, too, had been a comparatively weak state, controlling only a strip of Hungary to the east. By 1715 the position was very different. Following a series of brilliant victories against the Turks in the years after 1683, she gained control of the whole of Hungary. In the west, as a result of the settlements of 1713–14, she obtained the Spanish Netherlands. Milan, the Tuscan ports, Naples and Sardinia. This was a vast accession of territory and population. In 1715 Austria, like England, was unquestionably a great power.

Russia hardly counted in the European states system in 1680, but by 1715, as a

result of Peter the Great's victories against Sweden, she controlled the southern coastline of the Baltic Sea, a position confirmed by the Treaty of Nystadt in 1721. In 1715 Russia was by far the greatest power in northern Europe, though it was not until well on in the eighteenth century that the full impact of her new strength was felt in western Europe.

Among the other notable European states in 1715 the United Provinces was entering a period of relative political and economic decline, while Sweden, a great power in the 1680s, was well on the way to third-rate status. Spain, under its new Bourbon dynasty, was to witness something of a revival in the early eighteenth century but in 1715 was both poor and weak.

None of these changes, except the decline of Holland and, perhaps, the revival of Spain, boded well for France. In the age of Louis XIV she was the greatest international power. In the eighteenth century other nations challenged her for that title.

Chapter 10

France under Louis XIV

In March 1661 Cardinal Mazarin died. He had been the most powerful man in France for nearly twenty years, a position he owed partly to the considerable abilities which he displayed as the heir of Cardinal Richelieu and partly to his influence over the Queen Mother, Anne of Austria, who seems to have fallen in love with him. While he lived the young Louis XIV did not play an important role in state affairs, but on his death the king, then twenty-two years old, announced that henceforth he would be his own first minister. It was a promise he kept for the remaining forty-five years of his life.

Louis founded his government on two fundamental bases, a belief in hard work and a firm commitment to the idea of the divine right of kings. He devoted up to nine hours a day to affairs of state, and planned his work methodically. 'Give me an almanac and a watch', wrote the Duke of Saint-Simon, the greatest memorialist of the reign, 'and even if I am three hundred leagues away from him I will tell you what the king is doing.' This devotion, day in, day out, to the routine details of government, allied to an excellent memory, soon gave him great self-assurance in making decisions.

Louis firmly believed that he should work hard at government. His task, as he saw it, was to increase his own glory and the power of France. In doing this he would also benefit his subjects. Their role was to obey the king's commands without question. Louis' fervent belief in his right to rule as he thought best without interference from any human authority was one of the guiding principles of his life, and his reign saw the publication of the greatest of all statements of the divine right of kings, Bishop Bossuet's *Politique tirée des propres paroles de l'écriture sainte,* written to acquaint the king's heir, the dauphin Louis, with the true concept of kingship:

Princes . . . act as ministers of God and His Lieutenants on earth. . . . The royal throne is not the throne of a man, but the throne of God himself. . . . The prince may correct himself when he knows that he has done evil, but against his authority there is no remedy other than his own authority.

These words of Bossuet represent the ideas of Louis XIV.

A corollary of Louis' views on divine right was his belief in the need to rigidly subordinate every institution in the kingdom to the power of the Crown. This led to a long struggle with the papacy over the rights of the Gallican Church. In secular affairs it meant efforts to strip of effective power all those bodies in the kingdom which might have imposed practical restraints on royal authority. The Estates General, the French parliament, was not abolished, but it was never summoned. The *parlements,* the supreme judicial tribunals of the kingdom, which had played a notable role in resistance to the Crown's authority during Louis' minority, were deprived of effective political influence by a series of edicts culminating in a decree of 1673. The governors of provinces, provincial estates (where they continued to exist) and local towns were also deprived of many of the powers and functions which they had previously enjoyed and were increasingly subordinated to *intendants,* agents strictly controlled by the central government and sent to the provinces to impose its will there.

The splendour of Versailles

In the later stages of his reign Louis governed his kingdom from the great palace of Versailles, which still represents the apogée of divine right monarchy and which was designed to provide a glorious setting for the king and his court. Louis did not like Paris, for it reminded him of the troubles of the Fronde, the French civil war of 1649–53, when a mob had once forced their way into his bedroom in the Palais Royal. Moreover, at Versailles he could indulge his love of walking and hunting to the full. The construction of the palace was a gigantic task. Versailles, wrote Saint-Simon scornfully, was 'the saddest and most ungrateful of all places, without a view, without woods or water or good soil, for it all stood upon shifting sands or marshland'. Saint-Simon was always prepared to see the faults rather than the virtues in Louis' projects, but there is no doubt that the building of Versailles was immensely costly in human lives. Workmen died in their thousands of marsh fever. Their bodies, however, were removed from the local hospital at night and such unpleasant details were not allowed to interrupt the work of construction. This began on a large scale in the later 1660s, when fundamental alterations were made to the small country palace which Louis XIII had built in 1634. Building and decoration went on throughout most of the reign and the palace, set in magnificent gardens, soon became a splendid setting for the court, which moved there permanently in 1682, although there was hardly any provision for sanitation. After the move Louis seldom visited his capital, though it was only fifteen miles away.

Awed foreign ambassadors marvelled at the rigid etiquette which prevailed at court.

Above, the Galerie des Glaces *at Versailles, designed by Jules Hardouin Mansart. The walls are decorated with green marble and the ceiling with allegories of the apotheosis of Louis XIV.*

Opposite left, John Churchill, Duke of Marlborough (1650–1722), the English general who created an efficient English army, and won the independence to use it as he wished in the Blenheim campaign of 1704. As the war became unpopular, however, he suffered from increasing political attacks at home. National Portrait Gallery, London.

Opposite right, William III of England (reigned 1689–1702) and Stadtholder of the United Provinces, the implacable and ultimately successful opponent of Louis' schemes of expansion in the Low Countries. National Portrait Gallery, London.

The king's mistresses

His first notable affair, in the 1660s, was with Louise de la Vallière, blonde and pretty in a quiet sort of way, but torn between religious scruples and her genuine love for the king. Few could find ill to say of her. Even Saint-Simon spoke words of highest praise, describing her as 'modest, disinterested, gentle, good to the last degree, struggling unceasingly against herself'. In 1674, after she had finally lost the king's love, she took the veil and ended her life as Sister Louise-de-la-Miséricorde. She had been replaced some years before in the king's affections by the very lovely Madame de Montespan. With her fine blue eyes and splendid figure, she was a fitting consort for Louis during the triumphs of the 1670s, the decade of the Dutch war, which represented the high peak of his successes in Europe. She symbolized the high noon of his life, but her temperament did not match her beauty. She was spiteful and capricious and vented her temper even on the king himself. Louis confided his troubles to Madame Scarron, an attractive widow who had been employed to look after his illegitimate children. In 1680 he became completely alienated from Madame de Montespan after disclosures that she had dabbled in black magic. Within a year of the queen's death, which took place in 1683, he secretly married Madame Scarron, who is better known by her later title of Madame de Maintenon.

Besides his affair with Madame de Montespan, Louis had other, more fleeting liaisons in the 1670s, notably one with Mademoiselle de Fontanges, who was eighteen when she became his mistress in 1679. She was fabulously lovely, 'as beautiful as an angel' according to a contemporary who rather spoiled the effect by adding that she was also as 'stupid as a basket'. For a time the king seemed completely captivated, but when, after a year, she gave birth to a still-born child and became very ill she was sent to a convent. Louis, who visited her there when he was out hunting, wept when he saw her condition. She died in March 1681, a sacrifice to the king's pleasure and to the primitive medicine of the day. After his second marriage in 1684 Louis abandoned his pursuit of women. Under the watchful eye of Madame de Maintenon and surrounded by his children—most of them his illegitimate offspring by la Vallière and Montespan—he prepared for a worthy and dignified old age. Madame de Maintenon exercised some influence on royal policy, but she was the only woman who ever did. None of Louis' mistresses had any say in state affairs and the king's relationships with them never prevented him from devoting full attention to government.

The sole responsibility for deciding policy in both foreign and domestic affairs lay, of course, with the king. When he wanted advice he consulted the men who together

Each nobleman and attendant had his appointed place and duties. The finest distinctions of behaviour were of major importance to the hundreds of notables who formed the core of the ten thousand or so courtiers, servants and guards who lived in and around the palace. Elaborate etiquette covered such interesting questions as who should hand the king his shirt when he was dressing in the morning and the exact conduct of different dignitaries when they met in public. Such behaviour was much more than an expression of royal pettiness of mind. It reflected the ordered hierarchy on which Louis' whole system of government was built. Each man had his superiors to whom respect was due and his inferiors from whom he could expect due acknowledgment of his position. Only the king had no peer. He stood alone under God.

Louis' private life at Versailles, and earlier in his reign at his other palaces in and around Paris, revolved around his family and his mistresses. There were three great love affairs in his life, but his relationship with his wife, the Spanish princess Maria Theresa, whom he married in 1660, was not one of them. The queen adored her husband, but Louis, though he probably felt some mild affection for her, certainly did not return the feeling. He reserved his passion for his mistresses.

Rivals for power

This determination can also be seen in the way in which Louis encouraged the rivalry of the two great ministerial families of Colbert and le Tellier, which between them dominated the council for much of the reign. He regarded their rivalry as a guarantee of his own power. Between 1679 and 1683, for example, there were four ministers, Colbert and his brother, the Marquis de Croissy, and le Tellier and his son, the Marquis de Louvois. Their quarrels and jealousies ensured that the king had two independent and competing sources of information, ideas and advice. All his ministers from the 1660s to the 1680s were very able, some—Colbert, Lionne, le Tellier and Louvois—of quite outstanding capacities. The position was much less favourable towards the end of the king's life, when most of the ministers were unfortunately mediocrities.

The *Conseil d'en haut,* then, advised the king on the highest matters of state. Most of its members, however, also held one or more of the six greatest executive posts in the country. These were the offices of chancellor and controller-general of finances and the four secretaryships of state for foreign affairs, war, marine affairs and the royal household. The chancellor was the highest judicial officer of the realm, the controller-general of finances, as his title suggests, was principally concerned with state revenue and expenditure, and each secretary of state, besides his specialized duties, had general responsibility for a quarter of the provinces of France.

These six great officials were prominent figures on a number of other councils, less dignified than the Supreme Council, which were concerned with the general administration of the realm. The Council of Dispatches, which met every fortnight with the king in the chair, dealt with a mass of local government business. It was, in fact, the body responsible for the general internal administration of the country, and as such its principal members were the secretaries of state.

The importance of this council, however, must not be exaggerated. Its proceedings were largely formal, as the king decided almost all important questions in advance in individual consultations with each secretary of state in turn. Similarly in financial matters, Louis made his decisions after private discussions with his controller-general. The Council of Finances which held a meeting twice a week, performed largely routine duties.

There was also a Privy Council, under the presidency of the chancellor which was the supreme interpreter of law and privilege in the kingdom and a Council of Conscience, responsible for religious affairs. The king's Jesuit confessors, especially Père la Chaise and Père le Tellier, held, in turn, important places on the latter body.

formed the *Conseil d'en haut,* or Supreme Council. Before Louis' personal rule this inner council had contained members of the royal family and great noblemen. After 1661 there were drastic changes. All those who might claim political power by reason of birth were excluded. Membership of the council, and with it the coveted title of minister of state, was granted to those whose advice the king considered worth having. There were only sixteen ministers in all between 1661 and 1715, three, four or five at any one time. A man became a minister when he was first summoned to the council by an usher. He ceased to be a minister when the summons no longer came. The council met two or three times a week, always under the presidency of the king. The ministers, with two unimportant exceptions, were all men of middling rank, ennobled by the king for their services to the state. This 'reign of the vile bourgeoisie', which Saint-Simon and the old nobility so bitterly resented, demonstrated the king's determination to be complete master of his kingdom and government.

The decisions of the king and his councils at the centre were carried out in the provinces by the *intendents,* who were by far the most important officials in local government during Louis' reign. The functions of the *intendants* were summed up in their full title: they were *intendants* of justice, police and finance. As such they were responsible for preventing abuses in the administration of justice in the areas under their control, for superintending the maintenance of law and order, and for many functions in connection with the assessment and collection of the *taille,* the main direct tax in the country.

Colbert, the draper's son

Colbert, the man so largely responsible for creating the institution of intendant in its classical form, was by far the most important minister of the reign. He was the son of a draper and in his youth secured employment with a Paris notary. In 1640, when he was twenty-one, he took advantage of an uncle's marriage into the family of Michel le Tellier to enter army administration. In 1651 he transferred to the service of Cardinal Mazarin, managing the latter's household and business affairs with conspicuous success. Mazarin recommended him to the king with the remark that some of the debt which he owed to the Crown might be discharged in the person of Colbert.

Colbert won the king's confidence through his part in the destruction of Nicholas Fouquet, who in 1661 was one of the great powers in the kingdom as superintendent of finances, an office which gave him unrivalled opportunities for private profit at the cost of the state. Colbert showed himself utterly ruthless in a series of intrigues which led to Fouquet's arrest and trial, a trial which lasted for three years and ended in a sentence of banishment, which the king altered to one of life imprisonment. The office of superintendent was abolished on Fouquet's fall but Colbert exercised most of its powers, and in 1665 his position was confirmed when he was made controller-general of finances. He had other offices too. He became superintendent of buildings, arts and manufactures in 1664 and secretary of state for marine affairs in 1669. In fact he exercised influence over almost all internal affairs except the army, which was the province of le Tellier and Louvois.

Colbert's aim was to promote the power and glory of France by increasing the revenue and wealth of the country. He intended to do this by financial reforms, by the application of mercantilist principles to trade and industry and by the improvement of communications within the country. He had a passion for statistics, realizing that administrative reforms could best be based on a thorough knowledge of conditions in the country. In 1663 officials were instructed to provide detailed reports on all aspects of life in their localities which might possibly interest the government. Colbert received a mass of information on military ecclesiastical, financial and economic affairs, information which he used to good purpose in his reforms. He was, in fact, a protagonist of 'science' government, though the comparatively primitive nature of the statistics at his disposal meant that his calculations were open to very wide margins of error.

Colbert had very considerable success in the short run in increasing the effective revenue of the Crown. That was only thirty-one million livres in 1661, though the people paid eighty-three millions in taxation. Fifty-two millions were therefore lost in the process of collection, most of it going into the pockets of tax farmers and tax collectors. In 1667 the position was very different. Out of ninety-five million livres actually paid in taxation sixty-three millions

Above, Jean Baptiste Colbert (1619–83), who encouraged French industry and trade by introducing mercantilism and establishing high tariffs on imports; this policy led to conflict with the Dutch and, eventually, to cripplingly expensive wars. Château de Versailles.

Opposite, Madame de Maintenon (1635–1719), a close friend of Maria Theresa, the queen of Louis XIV, as well as the king's morganatic wife after 1684. She is said to have raised the moral tone of the court at Versailles by her devout Catholicism. Château de Versailles.

reached the Crown. The net revenue of the Crown had been more than doubled in six years, a remarkable achievement. He brought about this transformation mainly by a series of administrative reforms. He reorganized the budgetary system, bringing some order into the previously chaotic treasury procedure. He compelled tax farmers and tax collectors to disgorge their illicit gains and closely supervised their profits, and increased revenue from the Crown lands by improving their administration.

These and other measures were important, but they were essentially reforms of detail. No attempt was made at fundamental changes such as compelling the privileged orders, the clergy and nobility, to pay their fair share of taxation, admittedly an almost impossibly difficult task. In these circumstances revenue could be expanded only within certain limits.

Financial disaster

The outbreak of the war of devolution in 1667 and, above all, of the Dutch war in 1672 had a disastrous effect on Colbert's schemes. The need for large sums of money in a short space of time led to numerous financial expedients which hampered aims of increasing the prosperity of the country as a whole. In 1680, after peace had been restored and despite all Colbert's efforts, the net revenue was only sixty-one million livres against an expenditure of ninety-six million. The great improvement achieved in the country's financial position in the first decade of the reign had thus been halted, and after Colbert's death in 1683 things became very much worse.

Colbert's mercantilism, which was the motive force behind his commercial and industrial policies, was founded on the belief that France could expand her economy only at the expense of her neighbours, particularly of the Dutch. It was this idea which led him to impose heavy duties on foreign imports, especially his celebrated tariff of 1667 which was virtually a declaration of economic warfare against the Dutch. He also took positive measures to increase French trade by founding trading companies and encouraging the development of a French mercantile marine force. His four principal companies, the East and West India Companies, the Levant Company and the Company of the North, all failed during his own lifetime under the stresses of the Dutch war and over-detailed regulation of their activities by the state, but he had considerable success in his more general efforts to expand French shipbuilding through generous subsidies to shipowners. The resulting increase in the size of the French merchant navy led to a considerable growth in trade with northern Europe, Spain and the Levant.

Colbert's tariffs, which raised the price of foreign goods coming into France to prohibitive heights, were designed to stimulate native French industries and thus make the country as far as possible self-sufficient. He provided other help for industrial expansion. He set up a number of royal factories, owned by the state, such as the famous Gobelin tapestry works in Paris. State ownership was particularly successful in luxury industries, but more important from the point of view of general industrial development were the subsidies, monopolies and interest-free loans which Colbert granted to private entrepreneurs. By these he greatly increased the range and output of French industry from textiles to mining, metallurgy and the production of armaments. A large part in this expansion was played by experienced foreign workers who were encouraged to bring their skills from all parts of Europe, Germans and Swedes helped to build up the mining and metal industries, Dutchmen played important roles in the development of textiles, and Italians helped to revive the languishing silk manufactures of Lyons. Colbert's efforts to stimulate industrial development had permanent significance. Despite setbacks which took place after his death in the later years of Louis XIV's reign, he had provided a basis for French industrial advances in the eighteenth century.

One means of assistance which Colbert provided for industry was his development of internal communications. The road system remained bad, but he did a great deal to improve river transport and build canals. His most famous project of this kind, the *Canal des deux mers*, linking the Mediterranean and Atlantic, was completed in 1681, two years before his death. These improvements also benefited agriculture, which remained overwhelmingly the principal occupation of the people of France. Colbert did little else, however, to promote agricultural advance; industrial and commercial development brought quicker returns in revenue and international prestige than any agricultural improvements could possibly achieve.

Overall, Colbert was a good deal less successful than he had hoped. His commercial and industrial policies did not make France the dominant economic power in Europe and his financial work was first undermined and then ruined by Louis XIV's wars.

It would be wrong, however, to suppose that Colbert was irrevocably opposed to the wars which did so much harm to his plans. He realized perfectly well that his aggressive commercial policy might lead to armed conflict, and he accepted the possibility. He really had little choice in the matter. He always remained the king's servant and Louis always made his own decisions about war and peace. One must be careful, therefore, not to exaggerate

Colbert's achievement. Equally, one should not minimize it. The stimulus which he gave to French trade and industry had an enduring effect: the economic development of eighteenth-century France was built upon the work of Colbert in the seventeenth century.

During the years of Colbert's ministry religious affairs occupied a considerable part of the king's attention. Louis was faced with three major religious problems during his reign. These turned on his relations with the papacy, on the role of the Jansenists in the French Church, and on the position of the Huguenots in France.

Louis was always a conventionally devout Catholic, indefatigable in his attendance at mass, but he claimed to occupy a position of semi-independence in ecclesiastical affairs which the papacy found difficult to accept. Traditionally the Gallican Church (the Church in France) held views about papal authority which were anathema in Rome, especially the idea that a General Council was superior to the pope. Gallican claims were stoutly defended by the lawyers of the *parlements* who maintained that papal Bulls were not valid in France until they had been properly registered.

Louis took up some of the traditional Gallican positions, rejecting others when it suited his book, in the course of a conflict with the papacy which lasted for much of the reign. The Crown had long enjoyed the right to receive the revenues of bishoprics in the north of France during vacancies—the so-called *régale temporelle*. In 1673, however. Louis extended the claim to the whole kingdom and also demanded the *régale spirituelle*, the right to nominate during a vacancy to benefices without cure of souls. Two bishops refused to accept the decree and four years later appealed to Rome, where they received a sympathetic hearing from Pope Innocent XI. Deadlock ensured, as neither the pope nor the king was prepared to give way, and in 1681 Louis summoned a General Assembly of the French Clergy to consider the position.

The Assembly widened the split between Crown and papacy by voting the celebrated Four Articles, which were made an integral part of the theological teaching of the country by a royal order of March 1682. The first three asserted that kings were not subject to ecclesiastical authority in temporal affairs, that General Councils were superior to the pope, and that the customs of the Gallican Church were inviolable. The fourth admitted that the pope had the principal role in determining the content of the faith but also stated that his decisions were not irrevocable if they did not meet with the assent of the Church as a whole. The pope was furious at these pronouncements and refused to issue Bulls of institution to their Sees to those lesser clerics who had taken part in the Assembly and were later promoted to bishoprics by the grateful king.

Peace with the pope

In consequence, on Innocent's death in 1689, more than a third of the bishoprics of France were vacant. His successors Alexander VIII and Innocent XII were more conciliatory and in 1693 a compromise was reached by which the bishops who had taken part in the Assembly were confirmed in their sees after they had all sent letters of apology to the pope. Louis revoked his order that the Four Articles were to be generally taught throughout France, although the Articles themselves were not formally withdrawn. The conflict over the *régale,* which had started the whole struggle, was allowed to lapse, although in practice Louis had the better of the argument as he retained some of the rights which he had claimed in 1673.

Louis' readiness to compromise in 1693 was partly because of his increasing piety in old age. He was more and more reluctant to be at odds with the head of the Church. Also, on a more practical level, he needed papal assistance against the Jansenists, who caused the second main religious conflict of the reign. The Jansenists were named after a Flemish prelate, Cornelius Jansen, Bishop of Ypres, who died in 1636. Two years later came the posthumous publication of his book, the *Augustinus*, a commentary on the work of St Augustine, in which he claimed that men were so sinful that they could not cooperate with God in achieving their salvation but depended entirely on grace from on high. Thus, neither devotions nor good works helped to achieve entry into heaven. This teaching was very like the Calvinist doctrine of predestination and was fiercely assailed by other theologians within the Church, especially those in the Jesuit order. Both Richelieu and Mazarin attacked Jansenism and Louis continued their opposition. Under the influence of his Jesuit confessors he became firmly convinced that Jansenism was heretical and that Jansenists, suspected of believing in the legality of resistance to the Crown, were a political threat to his authority.

Jansenism already had been condemned at Rome in 1653. Innocent X had declared that four propositions ascribed to the Jansenists were heretical and another one false. The Jansenists conceded the pope's right to pronounce upon the orthodoxy of the propositions but at the same time denied that these propositions in fact appeared in the *Augustinus*. In 1656, however, Pope Alexander VII prohibited such evasions and Louis soon determined to impose discipline. Between 1661 and 1664 he tried to do so at the Convent of Port Royal des Champs situated near Versailles and the centre of Jansenist influence in France. The nuns, led by Mère Agnes Arnauld, a member of the great Arnauld family which provided the most notable leaders of the French Jansenist movement, refused to accept papal pronouncements without serious modification. Many of them were expelled

Opposite left, Louis and Colbert visiting the Gobelins tapestry factory, according to a tapestry produced by that very factory. Colbert bought the factory for the government in 1662, and it was the centre of production of both furniture and tapestries for the court until the 1690s, when furniture production there was ended. Musée des Gobelins, Paris.

Opposite right, a wax effigy of Louis XIV, surmounted by one of his wigs. Behaviour at Versailles became exceptionally refined, and it was considered rude to knock on a door; courtiers had to scratch the doorpanels instead to gain attention. By comparison, it was considered a great honour to assist the king with his morning toilet. Château de Versailles.

from the convent and a military guard was installed at Port Royal. These troops were, however, soon withdrawn, and in 1668, a result of the efforts of the newly elected Pope Clement IX, a settlement was reached which was in some ways a triumph for the Jansenists. They were merely asked to accept a formula renouncing the five condemned propositions 'sincerely' but not 'purely and simply'; that is to say, they were not required to admit that the heretical doctrines were to be found in the *Augustinus*.

The Jansenist dispute simmered down in the 1670s and 1680s under the influence of this truce but flared up again in the last decades of the reign. This was largely because of the work of the theologian Pasquier Quesnel, who in 1693 published his *Réflexions morales sur le Nouveau Testament*, which displayed the unmistakably Augustinian trends in his thinking and became the new basis of Jansenist theology. In 1703 Quesnel was arrested in the Spanish Netherlands. He escaped, but his papers were seized and sent to Versailles. They revealed a highly organized network of Jansenist sympathizers within France with whom Quesnel had corresponded for almost a decade.

This evidence, with its suggestions of a secret conspiracy, confirmed all Louis' old suspicions of the Jansenists and in 1705 he obtained a Bull from Clement XI which ordered the complete and unequivocal acceptance of all papal condemnations of Jansenism. The nuns of Port Royal des Champs, however, refused to comply without their customary qualifications. In 1709 they were forcibly removed and dispersed among hostile convents. The following year the king ordered the Port Royal buildings to be razed to the ground. It was a petty act, and he followed it up by obtaining from the pope in 1713 the celebrated Bull *Unigenitus* which defined and condemned as heretical 101 propositions from Quesnel's *Réflexions*.

The king did not succeed in extirpating Jansenism by these severe measures. Moreover, in his efforts to suppress it he depended more and more on papal support. In doing so he weakened his own claims and those of the French Church to a large measure of independence from Rome.

The Huguenots

The Jansenists at least claimed to be good Catholics, even though their opponents regarded them as , heretics. The French Huguenots, on the other hand, were openly separated from the Mother Church and as such were an obvious offence to a motto which Louis had made his own: 'one king, one law, one faith'. There were between one and two million Huguenots in France. They were among the most valuable and industrious of all the king's subjects, being particularly numerous among the financial, commercial and industrial sections of the population. In 1598, by the Edict of Nantes, which brought the French religious wars to an end, they had been granted permission to worship freely in many places throughout France and the right to hold all offices open to other citizens. They were also allowed to garrison several towns as a guarantee that these terms would be observed. In 1629 Richelieu deprived them of this last privilege but confirmed their other rights. During Louis' minority, at the time of the disturbances of the Fronde, they proved by their passivity that they were no longer any danger to the internal peace of France.

At first the king's attitude towards the Huguenots was moderate. He had high hopes that persuasion, especially financial inducements, would wean many of them away from their faith, and in 1676 an office known as the *caisse des conversions* was set up to give financial help to converts to Catholicism. This had some success, but after the end of the Dutch war Louis, motivated largely by a desire to show that his quarrels with the pope made no difference to his unimpeachable orthodoxy, decided to apply harsher measures against the Huguenots. Between 1679 and 1685 they were subjected to open persecution. Their churches were destroyed, their schools were closed down, and they themselves were deprived of state offices and civil rights.

From 1681 onwards physical violence was used against the Huguenots. Under the influence of Louvois it was decided to billet dragoons upon Protestant families in order to secure their conversion. The soldiers were told to make their stay as unpleasant as possible and torture was sometimes employed to persuade those who were reluctant to accept the Catholic faith. These methods were very influential in securing 'conversions.' Thirty thousand a year were made in Poitou where the policy was enforced with particular ruthlessness. Finally, in October 1685, by the Edict of Fontainebleau, Louis formally revoked the Edict of Nantes. All Protestant churches were to be destroyed, public and private worship by Huguenots was prohibited and Protestant ministers were ordered to leave the country within fifteen days. A solemn *Te Deum* was held at Rome to celebrate the revocation and the French clergy, headed by Bossuet, spoke of the king's action in terms of immoderate praise. The Protestant powers of Europe took a very different view; there was a tremendous revulsion of feeling against France in countries such as England and Brandenburg.

The economic consequences of the revocation of the Edict are less easy to assess. Although laymen were forbidden to emigrate, about 200,000 managed to leave France. They settled in many parts of Europe, especially in the United Provinces, England and Brandenburg. It used to be thought that their departure had a disastrous economic effect upon France, but recent research has tended to produce a rather different picture. The French economy in the latter part of Louis' reign was depressed by a complex series of factors such as unwise fiscal policy, wars, famines and currency revaluations. Among these the emigration of the Huguenots was probably only of secondary significance, even in the short term. Nevertheless, the exiles did enrich with their skills the countries where they found refuge, and all Louis' persecutions within France after 1685 could not completely stamp out Protestantism there. Huguenots continued to meet for secret worship and were a thorn in the government's side during the war of the Spanish Succession, when they conducted a guerrilla campaign in the Cevennes which had to be suppressed by regular French troops—the terrible war of the Camisards.

The Edict of Fontainebleau may have had less disastrous economic consequences for France than was once supposed, but the decade when it was issued, the 1680s, were surely the turning point in Louis' reign.

The victories of the Habsburgs against the Turks and William III's accession to the English throne radically changed the international situation, greatly to France's disadvantage, and the wars of 1688 to 1713 which followed had disastrous financial consequences for Louis' government. At the end of the war of the Spanish Succession annual expenditure exceeded receipts by forty-five million livres. Above all, at the end of the reign there was a debt of some

Above, a Dutch engraving of Protestants leaving France in the 1660s.

Top, the Revocation of the Edict of Nantes in 1685, when Louis withdrew the relative independence enjoyed by the Huguenots since the 1590s, so driving many Huguenot refugees to Holland and England, where they spread the image of Louis as a tyrant.

Opposite, an open-air meeting of Huguenots in the mid-seventeenth century.

107

DEMOLITION
DU
TEMPLE DE CHARENTON.

S. le Clerc   fecit

A magnificent age

It may be, however, that the true greatness of Louis' reign lies in the art and literature which the country produced. Versailles, the great monument of the period, was a mixture of Baroque exuberance and classical restraint which captured the imagination of Europe and has continued to fascinate the world. Few today might agree with the suggestion that by its construction Louis more than compensated for all the miseries which he imposed on Europe though his aggression, but it is certain that no man has ever left a more splendid or more characteristic monument. In the field of literature, the period from about 1660 to 1690 produced some of the great masterpieces of French and indeed of world literature— Molière's comedies and Racine's tragedies, Madame de Sévigné's *Letters* and la Fontaine's *Fables*, Bossuet's sermons and Boileau's poetry, and many other works.

The language in which that literature was expressed was one of the most effective instruments of French influence throughout the continent. The French tongue rose during the seventeenth century to the position of an international language, though its supremacy was only fully displayed during the eighteenth. Indeed, in the seventeenth century France became the arbiter of European taste, the great model for polite society almost everywhere.

The most permanent effects of Louis XIV's reign, then, lay in the cultural field. The supremacy of French manners and fashions in eighteenth-century Europe was not matched by a corresponding political supremacy. France, the strongest power in Europe when Louis began his personal rule in 1661, remained the most powerful single state at his death in 1715. It was then clear, however, that she could not hope to win the dominant position which had seemed within her grasp in the later 1670s and early 1680s. In the eighteenth century, before the revolutionary and Napoleonic interludes, her international power declined compared with that of Britain and Russia. In domestic affairs, Colbert's measures to build up French commerce and industry provided a basis for later economic growth, but nothing was done to deprive the nobility of their social privileges, and poverty, sometimes actual starvation, was the lot of the rural masses. Above all, on Louis XIV's death the Crown was burdened with a gigantic debt, largely the result of his wars. It never really overcame that burden in the eighteenth century. The causes of the French Revolution, which had its origins in financial crisis, can and should be traced back to the reign of Louis XIV.

3,000,000,000 livres compared with one of about 60,000,000 in 1661. France was on the brink of bankruptcy as a result of the king's ambitions.

In other respects as well, the last thirty or so years of the reign were a time of gathering gloom for Louis and his people. As the king became more and more devout after his marriage to Madame de Maintenon in 1684 the whole atmosphere of the court changed. The gaiety of the earlier days was replaced by a stately sobriety which made a more suitable background for the domestic tragedies which afflicted both France generally and the king personally from the 1690s onwards.

Peasant life

In seventeenth-century France the life of the average peasant was precarious in the extreme. It has been estimated that hunger and even possible starvation were a constant threat for over seventy-five percent of the population, a threat which rapidly became a reality in times of economic depression and bad harvests. The later seventeenth century was a time of prolonged agricultural depression and conditions became disastrous in 1693–4 and 1709–10. In these years, just when the country was fighting against European coalitions, bad harvests brought serious famine. Thousands of Frenchmen died of starvation: sometimes the population of villages was reduced by as much as a quarter. This was the harsh reality of life for the average man during the *grand siècle*.

In the midst of these trials the king suffered a series of appalling personal losses. Three dauphins of France died within twelve months: his only legitimate son Louis, the 'Grand Dauphin', of smallpox in 1711, and his eldest grandson, the Duke of Burgundy, and Burgundy's elder son, both of measles, in 1712. Burgundy's younger son, the future Louis XV, was probably only saved by the good sense of his nurse, who hid him away from the tender mercies of the doctors, who were preoccupied with his elder brother. Burgundy's wife, Marie Adelaide, the acknowledged darling of both the king and the court also succumbed to measles in 1712. and in 1714 another of Louis' grandsons, the Duke of Berry died. The king showed a dignity amid his sorrows which even Saint-Simon felt compelled to praise.

The king faced his trials amid mounting criticism of his rule. He had few distinguished servants to help him in later years— Torcy, a nephew of Colbert, was the only great minister at the end of the reign—and many contemporaries laid the failures of the end of the century squarely at the king's own door. A sign of the times was *Télémaque*, a remarkable book by Fénelon, Archbishop of Cambrai, which was published in 1699 and attacked the very bases of political autocracy. Louis died on 1 September 1715 after a painful illness, which he bore with great resolution. He said farewell to what remained of his family, thanked his ministers for their services and received the consolations of Church with all the signs of piety. He had reigned for over seventy-two years and had brought France to a very high peak of international power and influence.

Left, Pierre Corneille (1606–84), the French playwright. Corneille was one of the greatest exponents of a form of tragedy adhering to the three 'classical' unities – unity of time, of place and of action. His works included Le Cid *(1637),* Horace *(1640) and* Cinna *(1640). Château de Versailles.*

Opposite, the demolition of a Protestant church in the late 1680s; Louis had claimed that most Huguenots had by now converted to Catholicism, but many thousands still fled from the persecution.

FRANCE UNDER LOUIS XIV

Date	Domestic Affairs	Foreign Affairs	Rest of Europe	Date	Domestic Affairs	Foreign Affairs	Rest of Europe
1660				**1680**			
	Death of Mazarin (1661)	Marriage of Louis and Maria Theresa (1661)	Restoration of Charles II (1660)		Beginning of the *dragonnades* (1681)		Peter the Great becomes tsar (1682)
	Beginning of Louis XIV's personal reign				Death of Colbert (1683)	War with Spain (1683)	
	Disgrace of Fouquet	Occupation of Lorraine (1663)	Second Anglo-Dutch War (1665)		Revocation of the Edict of Nantes (1685)		Accession of James II (1685)
	Parlement loses its right to criticize edicts (1661)	War of Devolution (1667–8)				War of the League of Augsburg (1689–97)	Glorious Revolution (1688)
		Peace of Aix-la-Chapelle (1668)	Triple Alliance (1668)		Death of Louvois (1691)	Battle of La Hogue (1692)	
	Colbert controller-general of finance (1665)	War with Holland (1672–8)				Treaty of Ryswick (1697)	Charles XII King of Sweden (1697–1718)
	Louvois made minister (1672)	Treaty of Nymegen (1679)		**1700**			
			William III stadholder of the United Provinces (1672)		Destruction of Port-Royal	War of the Spanish Succession (1702–13)	Founding of St Petersburg (1703)
					Death of the Dauphin (1711)	Battle of Malplaquet (1709)	Act of Union between England and Scotland (1707)
						Treaties of Utrecht and Rastadt (1713–14)	
					Death of Louis XIV (1715)		Accession of George I (1714)
				1715			

Chapter 11

Russia of the Romanovs

Throughout the seventeenth century observers from the West found it difficult to think of Russia as part of Europe. Accounts of the country by foreign travellers and diplomats were almost unanimous in emphasizing its 'Asiatic' aspects, such as the arbitrary and despotic form of government and the subjection of women and their virtual exclusion from society. The obverse of the almost unlimited power of the ruler, the complete subjection of the Russian people, reinforced this impression of an oriental despotism.

By 1600 the idea of the 'slave-born Muscovite' was firmly enshrined in English literature—the phrase occurs in Sir Philip Sidney's poem *Astrophel and Stella*. Such ideas symbolized the fact that the new Romanov dynasty, which came to power in the early seventeenth century, occupied the throne of a country which seemed barbarous to the more sophisticated nations of western Europe.

The election of Michael Romanov to the throne of Russia in 1613 marked the end of a period of dramatic upheavals in Russian history. The 'Time of Troubles', as the years 1598 to 1613 are called, had witnessed Polish invasions and occupation of the country, several changes of dynasty and, above all, a gigantic social ferment in which the peasantry protested violently against the oppressions of the government and their landlords in general and the growing burdens of serfdom in particular. The origins of that revolutionary social movement can be traced back to the developments of the fifteenth century and earlier, but, despite its long antecedents and the extent and savagery of the storm in which it culminated, it left few permanent marks on the political and social structure of the country. The fundamental fact of previous Russian political life—the absolutism of the tsars—emerged virtually unscathed from the upheavals. The great majority of the peasants who had played a prominent part in the movement were returned to the tender mercies of masters whose one real remedy for discontented serfs was continuous and brutal use of the knout.

The Orthodox Church, endowed with enormous estates and vast privileges in 1598, retained both throughout these years of turmoil. It is true that the storms of 1598 to 1613 completed the downfall of the great influence previously enjoyed by the ancient Russian princely and noble families, but this was merely the culmination of a trend which had been continuing throughout the sixteenth century, and the fact that the nobility of birth was replaced by a 'service' nobility, which owed its rise to the influence which it derived from holding court and state offices, meant that the change was essentially merely one of personnel—there was certainly no remodelling of the social structure.

Michael, the first Romanov tsar, the man who had the task of maintaining internal peace and stability after the Troubles, was not well equipped for his task. A sickly youth of sixteen when he came to the throne, he was dominated first of all by his forceful mother and then, from 1619 onwards, by his father Filaret, who had previously been a prisoner in Poland. Filaret became patriarch or head of the Russian Church, was recognized as co-ruler with his son and, in practice, governed the country until his death in 1633. Michael himself died in 1645 and was succeeded by his only son Alexis, then sixteen years old.

The new tsar, a man of conservative mind, pious to the point of bigotry, showed few signs of real ability in matters of state—his main preoccupations seem to have been with complicated church and court ceremonies—and the conduct of government business was left to favourites and officials. When he died in 1676 his eldest son, Fedor, a delicate, unassertive boy of fourteen, succeeded to the throne. Fedor's early death in 1682 precipitated a struggle for power between rival branches of the imperial family, a struggle which was the prelude to the reign of Peter the Great.

Reforming the government

The conservatism of Michael, Alexis and Fedor, helps to explain the continuity between Russian political and social developments in the sixteenth and seventeenth centuries. Before the upheavals of the Time of Troubles the tendency had been towards increasing centralization and regimentation, a tendency which was resumed under the Romanovs. The central administration of the country was carried on through *prikazy*, government departments inherited from the sixteenth century. There were a large number of these in Michael's reign, perhaps as many as fifty in all. The authority of the different *prikazy* often overlapped and the whole system was both unwieldy and inefficient. During the seventeenth century improvements were made. Some *prikazy* were merged, while others were grouped together under the control of a single official. These reforms, though their importance must not be overrated, did help

Opposite top, the Palace at Versailles, set in a large formal garden designed by André Le Nôtre to combine formality, pleasing vistas and a regular appearance when viewed from the windows of the Palace itself.

Opposite bottom, a view of the Palace of Versailles, painted in the late seventeenth century by Jean-Baptiste Martin. Château de Versailles.

to prepare the way for the administrative reforms of Peter the Great.

The tendency towards centralization was more immediately obvious at local level, where administration in the seventeenth century was carried on by governors appointed by the central authorities and by elected officials. The elected local officials, who dated from the reign of Ivan the Terrible (1533–84), might seem at first sight to be exceptions to the rule of growing centralization. In fact, from the very start they were government agents rather than representatives of local interests, and this aspect of their role developed in the seventeenth century.

The main duty of such officials was the unpopular one of collecting taxes from their fellow-citizens, a task for which they received no pay from the government. Their good behaviour was guaranteed by heavy penalties for misdemeanours and by the fact that the local communities which elected them were collectively responsible for their actions. In these circumstances, 'local self-government' was a mockery. Local officials were simply unpaid agents of the central government. They functioned under the close supervision of the governors who were, for all practical purposes, the supreme masters of the territories under their control. Most governors exploited their position to the full, and a complaint of 1642 declared that they had 'reduced the people of all stations to beggary and . . . stripped them to the bone'.

Like the administrative history of seventeenth-century Russia, the social history can be viewed essentially as a continuation of sixteenth-century trends. The great themes of sixteenth-century social history were the development of serfdom and the increasing regimentation of the population as a whole in the interests of the state. Serfdom had originated in Russia long before 1500, but it developed rapidly during the course of the sixteenth century. There were two main reasons for this. First of all, the central government tried, for fiscal purposes, to keep peasants living on state land from moving away. Second, peasants living on private estates became increasingly indebted to their masters. In these circumstances, more and more peasants became tied to the land.

Serfdom

The great Code of Laws issued in 1649 confirmed the developments of the previous century and a half and restricted still further the rights of the peasants, reducing virtually the whole of the Russian peasantry to serfdom. Indeed, the framers of the Code embodied in it the idea of the complete subordination of all classes in the community to the interests of the state as they saw them. This applied just as much to the two other great classes, the burghers and the nobles, as it did to the peasants. Burghers

were forbidden to move from the towns where they were living when the Code was issued—a provision largely designed to prevent tax evasion—and the nobility, who were given the sole right to own estates farmed by servile labour, became a hereditary caste whose main duty was military service to the state.

The provisions of the Code were, of course, honoured as much in the breach as in the observance. Despite its failures, however, the main idea which it enshrined was to dominate almost the whole of later Russian history.

Alexis and Fedor, despite their conservatism, did, in one respect at least, show themselves to be less hidebound than many of their subjects. They accepted changes in church ritual and in the phrasing of certain religious texts which were anathema to large numbers of Russians and which produced an important and permanent schism in the Russian Church. The matters at issue seem incredibly trivial today, but minor points of ceremonial, such as the use of three instead of two fingers in making the sign of the cross, provoked the most ferocious cruelties from the authorities and the staunchest resistance and utmost heroism from the 'Old Believers', as those who resisted the changes came to be called.

The changes, which brought Russia into line with other Orthodox Churches, were approved by a great Church council which met in the autumn of 1666 and continued its work until 1667. This council, which was attended by the patriarchs of Alexandria and Antioch and by representatives of other important branches of the Eastern Church, anathematized all who refused to accept the revised texts and the new ritual. The extent of resistance to the decisions of 1667 bears witness to the attachment to traditional religious observances which characterized a large part of the population of Russia. For them, formal piety was the very essence of the faith and they saw in the changes the abandonment of Christianity itself. During the years up to about 1690, when the most

violent persecutions took place, thousands of Old Believers burned themselves to death to escape contamination by the new 'heresy.'

The schism of the later seventeenth century weakened the inner religious life of the official Church by depriving it of many of its more devout members. It also weakened its position in relation to the state. In its efforts to suppress the Old Believers it had to rely more and more on the power and goodwill of the tsar. This was the situation which, in the early eighteenth century, enabled Peter the Great to reduce the Church to the position of a department of state.

Russia begins to look west

The changes in the Church can hardly be regarded as 'progressive'—they were an attempt to return to the pure Orthodoxy of the past—but, despite the profoundly conservative ethos of Russian life at all levels, there were areas in which new ideas did break into the country. The so-called 'westernization' of Russia, itself a misleading term, started long before the reign of Peter the Great, who is traditionally regarded by historians as its most distinguished protagonist. In the sixteenth century Ivan the Terrible imported foreign artisans and craftsmen, and a special suburb of Moscow, the 'German' quarter as it was known, was set aside for them. This settlement was abolished during the Time of Troubles but was restored in 1652 as a result of the large influx of foreigners during the reign of Michael and the early years of Alexis. The government was afraid that native Russians might be contaminated by the habits and heresies of the foreigners, hence the attempted segregation, but it was impossible to keep foreign habits from influencing, at least to some extent, the upper classes in Moscow. Even the tsar himself was affected. He introduced foreign furniture into the palace, established an orchestra, instituted theatrical performances and developed a liking for the ballet.

The immigration of foreigners, which made possible the beginnings—at a very superficial level—of western cultural influence in Russia was, however, permitted and encouraged by the government for severely practical reasons. The Russian army was much inferior to those of its neighbours, especially to that of Sweden, both in the quality of its troops and in the weapons at its disposal. Many foreign soldiers of fortune were employed in the seventeenth century in an effort to improve the fighting standards of the army, and attempts were made to exploit Russia's natural resources in the service of the armed forces by encouraging the immigration of industrialists and craftsmen who were ordered to train native Russians in their skills. In this way it was hoped that Russia would eventually become independent of foreign technical aid. That, of course, was very much a long-term ambition; the country was not only sadly lacking in skilled manpower of every kind but also in the educational institutions which were the necessary prerequisite for technical advances.

The anxiety of seventeenth-century tsars to improve their armed forces reflected the fact that a very large part of their reigns was spent at war, almost half the total period between 1613 and 1682. These wars were fought against Sweden, Poland, the Tartars and the Turks, often on several fronts at the same time. The seventeenth century was the great age of Swedish power. That power was based on the genius of a series of warrior kings, Gustavus Adolphus, Charles X, Charles XII, on the efficiency and patriotism of her armies, on the exploitation of her natural resources of tin and copper and, above all, on the relative weakness of her neighbours, especially Poland and Russia. These temporary advantages were nullified by the growth of Russian power under Peter the Great, and when Sweden suffered a series of setbacks in the early eighteenth century she did not have reserves of population and natural resources (her copper industry was by that time in decline) to fall back on. In the seventeenth century, however, she was much too strong for Russia and kept her away from the shores of the Baltic, a traditional area for Russian expansionist ambitions.

Seventeenth-century Russia, which thus faced Sweden at the height of her power, fought against a Polish state which was already in decline.

The sixteenth century had been Poland's golden age. Then she was the predominant political power in east central Europe. In 1572, however, the great Jagellonian dynasty which had ruled the country since the fourteenth century died out and a process of progressive political disintegration began under a series of elected kings who were forced to concede more and more power to the land-owning gentry or *szlachta* who, by the middle of the seventeenth century, had gained a dominant voice in the country. That dominance received institutional form in 1652 with the introduction of the notorious *liberum veto*. By applying the veto any member of the Diet (the Polish parliament) —a body dominated by the *szlachta*—could not only defeat the legislation under consideration but also nullify all laws previously agreed in that session of the Diet and dissolve the Diet itself.

In the hands of the selfish *szlachta* the *liberum veto*—which was merely the most striking provision of a constitution which by the mid-seventeenth century had deprived the Polish king of all real power—was an instrument of anarchy. Against a Poland faced with such formidable internal political weaknesses, Russia had some military successes. Between 1654 and 1689 a complicated and bloody struggle took place between the two countries for control of the

Ukraine. Russia emerged with substantial territorial gains, including the city of Kiev, but she had expended immense sums of men and money in the process and her victories did not render her southern frontier more secure; that still remained at the mercy of the nomadic Tartars, backed by the power of the Ottoman Empire.

Peter the Great

The history of Russia in the seventeenth century, then, is a story of conservatism in both Church and state. The tsars and their advisers were suspicious of all outside influences which might contaminate the true Russian heritage. They were, it is true, prepared to accept changes in the Church which were anathema to large sections of the population, but these changes were merely

Above, Archangel in the seventeenth century; the town had been founded in 1584 and it was the main port of Russia until the early eighteenth century; the fact that it was on an inlet of the Arctic Ocean and was icebound for much of the year contributed much to the isolation of Russia. National Maritime Museum, London.

Top, Moscow in the seventeenth century, centred upon the Kremlin or citadel; an English trading mission, led by Richard Chancellor, had visited the city in 1553, but a hundred years later foreign visitors were still a rarity.

Opposite, Alexis Mihailovitch, Tsar of Russia (reigned 1645–76), whose reign saw the start of the creation of modern Russia, with the institution of serfdom and the union of the Ukraine with Russia.

a return to the stream of genuine Orthodox tradition from which Russia had departed through ignorance. The 'westernization' of the country—if the term must be used—was an attempt to introduce western technical and military expertise into Russia under strictly regulated conditions, an attempt to increase the power of the state, not to change the social milieu. The population as a whole was subjected to a regimentation which was never entirely effective but which aimed, as the Code of 1649 showed, at the subjection of the individual to the needs of the state.

In this situation general standards of personal behaviour were almost incredibly low. Tsar Alexis won the reputation of being a kindly man, but even he used his fists freely on the highest state dignitaries, and frequent and often sadistically violent beatings with the knout were not only commonplace but were the lot of high and low, young and old, women as well as men. Drunkenness was common, and incest and sexual perversion were rife, especially among the lower classes, where big families were often crowded into a single room.

Contemporary observers, both Russian and foreign, are unanimous about the brutality and general coarseness of conduct which were the rule rather than the exception in Russia. The country which Peter the Great was called upon to rule must have been a hell for those with sensitive natures, if any such were able to survive until maturity in the conditions just described.

Peter's formal accession to the throne came in 1682, on the death of Fedor. Fedor was survived by a brother Ivan, a half-blind, mentally defective youth of fifteen, by six sisters—all children of Alexis by his first wife Maria Miloslavsky and by a half brother, Peter, Alexis's son by a second wife, Nathalie Naryshkin. This situation was the signal for a series of intrigues between the rival Naryshkin and Miloslavsky clans. At first the robust, ten-year-old Peter was proclaimed tsar, but the Miloslavsky fought back under the leadership of Sophie, one of Alexis's daughters, a very ambitious woman of twenty-five. She conducted a skilful propaganda campaign, directed against the Naryshkin, among the *streltsy*, a semi-military organization which was stationed in the capital and whose members engaged in trading activities in addition to their military duties. By promising them increased pay and privileges she won their support, and on three successive days in May 1682 the *streltsy* invaded the Kremlin and put some of Peter's Naryshkin relatives to death in full view of the young tsar.

As a result of this coup d'etat Ivan and Peter were proclaimed joint tsars. Power, however, passed to Sophie, who became regent. The events of May 1682 must have been a traumatic experience for Peter. Some historians have used the bloody events of these days to explain the cruelties and contradictions of his later career. One thing at least seems certain. When Peter had to deal with a *streltsy* revolt in 1698, when he was in full control of the government, memories of the events of 1682 must have stirred in his mind. It is worth noting that the rebels of 1698 were treated with a cruelty which even Ivan the Terrible had never exceeded.

Sophie's rule lasted for seven years and was brought to an end largely by her own ambitions. She seems to have planned to get rid of her brothers and proclaim herself sole ruler. The *streltsy* refused to support her and she was deprived of power and locked up in a convent. After her downfall Ivan and Peter ruled jointly, although the former took no part in the actual business of government. He died in 1696.

When he became sole tsar, Peter's character was already fully formed. During Sophie's regency he had lived in a small village on the outskirts of Moscow. There he formed a miniature army and developed an interest in ships, an interest inspired by his discovery of an old English sailing boat in a barn.

This enthusiasm for maritime matters was

confirmed when he visited Archangel in 1693 and 1694. It was on the first visit that he first actually saw the sea. In the years immediately after Sophie's fall he seems to have taken little interest in affairs of state. He preferred to organize large-scale army manoeuvres and build boats. When he did visit the capital, he rarely went to the Kremlin, but spent most of his time in the company of friends in the German settlement. There, at the centre of a group of foreign and Russian companions headed by the Scotsman, Patrick Gordon, the Swiss, Francis Lefort, and the Russian, Alexander Menshikov, Peter was exposed to the influence of Western ideas as well as to the pleasures of drinking and hunting. By 1695, in fact, when he undertook his first campaign against Azov, a Turkish port on the Black Sea, Peter had already shown great interest in the three influences which were subsequently to dominate his reign: the army, the sea, and western Europe.

The 1695 campaign was a failure, but Peter returned to the fray the following year, when, with the aid of a hastily constructed fleet, he captured Azov. In 1697 he decided to visit western Europe in person, to find out what it was really like and to study navigation, shipbuilding and the military arts in general. The tsar travelled incognito throughout his trip, which included visits to Brandenburg, the United Provinces, England and Austria. The incognito, however, was loosely observed—it would have been difficult to maintain in any event in view of Peter's remarkable appearance; he was a giant of a man over six and a half feet tall. He returned to Moscow via Vienna, which he left earlier than expected in order to deal with a *streltsy* rebellion which had broken out in his capital. His bloody repression of the revolt was followed by the disbandment of the *streltsy* regiments stationed in the capital. The political power of what had been Russia's praetorian guard was thus broken once and for all.

As a result of his first visit to the west Peter brought to Moscow hundreds of western technicians and artisans. The journey had stimulated his curiosity about other countries and later in his reign he made further visits abroad, including a notable trip to France in 1717.

Military campaigns

Peter's reign was dominated by wars. During the entire period of his rule, from the downfall of Sophie until his death, only one whole year, 1724, was free from military activities. The needs of these very expensive wars determined not only his foreign policy but the domestic history of the reign as well. The great majority of his reforms were introduced with a view to making the country fight more effectively.

Above, the expansion of Russia during the reigns of Alexis I and Peter the Great.

Above left, the tsar's forces doing battle with the rebellious regiments of the Russian army known as the streltzy.

Opposite left, Sophie Alekseyevna (1657–1704).

Opposite top right, Peter the Great, Tsar of Russia (reigned 1682–1725), reviewing the Dutch fleet.

Opposite bottom right, the house in Saardam, in Holland, where Peter the Great stayed in 1697.

The military operations of the reign included campaigns against Turkey in 1695, 1696 and 1710–11 and a war against Persia in 1722–3. As a result of the campaigns against the Turks Peter gained and then lost the port of Azov on the Black Sea. In the Persian war he obtained territory on the western and southern shores of the Caspian Sea, lands which Russia lost soon after his death. These wars, however, were overshadowed by the great struggle against Sweden, which occupied the years from 1700 to 1721. Peter fought to gain territory on the Baltic which would give him an outlet to western Europe. In the struggle Russia was only one member—though certainly the most important member—of a coalition which included, at different times, Denmark, Poland, Brandenburg and Hanover. Each of these countries had its own ambitions and grudges against Sweden, which was still in 1700 the dominant Baltic power and a great European power as well.

At first Russia did very badly. She suffered an overwhelming defeat in 1700 at Narva, a Swedish fortress on the Gulf of Finland. In that battle a small army of Swedes under their young warrior-king Charles XII, a man of reckless courage and some military genius, defeated a Russian force perhaps five times as large. As a result of the defeat Peter for a time contemplated peace at any price. Soon, however, he recovered his nerve and set about reorganizing his army and building a fleet. His efforts were repaid in full measure in 1709 when, at Poltava in the Ukraine, the reformed Russian army, under Peter's personal command, inflicted a crushing defeat on the Swedes. It was the turning-point of the war. Charles XII took refuge in Turkey after his defeat. He later returned to Sweden but was never able to recover for his country her former dominant position. After his death in battle in 1718 peace became inevitable. The Treaty of Nystadt of 1721 recognized the changed power structure in the north. Russia gained from Sweden the Baltic provinces of Livonia, Esthonia and Ingria and a part of Karelia. Peter had obtained his window to the west, but it was at a heavy cost to the Russian people.

The Northern War was the great motivating force behind most of Peter's domestic reforms. He reorganized the army and created a navy in order to defeat Sweden; his financial measures were designed principally to secure enough money to pay for the vastly expanded military establishment; his administrative measures were intended to make the country's war machine more effective by strengthening the civilian government behind it; his encouragement of industrial development was chiefly designed to produce arms, equipment and clothes for his soldiers and sailors.

Peter began the war against Sweden with an army 35–40,000 strong, consisting mainly of inadequately trained volunteers. By the

end of the reign it had developed into a comparatively well organized regular force of some 200,000 men. In 1703, when the conquest of Ingria gave him access to the Baltic, he began to construct a fleet there. When he died in 1725 he had about 800 vessels of all types manned by nearly 30,000 seamen.

Peter was always desperately short of money to pay for his ever-expanding army and navy. War expenditure rose from about 2,300,000 roubles in 1701 to 3,200,000 in 1710, and even in 1724, a year of peace, the maintenance of the army and navy cost the state well over 5,000,000 roubles. The additional revenue required to meet these growing military needs was raised by debasing the coinage and by hand to mouth methods such as the invention of ingenious new taxes, like those imposed on hats, beehives, smokestacks, private bathhouses and beards. State trading monopolies—on salt and tobacco, for example—were established and towards the end of the reign a poll-tax. The poll-tax, levied on individuals, replaced a tax on households as the basis of the system of direct taxation. This reform in particular brought considerable additional revenue to the government—revenue from direct taxation rose from 1,800,000 to 4,600,000 roubles after its introduction.

The burden of these additional taxes fell, of course, on the peasants, who also provided the great bulk of recruits for the armed forces. Peter's quest for military glory certainly brought no obvious gains to the rank and file of his subjects, only added burdens.

The tsar's administrative reforms, some of them directly inspired by military problems, were all at least indirectly related to the needs of war; greater efficiency in civil government would help to produce a more effective military machine. The reforms introduced were of the greatest importance in Russian institutional history. The provinces, into which the country was divided by a decree of 1707, lasted, with modifications, until the fall of the Empire, as did the Senate, which was established in 1711. This became the chief organ of administrative control in Russia and the highest judicial authority as well. The central administration itself was reorganized in 1717 by the creation of nine colleges, based on Swedish models, to replace the old *prikazy*. Some of these colleges lasted until the nineteenth century.

The confusion almost inevitably created by the introduction of so many major reforms in a few years, together with the lack of properly trained staff for the

Above, the Battle of Poltava, in the Ukraine, at which Peter the Great gained his revenge over Charles XII of Sweden, who was forced to take refuge in Turkey. This victory ensured that Russia would be a permanent force in northeastern Europe.

Opposite top, Peter the Great, who modernized the Russian army and navy and reorganized the state administration in order to be able to support his aggression, winning important victories over the Swedes, and also attempting to expand Russia in the southwest. National Maritime Museum, London.

Opposite bottom, the Battle of Narva in 1700, at which Charles XII of Sweden decisively defeated Peter the Great of Russia. The defeat led Peter to reorganize the army and build new defences in the north, and it encouraged him to modernize Russia.

new institutions, meant that the measures had less success than Peter hoped in producing administrative efficiency. Their long life, however, bears witness to their great importance.

The development of Russian industry under Peter was largely a result of the great and growing need of the army and navy for arms and equipment. By the end of the reign there were about two hundred large-scale industrial enterprises in operation. Among the most important of these were armaments works and foundries—notably the iron industry of the Urals—and textile mills, which produced cloth for army uniforms.

Nobility and the Church

The chief duty of the nobility in seventeenth-century Russia had been military service. This remained its principal function in Peter's reign, though he imposed the obligation with a vigour which had previously been lacking. He also began large-scale recruitment of the nobility into the newly created organs of civil administration. Noblemen may have been angered by the growing duties imposed upon them by the state, but they had compensations. In Peter's reign they were allowed to maintain and even to increase their already firm hold over their serfs. The serfs, in contrast, had nothing to brighten the gloom of their lives. They had not only to contend with the cruelties of their masters but were faced with ever increasing demands from the

state: demands for their bodies, to be used as cannon-fodder in Peter's wars, and demands for more and more of their meagre earnings in taxation. It is no wonder that frequent peasant revolts, especially in southern Russia, were a permanent feature of the reign.

Peter, therefore, treated his subjects, nobles and peasants alike, not as individuals but as assets at the service of the state, assets to be employed in any way he thought fit. The Church, too, was firmly subordinated to his control. The Russian Church had traditionally been subservient to the tsars, and the schism of 1667 had increased its dependence on the state. Until Peter's reign, however, it had at least had its own head, the Patriarch, who enjoyed vast dignity and prestige.

After the death of Adrian in 1700, however, Peter left the patriarchate vacant. In 1721 the office was abolished altogether and the government of the Church handed over to a holy synod, which was headed by a layman appointed by the tsar. After this reform the Church became, much more clearly than ever before, a department of state, a position which it was to retain until the Revolution.

A new capital

In addition to his major reforms Peter introduced many minor changes which had a significant cumulative effect on the appearance and behaviour of the upper classes in society. Members of the nobility were ordered to wear western dress and to shave off their beards, and women of the upper classes were encouraged, even ordered, to attend social gatherings—a fundamental breach of the traditional seclusion in which they had been kept until then. These reforms meant that the upper classes had been westernized in dress and appearance by the end of the reign. The peasantry remained largely unaffected. Peter's reign marked, in fact, the beginnings of a decisive split in Russian society between the nobility and the rest of the population. This tendency was accentuated by and indeed was partly a result of the foundation of St Petersburg in 1703 on the shores of the Gulf of Finland. The new capital, which became the mecca of the Russian nobility, was, by its very geographical position exposed to the influence of western Europe as Moscow had never been.

Peter's creation of a new capital was one completely original and very important contribution which he made to Russian history. There were other original policies, such as the establishment of the holy synod and the creation of a navy, but much of his work was a development, at an accelerated pace, of trends already established by his predecessors. This was certainly true of his policy of 'westernization'.

Peter died in January 1725, at the age of fifty-two, of complications caused by chronic venereal disease. He remains an enigmatic figure. He combined enormous energy and great intellectual curiosity with a propensity for extreme cruelty which can only be explained, not excused, by the general brutality of the age and country in which he lived. There is no doubt about his importance in Russian and, indeed, in world history. In the mid-1690s, when he assumed personal control of the government, Russia was at best a second-, at worst a third-rate power. At his death in 1725 she was, as a result of his efforts, unquestionably the dominant state in northern and eastern Europe and a power of first-rate importance in the continent as a whole. She has retained both these positions ever since.

ENGLAND, THE UNITED PROVINCES AND RUSSIA DURING THE SEVENTEENTH CENTURY

Date	England	United Provinces	Russia
1600			
	James I (1603–25)	Truce with Spain (1609)	Tsar Michael Romanov (1613–45)
	Gunpowder Plot (1605)	Oldenbarneveldt executed (1619)	
	Charles I (1625–49)	End of truce with Spain (1621)	
		Frederick Henry, Prince of Orange and stadholder (1625)	Treat with Poland (1634)
	War with Scotland (1639)	Capture of Breda (1637)	
	Long Parliament (1640)	Marriage of William II of Orange and Mary Stuart (1641)	
	Execution of Strafford (1641)		
	Civil War begins (1642)		
	Laud executed (1645)		Tsar Alexis (1645–76)
	Battle of Naseby (1645)	Succession of William II of Orange (1647)	
	Execution of Charles I (1649)	Treaty of Münster (1648)	Code of Laws (1649)
1650			
	Charles II defeated at the battle of Worcester; goes into exile (1651)	Death of William II; birth of William III (1650)	
	Cromwell lord protector (1653)	First Anglo-Dutch War (1652)	
	Death of Cromwell (1658)	John de Witt grand pensionary (1653)	War with Poland (1654)
	Restoration of Charles II (1660)	Treaty of Paris (1662)	
	Act of Uniformity (1662)	Second Anglo-Dutch War (1665)	
	Conventicle Act (1664)		
	Great Plague (1665)		
	Fire of London (1666)	Treaty of Breda (1667)	Russian Church council (1666–7)
		Triple Alliance (1668)	

Date	England	United Provinces	Russia
1670	Treaty of Dover (1670)	Third Anglo-Dutch War (1672)	Peasant's revolt (1670–1)
		Invasion by French (1672)	
		Murder of de Witt brothers (1672)	
		William of Orange hereditary stadholder (1674)	
	Popish Plot (1678)	Mary Stuart marries William III (1677)	Tsar Fedor (1676–82)
1680			
	Accession of James II (1685)	League of Augsburg (1686)	Tsar Peter the Great (1682–1725)
	Landing of William III (1688)		Revolt of the *Streltsy* (1682)
	Declaration of Rights; William and Mary, king and queen (1689)		
	Battle of the Boyne (1690)		Building of Russian fleet (1696)
	Triennial Act (1694)		Capture of Azov (1696)
		First Partition Treaty (1698)	Massacre of the *Streltsy* (1698)
	Act of Settlement (1701)	Alliance with Holy Roman Empire against France (1701)	War with Sweden (1700)
	Accession of Anne (1702)		Defeat at Narva (1700)
		Suspension of stadtholderate (1702)	
	Act of Union with Scotland (1707)		Founding of St Petersburg (1703)
			Victory at Poltava (1709)
		Peace of Utrecht (1713)	Peace of Pruth (1711)
	Accession of George (1714)		Execution of Tsarevich Alexis (1718)
			Peace of Nystadt (1721)
	Accession of George II (1727)		Death of Peter the Great (1725)
1730			

Chapter 12

Rebellions and Revolutions

In the 1640s and 1650s there was a great series of rebellions and revolutions in Europe. In May 1640 the people of Catalonia in the northeast of the Iberian peninsula rose in revolt against the Madrid government of Philip IV and his minister, the Count-Duke of Olivares. In January 1641 the rebels elected Louis XIII of France as Count of Catalonia in place of Philip IV, and the struggle continued until 1652 when the Spanish government recaptured the town of Barcelona and brought the revolt to an end. Portugal also rebelled in 1640 against the demonination of Madrid, and the Duke of Braganza, a scion of the old national royal House of Avis, was proclaimed king, a decision which was ratified by the Cortes, the Portuguese parliament, in January 1641.

The war between Spain and Portugal which followed lasted intermittently until 1668, when Portuguese independence was formally recognized. The third great rebellion against Spain did not come until seven years after the outbreak of the Catalonian and Portuguese revolts. In July 1647 a young Neapolitan fisherman, Masaniello, led a movement against the oppressive government of the Duke of Arcos, the hated Spanish Viceroy of Naples. The revolt, however, was short-lived. It lasted only until March 1648, when Spanish authority was restored.

Besides the three rebellions against Madrid there were revolutionary movements in England, France and the United Provinces. By far the most important of these, of course, was the conflict in England. This can be said to have begun in 1640 with the calling of the Long Parliament by Charles I, who was desperate for financial assistance against his rebellious Scottish subjects. The subsequent civil wars of 1642–8 led to the eleven years' interregnum which preceded the restoration of Charles II in 1660.

Less prolonged and of less permanent significance was the movement known as the *fronde,* which took place in France between 1648 and 1653. This had its immediate origins in general discontent at the financial exactions of Cardinal Mazarin's government. In its early stages it was headed by the *parlement* of Paris, which imposed a comprehensive programme of reform on the Crown. Later, however, the leadership was taken over by members of the nobility, who showed only too plainly that they were motivated by selfish ambitions. As a result, Mazarin, who twice went into exile during the struggle, was able to return permanently in 1653. The reform programme which the government had accepted under pressure in 1648 was quietly forgotten.

The upheaval in the United Provinces, led to the establishment there of the republican régime of 1650 to 1672. In 1648–9, after the end of the Thirty Years' War, the States of Holland demanded substantial reductions in the army. William II, stadtholder of most of the provinces of the union and captain-general of its military forces, went some way to meet those demands but refused to go as far as the States of Holland wished. William and his opponents in Holland became more and more estranged as the months passed and civil war seemed a real possibility, especially as both parties took measures which overstepped the bounds of strict constitutional legality. In August 1650 William made preparations for a military coup d'état directed against Amsterdam, the centre of the opposition, but the city immediately made concessions. The general outcome of the struggle was, however, still uncertain in October when William caught smallpox. The following month he died. In the reaction which followed, the forces of centralization in the republic were left leaderless and the republican era, under the dominance of Holland, began.

Despite very great differences in the duration and importance of these six revolutions, their origins had some common features. All were to a considerable extent reactions against the financial demands of governments which were engaged in expensive wars. Spain, France and the United Provinces all took part in the Thirty Years' War. Spain fought against the Dutch between 1621 and 1648 and in 1635 found herself at war with France as well, a struggle which continued until 1659. The enormous cost of military operations led Olivares in Spain and Richelieu and later Mazarin in France to multiply the financial demands which they made upon their peoples. In Olivares' case, he was particularly determined that the non-Castilian parts of the Spanish Empire should pay a fair share of the cost of the war. He therefore made substantial financial demands upon Catalonia. Portugal and Naples, demands which led directly to rebellions.

Similarly, in France Mazarin's desperate need for money to carry on the war against Spain led to a series of financial expedients which in turn sparked off the *fronde*. In the United Provinces it was a combination of William II's determination to renew the war with Spain after the peace of 1648 and Holland's equally firm resolution to disband as many as possible of his expensive troops which produced the revolutionary situation in 1650. In England it was Charles I's need for money for an army to send against his rebellious Scottish subjects which compelled him to summon the Long Parliament.

The rebellions and revolutions of the 1640s and 1650s were, however, more than just political and constitutional conflicts brought on by war and fought out between governments on the one hand and the people and representative institutions of their countries on the other. This kind of interpretation, which, in a sophisticated form, satisfied many past historians, is now seen to be too simple. It tells us part of the truth about the conflicts of the mid-seventeenth century, but, if we want to discover the whole truth, we must dig deeper.

One explanation which has been widely publicized and widely accepted in recent years is the Marxist interpretation. According to Marxists and to some other economic historians who accept their arguments, the 'general crisis' of the mid-seventeenth century, which produced so many revolts and revolutions, was basically an economic crisis. The conservative forces in the rebellions, they believe, represented 'feudal' interests, whereas the revolutionaries, in some of the revolts at least, represented the 'progressive' ambitions of the bourgeoisie, hampered in their economic activities by the dominance of restrictive and obsolete governmental systems. It was only in England, however—so the argument goes on—that the 'progressive' forces, representatives of nascent capitalism, were able to triumph completely. Thus, in England alone the old structure of government was shattered and, within the new freer forms which were established, rapid industrial advances possible later. Such an interpretation, which sees the English Revolution of 1640–60 as a necessary precursor of the Industrial Revolution of the eighteenth century, is, on the face of it, a plausible hypothesis. It gives a clear, general explanation of the mid-century revolts and specific reasons for the widely held assumptions that the conflict in England was much the most important of all the struggles.

There is, however, a grave weakness in the thesis. Little solid evidence can be advanced to support it. It is difficult, if not impossible, to demonstrate convincingly that the economic ambitions of the bourgeoisie were a significant motive force behind the revolutions of the 1640s and 1650s, and the supposition that the Puritan triumphs of 1640–60 in England directly aided the growth of capitalism there is only a theory. It has not been positively proved. The Marxist account is, therefore, an interesting hypothesis, but it can at best only add to our understanding of the mid-century crisis, not provide a total explanation of it.

Another ambitious interpretation less narrowly based than that of the Marxist is the recent thesis of Professor H. R. Trevor-

Roper, who argues that the mid-century revolutions were the culmination of a general social crisis which had been developing in western Europe since about 1500. The whole period from about the beginning of the sixteenth to the mid-seventeenth century should, he argues, be regarded as the age of 'Renaissance' society and the 'Renaissance' state. During these years, he maintains, the societies of most European states were dominated by the increasingly magnificent and expensive courts of their kings and princes and by ever expanding bureaucratic machines staffed by greedy officials. Only a small fraction of the cost of these great bureaucracies fell upon the princes whom they served. Much the larger share, probably well over three-quarters of the cost, fell upon the population at large. This was because the salaries and fees which officials were paid by their governments for prescribed administrative duties tended to be small and remain fixed. On the other hand, officials could expect tips or gratuities from clients who hoped, by such gifts, to oil the wheels of the administrative machine to their own advantage. Gratuities were generally accepted as a necessary evil, but the line between the legitimate profits of office and open corruption was hard to draw. It seems plausible that, as the sixteenth century wore on and the seventeenth century opened, standards throughout Europe declined. They certainly did so in England, where the situation under King James I, when any adventurer might hope to make a quick profit at the expense of the subject, was a far cry from the position in the middle of the Elizabethan period when the queen and her chief minister, Lord Burghley, husbanded the resources of Crown patronage in the general interests of the nation.

This expansion of courts and bureaucracies and the corruption which accompanied it was only possible, Trevor-Roper maintains, because the general expansion of the European economy in the sixteenth century made the expense bearable to the population as a whole. Even so, by the 1590s the cost of Philip II's wars produced everywhere in Europe a growing volume of complaint, and popular anger was very often directed against bureaucratic extravagances. If peace had not come in the first decade of the seventeenth century, the whole system might soon have cracked under the strain.

Court and country

In these circumstances, when war was resumed in the 1620s, governments with larger and larger military expenditure to meet had to make continually increasing financial demands upon subjects who had to find the money, amid the dislocations of war, out of the proceeds of contracting economies. The inflated Renaissance courts and bureaucracies then became intolerable

financial burdens. The 1620s thus saw the creation of a revolutionary situation in which the main ingredient in many European states was the anger of the 'country'— those subjects who had no profitable contacts with the ruling courts and bureaucracies—at the demands and extravagances of their masters. The rebellions of the 1640s, Trevor-Roper believes, were fundamentally a result of this general resentment, though of course each revolt was sparked off by specific immediate grievances in its country of origin.

The Trevor-Roper thesis, brilliantly argued and presented, is open to detailed criticisms from specialists in the history of each of the individual countries concerned, but it surely adds to and deepens our knowledge of the mid-century rebellions. Tensions between 'court' and 'country' were certainly a very important factor in the history of early seventeenth-century Europe and though Trevor-Roper may be wrong in seeing them as the most important cause of the revolts of the 1640s his explanation of these conflicts as great social crises is a valuable and convincing complement to the more traditional stress on military and constitutional factors and to the theses of the Marxists.

The middle decades of the seventeenth century, the time of the rebellions, divide two different worlds. The reasons for the transformation of European life which took place at that time are many and complex. The political, constitutional, economic and social revolutions of the 1640s and 1650s—for the events of mid-century were all these combined—played a part in this transformation, but even more important were profound general changes in European thought. Basically, the world of 1700 was completely different from the world of 1600 because the seventeenth century saw a combined scientific and general intellectual revolution which had unparalleled consequences for human attitudes and, ultimately, for the physical life of man on earth.

Scientific and intellectual revolution

In the long run the scientific and intellectual changes of the seventeenth century were vital in producing our twentieth-century civilization with its generally accepted emphasis on rational calculations. We must remember, however, that, in the short term these developments produced a society in which to perhaps a greater extent than ever before, there was a profound gulf between the ideas and attitudes of the educated classes and of the ignorant multitudes. In previous centuries, although the gulf between educated men and the population in general was very wide, they shared to a considerable extent the same general assumptions about man and the universe.

Above, Johannes Kepler (1571–1630), the German astronomer who solved one of the important failings in the Copernican system by showing that the planets moved around the sun in ellipses rather than in circles. He published his findings in On the Motions of Mars *in 1609.*

Top, the trial of Charles I of England, conducted by the House of Commons in 1648. This event was the climax of the political upheavals in Europe in the 1640s.

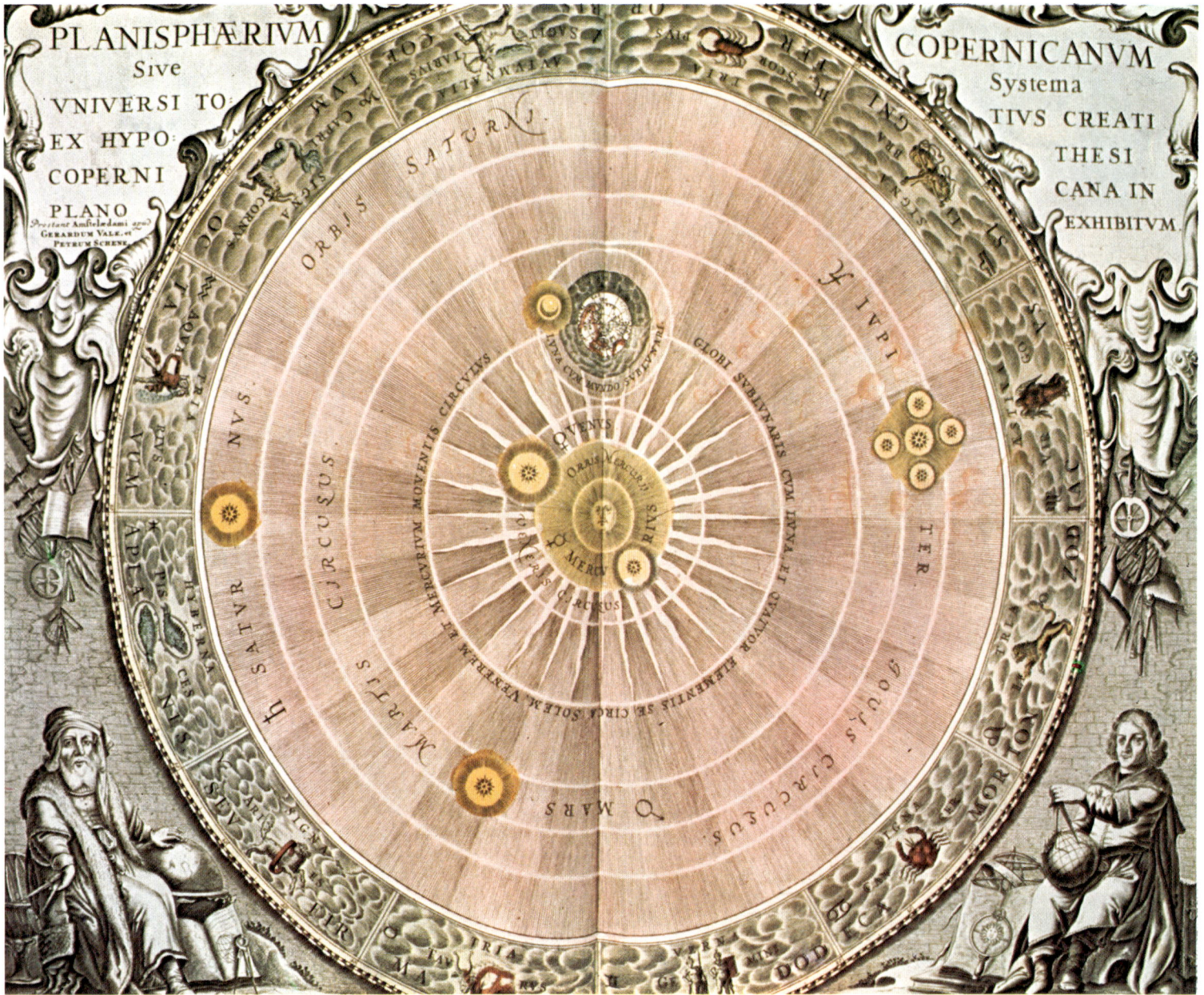

PLANISPHÆRIVM Sive VNIVERSI TO: EX HYPO: COPERNI PLANO

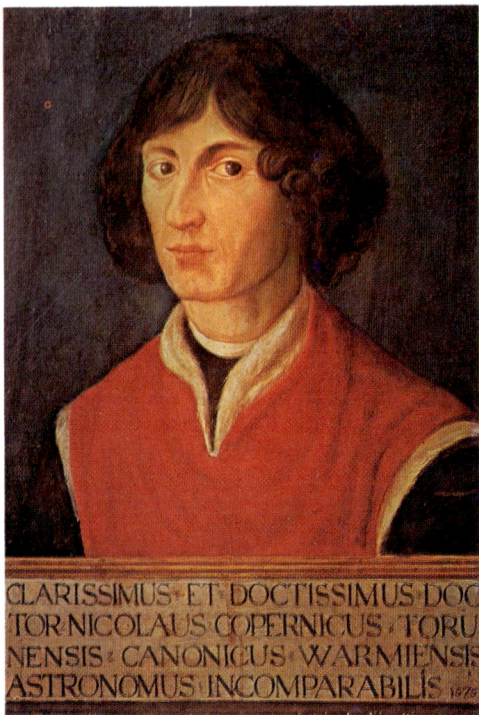

CLARISSIMUS ET DOCTISSIMUS DOC
TOR NICOLAUS COPERNICUS TORU
NENSIS CANONICUS WARMIENSIS
ASTRONOMUS INCOMPARABILIS

In the course of the seventeenth century this ceased to be true.

Between 1600 and 1700 the literate reading public of Europe fed itself on the flood of books in which those who were exploring the frontiers of knowledge propagated and sometimes even attempted to popularize their ideas. Of course, even the great majority of the educated men who read the books of the leading scientists and thinkers of the time did not fully grasp their arguments—how many men in the seventeenth century really understood the works of Newton?—but they absorbed enough to produce a radical change in their ways of thought. The profound difference between the educated and uneducated communities is one of the most fundamental and important facts of the time.

The great thinkers of the seventeenth century, with the notable exception of Leibnitz, rejected theological explanations of natural phenomena (that is, explanations in terms of an ultimate will and purpose which transcended scientific inquiry) and saw instead a universe which could be understood rationally by the analysis of carefully collected information. This was a change from a supernatural to a mathematical view of the universe. Mathematics was one of two fundamental sets of tools which gave man his new understanding of the universe. The other was the development of precision instruments, which could be used for assembling and measuring significant data. To take just one example, the telescope, invented in 1608 by two Dutchmen and improved and developed by Galileo and others, demonstrated beyond all doubt the validity of the Copernican system of astronomy which in the sixteenth century had rejected traditional views of the earth as the centre of the universe and postulated the idea that it revolved around the sun.

The growing emphasis on rational calculation received its greatest encouragement from developments in mathematics. The importance of mathematics in the seventeenth-century scientific revolution can hardly be overstressed. The century was not only one of the greatest periods of progress in the history of mathematics, it was also the period in which mathematical knowledge and methods had the greatest influence on the growth of knowledge in other fields, and consequently on the general development of human life. It is difficult to say why there should have been a great period in mathematics at precisely this time. The main reason is probably the emergence of a number of mathematicians of genius, each of whom built on the work of his predecessors to produce general rules about mathematical truths which previously had been understood only separately and not in their interconnections.

Mathematics

The mathematical advances of the century were made on the broadest possible front, but perhaps the greatest single mathematical achievement of the period was the calculus. The calculus should not be regarded as a sudden invention. It was rather the completion and synthesis by two great mathematical minds, Leibnitz and Newton, of the work of a number of other men. Newton and Leibnitz worked independently of each other, and much ink has been spilled in discussing their relative shares of the credit. Whatever the verdict, it is certain that both deserve a great deal of praise for their work on one of the most practically useful instruments of calculation that has ever been devised by man. It provides the means of solving the most endless variety of problems which turn on the relationship between changing quantities and can in fact be used for almost all difficult calculations.

One of the mathematicians whose work was of great importance in the pre-history of the calculus was the Frenchman René Descartes, whose even greater fame as a philosopher will merit attention later. As a boy Descartes acquired a liking for mathematics, 'because of the certainty of its proofs and the evidence of its reasonings'. This love remained with him for the rest of his life and led to the production of his most important scientific work, the *Geometry* of 1637, in which he laid the foundations of analytical geometry. He showed that geometric problems could be put into algebraic forms and in this way introduced a system by which problems about space (that is, geometrical problems) could be solved by numerical calculations through the application of algebraic and arithmetical methods.

Descartes, in fact, was the originator of *l'esprit géométrique*, 'the geometric spirit', which stressed calculation and number as a key to understanding. He provided the basis for a world founded on measurements and his ideas dominated much of the thought of the later seventeenth and eighteenth centuries. Fontenelle, the greatest popularizer of seventeenth-century scientific developments, stated that, 'the geometric spirit is not so attached to geometry that it cannot be disentangled and carried over into other areas of knowledge.' By 1700 Descartes had a legion of disciples who applied his ideas and methods to politics, philosophy, literature, medicine and religion.

One area of Descartes' thought which produced difficulties was his attitude to the relationship between reason and experiment. He believed that men, after discovering a few fundamental principles as a result of observation, could reason out the whole structure of the universe from these basic ideas. Although he lost his earlier confidence in this method before he died, many of his followers ignored these doubts, especially when they applied his ideas to non-scientific fields. There were, however, many exponents of *l'esprit géométrique* who laid the very greatest stress on the importance of experimentation. In this respect they followed in the footsteps of Galileo rather than Descartes.

Galileo

Galileo can claim to be the 'father' of modern mechanics and physics and the founder of modern observational astronomy. His contribution to mechanics and physics was founded on his work on the theory of motion. In the course of experiments he examined with meticulous care the behaviour of freely falling bodies and of bodies moving horizontally on the earth's surface. In these experiments he anticipated two of Newton's three laws of motion, including the law of inertia. That law—the idea that every particle continues in a state of rest or motion in a straight line unless compelled by a force to change that state—is the real foundation of the modern theory of motion. Galileo was in fact, the first man to see that mathematics and physics, previously kept in separate compartments, should be joined together.

No less important was his astronomical work. In the spring of 1609 he learned of the recent invention of the telescope. He soon built models for himself, making improvements which ensured that his telescopes were the first which could be used for observing the heavens. By 1610 he was able to announce a series of fundamentally important astronomical discoveries, published under the title *Sidereus Nuncius*. He observed that the Milky Way was composed of a collection of distant stars, saw spots on the sun, discovered the satellites of Jupiter, observed the phases of Venus and found that the surface of the moon was irregular rather than smooth, as had previously been supposed. In 1611 he visited Rome and demonstrated his telescope to prominent members of the papal court. He was flattered by the cordial reception he received and this encouraged him, two years later, in his *Letters on the Solar Spots*, to raise openly the issue of the Copernican theory. He maintained that the movement of the

Above, Galileo Galilei (1564–1642), the Italian scientist whose invention of the telescope, discovery of the abstract principles of physics and demonstration of the truth of Copernicus' theories of the solar system can be said to have been the turning-point in the scientific revolution. Biblioteca Marucelliana, Florence.

Opposite top, an illustration by Andreas Cellarius in 1708 of the Copernican system of the universe, showing the sun at the centre with the planets, including Earth, orbiting it. By this time, Newton had dealt with the last problems inherent in Copernicus' ideas.

Opposite bottom, Nicholas Copernicus (1473–1543), the Polish astronomer whose book De revolutionibus orbium coelestium (1543) was the first to suggest that the Earth was not at the centre of the universe. Museum Historyczne Uniwerstytetu Jagielionskeigo, Cracow.

OPTICKS:
OR, A
TREATISE
OF THE
REFLEXIONS, REFRACTIONS,
INFLEXIONS and COLOURS
OF
LIGHT.
ALSO
Two TREATISES
OF THE
SPECIES and MAGNITUDE
OF
Curvilinear Figures.

LONDON,
Printed for SAM. SMITH, and BENJ. WALFORD,
Printers to the Royal Society, at the Prince's Arms in
St. Paul's Church-yard. MDCCIV.

spots across the face of the sun showed that the earth revolved around it. Copernicus was right.

In 1616, however, the theologians of the Holy Office declared Copernicanism 'false and erroneous' and the pope admonished Galileo not to defend its doctrines. In 1632 he openly violated this papal command by publishing his *Dialogues on the Two Chief Systems of the World*, a compelling plea for the Copernican system. The work was greeted with acclaim throughout Europe, but the Church authorities decided to prosecute him on 'vehement suspicion' of heresy. He was compelled to stand trial at Rome in 1633 and, under threat of torture, to recant his opinions in a formula in which he 'abjured, cursed and detested' his past errors. He was sentenced to imprisonment during pleasure—immediately commuted by the pope to house arrest for the last eight years of his life on his own little estate near Florence—and ordered to recite the seven penitential psalms once a week for three years. The sentence was comparatively mild by the standards of the time and no other eminent scientist of the century was forced to recant his opinions, but the fate of the aged Galileo illustrates the fact that scientific freedom was newly and not easily won in the seventeenth century.

Galileo's fate at the hands of the Inquisition must have discouraged writers who would have liked to challenge traditional views of the universe, and although scholars were well aware of the inadequacies of ancient cosmologies it was some years before the Copernican system was generally accepted. In 1686, however, there appeared a book which was more influential than any other in making Copernicanism fashionable. This was Bernard de Fontenelle's *Entretiens sur les pluralitiés des mondes*.

Fontenelle is a most interesting man. Born in 1657, he died in 1757, a month before his hundredth birthday. He was never a scientist of great originality, but he kept abreast of all new scientific developments and corresponded with many European scientists. He was the great publicist of the seventeenth-century scientific revolution and recorded its achievements in innumerable books. Fontenelle presents a simplified version of Descartes' picture of the universe. This Cartesian cosmology—Descartes' ideas are described as Cartesian and his followers as Cartesians—accepted the basic Copernican thesis of the circulation of the earth around the sun and was also founded to a considerable extent on Descartes' theory of vortices. According to this, the whole universe consisted of a number of vortices fitting together like soap bubbles. In the centre of each vortex was a star. In the vortex containing the solar system the planets circled round the sun; some planets were surrounded by their own, subsidiary vortices containing satellites, like the moon. The whole universe was filled with a kind of celestial fluid, which kept the stars and planets in their places.

Fontenelle's book was popular but it was out of date the year after it was published, for in 1687 Newton's *Principia Mathematica*, one of the great scientific works of all time, appeared. Although the *Principia* was certainly Newton's masterpiece, it merely set the seal on a lifetime of scientific achievement. Isaac Newton was born in 1642 in the Lincolnshire village of Woolsthorpe. He went up to Trinity College, Cambridge, in 1661, taking his degree in 1665, when the university was closed because of the Great Plague. He thereupon returned to Woolsthorpe, where he remained until the spring of 1667. That year and a half, when he was twenty-three and twenty-four, was perhaps the most creative period in his entire life, as he himself recognized later, when he said that he was then in his 'prime . . . for invention, and minded mathematics and philosophy [i.e. science] more than at any time since.'

Newton

During that brief period, Newton made some epoch-making contributions to the history of science, including the foundations of the differential and integral calculus and the analysis of the composition of white light and the nature of colours, a piece of research which was the foundation of the technique of spectrum analysis. His great discovery was his conception of the force of gravitation extending from the earth to the moon.

Altogether, it was a series of scientific and mathematical advances unequalled in importance since the time of the Greeks. Newton's old Cambridge teacher, Isaac Barrow, himself a distinguished scientist, recognized his pupil's soaring genius and resigned the Lucasian chair of mathematics in 1669 so that Newton, then twenty-six years old, could succeed him.

Newton returned to the early work on light which he had done in 1666 and began researches which found final expression in his *Optics*, published in 1704. His theories about light gave rise to considerable controversy in his own time, notably with Robert Hooke, a fellow member with Newton of the Royal Society, and the protagonist of rival ideas on the subject. Hooke advocated a wave theory of light, according to which light consists of a series of pulses or waves transmitted through the ether pervading space. Newton, on the other hand, advanced a combination of wave and corpuscular theories. According to him, light consists of a series of corpuscles emanating from luminous bodies. These corpuscles give rise to waves as they pass through the ether. Newton's ideas have returned to fashion in our own time, in which there has been in scientific thinking a fusion of elements of both corpuscular and wave theories.

Newton set out the results of some of his early work on light in a paper which he presented to the Royal Society in 1672. The controversy which this aroused led him to explain his position. 'The best and safest method of philosophizing [that is, of conducting scientific enquiries] seems to be, first to enquire diligently into the properties of things, and of establishing these properties by experiment, and then to proceed more slowly to hypotheses for the explanation of them.' There could hardly be a clearer statement of the importance of the experimental method.

One very important by-product of Newton's work on optics was his invention of the reflecting telescope, a new form of the instrument which ultimately enabled very large telescopes to be constructed.

Important though Newton's work on optics was, his main claim to immortality rightly rests on his *Principia Mathematica*, begun in 1686 and published the following year. The fame it brought Newton inspired Alexander Pope to write his famous *Epitaph intended for Sir Isaac Newton*:

Nature and Nature's laws lay hid in night.
God said, Let Newton be! and all was light.

This tribute to genius should not, however, be allowed to obscure the fact that the *Principia* was a synthesis of advances made during the two preceding centuries and owed much to the researches of men like Leonardo da Vinci, Kepler, Galileo, Huygens, Hooke and Halley.

This is not, of course, to belittle Newton's achievement. It was he who produced the final proofs and in so doing created a picture of the universe as a rigid mechanism held together by absolute mechanical laws founded on the principle of gravitation, a principle which accounted for the movement of heavenly bodies, of the tides and of objects on earth. It was not until about fifty years later that Newton's explanation won general acceptance in preference to Descartes' theory of vortices. After that, however, Newton reigned supreme for some 200 years. It was only from the early twentieth century onwards, when Albert Einstein developed the special and general theories of relativity, that Newton's theory of the universe could no longer be regarded as final. The discovery that the mass of a body varies with its velocity changed the whole terms of reference of physics.

The publication of the *Principia* in 1687 marked a turning-point in the history of science in the short as well as in the long term. Nine decades of tremendously productive research were followed by thirty or forty largely barren years. It was as if the publication of Newton's masterpiece had exhausted the creative spirit of the age.

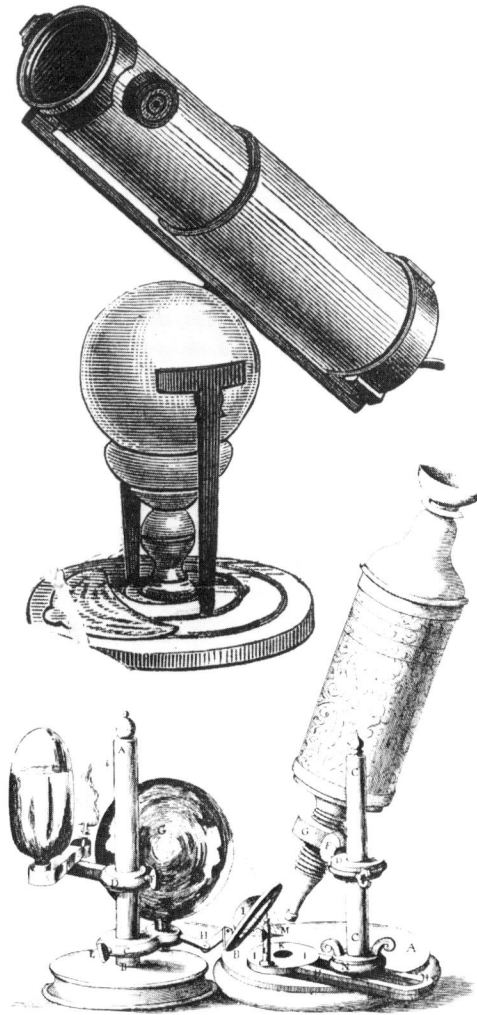

On first thoughts, this cessation of important discoveries seems surprising. There were many reasons why uninterrupted progress might have been expected. By 1700 European scholars formed an international community whose members exchanged information about their researches in voluminous correspondence and through the publication of learned periodicals. The new scientific learning was also slowly establishing itself in the universities, and, above all, *l'esprit géométrique* provided a favourable intellectual climate for continuing investigation and experiment. It also, however, provided a vehicle for the ideas of its founder, Descartes, and here perhaps lies a clue to the paucity of fundamental scientific discoveries between about 1690 and 1720. The authority of Descartes and Newton was so great that it cast a shadow over disciples who tended to feel that they had little to add to the words of masters, whose teachings they could only expound.

The eagerness of the generation of 1700 to apply the creative discoveries of the previous century to technology may also have left it less time for thinking about further fundamental advances. The years at the turn of the century saw many developments in applied technology: the improvement of pumps for mines, the application of the new mathematics and physics to the

Left, Isaac Newton's reflecting telescope, which he invented in 1668 and which allowed the astronomer to sit at the side rather than at the end.

Below left, Rupert Hooke's microscope, from his book Micrographia, *published in 1665. Hooke invented and improved several scientific instruments, including the microscope, the spiral spring in watches and a calculating machine.*

Opposite left, Bernard le Bovier de Fontenelle (1657–1757), the French popularizer of the ideas of Copernicus and Descartes. Between 1680 and 1720 the ideas of the scientific revolution became widely known for the first time. Château de Versailles.

Opposite centre, Isaac Newton (1642–1727), the English astronomer and phycisist whose theory of gravitation seemed to be able to explain the entire universe. National Portrait Gallery, London.

Opposite right, the title page of Newton's Opticks, *published in 1704. Much of his research was in the field of the refraction of light through prisms.*

problems of architecture, and the development of the steam engine are examples. Indeed, throughout the eighteenth century, engineers and other technicians continued the gigantic task of applying the 'pure' scientific achievements of the period 1600 to 1690 for the practical benefit of mankind.

Political philosophy

In the seventeenth century the influence of *l'esprit géométrique* made itself felt throughout the entire learned world. Almost all scholars shared the belief that the world could be understood by the aid of human reason and described in terms of mathematics. This belief influenced the style and content of their work in other fields, such as political thought, philosophy, literature, medicine and religion.

A name which can usefully be used to link seventeenth-century scientific and political studies is that of Sir William Petty, one of the early fellows of the Royal Society. Petty worked on figures of trade and population and expressed a firm belief in the benefit of applying the results to the problems of government. As such, he was the founder of what contemporaries called political arithmetic and we would call statistics. His ideas were to have a great future. The comparatively rudimentary calculations which he

made were developed in subsequent centuries into a sophisticated science which is the foundation of modern administration.

This general influence which the scientific spirit exercised on administrative and social problems can also be traced in the work of the three greatest political theorists of the century, the Englishmen Thomas Hobbes and John Locke and the Dutch Jew Benedict de Spinoza. All three shared the assumption that the same cause would always produce the same effect, one of the most fundamental of scientific theories.

Hobbes, who was born in 1588, grew to manhood and spent the middle years of his life at a time when the Elizabethan system of government was collapsing under the ineffective rule of James I and Charles I. When civil war broke out in 1642 the conflict turned largely on the question of sovereignty, on where, in other words, ultimate power in the English state lay. It was this problem of sovereignty which provided the central theme of Hobbes' most famous work, *Leviathan*, published in 1651, two years after England had executed her king. The title is metaphorical. Leviathan is the state and Hobbes chose the name because in the Vulgate version of the Book of Job we are told that no power on earth can compare with Leviathan. In that time of turmoil in England Hobbes turned, in fact, to the

idea of the supremacy in government of one selected man or assembly, preferably one man, who would exercise all legislative, executive and judicial power in both the secular and ecclesiastical fields.

Hobbes based his theory of the need for such a sovereign on a deterministic view of human nature. All human actions, he argued, were founded on self-interest. In such circumstances every man needed a guarantee of the good behaviour of his fellows, otherwise his life would be 'poor, nasty, brutish and short'. Such a guarantee could only be obtained by vesting all authority in a sovereign power which would be able to keep all men in order.

Hobbes' state was founded on a social contract. The ruler could treat his subjects in any way he chose as long as he was able to keep the peace, but 'the obligation of subjects to sovereign is understood to last as long as and no longer than the power lasts by which he is able to protect them.' These last lines explain why Hobbes' views failed to become an orthodox defence of monarchy. The Leviathan he conceived, with complete ability to overawe and at the same time protect its subjects, had seldom, if ever, existed. The arguments in *Leviathan* are, however, worked out with a rigid consistency which pays tribute to the scientific spirit of the age in which it was written.

Above, William Petty (1623–87), an English statistician who tried to set up a large-scale geographical survey and sought to establish the 'scientific' laws of political economy; such interests were typical of the intellectual milieu of Charles II's court in England, where the Royal Society was founded in 1661.

Above left, a Dutch astronomer of the second half of the seventeenth century. National Gallery, London.

Left, Thomas Hobbes (1588–1679), the English philosopher whose hatred of the English civil war led him to develop a political philosophy of absolute state power in his Leviathan of 1651; despite his conservative theme, his work was attacked for its materialist view of man and its denial of God as a formative influence in human society. National Portrait Gallery, London.

Opposite left, the Moon, according to a French book of 1685 describing the universe; the application of the telescope gave Europeans a new curiosity about the nature of the heavenly bodies and so brought the theories of Kepler and Newton to general prominence.

Opposite right, Christiaan Huygens (1629–95), the Dutch phycisist who discovered the pendulum clock. The accurate measurement of time was vital to the scientists of his day, who were much concerned with understanding the laws of motion.

Spinoza, one of the other two outstanding political theorists of the century, was also on the side of authority. He too denied any rights to individuals against the state. In his last work on politics, the *Tractatus Politicus*, published in 1677 after his death in the same year, he supported Hobbes' view that in a state of nature most men would strive for their own aggrandizement to the detriment of others. The only remedy was absolute government, which had the task of preserving the security and peace of its subjects. Unlike Hobbes, however, Spinoza saw that true peace was much more than just the absence of war. It meant, in fact, real concord among men, and a wise government, he argued, would preserve peace by granting, at its discretion, the maximum possible freedom to the people under its control, especially in matters of thought and religion.

John Locke had very different views from Hobbes and Spinoza. He was on the side of liberty rather than authority. It used to be thought that his most important work on political theory, his second *Treatise on Government*, which appeared in October 1689 (though dated 1690) was written specifically to vindicate the Revolution of 1688. We now know, however, that it was composed earlier in the 1680s. In it Locke gives his own theory of 'the true original extent and end of civil government'. Unlike Hobbes he assumed that man was naturally good and that he enjoyed inalienable rights to liberty and property which he retained when he made the original agreement which brought ordered society into existence. In making this 'social contract', in fact, men gave up their equality and natural 'executive' power with the specific objective of ensuring the preservation of their liberty and property. Rulers must therefore conduct their governments in the interests of their subjects. If they became tyrannical then the people were entitled to rebel and expel them from power.

Europe as a whole was at first more interested in Locke's philosophy than in his politics. Later on, however, in the eighteenth century, his political doctrines exercised very great influence abroad. He became the ancestor of much of the liberalism which played an important role in the life and politics of eighteenth-century America and France and is still such a powerful force.

Political theory, or political philosophy as it is sometimes called, can be regarded as a branch of philosophy as a whole, and two of the leading political theorists of the age, Spinoza and Locke, also wrote very important works of general philosophy. The seventeenth century is of the very greatest importance in the history of philosophy. In the words of Sir George Clark it 'contains the beginning of a chapter, the most abrupt of all the new beginnings since the rise of our philosophical tradition amongst the ancient Greeks'. The word 'philosophy' was used in the seventeenth century to mean what is now called science. We have

already discussed scientific developments and must now consider philosophy as the term is understood in our own time: the study of the ultimate problems which are raised in the search for truth and knowledge about man and the universe.

Medieval philosophical systems had been dogmatic: truth was the prerogative of authority, whether represented by the writings of Aristotle or the teachings of the Church. The new philosophy which developed in the seventeenth century was stimulated and indeed made possible by two great movements of thought, the Reformation and the scientific movement of the sixteenth and seventeenth centuries. The Reformation had little direct effect on philosophical speculation—it laid stress on faith rather than on learning and reason— but by flouting the authority of the Church in religious matters the reformers laid it open to challenge in other fields. The scientific movement, on the other hand, exercised a direct and powerful effect on philosophical thought. Copernicus, Kepler, Galileo and their successors presented new scientific views of the universe which led thinking men to speculate anew about the world and man's place in it. The influence of the new mathematics was profound—the greatest philosophers of the seventeenth century, with the exception of Locke, were all mathematicians of distinction.

Descartes

The man who can justly be called the 'father of modern philosophy' was a brilliant mathematician too. Descartes' methods were as important as the conclusions which he reached. The medieval schoolmen had gone about their work by systematically arranging all that was known about a subject and then arguing from the assembled material. That was induction, but clearly of a very different kind from the inductive methods based upon practical experiments which were later used by Galileo and Newton. Descartes, in contrast, stressed the importance of *deduction* in his principal philosophical works, like the French *Discours sur la methode*, published in 1637 and probably one of the two most influential books of the century (Newton's *Principia* was the other). His method was to begin by doubting everything and then to ask whether or not there was some truth which was so self-evident that it was not open to question. If he could find such a certainty he could then deduce other truths from it. It was clear, rational methodology, closely related to mathematics.

Descartes found his fundamental truth in the famous proposition, *Cogito, ergo sum,* 'I think, therefore I am', the idea that the processes which take place within the individual mind—such as understanding, calculating and doubting—prove beyond all question that the mind itself exists. From this starting point he went on to infer other

truths which, he maintained, necessarily followed. He constructed a universe which consisted of a world of experience and a world beyond experience. The existence of God, in the world beyond experience, was necessary because it was only from a being such as God that men could derive concepts which were outside their own experience: for example, eternity, immortality, omnipotence. The world of experience, the external world which men saw all around them, was not altogether as it seemed, because men's senses sometimes produced illusions about it. Still, it did have real qualities, which could be measured in mathematical terms.

In the Cartesian universe human reason was supreme. It led to a knowledge of God in the world beyond experience, and in the external world it seemed to make possible a mastery of man's environment.

Rationalists and empiricists

Descartes' works became the point of departure for both the opposing schools of thought into which philosophy divided during the seventeenth and eighteenth centuries, the rationalists and the empiricists. Those followers who stressed the rationalist side of his teaching and took the name 'Cartesians' were often men of considerable intellectual ability, though they were all far inferior mentally to another rationalist, Spinoza, whom we have already met as a political theorist but whose greater claim to fame is as a philosopher. Although far too distinguished simply to be labelled a Cartesian, Spinoza was in complete agreement with Descartes' methods and set out his own philosophical conclusions in the form of a deductive system in his greatest work, the *Ethics*, published in 1677.

Spinoza's philosophy is notoriously difficult to understand, but his conception of God, unlike Descartes', is not that of a pure spirit endowed with intellect and will. God, for Spinoza, combined attributes of matter and mind in a single substance, and was as much body as spirit. The physical laws which men knew were simply the operation of the divine mind: God and nature were one. Spinoza's philosophy, despite its frequent obscurity and difficulty, had a very practical purpose. It was designed to teach men how to live, as the title of his great work, *Ethics*, suggests. Only God was real, and all other beings and objects must be regarded in the context of eternity. This, however, did not preclude the need for human beings to try to live lives of virtue founded on reason and on intellectual love of God.

A few years after Spinoza's death John Locke arrived in Holland as a political exile. At that time he was already putting together the ideas which he published in 1690 as his *Essay Concerning Human Understanding*. Locke was the founder of a distinctively British philosophical school which exerted great influence on European thought in the eighteenth and nineteenth centuries, but he too owed much to Descartes, from whom he took his confidence in clear and distinct knowledge and his ideas about the fundamental distinction between mind and matter. However, he approached the problems of philosophy in a totally different way from Descartes. He used what he called a 'historical, plain method', an approach stressing the role of experience in the gaining of knowledge, in which he turned away from the construction of elaborate philosophical systems which had so preoccupied Descartes and Spinoza, to examine human ideas and their significance. In his *Essay* he took the contents of the individual mind and examined them one by one. The mind, he argued, was empty to begin with, but it soon filled up with simple data, impressed upon it by experience. It then worked upon these elementary ideas to form more complex thoughts. The whole of knowledge consisted of a collection and comparison of ideas.

Locke's work was much less ambitious in its aims than that of his predecessors. He

himself wrote 'it is . . . enough to be employed as an underlabourer in clearing the ground a little, and removing some of the rubbish that lies in the way of knowledge.' He also makes much easier reading. His work has none of their difficulties of mathematical form and hard vocabularies of technical terms.

In any survey, however brief, of seventeenth-century philosophy, it would be wrong to omit the name of Leibnitz, a man of many-sided genius, mathematician, historian, theologian and politician as well as philosopher. He never worked out his philosophy in a single, comprehensive treatise, but his ideas were systematized by others after his death. According to Leibnitz the universe consisted of an infinite number of simple substances, each complete in itself, which he called 'monads'. The highest monads were the souls of men, but all monads were spiritual realities. Material things did not, in the strict sense, exist: it was only at the confused level of sense perception that they seemed to be real. Harmony among the monads was maintained by God, who, having an infinite number of possibilities to choose from, created the best of all possible worlds. This is Leibnitz's famous optimism, which was so ruthlessly caricatured by Voltaire in *Candide*.

Of course, despite his genius, he was a man of his times, limited in his ideas by his own concepts and those of his fellow scientists. Just as Newton did not anticipate the idea of relativity, so Leibnitz, even though he stressed that the monads were always changing, did not really understand that the essence of anything lies in its development in time: the idea of evolution.

Pioneers of medicine

The influence of the predominantly mathematical and scientific spirit of the seventeenth century can be seen in medicine, literature and painting no less than in political and philosophical thought. In medicine one school adopted Descartes' view that the human body is a machine. Prominent among these iatrophysicists, as they called themselves, was the Italian Giovanni Borelli, who was particularly interested in the physical laws which govern the body's movements. The greatest medical pioneer of the century, however, was the Englishman William Harvey. In 1628 he set out his discovery of the circulation of the blood in his *De Motu Cordis et Sanguinis,* a fundamentally important work which was the result of accurate observations and careful experiments.

Harvey revolutionized medicine by proving a series of closely interrelated points: that blood is propelled from the heart at regular intervals and in a constant stream, that the same blood circulates in both veins and arteries and that the heart propels only blood and not 'air' as well, as had formerly been supposed. He made other important

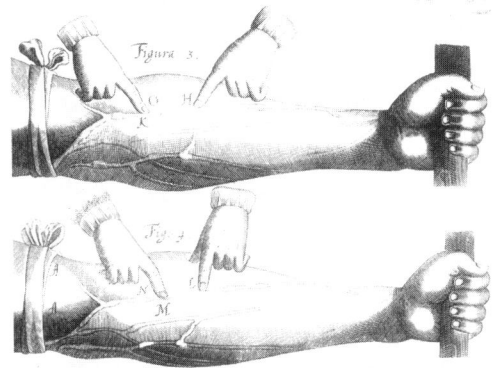

Above, the circulation of the blood, as illustrated in De Motu Cordis *of 1628 by the English physician William Harvey (1578–1657); this discovery was important in the development of modern medical science.*

Top, the title page of William Harvey's book of 1628 in which he outlined his theory of the circulation of the blood; his discovery owed much to the growing skill of surgeons in the previous century and also to the relaxation of the Catholic Church's ban on dissecting human bodies.

Opposite top, John Locke (1632–1704), the English philosopher whose theories of human knowledge led him to a political philosophy which was influential in justifying the Glorious Revolution of 1688; his belief that all men were born entirely ignorant, and that their ideas were the result of sensation and reflection, implied that society could only be organized for the benefit of all men equally. National Portrait Gallery, London.

Opposite bottom, René Descartes (1596–1650), the French philosopher and mathematician who is considered the founder of modern philosophy for his search for certain knowledge on which to base an understanding of the world. His system implied a sharp division between the material world and the world of ideas.

contributions to medical knowledge, especially in the field of embryology, and the new experimental methods which he used in his work were as important as the actual results he obtained. They pointed the way to the future, just as *De Motu Cordis* itself became the starting point for further research in physiology and anatomy, such as that of the Italian, Marcello Malpighi, Harvey's greatest immediate successor, who used the microscope to demonstrate the circulation of the blood in the capillaries.

In literature, the growth of the scientific spirit is revealed in stylistic changes which took place during the course of the century. Many early seventeenth century writers sought to impress by a difficult style—the poetry of John Donne and of his Italian and Spanish contemporaries is a good illustration of this—but as the years went by simplicity, lucidity and exactitude, mathematical ideals, became the fashion. They were exemplified during the century by the prose of Pascal and at its end by the works of Addison and Pope. The same kind of general tendency can be detected in painting. As the years passed there was a trend away from the Baroque grandeur and sumptuousness found in the early part of the seventeenth century in the works of Rubens towards the greater simplicity and restraint which characterized the art of Watteau at the end of Louis XIV's reign.

The Church opposes science

When we turn from art and literature to religion we find that the Church contributed little to the scientific revolution—in many ways it was a positive hindrance, witness Galileo—and that only one man made a front rank place for himself both as a defender of Christianity and a leader of the scientific revival. That was the Frenchman Blaise Pascal, a mathematician of great distinction who supported Jansenism in his *Lettres provinciales,* which appeared in 1656–7. His *Pensées,* published after his death in 1662, are fragments of a planned defence of Christianity.

The most important links between established religion and the scientific spirit in the seventeenth century are, in fact, to be found in the destructive effects which the latter had on the former. The Bible had previously been thought to be beyond criticism. Now, however, Cartesian sceptics argued that it should be subjected to textual analysis, just like any other document. Richard Simon, a Catholic priest, published several critical histories of the Old and New Testaments, works which revealed that the text of the Bible was full of difficulties of chronology and problems of vocabulary and meaning. His work was condemned by Catholics and Protestants alike, but, together with that of the great sceptic Pierre Bayle, it provided a great fund of arguments to support the Deists in the eighteenth century.

Indeed the end of the seventeenth and the beginning of the eighteenth centuries, the years roughly from 1680 to 1720, witnessed what has been aptly called a crisis in the European mind. Between these dates, large numbers of educated men, having absorbed the main ideas of the scientific revolution of the previous hundred years, began to question the very basis of traditional Christian teaching. Before 1680 only isolated thinkers had doubted that Christ was a Man-God who died on the cross for the salvation of mankind. After 1720 very many intelligent men questioned that belief. It was an intellectual revolution, a change from an attitude of mind which accepted traditional religious fundamentals to one which exalted scepticism and the secular spirit. The fact that the uneducated masses of Europe continued to adhere to old ideas only serves to highlight the change in attitude of so many intelligent men.

The new army

Besides vast political, social, scientific and intellectual changes, the seventeenth century also produced a military revolution. Professor Michael Roberts, one of the leading authorities on the subject, traces its beginnings back to the 1560s, but its main stages certainly came in the early seventeenth century and had profound effects not merely on military affairs in later years but on many other aspects of life as well.

In the mid-sixteenth century the dominant formation on west European battlegrounds was the Spanish tercio, or its equivalent. A tercio consisted of a square of pikemen and musketeers some 3,000 strong and epitomized the fact that infantry had replaced the heavy cavalry of the Middle Ages as the most important arm on the battlefield. The huge size of sixteenth-century infantry units made them difficult to manoeuvre quickly, with the result that tactics on the battlefield tended to be defensive rather than offensive. Commanders, in fact, usually avoided battles if at all possible.

The revolution which changed this situation took place in two stages between about 1590 and 1632, after an earlier, abortive start under Erik XIV of Sweden in the 1560s. The first stage, under the leadership of Prince Maurice of Orange, lasted until 1609, the second, under Sweden's Gustavus Adolphus, from about 1617 to 1632. Maurice returned to Roman models, with regard to both the size of his army units and their order of battle. His 'battalions' were about 500 strong—roughly the size of a Roman cohort—and he also favoured a linear order of battle as opposed to the square formation of the tercios. These changes made for much greater flexibility and manoeuvreability, but they did not win general acceptance in Europe, partly because they did not lead to any really striking successes against the tercios. It is notable that Maurice used the innovations chiefly in a

Blaise Pascal

defensive spirit. He fully shared the general contemporary dislike of battles.

This defensive attitude was completely changed by Gustavus Adolphus, who demonstrated the ability of the new linear formations to win successes in attack as well as in defence. He took over Maurice's smaller units but through a series of administrative and tactical reforms vastly increased their effectiveness on the battlefield. Junior officers and NCOs were given much greater responsibility and initiative on the field and musketeers and pikemen were linked together in the closest possible combination. This was greatly aided by Gustavus's exploitation of the salvo which he was the first to employ it at point blank range.

These changes, which were accompanied by important improvements in the mobility of the Swedish field artillery, demonstrated their significance in a series of victories during the Thirty Years' War, of which the Battle of Breitenfeld in 1631 was perhaps the most notable. The days of the tercio were numbered, and in 1643 the great Condé, then a young man, smashed once and for all the legend of their invincibility at the Battle of Rocroi. With that victory the military leadership of Europe, to which Gustavus Adolphus had aspired before his death in 1632, passed indubitably from Spain to France.

Changes in strategy

In the great battles of the Thirty Years' War, which marked the success of Gustavus' revolution, offensive tactics came back into favour after the long defensive interlude of the sixteenth century. At the same time, equally important strategic changes took place which transformed the whole scale of seventeenth-century warfare. In the sixteenth century, during the long Habsburg-Valois struggle, operations on several fronts

were common, but these were not usually planned in a systematic way. During the Thirty Years' War, however, with battles once more fashionable and hostilities ranging over the whole of central Europe, commanders began to look on the whole area of conflict as a single great theatre of war. Indeed, Gustavus himself planned to combine two types of strategy: offensive operations which were intended to defeat the enemy on the battlefield, and a gradual conquest of Germany by the systematic occupation of the country. His early death prevented any attempt being made to carry out the latter idea, but the grandiose nature of the scheme bears witness to the growing ambitiousness and scale of military operations.

The most noticeable result was a great increase in the size of armies. Philip II's Spain, the greatest military power in the later sixteenth century, had an army of perhaps 40,000 men. Louis XIV's France, the leading military power of the seventeenth century, had 400,000 men under arms during the king's later years. Throughout much of Europe, in fact, the seventeenth century saw the permanent establishment of armies on a scale which had not been approached before. In the 1620s Brandenburg's army was less than 1,000 strong. In the early eighteenth century, in the reign of Frederick William I, it consisted of over 80,000 men.

Navies too grew rapidly in size. Spain, the greatest naval power of the sixteenth century, declined in importance at sea as well as on land during the seventeenth. By the end of the war of the Spanish Succession, indeed, she had almost no navy left at all. In any event, even at the height of her power in the sixteenth century she had never had a large, organized royal navy, maintained by the state for the purposes of war alone. Neither, of course, had her enemies. All depended, as

Above, the Battle of Rocroi in 1643, at which the French army decisively defeated the Spaniards. The seventeenth century saw a revolution in warfare that resulted in armies numbering more than 100,000 men and an improvement in fortifications against artillery. Musée Condé, Chantilly.

Opposite, Blaise Pascal (1623–62), the French philosopher who studied barometric pressures and invented the modern study of probability. His Pensées were notes for a book outlining his belief that the scope of reason as a means of understanding the universe was limited – an unusual belief among scientists of his day.

131

the Armada campaign had clearly shown, on large numbers of hired and commandeered merchantmen to supplement small nuclei of specialized warships. In the seventeenth century England, Holland and France challenged for the position which Spain had previously occupied. The three Anglo-Dutch wars and the threats which Colbert's naval building programme posed to both the maritime powers led to a considerable increase in the number and of great improvements in the construction of specialized warships and to significant developments in the administration behind them.

This vast growth in the size of armies and navies helped to increase social mobility. It is true that few of the leading commanders in the seventeenth century were of humble origin, but below the very highest ranks, and especially perhaps in naval and military administration, poor young men of intrinsic ability could readily make a mark which enabled them to raise their status in the world. Of more fundamental importance for the history of the times was the strain which the upkeep of these enormous forces placed upon the finances of European states. Rulers were always desperate to raise more and more money to improve their war machines or even simply to keep them going. It is very significant, as we have already noticed, that the immediate origins of the mid-century revolutions, which affected France, England, the United Provinces and the Spanish dominions, lay in the financial demands which the rulers of these territories made upon their subjects in order to pay for the upkeep of military forces. In short, the military revolution of the seventeenth century had profound social, financial and constitutional consequences.

The shape of the future

In 1715 the military, political, economic, religious and intellectual situation in Europe was very different from what it had been a century before. In the political and military spheres France had replaced Spain as the greatest European power. In 1600 the Spanish Empire, with possessions in four continents, was the dominant power. It is true that Philip II had failed to conquer England or to subdue his rebellious subjects in the northern Netherlands, but he passed on to his son Philip III in 1598 a much larger empire than the one which he had inherited from his father, the Emperor Charles V, in the 1550s. The seventeenth century, however, saw a steady reduction in Spanish power, which had been founded essentially on the strength of the Castilian heartland of the empire. The rapid economic decline of Castile from the early years of the century onwards led to growing financial demands on the periphery, which in turn helped to produce the revolts of the 1640s. Soon Portugal was irrecoverably lost and by the last years of the century an impoverished

Spain under the rule of a mentally subnormal king, Charles II, had sunk to the status of a second-rate power. In the early years of the eighteenth century, with a Frenchman, Philip V, on the throne, she began to recover some strength, but Spain was never again to be one of the greatest powers in Europe.

The Treaty of the Pyrenees in 1659, a landmark in the decline of Spain, also marked the rise of France to the position of the leading power in Europe, a place which she owed mainly to the work of the great cardinals, Richelieu and Mazarin, whose victories against both Austrian and Spanish Habsburgs in the Thirty Years' War strengthened the position of their country abroad, just as their work in domestic affairs laid some of the foundations for Louis XIV's rule at home. By the 1670s France, with by far the best army and diplomatic service in Europe, was also rapidly increasing her economic strength, particularly her industrial potential. It seemed that she was in a position to threaten complete domination of the continent. By 1715 that danger had gone. France remained the most powerful single state, but changes in the international situation from the 1680s onwards, and particularly the growing power of England, which under William III was constantly hostile to France, ensured that there was a balance of power in European affairs.

Indeed, the years from 1680 to 1715 saw the emergence of England, Austria and Russia as great powers, able to play very important roles on the eighteenth century European scene. The rise of England in the period 1688 to 1715 is demonstrated by the predominant role she played in the coalition which finally set limits to Louis XIV's ambitions in the war of the Spanish Succession. Under Marlborough, Britain's

armies inflicted the first serious defeats on the French military machine which it suffered during Louis' reign, and her navy, as large as the French and Dutch navies combined, dominated the seas. This growth in Britain's military and hence in her political power was accompanied by a relative decline in the importance of the United Provinces. William III, after he became king of England in 1689, made it clear that he regarded Britain as the senior partner in the alliance of the two maritime powers, and in 1715 it was already clear to informed observers that the United Provinces had begun that long decline in her political importance which took place during the eighteenth century.

Austria's star in the later years of the seventeenth century was by contrast in the ascendant. Her great victories over the Turks in the 1680s and 1690s, leading to the reconquest of Hungary, together with the huge possessions which she obtained in Italy and the Netherlands in 1713, made her very clearly a great power in 1715. Russia too, under the enormously energetic rule of Peter the Great, increased her strength by leaps and bounds at the turn of the century. By 1715 and still more by 1721 she had replaced Sweden as the predominant power in northern and northeastern Europe, where she exercised great influence in the vast but declining Polish state.

Russia's power rested on her large population and vast natural resources, the basic elements in the economic and hence in the potential political power of any country. Actual power, of course, depended on how far governments were able to use the skills and abilities of their people to develop the natural resources of the country in the service of the state. France, which had a numerous and relatively skilful population and considerable natural resources, was in 1700 more powerful than Russia, which had superior resources but a slightly smaller and very much less skilful population. The Ottoman Empire, if one considers its European, Asiatic and African provinces together, had many more people even than France, but its real power was limited by technological backwardness. The United Provinces, by contrast, concealed the disadvantages of a small country and population by exploiting the very highly developed skills and energies of its people and its natural geographical advantages at the centre of European trade routes to make itself the leading commercial and financial power of the seventeenth century. It was a remarkable achievement, but, in the nature of things, it was bound to be temporary. Once Britain, with a similarly favourable geographical position, a larger population and greater natural resources, began to concentrate more and more efforts on financial and commercial development the days of Holland's supremacy were numbered. In 1715 the United Provinces were still the leading commercial and financial power, but they were being rapidly overtaken by Britain.

In the seventeenth century, as the Anglo-Dutch wars showed, economic conflicts played an increasing role in international affairs, a tendency which continued in later years. Religious differences, in contrast, played a less significant part in the international relations as the seventeenth century wore on. The Thirty Years' War was the last great conflict in western and central Europe in which religion played a really important role, though of course the war between Austria and the Ottoman Empire in eastern Europe in the 1680s and 1690s had strong religious overtones. From 1648 onwards, in fact, the religious frontiers of Europe were fixed. After that date, although religion continued to play a very important role in the internal politics of states, as the treat-ment of the French Huguenots and the career of James II in England showed very clearly, no European country changed its formal religious allegiance.

It was during these years too, however, that traditional religion, whether of the Catholic or Protestant variety, lost its hold over many educated Europeans. This intellectual revolution was preceded, accompanied and largely caused by the great developments in mathematics and science which characterised the seventeenth century and had ramifications throughout the whole field of thought. The intellectual climate among intelligent men was totally different in 1700 from what it had been in 1600.

These changes in thought were perhaps the most important of all the developments which took place during the period. It is traditional to see the great break in the century between the 1640s and 1650s, when so many political and social revolutions occurred. In the field of thought, however, the years 1680 to 1720 were crucial. It was in these years that great numbers of intelligent men who had absorbed the rudiments of the seventeenth-century scientific advances came to adopt a secular view of life and a sceptical attitude towards traditional authority which betokened a decisive breach with the past. It is perhaps at that time, rather than at any other, that we should place the dividing line between 'medieval' and 'modern' thought. The educated men of 1700 belonged in truth to a 'new Europe': they were the first generation to share a good many of the attitudes of the modern European mind.

Opposite, the formal gardens of an English country house at Stowe in Buckinghamshire, laid out in the 1690s; the passion for mathematical harmony overtook all the arts after the evaporation of the passions of the Baroque age.

THE CIVILIZATION OF THE SEVENTEENTH CENTURY

Date	Events	Arts	Sciences	Literature and philosophy	Date	Events	Arts	Sciences	Literature and philosophy
1600					1660				
	Accession of James I (1603)	El Greco: *View of Toledo* (1605)	Galileo: the telescope	Cervantes: *Don Quixote*		Restoration of Charles II	Rembrandt: *The Guild of Drapers*	Royal Society founded (1662)	Molière: *Tartuffe*
	Assassination of Henry IV	Birth of Rembrandt (1606) Monteverdi: *Orpheus*	Kepler (1571–1630)	Bacon: *Novum Organum*		Building of Versailles begins	Murillo: Decoration of the hospital of Coridad	Leibnitz: theory of movement (1670)	Milton: *Paradise Lost* (1667)
	Accession of Louis XIII (1610)	Rubens: *Last Judgement*	Harvey: circulation of the blood	Authorized version of the Bible (1611)					Pascal: *Pensées* (1670) Spinoza: *Ethics*
	Beginning of the Thirty Years' War		Harvey: working of the heart	Birth of Molière (1622) Birth of Pascal (1623) First Folio of Shakespeare published (1623)		Treaty of Nymegen (1679)	Sir Christopher Wren: Greenwich Observatory begun (1676)	Newton: theory of gravity (1682) Halley's comet (1682)	Bunyan: *A Pilgrim's Progress* (1678)
1630						Death of Colbert (1683)	Birth of Rameau (1683)		Leibnitz: *Systema Theologicum*
	Death of Gustavus Adolphus (1632)	Rembrandt: *The Anatomy Lesson* (1632)	Prosecution of Galileo (1633)				Birth of Watteau (1684)		Newton: *Principia Mathematica* (1687)
	Death of Richelieu (1642)	Inigo Jones' plan for Covent Garden Market	Birth of Newton (1642)	Birth of Locke and of Spinoza (1632)			Birth of J. S. Bach and Handel (1685)		
	Treaties of Westphalia (1648)	Van Dyck: *Portrait of Charles I*	Torricelli: the barometer	Donne's collected poems published (1633)	1690	William and Mary King and Queen of England (1689)	Purcell: *Dido and Aeneas* (1689)	Huygens: *Treatise on Light* (1690)	Birth of Voltaire (1694)
	Execution of Charles I (1649)	Velasquez: *Crucifixion*		Corneille: *Le Cid* (1636) Descartes: *Discours sur la méthode* (1637) Birth of Leibniz (1646)		Treaty of Ryswick (1697)	Birth of Chardin (1699)	Newton: *Optics*	Congreve: *The Way of the World* (1700)
	Death of Cromwell (1658)	Mansart: *Val-de Grace* Rembrandt: *Portrait of the Artist*	Creation of the Academy of Sciences in Paris (1658)	Pascal: *Les Provinciales* (1656)	1720	Death of Louis XIV (1715)	Birth of Boucher (1703)	Papin: experiments with steam	Leibnitz: theory of monads

Part III

THE STRUGGLE FOR SUPREMACY

Introduction

The civilization of the eighteenth-century, despite the outstanding impact of English habits of thinking on scientific inquiry and philosophy on the age was continental in character. And apart from the rich contribution of the Austrian and German courts to music and the stage, the culture of the Enlightenment, taken as a whole, was French and its metropolitan centre was Paris. It was French fashions of taste and thought and of governmental and diplomatic habit which permeated the more provincial centres of Europe, especially the more backward parts of Europe where standards and practices were set not by a mercantile middle class but by 'enlightened despots' in touch with France and each other.

The civilization of the eighteenth-century was, indeed, continental in another sense. It was continent-wide. One must always guard against the tendency of historical perspective to see uniformities and to shade out disparities and in our case to accept the polite and the articulate and to discount the disparate, the turbulent, the primitive, indeed the barbaric, aspects of life in the rural society which Europe essentially remained. Nonetheless, Europe in the eighteenth-century was culturally more homogeneous than she had been since the Middle Ages and was to be again until the present.

'The concert of Europe' is a post-Napoleonic term which previous generations had not found it necessary to invent because its reality was assumed. The relations between states continued to be governed largely by dynastic assumptions and the room to manoeuvre by limited objectives in which an element of whim or fantasy was only partially displaced by Frederick the Great's intrusion of an element of *Realpolitik*. The limited objectives of diplomacy extended to wars fought by small armies of mercenaries and pressed troops drilled to formal manoeuvre in campaigns limited by the seasons and by a primitive organization of supply. The concepts of national mobilization and of ideological crusade had not yet been born. These objectives were limited by a social and political order which held so stable that trade between enemies could thrive and the gentry could travel through enemy country without any threat of molestation; social communication among equals was unimpaired by war. This is not to deny that there were major shifts in the balance of forces such as the revolution in alliances of 1756 or that resulting from the inefficient but powerful new impact of Russia combined with the slackening hold of Turkey in eastern Europe. The latter, however, took place at the periphery of a Europe whose boundaries were extended to include a partially Europeanized Russia as part of the European system.

That system held not so much because of a common aristocratic and semi-feudal social order but because the personal rule of princes acquired new force from the rationalizing of administration: the erosion of medieval estates and privileges (including practices of self-government which were thought to be anachronistic) and the substitution of military, civil and judicial services responsible to the ruler. By such means the 'enlightened' despots of principalities created for themselves both the fact and the notion of 'states'. Kosciuzko's Poland apart, however, this notion did not extend to that of the 'nation', and the threat of a revolution which was both French and ideological forced the despots of the Enlightenment into a reactionary defensiveness which, until national self-consciousness, was no match for the French revolutionary elan. Against this new force—which produced so cataclysmic an event, or series of events, that the map of Europe, politically, governmentally, socially and ideologically, was never the same again—the civility of the Enlightenment, so urbane and, in a measure, so well-intentioned, collapsed; and the civilization of the eighteenth-century, as proud and seemingly as established as that of the Roman Empire which was so much admired, was shown to be shallow and inadequate in its thinking, its practices and its capacity for change.

Chapter 13

Central and Eastern Europe in the late Seventeenth Century

Until the nineteenth century, an area considerably larger than the two present-day German states was occupied by the Holy Roman Empire—not an empire in the modern sense, or even a state, but a patchwork of some 350 territorial units owing allegiance to a Holy Roman emperor. The majority of the inhabitants were Germans, but the empire also contained the Czechs of Bohemia, the Flemings of the Spanish Netherlands and other non-Germans.

The empire was religiously as well as politically fragmented; and the hatreds of Catholic, Lutheran and Calvinist were the occasion of the terrible Thirty Years' War (1618–48), in which most of the European powers became involved. Germany was the main theatre of the war and at its close was physically and morally devastated. Although not all areas were equally affected, suffering and impoverishment were very widely distributed. Law and order vanished; trade was disrupted and often re-routed to avoid Germany altogether; and the population of both town and country fell catastrophically. In many areas the material and human losses were not made good until the early decades of the eighteenth century.

The political results were equally serious. For a time during the war it seemed that the Emperor Ferdinand II might be able to weld the empire into a unified state comparable with France or Spain. His failure entailed the creation of new weaknesses and—of much greater importance—the perpetuation of all the existing weaknesses. In an age when powerful and unified nation-states were coming to dominate Europe, and when the authority of governments was being asserted with increasing success by ever larger bureaucracies, the empire remained as it was: a quasi-feudal agglomeration of more or less independent units.

The lay and ecclesiastical princes, free cities and imperial knights whose territories made up the empire owed formal allegiance to the emperor, but the more powerful were entirely beyond his control. Imperial authority was backed neither by an army nor by the ability to levy taxes. The deliberative assembly, the Diet, was a wrangling, ineffective body; the judicial institutions of the empire were antiquated and notoriously slow. The exercise of imperial power was restricted to arbitrating in disputes between German rulers and occasionally between rulers and their subjects; and even this applied only to small or weak states.

The emperor did not inherit his office: he was elected by the most important princes of the empire. In the late seventeenth century the electors were the ecclesiastical rulers of Mainz, Trier and Cologne and the lay princes of the Palatinate, Saxony, Brandenburg, Bavaria, Bohemia and Hanover. Every candidate for the throne had to buy the electors' support with cash or concessions, so that any continuous growth of imperial authority was impossible to achieve in normal circumstances. In fact, the Habsburg family succeeded in monopolizing the imperial office: with one exception (1742–5), every emperor from 1438 until the dissolution of the empire in 1806 was a Habsburg. This provided the empire with its only element of effective continuity; and it was the resources of the Habsburgs' large hereditary possessions that sustained such authority as the emperor possessed.

For practical purposes, then, the largest German principalities were independent states, able to make alliances with each other or with non-German powers, jealous of their neighbours and hostile to the extension of imperial authority. A certain vestigial imperial or German sentiment could persuade the princes to rally to the emperor, notably in campaigns against the Turks; but it was always of brief duration. From 1681 there was even an imperial army of sorts, though it was mainly provided by the western states of the empire, which felt threatened by the aggressions of Louis XIV.

Indeed, the diplomatic history of these German states in the late seventeenth and early eighteenth centuries was largely one of reaction to French initiatives. Louis' insatiable ambition and over-confidence gradually united the empire against him. The powerful league of Rhine princes, formed in 1654 as a satellite of France, was dissolved in 1668. French success in the War of Devolution (1667–8), the Dutch War (1672–9) and the legalistic aggressions by which Louis 'reunited' border territories with France made it progressively more difficult for the French to buy off German states or to play upon their mutual suspicions; France, not the emperor, came to be seen as the main threat to their security. In 1686 the princes of Franconia and the Rhineland formed a defensive alliance, the League of Augsburg, directed against France; and within two years Brandenburg, Bavaria and Saxony had joined the league. From the beginning of the War of the League of Augsburg (1688), most of the empire took part in the long struggles against France that ended only in 1713.

This unity was as factitious and devoid of significance for the future as the larger unity of the European states against France. The

Above, a German woodcut of 1643 showing robbers attacking a horseman; the Thirty Years' War brought devastation to many parts of Germany and, in its wake, a threat of social collapse and anarchy.

Opposite, Madame de Pompadour, the mistress of Louis XV of France, with the Duke of Choiseul. Waddesdon Manor. The National Trust.

On page 134, the Battle of Dettingen of June 1743, an English victory in the War of the Austrian Succession. It was the last occasion on which an English king led his troops in battle.

NORTH SEA

DENMARK

BALTIC SEA

POMERANIA

POLAND

EAST PRUSSIA

HANOVER

RAVENSBURG
HOLLAND
(UNITED
PROVINCES)
CLEVES

BRANDENBURG

MARK

SAXONY

SILESIA

BOHEMIA

MORAVIA

SPANISH
NETHERLANDS

FRANCE

AUSTRIA

HABSBURG HUNGARY

TRANSYLVANIA

SAVOY

MILAN

OTTOMAN EMPIRE

POLAND

Boundary of the Empire ▬▬▬

Ottoman Empire |||||

Swedish possessions ▓

Hohenzollern possessions ≡

Spanish Habsburg possessions ≡

Austrian Habsburg possessions ⋮

France and French possessions ⋰

---

less dramatic but more durable tendencies of the age reinforced the independence and power of the individual princes. The right of subjects to appeal to the emperor over the heads of their rulers was progressively curtailed. Several princes succeeded in weakening the representative estates in their dominions, or even in doing without them altogether, aping the absolutism of Louis XIV. Every petty ruler sought to emulate at least the trappings of the Sun King's greatness, building a miniature Versailles, making French the language of his court, creating a bureaucracy and maintaining a standing army.

The extra-imperial interests of the princes were emphasized by the dynastic ambitions that led them to seek thrones outside Germany, as when Augustus the Strong of Saxony became King of Poland (1697) and the Elector of Hanover became George I of England (1714). In the long run this kind of entanglement led to the neglect or overexploitation of the German state concerned; and it was partly because Saxony and Hanover became involved in Polish and British affairs that, as we shall see, Brandenburg-Prussia was able to become the leading German state.

German commerce had begun to decline in some places before the Thirty Years' War, and the war itself wrecked the German economy and left foreign powers in control of the mouths of the great German rivers. A highly centralized state like France, with large resources at its disposal, might have recovered fairly quickly; the hundreds of units making up the empire could not.

Division bred many weaknesses. The exactions of the princes were disproportionate to the resources of their states, which had to pay for the upkeep of a local court, a local bureaucracy, a local army. The burden was unevenly spread, since noble privileges were usually left untouched—a tacit repayment for noble acquiescence in princely absolutism. The means by which revenue was raised, though in accordance with the economic theories of the time, were inappropriate to a complex of small, impoverished states. Taxes, monopolies and excise duties discouraged manufactures:

customs duties levied at frontiers and along rivers drove away trade. Towns under princely rule were borne down by their rulers' exactions; the free cities, hemmed in on all sides by the territories of the princes, stagnated.

There were exceptions, notably Hamburg, Frankfurt and Leipzig; indeed, all generalizations about the empire—a miniature world of states and cities with varied resources and widely different socio-political structures—are subject to qualification. The situation of the peasants was even more various. In Saxony and western and southern Germany they were free and relatively prosperous. Elsewhere, and particularly in the northeast, they were still serfs, allowed to cultivate their holdings in return for various services, including work on the land which their lord farmed for his own use; and here the rigours of serfdom were if anything increased after the Thirty Years' War. Depopulation encouraged landlords to enlarge their own holdings, which entailed the imposition of greater labour services on a peasantry much reduced in numbers.

Thus all the facts of German life indicated prolonged backwardness, fragmentation and diversification. Germany was not to be united for two centuries, but the politics of central Europe were about to be transformed by the emergence of new forces. Religion gradually ceased to be a political issue; for most of the eighteenth and nineteenth centuries the main motif of German history was to be 'dualism', the domination of Germany by two states, the Habsburg dominions and Brandenburg-Prussia. This was foreshadowed by two developments in the late seventeenth century; the consolidation and extension of the Habsburg lands through the defeat of the Turks; and the forced growth of Brandenburg-Prussia under a succession of able Hohenzollern rulers.

Brandenburg-Prussia

The Electorate of Brandenburg was a poor, sandy, waterlogged land in north-east Germany. It had been ruled by the Hohenzollern family since 1415; under Frederick William, 'the Great Elector', it was to become the heartland of a formidable state.

The other Hohenzollern territories were scattered and difficult to defend. Only Pomerania, immediately to the north, was defensible; the duchy of East Prussia, for which the elector did homage to the king of Poland, was separated from Brandenburg by a wide belt of Polish territory; the duchy of Cleves and the counties of Mark and Ravensburg were in the distant Rhineland.

When Frederick William acceded in 1640, at the age of twenty, the Thirty Years' War was entering its final phase, and most of his possessions were occupied by foreign troops. He extricated himself from his difficulties by a combination of skill and good luck, and with French support secured relatively good terms at the Peace of Westphalia (1648). Sweden took western Pomerania, with the vital harbour of Stettin which controlled the River Oder, but as partial compensation Frederick William received several secularized bishoprics adjacent to Hohenzollern lands. Only after Westphalia was Frederick William able to begin the task which occupied the rest of his life.

The Hohenzollern lands were not a state: they were separate entities which happened to be ruled by the same man; each was represented by its own Estates, preoccupied with local problems and averse to voting money for the defence of other Hohenzollern possessions. The essential achievement of Frederick William's reign was to make this dynastic complex into a unified state, the total resources of which were at the elector's disposal.

The Brandenburg Estates were dominated by the Junkers, nobles who farmed their lands for profit with serf labour, mainly producing corn and beer for sale. They were a working nobility, by no means very wealthy, and they had none of the thirst for adventure and glory characteristic of great aristocracies. In 1650 they refused the elector money with which to fight the Swedes in Pomerania: Pomerania was no concern of theirs. In 1652, when Frederick William demanded a general excise that would have ended the Junkers' virtual exemption from taxation, he had to be content with a compromise. The Junkers' control over their serfs was strengthened; the elector was to consult the Estates on all matters of importance; and in return he was to have a grant of 500,000 thalers.

In the event, what mattered was the money. With money Frederick William could raise troops; and with troops he could impose his will on his recalcitrant subjects. The war between Sweden and Poland (1655–60) gave him the opportunity and excuse to execute this policy. In the war itself he judiciously changed sides at the right moment, thereby securing the complete independence of his duchy of East Prussia; but the internal repercussions were even more important.

Everywhere the elector's soldiers recruited and collected the taxes he imposed; resistance was simply met by force. In Brandenburg alone, which had granted 500,000 thalers over six years in 1652, 110,000 thalers a month was being collected by 1659. The excise, which was gradually made compulsory for all the towns, became a permanent tax; and without the power of the purse the Estates became insignificant. The Junkers, secure in their control over the serfs and exempt from payment of the excise, quickly accepted the situation.

Elsewhere the pattern of events was similar. East Prussia, with a relatively wealthy nobility habituated to the anarchy of Poland, put up a stiffer resistance than Brandenburg. Only in the 1670s was all opposition destroyed; the independence of the four locally elected governors was ended, and the duchy was integrated into the Hohenzollern state. The Rhineland territories preserved some independence, though they lost the exceptional liberties they had won earlier. They were simply too far away for the Hohenzollerns to control them autocratically.

It is difficult to assess how consciously Frederick William planned the development of the Hohenzollern state; but his rule undoubtedly possessed an inner logic, conscious or not. Given the scattered nature of the Hohenzollern territories, security could be gained only by strengthening the army. A bigger army had to be supported out of heavier taxes, which could be collected only by the army. Army and administration thus became closely identified. The General War Commissariat, created to organize supplies for the army during the Swedish-Polish war, took over the collection of taxes, and its officers became the most important executives of a centralized and militarized bureaucracy.

Above, Frederick William, elector of Brandenburg (reigned 1640–88), who won Brandenburg's independence from the Polish king, took Pomerania and created a unified and militarily strong Prussian state. Schloss Fasanenie, Fulda.

Opposite, the Holy Roman Empire after the Treaty of Westphalia in 1648.

The army, which had numbered less than 5,000 at the end of the Thirty Years' War, was 12,000 strong even after reductions made in 1660; and at Frederick William's death in 1688 a small population (about a million) was supporting a standing army of 30,000. The nobility increasingly valued state service as a means of advancement, developing an unshakable esprit de corps and unswerving devotion to the dynasty. Even under the Great Elector, army and state, officer and official were becoming synonymous.

The Great Elector had every interest in making his state prosperous, since prosperity entailed a larger tax yield. He encouraged immigration, granting favourable terms to Dutch farmers and Huguenot refugees from Louis XIV's persecution. He improved communications, building a canal that enabled barges to sail from the Oder to the Elbe via Berlin (thus avoiding the Baltic ports controlled by Sweden). A fleet of ten craft was equipped, and there were strenuous efforts to develop colonial trade—strenuous but misguided, since Brandenburg stood no real chance of competing with the maritime powers.

The negative side of Frederick William's economic policies (government regulation, heavy taxes and tolls) had much in common with that of his contemporaries; but its emphatic character derived from the need to support a disproportionately large army. Economic development was also inhibited by the disadvantages under which the towns laboured in competing with rural products sold by a privileged nobility. Recovery from the Thirty Years' War was slow, and Brandenburg-Prussia remained a poor land.

The army achieved its first notable success in the Dutch War by defeating the Swedes at Fehrbellin in 1675, though Sweden's ally,

France, bullied Frederick William into restoring his Pomeranian conquests. After this reverse the elector returned to the unheroic policy of taking subsidies from the seemingly invincible French. Only from 1685 did he ally with the emperor against France; and it was under his son Frederick (1688–1713) that Brandenburg took part in the great coalitions against France.

The wars brought the Hohenzollerns no acquisitions of any moment but Frederick acquired a new title. In return for his support in the imminent War of the Spanish Succession, the Emperor Leopold I agreed that Frederick should become King of Prussia, Prussia being chosen because it was outside the boundaries of the Holy Roman Empire. In January 1701 Frederick crowned himself and his wife with great pomp.

Frederick I of Prussia was not an outstanding king. Power was largely exercised by his ministers, while the king surrounded himself with ceremonial, spent lavishly, built palaces and patronized the arts. The Prussian Academy and the University of Halle were founded in his reign.

War and royal expenditure soon put Prussian finances in disarray, and it is likely that, had he lived, the king would have reduced the size of the army at the end of the war rather than sacrifice his pleasures. If this had happened, Prussia would have developed more normally, for better or worse; instead, his successor, Frederick William I, resolutely intensified the militarization of Prussia.

Habsburg lands

Although the Austrian Habsburgs failed to make the office of Holy Roman emperor an effective one, in the seventeenth century they prepared a new role for themselves by consolidating and extending their family possessions in central and southeastern Europe. From the eighteenth to the twentieth centuries they were to be most important as rulers of the state that it is convenient to call 'Austria'.

Its nucleus was formed when Charles V handed over the Habsburg lands in central Europe to his brother Ferdinand (1519–21) and Ferdinand secured his own election to the thrones of Bohemia and Hungary. But like the Great Elector's inheritance, the Habsburg lands were a dynastic complex rather than a state. In 1648, at the close of the Thirty Years' War, they comprised the German-speaking duchies of Upper Austria, Lower Austria, Styria, Carinthia, the Tyrol and Carniola; the kingdom of Bohemia, with Moravia and Silesia; and, outside the Holy Roman Empire, as much of the kingdoms of Hungary, Croatia and Dalmatia as the Habsburgs were able to defend against the Turks.

The process of state-building began early in the seventeenth century. Territories ceased to be apportioned among members of the

family, so that authority was concentrated in the hands of the emperor in Vienna; and the rights of the Estates were considerably reduced in the German-speaking lands. The crushing of the Bohemian revolt, which sparked off the Thirty Years' War, provided the opportunity for an even more forceful extension of Habsburg authority: the Protestant heresy was uprooted, the flourishing and self-assertive Czech towns ruined, and the Czech nobility replaced by Habsburg nominees (mainly German) who depended on the emperor for their continued security. The Bohemian monarchy, previously elective, became hereditary in the Habsburg family.

Although the servants of the emperor forged instruments of central control in the capital, they were never able to use them with the absolute authority of French or even Prussian administrators: there were too many differences of race, language and (in Hungary) religion, too many local laws, customs and institutions to permit the establishment of administrative uniformity.

The guardian—and beneficiary—of local privileges and immunities was the landlord. In the Habsburg lands, as elsewhere in central and eastern Europe, he was becoming more powerful—increasing his rights over the serfs, extorting more labour services from them, and successfully competing with the towns in selling the produce of his lands. Apart from the ravages of the Thirty Years' War, which had been terrible in the Habsburg lands north of the Danube, and the deliberate ruin of the Bohemian towns, the problem of depopulation had been accentuated by the emigration of persecuted Protestants. The backwardness of the Habsburg lands was perpetuated by neglect of the towns and by the drain of money, men and materials in the struggle against the two great enemies of the Habsburgs: France and Ottoman Turkey.

The Habsburgs' enemies

France and Turkey had been traditional allies since the early sixteenth century, just as France and the Habsburgs had been traditional enemies. At that time the Habsburgs seemed on the point of encircling and destroying France; from the mid-seventeenth century the situation was reversed. Spain, under another branch of the Habsburgs, was in decline; the Holy Roman Empire was weak and divided; Habsburg Austria seemed exhausted, remote and distracted by the Turkish menace. Louis XIV made France the greatest power in Europe, expanding her borders by a series of successful aggressions and even intriguing to become Holy Roman emperor.

Leopold I (1658–1705) was preoccupied with the struggle against the Turks in the first half of his reign and made no attempt to resist French aggressions until the Dutch War of 1672–9 (significantly, during a truce with the Turks). The great Austrian effort against France occurred only after the Turks had begun to retreat; from 1688 Austria took a most important part in the great coalitions that first checked and then humbled France.

The Turks were an even more pressing problem than Louis XIV. Their armies had menaced Europe for 200 years and had almost invariably defeated the armies of Christian states; only a strip of Hungary barred them from Vienna itself. Habsburg Hungary, hardly more than a quarter of the old kingdom, was effectively controlled by a turbulent nobility jealous of its liberties. The monarchy remained elective; the nobility claimed the right to resist the king if their privileges were infringed, legislated in their own interest through the Estates, paid no taxes and nominated the head of their own armed forces. Hungarian Protestants, plotters and nobles who believed their liberties threatened could look for protection to a powerful neighbour: Transylvania.

In origin Transylvania was a breakaway state from Habsburg Hungary. By 1648, thanks to the statesmanship of Bethen Gabor (1613–29) and Gyorgy Rakoczi I (1630–48), it occupied almost half the territory of old Hungary and was virtually independent of the Turks. Its Calvinist rulers tolerated Catholic and Protestant alike, adding an ideological element to the hostility of the devoutly Catholic Habsburgs.

The ambitious Gyorgy Rakoczi II led Transylvania to disaster. He joined the Swedish king, Charles X, in attacking Poland; and while he was being defeated there, the Turks invaded Transylvania. After a confused struggle Rakoczi was defeated and killed (1660), as was his successor Janos Kemeny (1662). The Turks overran Transylvania and prepared to attack Habsburg Hungary.

When they took the great fortress of Neuhausel in 1663, Christian Europe rallied to the defence of Austria with men and money—an indication that the medieval conception of a Christian community was still not entirely defunct; even Louis XIV sent 6,000 men. The subsequent defeat of the Turks at St Gotthard (1664), by an army under the imperial general Montecuccoli, was the first indication that military supremacy had passed to the Christian states.

The decisive nature of this event was obscured by the haste with which Emperor Leopold made peace—partly because Christian losses had been heavy, partly through caution and partly because he was becoming preoccupied with the Spanish succession problem. The treaty of Vasvar left the Turkish position in Hungary still unshaken.

The Hungarian magnates, incensed at what they deemed Habsburg treachery in not pursuing the defeated Turk, plunged into an orgy of incompetent conspiracy. Leopold made this the excuse for a military occupation of Hungary (1670), but the subsequent attempt to suppress Hungarian liberties, end toleration of Protestants and 'put the Hungarians into Czech trousers' was premature. Many Hungarians joined Imre Thokoly in northern Hungary, where, abetted by the Transylvanians and aided by the French, he conducted a ferocious and successful resistance. In 1681—just in time —Leopold realized his mistake and restored the Hungarians' lost liberties.

This action deprived Thokoly of much of his support and forced him to turn to the Turks, who were in any case preparing to march on Vienna. The Austrians appeared powerless to stop them, and in July 1683 the Habsburg capital was besieged by a great Turkish army. Again Europe came to the defence of Austria, all the more effectively since a great reforming pope, Innocent XI, ceaselessly exhorted and negotiated with the powers. Most of the German states sent contingents of troops and, largely through the pope's influence, in March 1683 Leopold secured the alliance of John Sobieski, King of Poland. In September, when Vienna was close to capitulation after a heroic defence, a cosmopolitan army of 70,000, commanded by Sobieski, swept down from the Kahlenburg and routed the Turks.

Vienna was saved, but the immediate fruits of victory were lost through dissensions among the victors. On this occasion Leopold decided to pursue his advantage. At Ratisbon (1684) he recognized all Louis XIV's gains since the War of Devolution in return for a twenty-year truce that left him a free hand in the east. The Turks were expelled from Hungary only after fifteen years of intermittent fighting, long periods of Austrian inactivity being enforced by the war against France (1688–97) which broke out despite the truce of Ratisbon. At last, in 1697, the brilliant Eugene of Savoy took command of the Austrian army and overwhelmed the last effective Turkish force at the Battle of Zenta. By the Treaty of Carlowitz (1699), the Turks ceded to the Habsburgs all of Hungary and Transylvania except Temesvar in the southeast.

The Danubian monarchy

The enlarged kingdom of Hungary became part of the Habsburg state in that the Hungarian Estates agreed to make the crown hereditary and renounced the right of insurrection (1686). But the Hungarians retained most of their privileges as well as their suspicion of the Habsburgs; despite the conciliatory tactics of the Austrians, there was a serious revolt under Francis Rakoczi (1703–11). Transylvania, where the tradition of independence was even stronger, was treated with equal moderation; it remained a separate Habsburg province, not subject to Hungary.

In the course of the eighteenth century it became clear that if the Habsburgs had

Below, an army from Brandenburg fighting the Turks in the seventeenth century; the Turks continued to be a real threat to the states of eastern Europe throughout the seventeenth century.

Opposite, Frederick I, Elector of Brandenburg (reigned 1688–1713), who won the title of King of Prussia in 1701 in return for his opposition to France and as a recognition of the reality of Brandenburg's power in eastern Europe.

failed to create a highly centralized state of obedient citizens like the Prussians, they had achieved a durable success. Despite its vicissitudes, the great Austrian-Bohemian-Hungarian bloc was to be one of the great European powers down to 1918.

Poland

The relief of Vienna was the last triumph of old Poland, and an appropriately chivalrous one. For although the largest state in Europe after Russia, late seventeenth-century Poland was manifestly in decline because of her antiquated political and social structure.

The monarchy was elective and therefore weak. Taxes and other important decisions required the approval of a parliament of nobles (the *Seym*) that was paralysed by increasingly strict application of the right of any member to use the 'free veto' which at once dissolved the *Seym*. In practice the local assemblies, also dominated by the nobility, were more powerful. Such a situation invited intrigues on the part of other states, while the Poles themselves, lacking any rational machinery for reaching decisions, frequently formed rival armed confederacies to forward the interests of the various factions. Civil war, or the threat of civil war, loomed at every crisis.

The nobles, who were the only beneficiaries of Polish 'liberties', resisted all reforms. About a tenth of the population was noble, though wealth and power were engrossed by a few great families, of whom the lesser nobility tended to become clients. The economy had been dominated by the nobility since the Turkish conquest of the Black Sea ports in the fifteenth century, which destroyed overland trade with the Baltic. In Poland, too, the position of the serfs was deteriorating, while noble privileges—above all the right of nobles to import and export without paying duties—made it impossible for the towns to flourish.

The impact of war on an anarchical and economically backward kingdom was bound to be disastrous; and Poland was almost constantly at war in the second half of the seventeenth century. In 1654 the struggle against the rebellious Dnieper Cossacks, which had dragged on since 1648, was transformed by the intervention of Russia; and the Russian example encouraged Charles X of Sweden to invade in the next year. In the course of the war the Swedes twice overran Poland, which was eventually saved by the help of Sweden's enemies, Denmark and Austria, and a volte-face by Brandenburg. At the Peace of Oliva (1660) Poland renounced her suzerainty over East Prussia; at Andrusovo, after seven more years' fighting against the Russians, she ceded the areas around Smolensk and Kiev.

The loss of territory was considerable, though mainly of areas that had long been in dispute; but the devastation caused by the war was much more serious. Before Poland could recover, she was at war with the Turks, who in 1672 invaded Podolia in southeast Poland. Despite John Sobieski's great victory at Chotin (1673), Podolia was ceded to the Turks in 1676.

The wave of national feeling provoked by the Turkish invasion led to the election of Sobieski as King of Poland (1673–96). He was a much more forceful ruler than his predecessors, John Casimir (1648–68) and Michael Wisnowiecki (1669–73), and it was he who led the Christian army that defeated the Turks before Vienna (1683). But he proved unable to cure Poland's internal ills; indeed, it can be argued that Sobieski became obsessed by his crusading zeal and sacrificed Polish interests to a war of which Austria was the main beneficiary.

The election of the Duke of Saxony, Augustus the Strong, as King of Poland (1697) inaugurated a long period of anarchy. Augustus's right to the crown was contested by the Prince de Conti and later by Stanislas Leszczynski, backed by Sweden. The civil war that ensued was ended only in 1717, with a treaty of exhaustion that solved nothing.

The Ottoman Empire

Turkish power, too, was declining, though the resources and manpower of the empire —stretching over North Africa, eastern Asia

and the Balkans—enabled it to sustain catastrophic losses and even to make spasmodic recoveries.

The seventeenth-century crisis was at first sight of the sort that many states had passed through and survived. The sultan ruled as a despot, usually through a grand vizier; and the fate of the empire depended on the abilities of one or the other. Weak sultans were governed by household and harem intrigue, and the empire suffered accordingly: the administration became corrupt and incompetent, there were provincial revolts, palace revolutions and military setbacks—very much the pattern of Ibrahim I's reign (1640–48), and the early years of Mehmed IV (1648–87).

An able grand vizier could soon put this right. When Mehmed Koprulu took office in 1656, he conducted a brutal purge of inefficient and hostile officials, restored Ottoman finances by rooting out corruption, put down two dangerous revolts and re-invigorated the armed forces. The navy defeated the Venetians and recaptured Lemnos and Tenedos (1657), which had been lost under Ibrahim; the army invaded Transylvania, defeated Gyorgy Rakoczi II and re-established Turkish suzerainty.

But the revival left untouched the fundamental weakness of the empire: the Turks had failed to make a satisfactory transition from nomadic warriors to masters of a settled empire. Warriors held land in return

EMERGENCE OF THE GREAT POWERS OF CENTRAL-EASTERN EUROPE

Date	Brandenburg-Prussia	Austria	Russia	Date	Brandenburg-Prussia	Austria	Russia
1640	Frederick William Elector (1640)			1740	Frederick I (the Great) (1740–86)	Maria Theresa (1740–80)	Elizabeth (1741–61)
	Peace of Westphalia ends Thirty Years War (1648)				First and Second Silesian Wars (1740–5)	War of the Austrian Succession (1740–8)	War with Sweden (1741–3)
			War with Poland (1654–67)			Austro-Russian alliance (1746)	
1660	Peace of Oliva (1660)				Convention of Westminster (1756)	Alliance with France (1756)	
		Battle of St Gotthard (1664)			The Seven Years War (1756–63)	The Seven Years War (1756–63)	
			Razin's revolt (1670–1)	1760			Catherine II the Great (1762–96)
	Battle of Fehrbellin (1675)				Alliance with Russia (1764)		War with Turkey (1768–74)
1680		Relief of Vienna (1683)			First partition of Poland (1772)	First partition of Poland (1772)	
		Reconquest of Hungary (1684–99)					Pugachev revolt (1773–4)
		War of the League of Augsburg (1688–97)			Austro-Prussian War (1778–9)		
	Frederick III Elector (1688)		Peter I the Great (1689–1725)	1780		Joseph II (1780–90)	
			Capture of Azov (1696)			Austro-Russian alliance (1781)	Crimea annexed (1783)
			Peter in Europe (1697–8)		League of German Princes (1785)		Charter of Nobles (1785)
1700			Great Northern War (1700–21)		Frederick William II (1786–97)	War with Turks (1788–91)	War with Turks (1787–92)
		War of the Spanish Succession (1701–13)				Leopold II (1790–2)	
	Frederick I of Prussia (1701)	Charles VI (1711–40)	Battle of Poltava (1709)		Prussia and Austria at war with revolutionary France (1792)		
	Frederick William I (1713–40)	Pragmatic Sanction (1713)	Loss of Azov (1711)		Second partition of Poland (1793)		Second partition of Poland (1793)
		War with Turkey (1716–18)			Third partition of Poland (1795)	Third partition of Poland (1795)	
1720		Alliance with Spain (1725)		1800			
		Treaty of Vienna (1731)					
		War of the Polish Succession (1733–5)					
		War with the Turks (1736–9)					

abandon battle cavalry. Social and cultural conservatism made decline inevitable.

Under Mehmed Koprulu's son, the able Fazil Ahmed (1661–76), Turkey managed to escape the consequences of St Gotthard and win fresh victories over weaker opponents: the Venetians were driven from Crete (1669) and Podolia was taken from Poland (1676). But Fazil Ahmed's successor, the grossly overconfident Kara Mustafa, led the Turks to the disaster before Vienna; and subsequent campaigns proved that, though the Turks might rally, European arms had acquired an unmistakable overall superiority. Two hundred and fifty years after the Turks had captured Constantinople, the Turkish threat to Europe disappeared, never to return.

for military service, and both they and the sultan looked to plunder from successful warfare to supply much of their needs. Commerce was despised and left to European companies and non-Muslim subjects (Greeks, Armenians, Jews); even the administration of the empire was largely run by the 'Phanariot' Greeks of Constantinople.

Both the system and the outlook behind it were anachronistic. Expansion had effectively ended, and fighting on ravaged borderlands provided little plunder. Administrative negligence only increased the difficulty of raising taxes from peasants who rarely used money. The hereditary principle began to undermine military organization: landowners evaded service and passed on their holdings to their children, whether or not they were of military age or inclination; and the famous regular army of Janissaries ceased to be recruited from the sons of Balkan Christians and became a hereditary caste.

The Ottoman crisis was doubly serious because the West was making important technological advances. This superiority quickly became apparent in the conduct of warfare: in 1664, at the Battle of St Gotthard, European professional infantry and mobile field artillery smashed the Turkish cavalry. The Turks used unwieldy heavy artillery for siege operations, but the mystique—and social predominance—of the mounted warrior made it unthinkable for them to

Chapter 14

The Age of Reason

of Christian dogma was absent—Deism, 'natural religion'—appeared in England very early in the eighteenth century.

England thus provided many fundamental elements of the thought of the Enlightenment, which in the eighteenth century was often called 'the English philosophy'. English influence was increased by the admiration felt for her 'free institutions', relatively fluid class structure and her policy of religious toleration, and all the more so since they were accompanied by a growing power and prosperity.

The Age of Reason or Enlightenment, the *siècle des lumières,* the *Aufklärung*: all terms commonly applied to the period from about 1715 to the outbreak of the French Revolution in 1789 and all expressive of a decisive shift in the way men thought. Until the Enlightenment, institutions and beliefs were largely determined by authority, custom and tradition, supported and sanctified by religious doctrine. Change could be justified only by appealing to the past, as Protestants appealed to Scripture and the practice of the primitive Church and English parliamentarians to the supposed liberties of the fifteenth century. The achievement of the Enlightenment was to substitute reason for tradition and the criterion of utility for authority and, in doing so, to create a secular humanitarianism and a secular conception of progress which have remained characteristic of modern man.

'The English philosophy'

Many of the ideas of thinkers and writers in the Age of Reason were not new, though they had previously been the property of the few. They had appeared in England as early as the 1680s, when John Locke (1632–1704) produced a political philosophy in which the government was a trustee for the people, who had the right to rebel if their trust was abused. His *Essay Concerning Human Understanding* examined the nature of the human mind and argued that ideas were not innate but derived from the experience of the senses. Both of these theories were subversive—of a divinely ordained human authority and of the religious idea of man as born in sin yet capable of distinguishing good from evil; they implied that the state should be rationally ordered for the benefit of its citizens and that man and society could be studied and altered.

The achievements of Sir Isaac Newton (1642–1727) held out the possibility of understanding the world by scientific investigation. They revealed a universe that functioned according to unvarying laws without divine intervention, making God a 'great watchmaker' who had created the universe, set it in motion and then withdrawn. Beliefs from which the apparatus

The *philosophes*

Just because of the greater freedom of English society, Enlightenment ideas never crystallized into a doctrine of opposition and attack. In France, an educated class as large as that in England confronted arbitrary rule, entrenched privilege and a powerful Church—all strong enough to oppress but no longer efficient or confident enough to suppress. It was therefore in France that the most articulate and rigorous criticisms of the old order were made; and it is the French writers called *philosophes* who epitomize the Age of Reason.

The *philosophes* were not an organized group and were by no means in complete agreement either theoretically or practically. They were not even 'philosophers' but rather popularizers and propagandists, explaining and applying scientific method—observation, experiment, generalization—to the different departments of human life and attacking prejudice, privilege and intolerance.

If they had no common programme, they did have many attitudes in common. The attack on religion occupied much of their energy—not unreasonably, since religion was the authority that justified all other authorities. They were in fundamental agreement in desiring a secular society in which men obeyed the law rather than an arbitrary power, in which there was freedom of speech, writing enquiry and dissent and in which cruelty was no longer part of judicial processes or punishments. Without necessarily being democrats or egalitarians, they disliked aristocratic privileges and the disabilities under which the peasants laboured. They shared an enthusiasm for practical improvements, whether industrial or political, akin to their devotion to the empirical methods of science and their contempt for metaphysics. Finally, almost all the *philosophes* assumed that, in principle, all men were capable of understanding the truth and wrote accordingly. It can be argued that their passion for lucidity, simplicity and order limited their profundity; whether or not that is so, it gave their writings an impact which can still be felt.

French society in the eighteenth century was an ideal one for the diffusion of subversive ideas. Paris was the intellectual

capital of Europe, and the Parisian salons, presided over by wealthy, fashionable and intelligent women such as Mme Geoffrin and Mme du Deffand, were arenas in which the ideas of the Enlightenment were tested and refined. They provided a receptive audience for manuscript works which the author dared not publish (frequently the case until the middle of the century) and a school for purity and clarity of language, the outstanding characteristics of eighteenth-century French prose.

The prestige of French literature facilitated the diffusion of the Enlightenment abroad. Under Louis XIV, France had become the cultural arbiter of Europe and French the language of polite society. Every German princeling built a miniature Versailles where only French was spoken and only French books were read. In the eighteenth century, France ceased to dominate Europe politically while retaining her cultural supremacy; but the salons replaced Versailles as the avant-garde of that culture. Both Frederick II of Prussia and Catherine II of Russia spoke French for preference, read the works of the *philosophes*, and claimed to be their disciples. Even as late as the 1770s, the great English historian, Gibbon, could assert that he thought and wrote best in French. Such was the European preoccupation with what the French did, said and wrote that the

German-born *philosophe*, Grimm, compiled a regular Parisian newsletter which circulated the courts of Europe.

Voltaire

In the 1720s the Enlightenment was still very much an underground movement, its attitudes expressed in published works only in indirect or ironical terms. Even at its height, criticisms of Church or state were guardedly phrased unless the work were published anonymously and/or abroad.

A full-scale attack on the Church appeared as early as 1697: Pierre Bayle's *Historical and Critical Dictionary*, published in Holland, provided ammunition against Scriptural history and theological dogmas that was still being used several generations later. Other published works were more cautious, notably Montesquieu's *Persian Letters* (1721), in which two Persian residents in Paris compare French customs with their own. The comparison implied not only that French society was riddled with absurdities and injustices but that its institutions had no universal validity.

At this date, however, the career of the greatest figure of the Age of Reason had already begun. François-Marie Arouet, known as Voltaire (1694–1788), was the universal genius of the age, by turns poet,

playwright, historian, scientific popularizer, anti-clerical polemicist and writer of picaresque or exotic 'philosophical' tales. His enduring fame rests upon his prose writings, which are unsurpassed models of clarity, economy and elegance, shot through with malicious wit and irony.

Voltaire knew the injustices of the existing order at first hand: he was beaten up by an aristocrat's bullies, some of his books were burnt by the public hangman, and much of his life was spent in flight and exile. During one such exile, passed in England, he wrote his *Lettres Philosophiques*, the most important piece of French propaganda for English thought and institutions.

Voltaire's best-known and funniest book is *Candide* (1759), one of the picaresque tales, in which the ingenuous Candide wanders the world, learning the hard way the inaccuracy of his tutor Pangloss's belief that this is 'the best of all possible worlds'. At last he determines to cultivate his garden —that is, to improve the world by practical activity. *Candide* was in part suggested by the terrible Lisbon earthquake of 1755, an event of some importance in generally undermining the doctrine of a beneficent providence.

Voltaire evidently came to the same conclusion as Candide, for his last years were spent in vigorous and often effective campaigns to right injustices. His most famous

The great *Encyclopaedia*

By the middle of the eighteenth century, Enlightenment attitudes were becoming established and widespread. Many of the *philosophes*—Helvétius, Holbach, Morelly, Lamettrie, Condorcet—took up increasingly radical positions, formulating atheist, materialist, determinist and even communist systems. Lamettrie, for example, called one of his books *Man the Machine* (1747).

A utopian element was also becoming more pronounced: if man had not fallen, if he was formed by his sense-experiences, he could be improved by changing his environment; if he was capable of reasoning, he was capable of virtue and happiness. All mysteries would be revealed in time by science, all injustice abolished by reason and good will: earth could be made a secular paradise.

The epitome of the age was the great *Encyclopaedia,* which appeared in twenty-eight volumes from 1751 to 1772, despite sporadic attempts to suppress it. Its editor was Denis Diderot (1713–84), one of the most important *philosophes*, initially with the collaboration of the mathematician d'Alembert.

The *Encyclopaedia* was at once a monumental work of reference and a polemic against absolutism, Christianity and privilege. Almost all the great figures of the Enlightenment contributed, providing what amounted to a thinly disguised summary of 'philosophical' ideas. It was also a compendium of scientific and technical information, describing and illustrating in careful detail the craft and industrial processes that had previously been jealously guarded secrets—a fine example of the *philosophes'* enthusiasm for empirical science and the improvement of life by practical means.

Nations other than France contributed to the Enlightenment, though readers outside England and France tended to be more influenced by the French *philosophes* than by writers in their own countries. Such were the Italian Cesare Beccaria, whose *Of Crimes and Punishments* (1764) advocated a more rational and humane penal system, and the German dramatist and critic Gotthold Lessing (1729–81) who, like Diderot, attempted to create a realistic middle-class drama. The Scottish Enlightenment was of particular distinction and in David Hume (1711–76) produced an outstanding philosopher. Another Italian, Giambattista Vico (1688–1744), outlined an evolutionary historical philosophy that cut across such Voltairean simplifications as 'reason versus fanaticism', providing insights that were only developed later: a significant comment on contemporary preoccupations.

The most substantial achievements of the age were of another kind, resulting from the

Above, Voltaire (1694–1788) dictating while dressing; he was the epitome of the Enlightenment in his resolute and witty opposition to superstition and privilege; his book Candide *(1759) demonstrates that he was even able to satirize the rational and optimistic beliefs that he himself championed. Musée Carnavalet, Paris.*

Left, an engraving from Diderot's Encyclopaedia *(1751–72), showing a cutler's workshop and tools; eleven of the twenty-eight volumes of the* Encyclopaedia *were made up exclusively of such engravings of industry, which were based on drawings done by Diderot himself.*

Opposite, a gathering at the salon of Madame Geoffrin in Paris in 1755, including many of the most famous names of the French Enlightenment, such as d'Alembert, Rousseau, Diderot and Condillac. Château de Malmaison.

success was the rehabilitation of Jean Calas, a Protestant victim of the religious prejudice of the French law courts.

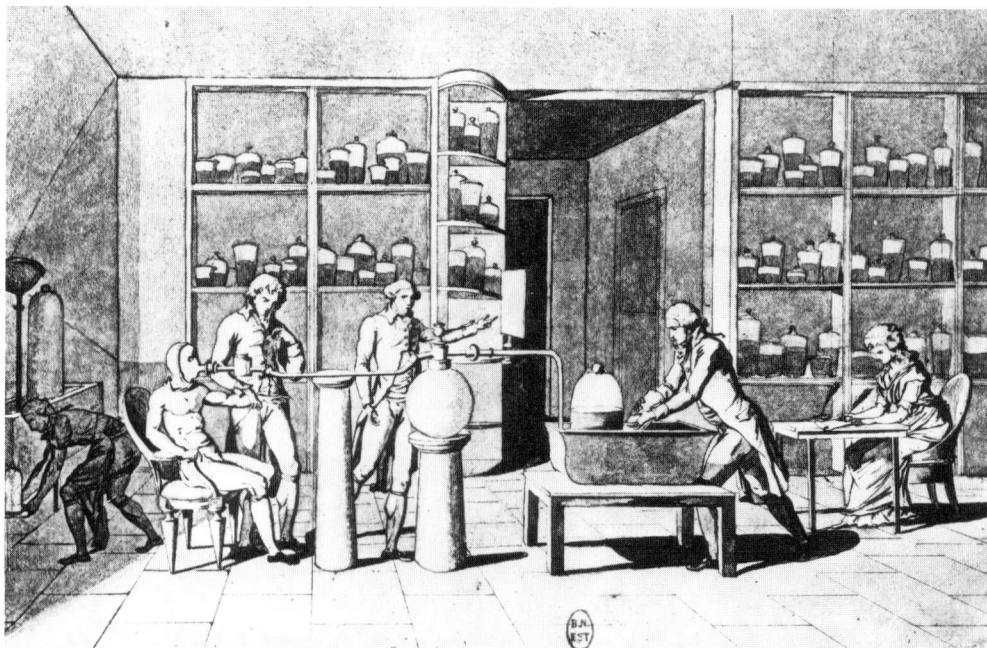

use of scientific empiricism to create mechanical 'Newtonian' models which operated according to immutable laws. This was particularly true of the study of man and society. Charles de Secondat, Baron de Montesquieu (1699–1755), already famous as the author of *Persian Letters,* was the effective founder of sociology and the study of comparative institutions. Despite its aberrations, his *Spirit of the Laws* (1748) represents the first attempt to analyse the interaction of religion, institutions, geography, climate and history in the formation of societies.

Similar developments were taking place in the study of history. In *The Age of Louis XIV* (1751) Voltaire abandoned the traditional narrative treatment of politics and war and presented a picture of French society as a whole, relating the manners, customs and beliefs of the period to the political, economic and administrative structure. The masterpiece of eighteenth-century historical writing was undoubtedly Gibbon's *Decline and Fall of the Roman Empire* (1766–88), a work of massive synthesis, written with urbane irony in rolling, balanced periods.

Experiments in improving agricultural and industrial production were one of the enthusiasms of the eighteenth century; and the larger questions of 'political economy' also became an object of systematic study. Theoretical advances were made by the 'Physiocrats' in France and, much more decisively, by the Scot Adam Smith. In *The Wealth of Nations* (1776) Smith analysed such fundamental processes as division of labour and provided the theoretical groundwork for the nineteenth-century belief in unfettered individual enterprise.

The natural sciences

Considerable progress was also made in the natural sciences, though the Enlightenment

was an age of solid advance rather than dramatic breakthrough. One example is the steady improvement of scientific instruments, which were essential to more exact and detailed research. Here it must suffice to mention the production of an accurate thermometer, to which the Swede Celsius, the Frenchman Réamur and the Danziger Fahrenheit all contributed.

Analysis and classification were characteristic activities of the Enlightenment scientist. In chemistry, the Englishman Henry Cavendish (1731–1810) isolated and described hydrogen, the Scotsman Joseph Black (1722–99) discovered carbon dioxide and another Scot, Daniel Rutherford (1749–1819), discovered nitrogen. Towards the end of the period, Antoine Lavoisier (1743–94), a French aristocrat, laid the basis for the modern system of classification into elements and compounds.

Biology too had its great classifier: the Swede Carl Linnaeus, whose *System of Nature* (1735) included some 12,000 living things, which were for the first time provided with precise names. The most influential and popular work of the period, however, was Georges-Louis Buffon's *Natural History* (1749–88), as much a work of literature as of science. Buffon, unlike most scientists of the day, had difficulties with the authorities, who censured his observations on fossils, which he rightly believed to be older than the date established for the creation of the earth by Biblical studies.

Other scientists' works can only be noted here: in electricity, for example, Pieter van Musschenbroek's Leyden jar (1746), Priestly's *History* (1767), Benjamin Franklin's experiments; in mathematics, Bernouilli, Euler, Lagrange. At the end of the period, the German-born English astronomer Sir William Herschel, also one of the great classifiers, made perhaps the most spectacular discovery of the age when he observed an unknown planet, Uranus (1781).

The impact of the Enlightenment

The Enlightenment created a climate of opinion in which 'the books that inspire benevolence are practically the only ones read' (Diderot). Pacifist sentiments began to be expressed among the educated classes; humanitarian feelings were manifested in disapproval of slavery, efforts to secure prison reform and the growth of Freemasonry as a secular religion of humanity.

Yet the immediate social and political results were negligible. The *philosophes* themselves looked to those already in power to introduce institutional changes. They admired and corresponded with the 'enlightened despots' of central and eastern Europe, and in France they cultivated the ministers and even the mistresses of the king. Such tactics could at best achieve only limited results; but all other avenues of advance were closed. The great monarchies contained no party, group or class to whom the *philosophes* could appeal in programmatic terms, which is probably the main reason why they never formulated a common policy and why not one of them produced a coherent political philosophy.

In the course of the century, however, Enlightenment attitudes did begin to appear outside the elite of court and salon. That is not to say that the works of the *philosophes* were read by the masses; but the diffusion of ideas, in a simplified and sometimes garbled form, can take place without popular acquaintance with primary sources. This was particularly true of France, but it could also be observed in most of western Europe before the French Revolution; and even as far away as Russia an intellectual minority disapproved of despotism and serfdom.

The *philosophes* did not think, and had no grounds for thinking, in revolutionary terms. Their ideas were to be one of the

elements that led to the French Revolution, but the Revolution was produced by a unique and perhaps improbable concatenation of circumstances and beliefs—the idealism generated by the American War of Independence, the quarrel between crown and nobility, the bankruptcy of the crown—which could not be foreseen in the mid-eighteenth century. Then, neither the resources nor the social structure of Europe were such as to promise rapid change.

Eighteenth-century society

Eighteenth-century society was still overwhelmingly agricultural, despite the growth of cities and the development of an urban middle class in western Europe. On the eve of the Revolution in France, the land of the Enlightenment *par excellence,* some twenty-two million out of a population of about twenty-six million were peasants. In central and eastern Europe the peasantry accounted for an even higher proportion of the population, towns were very small, and the only middle class of any importance was bureaucratic rather than mercantile. Only in Holland (properly called 'The United Provinces') had specific historical and geographical circumstances produced a mercantile society.

In the agrarian societies the dominant group was still the nobility. Nobles enjoyed great privileges, including tax exemptions and rights to payments and services from the peasantry; again, these tended to be very much greater in central and eastern Europe. They had a monopoly of the great offices of Church and state, even where (as in France) they wielded little collective political power.

There were wide differences in wealth and even status between nobles, since in most of Europe nobility was a matter of status—inherited by every child of a noble—rather than possessions; with the result that many were no more than small farmers, and a few were paupers. But when all the differences are allowed for, the aristocratic character of eighteenth-century Europe is undeniable.

The mercantile middle class was becoming increasingly prosperous and powerful in western Europe, particularly in England and France; and it is doubtless significant that it was in these countries, with a relatively large number of educated men and a rapid growth of literacy, that the Enlightenment was brought to birth and widely diffused.

The basis of middle-class wealth was trade, not industry, though the unprecedented expansion of trade in the eighteenth century provided the source of raw materials, the markets and much of the capital that made the Industrial Revolution possible. Trade between Europe and the rest of the world expanded continuously, and as Dutch maritime strength slowly declined a worldwide struggle began between France and England. Europe, North America, the West Indies and India were the main theatres of a conflict that continued in one form or another until 1815. Eighteenth-century governments if anything overestimated the importance of commerce and supported their merchants and colonists by subsidy and by force of arms. The wars of the period were not commercial wars, but commercial considerations powerfully influenced the way they were conducted. Hence the attention paid to the West Indies, the source of tobacco, sugar, coffee and dyestuffs. The Atlantic trade, of which the West Indies was the heart, brought prosperity to Liverpool, Bordeaux, Nantes and the other great ports of western Europe. Trade between European states, and with India, southeast Asia, the Mediterranean and the Levant, also expanded.

The commercial spirit touched life at many points. Commodities from overseas—tea, coffee, tobacco, muslins—changed European habits. Manufacturing areas in every mercantile nation became dependent on the prosperity of international trade. Merchants formed pressure groups that no government could ignore, and the wealthiest had little difficulty in marrying their children into the nobility.

Important as these developments were, they did not constitute a social or economic revolution. The harvest, not the trade figures, decided the happiness of nations. The most rigorous economic blockade could not reduce a nation at war: a bad harvest caused it to starve in peacetime. The agencies of transformation—rapid industrial growth and technological advance—were found only in England, and only very late in the century.

One fact that did make for change was population growth, which was substantial and steady in France, Spain and Italy and rapid (from about mid-century) in England, Ireland, the Low Countries, Scandinavia, Russia and parts of Germany. France remained the most populous country in Europe, with twenty-odd million inhabitants, until late in the century; then she was overtaken by Russia, whose population reached thirty-six million by the end of Catherine II's reign (1796). In England and Wales the increase in population (just over five million in 1700, nine-and-a-half million in 1800) was of great importance in providing the labour force and the market needed for an industrial revolution.

The agricultural revolution and the first phase of the industrial revolution in Britain are outside the scope of this book. They laid the foundations for a new kind of society, in which agriculture yielded pride of place to industry, the country to the town, the craft workshop to the factory. Even in Britain the transformation was effected only in the nineteenth century. The societies discussed in this book remained hierarchical and rural until the nineteenth and, in some cases, the twentieth century.

New modes of feeling

The consciousness of European man was changing more quickly than material reality. By the 1760s a new sensibility, in some respects hostile to the values of the Enlightenment, was beginning to manifest itself.

As inheritors of that sensibility we find the men of the Enlightenment 'rational' to the point of aridity: rather superficial and complacent in their belief in reason as the answer to all problems and lacking in warmth if not in light. This is partly an illusion created by the formal manners and polished conversation of the period: Voltaire, for example, fought intolerance and injustice with unmistakable passion. But it is also true that the *philosophes* were concerned with man as a social rather than an individual and unique being and that their writings display almost exclusively what may be called public feelings.

In the second half of the eighteenth century, the revulsion against reason, restraint and formality—already apparent somewhat earlier—became marked. The cult of sentiment, of spontaneous and passionate individual feeling, was the direct precursor of the Romantic movement, which is usually dated to the very late eighteenth and early nineteenth centuries. Indeed, most of the characteristics of Romanticism—love of nature, childhood, the remote and mysterious past, the exotic, the wild and irregular—appeared in some form quite early in the eighteenth century.

The new sensibility was expressed in many different ways. The English landscape garden replaced the formal French garden. A quasi-oriental style (*chinoiserie*) became the rage in furniture and interior decoration; Sir William Chambers built a pagoda at Kew. Ruins became collectors' items, and in 1747 the dilettante and letter-writer Horace Walpole—in many respects a typical figure of the Age of Reason—began to build himself a 'Gothick' house, Strawberry Hill. In painting, the graceful Rococo style of Wattau, Boucher and Fragonard gave way to Neo-classicism, in part a response to the growing cult of sentimental republican virtue—another of the obsessions of the age, given impetus by excavations at Pompeii and Herculaneum, which provided a wealth of information about everyday life in antiquity. In the 1760s, Greuze's oversweet paintings of maidenly distress and domesticity were acclaimed in France, where the attractions of the simple life prompted Marie Antoinette to play the sheperdhess in her dairy at Rambouillet.

Literature provided the fullest expression of the new attitudes in all their complexity. Here only a few landmarks can be indicated. In France, Galland published a translation of *The Thousand and One Nights* (1704–17) which gave a fillip to the taste for the exotic. In England, Edward Young's *Night Thoughts* (1742–45) were filled with a satisfactorily gloomy introspection, Thomson's *The Seasons* (1726–30) with an exalted love of nature, and Walpole's *Castle of Otranto* (1764) with supernatural horror in a mysterious 'medieval' setting. Thomas Percy, the Bishop of Dromore, collected and published old English ballads in his *Reliques* (1765), and the European vogue for the supposed poems of the Gaelic bard Ossian (in fact the work of their 'discoverer', James Macpherson) was such that they survived Dr Johnson's denunciations and were still being declaimed by Napoleon at the beginning of the nineteenth century.

Many of the extravagances of this 'pre-Romantic' period were somewhat tongue-in-cheek or were at least not felt profoundly enough to impinge on social mores. Horace Walpole lived in a quaint house and wrote a thriller; but his behaviour remained that of a cultivated English gentleman. That is not to say that fads and fashions are arbitrary: in this period they indicate (among other things) a certain restlessness and dissatisfaction with the ordinary course of social life. But the dissatisfaction remained on the fringe of consciousness, not at its centre: it appeared in night thoughts rather than daylight actions.

The 1770s witnessed the brief emergence of the German 'Storm and Stress' writers, who displayed in their own lives an agonising inability to adjust to everyday realities that was to be one of the characteristics of full-blown Romanticism. Paradoxically, it was the most balanced—and by far the greatest—of the school, Johann Wolfgang Goethe (1749–1832), whose work had the most 'Romantic' impact: the suicide of the hero in *Young Werther* (1774) was imitated by many young men who fancied that they were profoundly introspective as well as unsuccessful in love.

Much more characteristic of the period, and probably much more deeply felt, was 'the cult of the heart'—of spontaneity, sincerity, love, sentimental virtue. Its special feature was that sincerity rather than actions increasingly became the criterion of virtue; hypocrisy became the worst of vices. In England, the heartless rake of Restoration comedy gave way to the likeable scamps of Fielding, Sheridan and Goldsmith. The new heroes got into scrapes hardly better than those of the rakes but were always saved by their transparent good nature.

A more religious morality was upheld by Samuel Richardson, whose multi-volume epistolary novels set all Europe weeping. *Pamela* (1740–41) and *Clarissa Harlowe* (1747–48), with their portraits of maidenly virtue under assault and protracted deathbed scenes, let loose a flood of sentimental novels, of which the most important was *The New Heloise* by Jean-Jacques Rousseau.

Society and the noble savage

Rousseau (1712–78) wrote few works, but every one made a profound impression on his own and following generations. He was the son of a clockmaker in Geneva, a city with powerful traditions of puritanism and independence, and both his social origin and place of birth influenced the attitudes of his maturity. So must his youthful experiences as a timid hanger-on, always on the fringes of good society.

Unlike the *philosophes*, Rousseau regarded the very existence of society as objectionable; it was not badly constituted, but bad in any form. In his first published work, the *Discourse on the Arts and Sciences* (1750), he argues that progress and society have corrupted man, that in his natural state man is virtuous and happy. Though he never used the phrase 'the noble savage', Rousseau is rightly associated with the idea behind the words, for it was largely the extraordinary eloquence of his prose that made the idea of unspoiled primitive man (already of literary commonplace) into a potent myth.

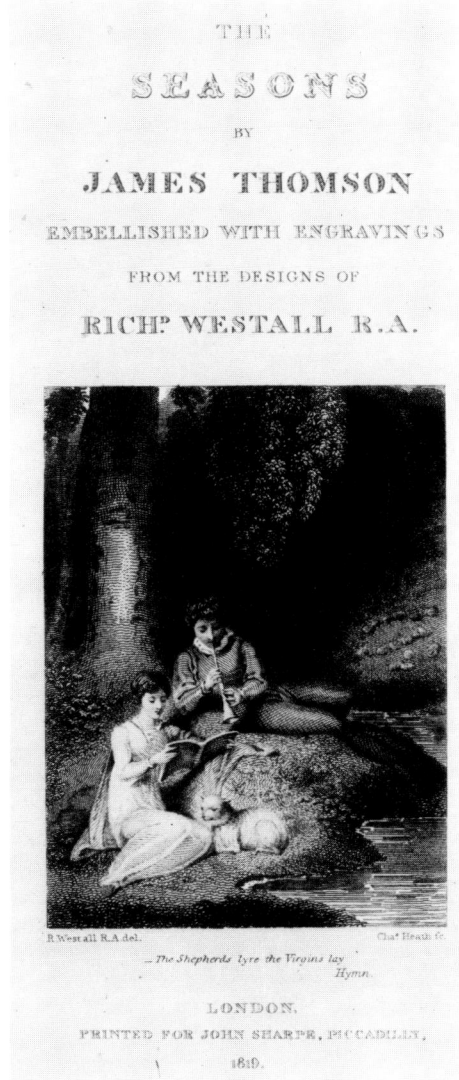

Above, the title page of The Seasons, *by James Thomson (1700–48), a typical expression of the interest in the moods and lyricism of nature common in the romantic era.*

Above left, an engraving of Strawberry Hill, in Twickenham, Middlesex, which was built in 1747 by the English author Horace Walpole (1717–97) in a medieval style. Interest in exotic, curious and charming architecture and landscape replaced the formal and classical styles of the late seventeenth century.

Left, a painting of a scene from Pamela *(1740–41), the story of a maidservant and the son of her employer, written by Samuel Richardson (1689–1761); virtue and sexual morality was an important theme of eighteenth-century literature. Tate Gallery, London.*

The New Heloise (1761) was probably the most popular novel of the century, running to scores of editions. Like *Clarissa Harlowe*, it is written as a series of letters and now seems intolerably long and diffuse; but eighteenth-century readers were enchanted by extended descriptions of the struggle between passion and duty and by Rousseau's enthusiasm for nature, simplicity and children.

In *Emile* (1762), a tract on education thinly disguised as a novel, Rousseau takes the same line: the child Emile must be shielded from contact with society. Rousseau recognized that children were not miniature adults and that their capacities and needs differed at each stage of development. He insisted that the child must learn only what and when he needs to learn and that direct sensory experience was at least as important as learning from books. These doctrines were taken up enthusiastically, since the eighteenth century was one of growing emphasis on family life and the role of parents—not tutors or servants—in bringing up children.

The message of *The Social Contract* (1762), one of the most influential books ever written, is that the only legitimate foundation for political authority is 'the general will', not inheritance or force. The by and large passive and heavily qualified conception of popular authority proposed by Locke was now expressed in active terms. Rousseau understood that majority decisions might not be in the general interest (which is in fact one of the problems of democratic theory), and some of his speculations can be regarded as justifying dictatorship by a minority representing the 'true' will of the people. But despite its confusions and ambiguities, the central idea of *The Social Contract* is unmistakably that of government not only in the interests of the people—which an enlightened despot claimed to provide—but government directly answerable to their will.

Rousseau's posthumously published *Confessions* began the whole modern tradition of confessional literature. Here he attempted to tell the whole truth about himself, including his social failures, low actions and sexual peculiarities; unintentionally he also chronicled his growing persecution mania, which led him to believe that his friends and acquaintances were part of a vast conspiracy against him. The *Confessions* exhibit in its least attractive light Rousseau's assumption that sincerity excuses everything; but they also comprise a wonderful self-portrait, opening up a wide avenue by which man's knowledge of himself could be increased.

Reason, sentiment, revolution

The relationship between the rationalism of the Enlightenment and the new modes of feeling is complex and obscure. In some respects they were complementary: the attack on accepted beliefs and institutions, above all the attack on institutional religion, was certainly instrumental in the development of a new sense of individual uniqueness and new emotions towards man, society and nature. Even those who were consciously hostile to the *philosophes* absorbed much of their teaching: when Rousseau rejected the legitimacy of authority based on inheritance or prescriptive right, he was adopting the central position of the Enlightenment.

It would nevertheless be wrong to ignore the element of deliberate reaction against the Enlightenment in these emotions, especially since it became more prominent in the nineteenth century. In the immediate future, however, all the main currents of eighteenth-century thought and feeling were to mingle in the French Revolution, that amazing phenomenon which was at once rational, romantic, individualistic, utopian and severely practical.

Toi qui veux usurper le Sceptre du Parnasse,
Qui contre mes écrits parlas avec audace,
Sur toi de mes malheurs. ces poings me vengeront...
M'attaquer sur tes pieds! eh! bon Dieu! que diront
Les quadrupedes tes confreres,

Te voyant des humains prendre ainsi les manieres?
Mais, l'épée au coté, se battre en porte-faix!...
Pourquoi non? les brocards te causent des allarmes?
Un Sage, si tu l'es, ne s'écarte jamais
Des loix de la nature, et nos poings sont ses Armes

Chapter 15

The Enlightened Despots

During the eighteenth century, very considerable changes were introduced from above in the monarchies of central, southern and eastern Europe. The rational-humanitarian aspect of the changes and the fact that they were conceived and executed by monarchs or their chosen ministers (and not in response to public opinion) has made it natural to call this phenomenon 'enlightened despotism'. The image thus created, of the philosopher enthroned, was precisely that achieved by the sedulous self-advertisement of Frederick II of Prussia and Catherine II of Russia, the most glamorous rulers of the age.

In fact, 'enlightened despotism' was essentially the eighteenth-century phrase of a more extended process: the development of the modern state, served by a large bureaucracy, able to make heavy demands on the energies and resources of all citizens and intolerant of rival authorities. In this sense, eighteenth-century monarchs were imitators of French absolutism, concerned with the rationalization of functions, centralization and the destruction of class, regional and clerical privileges. Extensions of government activity and the increasing cost of waging war necessitated a larger revenue; and that in turn necessitated more civil servants, revision of the tax structure and measures to encourage agriculture, industry and trade.

But 'enlightened' is not an inappropriate description of this eighteenth-century phase of the process. Being well-informed and well-educated, monarchs and ministers could not avoid being influenced by the Enlightenment, and many characteristic measures of the period—freedom of speech and writing (albeit limited), abolition of judicial torture, codification of laws, various degrees of religious toleration—can scarcely be dismissed as acts purely in the interest of the state. Many extensions of state activity were in any case welcomed by the *philosophes*. They too hoped to see the wealth of nations increase and disliked privilege and clerical power, though their motives were different from those of the monarchs they admired.

Within the general pattern of 'enlightened despotism' there were numerous deviations and permutations. Frederick William I

of Prussia greatly strengthened the state without being influenced by the Enlightenment. Catherine II proclaimed her 'enlightened' convictions but failed to translate them into action. Frederick II acquired religious scepticism from Voltaire, called himself the first servant of the state—and upheld aristocratic privilege in every sphere. It was, paradoxically, Austria—usually thought of as a highly conservative state—that produced the very type of the enlightened despot in Joseph II.

Enlightened despotism was confined to 'backward' Europe; the great mercantile states (Britain, France, Holland) were unaffected. The absence of a powerful middle class in central, southern and eastern Europe made the monarchy the initiator of change; but it also deprived monarchs of the effective support with which they might have curtailed noble privileges. As a result, the monarchy was in the last analysis dependent on noble support; and the price of that support was the perpetuation of privilege.

Despite the developments which have been described, the pre-industrial state had only limited instruments of control: there was no possibility of a state apparatus holding down a country without at least the acquiescence of the wealthy and socially powerful classes. 'Despots' and 'absolute' rulers could introduce only limited changes, though their limitations would seem less marked had the age of enlightened despots not been succeeded by the age of political and industrial revolutions.

The idea of 'the state'

The personal qualities of a ruler were still decisive: the most highly developed bureaucracies remained geared to personal control

Above, Frederick II of Prussia (reigned 1740–86) reviewing his troops; for him and his contemporaries war was the extension of the abstract art of diplomacy, and he believed that the army should be a professional body, independent of the rest of the population.

Opposite, an imaginary encounter between Voltaire and Rousseau, the two greatest exponents of Enlightenment thought; whereas Voltaire believed in reason and civilization, Rousseau advocated passion and freedom from artificial constraints on man's nobility.

NORTH SEA

BALTIC

EAST PRUSSIA

Königsberg

HOLSTEIN

WESTERN POMERANIA

POMERANIA

Danzig

MECKLENBURG

Hamburg

Stettin

WEST PRUSSIA

Elbe

BRANDENBURG

Vistula

Minden • RAVENSBURG

Berlin

CLEVES

Magdeburg

Warsaw

MARK

SOUTH PRUSSIA

Rhine

Oder

SILESIA

Frankfurt

Mainz

FRANCE

Nuremburg

Prague

Danube

Vienna

Legend:
- Hohenzollern possessions in 1713
- Territories acquired in 1720
- Territories acquired 1748-63
- Territories acquired in 1772
- Territories acquired 1793-9

by monarch or minister. If a ruler was feeble or entrusted the government to incompetents, the state stagnated or declined.

Nevertheless, in the eighteenth century, perhaps because administration was bureaucratized, the conception of monarchical government tended to become more impersonal. Kings increasingly thought in terms of state interests rather than family interests and identified themselves with the state rather than vice versa. On the other hand, when Frederick II (The Great) or Joseph II spoke of themselves as servants of the state, they meant the state and not the people; they remained very much masters of men. The idea of 'the state'—an abstraction for which any sacrifice could be demanded —came into existence even before technology and communications made its power all-embracing.

If the king were becoming the state's servant, he showed no sign of becoming redundant. The eighteenth-century conviction that a strong monarchy was the best form of government seemed to be supported by experience: republics like Holland and

Venice were declining, and the elective monarchies of the Empire and Poland were clearly incapable of governing effectively; only the constitutional monarchy of Britain provided a partial exception.

For most of the period, representative institutions were regarded as medieval anachronisms—obstacles to the unity and effectiveness of the state. The only enlightened despot to display any interest in representative institutions was Leopold of Tuscany (Leopold II of Austria) in the late pre-Revolutionary period, when the cult of Roman republicanism, the teachings of Rousseau and the practical success of the American Revolution had all combined to begin a revival of interest in representative government.

The French Revolution ended any possibility—and at best it had been only a possibility that enlightened despots might collaborate with this new force. Instead, monarchs were frightened into alliance with the nobility and the Church, and enlightened despotism passed into reaction pure and simple.

The 'drill-sergeant' king

Frederick William I of Prussia was far from the conventional idea of an enlightened despot. He was pious, uncultivated and subject to terrible rages in which he thrashed anyone within reach. Yet he gave the Prussian state a unique character, leaving his successor the means with which to make Prussia a power in Europe.

The army was the king's ruling passion. He hired or kidnapped men over six feet tall from all over Europe for his famous 'regiment of giants' at Potsdam. More significant was the increased size of the army, which by Frederick William's death comprised some 83,000 men, making it the fourth largest in Europe. It was supported by what was in fact one of the lesser European states in both population (about two-and-a-half million in 1740) and economic resources.

Like most European armies, it consisted of pressed men or mercenaries, many of them foreigners. Savage discipline and endless drills and reviews transformed it into an efficient fighting force but did not prevent large-scale desertion. It was to remedy this that in 1733 Frederick William assigned to each regiment a Prussian district ('canton'), which was obliged to make up the regiment's numbers. Foreigners continued to be recruited in large numbers—even under Frederick the Great about a third of the total strength of the army was foreign-born —but the basis of a national fighting force had been created.

By providing peasant soldiers, the cantonal system speeded the transformation of the Junker class into a military service nobility. The king himself set an example by always wearing uniform. He created a cadet corps in Berlin for the sons of Junkers; membership became a much sought-after privilege that reinforced the attractions of a military career. The officer corps became the virtual monopoly of the nobility, and by 1740 the fractious Junkers, only half-tamed by the Great Elector, were devoted servants of the crown.

The other features of Frederick William's reign were bureaucratic control over the state and royal control over the bureaucracy. In 1723 the collection of taxes and crown revenues was concentrated in a new institution, the General Directory, which also supervised all the activities of provincial authorities through local committees. In the towns, elected local officials were replaced by salaried state officials. Bureaucratic control, originating in the need to raise large sums to support the army, became all-pervasive.

Royal control was maintained by a system unique to Prussia. Most rulers took decisions in council; Frederick William took them in his 'cabinet', alone with his secretaries, on the basis of reports submitted severally by his ministers. To avoid the concentration of power in the hands of any single official, the specialized 'colleges' into which the administration was divided never had a single head.

The main concern of king and bureaucrats alike was to increase revnue, most of which (about three-quarters) was used for the upkeep of the army. Frederick William made strenuous efforts to collect every sum that could possibly be interpreted as his due. He reformed the leasing arrangements for properties on the royal estates, on which about a third of the Prussian peasantry lived, and practised rigid economy. The measure of his success is that the income of the crown more than doubled during his reign.

Trade and industry continued to be strictly regulated, and immigration was encouraged by every possible means. Refugees arrived from France and Salzburg (from which Protestants were expelled in 1732), and many foreign recruits who joined the Prussian army settled in the Hohenzollern lands when they retired.

Despite Frederick William's idiosyncracies, the state that he created displayed many essential characteristics of an enlightened despotism. The functions and powers of the bureaucracy grew; intermediate authorities—elected urban officials, guilds—were destroyed or emasculated; tradition was overridden in the interests of efficiency. But the Hohenzollern state also possessed unique features which derived from the maintenance of a disproportionately large army. Troops were billeted on the civilian population, and much local trade was concerned with supplying their needs; prices were fixed and enforced by garrison commanders; soldiers received a rudimentary education and staffed the lower grades of the civil service. Close government supervision accustomed the

Above, Frederick William I of Prussia (reigned 1713–40), who spent much of his reign building up the Prussian army and reorganizing the finances of the state in order to be able to support it. Yet he fought only one limited war during his reign. Schloss Charlottenburg, Berlin.

Opposite, the growth of Prussian and Hohenzollern power in eastern Europe in the eighteenth century.

citizen to obey soldiers or authorities that were military in origin or style; respect for the landlord blended with respect for the officer. Other states, it has been said, possessed armies; only the Prussian army possessed a state.

Frederick William accumulated troops and treasure, but he made little use of them. The solitary Prussian acquisition during his reign was part of western Pomerania, with the port of Stettin (1720), a reward for helping to end the Great Northern War. Because of Frederick William's diplomatic ineptitude, Prussian influence in Europe was negligible—in the event, no great misfortune, since the wars and diplomacy of the period were singularly wasteful and inconclusive.

The philosopher prince

It was Frederick William's successor who revealed Prussian might to an astounded Europe.

Frederick II (1740–86) had a troubled adolescence and young manhood. His addiction to the flute, books and elegant conversation enraged Frederick William, and relations between father and son reached breaking-point in 1730, when the eighteen-year-old Frederick decided to flee abroad.

His plan was discovered, he was imprisoned and forced to witness the execution of his confidant, Katte; and for a time his own life seemed in danger, In fact, he was kept under supervision while he performed routine administrative and military duties— an invaluable apprenticeship despite its punitive aspect. The incident was a valuable lesson in patience and self-control; henceforward Frederick obeyed his father without question.

Neither now nor later did he abandon his cultural pursuits. He was a skilful flautist, a competent composer, read voraciously, and poured out odes, tragedies, prose arguments and, in later life, histories and memoirs. All his literary works were written in French; he thoroughly despised German, which he wrote abominably. When his father allowed him more freedom, Frederick gathered about him a company of wits and scholars, while his correspondence with Voltaire provided Frederick with good literary advice and both correspondents with opportunities for relentless mutual flattery.

Those who expected Frederick to be a peaceable philosopher-king had mistaken his character. He absorbed the rationalism of the Enlightenment rather than its humanitarian idealism. As early as 1731 he was discussing the expansion of Prussia without reference to legality or diplomatic fictions. He regarded himself as the first servant of the state; but Frederick's state was an abstraction with strategic necessities and appetites: it was by no means synonymous with 'the people', whose welfare could in fact be sacrificed to its interests. If it did not

originate with Frederick, this impersonal conception of the state was first consciously formulated by him.

Frederick's first acts as king displayed his allegiance to the Enlightenment: judicial torture was abolished, censorship of the press ended and religious toleration proclaimed. The difference between Frederick's conception of kingship and his predecessors' was clearly shown in the deforestation of royal hunting-grounds for agriculture: the state came before royal pleasures.

Meanwhile, Voltaire hurried the king's *Anti-Machiavel* through the press, believing that Frederick might now prefer to suppress his criticisms of the great analyst of political ruthlessness. Events proved Voltaire right: Frederick's first major act of policy was to attack Austria without provocation.

The Austrian emperor, Charles VI, had been succeeded by his daughter, Maria Theresa. The disputed succession of a woman gave Frederick his opportunity: at the end of 1740, with 40,000 Prussian troops, he marched into Silesia, confident that although the powers (including Prussia) had formally accepted Maria Theresa's accession their greed would soon lead them to follow his example.

Frederick's calculations proved correct: his action began the War of Austrian Succession (1740–8). Prussia's part in it was limited to two relatively brief struggles against Austria (1740–2 and 1744–5), generally known as the First and Second Silesian Wars. Prussian victories astonished Europe and made it clear that she had joined the ranks of the great powers. Many of these victories—Chotusitz, Hohenfriedberg, Soor —were gained under Frederick's command. and even before the end of the war he had begun to be called 'Frederick the Great'. At its end, all the powers recognized Prussia's acquisition of Silesia.

Silesia was a wealthy and populous province, with a thriving woollen industry and

deposits of iron, coal and lead that were invaluable to a militaristic state. It is indicative of the limited aims (and means) of eighteenth-century rulers that this single acquisition was to be at risk for most of Frederick's reign.

This was in part a result of Frederick's methods. His wartime diplomacy—ceasing to fight when his French allies seemed about to overwhelm Austria, taking up arms when Austria grew too strong—had been successful; but they left him friendless. Maria Theresa burned to recover Silesia; Russia coveted East Prussia; and France, formally still Prussia's ally, no longer trusted Frederick.

The Seven Years War

Frederick was aware of his isolation; after the Second Silesian War he declared that henceforth he 'would not disturb a cat'. However, eight years of uneasy peace revealed Frederick's weaknesses as a diplomatist: a tendency to credit others with his own rationality and subtlety, and a temperament bias towards 'action'. In January 1756, alarmed by an Anglo-Russian rapprochement, Frederick signed the Convention of Westminster with Britain—which simply convinced France that she should accept Austrian offers of a defensive alliance. Believing that he was about to be crushed by a Franco-Russo-Austrian coalition, Frederick decided to move first.

In August 1756 he attacked Saxony, a strategically important state because its borders were only a few miles from Berlin. The Saxon army was defeated and incorporated into Frederick's forces and the resources of Saxony harnessed to Prussia's needs. In return for these advantages Frederick had precipitated war with Russia and Austria and—by attacking instead of waiting to be attacked—had ensured that

Left, the Battle of Leuthen of 1757, at which Frederick the Great defeated the Austrians in the Seven Years War; he began to be driven back by the alliance of Russians and Austrians two years later.

Opposite, the Promised Land of Frederick William, *shown here as the refuge from tyranny.*

France would join them. Sweden also declared war, and Frederick found himself encircled by enemies determined to dismember his kingdom.

For Prussia, the Seven Years War was a struggle for survival only. Frederick's sole ally was Britain, which paid him yearly subsidies and maintained an army in western Germany. Despite brilliant victories—at Rossbach (1757) over a Franco-German army, at Leuthen (1757) over the Austrians, at Zondorf (1758) over the Russians—the coalition drove Frederick's armies back by sheer weight of numbers. Against this, victories brought only temporary relief; and there were as many defeats as victories. The king was tireless and endlessly resourceful and his army had the advantages of interior lines and unity of command; but the situation several times reached a point at which Frederick contemplated suicide.

From 1760 the war was mainly one of attrition, siege following siege, while both sides became increasingly war-weary. The coalition began to break up—possibly saving Frederick from ultimate defeat— with the succession of Frederick's fanatical admirer, Peter III, as Tsar of Russia. When peace was made in 1763, Prussia—including Silesia—remained intact.

Prussia had survived, thanks to Frederick's genius and determination; but even more of the credit lay with the army and bureaucracy created by his predecessors. In particular, the efficiency of the civil service provided a revenue proportionately greater than that of the other European states and actually as great as that of Russia.

In most respects Frederick was content to follow the same methods as his father. He attempted to keep down imports and encourage exports; waged tariff wars against Austria and Saxony; reduced internal tariff barriers; built canals; drained marshes; and established hundreds of new villages. Silesian ores were vigorously exploited. The production of silks and woollen cloths increased so rapidly that they became the chief Prussian export. There were inevitable conflicts between the state's need for revenue and the needs of production and inevitable defects in a system so highly regulated and inimical to initiative; but on the only meaningful basis of assessment—comparison with other states—Prussian economic policy worked well.

Frederick was an ubiquitous presence, supervising, directing, checking. Unlike his father, he interfered even in routine matters. He would set up specialized agencies, correspond with local officials over the heads of their superiors and set one official to spy upon another. Such methods did often get things done more quickly, but they disorganized the machinery of the Prussian administration and made civil servants reluctant to act on their own initiative. These defects were tolerable while the king was a man of exceptional industry and intelligence—that is, while Frederick was king—but inevitably he had no successor as a one-man state supervisor.

During the Seven Years War, Prussia was devastated by the hostile armies and population declined by about a tenth. Frederick redoubled his efforts: the peasants were kept going by credits and supplies from the war magazines; the currency was restored; a state bank was opened; the growing of potatoes and sugar-beet (preventatives of famine) was encouraged despite opposition from the conservative peasantry. Despite some dubious experiments, state regulation was conspicuously successful in bringing about economic recovery.

The social and economic privileges of the nobility remained untouched; indeed Frederick, unlike his father, preferred to appoint men of noble birth to posts of any importance. In this as in other respects, Frederick became less and less 'enlightened'; in fact, the only notable reforms of his reign

were judicial. His efforts to increase the peasant's security of tenure are perhaps another exception; but it is more like that they were prompted by concern for the availability of cannon-fodder.

Frederick's later years

Between the wars Frederick was still the patron of art and letters, for whom Knobelsdorff built the Berlin Opera House, the east wing of the palace at Charlottenburg and the Rococo palace designated by Frederick for relaxation—the famous Sans-Souci at Potsdam. Frederick wrote a long poem, *The Art of War* (extensively revised by Voltaire), and a *History of My Times* about the Silesian wars—the first of several such histories. Voltaire himself became a guest of Frederick (1750–3), though the king's treatment of him after they quarrelled indicated

that the tyrant was close to the surface in the philosopher-king.

The stress of the Seven Years War strengthened the misanthropic and conservative elements in Frederick's make-up. The brilliant young prince, the glamorous king, were gradually replaced by a bent figure in a shabby, snuff-stained coat, remote from other men in his dedication to the state.

The conservatism of Frederick's foreign policy was less a matter of choice. Prussia could not afford another war and had no friends. France and Austria remained allies. Britain, Frederick believed, had let him down. He made the only possible alliance open to him, with Russia (1764–80). Frederick had no wish to see Russia expand, and much of his diplomatic activity was in fact designed to prevent his ally from exploiting her victories over the Turks. Poland was

another matter: Frederick was enthusiastic in seconding the Empress Catherine's suggestion that Russia, Prussia and Austria should each take a slice of Polish territory. The first partition (1772) fulfilled one of Frederick's long-cherished ambitions: the acquisition of West Prussia. This territory contained a large German-speaking and Lutheran element, easily absorbed into a German state; and East Prussia, hitherto indefensible, was joined to the main block of Hohenzollern lands.

This was Frederick's last coup: henceforth his postures were defensive. The war between Prussia and Austria (1777) was a halfhearted affair, but Frederick succeeded in preventing Austria from acquiring a large part of Bavaria. Perhaps the crowning irony of his career was his leadership of the League of German Princes, formed in 1785 to oppose Joseph II's Bavarian exchange scheme. Frederick, the unscrupulous aggressor who had twice broken the peace of the Empire, now marshalled German opinion against the radical schemes of the emperor himself.

Frederick's legacy

Under Frederick the Great, Prussia became recognized as a great power and acquired the territory and population (over 5 million by 1786) to support her new status more effectively. In immediate political terms his aims and methods were justified by their success; but their long-term effects were more questionable.

The military aspect of the Prussian state was decisively strengthened. The prestige of the army became unshakeable, and its influence was felt everywhere in Prussia. Frederick has, with some justification, been accused of beginning the European arms race: after the Seven Years War the army remained at its wartime size of just under 200,000 men (about four percent of the population), and habits of obedience and belief in force as a method of solving disputes became deeply ingrained in the citizens. In this sense it is possible to blame Frederick and his father for some of the disasters of modern German history.

In the immediate future Prussia continued to expand: Frederick's successor, Frederick William II (1786–97), took part in the Polish partitions of 1793 and 1795. But the penalties of rigid structures and unthinking obedience were soon to be visited upon Prussia in the Revolutionary and Napoleonic Wars, in which Frederick the Great's army was smashed and the state itself almost destroyed.

Austria under Charles VI

The reign of Charles VI (1711–40) coincided in time almost exactly with that of Frederick William I of Prussia; but whereas Prussia steadily grew in strength, the Austrian Monarchy struggled with financial difficulties, military reverses and internal disaffection.

The early years of the reign were promising. The long War of Spanish Succession came to an end, and if a Habsburg no longer sat on the throne of Spain the Austrian branch of the family acquired most of Spain's possessions in Europe: the Spanish Netherlands, Milan, Naples, Sardinia. In the war against the Turks (1716–18) Eugene of Savoy crushed the Turkish armies and captured Belgrade; and when peace was made at Passarowitz (1718), Austria gained Temesvar and considerable territory to the south and east of Hungary.

The most pressing internal problem appeared to have been solved when agreement was reached with the Hungarians. The Rakoczi revolt ended in 1712, and Charles was able to negotiate a settlement that was satisfactory to the dynasty, if not entirely so to the state. The Hungarians continued to enjoy a very considerable degree of self-government and to pay little in taxes (the nobility paid nothing); but they accepted the succession of Charles's daughter and the principle that Hungary was an indivisible part of the Habsburg Empire.

The fact that Charles had no male heir complicated both his internal and external policies. In a declaration of 1713—the 'Pragmatic Sanction'—Charles willed all his dominions to his eldest direct heir, whether male or female; and over the years it became clear that he would be succeeded by his daughter, Maria Theresa (born in 1717). After he has secured the agreement of the Hungarians and his other, more tractable subjects, Charles formally promulgated the Pragmatic Sanction in 1724; but he still needed the acquiescence of the other great powers. This was necessary not because women were regarded as inevitably feeble rulers—though that conviction had not entirely disappeared despite examples to the contrary—but because Maria Theresa had possible rivals. Charles's elder brother, Joseph I, had left two daughters who had married the electors of Bavaria and Saxony; and it seemed likely that other powers would support their claims in order to weaken and possibly to dismember the Austrian Empire.

Charles's tortuous and otherwise ineffective foreign policy was primarily intended to avoid this contingency by securing international recognition of Maria Theresa. In this at least he succeeded: by the end of the War of Polish Succession (1733–5) all the great powers—even the hereditary enemy, France—had guaranteed the Pragmatic Sanction.

It was an ill-advised policy: in return for paper guarantees Charles sacrificed real advantages. Austrian strength and prestige. —the only real guarantees of the Pragmatic Sanction—steadily declined. Charles's wars exhausted Austrian finances yet produced military results that were at best unimpressive. In a new war (1737–9) against the Turks, they were disastrous: Austria was heavily defeated, and all the gains of Passarowitz were lost except Temesvar. The prospect of expanding overseas trade through the Ostend Company had been sacrificed to placate the maritime powers, and the small fleet built at Trieste was sold. Economic growth remained slow, and—as if to punish Austrian weakness with the maximum irony—the most rapidly developing province, Silesia, was lost as soon as Charles died.

Maria Theresa

As soon as Maria Theresa came to the throne, Frederick the Great attacked Silesia, and the electors of Bavaria and Saxony asserted their wives' claims to the Habsburg inheritance. By the summer of 1741, France, Bavaria and Spain had formed an alliance against Austria, and by October the ill-prepared Austrian army had to face a Franco-Bavarian force in Bohemia as well as Frederick's army in Silesia. The beginning of the War of Austrian Succession appeared to foreshadow the dissolution of the Habsburg state itself.

Above, Charles VI, Archduke of Austria and Holy Roman Emperor (reigned 1711–40), whose reign was mainly taken up with his unsuccessful attempt to become king of Spain, and to secure a peaceful accession of his daughter Maria Theresa to the Austrian throne on his own death.

Top, the Opera House of Berlin in 1742; Frederick himself was a skilful flautist and composer and was an eager patron of music, including opera.

Opposite left, Frederick II of Prussia (reigned 1740–86), known as Frederick the Great. He combined an interest in learning and music with a determination to expand Prussia to be the dominant state of eastern Europe. Schloss Hohenzollern.

Opposite right, Frederick the Great at the Sans-Souci castle near Potsdam, with a number of guests, including Voltaire, in the early 1750s.

At this crisis the twenty-three-year-old Maria Theresa behaved with courage and resolution, making a dramatic appeal to the Hungarian nobility which won their support. More immediately important, Frederick the Great effectively dropped out of the war: he had no wish to see his ally France destroy Austria and dominate Europe. The French and Bavarians were driven from Bohemia, and the initiative passed to Austria. The crisis had passed: the fortunes of war fluctuated, as Frederick again intervened (1744–5) to prevent an Austrian triumph; but the existence of Austria was never again threatened.

After the peace of Aix-la-Chapelle (1748), Austrian policy was almost exclusively directed towards revenging her defeat by Prussia and recovering Silesia. Even during the war Maria Theresa would have preferred to make peace with France in order to face Prussia alone; but she had been hindered by her British allies (who were only interested in fighting France) and by the French obsession with their traditional anti-Habsburg policy. Now she set about winning the friendship of France in earnest.

The architect of this policy was Prince Wenzel von Kaunitz, the outstanding diplomatist of his generation, who became chancellor of Austria in 1753. Kaunitz believed that the Bourbon-Habsburg struggle was no longer relevant to European politics and that only the destruction of Prussia could restore Austrian primacy in Germany. A new policy required a new partner. Britain had neither the desire nor the ability to intervene in eastern Europe, whereas the support of France, still the most powerful nation in Europe, would ensure victory, and French subsidies would keep the Russian (as well as the Austrian) armies in the field.

While Kaunitz negotiated with France, another of Maria Theresa's advisers, Count Ludwig Haugwitz, was organizing the military, administrative and financial reforms which might enable Austria to match the Prussian war machine. The army was subjected to a more rigorous training; conditions of service were improved; and administrative and tax reforms greatly increased revenue. Austria and Bohemia, the most docile Habsburg possessions, were the chief targets, and Austro-Bohemian institutions were streamlined and integrated. Now, as later, Hungary in particular was handled with tact. Maria Theresa had won the devotion of the Hungarian nobles in 1741 and she retained it by giving them preferential treatment and respecting their privileges.

Meanwhile, Kaunitz's diplomacy met with limited success. Austro-French negotiations were cordial but showed little sign of reaching a conclusion. Only Frederick the Great's miscalculations angered the French into making a defensive alliance with Austria (1756) and then brought them into the coalition against Prussia.

Kaunitz's diplomacy triumphed, but the Austrian and other coalition armies failed to give Prussia the coup de grâce; and Austria emerged from the Seven Years War with nothing to show for her expenditure of blood and treasure.

After the disappointment of the Seven Years War, Maria Theresa avoided adventures in foreign policy and determined upon a more thoroughgoing reorganization of her dominions. All internal policy was brought under the direction of a single Council of State; and a central bureau, the Directorium, controlled the administrative system. A beginning was made in efficient budgeting, while the functions of the provincial estates were largely taken over by royal officials, and further military reforms were introduced by the empress's son, Joseph.

Maria Theresa's agrarian reforms were more radical still. Their original motive was financial: a peasant who performed heavy services for his lord could not make his own land productive; so he could not pay much in taxes. But the investigations of royal commissioners revealed a degree of peasant misery that produced a genuine humanitarian revulsion in Maria Theresa, who was only with difficulty persuaded not to abolish serfdom entirely. Maximum labour services were established in successive provinces over a period of years (1767–78) and the result was a definite improvement in the lot of the peasantry. The direction in which the government hoped to move was made clear by their treatment of peasants on crown lands, who were freed from all servile obligations and became simple tenants. By and large, however, landowners failed to follow the government's lead.

These measures demonstrate the extent to which 'enlightened despotism' sprang from the needs of the state rather than the personality or convictions of the ruler. Nobody could have been less the received image of the enlightened despot than the pious, conservative, sturdily sensible but scarcely intellectual Maria Theresa; yet she proved willing to override custom and tradition in the interests of the state and to tax the clergy and dissolve monasteries in the face of papal opposition. She, much more than self-conscious Enlightenment intellectuals like Frederick II and Catherine of Russia, deserves a place among the enlightened despots.

The radical emperor

Maria Theresa's successor was her son, Joseph II (1780–90), who intensified the programme of radical reform. Joseph lacked his mother's caution and common sense; he was a doctrinaire Enlightenment prince who meditated profound changes in the structure of the state regardless of social, regional or religious difficulties. He proceeded at a pace that was dangerous in itself and madness

when combined with an adventurous foreign policy.

Joseph's hankering after military and diplomatic success became apparent even in his mother's lifetime. It was mainly he who convinced Maria Theresa that Austria should take part in the first partition of Poland (1772); and it was he who championed the Bavarian succession scheme which led to war with Prussia (1778), a fiasco that drained the Austrian treasury without achieving anything. Similar adventures were to ruin all Joseph's attempts at internal reform.

In the early years of the reign all went well. Administrative centralization was carried to its logical conclusion, and the empire was divided into administrative areas that ignored local and regional differences (a characteristic Enlightenment attitude, with both strengths and weaknesses). Equality before the law and religious toleration were introduced. The peasants were given personal liberty (that is, they were no longer forbidden to leave the estates on which they worked) and security of tenure for themselves and their descendants.

Joseph made the first sustained effort to end Austrian economic backwardness. No consideration other than utility was allowed to influence policy. For example, several hundred monasteries were dissolved because they were non-productive; as Joseph proclaimed (in the characteristic accents of the Enlightenment), 'orders which are absolutely useless to their fellow-men cannot be pleasing to God.' Internally, restrictions on trade were removed. The state ceased to subsidise industry, and the guilds lost much of their power to restrict production and commerce. External commercial policy remained mercantilist: tariffs were imposed on foreign goods in order to stimulate production in Austria, and Joseph concluded a number of advantageous trade agreements with other states.

Interference with the economic and social systems prevailing in the countryside—still, of course, the heart of the Austrian economy—went even further. During the 1780s a comprehensive census and land register was compiled for all Joseph's dominions; the feudal obligations of the peasants were swept away and replaced by fixed money rents; and finally, in 1789, a land tax representing twelve percent of yearly income was imposed on landowner and peasant alike, who now became equal before the tax collector as well as the law.

The magnitude of the changes introduced by Joseph—changes that would have transformed Austria into a modern state—was bound to arouse opposition. They quickly justified themselves in terms of economic growth and increased state revenue; but they offended most sections of the population in some respect—religious belief, regional independence, financial advantage, social superiority. Nor should the 'despotic' (as opposed to the 'enlightened') aspect of

Joseph's policies be ignored: the destruction of local liberties, the use of secret police, the imposition of German as the official language of the Habsburg dominions. Even without foreign entanglements Joseph would have encountered difficulties; military defeat completely destroyed his policies.

Joseph's early foreign policy failed; but its failure was not vital. The Austrian Netherlands were difficult to control and of limited commercial value, since the 1648 treaties had given Dutch shipping exclusive use of the River Scheldt. Joseph first attempted to force the Dutch to open the Scheldt and then elaborated a scheme to exchange the Austrian Netherlands for Bavaria, the acquisition of which would have enlarged the main block of Habsburg territory. But his Russian allies let him down, and in the face of French opposition and Frederick II's League of Princes (1785) Joseph had to abandon both his objectives.

His real misfortunes began with the war against the Turks (1788), into which he allowed himself to be led by Catherine. The war was a disaster: Russian strength proved an illusion and the Austrian armies again failed in the field. The exorbitant cost of the war wrecked Austrian finances, trade was disrupted, and prices rose steeply. New taxes to pay for the war made Joseph even more unpopular with all classes. The absence of the army made it impossible to suppress discontent, and Hungary and the Netherlands rebelled. Disillusioned, Joseph cancelled most of his reforms before he died, leaving the monarchy again in a state of crisis.

His successor, the able Leopold II (1790–2), had been an outstanding reformer as Duke of Tuscany and struggled to preserve some of the advances made under Joseph. He made peace with the Turks, managed to stabilize the internal situation and ·even began to elaborate plans for constitutional reforms involving popular representation; but his death ended any prospect of continued reform. The increasing radicalism of the French Revolution panicked Leopold's successor into blind reaction: the Austrian experiment in enlightened despotism was over.

German reawakening

Eighteenth-century Germany remained provincial and backward. Limited agricultural advances were made, but, with the partial exceptions of Prussia and the Rhineland, industry was of minimal importance. Urban development was slow and the urban middle class small and uninfluential.

German artistic and cultural development was nonetheless remarkable. The princely craze for culture, initially prompted by envy of Louis XIV, led to court patronage of architects, musicians and writers. Catholic Germany and Austria produced a sumptuously decorative Baroque architecture that reached its apogee in spectacular churches and monasteries. The Germans became the leading musical nation with the appearance of the composers, Johann Sebastian Bach (1685–1750) and Handel (1685–1759) and the Viennese masters Gluck (1714–87), Haydn (1732–1809) and Mozart (1756–91); Vienna, where Beethoven lived and worked from 1792 as pianist and composer, was to be the musical capital of Europe right down to the late nineteenth century. Literature, though held back for a time by imitation of French models, produced a dramatist and critic of the first order in Lessing (1729–81) and a universal genius in Goethe (1749–1832), who was followed in the 1790s by a galaxy of talents. The foundation of Halle (1694)

Above, Joseph II, Holy Roman Emperor (reigned 1765–90) lending a hand at the plough. His primary concern was with the lot of the peasantry, and in 1781 he abolished serfdom and permitted the peasants to buy their own land.

Top, a view of Vienna in 1785, one of the main cultural capitals of central Europe at a time when the cities were vying with each other to attract the best artists and musicians.

PETRVS LEOPOLDVS
Imperator Romanorum &c.

and Göttingen (1736–7) began the European pre-eminence of German universities and the writings of Immanuel Kant (1742–1804) that of German philosophy. Culturally, if not yet politically, Germany had become one of the great nations of Europe.

Though Charles Albert of Bavaria had a brief moment of glory as Holy Roman emperor (1742–5), the political history of Germany was dominated by Austro-Prussian dualism. The German princes became, even more markedly than in the previous period, dependants and auxiliaries of greater powers. Some were even content to supplement their revenues by hiring out their troops, providing Britain in particular with a convenient method of responding to continental emergencies.

Such conditions did not offer much incentive to the would-be enlightened despot; and for that matter the smallness of most states precluded ambitious undertakings. The only prince who instituted radical reforms comparable with Joseph II's was Charles Frederick of Baden, who imposed a uniform tax on land and abolished serfdom. But 'Josephism', as the emperor's anti-clerical policies came to be called, was adopted by a number of Catholic rulers, including ecclesiastical princes.

Towards the end of the pre-revolutionary period, there were indications that Enlightenment attitudes towards politics and society had begun to filter down to a wider public. (In Austria this had been deliberately fostered by Maria Theresa and Joseph, who had encouraged the production of books and pamphlets attacking the privileges of landowners and clergy.) The abolition of serfdom and noble privileges, religious toleration and political freedom became widely discussed as news of the French Revolution arrived. Enlightened despotism, it now became clear, involved an internal contradiction: to gain public support the despot had to spread enlightenment—which, however, led men to question despotism.

Even before the French Revolution, German rulers had become alarmed by the development of a German public opinion. Freethinkers had begun to be persecuted in Bavaria and Prussia; the limited freedoms characteristic of enlightened despotism had begun to be curtailed. Whether or not these events were part of a more general European 'revolutionary crisis', as some historians believe, is difficult to determine. After 1789, opinions in Germany (and everywhere else in Europe) were determined not by internal events but by reaction to the French Revolution.

Russia

By the time of Peter the Great's death in 1725, Russia had begun to emerge from the semi-oriental seclusion of previous centuries. Peter had imported Western technology and developed industries, created a large and formidable army and won for Russia a 'window on the West' in the Baltic provinces wrested from Sweden. To set the seal on his achievements he had built a new capital, St Petersburg, on the newly acquired coastline, where it faced Europe.

The work begun by Peter was far from complete. Russia was still technologically backward, with an almost wholly illiterate population engaged in agriculture and hunting. The furs and timber of the far north were still the chief source of wealth. Industry and overseas trade grew in the eighteenth century—particularly the iron industry in the Urals, which dominated the European market until coke-smelted British iron began to overtake it in the 1760s. But in general, capital remained short, techniques were rudimentary and communications poor. Lacking another Peter the Great, and handicapped by the inherent disadvantages of a serf-economy, Russia continued to lag behind the West.

Even at the beginning of the century Russia was the most populous state in Europe apart from France, with more inhabitants than Austria and Prussia combined. It was this fact that enabled her to become a great power despite her backwardness (though, ironically, abundant manpower may have helped to perpetuate that backwardness by providing a temporarily adequate substitute for technological development). By the end of the eighteenth century the population of Russia, swollen by natural increase and acquisitions of territory, stood at thirty-six million, far surpassing that of France.

The majority of this population were serfs, engaged in cottage industries or agriculture, who paid rent in money or kind or worked so many days a week on their lord's land. The serf was little better than a slave: he worked, married and travelled as and when his lord determined and was liable to be sold and taken to his new owner's estates without his family. During the eighteenth century the serf's position deteriorated further as landlords increased their demands and strengthened their legal rights; ultimately, under Catherine II, they acquired authority to send serfs to Siberia as convicts without public trial. Not surprisingly, the eighteenth century was a period of peasant unrest.

By contrast, the position of the nobility was improving. As well as increased control over their serfs, they won greater personal freedom and a privileged status. Peter the Great had instituted compulsory state service for life, controlled their movements and forbidden them to divide their estates; but under his successors these measures were relaxed or reversed.

The tradition of state service remained strong, but a large section of the nobility took the opportunity to become a leisured class, comparable with—and imitative of—their Western counterparts. Only political power was denied them: in Russia too, privilege was a tacit return for noble acquiescence in the continuation of the autocracy. The only serious attempt to limit imperial power—the conditions imposed by the Privy Council on Anne when they offered her the crown in 1730—did not survive her accession.

Peter the Great's successors had little of his ability and none of his determination. Under Catherine I (1725–7), Peter II (1727–30), Anne (1730–40) and Ivan IV (1740–1), the government was an indolent autocracy largely at the mercy of opposing factions. The coup d'état that replaced Ivan IV by Peter the Great's daughter, Elizabeth (1741–61), began a period of relative stability, though the intrigues of lovers, favourites, ministers and diplomats were still the determinants of public policy. In the eyes of Western observers, habituated to dynastic stability and a bureaucratic absolutism, Russia continued to be a barbaric 'Eastern' state, ruled through the seraglio.

However badly governed, Russia had become a force in Europe, albeit an erratic one which was liable to be paralysed by a coup or change of ruler (as happened in 1741 and 1762) and which could often afford to take the field only with the help of subsidies from another power. The War of Polish Succession (1733–5) made it clear that Russia, not France, was now the paramount influence in Polish affairs. The war of 1736–9 against the Turks revealed that Russia was stronger than Austria, her ally in the struggle after 1737. Whereas Austria was forced to make a humiliating separate peace, Russia at least regained Azov, which Peter the Great had lost in 1711.

In addition, easy victories over Sweden

Above, Maria Theresa, Queen of Bohemia and Hungary (reigned 1740–80), and ruler of the Habsburg territories of Austria and the Netherlands.

Left, a view of Moscow in the late eighteenth century, which was increasingly, though to a lesser extent than St Petersburg, dominated by western fashions and culture.

Opposite left, Leopold II, Holy Roman Emperor (reigned 1790–92), who reversed many of the policies of his brother Joseph II in order to restore peace to his lands.

Opposite centre, Joseph Haydn (1732–1809), the Austrian musician who played an important role in the development of the symphonic form.

Opposite right, Wolfgang von Goethe (1749–1832), the German philosopher, poet and statesman who became the epitome of the civilization of Germany in the late eighteenth century, combining the classical and the romantic traditions.

(1741–3) showed that here too the balance of strength had altered decisively in Russia's favour. In the West fear of 'the Russian colossus'—a fear that was to become irrational and obsessive in many nineteenth-century statesmen—had already begun to be expressed. Frederick the Great warned his successors that it was imperative to 'cultivate the friendship of these barbarians'. As yet, circumstances—and ineptitude—prevented Russia from reaping the harvest of her victories.

The Seven Years War followed the same pattern. Russia took her part in a great European coalition, held East Prussia for the duration of the war and even briefly occupied Berlin (1760), making her status as a great power indisputable. But the war also revealed the eccentricity of the new tsar, Peter III (1761–2), who took Russia out of the war because he admired Frederick the Great too much to fight against him.

Much of our information about Peter is untrustworthy, since it derives from his wife, Catherine, who supplanted him. But, if not quite the ignorant lunatic described by Catherine, he displayed an eccentricity that was little short of madness in an occupant of the dangerous throne of Russia. Peter, the half-German Duke of Holstein, ended the war against Prussia, openly displayed his preference for his Holstein troops, paraded his Lutheranism and insulted the Orthodox Church.

The outcome was inevitable. Catherine won over the guards regiments and, abetted by her lover, Grigory Orlov (a guards officer), deposed her husband.

Catherine II

The new empress was even less Russian than Peter. Sophia of Anhalt-Zerbst, who had been renamed Catherine on her reception into the Russian Orthodox Church, was the daughter of a Prussian noble family. In 1745 she became the bride of Peter, at that time heir to the throne, as part of one of Frederick the Great's diplomatic manoeuvres.

Catherine's early years in Russia were dangerous and difficult, and on occasion she was almost caught in the web of intrigue and counter-intrigue that characterized Elizabeth's reign. In this hard school she learned political realism. Unlike Peter, she adopted Russian manners, learned the language and professed Orthodoxy. When her hour struck, she was able to put herself forward as the representative of the Russian people, Orthodoxy and the army. First Peter, then Ivan IV (who had survived in confinement since 1741) were murdered, and Catherine was able to remain the undisputed ruler of Russia until her death in 1796.

Before she became empress, Catherine educated herself in the philosophy of the Enlightenment, becoming familiar with the

Pierre III, assassiné par les ordres de Catherine II son épouse.

works of Bayle, Montesquieu, Voltaire and Beccaria. Later, when she corresponded with Voltaire, Diderot and others, she took the opportunity to picture herself as an enlightened ruler and Russia as a well-administered land of plenty. Catherine herself laid the basis for her European reputation and began to be called 'the Great' as a result of her own propaganda.

Russian realities were very different. Catherine toyed with schemes to create a legislative assembly and codify the laws and made some efforts to revive Peter the Great's educational programme; but at heart she cared more for the triumphs of war and diplomacy. Besides, any reform would jeopardize the tacit alliance between the autocracy and nobility. Catherine loved power too much—and for that matter shared too many aristocratic prejudices—to take the risk. Only in secularizing Church property—a measure foreshadowed by her predecessors—did she act in a manner of which *philosophes* and enlightened despots alike would have approved. One incident illuminates her real position. In 1769 she began publishing a journal designed to improve Russian manners and morals; but when the numerous periodicals that flattered her by imitation were joined by Nikolai Novikov's *The Drone*, which attempted serious social analysis, it was promptly suppressed.

The gulf between privileged and unprivileged was in fact deliberately widened. In the few months of Peter III's reign, the emancipation of the nobility had been completed. Under Catherine they were loaded with privileges, culminating in a Charter of the Nobility (1785) which confirmed all their gains over the century and

gave them a share in local government. Hundreds of thousands of state peasants passed into serfdom as gifts to her noble supporters from the prodigal Catherine, and many of the peasants in lands conquered by Russia also become serfs. The condition of the peasantry continued to deteriorate as masters increased their demands in order to set up manorial industries or share the pleasures of life in St Petersburg.

Catherine's court was more sophisticated than that of her predecessors. To superficial observers St Petersburg appeared 'the Athens of the North', for which foreign architects designed beautiful new buildings —the Winter Palace, the Hermitage, Tsarskoe Selo. Its society was dominated by the spirit of the Enlightenment in its more superficial aspects: use of French and displays of wit, cynicism and polished manners. In this respect, too, Catherine's reign was a pseudo-Enlightenment—a tribute to the French culture which contemporaries were prone to identify with the Enlightenment.

Pugachev

The great rebellion of 1733–4 can be regarded as the peasants' verdict on Catherine and previous rulers. The rebels were led by Emelian Pugachev, a Don Cossack adventurer who claimed to be the dead Peter III (a type of imposture frequently adopted by Russian rebels). Exploited serfs, persecuted members of the sect of Old Believers, discontented non-Russian peoples and all who resented control by distant St Petersburg joined Pugachev, who was soon in control of much of the Volga region.

At first the rebellion was not taken very seriously, but when Pugachev laid siege to Orenburg and repulsed a relieving force, Catherine ordered a full-scale campaign to be mounted. Orenburg was relieved, but Kazan fell, and for a time Moscow itself seemed threatened. The arrival of Russian forces released by the Russo-Turkish peace (1774) sealed Pugachev's fate. His followers were hunted down, areas which had supported him were subjected to terrible reprisals, and Pugachev himself was captured and executed.

Pugachev's rebellion increased Catherine's conservatism. Her reaction was to create a uniform system of provincial administration (1775) with which the nobility were associated. In theory at least it should have led to better government; but its main object was to increase control over the countryside. Repression and vigilance, not reform, was Catherine's formula for the peasant problem.

Catherine's conquests

Catherine's claim to greatness lies in her conduct of war and diplomacy: she made Russia more powerful, if not happier. At the beginning of her reign Catherine entertained Nikita Panin's scheme of a 'northern

alliance' with Prussia, Poland, the Baltic states and Britain against the French and Austrians; but, apart from an alliance with Prussia (1764), the plan came to nothing. Catherine proved wise enough to concentrate on the problems at hand: Poland and Turkey.

Agreement to 'maintain Polish liberties' was an important motive in the Russo-Prussian alliance; but, in spite of the election of one of Catherine's lovers, Stanislas Poniatowski, as King of Poland, the Poles continued to be troublesome. The activities of the Polish confederacies tied down a large number of Russian troops—a situation made the more serious by the outbreak of war between Russia and Turkey (1768).

Despite Russian commitments in Poland, the war was prosecuted with success. However, Austria was ready to fight rather than see Russia gain territory in the Balkans, while Frederick II—ally or not—was unprepared to back Catherine against Austria but very willing to reconcile all three parties at the expense of Poland. In effect, the first partition of Poland (1772) was Catherine's way of buying off Austria and Prussia and of compensating herself for the Balkan gains she had been forced to renounce.

The Turkish war was brought to a successful conclusion at Kutchuk-Kainardji (1774), though Catherine might have pressed for greater advantages but for the Pugachev rebellion. Russia acquired a foothold on the Black Sea and right of passage through the Dardanelles for her merchant shipping.

Above, a Russian embassy at the court of the Ottoman sultan in 1775; after the treaty of Kutchuk-Kainardji the Russians were able to begin to dominate their southern neighbour, a policy that would cause diplomatic problems to Europe throughout the nineteenth century.

Top, a view of St Petersburg in 1753; founded by Peter the Great earlier in the century, the city was by this time the centre of Russian society and cultural life.

Above left, Catherine the Great, Tsarina of Russia (reigned 1762–96), walking her dog in 1794; as well as her luke-warm attempts at reform on enlightened principles, she was concerned with the expansion of Russian authority.

Below left, the execution in 1775 of Emelian Pugachev, the Cossack whose rebellion of 1773–74 expressed the social strains of the growing Russian state. Pugachev was able to control the Ural region and take Kazan before being defeated.

Opposite, the murder of Peter III, Tsar of Russia (reigned 1762); his wife, later Catherine II, forced him to abdicate on the grounds of insanity, and may have ordered the murder a few days later.

The Crimea became independent of Turkey (the first step towards its incorporation into Russia), and Russia gained vaguely worded rights to make representations on behalf of the sultan's Christian subjects. (In the nineteenth century this clause was the pretext for repeated Russian interference in Ottoman affairs.) The Treaty of Kutchuk-Kainardji was a landmark in Russian history: under Peter the Great, Russia had gained access to the Baltic; under Catherine, she gained access to the Mediterranean.

The second half of the reign was a sort of repeat performance. When the alliance with Prussia lapsed, Catherine chose a new partner who would be of more direct help against the Turks: Joseph II of Austria. With Joseph's support she annexed the Crimea (1783); but characteristically she made no effort to help Joseph to reestablish Austrian supremacy in Germany. On this, as on other occasions, Catherine posed as the arbiter of Europe—a flattering and undemanding role—but refused to commit her forces outside eastern Europe.

In the 1780s she dreamed of overthrowing the Ottoman Empire completely and re-establishing the ancient Byzantine Empire (the 'Greek project'). In the war that began in 1787, Austria quickly collapsed; and though the Russian performance was better, it hardly justified such extravagant ambitions. At the Peace of Jassy (1792) the Sultan of Turkey accepted Russia's acquisition of the Crimea and ceded the rest of the northern shore of the Black Sea.

Catherine led the way in destroying the Polish state by the partitions of 1793 and 1795. Her troops did most of the fighting and she took the largest single share. Her partners, Austria and Prussia, were also engaged in the struggle against revolutionary France, in which Catherine had promised her aid. Whether she would have intervened on any scale is debatable: it seems more likely that she would have launched another attack on the Turks. Her death left the question open.

In Russia, the French Revolution was greeted with enthusiasm in some circles, influenced by the Enlightenment culture that Catherine had favoured. But from the fall of the Bastille in July 1789, Catherine herself loathed the Revolution, and any of her remaining pretensions to liberalism disappeared. Russian students in the West were ordered home; the imports of French books and journals—including Catherine's favourites—was prohibited. Novikov, whose *The Drone* had got him into trouble some twenty years before, was imprisoned as a subversive publicist and freemason. Alexander Radishchev, who can be regarded as the first figure in the great tradition of Russian literature of social conscience, was sent into Siberian exile.

Catherine's triumphs were bought at a high price. The cost of her wars was enormous, and she financed them by issuing ever greater quantities of paper money. This

rapidly depreciated, dislocating the whole Russian economy and wrecking many of the real industrial advances that had taken place. Other negative features—the growth of noble privileges, the deterioration in the lot of the peasantry—have already been noticed.

The positive features were by no means negligible. Russia gained six million new subjects (though not all of them accepted Russification with docility) and vast territories in the south. These were to become the granary of Russia, and made possible

the population explosion of the nineteenth century.

The Baltic states

The conclusion of the Great Northern War (1721) marked the end of Sweden's bid for supremacy in the Baltic. Russia took Sweden's territories on the eastern shore of the Baltic, and Prussia acquired western Pomerania. It soon became apparent that they had also replaced Sweden and her old antagonist, Denmark, as great powers; and

Territories taken from Sweden

Territories taken from Poland

Territories taken from Turkey

Pugachev rebellion

from the eighteenth century Scandinavia was on the periphery of international affairs.

The situation in the Baltic itself was stabilized. Sweden remained in control of Finland, Denmark of Norway. The Danes accepted the loss of what had become southern Sweden; the Swedes gave up their attempts to conquer Norway and reconciled themselves to paying the Danes customs duties for passage through the Sound. The two powers were comparable in population and resources, and the balance between them lasted the rest of the century.

The disasters of Charles XII's reign (1697–1718) had destroyed Sweden's Baltic empire and with it the justification for absolute royal authority. When Charles died leaving no direct heir, the aristocracy seized their opportunity: the crown was offered to Charles's sister, Ulrica, on condition that she accepted a constitution drawn up by the Swedish Estates. Her agreement initiated what came to be known as 'the Age of Freedom'. The council that ruled Sweden was selected and controlled by the Estates, which met regularly and took decisions by majority vote.

The 1720s and 1730s were dominated by Count Arvid Horn, whose policy of avoiding foreign adventures while Sweden recovered her strength resembled that of Walpole in Britain and Fleury in France. This unheroic policy led to the formation of the opposing 'Hat' party, which advocated resuming Sweden's traditional alliance with France and dreamed of recovering the lost provinces from Russia.

Horn and the 'Caps' were ousted in 1738; but, though the Hats managed to hang on to power until 1765, the period that followed was one of intense party conflict which gave foreign powers unlimited opportunities for interfering in Swedish affairs by intrigue and bribery. The overambitious policy of the Hats led Sweden into war with Russia (1741), from which she was fortunate to escape with only the loss of a strip of Finland, and to join the coalition against Prussia in the Seven Years War, with equally negative results.

After a brief period of rule by the 'Younger Caps', the twenty-five-year-old Gustavus III (1771–92) staged a coup, overthrew the constitution, and recovered most of the powers that the crown had possessed before the Age of Freedom. He introduced many of the reforms characteristic of the enlightened despot—abolition of judicial torture, religious toleration, freedom of the press, lifting of internal tariffs etc.

Noble opposition revived in the 1780s, provoked in particular by the king's heavy military expenditure, culminating in a fruitless war with Russia and Denmark (1788–90). With popular support Gustavus was able to reinforce and extend his powers by a second coup d'état (1789), but his triumph was brief: in 1792 he was assassinated by a group of nobles.

Left, Gustavus III of Sweden (reigned 1771–92), who instituted many reforms; but, like those of most of the 'enlightened despots', his policies tended to increase taxation and the power of the state, and he lost the support of the nobility. Historisches Museum, Dresden.

Opposite, the expansion of Russia during the reign of Catherine the Great.

Left, the arrest of Johann Struensee (1737–72) in 1772 on the charge of adultery with the Queen of Denmark. In the previous year he had managed to begin lasting reforms including the support of commerce and freeing the educational system.

From the reign of Frederick III (1648–70), Denmark was ruled absolutely by his dynasty, the Oldenburgs. The old nobility was carefully controlled, and royal power was exercised through a new nobility and a civil service, of which many members were Germans who owed everything to the crown. During the eighteenth century, however, a series of weak kings allowed the royal council to engross more and more power—a trend briefly reversed by Johann Friedrich Struensee.

Struensee, a German, was the insane Christian VII's physician and the queen's lover. In 1770 he became virtual dictator of Denmark, broke the power of the council, and launched a programme of enlightened reforms. The pace at which they were introduced, and above all Struensee's attacks on noble privileges, led to his fall and execution (1772). But not all his measures were cancelled; and a few years later even more important reforms were initiated by Andreas Bernstorff, culminating in the effective abolition of serfdom in 1788.

Poland

Poland failed to overcome her difficulties until it was too late. Under the Saxon kings, Augustus II (1697–1733) and Augustus III

(1733–63), economic and social problems went unsolved, and the *Seym* was constantly sabotaged by use of the free veto. Foreign intervention became blatant, and the disputatious Poles easily formed the habit of appealing to outsiders. Interested powers—Russia, Prussia, France—corrupted members of the *Seym*, decided who should be king and violated Polish territory with impunity.

The full extent of Poland's weakness became apparent on the death of Augustus II. Stanislas Leszczynski, once Augustus II's rival, was elected by the Poles with enthusiasm. But Leszczynski was also the French candidate; and Austria and Russia had decided that the Saxon line should continue. A Russian army compelled the Poles to change their minds and drove Leszczynski from the country.

During Augustus III's reign Poland sank deeper into anarchy. Internal politics revolved around the struggle between two great families, the Czartoryskis and the Potockis, both of which attempted to form connections with the great powers. During the Seven Years War, Russia used Polish territory as a base from which to attack Prussia, and Prussian troops counterattacked across the border while the Poles themselves remained in a state of near civil war.

The long overdue reformation began under Stanislas Poniatowski, who became King Stanislas Augustus in 1764. Poniatowski had been one of Catherine II's lovers and was placed on the throne by Russia and Prussia; but he refused to be a puppet and had already made some progress towards reform when the first great crisis of his reign occurred.

Religious dissensions in Poland had provided a pretext for Russian and Prussian diplomatic pressure for several decades. Poland was a Catholic state but contained a large Lutheran minority (mainly German) in the northeast and an even larger Orthodox minority (mainly Ukrainian and Russian) in the east and southeast. Both had very limited civic rights and were subject to strong Catholic pressure. Their natural defenders were Lutheran Prussia and Orthodox Russia; and Frederick II and Catherine II—both religious sceptics—were quite prepared to exploit the issue.

Catherine first encouraged the 'dissenters' to form confederacies, then (1768) bullied the *Seym* into ending their religious disabilities. The reaction was swift: confederacies sprang up all over Poland and harried the Russians, who were further embarrassed by a border incident which sparked off the Russo-Turkish war of 1768–74.

Catherine solved her ensuing difficulties by joining Prussia and Austria in partitioning Poland. In 1772 about a quarter of the kingdom and more than a third of its inhabitants were taken over by new masters.

The first partition shocked the Polish nobility out of their complacent absorption in 'Polish liberty'. Encouraged by the king, the *Seym* passed a series of measures designed to modernize and strengthen the state, culminating in the constitution of 1791. The crown became hereditary; the free veto and confederacies were abolished; a centralized administration was set up; the system of taxation was revised and made more equitable; and the privileges of the nobility were reduced. Intellectual life quickened under the impact of educational reform, and even the Polish economy, half-strangled by concessions to Prussia and Russia, showed some improvement.

Catherine was less than ever inclined to allow a Polish revival. The constitution of 1791 decided her: in 1792 the conservatives, who had opposed the constitution, were stirred into activity, and Russian troops again invaded. Poniatowski was forced to agree to a second partition (1793), Russia taking a huge slice of eastern Poland and Prussia a smaller area in the west. All that remained of the ancient kingdom was a small and defenceless state under Russian control.

The disappearance of Poland now seemed only a matter of time. The Polish leaders, partly inspired by the successes of 'the people in arms' during the French Revolution, decided to act before the Russian grip tightened; and in 1794 Poland rose in revolt.

The leader of the rebels was Tadeusz Kosciuszko, an enthusiast for liberty who had already fought in the American War of Independence. Under Kosciuszko the revolt took on something of the nationalist fervour that characterized Polish revolutionary activity throughout the nineteenth century. The peasants, promised their freedom, went into battle with scythes; and against all expectations they defeated the Russians at Raclawice.

Lacking help from outside, the revolt was nevertheless doomed to failure. Prussian troops arrived to support the Russians, and after a few months the redoubtable Suvorov took Warsaw. Kosciuszko was captured and later went into exile.

The failure of this gamble brought about the third partition that the Poles had striven to avoid: in 1795 Russia, Prussia and Austria completed the destruction of the Polish state.

The Ottoman decline

After 1700 the decay of the Ottoman Empire proceeded with seeming inevitability. The instability of authority at the centre, where seraglio intrigues continued to determine the fate of viziers, or prime ministers, (and sometimes of sultans), encouraged the ambitions of provincial governors and local warlords. In most of north Africa the sultan's authority became merely nominal, and from about 1750 to 1820 there were even semi-independent principalities in the Anatolian heartlands of the empire. The Balkan peoples grew uneasy under Turkish rule, and the Balkan bandit began to take on full heroic stature in legend and folklore.

Cultural and religious conservatism kept the empire backward, and maladministration, political disorder and epidemics made it poor. But what made eighteenth-century Ottoman stagnation more than an episode in the empire's history was the impact of the West, whose technological superiority was increasingly manifested in economic as well as military terms. Western factory products, especially western textiles, crippled the traditional handicraft industries, inhibited the growth of towns and perpetuated Levantine economic and technical inferiority.

It was hard for the Turks to learn from the West. They were by tradition a military race, and centuries of success in war appeared to justify contempt for commerce, administration, diplomacy and their Christian subjects. Intelligent Turks at least grasped the necessity of military reform; the unintelligent could not grasp even that. Several Turkish rulers attempted to refashion the army on western lines, but even the most sustained effort—made under Selim III (1789–1807)—achieved little against the opposition of the Janissaries and the protests of the faithful. Distrust of change had become ingrained.

This attitude might have been more difficult to sustain had the empire's international position declined more rapidly; but for most of the eighteenth century it was maintained with surprising success. The war of 1736–9 against Austria and Russia was, if anything, victorious: Azov was finally lost, but all the Balkan territories ceded at Passarowitz were recovered. Apart from a setback in Transcaucasia. Turkey held her own against her old eastern antagonist, Persia (also beginning to decline); and the long wars in Europe provided her with a breathing-space in the middle decades of the century.

The war of 1768–74, the loss of the Crimea and the war of 1787–92 revealed the full extent of Turkish weakness. They also revealed that the result of the 1736–9 war had not been fortuitous: Russia had replaced Austria as Turkey's main antagonist and, having occupied the northern shore of the Black Sea, was certain to attempt the penetration of the Balkans.

Two elements of the nineteenth-century 'Eastern Question' were now present in southeastern Europe: a decadent Turkey and an aggressive Russia. The diplomatic exertions of France on Turkey's behalf, and Austrian hostility to Russian gains in the Balkans, prefigured the jealousies and anxieties of the other powers, which were to complicate the Russo-Turkish conflict. It required only the eruption of Balkan nationalism in the nineteenth century to create a problem of European magnitude and labyrinthine complexity.

Above, Selim III, Sultan of Turkey (reigned 1789–1807), who tried to reform the Ottoman state along western lines, but was defeated by the conservatism of the Janissaries, who deposed, imprisoned and eventually assassinated him.

Opposite left, Stanislaus II of Poland (reigned 1764–95), who was put on the throne as a Russian puppet but who attempted to reform the Polish government and improve the condition of the peasantry. He was forced to abdicate after the third partition of Poland in 1795.

Opposite right, Tadeusz Kosciuszko (1746–1817), the Polish patriot who rebelled in 1794 against the second partition of Poland the previous year; after his defeat he went into exile in America, where he had earlier helped the colonies to win their independence from Britain.

Chapter 16

War and Diplomacy in eighteenth-century Europe

The period between the late seventeenth and late eighteenth centuries was one of diplomacy and warfare conducted without ideological passion. The wars of religious fanaticism had ended; the wars inspired by revolutionary or nationalistic ideologies had not yet begun. Before the French Revolution of 1789, diplomatic activity had a single motive: to advance the interests of the dynasty or state.

In this sense, eighteenth-century rulers were immoral or (more accurately) amoral. But the politics of self-interest do not necessarily cause more suffering than the politics of religion or idealism: and this was a period when self-interest in fact led to a diminution of the scope and intensity of warfare.

Most eighteenth-century wars were fought without antagonism and for limited objectives. The aggressor hoped to win a province; and if he was defeated he expected to pay with one. Monarchs respected one another's property, if only to avoid retaliation: towns were no longer sacked and soldiers were forbidden to loot and pillage. War became conventionalized—an occupation for professionals which for much of the time did not affect civilians. Trade between belligerents might well continue without interruption, and a gentleman could travel freely in a state with which his own was at war.

The bulk of almost every army was drawn from the dregs of the population, bribed or bullied into the ranks by recruiting sergeants. There were usually also large contingents of foreign mercenaries or soldiers conscripted in occupied territories. Such troops had to be endlessly drilled and savagely disciplined until they were more afraid of their officers than of the enemy. Naturally, when they got the chance, many of them deserted.

Desertion was a major problem for commanders, whose need constantly to supervise their own troops limited the striking power of their armies. Soldiers liable to desert could not be sent out in scouting parties, so information was inadequate. They could be deployed only in open country, so that freedom of manoeuvre was restricted and the line of advance irregular. Armies operating *en bloc* had to be supplied from large war magazines and could not

easily sustain long campaigns at a distance from their base area. Finally, large baggage-trains and poor communications further impeded rapidity of movement.

Even the greatest eighteenth-century commanders—Marlborough and Frederick the Great—only partly transcended these limitations. Decisive victories of the Napoleonic type, in which a mass national army penetrated deep into enemy territory, lived off the land and destroyed the opposing army with a single knockout blow, were unthinkable. Most wars involved long sieges, prolonged manoeuvring, set-piece battles and inefficient pursuit of a defeated enemy. In western Europe, defensive tactics were highly developed, and only minimal advantages were sought. Peace was generally made when one or both of the contestants were financially exhausted rather than defeated.

Diplomatic realities and illusions

Such conditions necessarily imposed limited aims; but statesmen did not always think so. The eighteenth century was a period of overelaborate and sometimes fantastic schemes: the improbable combination of Swedes, Jacobites and Spaniards projected by Charles XII's minister Goertz, the plans for dismembering France entertained by the Spanish queen, Elizabeth Farnese, and Charles VI of Austria, Panin's northern alliance, and Catherine's 'Greek project'.

In part, the prevalence of diplomatic fantasies resulted from uncertainty about the direction which European affairs were taking. Until the early decades of the eighteenth century, certain constant diplomatic factors had guided generations of rulers. The conflict between France and the Habsburgs had polarized European diplomacy for two centuries, offering other states the clear alternative of joining one side or

the other; and in eastern Europe, the struggle against the enemy of Christendom, Ottoman Turkey, was still older. Even the Swedish attempt to dominate the Baltic (and perhaps central and eastern Europe) dated back to the 1640s.

By 1713 the familiar patterns had begun to disappear. France, exhausted by Louis XIV's wars and ruled in turn by a pacific regent, a pacific minister and a feeble king (Louis XV), ceased to dominate Europe. With Spain no longer ruled by a Habsburg, and imperial power negligible, Austria became a mainly east-European power. The liberation of Hungary ended the Muslim threat to Christendom, and Turkey became more or less another member of the European state system. And at the battle of Poltava (1709). Sweden was once and for all destroyed as a great power by the armies of Peter the Great. The traditional alliances were no longer satisfactory, though it was more than half a century before they were abandoned. For at least a generation, Austria, Britain and Holland had combined to resist France, whose traditional allies were Sweden, Turkey and Poland. By 1748 the Dutch, like the Swedes and Turks, were no longer a force in Europe, while Britain and France were increasingly absorbed in a struggle for empire outside Europe. Even more important was the rise of two new states: Prussia, which rivalled Austria for primacy in Germany, and Russia, which established a virtual protectorate over France's old dependant, Poland.

The Franco-Austrian rapprochement of 1756 was the first drastic realignment prompted by the changed balance of forces. It was the prelude to an even greater change: the division of Europe into separate diplomatic spheres: the west, where Britain, France and Spain fought intermittently for colonies; and the east, where Russia, Prussia and Austria manoeuvred or combined to decide the fate of their weaker neighbours. Europe only became a single theatre of diplomacy and war with the French Revolution and its Napoleonic sequel.

The Peace of Utrecht

The War of the Spanish Succession (1701–13) was effectively ended by the Peace of Utrecht (1713). Its chief results were that France, though almost brought to her knees in the last years of the war, secured the Spanish throne for Louis XIV's grandson, who became Philip V; and that Spain lost all her European possessions, most of which were taken over by Austria. Thus Spain passed from the Habsburg family to the Bourbons, and Austria became the paramount power in Italy as well as acquiring the Spanish Netherlands. The Duke of Savoy gained Sicily and some territory in mainland Italy; and various other provisions were made to contain France and reward members of the anti-French coalition. Britain's gains were mainly colonial, but her retention of Gibraltar and Minorca increased her power in the Mediterranean and ensured future conflicts with Spain.

Peace-making and peace-keeping

In 1716 the Austrian armies under Eugene began a war against the Turks that culminated in the victorious peace of Passarowitz (1718). The most important event of 1716 was, however, the Anglo-French alliance, to which the Dutch also adhered (1717). Neither Britain's new Hanoverian king nor France's regent was entirely secure: and both countries were war-weary. They had a shared interest in maintaining European peace.

It was partly Anglo-French diplomacy that brought the Great Northern War (1700–21) to an end, though it did little to affect its outcome: Sweden ceded her eastern Baltic possessions to Russia and fell from the ranks of the great powers; Russia, as later became apparent, joined them.

Before the pacification of the Baltic had been completed, the western Mediterranean became the potential centre of a new European war. Under the direction of Elizabeth Farnese and her adviser, Alberoni, Spain attacked and captured Sardinia (1717) and Sicily (1718). The powers reacted swiftly. The emperor adhered to the British-French-Dutch system (Quadruple Alliance, 1718); and a few days later a British fleet defeated the Spaniards off Cape Pessaro. Philip was compelled to make terms by a French

invasion of Spain (1719). The immediate (and irrelevant) result of the crisis was that the Duke of Savoy was compelled to cede Sicily to the emperor in return for the poorer island of Sardinia, of which he became king. The self-imposed peace-keeping mission of France, Britain and Holland appeared to have succeeded.

In fact, nothing had been solved. Spain, fobbed off with promises of territory in Italy for Elizabeth Farnese's sons, remained dissatisfied. Charles VI of Austria, resenting his dependence on the maritime powers, attempted to get a share in overseas trade for Austria through his Ostend Company (1722). In 1725 Spain and Austria became allies—the outstanding geopolitical absurdity of a period marked by halfhearted attempts to adjust to changed conditions. Faced by a British-French-Prussian combination, Austria backed down. Spain fought a brief war against Britain (1727), unsuccessfully besieging Gibraltar, until French diplomatic pressure forced her to make peace. By the treaties of Seville (1729) and Vienna (1731), Elizabeth Farnese's son Charles became Duke of Parma and was recognized as heir to Tuscany. Charles VI abandoned the Ostend Company and collected British and Dutch guarantees of the Pragmatic Sanction, which had now become his chief diplomatic aim. The ultimate success of Spanish policy demonstrated that, in a period when the great powers were concerned to preserve peace, a second-class power could exploit its nuisance-value to make limits gains.

In the 1720s and 1730s British policy was directed by Walpole and French policy by Cardinal Fleury, men of similarly pacific outlook. While they stayed in control, Anglo-French relations remained good, though in the decade after 1731 Britain played little part in European affairs. The French war party, on the other hand, dragged the reluctant Fleury into yet another round of the Bourbon-Habsburg conflict.

The War of the Polish Succession

'War of the Polish Succession' is a misnomer for the conflict of 1733–5. France had no serious chance of opposing the Austro-Russian candidate, Augustus III; and she embarked on what was primarily a war against Austria in order to compensate herself for loss of influence in Poland.

The French overran Lorraine, but Italy, where France, Spain and Sardinia fought in alliance, was again the chief theatre of war. The Austrian armies suffered several defeats, and the peace terms were unfavourable to the Habsburgs. Stanislas Leszczynski, the unsuccessful French candidate for the Polish throne (and Louis XV's father-in-law), received Lorraine, which was to become French territory at his death; Francis of Lorraine, Maria Theresa's husband-to-be,

received Tuscany in compensation. Charles VI received Parma; Charles of Parma became ruler of Naples and Sicily. One major objective of Habsburg policy was achieved: France joined the other great powers in guaranteeing the Pragmatic Sanction.

The war was important for several reasons. Russia supplanted France in Poland; and in the virtual acquisition of Lorraine the French monarchy won its last great triumph before the Revolution. Franco-Spanish cooperation began an enduring pertnership that was geographically and dynastically appropriate—and, incidentally, the first permanent feature in European diplomacy since Utrecht. And the situation in Italy was stabilized: henceforward the south was to be ruled by a Bourbon dynasty and most of the north by Habsburgs. This arrangement too was sound and lasted without material alteration until the second half of the nineteenth century.

The War of the Austrian Succession

In the Turkish war of 1736–9 Austria lost all the territory outside Hungary that she had gained at Passarowitz, whereas her Russian ally was at least nominally victorious. The most serious aspect of this reverse was that Austrian weakness was revealed at a moment of dynastic crisis. The accession of Maria Theresa, Frederick the Great's invasion of Silesia, the invasion of Bohemia by a 'Bavarian' (in fact Franco-Bavarian) army and Spanish attacks on Habsburg possessions in Italy seemed to prefigure the disintegration of the empire. Austria's only ally, Russia, was paralysed by the crisis attendant on Elizabeth's accession and the simultaneous Russo-Swedish war. Even the German imperial crown was lost, for in January 1742 Charles

Albert of Bavaria was elected Holy Roman emperor—the first non-Habsburg to sit on the throne since 1438.

Then Austrian fortunes revived. Frederick the Great agreed to a brief truce (October 1741) which enabled him to occupy the rest of Silesia while the Austrian army rallied to defend Bohemia. Britain helped Maria Theresa with subsidies and began to form an auxiliary 'Pragmatic army'. In 1742 Prussia inflicted heavy defeats on Austria but made peace in return for Silesia, while the French and Bavarians were driven from Bohemia with heavy losses and Bavaria was occupied by Austrian troops.

In real terms this ended the War of the Austrian Succession. The Austrian monarchy was saved and Silesia lost; and what followed was a futile European war on the old pattern. Ties between Britain and Austria were strengthened, and in 1743 the Pragmatic army under George II defeated the French at Dettingen. In 1744 France declared war on Britain, entering the Anglo-Spanish colonial war that had been in progress since 1739. She also declared war officially on Austria and invaded the Austrian Netherlands. Frederick the Great, alarmed by Austrian successes, re-entered the war (1744–5) long enough to obstruct an Austrian invasion of France and then left it for good, still holding Silesia. In 1745 the French, under Maurice de Saxe, won the great Battle of Fontenoy over the British, Austrians and Dutch and in the next two years overran the Austrian Netherlands and part of Holland. Fontenoy was to be the military counterpart of the acquisition of Lorraine—the last great victory of pre-Revolutionary French arms but for the moment it seemed as if France was again 'the great nation' in Europe.

Faction and financial difficulties hampered the diplomatic exploitation of French victories; and France, like most of the other combatants, lacked intelligible war aims. When peace was at last made, at Aix-la-Chapelle (1748), it was on the basis of a restoration of all conquests. European or colonial. The imperial crown had already returned to Habsburg control on the election of Francis of Lorraine as Holy Roman emperor (1745). The only gainers at the peace were Elizabeth Farnese's second son, Philip, who became Duke of Parma, and the King of Sardinia, who was rewarded with territory for helping Maria Theresa.

All the same, the war registered important changes in the European situation. The Dutch were clearly no longer a great power. The emergence of Prussia signified that European wars would never again assume the aspect of straightforward Austro-French struggles for supremacy in Germany, Finally, the renewal of Anglo-French antagonism, based on commercial and colonial rivalry, became a permanent feature of European diplomacy until the end of the Napoleonic Wars.

Kaunitz made the decisive break with

diplomatic tradition. He initiated negotiations for an Austrian alliance with France. The French were sympathetic towards the idea of an understanding that would leave them free to concentrate on the unfolding colonial struggle against Britain but for that very reason were unwilling to participate in an Austro-Russian attack on Prussia.

Agreement was precipitated by a series of misunderstandings and miscalculations. A subsidy treaty between Britain and Russia (1755) convinced Frederick II that he should himself reach an accommodation with Britain. By the Convention of Westminster (January 1756) Prussia and Britain agreed to neutralize Germany: foreign troops were to be kept out and peace maintained. Frederick protested that the Convention did not affect the Franco-Prussian alliance, but Louis XV and his ministers regarded Frederick's action as the blackest treachery. Elizabeth of Russia, who had viewed the treaty of 1755 as a preliminary to attacking Prussia, was equally angry with Britain, and egged on Austria to bring France into an anti-Prussian coalition. As a result, France hurriedly concluded the first treaty of Versailles with Austria (May 1756). The diplomatic revolution had taken place.

The treaty was only a defensive one, however: each party agreed to help the other if attacked in Europe—a provision that kept Austria out of the Anglo-French colonial war, which had already begun (1755), but gave France the continental security she needed in order to win it. That, at least, was France's position in May 1756. Whether Austria could have tempted her into an aggressive war against Prussia remains in doubt; for Frederick, obsessed by the spectre of a French-Austrian-Russian coalition, determined to launch a preventive war. His attack on Saxony activated the defensive alliance between France and Austria and brought into being the coalition that he dreaded most of all.

The Seven Years War

The central drama of the Seven Years War in Europe was Prussia's fight to survive against the armies of Austria, Russia, Sweden and the German states, which has been sketched out in the section describing Frederick the Great's career. There were a number of reasons for the failure of the anti-Prussian coalition: Frederick's meticulous preparation, military genius, ruthlessness, resourcefulness and luck; suspicion and lack of coordination between his enemies, the Austrian preference for titles rather than talent in commanders; Russian slowness in mobilizing and intervening (1758); and, possibly decisive, the change of ruler that took Russia out of the war in 1762.

It is unlikely that Frederick could have survived until 1762 if France had been able to add her weight to the coalition. In this respect Frederick's British alliance proved invaluable. Under the elder William Pitt, Britain subsidized Frederick and undertook a holding operation in western Europe. From the British point of view the object was to frustrate a French victory in Europe and thereby prevent France from concentrating her resources on the colonial struggle. In pursuance of this policy, regular naval-cum-military attacks were made on the French coast; but Frederick's effective

Above, the Battle of Fontenoy in 1745 at which the French Count de Saxe defeated the British in the War of the Austrian Succession; such battles had little effect on the economies or fortunes of the nations concerned, beyond the territorial ambitions of their rulers. Château de Versailles.

Opposite, Stanislaus I of Poland (reigned 1704–09; 1733–35). who relied for his throne on Swedish support during the Northern War and regained his throne with French help in the 1730s; Poland, though a sovereign state, was never independent from foreign interference in the eighteenth century.

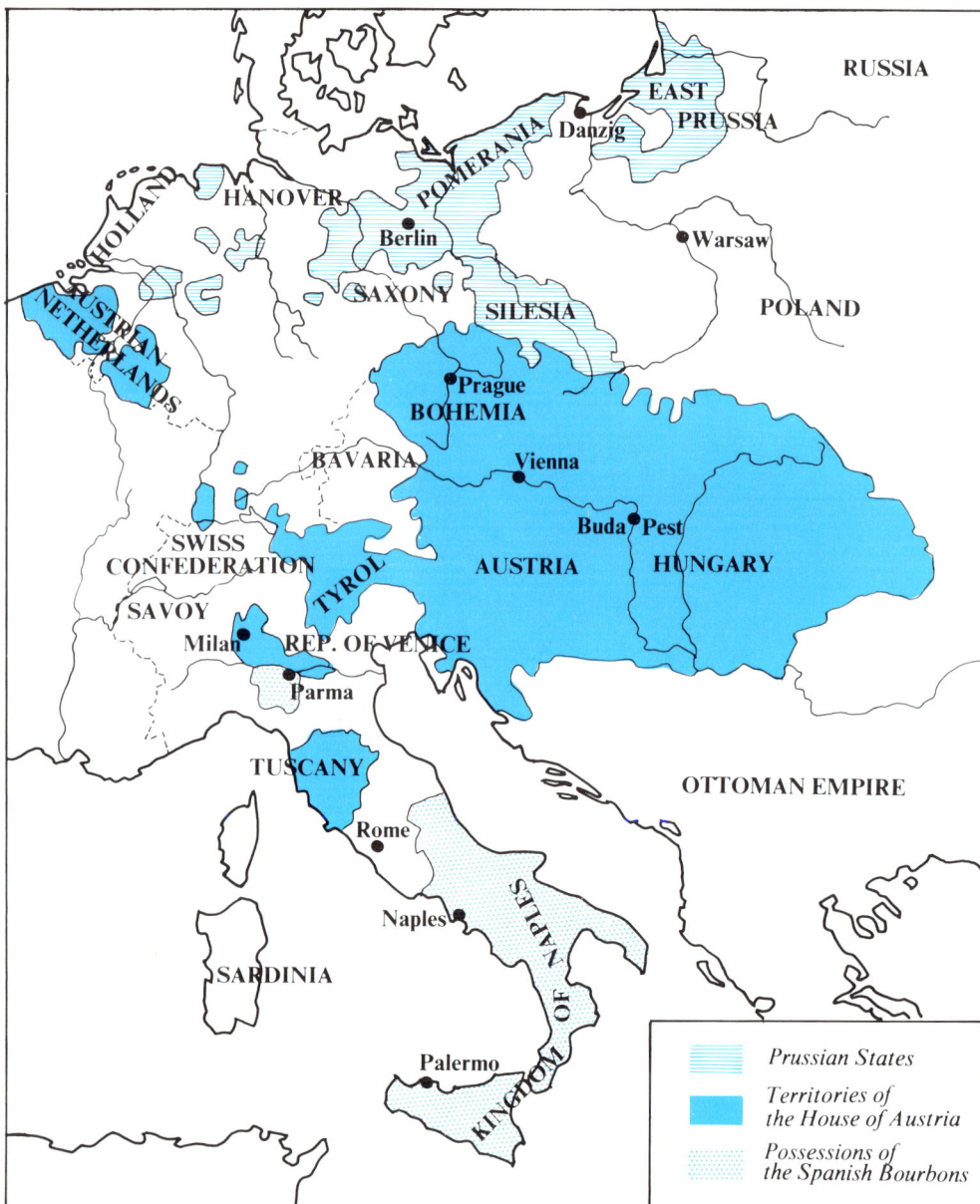

RUSSIA

EAST PRUSSIA

Danzig

POMERANIA

HANOVER

HOLLAND

Berlin

Warsaw

SAXONY

SILESIA

POLAND

AUSTRIAN NETHERLANDS

Prague
BOHEMIA

BAVARIA

Vienna

Buda Pest

SWISS CONFEDERATION

TYROL

AUSTRIA

HUNGARY

SAVOY

Milan

REP. OF VENICE

Parma

OTTOMAN EMPIRE

TUSCANY

Rome

Naples

SARDINIA

KINGDOM OF NAPLES

Palermo

Prussian States

Territories of
the House of Austria

Possessions of
the Spanish Bourbons

protection was the mixed army of British, Hanoverian and hired German troops maintained by Britain in western Germany. After his victory at Rossbach (1757), Frederick never had to face a French army; the French were contained and even defeated at Crefeld (1758) and Minden (1759) by the Anglo-German force under the command of Ferdinand of Brunswick.

British policy was triumphantly successful. By 1759 France was compelled to reduce her subsidies and other commitments to Austria, while British naval and colonial victories multiplied. The 'Family Compact' between France and Spain led to Spain's entry into the war against Britain (1762) but failed to shake British maritime supremacy. The war overseas was ended by the Peace of Paris (1763), and French withdrawal from the European war, following upon that of Russia, left Austria no alternative but to make peace with Prussia at Hubertusburg (1763). Britain's colonial gains were substantial; continental Europe, after seven years of exhausting struggle, remained as it had been before the war.

Two diplomacies

After 1763, France remained in close alliance with Spain and more loosely connected with Austria; but she carefully avoided continental entanglements. Lorraine became French in 1766, and France bought a rebellious Corsica from Genoa in 1768; for the rest, she bided her time until she could revenge herself on Britain. Britain, shunned by Frederick, was unable to find a continental partner. Though they were not always fully conscious of the fact, the western European powers had few interests and no influence in central and eastern Europe.

Russia, Prussia and Austria were equally preoccupied. The Prusso-Russian alliance (1764) operated to maintain the Polish and Swedish constitutions until the question of the dissenters embroiled Russia in Poland and led her into war with Turkey. While Gustavus III seized the opportunity to re-establish absolutism in Sweden, Austrian hostility forced Russia to forego gains in the Balkans and, with the connivance of Frederick the Great, led on to a three-way reconciliation based on the partition of Poland (1772). Russia was left free to make a highly advantageous peace with the Turks at Kutchuk-Kainardji (1774).

In the west, the American War of Independence (1775–83) enabled France and Spain, at last unhindered by continental commitments, to take their revenge on Britain. The thirteen colonies became independent, and Britain ceded some of her colonies to France and Spain. In Europe, the British navy was defeated in the Mediterranean and Minorca was lost; but a Franco-Spanish force failed to capture Gibraltar. The other powers were not involved, though Catherine II organized the League of Armed Neutrality (1780) to

oppose the British practice of searching neutral vessels on the high seas.

The resurrection of Austrian ambitions in central Europe prompted France to diplomatic if not military activity. Austrian claims to Bavaria provoked a brief and half-hearted Austro-Prussian war (1778–9) and aroused the hostility of France, which had no wish to see the Austrian border expand westwards. Completely isolated, Austria was forced to back down.

Joseph II continued the Austrian forward policy and, since Prussian hostility was inevitable and French friendship had been found wanting, allied with Russia (1781). But whereas Joseph wanted Russian backing in central Europe, Catherine viewed Austria as an ally against the Turks. Catherine got the best of the bargain: Austrian diplomatic pressure enabled Russia to annex the Crimea without difficulty (1783), but Russian help for Austria never went beyond verbal support. Joseph failed to compel Dutch agreement to the opening of the Scheldt and was equally unsuccessful in his scheme to exchange the Austrian Netherlands for Bavaria. France opposed both schemes, and Frederick the Great was able to crown his career by organizing a League of German Princes (1785) which effectively quashed the Bavarian project.

Into the age of revolutions

In the late 1780s two of the great powers were in a state of collapse. France was paralysed by the chronic financial difficulties of the crown and the violent opposition of the privileged classes to any kind of reform, Austria by military disaster against the Turks and rebellions in Hungary and the Austrian Netherlands.

The other powers took surprisingly little advantage of this situation, though Prussia, backed by Britain, did break the pro-French party in Holland (1787), which then joined a Prusso-British alliance (1788). Surprisingly Prussia let slip the opportunity of crippling or even destroying Austria, and Leopold II was able to make peace with the Turks and put his house in order.

Russia brought her war with the Turks (1787–92) to a victorious conclusion, despite a Swedish declaration of war. The hostility of other powers towards the Russian advance proved ineffective. Britain's prime minister, the younger Pitt, protested at the Russian seizure of Ochakov, thought about sending an ultimatum and then changed his mind. Eastern Europe remained the preserve of Russia, Prussia and Austria, with Russia very much the leader.

This was confirmed by the second and third partitions of Poland, the most enduring effect of which was to make the three great eastern powers partners in crime. Whatever their differences, they had a shared interest in holding down the Poles. The post-Napoleonic Holy Alliance was already prefigured and was to last in one form or another until the late nineteenth century. So, as we have seen, was the Eastern Question, posed by the decline of Turkey.

Elsewhere in Europe, diplomacy was dominated by a new phenomenon—the French Revolution, which ushered in a new age of ideological conflicts, created new diplomatic patterns and, in power-political terms, enabled France to reorganize her resources and resume her primacy in Europe.

Chapter 17

England in the Eighteenth Century

The eighteenth century saw the culmination of the great Anglo-French struggle for colonial empire. The outcome was profoundly affected by the domestic history of each country during the same period. France had undoubtedly greater resources, and both nations saw a large influx of commercial wealth. But whereas the British adapted their institutions to utilize such riches, the French were continually straining within the archaic straitjacket of the *ancien régime*. The result was that the most remarkable event of the century in each country was a revolution, but whereas the British upheaval was industrial that of the French was political. The French Revolution ultimately released the long-constrained energies of that nation, but by 1789 Britain had already won the duel for empire and had established an ever-growing hegemony of the world outside Europe.

The Glorious Revolution

On 5 November 1688 William of Orange landed in England, and a month and a half later King James II wisely fled the country. An observer of the time might have thought these occurrences were typical of the English. For over a generation, England had appeared to be one of the most unstable states in Europe. One king had been executed and another driven from his throne. The country had lurched wildly from monarchy to republic and back to monarchy again. A great civil war had been fought. It was anything but clear in 1688 that this chaotic phase was over, but it had in fact passed for ever. The next era would be one of great political stability compared with other nations. During this period, the English would show a positive genius for the creation and sensible use of their national wealth. Internal peace and orderly government would allow the nation to develop commerce, extend its empire and defeat its largest imperial rival, France. The wealth so accumulated would then be ploughed into manufacturing to create the Industrial Revolution. Thus England would eventually transform the world in a way that no single nation has ever done again.

The English accepted their new ruler with some misgiving. Though a Protestant the lean and tubercular Dutchman was not much more attractive personally than his predecessor. The best thing about him was his wife Mary, who at least was of pure Stuart lineage. They were to reign together as William III and Mary II.

As it was felt necessary to bridle somewhat the powers of the monarchy, the two new rulers did not ascend the throne without conditions. Before their arrival, a convention had met and produced a declaration of rights which was later converted into the Bill of Rights. By this it was maintained that parliament should be called frequently, while William was deprived of the power to maintain a standing army in time of peace on his own authority.

To all this the king agreed. Of course his freedom of action was somewhat limited, but then so was his interest. William was a constructive monomaniac. The sole driving passion of his life was his hatred of France. But at least this was not simply an empty obsession, rather he saw more clearly than others the magnitude of the threat to Europe of French hegemony. For aid against France he was willing to sacrifice some of his powers as a domestic monarch.

So England entered the War of the League of Augsburg which was waged until 1697. Despite few victories and many defeats, the great confederacy of European nations that William had scraped together was ultimately successful in curbing the expansionist activities of Louis XIV. Yet Englishmen at home became dissatisfied. They did not see the need for the fighting in quite the same lucid clarity as did their leader, and it certainly brought little in the way of glory. True, William decisively trounced James II in the Battle of the Boyne when the latter landed in Ireland, but the country was beginning to get restive.

William did little to counteract the growing mood of disenchantment with himself. Though he was willing perforce to share some of his power with parliament, he did his best to avoid placing much of it in the hands of a single political party. This annoyed the Whigs, who had done most to bring him to power. Between 1694 and 1698, in control of parliament, they forced themselves upon him, but their own avarice for power and place soon made them much disliked, while the king's popularity also continued to decline, especially after the death of Queen Mary in 1694.

More and more, politics fell into a state of confusion, and more and more political leaders began opening up secret correspondence with James, 'the king across the water'. By the time of the election of 1698, James II was hoping to return to his country not by conquest but as a result of dutiful recall by his loyal subjects. The election itself brought heavy gains for the Tories, led by the shrewd and devious Robert Harley, and these were pushed further in the election of 1700. Then, as the House of Commons became more resolutely hostile to the king, the succession problem created yet another crisis. William and Mary had left no offspring, and all the many children of the heir apparent, the Princess Anne, had died. This necessitated an Act of Settlement, which stated that in the event of both William and Anne dying without heirs the throne was to pass to a member of the Protestant ruling family in Hanover, which was related to the Stuart house by marriage.

Meanwhile, in Europe, the dynastic ambitions of Louis XIV and the imbecility of the dying King Charles II of Spain had created a situation which raised the spectre of a future in which the mighty empires of both France and Spain would be ruled by a single monarch. In order to forestall this, William began laboriously to construct a new grand alliance, which was completed in September of 1701. In England the idea of a new war brought great consternation, but Louis XIV managed to play directly into the hands of his enemies. When James II died a few days after the alliance was negotiated, Louis stupidly recognized James' son, the 'Old Pretender' as King James III of England. This ended divisions in the country completely. And when William III died a few months later, the country cheerfully embarked on the war he had begun under the leadership of its new sovereign, Anne, and her general, John Churchill, Duke of Marlborough.

War costs money. Between 1688 and 1815, England was to fight no less than five colossal wars with her great enemy, France. The ultimate success of the British was owing in no small measure to the fact that in the very first of these conflicts they developed sophisticated methods of finance. King William's War of the Grand Alliance placed immense strains on the nation, but British business proved equal to the occasion. The most important expedient devised was the Bank of England. The new bank raised £1,200,000 from the public in twelve days and loaned it to the government at eight percent. So long as the interest was paid annually, the original loan was allowed to remain, and thus the National Debt came into being. The bank was incorporated and allowed to issue notes, although not at first as legal tender. Despite an early run on it, and a moratorium, the bank survived, prospered and was able to declare a dividend of twenty percent after the war. It proved to be one of the most important steps in England's march to world empire.

Whigs and Tories

The reign of the homely and rather inept Queen Anne was both enhanced and dominated by the War of the Spanish Succession, marked by the incomparable victories of the Duke of Marlborough. During the period domestic policies were noted for strife between the Whigs and the Tories, which

rose and fell in bitterness erratically, reflecting the fortunes of the war itself. At the beginning, however, the nation was united and led by a coalition government headed by the two great non-party ministers, Lord Godolphin and Marlborough himself. Behind the scenes the queen was greatly influenced by her intense friendship with the Whiggish Sarah, Duchess of Marlborough, though Anne's own bias lay towards the Tories, principally because of her love of the Church of England in its High Church form.

It did not take long for the early harmony to disappear, and discord erupted between the Tory-controlled House of Commons and the Whig-controlled House of Lords as early as 1702.

The high Tories now became more and more critical of the conduct of the war, but this proved to be a disastrously wrong move. Soon the Duke of Marlborough was winning victories of greater magnitude than the English had enjoyed for over a hundred years. The country was swept with patriotic ardour, and in the election of 1705 both the Whigs and a group of Tories—led by the too-clever Harley—who supported the ministry made substantial gains. For the next four years the Whigs steadily increased their position but at the same time managed thoroughly to overplay their hand. Their arrogant pursuit of power alienated the queen, who was also beginning to tire of the Duchess of Marlborough. In 1707 Abigail Masham, a relative of Harley's, began to replace Sarah in Anne's favour. This lured Harley himself into making a premature coup to secure the dismissal of Lord Godolphin. But Marlborough's threat of resignation temporarily ended the matter, and it was Harley himself who resigned.

Nevertheless, 1709 saw the beginning of the Whig downfall. In November, a controversy over the sermon of one Dr Sacheverell led many people, including the queen herself, to feel that Godolphin and the ministry were attacking the Church. Moreover, dissatisfaction with the seemingly interminable war was now rapidly increasing. Finally, the friendship between the queen and the Duchess of Marlborough broke down completely. In 1710 Robert Harley persuaded Anne to turn out Godolphin himself. The elections held later in the year resulted in a huge Tory majority.

Above, the Duke of Marlborough at the Battle of Malplaquet in 1709; despite this and other victories, Marlborough was not able to finish the war decisively and its expense gave rise to a strong Tory opposition. National Army Museum, London.

Top, Blenheim Palace in Oxfordshire, built by John Vanbrugh in the early eighteenth century and given to the Duke of Marlborough by the English nation in gratitude for his military services against Louis XIV.

Shortly afterwards even Marlborough was curtly dismissed, and the greatest English military hero since the Middle Ages retired to Holland. Anti-war feeling was sweeping the country, and the queen now created twelve Tory peers, to give that party control of both Houses of Parliament. After long negotiations, the Peace of Utrecht was signed in April 1713.

Yet the Tory triumph was to be a brief one. In December 1713 the queen became seriously ill and this raised the vexing problem of succession. Many Tories would have preferred to see James Stuart, the 'Old Pretender', called to the throne, and a leader of this group, the young Viscount Bolingbroke, secured the overthrow of Harley, now Earl of Oxford, on 27 July 1714. But instead of power going to Bolingbroke himself, it fell to the enigmatic Duke of Shrewsbury, a moderate Tory who gave the casting vote in support of the Hanoverian succession on the very day before Queen Anne died on 1 August.

One important aspect of her reign remains to be mentioned. The dead queen had begun by ruling over two nations and had ended by reigning over one. It had long been obvious that England and Scotland, separate kingdoms although ruled by the same monarch, must move either further apart or closer together. The English had been worried over Scottish loyalty, the Scots attracted by opportunities of participating in England's colonial empire. So, after some serious bargaining, the Scots gave up their own parliament and agreed to the Hanoverian succession. On 1 May 1707 the Act of Union was settled, and both Scotland and England merged into the United Kingdom of Great Britain.

George I

George Lewis, Elector of Hanover, the gross, concupiscent and somewhat vicious man who had become king of Great Britain, arrived in the country in September 1714. His reign was to mark something of a decline in the effective powers of the monarchy. It was not that any constitutional changes took place or that the new king was uninterested in British politics. But he was absent in Hanover for long periods, and he did not have the mentality to grasp the structure of the British system sufficiently to manipulate it. His accession to power, however, was remarkably uneventful, owing to the good management of Shrewsbury.

One thing that became rapidly clear was that the day of the Tories was over. Those who had any dealing with the Stuarts were brutally snubbed; even those who had not, like Shrewsbury, soon faded away. The Tory downfall was completed when Bolingbroke and the Duke of Ormonde fled to France and joined the court of the Old Pretender. This resulted in the abortive and mismanaged Scottish rebellion of 1715, after which most Tories seemed tainted with Jacobitism.

The hour of the Whigs had therefore arrived and was soon confirmed by their resounding election victory in 1715. Who would lead them? The man who quickly shouldered his way to the top was Marlborough's former general, Lord Stanhope. Stanhope's principal policy was to restore Britain's proper position in Europe after the diplomatic isolation which had arisen from the Peace of Utrecht, when Harley's Tory administration had abandoned the nation's allies in its indecent haste to end the war. In the next six years Stanhope worked towards this end, conducting a brilliant diplomacy.

But dissensions soon appeared within the Whig Party itself. Robert Walpole, the able chancellor of the exchequer, backed by Viscount Townshend, was intent on economy. The Earl of Sunderland supported Stanhope, whose diplomacy, with its expensive subsidies to various continental nations, was costly. The two factions had more or less fought each other to a draw when the whole country was rocked by the famous South Sea Bubble crisis. In 1720 the South Sea Company came up with a plausible proposal to take over the whole of the National Debt on remarkably favourable terms. This was eagerly accepted by Sunderland and resulted in a wild rise in the value of the company's shares, which had increased by 1,000 per cent in August of 1720. Then the inevitable reaction set in; the shares slumped, and thousands of people were ruined. A storm of indignation broke over the government, with charges of bribery and corruption. Walpole, who had earlier established public financial confidence with a sinking fund, was hastily called in to save the situation. He did his work well. By December 1720 parliament had accepted his schemes for reform and Walpole's prestige rose immensely. Then, at the same juncture, his rivals miraculously disappeared. Stanhope dropped dead during a debate in the House of Lords, and Sunderland, too, died shortly afterwards. Walpole and Townshend emerged supreme. The result was to be forty years of remarkably stable government.

Walpole and the supremacy of the Whigs

Robert Walpole was a man of great ability and a remarkable judge of character. He was also very greedy. Yet the greed of the new 'prime minister' (as Walpole was coming to be called)—especially his greed for power —would ultimately be to the nation's benefit, for Walpole wished to exercise his power in the directions in which he was most talented—those of finance and of building commercial prosperity. Fortunately, there was possibly no period in Britain's history when such talents could

bring greater national rewards.

It has been said that Sir Robert could never brook a rival and surrounded himself with mediocrities. This assertion is only half true. Certainly, he eliminated his rivals. Together, Walpole and Townshend managed to outmanoeuvre Lord Carteret, the last and most brilliant leader of Stanhope's faction, and edge him out of the government. But even Townshend, Walpole's brother-in-law and confederate, was deemed too much of a threat and was forced to resign in 1730. On the other hand, Walpole's 'friends'—Harrington, Hardwicke and especially the brothers Pelham, Henry and Thomas, Duke of Newcastle—were scarcely nonentities. Rather they were formidable men, but with limited capacity for leadership. Therefore they could greatly assist Walpole but were unable to challenge his own position until he was greatly past his prime.

Nevertheless, although Walpole swiftly emasculated his rivals, a strong opposition of Tories and discontented Whigs always dogged his footsteps. To these were eventually added the formidable talents of Bolingbroke, who had finally forsaken his Jacobitism and returned to England. Yet, for all of this, Walpole was able to keep his position intact for nearly twenty years. Not only did he usually have a parliamentary majority in his pocket but he also had the support of the monarchs. George I came to rely upon him; so did George II, while the latter's wife, Queen Caroline, proved to be the staunchest of all his many adherents.

Walpole also played parliament and Crown off against each other. The usually sound majority for Walpole in parliament was really the creation of the Duke of Newcastle. Newcastle was a dithering, eccentric and neurotic man, who lived in a state of constant agitation, often bordering on panic. But he possessed shrewd common

sense and made political patronage into a fine art. He was the man who knew everybody in all the constituencies, understood where money was to be applied in order to win elections and forced every civil servant in however minor a position to support the government with his votes and influence or forfeit his job. Even so, Walpole's hold on parliament sometimes failed, and on these occasions he was quite willing to use against it the considerable powers of the Crown—powers which George II did not have the skill to use in his own right.

Thus was set the pattern of politics for a long time to come. A Whig government, consistently but impotently opposed by the Tories, but occasionally in danger from other Whig factions which rose and fell around outstanding personalities and orators. Of course, parliament was the old unreformed parliament in which the House of Commons suffered from a proliferation of 'pocket boroughs', where the electorate was controlled by some landed magnate, and of 'rotten boroughs' which returned members although the constituencies contained no real electorate. It represented the lower classes hardly at all and even the upper classes most unevenly. Nor did representation even remotely relate to distribution of population. Yet, despite its peculiar nature, the British legislature was far more responsive to the wishes of the nation as a whole than that of any other European country. When Britain fell on more evil days in the reign of George III, a demand arose to reform its basic institutions; but in the mid-eighteenth century parliament's prestige was high, perhaps the highest it has ever been.

Under Walpole, the system certainly managed to work to the nation's benefit. Striving to maintain peace abroad, in domestic affairs he reformed the system of taxation, reduced the National Debt and

Above, George II (reigned 1727–60); he was a strong supporter of Walpole's government. National Portrait Galley, London.

Top, the Battle of Culloden in 1746, at which the English destroyed the supporters of Bonnie Prince Charlie and which led to permanent Scottish subjugation to English rule.

Top left, Robert Walpole (1676–1742), the leader of the Whigs in parliament and the king's first minister between 1721 and 1742. His control over the government was exerted through a cabinet of colleagues and relied more on his power in parliament than on the support of the king. National Portrait Gallery, London.

Opposite left, Queen Anne (reigned 1702–14) accepting the Articles of Union of the kingdoms of Scotland and England in 1707.

Opposite right, George I of England (reigned 1714–27), also Elector of Hanover, made king according to the Act of Settlement which was intended to bar the Stuarts from the throne. George himself was scarcely interested in England, but his Protestantism made him acceptable to most, and the Tory party, which supported the Stuarts, was eclipsed on his accession. Royal Collection.

increased commercial prosperity. He did suffer some defeats, notably his failure to impose an excise tax in 1733, but on the whole his long ministry succeeded in transforming the national outlook. By the time he retired, the political realities of the not so distant past—religious controversies, battle to the death between Whigs and Tories, the putting up and the casting down of kings, the possibility of great civil wars—seemed like memories of a bygone age. Perhaps the greatest tribute to his ministry occurred in the year of his death, when Charles Edward Stuart, the 'Young Pretender' landed in Scotland in the hope of capturing the throne for his father. Backward Scottish Highlanders would rally in numbers to the romantic banners of Bonnie Prince Charlie; the English would have none of him—to them he represented danger and the return of pointless strife.

After 1733 it became increasingly clear that Walpole's power was declining. With growing age, he began to lose his grip, and at the same time his enemies were waxing stronger. Eventually, even Walpole's friends were beginning to have their doubts. The crisis came in 1739 with the outbreak of the War of Jenkin's Ear against Spain. Walpole wished to avoid it, but the nation's mood was strongly bellicose and he was pushed aside.

Sir Robert's departure was followed by some turmoil. The brilliant Carteret succeeded him, but the miseries and failures of the war increased and Carteret, too, was turned out of office.

Yet no sooner had Carteret been removed than the nation had to reckon with rebellion and invasion. In 1745 Bonnie Prince Charlie landed in Scotland; the Highlands rallied to him and he had soon captured Edinburgh. But the 'Forty-five' was a forlorn hope without English support and this was not forthcoming. The invasion of England failed and King George's son, the Duke of Cumberland, slaughtered the Scottish army in the Battle of Culloden. The Highlands were ruthlessly scourged and subdued, and Charles Edward fled the country never to return again.

Meanwhile, Walpole's friends were re-establishing their power, and Henry Pelham, a sort of diminutive Walpole, now stepped firmly into the shoes of his great predecessor. It was natural that the Pelhams should wish to carry on Walpole's system, but one might wonder why the nation would want such uninspired leadership. Walpole's government without Walpole somewhat resembled an orchestra without a conductor. Yet somehow the brilliant alternatives to him in the House of Commons seemed dangerous. The orchestra, therefore, was willing to try to continue under the leader, so to speak, and Henry Pelham provided a sound, if dull, administration until his death in 1754, and then Newcastle himself carried on. But colonial conflicts

were already beginning to involve the country in yet another war. And when that, too, began to go badly, the foundations of the old system began to shake. It was then that the king called William Pitt to take command.

Methodism

John Wesley was born in 1703, the son of a Church of England clergyman. Oppressed by a deep sense of sin, he entered the Church himself but found little solace there until 1738, when he underwent a deep mystical experience. From this he emerged preaching the necessity of every individual to attain a personal and highly emotional relationship with Jesus Christ, his Saviour. Wesley never intended to break from the Established Church but hoped to transform it. The Church, however, resisted him bitterly, and connections were finally severed in 1784.

In the intervening years, Wesley had uncovered a dark facet of English life which had remained unremarked. Following its victory over the Puritans, the Church of England had more and more lost contact with the lower classes of the nation. The souls of the ordinary people were truly a house swept and garnished and now dominated by a massive purposelessness which so often found its outlet in gambling, cheap gin and in the more brutal sports of the day, such as cock-fighting and bear-baiting.

Preaching a violent mixture of damnation and salvation, the Wesleyan movement swept through England and indeed on to America. The Methodists were drawn from the poor but were extremely well organized, and in fact Wesley had without knowing it constructed a machine of great revolutionary potential. But it was not to be used for revolutionary purposes; Wesley had no wish to overthrow existing institutions. Nevertheless by the time he died Wesley and his God had enabled hundreds of thousands of people to find a vital core of meaning to their existence which had been lacking hitherto.

Wesleyan Methodism was but one of the illustrations of the growth and ferment in

Above, a cartoon of gamblers in The Hazard Room by Thomas Rowlandson (1756–1827), done in about 1729. Victoria and Albert Museum, London.

Left, a cartoon of stockjobbers by William Hogarth (1697–1764); the early eighteenth century was an age of commercial investment and saw several scandals, such as the South Sea Bubble in 1720. Guildhall Art Gallery, London.

Opposite, John Wesley (1703–91), the English evangelical preacher. He was opposed by the Church of England and set up the Methodist Church, gaining widespread support in the industrial regions of the north and of Wales. National Portrait Gallery, London.

the society that lay behind the stately facade of Georgian politics. From about 5,500,000 at the beginning of the century, the population of the country had risen to about 9,000,000 at the end. Throughout the century the majority of the people remained rural, but London, the largest city in Europe, doubled its population to over a million in the same period. Similarly, the seaport towns of Bristol and Liverpool began their remarkable rise in size and prosperity with the growth of colonial commerce, especially the slave trade. Moreover, the face of the land was changing and more people were being driven to the towns. New ideas about agriculture and stock raising led to much larger farms; commons and waste lands were enclosed, and many small farmers were forced to become agricultural labourers or to seek different work in the towns.

There was also much influx and change on the intellectual scene. Sir Isaac Newton, the nation's greatest scientist, died in 1727 after profoundly changing the whole of man's picture of the universe. Locke, Hume, Gibbon and Adam Smith extended the fields of philosophy, history and political economy. The fine arts boasted a galaxy of great names from Reynolds to Hogarth. Literature enjoyed a splendid age, and the century that opened with the acerbic satire of Swift and Pope closed as Jane Austen was beginning to write.

Behind all this lay the rising wealth of the commercial revolution which preceded the industrial one. Commerce in eighteenth-century England laboured under many hindrances, but from Walpole onwards England was blessed by a series of governments that put the increase of the nation's wealth before everything else. This dominance of the profit motive affected everything— commerce itself, agriculture, industry and also the institution of war.

Throughout the first half of the century agriculture and industry were moderately prosperous. They would become more so once it was demonstrated how more money could be made from them. For the moment, however, the best investment was trade and commerce, and it was there that the national energies were directed. Britain's trade was

increasingly colonial. The mercantile system had apparently paid off; the East India Company, the great consumer market in America, the African slave trade, above all, the sugar, rum and molasses trade of the West Indies—these all filled the nation's coffers.

Commerce also greatly affected British warfare. In an old Scottish folk song the English commander, Sir John Cope, challenged Bonnie Prince Charlie to battle with the words: 'I'll larn you the arts o' war.' On this occasion, Sir John was swiftly defeated. Nevertheless, despite this and dozens of other exceptions, Britain had a great deal to teach the Continental dynasts (of whom Charles Edward Stuart was a representative) about methods of waging war in the mercantile age. Of course the country was helped by its insular position, which meant that more concentration could be placed on the navy than on the army. Armies were expensive and their officers often incompetent. The navy was also expensive, but its value in relation to the greatest single producer of wealth that Britain had—the merchant marine—was indisputable. Britain could let other nations fight on the continent, while her navy swept

the commerce of her enemies from the sea and gobbled up their colonies. Of course, all this required qualities of leadership in which British governments were often sadly lacking. But when good management was available, as when the elder Pitt was directing affairs, half the world could be brought within Britain's grasp.

Pitt and George III

The political upheaval which marked the end of the long era of Walpole-Pelham domination is associated with the names of two men—William Pitt the Elder and George III. These two had much in common; both were naively idealistic, both hated parties and party politics; Pitt was mentally ill, and in the king's later days his mental faculties were gravely impaired.

Pitt, the member of a family which had made its fortune in the East India trade, naturally thought in commercial and colonial terms. He saw clearly that it was by concentrating on these spheres that the country might triumph in its great conflict with France. But he was too brilliant, too aloof, too erratic; indeed, any man who could say, 'I know that I can save the

country and that I alone can', must have been either a genius or a madman, and there was undoubtedly something of both in this remarkable man. It was only the disasters at the beginning of the Seven Years War that resulted in his call to high office. But when Pitt was lucid he saw much further than most people. A war-winning combination was quickly worked out—Newcastle kept matters quiet at home, while Pitt directed the conflict abroad. Soon the church bells of London were ringing for victory with a happy frequency.

In 1760, however, George II died, and the young and inexperienced George III ascended the throne. George, encouraged by his tutor, the Earle of Bute, had long looked forward to the day when he could rid the country of the greedy, self-seeking, corrupt men whom he thought were running it. In this group he included Pitt, since the latter was now collaborating with Newcastle. For the moment he did nothing but bring Bute into the ministry, but soon both Pitt and Newcastle were turned out. The king then called in Henry Fox to handle the grosser side of politics, and Fox forced all Newcastle's adherents throughout the land, from the highest to the lowest, either

John Wilkes Esqr.
Drawn from the Life and Etch'd in Aquafortis by Willm Hogarth,
Price 1 Shilling.
Publish'd according to Act of Parliament May ye 16. 1763.

to support the new ministry or to forfeit
their positions.

This 'massacre of the Pelhamite inno-
cents' destroyed Newcastle's power, but
it did not help the king much. Bute soon
found that he lacked the resolution to
remain prime minister; Fox did not have
the ambition and the king was left alone.
Nor could he get Pitt and Newcastle back
again—they were estranged from one another and would not cooperate. For ten
years there was great political instability
marked by rapidly changing ministries.
During this period the storm which was to
rob Britain of much of her American
empire was steadily growing.

Wilkes and Lord North

It was in 1770, with the emergence of
Lord North as prime minister, that the
country once again saw strong and stable
government. Moreover, George III had
at last learned, as neither of his predecessors had, how a king could still play
a predominant role in British politics by
building up his own party in parliament.
Much of Lord North's support came not

from the old Whig factions, but from a new group, the 'King's friends', who were willing to vote for the ministry that the king himself supported. But such halcyon days for king and parliament were not destined to last for long.

Even before North came to power, John Wilkes was challenging the whole system. Wilkes was a rather unsavoury character who nonetheless managed to leave important landmarks on the road to individual and national political liberty. Starting with criticisms about the Peace of Paris which ended the Seven Years War in 1763, over the next decade Wilkes, by his fierce audacity, managed to provoke a series of governments into persecuting him in ways that were sometimes constitutional, sometimes unconstitutional, but generally rash. Always fighting back, whether in jail, the law courts or in parliament, Wilkes not only established some fundamental principles of justice but also heaped great disrepute on several governments and on the whole unreformed system of parliament itself.

The Wilkes debacle was soon followed by the wars of the American Revolution, during which the ineptitude of government by the king and Lord North became increasingly evident. There were many triumphs and defeats for the ministry along this long road, but by 1783 the country was in desperate straits, fighting not only its own colonists but also France, Spain and Holland as well, and it had temporarily lost the vital command of the seas. In that year, the king's system collapsed, the Treasury benches were stormed, Lord North was driven from power and replaced as prime minister by the Marquis of Rockingham, an old associate of the now deceased Duke of Newcastle.

For the moment, however, it did not seem as though any national regeneration had taken place. Although some good work was done, notably Edmund Burke's reform of the Civil Service, a period of ministerial instability returned which culminated in the assumption of power by the cynical political coalition formed by Lord North and his arch-rival, Charles James Fox.

George III was by now quite distracted. Where could he find an honest man? The one he finally produced was the second William Pitt, the younger son of the former great minister. The king had chosen well. Only twenty-four years of age, Pitt, with one brief interruption, would rule the country until his death. At first he was in a minority in parliament, but in 1784 he won a great election victory. Pitt then set to work quickly, but many of his more important measures were forced into abeyance by the next great storm that broke over the country. In 1789, the French Revolution began. This not only profoundly altered politics within Britain itself but meant that once more the country would have to enter into another long struggle for

survival. When the Revolutionary and Napoleonic Wars finally ended, so did the world of the eighteenth century. The age of Walpole, the Pelhams, the Pitts and the Foxes had dissolved, and the era of Grey and Peel, of Gladstone and Disraeli, was about to begin.

The New Jerusalem

The closing years of this period saw the start of the most important changes ever to take place in Britain and perhaps in any other country. The colonial-commercial revolution of the early part of the century was followed, after 1760, by the beginning of the Industrial Revolution. Why this happened is a very complex question, and there were many contributory factors, such as the abundance of coal and the cheapness of water transportation within Britain itself. Basically it was a question of wealth; of having the wealth and of knowing how to use it. Above all, British business men saw industrial production as a better way of making money than such things as floating loans to governments or purchasing offices. Moreover, the British government supported

them wholeheartedly in this, and, unlike those of other nations, the upper classes did not despise investment in commerce and industry. For a hundred years the country had accumulated wealth through commerce, and commerce pointed in directions where more wealth could be made. For instance, if you were shipping Indian-made textiles from Britain for sale in Africa or the West Indies, it did not take much sense to understand that it would be a great saving to ship them directly from England and that immense profits might be made by any Englishman who could devise means of manufacturing textiles as cheaply and as efficiently as the Indians. Small wonder, therefore, that the capital was found to back the series of inventions that revolutionized the British textile industry in the eighteenth century. And, of course, once the Industrial Revolution began to gather momentum, invention begat invention. Soon Britain was well on the road to the new world of vastly increased industrial production and material prosperity as well as that of sweated workshops and child labour. In 1789, these unfamiliar and undreamed of horrors and benefits lay just beyond the horizon.

Chapter 18

The Reign of Louis XV

'I am leaving you, but the state will always remain.' So spoke Louis XIV, the grand monarch, on his death-bed. But would it? Cardinals Richelieu and Mazarin and King Louis himself had certainly created the most formidable nation in Europe. The terrible divisive elements of former centuries had been dissolved; the religious wars had ended, the power of the great nobles had been broken and the aristocracy as a whole reduced to impotence. Yet much of the substance of the newly great nation had been wasted on Louis' own wars and in the expulsion of the Huguenots. Despite the administrative centralization, a sound financial structure had not been achieved and the taxes were still concentrated on the poorer parts of the community. Nevertheless, there was still much to be optimistic about in 1715. The disastrous War of the Spanish Succession had not ended nearly as badly as might have been expected. The confused aims of the allies, a last victory by Marshal Villars, a skilful negotiation of the peace treaty had kept losses to a minimum at the treaties of Utrecht. France had been weakened but was undoubtedly still the most populous and the greatest power in Europe. The most urgent problem was that of the succession. The quality of absolute monarchies necessarily depends on the character of the monarch. The new king was a child of five.

Regency and *Polysynodie*

The extreme youth of Louis XV required a regency, and by custom the regent would be the man next in succession to the throne. This meant that power would fall into the hands of Philip, the Duke of Orléans, a man of many accomplishments and of good political sense. But Philip was also a person whose private life was marked by impiety and a total disregard of the obligations of his rank; he lived in the midst of a vast bevy of loose women and degenerates who staggered through an endless series of orgies and gargantuan drinking bouts in the fashionable underworld of Paris.

The old king had cordially detested Philip and in his will had attempted to reduce the regent to a cipher. Real power was to reside in a council made up of the royal bastards—Louis' sons by the Marquise de Montespan. But the nobility, long wearied by monarchial absolutism, looked to Philip as their champion and helped him to free himself from the dead hand of Louis XIV. All turned to the *parlements* as the repository of the French constitution. The *parlements*, basically aristocratic law courts (and not to be confused with the English parliament, the French equivalent of which was the Estates General), had kept their authority intact in theory under the grand monarch by not exercising it in practice, but they, too, now hoped that their hour had come. The dead king's will was duly and swiftly quashed.

Philip soon made other changes as well. The court was moved from Versailles to

Above, Philip, Duke of Orleans who acted as a regent during the minority of Louis XV and who attempted to restore the French economy by traditional means.

Opposite, William Pitt the Younger (1759–1806), the British Prime Minister whose ministries of 1783–1801 and 1804–06 saw Britain's development into the first industrial nation.

Paris, where the nobles would be more comfortable and the regent more free to indulge his tastes. Next came a major administrative reform. The nobility, who had placed Philip in real power, hoped he would dismantle the structure of royal absolutism. The regent's answer was the creation of the *Polysynodie*. Instead of the old system where all business was conducted by the king through his secretaries, a new organization came into being consisting of six councils, staffed largely by nobles. But the foundations of royal government, arduously created by Louis XIV, were not to be cracked so easily. After a generation in which they had been allowed to devote themselves only to war, the conduct of their own states and the petty intrigues of Versailles, the nobles found themselves unfit for anything else. They were unable to govern, and consequently government nearly came to a halt. The *Polysynodie* was about as bad a failure as it could have been. It was abolished, unlamented, in 1718.

Yet somebody had to govern. It was clear that the regent, preoccupied as he was with sex, wine and the nature of the universe, already had enough to do. But Philip did have a certain grasp of the problems of his country as well as a mind that was totally untrammelled by orthodox modes of thinking. When a young Scottish adventurer whom he had met in one of his nightly escapades announced that he could cure the ills of France, the regent paid attention.

In retrospect the career of John Law, emerging from a gambling den, briefly taking over the whole economy of France, then fleeing to Britain leaving ruin and disgrace behind him, seems like some monstrous sort of a confidence trick. Yet Law had real insight into some of the problems of the day. The main point, he realized, was that true national wealth depended on population and production. Money should not be an end in itself but merely a means of exchange to promote trade. France, without adequate credit facilities, could be outrun by lesser states like Britain and Holland, which had better developed their smaller resources. His remedy was a royal bank, which would use the king's credit to print paper money, which in turn would be used to finance the exploitation and the development of all of the country's undoubted resources.

Philip, pleased with such radical ideas, gave Law encouragement, and in 1716 the Scot was authorized to establish a private bank. This proved a great success, and a year later Law obtained control of the languishing Mississippi Company with its monopoly of the trade of Louisiana. This he reorganized into the Company of the West, and within two years Law's bank became a royal bank and his company had absorbed all of the other rather derelict colonial companies dealing with the trade of Senegal, the East Indies, Africa and China. Orthodox financiers were aghast and opposed him, but Law was not to be brooked.

When the farmers general, who collected all the indirect taxes of the country, attacked him, Law outbid them and gained control of the raising of taxes himself. His rise continued with breathtaking speed. He took over the coinage of money and then assumed the national debt, asking only three percent interest. Finally, he received the office of comptroller general of finances, bringing the whole of the French economy under his direction.

Law then sketched out a programme of badly needed reform. Direct and indirect taxation was to be reorganized in a unified system. All sorts of unnecessary offices were to be abolished, capital was to be advanced to manufacturers, and a large programme of public works begun. Most important, a new tax was to be introduced that would be paid by all classes of the community and from which the nobles and the clergy were not to be exempt.

But the foundation of Law's prestige was a shaky one, and the speculative nature of the Company of the West—renamed the Company of the Indies in 1719—was to prove fatal to his programme for reform. Much of Law's success was owing to the fantastic boom of the company's shares. In fact the company had good potential and given a generation or so of hard work might have paid off handsomely. But Law's agents issued propaganda grossly misrepresenting Louisiana, which was pictured as a veritable land of gold. Share prices began to rise amazingly. By the middle of 1719, there were such wild scenes of buying in the Rue de Quincampoix in Paris that police had to clear the streets because of bloodshed, while the shares were inflated to forty times their face value. This could not continue, given the discrepancy between the share values and the immediate real potential of Louisiana. By 1720 a panic had begun. Law attempted to stem it by means of

a controlled deflation, but now his enemies showed themselves. The *parlement* of Paris refused to register the edict cutting the value of all notes in circulation by one-quarter. Law's empire of paper money collapsed completely, and he himself fled the country.

Law's schemes for financial reform disappeared with their projector, but the failure of the miracle worker did not mean the fall of the regent. France, even under its old system of financial mismanagement, could still manage to stagger on so long as there was peace. And this was provided by the skilful diplomacy of the Abbé du Bois, Philip's old tutor. But in 1723 the regent died; the raffish epic of society to which he had given his name perished with him, and a new era began.

Cardinal Fleury and the old regime

Philip of Orléans was succeeded as regent by the next prince of the blood, the ugly and stupid Duke of Bourbon. The latter's one action of note lay in the field of royal matrimony. It was decided that it would be for the best if the young Louis XV were to marry and produce an heir to the throne as soon as possible. Therefore, his present fiancée, the five-year-old Spanish infanta, was bundled back to her homeland to the fury of the Spanish court, and Louis was quickly married to Marie Leczinska, a daughter of the ex-King of Poland.

Bourbon shortly afterwards brought about his own downfall by attempting to remove a potential rival—André Fleury, Bishop of Fréjus, and tutor to the king. But this incident brought together Louis' two most pleasing characteristics—an eye for talent and loyalty to his friends. The sixteen-year-old king stood his ground, dismissed Bourbon and made Fleury the virtual ruler of France. Not until nearly the end of his reign did the king again exert himself so decisively and to such good effect.

When Fleury, soon to become a cardinal, assumed the reins of government, few people other than the deposed Duke of Bourbon were upset or worried. After all, the new minister was a mild and inoffensive little man and at the age of seventy-three did not seem destined to pursue the arduous labours of government for very long. In fact he soon showed himself to posses great reserves of energy, determination and political skill, and he went on ruling the country for the next thirteen years. Strongly conservative, Fleury was not temperamentally suited to undertake any of the revolutionary changes needed to revivify the ailing structure of government. But by practising honest administration at home, and by cultivating peace abroad, he could at least stop decline, and this he managed to accomplish.

In the first place, he built up a strong team of assistants and gave them the security of tenure that was necessary for them to do their work well. D'Aguesseau was made chancellor and continued the vast work of legal codification. Maurepas built up the navy, and D'Angervilliers showed much industry in his long tenure as secretary of state for war from 1728 to 1740. Orry was an orthodox and efficient comptroller general from 1730 to 1746. Owing to this remarkable period of stability in the heads of departments, and to the abilities of the men themselves, Fleury's administration marked a period of peace and prosperity—the flowering of the old regime.

Given the precarious state of French finances, the sine qua non for the success of Fleury's policy was the keeping of peace. He was fortunate in that his long term of office coincided with the rule in England of the equally pacific Sir Robert Walpole. Towards the rest of Europe, he conducted a skilful diplomacy. Yet Fleury could not always have his own way, even in France. Here, his main obstacle was the old aristocracy who still persisted in seeing their main reason for existence in getting killed or in cutting heroic figures in foreign wars. He was therefore always dogged by the war party, which in his ministry centred around Chauvelin, the keeper of the seals. Eventually the hopes of the queen's father regaining his throne allowed Chauvelin to lead the country into war in the dispute over the Polish succession in 1733.

Even then, Fleury managed to keep the campaign to a minimum, secure some diplomatic triumphs and all the while give Chauvelin enough rope to hang himself. The latter was disgraced and dismissed in 1737. The nation had another breathing space, but it was not to last for long. The decline of Walpole changed the attitude of Britain, while the bellicose young nobles of France soon found a new, stronger leader in the Count of Bellisle. When Fleury died at the age of ninety in 1743, the country had stumbled into the much more ruinous War of the Austrian Succession.

Madame de Pompadour

Cardinal Fleury was not to be replaced. Like Louis XIV on the death of Cardinal Mazarin, Louis XV determined to be his own prime minister once his old tutor had passed from the scene. Unlike Louis XIV, however, he did not have the qualifications for such a rôle. Louis was intelligent enough, but he had an almost pathological lack of faith in his own judgment. Consequently, he rarely exercised it. The result was that councils would meet, the secretaries of state and the heads of departments would argue their points of view, the king would listen to it all in silence, and then the meeting would break up and the ministers struggle on as best they could without any sort of co-ordination. In the circumstances, government lost all sense of direction.

Perhaps it was a bad conscience about his own inability to govern that led Louis to indulge so remorselessly and so compulsively in his other two main pastimes— hunting and women. Year after year, vast numbers of slaughtered animals filled up the royal larder and a long procession of mistresses wandered in and out of the royal bedchambers. Most of the latter were quick and easy conquests, whose time in the royal favour might last only a few nights or weeks, but in 1744 a woman of different calibre appeared on the scene. Jeanne Antoinette Poisson was the daughter of a servant in one of the great French banking houses and was married to the nephew of one of the farmers general. She understood the mysteries of high finance and of many other things as well. In September of 1745 she became Louis' recognized mistress and was given the title of Marquise de Pompadour. Then something curious happened. Louis and his new beloved failed as lovers but became close friends. For a quarter of a century, first as actual, then as titular mistress, Pompadour ruled the glittering society of the court.

It is with Pompadour that the elegance of the period is associated. An exquisite beauty, she wished to be surrounded with

Above, a masked ball at Versailles in 1745; the cost of the court was becoming an expensive luxury to the stagnant French economy. Musée du Louvre, Paris.

Top right, Cardinal Fleury (1653–1743) who acted as tutor to Louis XV and who attempted to restore the French economy by more traditional means.

Top, Cardinal Fleury (1653–1743), who acted as tutor to Louis XV and who attempted to restore the French economy by more traditional means. The Wallace Collection, London.

Opposite, John Law (1671–1729), the Scottish financier who won the support of the Duke of Orléans in 1716 to establish a national bank of France and give widespread credit. His scheme led to a wave of speculation and subsequent financial disasters.

objets d'art, and taste became everything. Armies of craftsmen—jewellers, goldsmiths, bookmakers, makers of porcelain, furniture and tapestries—laboured to meet the inexhaustible demand of the king's great mistress. Buildings were built and gorgeously decorated, musicians and artists patronized. It used to be thought that this was the extravagance that ruined French finances and hastened the Revolution. And it is true, of course, that the lavish French court, which plumbed depths of inanity as often as it reached heights of elegance, can hardly have presented an edifying spectacle to starving French peasants. Nevertheless, the country was basically rich enough to have carried such expenditure, vast though it was, with relative ease. To discover the ills of France, it is necessary to look further than the frivolous court.

Wealth and taxation

The story of France in the eighteenth century is by no means one of continuous decline. The population was certainly increasing. By mid-century it had reached about 22,000,000, and one European in every five was French. Wealth, too, especially commercial wealth, was on the upsurge. The wars of Louis XIV had proved destructive to overseas trade. But the period of peace after 1715 and Fleury's stabilization of the currency in 1726 had made new beginnings possible. Successful French diplomacy in the Ottoman Empire brought a large upsurge of trade with the Levant. At the same time the traditional export of wine and brandy from Bordeaux to the rest of Europe continued.

The most significant part of French commercial expansion, however, was her colonial trade. While the huge areas of Canada and Louisiana did not really amount to much economically, and while her trade in India showed but modest gains, France had discovered a fountain of wealth in the West Indies. Her sugar islands, Martinique, Guadeloupe and Saint Domingué and the trade in slaves attendant upon them, were soon employing over 500 ships a year and causing great envy to the rival West Indian power of Britain. A rise in prosperity in such ports as Marseilles, Dunkirk, Le Havre and, above all, Nantes testified to the growing opulence of overseas commerce.

So wealth certainly came into France. But what was it used for? Much found its way into the hands of the great bankers and financiers like the Paris brothers. These men, who also farmed the indirect taxes, found that their easiest profit came from loans to the king to finance wars and to meet deficits. They did not invest much in commerce, despite its potentiality.

The picture regarding industry and agriculture was even worse for, with the population increase pressing on the land, revolutions in industry and agriculture became necessary. They did not take place. The fact that the Industrial Revolution began in Britain in the eighteenth century and not in France does not testify to the greater inventiveness of the British but rather to the fact that the British were willing to capitalize the inventions. By 1789 there were some 20,000 spinning jennies in Britain and less than 1,000 in France. French industry did improve in the eighteenth century but at a modest rate, held back by the regulations of guilds and by state control. Even worse was a system, of an almost incredible number, of hindrances on domestic trade caused by internal tolls, customs and excise dues. This system produced both armies of smugglers and armies of officials attempting to prevent smuggling. Yet all efforts to change it came up against a blank wall of vested interests.

But the most glaring abuse in old France was the system of taxation. Louis XIV had created a centralized state administratively but left it to be financed by machinery that was positively medieval. The principal tax in France was the *taille*, a relic of fuedal times that was placed on people who did not perform military service. The sum to be raised by it each year was annually determined by the Council of Finances. The *taille*, and a few other direct taxes, were supplemented by an impossibly vast and complex system of indirect taxation, the proceeds of which were gathered by the farmers general. From the direct taxes the nobility were exempt and the clergy, immensely wealthy, were nearly so. With an income of between 100 and 200 million livres a year, the Church paid out a 'free gift' of two or three millions. Nor were the taxes levied or gathered with much sense of equity. Many people, locally and nationally, could secure exemptions. It was always the poor and defenceless sections of the community that bore most of the burden.

Under such a system, the structure of French society was clearly in danger. Yet there was a surprising quiescence throughout the land. The peasantry, vast and inarticulate, caused surprisingly little trouble. Even during the Revolution, it was moved only once to radical action. The middle classes were more powerful and hence more dangerous to the established order; but middle classes are not by nature prone to really violent revolution. The working class seemed too small to count. If the French government could have managed to stagger on without financial crises, the old regime would probably not have ended in the holocaust that it did. But for the government to make ends meet, the system of taxation had to be reformed or involvement in wars had to be absolutely avoided. Astride both of these paths stood the aristocracy. The nobles were as eager as ever for warfare, but they would not give up their privileges, which included exemption from taxation. Thus they marked out the path of their own destruction, but for them the road to hell was not paved with good intentions.

During the days of Fleury's rule, the comptroller general of finances had been Orry. The latter's methods of extreme economy had succeeded in keeping things going, but the War of the Austrian Succession proved to be too great a strain and in December of 1745 Orry was dismissed. The man picked to replace him was Machault D'Arnouville, the former intendant of Valenciennes. The appearance of this icy but rigidly honest administrator in Louis' gay court again testifies to the king's good judgement of men. Working with great energy Machault somehow managed to finance the war—using every immediate expedient he could think of. But he was not content to rest on such laurels and as soon as peace returned he began digging towards the roots of all France's problems. In 1749 he produced his solution—the *Vingtième,* a tax of one-twentieth on all income without

exception. Then, as Machault began to organize the new administrative personnel necessary to collect it, the astonished forces of reaction began to prepare their resistance.

The *parlements* and the provincial estates at first refused to register the edict of taxation. However, the king compelled them to do so. Then the clergy took the lead in opposition. The campaign they waged was so powerful that at last the king began to waver. In his court, the *dévot* Catholic party, including the king's own daughters, pushed the claims of the Church. Pompadour gave her support to Machault, but in the end the bishops triumphed. In December of 1751 Machault gave up, and all hope of financial reform was lost for the time being.

Jansenists and *parlements*

It was in the 1740s that another problem began which caused much consternation throughout the country. It commenced as a religious struggle between the Jesuits and the Jansenists and was transmuted into a political conflict between the *parlements* and the king. By the mid-eighteenth century, Jansenism, as it had existed fifty years before, had more or less died out. But the name was still used to describe those who championed the Gallican rights of the Church in France against papal authority in Rome. Opposed to these were the Jesuits and the *dévot* party in the court, which included the queen. It was in 1713 that the pope had issued the famous Bull, *Unigenitus,* condemning supposed Jansenist proportions. But it was not until 1746 that the new Archbishop of Paris, Christophe de Beaumont, took the extreme step of threatening excommunication against those who refused to accept the Bull and began forbidding the last rites to those who had not obtained a ticket of their acceptance from a priest. At this point the *parlements* objected. The French *parlements* were law courts which

also had wide police powers over various matters such as religion, trade and industry, and morals. The most important of them was the *parlement* of Paris with a jurisdiction stretching over one-third of the country. Membership in all the French *parlements* was less than 2,000. Originally recruited from middle-class lawyers, heredity and money had since become the requirements of office. By the eighteenth century, the *parlements* were a stronghold of aristocratic reaction. In fact they were more reactionary than the king himself and wished only to replace his power with their own. But the people were not fond of the Jesuits nor of the *dévot* party, and by emerging as the protectors of Gallicanism the *parlements* could hope to gain much popular support.

When the Archbishop of Paris took his position on the Bull, *Unigenitus,* the Paris *parlement* threatened to imprison priests who refused to allow confession or to give the last rites. In 1735, when sacraments were denied to a seventy-eight-year-old nun, the *parlements* even threatened to bring the archbishop to trial. At this point the king intervened. In the court, Pompadour had been supporting the Jansenists, but Louis was more influenced by the bishops and by the *dévot* party.

The king now ordered the Paris *parlement* to cease its attack on the archbishop. Instead the *parlement* replied by drawing

Above, The Oyster Luncheon, *painted in 1737 by de Troy in pre-Revolutionary France; the French nobility were more concerned with sensual pleasures, and with protecting their own privileges, than with the well-being of the country as a whole. Musée Condé, Chantilly.*

Above left, Jean Baptiste de Machault d'Arnouville (1701–94), who attempted to tax the nobility and clergy in the late 1740s to pay for the War of the Austrian Succession but who had to abandon the policy in 1751. Musée de Versailles.

Opposite, the port of Bordeaux in the eighteenth century, one of France's largest ports, particularly enriched by its association with the slave trade.

up the *grandes remonstrances* of 9 April 1753. Remonstrances were a traditional right that the *parlements* had, but they usually delivered them to the king in private. In this case, they were printed and soon sold 20,000 copies. Now the *parlements* were claiming not only to be the protectors of the Gallicans and the Jansenists but were also debating the king's absolute power, sometimes using the arguments of Montesquieu and Locke; it was claimed that the king was a constitutional monarch bound by the fundamental laws of the realm of which the *parlements* were the guardians. Soon, placards were appearing reading 'Long live the *parlement*! Death to the king and the bishops.'

The king was not certain of what to do and, bedevilled by divided counsels, he pursued a wavering course. In May 1753, he exiled the members of the Paris *parlement* to other parts of the country. A year later, he was forced to bring them back, after no one would do business in the temporary royal court. They returned to bonfires and celebrations, and public opinion was greatly aroused. The struggle continued, in a tortuous way, over the next few years, but a truce occurred in 1757 when an attempt on the king's life briefly induced moderation on both sides.

The prestige of the king, which had suffered from his battle with the *parlements*, was soon to sink still lower. In the Seven Years War, a long series of defeats, inflicted by the British and the Prussians, brought the repute of the government to its lowest ebb. The country needed some sort of a saviour and Madame de Pompadour felt she could produce one. In 1758 a friend of hers, then at the embassy in Vienna, was hastily recalled, made Duke of Choiseul and created secretary of state for foreign affairs.

The indefatigable yet lighthearted Choiseul was perhaps not as great a man as he appeared at the time, but nevertheless he quickly set to work, re-establishing some measure of royal authority and of the country's prestige. Little could be salvaged from the war, but at the Peace of Paris Choiseul did as well as could be expected. French losses were grievous but not as bad as they might have been.

If he could not save one war, Choiseul could at least prepare for victory in the future. His foreign policy was sound, shoring up the Austrian alliance and creating the Family Compact with Spain. He then began to overhaul the army, buying out and retiring many officers and placing recruitment and equipment in the hands of civil servants. The artillery was integrated within the army as a whole; the better military schools were begun. More important, he rebuilt the French navy. The number of capital ships was doubled, and naval administration as a whole was overhauled. His term of office also saw two important accessions to French territory in Europe. In 1768, Choiseul purchased

Corsica from the Republic of Genoa, suppressing the nationalist rebellion of Paoli. Two years before, Lorraine had become incorporated within France as the result of the death of Stanislaus Lesczinski, although this was really a long-term result of Fleury's foreign policy.

Although Choiseul thus strengthened the military sinews of the nation as a whole, he did not take action at home to bolster the king's authority over the *parlements*. On the contrary, he believed in the necessity of coming to terms with them and gained much of his freedom of action from his cordial relations with the Paris *parlement*. And it was during his term of office that the *parlements* finally gained their victory over their most hated enemy—the Jesuits. In Martinique, a large commercial enterprise built up by a Jesuit priest went bankrupt and the creditors obtained judgment against the Society as a whole. With truly heroic folly, the Jesuits appealed to the *parlement* of Paris. That body immediately and gleefully proclaimed the Society responsible for all the debts incurred and then set up a commission to examine and report on the Jesuit Order as a whole. As a result, the *parlement* declared against them as strongly as possible, and it was decreed in 1762 that the Society of Jesus should be suppressed.

Louis XV, inspired by the *dévots*, attempted halfheartedly to protect the Jesuits. But in the midst of the defeats of the Seven Years War, he simply did not feel strong enough to challenge the *parlements*. In the end, he consented to a royal edict which abolished the Society and confiscated all its property.

The *parlements* and the king

With the suppression of the Jesuits, the overweening pride of the *parlements* was becoming boundless. They persisted in their obstruction of all types of financial reform. Following its victory over Machault, the Paris *parlement* waged war against successive comptrollers general, while the provincial *parlements* followed its example in respect to the royal intendants. By 1763, they had managed to get one of their own members appointed as comptroller general, and all further hope of financial reforms seemed permanently lost.

Then events in Brittany took them one step further. There a controversy over who had the right to build provincial roads grew out of all proportion and resulted in the arrest of the leader of the Rennes *parlement* by the royal governor. For the first time, all the other *parlements* in the country joined together in the support of Rennes and in denunciation of an act carried out with royal authority. Soon their statements were close to denying the sovereignty of the king. But then, with unexpected determination, Louis bestirred himself and suspended the *parlement* of Rennes. In 1766, in a *lit de justice* the king appeared before the Paris *parlement*, ordered it not to concern itself with the fate of its sister at Rennes and declared: 'I am answerable to no one. In my person alone resides the sovereign's power; from me alone my courts take their existence and authority.' Even Louis XV had at least been stung to action.

Given that Louis was at last contemplating action against the *parlements*, the position of their ally, the Duke of Choiseul, was necessarily weakened. The loss of his protector, Madame de Pompadour, who died in 1764 at the age of forty, does not seem to have hurt his standing, but his violent dislike of her successor, the ravishing beauty, Madame du Barry, did. Then, in 1768, Maupeou, a man known to be hostile

ENGLAND AND FRANCE TO THE DEATH OF LOUIS XV

Date	England	France	Europe	Date	England	France	Europe
1600	Publication of Newton's *Principia* (1687) Accession of William of Orange (III) and Mary II (1689)		Peter the Great assumes the government of Russia (1689)	1725	Death of George I. Accession of George II (1727) Founding of Methodist Society (1730)	Réamur's thermometer (1730)	Death of Peter the Great (1725)
	Battle of the Boyne (1690) Death of Mary II (1694)	French take possession of Nice and Savoy (1696)	War of the League of Augsburg (1697)			*Corvée* (public works) instituted by Fleury (1733)	War of the Polish Succession (1733)
1700			Death of last Habsburg, Charles II of Spain (1700) War of the Spanish Succession (1701)		War of Jenkins' Ear (1739)	French East India Company established (1735) Famine in Paris (1740)	Accession of Frederick the Great (1740)
	Act of Settlement—English crown to Hanover (1701) Death of William III Accession of Anne (1702)				Bonnie Prince Charlie (1745)	Pompadour becomes Louis XV's mistress (1745) Machault's *vingtième* tax (1749)	Accession of the Empress Elizabeth (1741)
	Union of England and Scotland (1707) Dismissal of Marlborough (1710) Death of Queen Anne. Accession of George I (1714)	Papal Bull *Unigenitus* (1713)	Battle of Blenheim (1704) Peter the Great's defeat of Swedes at Poltava (1709) Treaty of Utrecht (1713)	1750	Death of George II. Accession of George III (1760)	Suppression of the Jesuits (1762) Purchase of Corsica (1768) Birth of Napoleon Bonaparte (1769)	Seven Years War opens (1756) Death of the Empress Elizabeth. Accession of Catherine the Great (1762) Peace of Paris (1763)
		Death of Louis XIV. Accession of Louis XV. Regency of Duke of Orléans (1715) John Law's Bank (1716)			Expulsion of John Wilkes from the House of Commons (1764) James Watt's steam engine (1765) Hargreaves' spinning jenny (1767) Cook's first voyage (1768) Repeal of the Stamp Act (1776)	Lorraine incorporated into France. Louis XV breaks the power of the *parlements* (1770)	Jesuits expelled from Spain by Charles III (1767) Linnaeus publishes his *Systema Naturae* (1768) First Partition of Poland (1772)
	South Sea Bubble. Rise of Walpole (1720)	Collapse of Law's financial system (1720)	Treaty of Amsterdam. Russia as a European power (1717)				
		Death of Duke of Orléans (1723)	Proclamation of Russian Empire (1721) Maria Theresa named as Habsburg heiress (1723)	1775	Cook's second voyage (1772) 'Intolerable Acts' (1774)	Death of Louis XV. Accession of Louis XVI (1774)	Cossacks' Revolt under Pugachev (1774)

to the powers of the *parlements*, was made chancellor. The following year, Maupeou's friend, the Abbé Terray became comptroller general. In 1770 Choiseul clashed with the new comptroller and lost. Louis supported Terray, and Choiseul was dismissed and stripped of all his offices.

Power now passed into the hands of Maupeou, Terray and the new secretary for foreign affairs, d'Aiguillon, who became known as the triumvirate. Maupeou quickly set to work against what he clearly saw was his greatest adversary and cleverly managed to provoke the *parlement* of Paris into an open rejection of the king's authority. On Maupeou's advice, the king acted. The magistrates of the *parlement* were exiled to remote counties. Their privileges and their offices were abolished without compensation. The huge territory under the jurisdiction of the Paris *parlement* was broken up into six areas, each of which was given a new royal court.

With one swift stroke it appeared that the king and Maupeou had struck off the head of the enemy. His part in the action made the chancellor decidedly unpopular, but then an ugly, bad-tempered little man like Maupeou would hardly have expected to be loved anyway. Following his victory, he then proposed a fundamental reform of the whole judicial system of France.

The downfall of the *parlements* at last opened the way for Terray to begin the much-needed financial reforms. Machault's old edict of 1749 establishing the *vingtième* was put into operation. At the same time, Terray ironed out many of the inequalities of the taxation system and came to a new arrangement with the farmers general which increased the yield of indirect taxes. New forces were clearly at work that in a few years might have ended many of the anomalies of the old regime. Such was not

to be. In April of 1774 Louis XV contracted smallpox. A month later he was dead.

The death of Louis XV did not end all attempts at reform. Yet under his successor, a better man but a weaker king, the aristocracy and the *parlements* were able to fight back, regain their position, and once again flout all further attempts at progress. Choiseul's efforts gave France a chance for victory in the next war with Great Britain, but in winning it the French monarchy lost everything. Once again the royal finances were overwhelmed and this time there was no remedy but to summon the Estates General, a ghost that had not been seen since 1614. In doing so, the king and aristocracy raised a spectre that eventually destroyed them all.

When the corpse of Louis XV was taken to Saint Denis for burial there were few signs of mourning. No mass had been said in Paris for his recovery. At the funeral, contemptuous shouts deriding the dead king's main interests were heard: '*Voilà, the pleasure of women*' and '*Taiaut! Taiaut!*'—the French equivalent of 'tally-ho!'—were the cries. From the point of view of the ordinary people, this was not unfair. Louis had done little enough for them. But the nobility who also rejoiced should have mourned him. Had he lived, the seedy old king might have just managed to break their power—and saved them in spite of themselves.

Above, Louis XV with his sister; Louis was probably not greatly interested in solving the problem of financing the government nor with France's loss of prestige in European politics. Palazzo Pitti, Florence.

Opposite, a meeting of the Paris parlement *in 1723, known as the* lit de justice, *so-called after the seat on which the king sat to attend its official sessions. The* parlement's *authority was primarily judicial and was limited to a small area of France. Musée du Louvre, Paris.*

Chapter 19

The Western Mediterranean and Italy

The treaties which ended the War of Spanish Succession changed the western Mediterranean in two important respects: Spain lost her predominant position in Italy to the Austrian Habsburgs, and Britain became a Mediterranean power through her acquisition of Gibraltar and Minorca. The partial re-establishment of Spanish influence in Italy (1715–48) marked the end of territorial instability, since it was followed by alliances between all the great Mediterranean land powers. War at sea, where Britain was opposed by France and Spain, continued throughout the period, but its effects on the Mediterranean lands were slight.

Stability provided an opportunity for reform, and several more or less enlightened despots duly appeared. They had to combat peculiar difficulties: the fragmentation of the Italian peninsula into numerous small states; regionalism in Italy and Spain, created by geography and history; the numbers, wealth and privileges of the clergy in the traditionally devout Mediterranean lands; and psychological and economic inertia, induced in Spaniards and Portuguese by recently vanished greatness and long dependence on silver and gold from colonies in the Americas.

Italy was already a tourist's paradise, and the high court of the English aristocrat's 'grand tour'. The pleasures of Venice and the splendours of Rome could be enjoyed in a warm climate, and the more discriminating tourist relished the art treasures in which Italy abounded. Remains of Roman antiquity were still to be seen, and the hardy and serious-minded might risk being attacked by southern brigands to visit newly excavated Pompeii and Herculaneum.

What the tourist found picturesque was merely squalid in the eyes of intelligent Italians. The gap between rich and poor was even greater than elsewhere in Europe. Crime and violence were endemic, and law-enforcement corrupt and arbitrary. Economic fragmentation, clerical privileges, the dominance of the feudal nobility in the south, all aggravated the pressure of a growing population on the resources provided by a backward agriculture.

The states ruled by Italians failed to meet the challenge. Venice lived on her great commercial past and her tourist present; her trade declined, her fleet decayed and the fabled stability of her constitution became *rigor mortis*. Genoa, like Venice, practised neutrality as the only means of survival; her forces proved inadequate to control rebellion in wild and primitive Corsica, which was sold to the French (1768). The kingdom of Sardinia-Savoy, no longer able to profit by the quarrels of France, Spain and Austria, ceased to expand, remaining in the grip of a feudal nobility governed by an intermittently despotic king. The Papal States were worse governed still; a few reforms were introduced in the eighteenth century, but popes were hardly in a position to attack clerical privileges. Only in states attached to foreign powers—the villains of the nineteenth-century drama of Italian unification —was a serious effort made to cure Italy's ills.

Habsburg and Bourbon

The Habsburgs in the north were the most successful. Under Maria Theresa and Joseph, Lombardy (as the Duchy of Milan began to be called) became the most prosperous area in Italy, largely thanks to financial reforms culminating in a fixed tax on land (1757). Many of the Austro-Bohemian reforms were later introduced in Lombardy, including the reduction and regulation of feudal obligations, the suppression of monasteries and the partial abrogation of clerical tax exemption.

In Grand Duke Leopold (later Leopold II of Austria), Tuscany had perhaps the most enlightened ruler of the age. During his twenty-five year reign (1765–90), Leopold reformed the prison system, abolished torture and the death penalty, introduced tax equality, suppressed the guilds and (without complete success) struggled to diminish clerical privileges. The army was disbanded and the entire Tuscan navy (two ships) sold to Russia. But Leopold's most important achievement was to abolish all restrictions on trade, internal and external, including the internal tolls and customs barriers that survived from the age of Italian city-states.

Naples and Sicily provided more intractable problems. The Italian south was impoverished, infertile and malarial. Vast areas had not been brought under cultivation; almost all land was owned by the nobility, the Church and the king. The nobility, backed by armed retainers, existed in a state of feudal semi-independence, wielding powers of life and death over the peasantry. The Church was enormously wealthy and, like the nobles, exempt from most taxes.

The enlightened despot was not equipped to solve a problem of this magnitude; it is by no means solved today. Under Elizabeth Farnese's son Charles and (after 1759) his minister Tanucci, some clerical abuses were remedied, feudal obligations were reduced, the number of noble retainers was limited and an attempt was made to civilize and tame the nobility. The struggle to control the Church assumed an anti-papal aspect with the expulsion of the Jesuits (1767) and Tanucci's refusal to acknowledge the vague papal overlordship of Naples. Such measures made an admirable beginning, but only a beginning; and Naples was to be denied the generations of firm and enlightened rule that alone could have given her order and prosperity.

The papacy

Even in the seventeenth century, the papacy retained a not inconsiderable influence in international affairs, and, but for Innocent XI, Austria might not have chased the Turks from Vienna. In the eighteenth century this influence disappeared, along with the intense politico-religious quarrels that had sustained it. For diplomatic purposes, the pope was an insignificant Italian prince, with no army to speak of, whose territory could be violated with impunity.

The Church—and papal power over the Church—was regarded with increasing hostility by Catholic rulers. The papacy was constantly on the defensive. New concordats with Catholic powers increased the state's rights of appointment and taxation; monarchs dissolved monasteries and forbade the unlicensed publication of papal edicts. Habsburgs and Bourbons carried the war on the Church into Italy itself.

Catholic anti-clericalism was not new; nor was the struggle between Church and state. But it had entered a new phase of intensity with the development of bureaucratic state power and the state's growing need of revenue. And it was strongly coloured by the anti-clericalism of the Enlightenment, which tended to see the Church, and above all the Jesuits, as a sort of international conspiracy. For the Jesuits this meant temporary extinction. They were expelled from Portugal (1759), France (1764), Spain, Naples and Parma (1767). Finally, when the Bourbon powers united to coerce the pope, the order was dissolved (1773). This conflict, like so many others, was curtailed by the French Revolution, which united Church and king against the common enemy.

The revival of Spain

In the sixteenth century, Spain drew recklessly on the resources of her mighty empire in an attempt to dominate Europe and extirpate Protestantism. The legacy of that effort was a countryside drained of its manpower; an economy disrupted by the expulsion of heretical Jews and Moors and by the quantities of bullion that had poured in from the American colonies; a backward-looking, pious society, with a vast number of gentlemen (*hidalgos*) who considered most forms of work beneath them; and a mass of malpractices, useless honorary offices and antiquated institutions and regulations. The decline of Spanish power and prestige, visible throughout the seventeenth century, reached its nadir in the reign of the last Spanish Habsburg, the degenerate Charles II (1665–1700), and the subsequent War of Spanish Succession. At the end of the war the Bourbon dynasty (in the person of Philip V, grandson of Louis XIV of France) occupied another throne; but Spain had lost all her European possessions.

The disaster was less complete than it seemed. Spain was no longer obliged to overtax her resources by trying to defend the Netherlands, Milan and Naples; and the Bourbon administration displayed a reforming spirit that was, by Spanish standards, remarkable. Most of the credit belonged not to Philip V, but to his wife, Elizabeth Farnese, who controlled Spanish policy down to Philip's death in 1746.

Elizabeth was Philip's second wife, and her sons were unlikely to succeed to the throne; so she determined to carve out an inheritance for them in Italy. Over a period of years, she succeeded in making Charles King of Naples and Philip Duke of Parma. The triumph was dynastic rather than national, since these acquisitions were not under Spanish sovereignty; and Elizabeth's initial successes were gained through making Spain a nuisance rather than a terror to the great powers. All the same, Spanish prestige was undoubtedly increased.

When Philip arrived to fight for his Spanish crown (1701), he brought with him French experts who remedied some of the more obvious abuses. Their reforms played an important part in winning the war in Spain. Reform continued under Elizabeth, and for the same reason: an ambitious foreign policy necessitated an improvement in revenue and the creation of an efficient army and navy. Economic and fiscal reform did not go deep; energy and efficiency in exploiting resources, not structural change, was the rule; but the result was not unimpressive.

The death of Ferdinand VI (1746–59) brought one of Elizabeth Farnese's sons to the throne after all. Charles III (1759–88) was a competent and serious ruler, and at his accession he had already had twenty-five years' experience of governing Naples. Under Charles, as under so many supposedly enlightened despots, the needs of the state were paramount; but in attempting to satisfy those needs he instituted more fundamental changes than his predecessors.

Many of the reforms followed the familiar pattern of strengthening ministerial and bureaucratic control and ensuring efficient collection of revenue; but there was also a

sustained attempt to revitalize the economy. The Spanish Empire in America was reorganized and its commerce stimulated through reforms. As regards Spain, colonial trade ceased to be the monopoly of Cadiz and Seville and was opened to most Spanish ports and all Spanish nationals. The heavy sales tax that crippled commerce was drastically cut. Industry was encouraged by the abolition of guild restrictions and protected by tariffs, with the result that Spanish production of cotton cloths was surpassed only by that of Britain, and the silk and iron industries made considerable progress. There was no question of Spain becoming a great industrial nation, but Spanish manufactures at least took a respectable share of the internal and colonial markets.

The reform of agriculture, still the occupation of the overwhelming majority of the population, entailed a social revolution that few rulers were prepared or able to face. Charles attracted some foreign Catholic immigrants to work on uncultivated royal lands, distributed waste and other unused lands and introduced free trade in grain—a creditable record. But the deep-seated problems—farmers' lack of capital, unequal distribution of land, infertility, wasteful use of land for pasture instead of arable, ignorance and conservatism—remained unsolved.

The most dramatic event of the reign was the expulsion of the Jesuits in 1767. Charles and his ministers had no intention of introducing religious toleration, but they wished to complete royal control of the Church, which had been attained in most respects by the Concordat of 1753. Jesuits had been prominent in the riots of 1766, and Charles took the opportunity to subject the whole order to a biased enquiry whose findings gave him an excuse for expulsion. A reduction in the powers of the Inquisition completed the subjugation of Church to state.

Reform released energies which had been accumulating under the earlier Bourbons. With official approval, societies for economic improvement were formed in many Spanish towns. Despite colonial wars with Britain, which disrupted trade and brought the government to the verge of bankruptcy, the fruits of Charles's policies became apparent in the rapid industrial and commercial growth of the 1780s. An age of prosperity and expansion seemed to have begun.

Instead, the accession of a feeble king, ruled by his wife and her favourite, restored the rule of incompetence; and the French Revolution and Napoleon inspired crown and people alike with a reinforced attachment to the values of the past. Despite the achievements of Spain's enlightened despot, Charles III, the next century was to be one of internal paralysis and external impotence.

Portugal

Portugal lay in an even deeper slumber, despite the national upsurge that terminated the brief period of Spanish rule (1580–1640). Like Spain, Portugal looked back on a glorious epic of exploration, colonial empire and commercial expansion. In the eighteenth century their only relics were the gold and diamond mines of Brazil and the complementary Angolese slave trade.

Brazilian gold bore up a state in which a small population (only about three million by 1800) supported droves of idle gentlemen and a priesthood whose wealth, privileges and numbers were probably in relative terms the greatest in Europe. Gold was also used to make up Portugal's balance of payments deficit, for whereas manufactured goods poured into Portugal, from Britain in particular, the sole Portuguese product for which there was any demand was port, one of the vices of the English gentry.

The only man who tried to change this state of affairs was the Marquis of Pombal, who dominated Portugal throughout the reign of Joseph I (1750–77). Pombal was consistently brutal in suppressing actual, potential or imagined opposition; he was a dictator first and a reformer second. An attempt on the king's life (1758) provided him with an opportunity to break the great noble families and move against the Jesuits. Jesuit property was sequestered and the order expelled (1759), an action that was to be imitated by the Bourbon courts. Portuguese obedience to Rome was withdrawn until the final suppression of the order.

These actions were performed in the interests of the state and Pombal's own power: neither noble privileges nor the religious monopoly of the Church was ended, and the works of the *philosophes* continued to be banned. Apart from his Brazilian policy Pombal's reforms were mainly designed to secure administrative and judicial efficiency, which had social implications only in so far as it entailed the abolition of sinecures. Much of his energy was employed in attempting to combat British domination of the Portuguese market —with inevitably limited success, since Portugal had not even the beginnings of a manufacturing economy able to supply her needs. Pombal's revolution was largely political; and as such it was quickly reversed when the pious Maria I (1777–1816) succeeded Joseph.

With or without Pombal, Portugal remained a backwater of Europe. The great conflicts of the period concerned her directly only once, when Spain invaded in an unsuccessful attempt to close Portuguese harbours to the British (1762). One event made a European sensation: the terrible earthquake which destroyed Lisbon (1755). Lisbon, thanks to Pombal, was built again (and built better), but the shock—actual and psychic—was felt throughout Europe.

Above, Lisbon in the mid-eighteenth century, shortly before the great earthquake of 1755 which destroyed most of the city.

Top, the port of Seville in the eighteenth century; after losing its monopoly of Spanish colonial trade in 1718, the town suffered a chronic decline.

Above left, the expulsion of the Jesuits from Spain by Charles III in 1767; Charles was an 'enlightened despot' who saw the Jesuits both as enemies of the truth and as opponents of his complete control over his kingdom.

Opposite left top, Charles of Bourbon visiting Pope Benedict XIV (reigned 1740–58) at a coffee-house in Rome; despite Benedict's patronage of the arts, he was unable to restore the papacy to the majesty and respect of former times. Palazzo di Lapodimonte, Naples.

Opposite left bottom, Philip V of Spain (reigned 1700–46), the first Bourbon king of Spain, painted with his family by Van Loo. During his reign, Spain's economy began to develop more successfully than at any time since the sixteenth century. Museo del Prado, Madrid.

Part IV

NEW WORLDS TO CONQUER

Introduction

Less than five hundred years ago the cloistered universe defined by Ptolemy was shattered, as inquisitive explorers of the Renaissance reached out over unknown waters and found strange lands on the other side of a round world. Although it was not realized at the time, the European struggle for power on the North and South American continents had opened when Columbus, by linking a New World to the Old in 1492, laid the foundations of the Spanish overseas empire. Five years later the ambit of European ambitions was once again widened when Vasco da Gama rounded the Cape of Good Hope, establishing a route to the East that has been followed to this day. Ranged along the Atlantic seaboard, Spain, Portugal, France, Holland and England sought in turn to exploit the discoveries, and the colonial rivalries of these western powers occupy a significant part of seventeenth- and eighteenth-century history. As competition for overseas wealth gradually superimposed itself on the traditional pattern of continental relationships, European states had to revise their calculations on the sources of national power. Age-old policies of continental conquest and expansion inevitably conflicted with new and inviting dreams of riches to be found in ancient and vulnerable empires beyond the horizon.

Spain had the advantage of a head start, but she failed to develop a stable administrative and economic basis from which to exploit her new-found riches. Nonetheless, despite her decline from European heights, in part owing to the savage aggressiveness of rivals, her empire in Central and South America remained intact. Remoteness was probably the key to immunity, for the area of competitive colonization had shifted by the middle of the seventeenth century northward of the Caribbean. Successive Spanish governments continued a vain struggle to monopolize the commerce of resentful colonial dominions. Vast discoveries of silver, gold and diamonds brought settlers, soldiers and administrators, but embittered natives and corrupt officials combined to defeat the mother country's regulations. Only in the second half of the eighteenth century did Spain's governors cautiously relax trade restrictions and, like the Marquis of Pombal in Protuguese Brazil, try without success to eliminate excessive abuses that were to lead, early in the nineteenth century, to armed revolt and the establishment of independent Latin American republics.

Meanwhile, a small, fiercely ambitious and loosely federalized republic, recently relieved of Spanish control, sought command of the world's sea routes. In Indonesian seas the Dutch ousted the Portuguese and took over the greater part of their empire. Although far more businesslike than Spain, Holland had not the financial strength to maintain, in addition to a first-class navy, an army sufficient to withstand the invading forces of Louis XIV. By 1674 she had lost for a second time, and finally, her one strategic base in North America, New Amsterdam (New York).

Rivalry for empire became thereafter essentially a long-drawn-duel between France and England, which became, in the eighteenth century, a struggle that embraced Asia as well as North America. In America the French saw from the beginning the strategic points that are vital to this day. They recognized the possibilities of a great circle of river and lake stretching from the St Lawrence River to Lake Michigan and thence southward by the Mississippi to the Gulf of Mexico. A successful policy of encirclement would enable them to shut the British behind the Appalachian chain of mountains and would ultimately give France the continent.

But only the most constant support in terms of men and supplies from Europe could have made the grand project feasible. Without secure communications French possessions in North America were bound to be hostages of the British navy, which after the Battle of La Hogue gradually achieved an overall command of the seas. Determined to maintain her European hegemony, and at the same time to build a great overseas empire, France fell between the two stools of imperial dreams and continental attachments.

In North America, the issue was fundamentally one of manpower. Had 50,000 Huguenots been forced, like the Puritans, to take refuge in Canada (instead of being barred from that country), French ambitions might have stood a chance of fulfilment. Had a mere half of one percent of the French population of some 18,000,000 been persuaded to emigrate to Canada at the beginning of the eighteenth century, the colony would have gained the numerical strength which alone could justify imperial policies of expansion. Against the weight of more than 2,000,000 British settlers, hemmed in the Atlantic coastal strip east of the Appalachian Mountains, a French colony of under 50,000 in 1755 could scarcely fulfil the designs of its explorers and governors. That New France was able to endure as long as it did was principally owing to professional troops and good organization. Although unrecognized at the time, the beginnings of the 'Second Hundred Years War' for empire foretold the twilight of French American domination.

The rivalry of France and Britain revealed itself as dramatically in India as in North America. When the English East India Company was incorporated on the last day of the sixteenth century, the power of the Muslims in India was reaching its zenith under the Moguls, invaders of Mongolian origin who under Babur had in the early years of the sixteenth century swept through the passes of the northwest frontier into the plains below. Under sovereigns like Akbar, English traders could do no more than cling precariously to the coastline in little factories whose existence depended on the favour of the local ruler. The Portuguese had long retired before the competition of the Dutch, whose concentration on the East Indies archipelago alone enabled the English to stick to such mainland trading outlets as Fort St George (Madras), Fort William (Calcutta) and Catherine of Braganza's dowry gift to Charles II, Bombay.

As a consequence of mounting corruption and inefficiency, the Mogul Empire was tottering long before French and English rivals for the spoils launched their Lilliputian forces against its imposing hulk. When the last great Mogul emperor, Aurangzeb, died in 1707, both the power and the glory had departed, and the way was open for France and Britain to struggle for an oriental heritage that neither Muslim nor Hindu was capable of sustaining.

As in North America, so in India, France lost out to Britain. Less skilful in native diplomacy, the British were able to combine land and naval power effectively and allow to leadership an initiative that was denied the French paladins—Dupleix, Bussy, Lally and Suffren. In romance and wonder, the British conquest of a subcontinent with handfuls of European soldiers equals the Spanish triumphs in Central and South America. Nearly a million square miles containing some 200,000,000 people—an area embracing religions and customs reaching back to fabulous antiquity—fell to an English company's arms.

By the terms of the Treaty of Paris in 1763, practically the entire French Empire in the East and West had disappeared. Half the world, so it seemed to a later generation, had slipped through French hands like sand between the fingers. With the exception of some West Indian sugar islands and a few isolated posts on the Coromandel coast, France had been dispossessed of her imperial domain. Only if Britain, through some catastrophic upset of the balance of power, lost command of the sea, could France hope to wipe out her painful humiliation. As it happened, in 1778 a resuscitated French nation, subsequently joined by Spain, was in a position not only to challenge British superiority but for a moment actually to win command of the sea. Bereft of allies and occupied with powerful enemies elsewhere, Britain had neither the ships, the materials, nor the men to subdue thirteen rebellious American colonies some 3,000 miles away. Nonetheless, by the end of the Napoleonic Wars the second British Empire overseas had not only survived, it had grown and consolidated itself into a world-wide business concern, which for the greater part of the nineteenth century European nations were content to accept.

Unlike the Americas, where, with the exception of Mexico and Peru, no organized states offered serious resistance to European arms, both China and Japan were able to withstand, and until the nineteenth century even to reject, the advances of the acquisitive West. Although European traders had tried in the seventeenth century to breach the portals of China, they had little success. Apart from occasional loopholes like Canton, China remained impenetrable; her Manchu conquerors and rulers refused admission to the profit-seeking barbarians of the outer world except under humiliating restrictions.

The first openings had been made in 1521 when the Portuguese, who had occupied Malacca in 1511, sent a representative to Peking. Although expelled within a year, they were able in 1557 to establish a settlement in Macao, not far from Hong Kong. It remained a European lookout and trading entrepôt for the China coast long after the Portuguese commercial empire had succumbed to the Dutch, who (five years after founding Batavia) established their Formosan base in 1624. The Jesuits had begun to trickle in, led by the famous Matteo Ricci (1552–1610). But unfamiliar enthusiasm for converts resulted in their deportation to Macao. They returned in about the middle of the century to enjoy the favour of the new Manchu dynasty and to make their great contributions to scientific learning. The Jesuit success represented a unique partnership of East and West which was unhappily broken some fifty years later.

The Jesuits under St Francis Xavier (1506–52) had also introduced Christianity into Japan, and pioneer Portuguese traders were followed early in the seventeenth century by Dutch, Spanish and English. By 1620 it was estimated that some 300,000 Christians were living in the main Japanese islands. A few years later, however, a policy of national isolation was adopted, accompanied by a period of savage repression which saw the consolidation of Tokugawa rule. From about 1640 to the end of the century, a handful of Dutch and Chinese traders at Nagasaki represented Japan's only connection with the outside world.

Not until after the middle of the nineteenth century was Japan compelled to open her ports to foreign commerce and, with the collapse of the old feudal structure, to organize a national state on the Western pattern as the best means of ensuring freedom from Western domination and conquest.

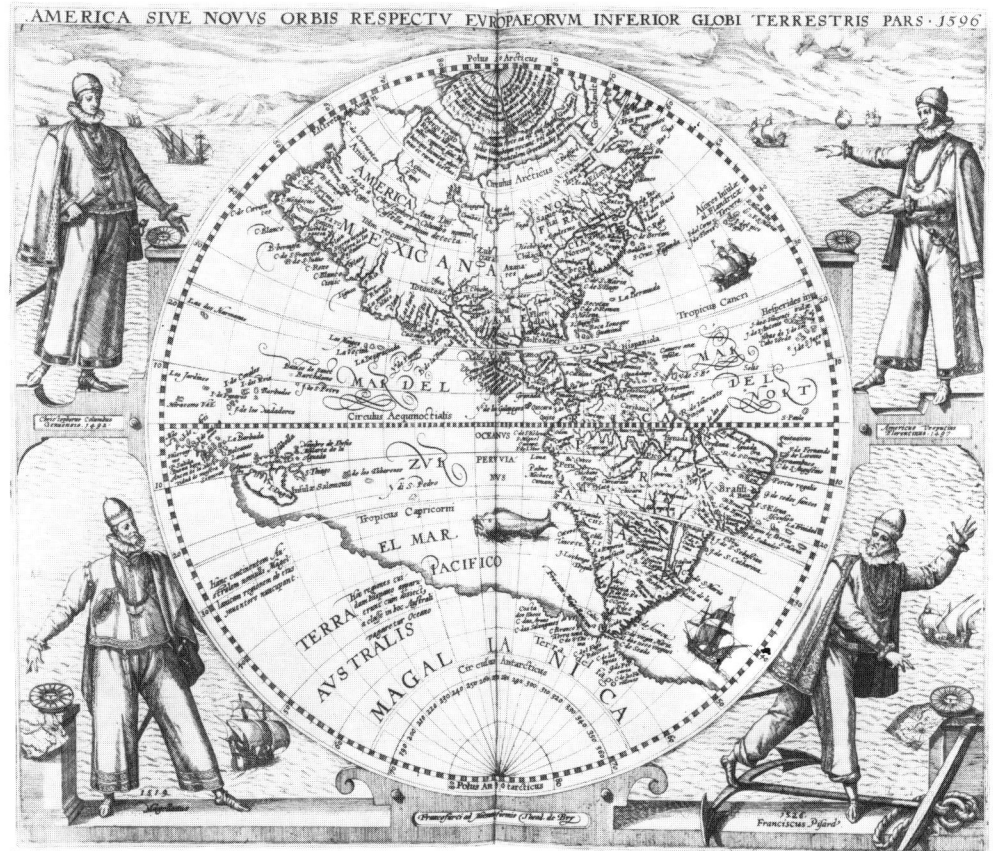

AMERICA SIVE NOVVS ORBIS RESPECTV EVROPAEORVM INFERIOR GLOBI TERRESTRIS PARS · 1596

When Hong Kong fell to the British navy, and 'Treaty Ports' opened the way to European commerce in 1840–42, it seemed certain that China too would copy the manners and methods of the West. But the very nature of the Treaty Ports provoked reaction—they were in every case territorial concessions extracted by force, or the display of force, by the European nations strong enough to make a bid for influence in the Far East. The principal reason for establishing these bases was the pursuit of trade, the benefits from which seemed unlikely to be mutual. After the experience of the Opium Wars, the Chinese saw in foreign commercial enterprise the chief menace to her security and way of life. As subsequent events were to prove, their fears were more than justified. China had neither the will nor the aptitude of Japan for emulating and keeping step with the West. As a result China had to endure her 'century of humiliation' at foreign hands. The result was the rise of a bitter anti-foreign sentiment and, with the triumph of Communism, the closing of the doors once again. Today China remains the one civilization outside the boundaries of the present international order and one that is largely beyond Western comprehension.

Above, the Western Hemisphere as it was known, or imagined to be, in 1596; around the map stand the great sixteenth-century explorers, Columbus, Vespucci, Pizarro and Drake.

On page 196, an illustration of William Penn's treaty with the Indians of 1681, painted by Edward Hicks in the early nineteenth century. Thomas Gilcrease Institute, Tulsa, Oklahoma.

Chapter 20

America in the Sixteenth and Seventeenth Centuries

The discoveries of Columbus and the feats of Cortes and Pizarro excited the imagination of all Europe. Soon other nations were sending expeditions across the Atlantic in the wake of the Spaniards. Extravagant hopes of finding new kingdoms built of gold rapidly faded, but settlers quickly accommodated themselves to exploiting the more durable wealth of forest and soil. Throughout the seventeenth century Britain, France, Spain and Portugal steadily developed their colonies in North and South America. Competition inevitably brought friction, and by 1700 the European powers were already beginning a titanic struggle for the control of a hemisphere.

Latin America after the Conquest

There is no other event in human history quite like the Spanish discoveries and conquests in the western hemisphere. Unknown continents, hidden empires, fabulous wealth —it all seemed much more like fantasy than reality. But it was reality, and the Spanish monarchs were faced with the task of ruling over vast new lands, greater in area and more populous than Spain itself. How were the new territories to be governed?

It was the system first developed for ruling over conquered Spanish Muslims that the conquistadores now extended to the American Indians. By royal grants, specified numbers of Indian households were 'entrusted' to individual captains, officers and even foot soldiers in the conquering Spanish army. These grants were called *encomiendas*, and the *encomendero* who received one would then build his estate and maintain his family and his personal following from the tribute in produce and in labour that the Indians entrusted to him would be forced to pay.

Many such grants were of truly princely extent. Cortes, for instance, received a domain containing over 100,000 Indians and sprawling over 25,000 square miles. Pizarro's was equally magnificent, and the other Spaniards were rewarded in accordance with their ranks. But the *encomiendas* were basically allotments of people rather than feudal grants of land. Indeed, the conquistadores did not usually desire a rural life and,

in true Spanish fashion, began laying out cities and villages almost as soon as they had arrived. The *encomedero*, therefore, often lived in a town and simply informed the various Indian head men of his *encomienda* how much tribute he expected to receive. The headmen, or *caciques* as they were known, would then have the onerous duty of raising the produce and labour for their overlords, as well as a little extra to keep for themselves. This, then, was the manner in which the conquering Spanish army spread its authority over the native population of the New World.

Despite the great distance of the Indies from Spain, and despite their own relative ignorance about their new dominions, the Spanish monarchs were from the beginning quite determined that royal authority in those territories should be real and not merely titular. They therefore regarded the early adventurers like Cortes and Pizarro with extreme suspicion—as men who might be tempted into becoming over-mighty subjects.

Thus, in the wake of the conquistadores, came the king's men, who were to rule the two huge viceroyalties of New Spain and Peru on behalf of their royal masters.

In Spain itself, various organs of government were hastily established. The *Casa de Contratación*, or Board of Trade, was set up in Seville to supervise all commerce between the homeland and the new colonies. But the Casa was soon placed under the aegis of another, more powerful, body, the Royal and Supreme Council of the Indies, subject only to the king and created by Emperor Charles V in 1524. The Council, consisting originally of only four or five members, continued in existence until 1834 and throughout most of this long period was an efficient and hard-working body of high prestige.

In America the viceroys arrived to set the king's recently won domains in order. Antonio de Mendoza arrived in Mexico in 1535, after an unruly period marked by the

atrocities of the ferocious Nuño de Guzmán and by the attempts of Cortes to exercise real power. In his long administration of fifteen years Mendoza ruled well, consolidating Spanish imperial authority and attempting to protect the Indians from the abuses of many *encomenderos*. At a slightly later date, from 1569 to 1581, Francisco de Toledo played a similar role in Peru. Both men laboured ably to bring order out of a relative chaos and both men left behind them an established system of government that was hardly to be altered until the end of the colonial period. It was a cleverly designed system of checks and balances constructed to limit the accumulation of power in the hands of any one man or body of men and to ensure that royal authority was felt down to the very lowest levels of administration. In this it succeeded. The whole complex structure will be dealt with in a later chapter. For the moment suffice it to say that other colonial empires were more successfully administered from the point of view of the colonists, none better than the Spanish from the point of view of their kings.

The wealth of the Indies

It was the Spanish discovery of precious metals that first convinced the world that America was something more than just a colossal barricade astride the sea route to the Orient. And the wealth that was found there was truly astonishing, arousing the

cupidity and wonder of all Europe. Some alluvial gold was early located on the island of Hispaniola. After that came the accumulated treasures of the Aztec and Inca domains, then the discovery of the great silver mines. In 1545 took place the most stupendous mineral discovery ever made by man. At Potosí, in Bolivia, an actual mountain of silver was uncovered. And by 1558 the three most important mines in Mexico were in operation.

But the wealth of the Indies was by no means restricted to minerals. Pearls and cochineal were important, but in the long run agricultural produce proved the most valuable of all. Not only were numerous varieties of crops of both New and Old World origin grown throughout the Spanish Empire, but also cash crops for export. Cotton, tobacco, sugar and dye-woods eventually produced more money than the mines.

To bring such riches home, the Spaniards evolved their famous trading system. Once or twice a year, two great fleets, laden with European manufactures, would leave Spain for the New World. One of these would proceed to Vera Cruz, the chief port of New Spain; the other would sail to Nombre de Dios (or later to Porto Bello) on the north coast of South America, whence the goods it carried would be shipped overland to Peru. Then, laden with the produce of the New World, the southerly fleet would refit in the great fortified harbour of Cartagena before keeping rendezvous with the other,

returning from Vera Cruz, in the equally fortified Havana. From there, the combined fleet would continue, under escort of galleons, back to Spain. There were other trade routes as well; Peruvian silver went to the Philippines, and there was inter-colonial trade between Peru and New Spain. But, of course, it was the transatlantic fleets, laden with silver, which were the most famous and which aroused the greed of pirates, privateers and men-of-war from the time of Drake until the latter part of the eighteenth century.

The Church and the Indians

All European nations colonizing the New World claimed that one of the principal objects was the Christianization and civilization of the Amerindians, but only the Spaniards took this seriously. This was partially owing to the character of the Indians they encountered. Once settlers were fighting them for their lives, they

Above, the silver mines at Potosí, in Peru, which provided fabulous wealth for the Spaniards; the mines were worked by the Indians, many of whom died in the airless conditions underground.

Above left, the Aztec god Huitzilopochtli being worshipped, according to a Dutch book of 1671 describing the wonders of the New World.

Opposite, Mexico City in the sixteenth century; the city, which was built on a lake, had been the Aztec capital and was taken over by the Spaniards as their headquarters.

quickly lost all ideas of converting the red men. Even in the Spanish Empire, so-called 'wild' Indians, like the Araucanians of Chile, received short shrift. But the conquest of the great Aztec and Inca domains produced a different type of situation. Here, after a brief resistance, large populations of settled Indians were completely helpless and at the mercy of their conquerors. How should these people be treated? There were two main alternatives: that they should be forced to support their rulers and to labour for them in field and in mines—for if the Spanish settlers were clear about nothing else, they were determined to avoid manual labour—or on the other hand the Indians could be looked upon as a harmless people whose welfare had been entrusted to the Spaniards by God. The first of these points of view was generally adopted by the settlers; the second by the majority of the priests and missionaries. Between these alternatives, the Spanish monarchs vacillated, their consciences genuinely torn.

Even before the mainland conquests, the Spanish settlers had been committing atrocities against the Indians on the island of Hispaniola. As early as 1511 the Dominican friar, Antonio des Montesinos, had spoken out. Using the text 'I am a voice crying in the wilderness', he denounced his own congregation, declaring: 'You are in mortal sin for the cruelty and tyranny you use in dealing with these innocent people.' After the exploits of Cortes and Pizarro, the problem was immensely sharpened. Bishops like Juan de Zumárraga and Vasco de Quiroga gained control of the *audiencia* of New Spain and overthrew the atrocious rule of Nuño de Guzmán. Others denounced the *encomiendas*, which in fact if not in theory made Indians into slaves. Worse still was the *repartimiento* or forced labour system. Friar Motolinía described with horror the scenes near the mines of New Spain where, 'it was hardly possible to walk except over dead men or bones and so great were the numbers of birds and the buzzards that came to eat the bodies of the dead that they cast a huge shadow over the sun'.

The most heroic champion of the Indians was the great Bartolomé de las Casas. Born in 1474, las Casas had arrived in America as a soldier of fortune as early as 1502. He prospered and gained control of much land and many Indians, but at the age of forty, when ordained as a priest, las Casas came to feel that he had been taking part in a monstrous crime. A vigorous, astute man, he made most of his appeals directly to the Crown, which held supreme jurisdiction over both the Indians and the Church.

Through the influence of the Crown, las Casas and his allies gained significant victories for their cause. The Inquisition, although extended to Spanish settlers in the New World, was given no authority over the Indians. Their denunciation of the abuses of the *encomiendas* resulted in 1542 in a series of new laws for the Indies

promulgated by Charles V. These insisted that all forms of Indian slavery should be ended, while other provisions, if acted upon, would have virtually abolished the whole *encomienda* system. However, as might be expected, this called forth stubborn resistance from the settlers. In New Spain, even the conscientious Mendoza advised that the colony might be lost if the laws were enforced. In Peru, the clumsy attempt to institute them immediately made by the first viceroy, Vasco Núñez, resulted in a full-scale rebellion led by Gonzalo Pizarro, one of the two surviving brothers of the old conquistador. Pizarro was quickly defeated and beheaded and royal authority restored, but it was clear the new laws would have to be revised. In 1547, another series of decrees restored the *encomiendas* although curtailing rights of inheritance associated with them, but the prohibition of Indian slavery was allowed to stand.

In 1547, las Casas, aged 72, finally left America to battle against any reversal of policy and to argue against Juan Gines de Sepulveda, a theologian who was insisting that the Indians were an inferior people and were 'natural slaves' in the Aristotelian sense. Las Casas was immediately aroused. In the first place, he was in no way intimidated by Aristotle whom he described as a 'gentile burning in hell, whose doctrine we do not need to follow except in so far as it conforms with Christian truth'. In the second place, he claimed that even if one accepted Aristotle's ideas they did not apply to the Amerindians who were clearly rational beings. In 1550, las Casas and Sepulveda met in Valladolid in a great debate on the issue, and until it was decided Charles V forbade all further Spanish conquests in America.

The debate itself was a moral victory for las Casas, and Sepulveda was not allowed to publish his own doctrines afterwards. Yet the problem was never to be resolved by a clear edict from Charles V or from any of his successors. The Spanish monarchs were indeed in a cleft stick. Their consciences took the side of the Indians, but their minds could not forget the silver. And to the kings the wealth of the Indies had an important religious use—they saw themselves as the secular champions of Roman Catholicism, and the riches of the New World helped to create the armies with which they fought both Protestants and Turks. What they really wanted was a world that could never be—one where the Indian would not be exploited and would gently be led to Christianity and where the silver would mine itself. Since they could not have this, the kings temporized and attempted both to please the settlers and to protect the Indian. They failed in each case.

It was only in a land where no great mineral wealth was to be found that the Spanish Church in America was temporarily able to achieve its ideal. In the La Plata basin, from 1605 on, Spanish Jesuits built up a huge mission centre containing some 100,000 Indians. Here they constructed a benevolent, theocratic despotism where every aspect of the daily life of the Indians was conducted under the strict supervision of the priests. The Paraguay mission was the only really large area conducted under such principles, but numerous other missions on the frontiers of New Spain and Peru created similar communities on a smaller scale. The rigid and narrow paternalistic rule of the priests meant that these areas were hardly idyllic, but they certainly constituted a nobler form of experiment than that of the *encomienda*.

There was one curious way in which the dilemma of Spanish-Indian relations could be resolved—by the exploitation of a third race. Within a few years of the discovery of America the infamous Atlantic slave trade had begun. To relieve one people from oppression by oppressing another seems

strange logic, but the Spaniard of the time saw a difference. The American Indians he had conquered were clearly his own responsibility; but, owning no possessions in continental Africa, he was only indirectly concerned with the negro. He did not enslave negroes himself but merely bought people already captured by the Portuguese. The ageing las Casas and a few others raised their voices against the iniquity of such fine distinctions, but on the whole Spanish opinion in all circles was overwhelmingly indifferent to the plight of the negroes.

The enslaving of the negro, however, did not save the American Indian. Nothing saved the Indian. Shortly after the conquest, the whole population structure of New Spain began to tremble, to shake and, finally, to disintegrate. The main cause was disease. Smallpox, measles, consumption, malaria and yellow fever, all these were brought to the New World from the Old by Europeans and Africans and ravaged a people who had no natural immunities to them. Perhaps 25,000,000 Indians dwelt in New Spain in pre-conquest days. By the mid-sixteenth century this figure had slipped to 6,500,000; by 1580, it was perhaps 1,900,000. Whole villages died out, vast areas went out of cultivation, and the whole of New Spain seemed destined to become a desert. Finally, in the seventeenth century, this horrific population decline was halted and reversed, but the new population was

largely of mestizo, or half-breed, rather than of pure Indian stock.

Much of the cultural heritage of the Indians of New Spain disappeared even faster than the peoples themselves. By the mid-seventeenth century, it was at last clear that the Catholic missionaries were winning great successes in the conversion of this vanishing people. In their vast desolation of soul, the Indians turned to the new religion, although keeping many of their own customs and rituals. Soon only monuments to the past remained—and the great statues and temples built to the various gods of the old Aztec pantheon would stare dumbly through the centuries over the people whom they had not saved and who increasingly knew them not. The Indian heritage of the Mexican people would reassert itself in the nineteenth and twentieth centuries. At the end of the seventeenth it seemed to have been buried for ever.

Decline of Empire

The tremendous decline of the American Indian population, and consequently of the New World labour force, was naturally reflected in all facets of colonial life. But the problem did not stop there, for the whole of the Spanish Empire, in the Old World as well as in the New, underwent a truly precipitous decline. In the sixteenth century, Spain had not only been the greatest power in Europe but had had only one conceivable rival for world empire—Portugal, which was finally absorbed by Philip II in 1580. Yet, in less than eighty years, all the power and glory of the Spain of Philip II had shrunk to the cardboard kingdom of Charles II—perhaps the most pathetic reversal of national fortunes in the whole of European history.

Of all of the manifold causes of the decline of old Spain, two stand out sharply: war and the lack of economic development. The seemingly inexhaustible stream of wealth from America encouraged the aggressive tendencies of the Habsburg monarchs, and their wars soon ate up that wealth and much more besides. Similarly, the inflow of silver at first stimulated the Spanish economy, but soon rising prices and costs ruined Spain as an economic competitor in Europe; Spanish industry first stagnated and then fell into complete decrepitude. Things were bad even at the end of the sixteenth century when silver imports from America were at their height, but soon the supply of silver began to dry up and Spain slipped from periodic to hopeless bankruptcy.

Everything seemed to work into a vortex spiralling downwards. Spanish mercantile policy, like that of the other European nations, had aimed at keeping the whole of the colonial trade in the hands of the mother country, but Spain simply could not manufacture the goods that the colonists wanted in exchange for their silver and agricultural produce. This increased costs enormously and encouraged smuggling by the English, French and Dutch. As Spanish power and commerce declined, so did the Spanish navy, and the smuggling could not be checked. By the seventeenth century, the Spanish concept of mercantilism had proved a complete failure.

In the New World, the depopulation at least solved the old controversy over the *encomiendas*. As the Indians disappeared so did the tribute on which the *encomienda* system was based. The new economic order that emerged was based on the *hacienda* and on peonage.

There was also a decline in government and administration in the Indies. Philip II had taken a close and consistent interest in his colonial empire; his increasingly weaker successors, Philip III, Philip IV and Charles II, cared less and less. More and more considerations of merit disappeared with regard to appointments, and offices were bought and sold like any other form of property. Nevertheless, the decline in the Indies did not proceed nearly so far, nor so rapidly, as the decline in Spain itself. Similarly, when a period of recovery came in the eighteenth century the Spanish possessions in the New World advanced much more rapidly than those in the Old.

Portuguese Brazil

By the Treaty of Tordesillas in 1494, Portuguese territory was to include all land within 370 leagues of a line drawn west of the Cape Verde islands. The Portuguese hoped that this area would contain the mythical continent of Atlantis. It did not, but in April 1500 Pedro Alvarez Cabral discovered, within the demarcation limits, the coast of Brazil and claimed it for Portugal.

Devoting most of her overseas energies towards the Indian Ocean, Portugal did little at first to develop her new colony. Indeed, she managed to keep possession of it only because it seemed so unimportant economically, producing little more than some dye-woods. Even so, English and especially French interlopers gave trouble but were finally evicted. Then came a modest boom in sugar cultivation. Portuguese sugar planters had long been prospering on the African island of São Tomé, but in the 1570s slave revolts led many of them to emigrate to Brazil. This greatly encouraged the Atlantic slave trade and also made Brazil look more attractive to alien powers. When, in 1580, the Portuguese Empire was swallowed by the Spanish this event not only demoralized Portuguese Brazilians, it also meant that Spain's enemies descended upon them as well.

Further French incursions were finally ended in 1615, but the Dutch were more successful. After a few abortive attempts in the early part of the seventeenth century, they gained a firm foothold at Recife in 1630. Within a few years they managed to gain control of some 1,200 miles of Brazilian coastline. The Dutch, particularly during the wise administration of John Maurice of Nassau, guaranteed the property rights and religious liberties of the Portuguese planters. The colony therefore prospered during the period of occupation, but when

Portugal freed herself from Spain in 1640 this provoked a nationalist reaction in Brazil as well. Revolts broke out against alien rule, and after fourteen years of warfare the Dutch withdrew.

Once again under Portuguese dominion, Brazil continued to prosper on the basis of sugar and cotton. It was not until the eighteenth century, however, with the discovery of gold and diamonds, that the colony was to attain its real importance.

North America

In the seventeenth century, the English, French and Dutch infringed the Spanish monopoly of the western hemisphere and eventually established colonies in the West Indies that were to grow rich on the labour of African slaves. Further north, attracted by the fur trade, the French founded an immense empire that stretched from Quebec to the Gulf of Mexico. The English moved more slowly so far as territory was concerned but much more rapidly with regard to settlement. By the end of the century, they had heavily populated the eastern seaboard of North America from Maine down to the Carolinas.

The Cabot voyage of 1497 had given England some claim to North America. That of Verrazano in 1523 did the same for France. Then, between 1534 and 1541, the French seaman, Jacques Cartier, made a remarkable series of voyages that carried him up the St Lawrence river as far as Montreal. Throughout the sixteenth century, a number of English navigators searched unsuccessfully for a northwest passage to Asia in the wastes of the Canadian Arctic. The purpose of all these early explorations was to find a sea route to the east or to discover rich Indian empires, thus duplicating the Spanish feats in Mexico and Peru. As such hopes faded, thoughts turned more

soberly to projects of colonization. During the last of Cartier's voyages Roberval, a French nobleman, brought out a party of settlers to Canada. But this attempt at colonization proved an ignominious failure, and twenty years later a settlement of French Protestants in Florida was cruelly exterminated by the Spaniards.

The next series of attempts was made by the English. The half-brothers Sir Humphrey Gilbert and Sir Walter Raleigh had experimented with planting settlements in Ireland and hoped to apply their experience to the New World. In 1583, Gilbert formally claimed Newfoundland for the English, but his attempt at settlement farther south was ended when storms wrecked his ships and Gilbert himself was drowned. Raleigh took up Gilbert's project and in the next few years three small groups of settlers were placed on or in the neighbourhood of Roanoke Island, in the area that he named Virginia. But all of them were to perish, and it was not until the next century that the English, French and Dutch established themselves successfully in North America.

Above, a Brazilian sugar mill of about 1640; sugar became the most important crop of the New World in the eighteenth century, as Europe's demand for it grew dramatically. Oliveira Lima Collection, Catholic University of America, Washington D.C.

Top, Sebastian Cabot (1483–1557), the Genoese sailor, towards the end of his life. He helped his father to discover Newfoundland in the 1490s and later explored the coast of South America.

Top left, an Indian village in Brazil in about 1640; the Indian populations of Central and South America fell dramatically in the sixteenth and seventeenth centuries. Oliveira Lima Collection, Catholic University of America, Washington D.C.

Opposite, negroes imported to work in the silver mines in the 1590s; it was discovered soon afterwards to be equally profitable to use these negro slaves on sugar plantations in the Caribbean and in North America.

French interest in the New World lagged for some time after Roberval's fiasco, but there were always those who thought of the possible profit that might arise from a monopoly of the fur trade. After an experiment in Nova Scotia, in 1608 Samuel de Champlain founded the city of Quebec on the St Lawrence river. With its citadel strategically built on the top of a cliff and commanding the one great river system penetrating from the Atlantic to the heart of the continent, Quebec was to be the stronghold of France in the New World.

Champlain was one of the greatest inland explorers of modern times. Driven by idealistic visions of empire, yet immensely practical as well, he pushed inland as far as the Great Lakes and southward down the Richelieu River, organizing the fur trade as he went. He also engaged deeply in Indian diplomacy and in 1609 formed the alliance between the French and the Hurons and Algonquins against the Iroquois, thus beginning the century and a half of conflict between the French and the latter formidable tribal federation.

At first, the fur trade was run in a haphazard manner, but in 1627, Cardinal Richelieu organized the famous Company of New France. The new association had great ambitions but was involved in immediate disaster. War broke out with England, and the buccaneering Kirke brothers both captured Quebec and destroyed the expedition bringing settlers and provisions in which the company had invested most of its initial capital.

Quebec was given back to France in 1632, and Champlain returned as governor. But the great explorer died three years later, and the Company of New France had been greatly weakened. It was reorganized in the 1640s, however, and began to show a profit. Nevertheless, the number of settlers in New France was miniscule, and the colony was soon racked by disastrous wars with the Iroquois. Not until the reign of Louis XIV did the fortunes of New France revive.

Raleigh's interests in the New World were eventually taken up by an organization which ultimately became known as the Virginia Company and was placed under the presidency of Sir Thomas Smyth, a great merchant adventurer. In 1607 Captain Christopher Newport took out a group of settlers on behalf of the company and near the mouth of Chesapeake Bay founded Jamestown, the first permanent English settlement in America. In the first year of its existence the new colony nearly perished through starvation and malaria, but the energetic Captain John Smith managed to keep things going, while his own life was saved, on the occasion of his capture by the Indian chief Powhatan, by the famous and timely intervention of Pocahontas, the chief's daughter, who later married an Englishman and came to England, where she died.

Opposite above, Samuel de Champlain (1567–1635), the French explorer of New France, allied with the Huron Indians and in battle with the Iroquois; as well as exploring the St Lawrence as far as the Great Lakes, he set up the colony of Quebec.

Opposite below, an Indian village in Virginia as recorded on Raleigh's expedition of 1585.

Map labels:

BEAUFORT SEA

GREENLAND

ICELAND

Yukon

Mackenzie

Great Bear Lake

Great Slave Lake

Lake Athabaska

HUDSON BAY

JAMES BAY

Nelson

Lake Winnipeg

NEWFOUND LAND

GULF OF ST LAWRENCE

NOVA SCOTIA

Columbia

Lake Superior

St Lawrence

Lake Huron

Lake Michigan

Lake Ontario

Lake Erie

Great Salt Lake

Missouri

Ohio

Allegheny Mts

BERMUDA

CALIFORNIA

Colorado

Rio Grande

Mississippi

FLORIDA

GULF OF CALIFORNIA

BAHAMAS

HISPANIOLA

GULF OF MEXICO

CUBA

I. DES PINOS

JAMAICA

CARIBBEAN SEA

Legend:

- English
- French
- Spanish

The Virginia Company had aspired to quick profits through the discovery of gold mines or from the production of wine and silk. These hopes proved illusory, but in 1612 a settler named John Rolph, who had married Pocahontas, began to grow tobacco. To the horror of King James I, the production of this 'vile weed' proved the salvation of the colony and the foundation of its future prosperity. The harsh but necessary period of stern military rule and of communal ownership of land was finally brought to an end. Settlers were given their own allotments and the government placed in the hands of a civil governor and council responsible to the Virginia Company. The colonists themselves were allowed representation in an elected House of Assembly. The establishment of this form of administration, which became a pattern for all the British colonies, was ultimately to be of immense importance.

207

The manner of their fishing.

A few Dutch traders and settlers had been active on the Hudson River since Henry Hudson had explored that area on their behalf in 1609. The original New Netherlands Company was slow in taking up any advantages, but the great Dutch West India Company, founded in 1621, began to activate matters. In 1626, Peter Minuit bought Manhattan Island from the local Indians; shortly afterwards an embryonic Swedish colony was swallowed up, and the New Netherlands came into being.

The settlement was basically a fur trading colony, centred around New Amsterdam (now New York), with its protective bastion at Wall Street and its acquisitive inhabitants straggling along the Hudson River. Trade with the Indians occupied most of their energy from the beginning, although there was also some agricultural settlement including grants of land over which the patron, or patroon, held manorial rights and where he wielded almost absolute power. By the time of the English conquest in 1664, there were about 7,000 souls in the New Netherlands, and a long period of good government under Pieter Stuyvesant had encouraged settlement. Even so, the colony had always been a minor concern of the West India Company and there were few Dutchmen who felt that their country had made a bad bargain when it eventually gave up all claims to the area in return for the confirmation of its rights in Surinam in South America.

At the same time that Virginia was finding its feet in the tobacco fields, a series of new English settlements with a radically different outlook from their southern neighbours were appearing in the north. The Pilgrims were a small and humble religious sect which had been driven from England by an intolerant establishment. Sailing in the *Mayflower* from Plymouth in September of 1620, they arrived off Cape Cod, Massachusetts, two months later. Far away from any government, they drew up their own political contract on board ship and indeed thus produced the first written constitution of any English-speaking people. They were diligent and hardworking and soon established the colony of New Plymouth.

This first English settlement in the north was soon followed by a much more important project. In England many Puritans found themselves despairing of the government of Charles I and were harried by the High Church party. A group of them managed to get a grant of land in North America and formed the Massachusetts Bay Company, under charter from the Crown. Ostensibly designed as a commercial organization, the new company had settlement in mind from the beginning. In 1629, all shareholders not intending to emigrate to America were bought out. A year later the vanguard, led by John Winthrop, sailed to found a new colony. Further emigration increased their numbers, and by 1640 there were some 14,000 Puritans in Massachusetts.

The Virginia Company was not destined to be as successful as the colony itself. Despite several reorganizations and schemes for raising capital, it began to founder financially. In 1624, King James I assumed royal responsibility for the colony; company rule had ended. Meanwhile, Bermuda had been discovered by accident when settlers going to Virginia were shipwrecked on the island. More important was the founding of Maryland in 1632, by Cecil Calvert, the second Lord Baltimore. Maryland, established on the side of Chesapeake Bay opposite Virginia, was granted as a proprietorship, and this gave Lord Baltimore wide feudal powers over the land. He hoped that the colony would be commercially successful and also a haven for his fellow Roman Catholics, and in a small way it proved to be both. Marylanders were soon cultivating tobacco, and economically the colony resembled a miniature Virginia. Roman Catholics were never in a majority among the settlers; however, there was no established Anglican Church and, distinct from their position in any other English dominions at the time, the Catholics enjoyed equal rights and freedom of religion.

The fact that Massachusetts was originally a company or corporate colony somewhat influenced its form of government. Governor, council and assembly were all elected in the way that shareholders might elect a chairman and a board of directors. This did not mean that Puritan Massachusetts was a democracy. The electorate was small and strictly confined to carefully scrutinized church members. The Puritans enforced their own brand of religious orthodoxy with rigid insistence, and those who dissented from it were persecuted almost from the beginning. Massachusetts was also fiercely determined to remain politically independent and had as little to do with the mother country as was possible.

The very intolerance of Massachusetts soon created new colonies. The Puritans rapidly drove out from their ranks people like Roger Williams, who believed in full freedom of conscience, and Anne Hutchinson, who followed her own mystical brand of theology. These two, and others like them, journeyed south, where Williams eventually founded the tolerant province of Rhode Island. Still others sought unsettled regions and brought into being the colonies of Connecticut and New Haven.

If the Puritans had so little tolerance for such godly radicals as Roger Williams and Anne Hutchinson, it may be imagined they had even less use for the more ruffian-like types of settlers. In nearby Quincy, a renegade lawyer called Thomas Morton had settled with a tough and lusty group of traders. There they sold liquor and firearms to the Indians and passed their leisure hours in drinking and in dancing with naked Indian girls around a maypole decorated, it was said, with obscene verses. The Puritans hastily packed Morton off to England, but the latter very nearly had his revenge. From the Crown's point of view Massachusetts had only been a sub-settlement in an area already granted to a body known as the Council of New England, under the presidency of Sir Ferdinando Gorges. Gorges had originally looked with favour on the Puritan settlements which he considered were under his jurisdiction. Later, influenced by Morton, he decided to take action against them. On Gorges' instigation, Charles I declared that he would take over New England as his father had taken over Virginia, and Gorges was appointed as first royal governor. But Gorges' ship was wrecked on the voyage to America, and then the outbreak of civil war in England ended forever any hopes of Charles I about strengthening his authority in the lands beyond the ocean.

The Red Indians

Conversion of the Red Indians to Christianity was always high amongst the avowed aims of all the European powers who colonized the New World. In practice, the Spaniards took this very seriously, the French less so, the English and Dutch hardly at all. After the brief period of good relations established under the auspices of Pocahontas and her kinsmen, the settlers of Virginia were forced to fight a series of border wars with Indians who rightly feared that their hunting grounds were disappearing forever. The northern Puritans believed that they were God's chosen people come to His chosen land and treated the Indians as the Israelites had treated the Canaanites.

As for the Indians themselves, most were hunting and fishing people, practising a little shifting agriculture. They were fierce fighters, but they were soon outnumbered and were usually incapable of any widespread coordination of their efforts. Many were killed, more died through disease, and by the end of the century most had been pushed back from the seaboard to the Alleghenny Mountains. On the upper Hudson River and north of Lake Erie, however, lived more formidable and more settled tribes who had large villages and who cultivated maize. The more southerly of these were banded into a confederation, the famous League of the Five Nations, and were called by the French the Iroquois. They were often at war with their northern neighbours, the Hurons. The fur trade soon exacerbated this conflict, the Iroquois acting as middlemen for the Dutch, and later the English, on the Hudson River and the Hurons allying themselves with the French. The Hurons, less organized, were nonetheless more numerous and good fighters. Into their land, in the wake of the fur traders, came Jesuit priests, the spearhead of French diplomacy, and it briefly appeared that this area might turn into another Jesuit theocracy. Unhappily, an epidemic greatly reduced the Hurons, and a deep factional struggle between Christians and pagans grew up within their ranks. At this fatal juncture the Iroquois began their great offensive of the 1640s. The Hurons were virtually exterminated, the French fur trade came to a halt, and soon even the settlements of the St Lawrence were placed in peril. It was to be some time before the French were able to regain the initiative in North America.

The West Indies

The enthusiasm aroused by their mainland discoveries had diverted the interests of the Spaniards from the Caribbean. By the seventeenth century they had settled only the larger islands and even these very sparsely, while the numerous small islands of the sea were still virgin territory. In 1622 Thomas Warner discovered St Kitts. Three years later an English settlement under Warner and a French one under the Sieur d'Esnambuc were cooperating peacefully on the tiny island.

From St Kitts colonization spread. The English occupied nearby Nevis and Montserrat, while in 1625 John Powell discovered

Above, Cecilius Calvert, the second Baron Baltimore (c. 1605–75) who became proprietor of the colony of Maryland in 1632 and organized it as a refuge for religious refugees of all faiths. Enoch Pratt Free Library of Baltimore, Maryland.

Top, the first houses being built in 1607 at Jamestown, Virginia, the first successful English colony in North America; regular support for the new colony from Europe enabled it to survive. Library of Congress, Washington.

Opposite, drawing of Indian methods of fishing in Virginia, made by a member of Walter Raleigh's expedition of 1584; Indian hostility to the first colonists added to the hazards of the dangerous journey and severe winters. British Museum, London.

the larger more fertile and uninhabited island of Barbados. Meanwhile, d'Esnambuc had sent settlers to occupy the more important island of Martinique. France later added Guadeloupe and St Lucia to her list of possessions, and in 1635 a chartered company was formed to be responsible for the French West Indian colonies.

Prior to this, an attempt by English Puritans to found a settlement on the island of Providence had failed when the colony degenerated into a nest of pirates and was removed by the Spaniards. However, the idea of plundering the Spaniards on the one hand and trading illegally with their colonists on the other was by no means exclusive to the Puritans of Providence. In these fields it was the Dutch who first achieved success. In 1628, in the sea battle of the Matanzas, the Dutch admiral Pieter Heyn forever enshrined himself in the history of the Caribbean by capturing intact the Spanish treasure fleet. This fabulous success, which allowed the Dutch West India Company to declare a fifty percent dividend to every shareholder, set a goal for generations of other seamen but was only twice repeated during the colonial period. The Dutch also claimed island colonies for themselves—Curaçao, Aruba and St Eustatius. These, however, were mainly used as trading entrepôts where

Dutch goods could be sold illegally to Spanish colonists.

So far as the English and French islands were concerned, the main event which overtook them was the sugar revolution of mid-century. Once the knowledge of how to raise sugarcane was imported from Brazil, it transformed the whole economic basis of the area. By the 1650s most of the smaller islands had switched to sugar, Barbados leading the way for the English and Martinique and Guadeloupe for the French. Such a change was to have an immense effect on the demography of the West Indies. During the early period the islands had absorbed large numbers of white immigrants as small farmers. But sugar cultivation required much capital, large plantations, and huge labour forces. Soon large sugar planters were buying out the small tobacco farmers, while the white population of the islands fell dramatically and the number of negro slaves soared. This both encouraged the slave trade enormously and also brought much wealth to the white planters and ultimately to the merchants of France and England. It was not until the next century, however, that the two colossi of Caribbean sugar producers—British Jamaica and French St Domingué—emerged as the most important colonies in their respective Western empires.

The great Civil War in England temporarily ended the English monarchy and replaced it with the Commonwealth. At first, some of the English colonies, both in the Caribbean and on the mainland, retained royalist sympathies, but a Puritan squadron sent out from England soon brought them to heel. However, provinces such as Massachusetts, which gave lip service to the Commonwealth, were left virtually independent.

The accession of Oliver Cromwell to full power in England again focused events on the West Indies. Cromwell's policy harked back to archaic ideas such as a league of all Protestant powers against Catholic Spain, and a new assault on Spanish America was planned and given the grandiloquent title of 'the Western Design'. In the event, this resulted in one of the most thoroughly wretched expeditionary forces ever to leave English shores embarking upon the attempted conquest of Hispaniola in 1655. The Spaniards proved more than a match for their adversaries, but the disgruntled English commanders did manage to capture weakly garrisoned Jamaica as a sort of consolation prize. Cromwell was thinking in terms of a foreign policy half a century out of date, yet he accidentally stumbled in the direction of the future. Jamaica, little regarded at the time, was to become the sugar queen of Britain's mercantile empire a century later. In the meantime, the island proved to have a modest usefulness of a different kind—it provided a base for the buccaneers who now entered upon their heyday of plundering and pillaging Spanish shipping and settlement.

The term 'buccaneer' originated from a group of Frenchmen who lived by curing meat or *boucan* on the uninhabited coasts of Hispaniola. They were peaceable enough until the Spanish cruelly scattered their settlements and hunted them down like animals. Taking to the sea, the buccaneers exacted a terrible revenge. Soon joined by many English and Dutch adventurers, they built up large fleets and irregular armies. For a generation they terrorized the Caribbean; the most famous of them all was the Englishman, Henry Morgan—he who amassed a fortune by sacking three of the richest Spanish settlements, who forced prisoners to walk barefoot over hot coals in order to get them to reveal their wealth, who made captured monks and nuns advance ahead of his troops and be shot down by their fellow Spaniards, who led armies that slaughtered men and raped women throughout the whole of the Spanish Main. Eventually, by the Treaty of Madrid in 1670, the Spaniards agreed to recognize the English settlements in the Caribbean and the English agreed to suppress the buccaneers. Morgan was retired, knighted, created lieutenant governor of Jamaica and quietly allowed to drink himself to death.

Mercantilism

Mercantilism was an economic doctrine that provided the whole theory for imperial expansion up until the end of the eighteenth century. Basically, mercantilists believed that all the European powers were engaged in a life and death struggle over controlling the natural wealth of the world. Those nations that gained most of this wealth would wax ever stronger; those who were shut out from it would inevitably weaken and perhaps perish.

Early economists thought of natural wealth in terms of amassing precious metals and bullion. Later on the mercantile concept was widened to include commodities as well. The major aim was to build a self-contained state that could produce all it needed and could free itself from dependency on rival powers. This was the motivating force behind the European imperial expansion of the time, although matters rarely worked out exactly as planned. In the long run, geography and consumer demand rather than mercantilist theories dictated what was produced. In fact, the Europeans stumbled across commodities like sugar, tobacco, coffee, cotton, cocoa and indigo which proved capable of producing immense profits, even though the demand for them in previous centuries had been nonexistent or severely limited. Of these, sugar was the most valuable, and thus, for both the English

and the French, the West Indies became the focal point for their American empires.

By the end of the seventeenth century, the tiny island of Barbados was becoming the jewel in Britain's imperial crown, with a trade turnover greater than most of the much larger mainland colonies put together.

Mercantilism had many interesting implications. Since the wealth of the nation was the first consideration, it was taken for granted that the state would interfere heavily in overseas economic affairs. The Dutch showed the way with the development of the two huge, monopolistic, chartered companies, the East India Company and the West India Company, which were almost departments of the government itself. But the most famous legislative expression of the mercantile system was Britain's Acts of Trade and Navigation, begun in the mid-1650s. These attempted to lay down the principles that all important commodities produced in the colonies should be shipped directly to Britain and not to other countries; that all goods which the colonists bought in exchange should be shipped directly from Britain; that all shipping should be carried in British or colonial ships. Since mercantile commerce was overseas commerce, the system enormously enhanced the value of sea power and encouraged all nations to build large navies and merchant marines. Mercantilism also meant that colonies existed for the sake of the mother country and not the other way around. Thus the colonists, although expected to gain their fair share from the wealth of empire, were nonetheless politically and economically subject to the dictates of European governments.

Above, English sailors trading with the natives of the West Indies in the late sixteenth century; a hundred years later these natives had been swamped by European and negro immigrants, who had come to work on the sugar plantations. Conversely, the West Indies gave the disease syphilis to Europe.

Opposite, a chieftain in Florida in the sixteenth century showing settlers a column erected by earlier European explorers. In places where the Indians did not fear the loss of their hunting grounds, Europeans and native Americans often cooperated amicably. Chicago Historical Society, Chicago, Illinois.

t' Fort nieuw Amsterdam op de Manhatans

SIGILLUM·CIVITATIS·NOVI·EBORACI
·1664·

The Stuart Restoration and further expansion

The return of the Stuarts to power in England in 1600 was accompanied by a new outburst of enthusiasm for colonial activities, of which the Navigation Acts were only one expression. A large new colony was planned immediately south of Virginia when, in 1663, Charles II issued a proprietary charter covering the territory which was to be known as Carolina. But this venture was chiefly noted for the absurd expectations of the proprietors of quick financial returns and for the ridiculously authoritarian constitution for the colonists drawn up by the philosopher, John Locke, mainly known for his anti-authoritarian political ideas. Most of the area remained uninhabited until the following century.

Nevertheless, other new English colonies came into being farther north along the Atlantic seaboard. In 1664, when England and Holland were at war, King Charles' brother, the Duke of York, organized the expedition which conquered the New Netherlands. The duke then turned this area into his own proprietary colony and renamed it after himself. Soon, however, he sold off the more southerly portions to another group of proprietors, and thus the separate colonies of East and West New Jersey came into being.

More important was the large colony established by the Duke of York's friend, William Penn. As a haven for his fellow Quakers, Penn acquired proprietary rights in what became Pennsylvania as payment for a debt owed to him by the Crown. When Charles II died and the Duke of York ascended the throne as James II, New York then became a royal colony. Pennsylvania, however, was a proprietorship until the American Revolution.

The Restoration era also saw the formation of two large chartered companies, with members and associates of the royal family among the shareholders. The Royal African Company was organized to put the slave trade on a better footing, while the Hudson's Bay Company was designed to exploit the wealth in furs available in the Canadian Arctic. The latter company was to suffer many vicissitudes during the following years of war with France, but in contrived to survive and is still operating.

Besides founding colonies, Restoration statesmen grappled with the problem of making royal authority more effective. The notoriously independent colonies of New England were eventually brought to heel by an English naval squadron and by their own fear of the French power growing up behind them. Ultimately, they acquiesced in acknowledging the sovereignty of the Crown and in promising obedience to the Navigation Acts. When James II became king, however, he attempted to push this trend still further. The former Puritan colonies were then deprived of their charters and forced to join together in the new Dominion of New England along with New York and New Jersey. However, the revolution of 1688 which drove James off the throne of England was immediately followed by the break-up of his embryonic Dominion. Nevertheless, William III did not allow the clock to be turned back completely. While New York, the New Jerseys, Connecticut and Rhode Island all regained their former status, Massachusetts remained a royal colony.

But the most remarkable development in the English American colonies had nothing to do with the deeds of Stuart statesmen; this was the astonishing growth of population. Through immigration and natural reproduction the number of English settlers had grown from the few hundred who landed at Jamestown to about 350,000 by the end of the century. This growth was to continue and was to be the most important single factor in deciding which power would ultimately rule in North America.

New France and the fur trade

In pursuit of the fur trade the French, as we have seen, had penetrated to the region north of the Great Lakes and allied themselves with the Huron Indians. But when the Iroquois hit back and destroyed Huronia, the whole existence of New France was placed in jeopardy. The threat of physical extinction had passed by the 1660s when a great Iroquois drive on Montreal was halted by the famous last stand of Adam Dollard at the Long Sault. Nevertheless, with the fur trade totally disrupted by the Iroquois, the colony must necessarily have withered unless help were forthcoming from France itself. This materialized in the reign of Louis XIV. Louis' great minister Colbert, was an avowed mercantilist and determined to retrieve the fortunes of the colony. Under his auspices the old and inefficient monopoly companies were replaced with a system of direct royal control, with a council headed by a governor, a bishop and an *intendant*. In 1665, the Marquis de Tracy arrived in New France with detachments of a crack French regiment—the first regulars who served in the colony. A year later, the French marched out to the Iroquois country and destroyed the villages and strongholds of the Indians. The latter avoided a pitched battle but were obliged to sue for peace.

Once this external threat was removed it was possible to overhaul the colony itself. The new system, with the governor as military and administrative head, the *intendant* handling economic and financial affairs, and the bishop dealing with the very important ecclesiastical side of life (for New France was a very Catholic colony), was designed to be a powerful 'troika' working to establish the settlement's welfare. Great strides were certainly made, particularly during the period of the zealous *intendant,* Jean Talon (1665–72), who devised methods of raising the population; there was a great increase in the area of land under cultivation and even the establishment of some modest industries.

Eventually, life in the colony took on a settled and permanent character. Its basis was the seigneurial system, a structure of feudal land-tenancy and of feudal dues, and despite its antiquated nature the system worked well. The seigneur acted as the local squire, magistrate, perhaps militia leader. But he was rarely much wealthier than his tenants and often worked in the fields with them. The tenants were assured of the full possession of land so long as they paid small dues and contributed minor labours, and they were free to sell their tenancies at will. Neither tenants nor seigneur had any political power—all this was invested in the council in Quebec.

Unfortunately, governor, bishop and *intendant*—designed to complement each other—might also oppose each other and paralyse administration. The most famous of the many such controversies was between Frontenac, the formidable governor who wished to extend the fur trade as rapidly as possible, and Laval, the greatest of the bishops, who was appalled at the way brandy debauched the Indians and brutalized life in the colony in general. It was inevitable that it should have been Frontenac's point of view that ultimately carried the day. To the government in Paris, if New France did not mean the fur trade, it meant nothing at all, for the sales of beaver pelts sustained the colony. But the fur trade was antipathetic to settlement; farmers ploughed land and cleared forests, thus driving away the Indians who trapped the beavers—and the beavers themselves who provided the furs. Moreover, many young men needed to work on the farms were drawn off into the more adventurous life of *coureurs de bois*— roaming the forests, trading, living with the Indians and on many occasions intermarrying with them.

It was the fur trade that also accounted for that other main characteristic of the French Empire in North America—its sprawling size. As old areas were denuded of furs new ones had to be found, so the empire expanded. Frontenac built a fort on Lake Ontario and by the end of the century the French were pushing towards Lake Superior. In the south, Marquette and Joliet reached the Mississippi in 1673; La Salle followed the great river to its mouth in the Gulf of Mexico in 1682, and Iberville founded a colony there in 1699.

But the occupation of this vast area inevitably led to conflict with the English settlers, who, their numbers steadily increasing, were already trickling over the mountains and eyeing the fertile lands to the west. In the whole of the French dominions in North America in 1700 there were scarcely more than 10,000 people. Thus, the fur trade

created a huge empire for France and staffed it with men—hardy fur traders and their Indian allies—who could defend it with great skill and courage. But it also ensured that these men were very few in number.

The first conflicts

The War of the League of Augsburg which began in 1689 was mainly a European affair, but for the first time colonial fighting was of some importance. Indeed skirmishes occurred in America even before the formal declaration of war. The French had captured posts on Hudson Bay, while the Iroquois Indians, allied to the English, had annihilated the town of Lachine, six miles from Montreal.

When real war began, the old Count Frontenac was sent back as governor of New France. He immediately organized savage Indian raids against the frontier of New England. In 1690, however, the French were placed on the defensive. In May a New England force, commanded by Sir William Phips, easily captured Port Royal in Nova Scotia.

In August, Phips set out with 2,000 men and thirty-four ships against Quebec itself. But the expedition did not reach its objective until October. Nor did the French simply capitulate in the face of enemy power as Phips appears to have expected. Frontenac answered his demand for surrender 'from the mouths of my cannon', to use his own words, and after some skirmishing and shelling the New Englanders gave up and withdrew.

The French next launched an offensive in 1696. Frontenac himself commanded the

QUEBEC, *The Capital of* NEW-FRANCE, *a Bishoprick, and Seat of the Soverain COURT.*

1. The Citadel. 2. the Castle. 3. Magazine. 4. ÿ Recolets. 5. Ursulines. 6. Jesuits. 7. Cathedral of Our Lady. 8. The Palace 9. ÿ Seminary. 10. The Hôtel Dieu. 11. S.t Charles River. 12. The Common Hospital. 13. The Hermitage of the Recolets. 14. The Bishop's House. 15. The Parish Church of the Lower Town. 16. The Upper Town v. ÿ Lower Town. 18. The Platform & Battery of Cannon. 19. The Ihe of Orleans. 20. Point Levi.

Above, Quebec in the mid-seventeenth century. The city became the administrative centre of the French province of New France in 1663, and was subject to regular attacks by both the Iroquois and the English until 1759, when it was permanently lost to the English.

Opposite left, the colony of New Amsterdam on the southern end of the island of Manhattan in the 1620s. The first colonists arrived there in 1624, and the island was bought from the Indians for a few trinkets two years later.

Opposite right, the seal of the city of New York, inscribed with the date 1664, the year in which the English won it from the Dutch. The colonies of New England had been founded in the 1630s and 1640s, and the conquest of New York, giving access to the Hudson River, increased English security in this region.

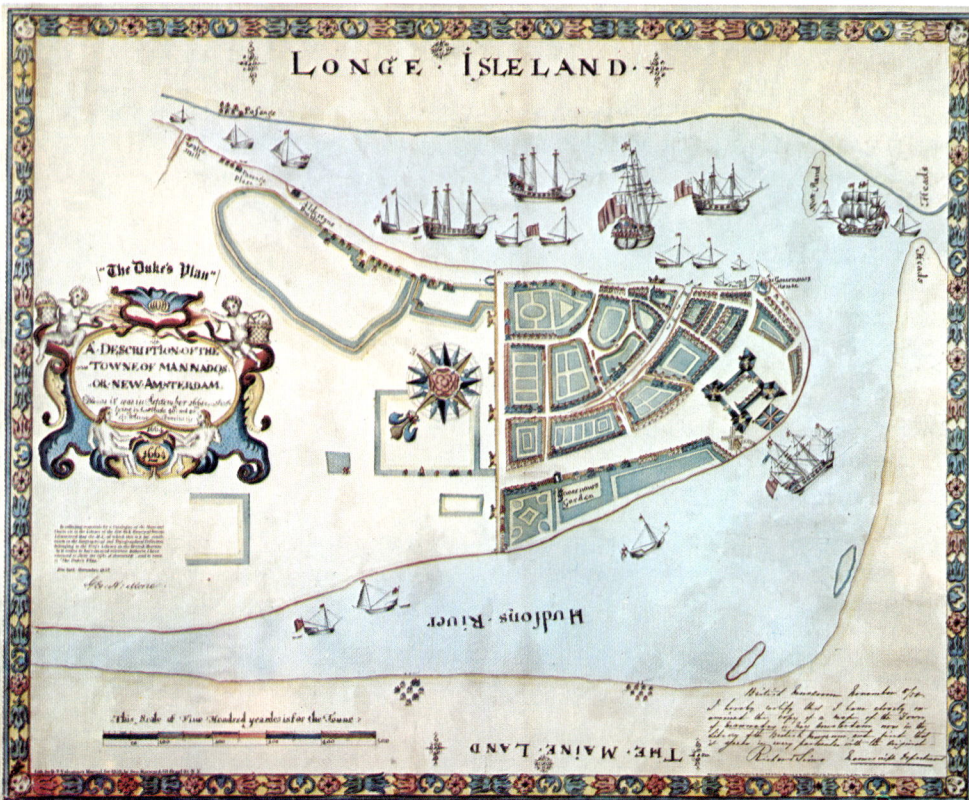

expedition striking at the Iroquois, while in an astonishing campaign the remarkable Sieur d'Iberville captured Pemaquid in Maine, attacked the English settlements in Newfoundland and in a single vessel bested three English warships on Hudson Bay.

In the West Indies the several operations of the war ended in a draw. Du Casse ravaged Jamaica but could not hold it. A French assault from St Domingué on Spanish Hispaniola was halted by the Spaniards in the battle of Limonade, but an Anglo-Spanish counter-attack failed when the troops perished from disease.

The Treaty of Ryswick, which ended the war in 1697, made few alterations in the West Indies, but in the north the French gained some advantages. Nova Scotia was returned to them, and they kept all but one of the English forts on Hudson Bay. By separate agreement, the Iroquois promised Frontenac to remain neutral in future conflicts. So the first, rather small, clash of empires had seen the English somewhat worsted by their rivals. Ryswick, however, was not the end of the story, only the beginning.

Chapter 21

Colonial Conflict in the Eighteenth Century

Just as the seventeenth century had been an age of primitive empire-building, so the eighteenth was to be one of imperial conflict. The economic doctrine of mercantilism, which had provided the impetus for colonization, also greatly influenced the institution of European warfare. On the one hand, it helped to temper it. Commercial wars were much less ferocious affairs than religious or nationalistic ones. On the other hand, mercantilist attitudes made the occurrence of war much more likely. The necessity of controlling ever more of the world's natural wealth inevitably led to the desire to destroy or swallow up the colonies owned by rival nations. Fighting was conducted on a world-wide basis. In the War of Jenkins' Ear, Britain made a great assault on Spanish America and utterly failed. But against their more formidable French enemies, the English were ultimately successful. A long series of colonial campaigns, reaching their climax in the Seven Years War, saw Britain wrest from France control of both India and North America.

Latin America

The seventeenth century, as we have seen, was a period of catastrophic decline, both for Spain and for her imperial possessions. The following century, however, saw an upward trend; the new Bourbon dynasty, arriving in Spain in 1700 in the person of Philip V, brought more brisk, French-inspired ways of thinking to the decrepit empire. This trend continued for most of the next hundred years and found its best expression during the reign of Charles III, from 1759 to 1788. Charles was an enlightened despot, whose motto was 'Everything for the people, but nothing by the people'. Although not over intelligent, he was sincere in his good intentions and ailing Spain saw a marked, if only partial, revival in her fortunes.

This upsurge was also evident in Latin America. This was partially owing to natural circumstances. By 1700, the dreadful population decline had been halted and reversed and so gave hope that reforms would enjoy a measure of success. At the same time the secret report of two Spanish naval officers, Antonio de Ulloa and Jorge Juan, clearly depicted the large amount of corruption and indolence that existed in Spanish colonial administration.

Latin America was much larger in the eighteenth century than it is today. Below the English and French settlements on the east coast of North America, almost the entire continent belonged to Spain and Portugal, who excluded all colonists but their own nationals. The only exceptions on the mainland were French Guiana (Cayenne), Dutch Guiana (Surinam), and the logwood-cutting camps of the British

Above, Latin America in the late colonial period, at the end of the eighteenth century. Apart from Portuguese Brazil, most of Latin America was ruled from Lima, in Peru.

Opposite top, William Penn's Treaty with the Indians, painted by Benjamin West (1738–1820). The Pennsylvania Academy of Fine Arts, Philadelphia, Pennsylvania. Joseph and Sarah Harnson Collection.

Opposite bottom, a Dutch plan of the early 1660s showing the layout of Mannados or New Amsterdam, founded in 1647.

in Honduras, which the Spanish made a few attempts to evict. The Caribbean, a vital area because of its sugar, indigo and tobacco, was divided between France, Britain and Spain. It was one of the main theatres of colonial warfare.

The Portuguese share of Latin America was Brazil; all the rest belonged to Spain. And the area of Spanish sovereignty was still growing. Texas was permanently occupied (1720–22); Spanish colonists settled Upper California from 1769, founding San Diego, Monterey, San Francisco and Los Angeles; Spanish explorers penetrated further up the west coast in an effort to pre-empt the British and Russians. Spain acquired Louisiana (the territory east of the Mississippi) from her ally France as compensation for Florida, which was ceded to Britain in 1763 but regained in 1783. Thus, over the century, Spain even made a territorial profit from her dealings with her stronger rivals.

The keynote of the century in both Spanish and Portuguese America was expansion, in most senses of the word. Spanish settlers moved into Uruguay in the 1720s, founding Montevideo, and into Patagonia in the 1770s. The Portuguese expanded to the south and west of Brazil. Cities, above all Mexico City, grew in size and splendour; trade boomed; new sources of wealth were tapped; and wealthy colonials began to visit the Old World.

Much of this was made possible by reforms in Spain and Portugal; but their success in fact brought forward the date when the colonies would seize their independence. Mercantilist economics encouraged all states to exploit and restrict the development of their colonies. The fact that Latin America was ruled by states poor in resources and militarily weak made the growth of colonial self-confidence a dangerous phenomenon.

Administrative reform

In the years of the Bourbon era, many salutary administrative experiments with regard to the colonies were made at both metropolitan and local levels. In Spain itself, the year 1714 saw the creation of a new Ministry of Marine and the Indies.

This body proved much more modern and efficient than the old Royal and Supreme Council, which had done good work in its time but was now past its prime. The old council still remained, however, rather obstructing the work of its younger rival, but most of its powers were gradually shifted to the new ministry in the course of the century. Another improvement occurred when all of the administrative institutions regarding the colonies were moved from Seville to Cadiz, a much more satisfactory port.

In the colonies themselves dramatic changes also took place. In the course of the century, the huge and cumbersome Vice-Royalty of Peru was split into three. In 1717, modern Colombia and Venezuela were detached from Peru, and the Vice-Royalty of New Granada was created. To the south, the area comprising much of present-day Argentina, Uruguay, Paraguay and Bolivia was turned into the Vice-Royalty of La Plata in 1776, with its capital at Buenos Aires. This area, originally ruled from Lima, thousands of miles away and behind the mountains of the Andes, now saw a period of rapid growth, testifying to the usefulness of the change. At the same time, the quality and ability of the viceroys themselves was improved, and in the late eighteenth century we have men like Bucareli and Revillagigedo, whose names and deeds are worthy to be compared with such notables from earlier days as Mendoza and Toledo.

Spanish government in the New World had originally been designed to ensure that royal authority was felt down to the lowest levels of administration. Its fundamental unit was the *cabildo* or town council. *Regidores*, or councillors, and *alcaldes*, or mayors, were the centres of power in their own small communities. They collected taxes, supervised police, sanitation and all the other duties of a municipality. The members of *cabildos* were ostensibly forbidden to use their positions for private gain, and all their acts were in theory reviewed, by higher officials.

Supervising the conduct of the *cabildos*, and of all other inferior magistrates, were the *audiencias*, or royal courts, whose judges were known as *oidores*—'those who hear'. The latter individuals were very highly paid, and their lives were circumscribed by rather monastic restrictions to guard against perversion of justice. Some ten *audiencias* had been created in the sixteenth century, each exercising many judicial, administrative, military and financial functions in its section of the empire. They were also designed to ensure continuity of administration and automatically took the place of a viceroy should he die or be recalled.

A viceroy was, of course, the direct representative of the king, and he lived in a palace with an establishment that many European monarchs might have envied. His powers were huge; so was his salary—in an effort to place him above corruption. His term of office, however, was generally short—in theory only three years. He was forbidden all private business, was not allowed to marry within his own realm and was always subject to instant recall from Madrid. He and all other officials were open to the periodic examinations of a royal visitor, who might appear when he chose, investigate all records and listen to complaints which anyone might bring. At the end of his term of office, every viceroy had to undergo a *residencia*, where a judge appointed by the crown would examine his whole record in public.

In some ways this cumbersome and complex structure of government had worked remarkably well. But during the lax period of the seventeenth century many abuses had grown up. The most important remedial measure of the eighteenth century was the introduction of the *intendencias*, again borrowed from French models. The greatest failure of the old system of administration had been the gap between the

extremely well paid viceroys and members of the *audiencias* on one hand and the local administrators such as the *alcades* and *corregidores* on the other. Owing to their small salaries, the latter had derived most of their income from bribery or exactions, while their pettiness and their distance from the seats of power had largely protected their corruption from investigation by the higher organs. Now, however, the viceroyalties were subdivided into dozens of *intendencias* ruled by professional administrators with good salaries. Beneath these were further subdivisions, administered by *sub-delegados*, who were appointed by the intendants. This extended to the majority of the populace at least some hope of real justice.

Economic revival and colonial defence

One of the reasons for the seventeenth-century decline of both Spain and the Indies was the tremendous falling off in the production of precious metals during this period. Similarly, the eighteenth century revival was accompanied by a remarkable increase in bullion production, especially in Mexican silver, greatly aided by the recoinage of the clipped and debased colonial currency undertaken in 1728 under the aegis of Philip V. Other factors as well—a decrease in the labour shortage, better mining techniques, and the more sensible management of the mining companies themselves—helped to double the Mexican silver output.

The Indies were also becoming important as exporters of other commodities. An increased demand for leather in Europe strongly stimulated the production of hides, taken from the wild cattle that roamed the pampas of the Argentine. Hitherto there had been little demand for meat, and the carcasses of these slaughtered cattle had been left for the vultures. But the discovery of huge salt mines near Buenos Aires meant that this area could begin to produce the

Above, a French indigo factory in the West Indies. Indigo, like many other vegetable dyes, was a valuable export to Europe until the nineteenth century.

Opposite left, Port St Jacques in Cuba in 1691; rich in both minerals and agriculture, this Spanish island was sought by the other imperial powers in the eighteenth century, but, apart from the years 1762–63 when it was held by Britain, the island remained firmly Spanish.

Opposite right, the title page of a history of the New World, published by Spain in 1730 as part of an attempt to revitalize interest in Spain's empire.

salted beef which was in such demand by the navies of the world. Agricultural exports, especially cash crops like coffee and cocoa, also saw an astonishing period of growth. Spanish lethargy had originally left the immense profits of sugar cultivation almost exclusively in the hands of other nations. But by the eighteenth century it was being grown in many places, both on the mainland and on the Caribbean islands. In Cuba, sugar production increased ten times within forty years. By the end of the century, that island was the greatest of the Caribbean exporters.

To manage their colonial wealth better, the Bourbons created a number of state monopoly companies modelled after the British and Dutch East India companies. The most important of these were the Honduras Company, the Havana Company, the Santo Domingo Company and the Caracas Company. But only the last-named was ever really an important success or paid good dividends.

The return of economic prosperity to the Spanish dominions was naturally accompanied by an important revival of trade and a significant growth of shipping. It was during the reign of Charles III that sensible attempts were made to increase this trend by the promotion of a freer trade within the Spanish Empire itself. In 1765 the monopoly of Cadiz was at last breached, and the Caribbean islands were opened to virtually unlimited trade with nine of the chief Spanish ports. This type of concession was later expanded, between 1768 and 1778, to all Spanish America excepting New Spain (Mexico) and Venezuela.

As her empire once again became so valuable to Spain it was necessary for the mother country to devote more thought and energy to protecting it. The old *encomienda* system had provided levies of soldiers to defend the empire in a manner similar to the Scottish clan system. But the decline of the Indian population on which it was based had led to the virtual disappearance of the *encomienda* by 1700. For a period, it was only detachments of regular soldiers that gave military protection to Spanish America. After 1760, however, a colonial militia system was introduced and organized with reasonable efficiency. Earlier,

a coastguard had been created in an attempt to end the huge illegal trade carried on between the Spanish colonists in the Caribbean and the foreign possessions there. Against smugglers, the *guarda costas* proved remarkably efficient, indeed almost too much so; the over-enthusiastic seizures made by their captains were among the chief factors promoting war with England in 1739.

To guard her trade and commerce with the colonies, Spain in earlier years had relied on the convoy system, on the vast complex of fortresses guarding the harbours of Havana in Cuba and Cartagena in Colombia and on her navy, at one time the finest in the world. In the seventeenth century, however, the convoys had ceased to sail, the fortifications had fallen into disrepair, the navy was virtually nonexistent. During the reigns of the Bourbons, new efforts were made in all three of these directions. In 1720, a 'project for Galeones and Flotas' was promulgated, ordering that regular convoys be resumed. But the system did not prove very adequate and worked only intermittently. It was abolished in 1789. The fortifications, however, were repaired to good effect—as the war of 1739 would show. Work on rebuilding the navy was begun in 1717 under Philip V. It was perhaps not as successful as the Bourbons had hoped, but within twenty years Spain could put some formidable fleets to sea.

Another important factor in terms of colonial defence was the alliance between Spain and France which existed for most of the century. France and Spain together could hope to equal or surpass British power at sea, and the Spanish Empire was secure from the French assaults on its territorial integrity that had occurred so frequently in the seventeenth century.

The War of Jenkins' Ear

The renewed attempts of Spain to strengthen her empire came none too soon. Her rich possessions always incited the cupidity of her enemies, and British statesmen were certainly giving serious thought to the prospect of seizing or destroying her dominions. Indeed, the Anglo-Spanish conflict which

broke out in 1739 was almost purely colonial in its origins.

One of Britain's chief gains at the Treaty of Utrecht in 1713 had appeared to be the *asiento* contract. This had assured the South Sea Company of the right to deliver 4800 slaves a year for sale in the Spanish colonies, to keep factors in several Spanish American ports, and to send one shipload annually of British merchandise to the Spanish trade fairs in the New World. It was expected that all this would be extremely lucrative. Yet great profits were not in fact forthcoming, and for one reason or another many of the annual voyages did not take place. Nevertheless, the Spaniards felt they, too, had grounds for complaint in that the British annual ships carried far more goods than the treaty had projected.

Worse still from the Spanish point of view was the constant smuggling of merchandise from the British Caribbean islands to the Spanish colonies. The introduction of the *guarda costas* somewhat checked this, but the over-enthusiastic seizures made by those vessels provoked great cries of rage in England against all sorts of real and supposed atrocities. Indeed the war of 1739 received its odd name when a Captain Jenkins produced his pickled ear in the British parliament, claiming it had been cut off by the Spaniards.

Relations between the two nations reached a crisis in 1738. The Spanish government wished to avoid conflict, as did Robert Walpole in England. Other British statesmen were, however, already mentally carving up the Spanish Empire. When negotiations foundered in 1739, the English decided to open hostilities with a surprise attack in the Caribbean.

British statesmen seemed sure that the Spanish Empire was ready to fall like some overripe fruit; but ideas differed about the best way to shake the great tree. Some thought in terms of conquering territory, others of seizing strategic ports. Others still surmised that the best idea might be to aid the Spanish colonists in seeking independence, because afterwards they were certain to trade mainly with Britain. In the end, much was left to the discretion of the commanders on the spot. Admiral Edward Vernon was despatched to the Caribbean

with one fleet; another was to follow, transporting a large army under Lord Cathcart. Simultaneously, Commodore George Anson set sail on an epic voyage to raid the Spanish possessions in the Pacific, equipped with dozens of proclamations urging the colonists to revolt. Vernon arrived at Jamaica in October of 1739; a month later, and without declaration of war, he stormed and took Porto Bello in Panama with only six ships.

The Spaniards now looked to their defences. One good fleet lay in Cartagena harbour under the astute command of Don Blas de Lezo; another commanded by Admiral Torres was on its way to the Caribbean. Then came an intervention. In 1740, a French fleet under the Marquis d'Antin arrived at St Domingué. Though France was at peace with Britain, d'Antin had secret orders to attack; but before anything could happen sickness had ravaged the French and d'Antin sailed home. England and France remained at peace. Spain was left to make the best of her own resources.

It soon became clear that the first blow would fall on the great fortified harbour of Cartagena, on what is now the north coast of Colombia. There the one-eyed, one-armed, lame Don Blas de Lezo was skilfully preparing defences. But in March 1741 the British arrived in apparently overwhelming numbers—twenty-nine ships of the line, over a hundred smaller vessels and some 23,000 men, of whom 15,000 were sailors. Despite the massive fortifications of Cartagena, the odds seemed against Don Blas and his 4,000 defenders. Yet it was time rather than numbers that was of the essence. A stubborn and drawn-out defence could

allow Spanish America's two greatest weapons—malaria and yellow fever—to begin their deadly work.

The pattern of the campaign quickly became clear. The two admirals, Edward Vernon and Sir Chaloner Ogle, both old Caribbean hands, urged and themselves took quick action. But General Thomas Wentworth, who succeeded in command when Lord Cathcart died, proved constitutionally incapable of hastening matters. With the navy leading, the outlying Spanish forts were taken and the harbour entered, while Don Blas carefully withdrew. At last only a single castle remained to the defenders, but it was beyond reach of naval bombardment. Wentworth now began, with exasperating slowness, to make dispositions for attack. His men were soon dying off from disease while the admirals fumed about 'gentlemen of parade . . . trained to nothing but reviews'. At last Wentworth attempted to assault the fort but was repulsed with 650 casualties. By then hundreds of men were collapsing daily, and soon there were only 3,500 effective soldiers left of a force of 8,000. In May the British ignominiously withdrew.

Eyes now turned towards Cuba, but the Spaniards meanwhile had been hastening the reinforcement of Havana. With their

Above, an encounter between the ship of Commodore George Anson and a Spanish ship from Manilla during the War of Jenkins' Ear.

Top, the capture of Porto Bello in November 1739 by the English in the War of Jenkins' Ear; this commercial war was fought entirely in the West Indies and it helped to speed the decline of Spanish colonial power.

Above left, a satire on the treaty between England and Spain made by Walpole in 1738; the interests of commerce had overtaken the old fears of Catholicism.

Opposite left, the port of Santa Domingo, on the island of Hispaniola. Like the other Spanish colonial ports this stronghold against pirate attacks in the sixteenth century was opened to English and French shipping in the eighteenth century.

Opposite right, the city of Cartagena, in Colombia, painted in 1786. Formerly twenty-nine forts had protected its treasure houses, but by this time its importance to the economy of Spain and the politics of Europe had declined. Museo del Palacio Real, Madrid.

own forces so depleted, the British therefore decided to destroy Santiago on the southern shore of the island. The troops disembarked in July, but Wentworth again sat and deliberated about whether or not to advance. At last he decided to await promised reinforcements from England and again his men began to sicken and die. Finally, with over 2,000 dead or ill, he withdrew from the island in November.

When 3,000 British reinforcements did arrive at Jamaica, one last assault was planned against the Spaniards—a surprise landing at Porto Bello, followed by a rapid march across the isthmus to Panama City. On this occasion, Vernon, in bad temper, spoiled the surprise element, whereupon Wentworth refused to march.

When the remnants of the three successive disasters reached Jamaica for the last time, the irritation and lack of trust between the commanders had reached such proportions as to doom all further efforts. Vernon and Wentworth were either not speaking or were quarrelling: Vernon and Ogle became involved in a physical brawl with the governor of Jamaica; councils of war could not be held. At last the Duke of Newcastle recalled both army and navy. Meanwhile, in the Pacific, Commodore Anson had fared better, attacking Spanish settlements and spectacularly capturing the richly laden Manila galleon. But the loss of two-thirds of his men from scurvy precluded his efforts to raise the Spanish colonies in rebellion.

The campaigns of the War of Jenkins's Ear are little remembered today, yet they are extremely important in the history of both the western hemisphere and the world. During the Seven Years War, Britain had more success in wresting colonies from Spain, but the campaign she planned at that time was much more limited and less deadly in its scope. The Vernon-Wentworth expedition was the only one launched by Britain which might conceivably have destroyed or crippled the Spanish Empire and placed large areas of Latin America under British rule. The walls of Cartagena, the skill of Don Blas and the valour of his men and the mosquitoes that carried tropical diseases had all cooperated to preserve Spain's dominions intact.

The fall of the Jesuits

Within the Spanish Empire, the Roman Catholic Church in the colonies was well controlled by the Church in Spain, and virtually all of the most important positions in its hierarchy were in the hands of Spanish-born clergy. It was also immensely opulent in the things of this world. By now, too, most of the Indians had been converted to Christianity, although observers had felt that while they had lost their old faith they had not truly grasped the new. At any rate, during the eighteenth century the Church remained a bastion of the establishment.

The chief exception to this rule was the Jesuits. Through shrewd investments, the order grew rich, but not so its individual members, who remained poor and dedicated and worked under a rigid discipline. Following their secret investigation in the 1740s, Juan and Ulloa reported, 'one does not see in them the lack of religion, the scandals and the loose behaviour so common in the others.' But the Jesuits, through championing the Indians, had always been disliked by the settlers. In 1767 they fell foul of the Crown as well. Charles III, annoyed by an order which was more loyal to Rome than to himself, ordered their expulsion. Whatever the merits of the case against them in Spain, the expulsion of the Jesuits was something of a disaster for the colonies. Missions fell apart, schools declined, hospitals and houses of charity disappeared. Especially pathetic were the results in the huge mission centre of Paraguay. There the rigid, theocratic sway that the Jesuits had exercised over the Indians might not have produced the best of all possible worlds; it was far better, however, than the breaking-up of the missions, the sale of land to rich planters and the exploitation of Indian labour which followed it.

Land and labour

The decline and disappearance of the *encomiendas* in the late sixteenth and seventeenth centuries necessitated a new type of basic agricultural organization. They were in fact replaced by the *haciendas*, or great estates, and by the system of peonage. The *haciendado* was the landowner, the peons his labour. This was not a system enforced or devised by any laws but one which grew up informally. In theory, the peon was a free agricultural labourer who received wages for his work. And indeed, if he could somehow save any money, this was his position in reality. In fact most peons lived out their lives in a form of debt-slavery. They fell into debt for rent they could not pay, for clothing or food advanced them by their estate owner, for many other reasons; and their wages rarely overtook their debts. They were tied to the estate and could not go elsewhere. Soon, almost all of the settled land was divided up amongst the huge *haciendas* and one employer would not usually accept the services of a runaway from another. Moreover, debts were continuous and inherited from father to son. Thus, throughout much of the Spanish Empire, a great deal of the population lived in a serf-like state, bound to their *haciendas*, and were often bought and sold with them.

Although it was the Indians who suffered most from the iniquities of the colonial system, they constituted the least threat to Spanish rule. Ignorant, illiterate and with little contact beyond their immediate neighbours, they had scant hope of making any sort of organized resistance. Their occasional, small-scale revolts of desperation

were easily crushed. On one single occasion, however, the vice-royalty of Peru was shaken to its roots.

José Gabriel Condorcanqui was a *mestizo*—one of mixed Spanish and Indian blood—who was also a direct descendant of the last great Inca. The Spaniards recognised him as the legal heir of the Incas and gave him the title of Marquis of Oropesa and a prominent position within the community. He may have been educated by the Jesuits, but his sympathies lay with his Indian relations. Taking the Inca name of Tupac Amaru, he carried the Indian cause to viceroys and governors. Unable to obtain any legal redress for the wrongs of his people, he raised a rebellion in November 1780. Thousands of Indians flocked to his banner; the authorities were unprepared, and briefly he found himself in control of a huge empire.

Naively believing that the local administrators were his only real enemies, Tupac called on the creoles to join in his revolt and proclaimed himself a viceroy ruling loyally on behalf of the Spanish king. After six months, however, regular soldiers and colonial militia dispersed his followers and Tupac himself was hideously tortured to death after witnessing the execution of his wife and family. But this only provoked another rebellion and more guerila warfare. When it ended, over 80,000 Indians and settlers had perished. This, however, proved to be the one great, blind and hopeless revolt of the masses; the ultimate danger to Spanish rule came from the higher orders of society.

Creoles and *gapuchines*

The varied peoples of the Spanish Empire were grouped in six great divisions derived from race of origin. There were Negroes, mulattoes, Indians, *mestizos*, white Americans of Spanish descent and, lastly, Spaniards born in Spain. It was the growing enmity between the last two groups that caused the greatest hazard to Spanish rule. Those Spaniards born in America called themselves *americanos* and were called by others creoles. Those born in Spain were known as *peninsulares* or more derisively as *gapuchines*. The creoles had many reasons for their discontent. Politically, despite a few exceptions, they were consistently excluded by the Spaniards from the highest offices of Church and state. Economically, the creole wholesalers of Mexico and Lima resented the privileges of the Spanish shippers in Seville and Cadiz. In the army and militia, creole officers were slighted by those of Spanish birth. Most irritating of all, perhaps, was the social distinction. Invariably, people of Spanish origin, whatever their background, looked down on even the wealthiest creoles of good family standing as being uncultured provincials. The creole upper classes greatly resented this; they were

Little of true originality was produced, however, except for the poetry of Sor Ines de la Cruz, a nun with strange genius who became world famous.

Architecture, however, was a different matter, and here was found the most distinctive creativity of the Indies. The inspiration came from Alberto de Churriguera, a Spanish architect belonging to a school whose members extended the extravagance of the Baroque style to such extremes that they became known as 'the delirious fools'. In the colonies this extravagance was pushed even further, with predictably varying results, but it is generally agreed that Mexico now boasts perhaps as many masterpieces of the late Baroque as all the rest of the world put together. Indeed, it could be said that a gorgeous Mexican cathedral, wherein great men and ladies knelt to pray beside crowds of wretched and unshod Indian peons, provides the most apt symbol of the Spanish Empire as a whole—a breath-taking edifice, beautifully adorned, containing within its walls extremes of squalor and splendour.

Brazil

Compared with the glitter of the Spanish colonies, Portuguese Brazil appears more like some vast charnel house containing all of the vices of mankind, somewhat tempered by a certain tolerance and cheerful indolence. Urban life was neglected. Cities were small and unimportant and churches unimpressive. Illiteracy and cultural ignorance were colossal; no printing press was set up, few books were imported, no universities were built. Life was rural, centring on the *fazenda*, or plantation, which sprawled over huge areas. One was larger than the whole kingdom of Portugal itself. Here the planter ruled from his great house like an absolute monarch over his hundreds or thousands of subjects. Labour conditions were often atrocious.

Unlike the Spaniards, the Portuguese showed no qualms of conscience about the fate of the aboriginal inhabitants of the continent. From the beginning, Indians were brutally kidnapped and worked to death as slaves on the plantations. But there were never enough of them, and huge numbers of negroes were imported from Angola and West Africa. Theoretically, Brazilian society was divided into a rigid caste system based on race. In practice, however, it was usually economic status that made the difference. The mulatto off-spring of the planters and their slaves were often treated as whites and sometimes rose to high positions. And there were certainly plenty of mulattoes and *mestizos*. Miscegenation proceeded at an incredible rate. Quite unashamedly, the Portuguese planters displayed their large broods of white, coloured and illegitimate children as a proof of their virility. This tremendous racial mixing was only partially caused by a relative lack of

Above, a Brazilian mulatto, the child of a European father and a negro slave mother; mulattoes were often able to attain positions of importance in colonial Brazil.

Left, a Brazilian Indian; although he appears here to reflect the Enlightenment's interest in the noble savage, the Brazilian Indians never in fact received any such respect from the Europeans.

willing to respect the viceroys and the *oidores* but not the numerous minor Spanish officials. Between these groups a marked resentment grew. But the creoles did not have the type of political institutions, as the Americans in the British colonies had, through which to voice their grievances. Moreover, they were intensely loyal to the Spanish monarchy. And, in the last analysis, it was not until that monarchy itself fell into grave disrepute during the Napoleonic Wars that the New World decided to break with the Old.

Spanish American culture

Culture and the fine arts were respected in Spanish America. Mainly they took the form of provincial versions of the culture of old Spain, deriving a strange fascination from their setting in a new and luminous land. Although sporadic efforts were made to educate the Indians, these were usually discouraged on the correct assumption that they constituted a danger to the establishment. Culture, therefore, was mainly upper-class culture, but it was widespread. Books were in great demand in the colonies, almost from the beginning of the conquest, and printing presses were early established in the Indies. Soon a stream of literature about New World subjects enriched that of the Old. Universities, modelled after the famous Spanish institution of Salamanca, were founded at an early date. Classes began in the University of Lima in 1572 and in Mexico in 1663. Some twenty-five institutions of higher learning had been organized by the end of the eighteenth century. The fields of drama, music, poetry, painting and sculpture all aroused enthusiastic interest.

white women. Portuguese men had a positive preference for the exotic. Whereas Portuguese women were kept in seclusion and treated as an inferior species, a handsome mulatto mistress might obtain a position of power in the household. One contemporary observer noted 'Brazil is a hell for blacks, a purgatory for whites and a paradise for mulattoes.'

Portuguese colonial government was rather haphazardly modelled on that of Spain. An overseas council, set up in Lisbon, was somewhat analogous to the Supreme Council of the Indies. After Portugal itself became free from Spain in 1640, a viceroy was appointed to rule Brazil, but this position was soon dropped in favour of the less royal title of captain-general. Under the captain-general the vast area of the colony was subdivided into several captaincies, while in the north the state of Maranhão was ruled independently from Lisbon. Portuguese government, however, never attained the same degree of centralized authority and control as did its Spanish counterpart. How could it? Portugal was a tiny nation with a population of less than two million. In the seventeenth century, when the empire extended over large areas of Africa and the countries bordering the Indian Ocean, it has been estimated that there were only about 10,000 Portuguese active throughout the whole of it. As the eastern empire declined, however, interest in Brazil increased. This became especially true after the discovery of gold and diamonds in the early eighteenth century. When, in this era, the King of Portugal could describe Brazil as his 'milch cow', royal authority was effectively extended somewhat further. Yet by Spanish standards Brazil was always lightly ruled.

The beginnings of the history of the Church in Brazil commenced with the arrival of six Jesuit priests in 1549. In 1551 the Portuguese king was made Grand Master of the Order of Christ by the pope and given much the same exclusive control of the Church in his realms as the Spanish monarchs exercised in theirs. The growth of Church organization in Brazil was slow, but Roman Catholicism was always of great importance in the social development of the colony. The numerous secular clergy, however, quickly identified themselves with the planter class and came under the influence of the great estate owners as much as anyone in the colony. Again, the Jesuits were an exception. Alone, they saw their main duty in protecting and Christianizing the Indians. They learned Indian languages, built dozens of mission villages and generally protected their charges (sometimes behind barricades) from the rapacity of slave hunters. In doing so, they earned the antipathy of virtually all other white people in the colony.

It was in the seventeenth century that the Portuguese began to move inland from the coast. The absorption of the Portuguese Empire by the Spanish between 1580 and

1640 had one advantage for Brazil. The Spaniards allowed the colony's boundaries to be extended further westwards than the line originally drawn by the Treaty of Tordesillas. The initial agents for this expansion were the ferocious Paulistas of the south from the area around São Paulo. These wild men, usually of mixed Portuguese and Indian blood, began to roam the hinterlands, hunting down Indians whom they sold as slaves. Their horrible raids destroyed many Indian tribes, but they also opened up much country which was eventually filled by the *vaqueiros*—the cowboys and stockmen who came after them.

In the 1690s roaming Paulistas discovered large deposits of alluvial gold in the area that came to be known as the Minas Gerais. Soon the first great gold rush of modern times had begun. People flocked in from all parts of the colony and from Portugal itself. They came from all walks of life: planters

deserted their plantations, merchants their shops, priests their churches and monasteries. Soon these newcomers were fighting a civil war with the Paulistas—the War of the Emboabos. The Paulistas were defeated but pushing further inland eventually discovered diamond fields as well.

The Portuguese court rejoiced. With his new-found wealth the king was able to improve his political position by ceasing to call his parliament, while his display of opulence astonished Europe. In the long run, however, the gold rush brought little of lasting good to either colony or kingdom. In Brazil itself, it marked the blackest period of its history. Gold was everything; and to get it out thousands of Indians and negro slaves were viciously worked to death. Plantations were neglected. Agriculture declined and many observers of the time felt that the colony was ruined and would sink into barbarism. Nor did the quantities of gold shipped across the ocean bring much that was lasting to Portugal. It caused inflation, was squandered by the king, and ultimately almost all of it disappeared from the nation into the shrewder hands of the English and Dutch.

During the eighteenth century, Portuguese colonial administration saw one brief period of enlightened rule reminiscent of the era of Charles III in Spain. During the reign of Charles's Portuguese contemporary Joseph I, virtually dictatorial powers were given to the able and energetic Marquis of Pombal. Pombal's most important reforms took place within Portugal itself, but he also attempted to deal in a like manner with the colonies. In Brazil there was a further effort made to strengthen and centralize royal authority. At the same time, several monopolistic trade companies were incorporated in an attempt to encourage colonial commerce. Pombal was also interested in humanitarian ideas. Little was done for the negroes, but a serious attempt was made to establish equality for the American Indians. Not only was Indian slavery prohibited, but also all forms of forced labour. Intermarriage between Portuguese and Indians was encouraged and all, except negroes, were to be considered equal.

Pombal's reforms are more interesting for their intention than for their achievement. The attempt to improve administration mainly disappeared in the bogs of bureaucratic inefficiency. The chartered companies were never a great success, and the enlightened legislation regarding Indians fell into abeyance after Pombal's death. In the long run his most lasting reform was for the worst. He, too, suppressed the Jesuits, a measure which pleased the planters but, as usual, had catastrophic results for the Indians.

Brazilian colonial history was more notable for the number of revolts by the servile and oppressed classes than was that of the Spanish possessions, although none was as serious as the great rebellion of Tupac Amaru. Many negro slaves rose against their masters on isolated plantations, and thousands escaped to the backwoods where they sometimes formed independent communities. One of these, the so-called Republic of Palmares, maintained itself for a decade against bands of Paulistas hired by the captain-general to destroy it. One of the major factors leading to the expulsion of the Jesuits had been a three-year war against Indians who had been ordered to evacuate their mission villages when Brazil took over a piece of territory formerly occupied by Spain. But the most interesting uprising occurred in the late eighteenth century in the area of the Minas Gerais. There the mineworkers, outraged when the government attempted to raise its profits from gold by increasing their taxes and lowering their wages, found a leader in one Joaquim José da Silva Xavier, a jack-of-all-trades, who had at one time worked as a

dentist and was nicknamed Tiradentes, or 'the tooth puller'. After organizing the workers and voicing their protests, Tiradentes called for large measures of social reform including the institution of a university, the abolition of slavery, the establishment of factories and, most important, the independence of Brazil from Portugal. The armed rebellion which he led was, however, quickly suppressed. Tiradentes was beheaded in 1792 but became a martyr and subsequently a national hero.

By 1800, the colony of Brazil had staked out what are roughly the boundaries of the Brazilian nation of today, sprawling over half a continent. Much of it was, and is, unoccupied. Other areas proved rich in agricultural and mineral resources. Its history was marked by unheard of atrocities against Indians and negroes and yet also by a less rigid colour bar between races than proved typical in most of the western hemisphere. In the ranks of the upper classes, there was something of the same cleavage between creole Brazilians and people born in Portugal that existed in the Spanish dominions. On the other hand, these differences were muted by the relative lightness of Portuguese rule. Brazil, however, had grown into a much more important community than Portugal itself and was unlikely to endure a second-rate status for ever. In the end, the Portuguese American Empire, like the Spanish, fell as a direct result of turmoil in Europe. Yet in Brazil Portuguese power was to subside by means of a series of gentle collapses rather than disappear precipitately by spectacular revolution.

Above, the Marques of Pombal (1699–1782), the Portuguese statesman who tried to reassert Portuguese authority over Brazil, stimulate its economy and improve the conditions of the Indians. He introduced many similar enlightened reforms in Portugal itself.

Opposite, Tupac Amaru, the leader of a violent Indian attack on European rule in Bolivia in 1780. He was executed in 1782 and his revolt brutally suppressed.

Chapter 22

The Struggle for North America

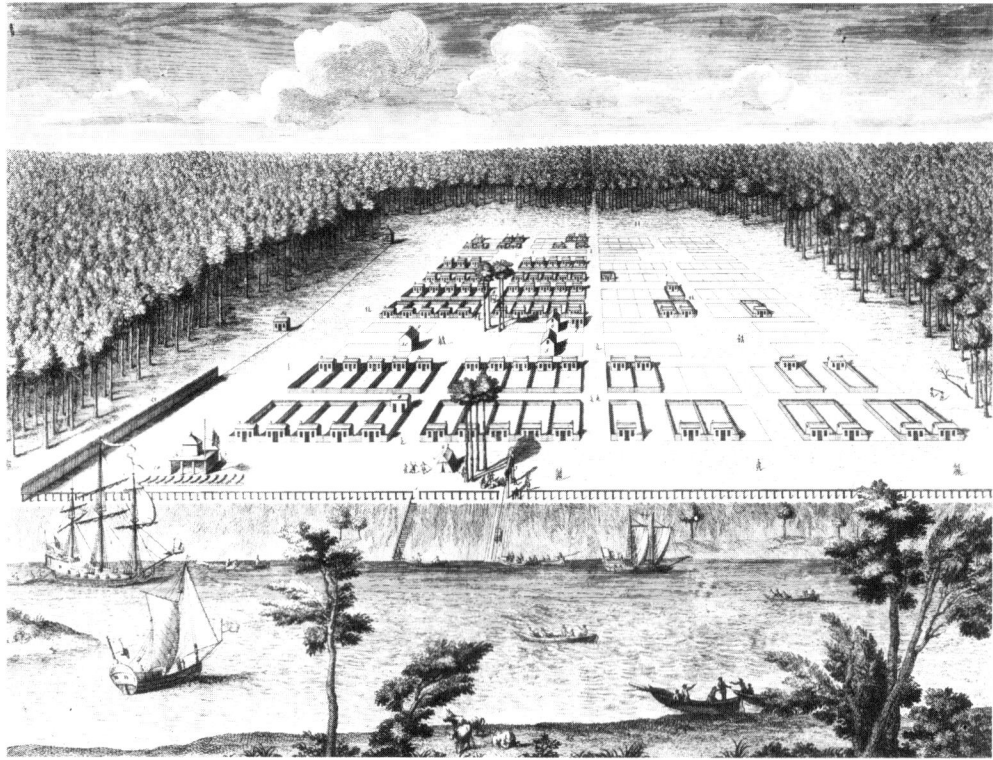

In America France, Spain and Britain struggled for the control of a hemisphere. Three factors can be named as most important in determining who won or lost in the American conflict—sea power, settlement and disease. The nation that controlled the sea could destroy harbours and capture islands with ease. More important, it could keep vital supplies from reaching the colonies of its rivals. On the other hand, areas that were well settled could support large bodies of regular troops and militia and were invariably difficult to subdue. The role played by disease has rarely been stressed but was of immense importance. Certainly malaria and yellow fever were prime factors in determining the course of warfare in the tropical regions of America.

In continental North America, disease was not of great importance, and here it was Britain that had both settlement and sea power working in her favour. Her colonists on the eastern seaboard were in such great numbers that, by the eighteenth century, there was no real chance of their being driven from the continent; it was simply a question of whether or not they could be contained. At the same time, the power of her navy made it easy for Britain to protect and nourish her own possessions while striking against the enemy either in the Caribbean or up the St Lawrence River.

France was somewhat, though not completely, lacking in all three essentials. Disease could protect her West Indian colonies from attack to a certain extent; in Quebec, she had a small area that was well settled: her sea power was by no means weak, especially when joined to that of Spain. But she suffered from grave disadvantages, and these would prove decisive in the event of major clashes with Britain. She attempted to make up for these as best she could. It was impossible to maintain large armies in North America because they could not be supplied, but she could and did send small bodies of very good troops and some excellent officers; she could build strong fortresses like Quebec and Louisbourg; she could practise Indian diplomacy astutely; she could count on a divergence of interests between the various British colonies and between the colonies and Britain herself. Lastly, she could hope that victories won by

her fine armies in Europe might counterbalance defeats in America. Yet, despite a gallant struggle, French weakness in sea power and settlement was ultimately fatal.

The British and French Empires

The Anglo-French duel for North American supremacy, which had begun in William III's time, continued for the next half century and reached its climax in the 1750s. During the same period, both empires continued to expand after their own fashion. For the English, growth was primarily demographic. Although the population of New France made the startling leap from about 7,000 to about 60,000 in this time, it remained absolutely dwarfed by that of the English colonies, which was rapidly pushing on towards the number of 2,000,000. Territorially however, driven by the needs of the fur trade, the French Empire continued to spread its borders west and south. In the score of years after 1720, a chain of forts, such as Niagara and Detroit, was built in the Great Lakes region, south into Ohio and Illinois territory and then far to the west when la Verendrye pushed deep into the Canadian prairies. In the extreme south, Iberville's brother, Bienville, founded New Orleans in 1718, and the French began moving up and down the River Mississippi in an attempt to connect New France with Louisiana.

British territorial expansion in the same period was more modest. In the north, Fort Oswego was built on the southeast shore of Lake Ontario, and Nova Scotia was conquered from the French. In the south, the uninhabited territory between Carolina and Florida was penetrated in 1733 when

General James Oglethorpe founded the colony of Georgia. This settlement was designed as a philanthropic venture which, it was hoped, would provide a new life for worthy but insolvent debtors. Such things as slavery and the trading of rum to the Indians were prohibited, but most settlers soon left the colony for the easier life of Carolina. In 1752 the restrictions were finally removed, normal colonial government instituted and the colonists granted 'the one thing lacking'—the introduction of slavery.

Even during wartime, the English colonists were inhibited from directing all of their energies against their French enemy by their quarrels and discords with each other. Moreover, trouble was brewing between the colonists and Britain herself over the question of how much political power should reside in the elected colonial assemblies and how much should be exercised from London. But one thing was clear: the English settlers were increasingly ready to burst the boundaries set by the Allegheny mountains and spill into the Mississippi valley where they would collide with the rapidly expanding French.

Spanish Succession and Austrian Succession

The War of the Leage of Augsburg had ended in 1694 with the French gaining certain advantages in North America. The War of the Spanish Succession (1702–14), which soon followed it, again saw colonial campaigns which were waged over thousands of miles along the eastern coast of the hemisphere. In the south, the French began well, their forces ravaging the settlements of England's Portuguese ally in Brazil. In the Caribbean, Iberville took the offensive once more, capturing St Kitts and Nevis before he died of fever. The English, however, soon recaptured the former island, although disease and stubborn French resistance ended their attempted conquest of Guadeloupe.

Further north, Governor James Moore of Carolina moved south into Florida and devastated a dozen Spanish mission villages. At St Augustine, however, Governor Zúñiga successfully defended the fort for seven weeks until Moore was forced to retreat. In 1706, it was the Carolinians who were on the defensive when a major Franco-Spanish expedition failed to take Charleston. The British then struck back, but two sorties against Pensacola also miscarried.

It was further north that the most important fighting of the war took place. Oddly enough, the exposed area of New York saw little action owing to the neutrality of the Iroquois Indians, who remained faithful to their treaty with Governor Frontenac. New England, however, suffered severely from raids by French Indians, the most famous of which was the sack of Deerfield, Massachusetts in 1707. But New England proved able to retaliate. Two militia attacks on Port Royal, Nova Scotia, failed in 1708, but two years later the energetic Francis Nicholson at last seized the ill-defended fort, and Nova Scotia fell into British hands.

In 1711, it was decided that Nicholson should advance overland to Montreal, while a major British amphibious expedition should strike down the St Lawrence River directly to Quebec. The military commander on this ill-starred venture was to be Brigadier Jack Hill, a brother of Abigail Masham. He commanded seven veteran regiments of British regulars, and the English Tories hoped he would win a great victory to offset the triumphs of the Whiggish Duke of Marlborough. He did not get the chance. The fleet transporting his men was commanded by Admiral Hovenden Walker, an old nonentity. Walker was not entirely destitute of all qualities of seamanship but was unfortunate enough to make the egregious error of attempting the ascent of the St Lawrence without good pilots. As a result, on the night of 23 August, many of his ships piled up on the north shore. Seven transports, one stores ship and about 900 men were lost, and English hopes of capturing Quebec ended in tragedy.

In the Peace of Utrecht, which ended the war, England made substantial colonial gains. Nova Scotia became hers, and her sovereignty over Newfoundland was recognized as well. All fur trading posts commanded by the French on Hudson Bay were given up, while in the Caribbean the island of St Kitts at last became a firmly established British possession. Finally, Spain granted to Britain the *asiento*—the sole right to carry slaves from Africa to the Spanish colonies—for a period of thirty years. Concessions such as these, however, owed less to the feats of British arms in North America itself than to Marlborough's splendid victories in Europe. But it was during this war that Britain emerged as the most formidable sea power in the world, and this was to have an inestimable effect on the future.

The major colonial theatre of operations in the War of Jenkins' Ear (which merged into that of the Austrian Succession, 1739–48) was the Caribbean, and the defeat of Britain's great offensive in that area has already been described. But there was also important fighting on the continent as well. In the south British forces, now commanded by Oglethorpe, failed twice more in attempts to take St Augustine. Nevertheless, in 1742, Oglethorpe, with only 600 men, skilfully cut to pieces a Spanish army of 3,000 intent on conquering Georgia.

This important defensive success was matched by an offensive victory in the north. Despite the loss of Nova Scotia, the French position in that area had actually grown stronger rather than weaker. On the island of Cape Breton they had built the huge fortress of Louisburg to command the Gulf of St Lawrence. Moreover, the majority of the inhabitants of Nova Scotia itself were still French Acadians (original settlers of the maritime provinces), who remained stubbornly hostile to their English rulers. Thus, the threat to New England from the area was at least as strong as ever, and in Massachusetts Governor William Shirley began to plan an audacious project— the capture of Louisburg itself. A force of 4,000 New England volunteers was organised under Sir William Pepperrell.

Fortune seemed to favour the efforts of the Americans. Louisburg was weakly garrisoned. From the far away West Indies, Commodore Peter Warren offered to escort and support the colonists with three warships. On the other side of the ocean, in Brest, the main French fleet which could have relieved the fort was blockaded by British squadrons. Lastly, as the attackers neared Louisburg, Warren managed to capture twenty French vessels which were heading for the fortress laden with provisions and ammunition. While attempts at direct assault failed, starvation soon took its toll and reduced the French garrison to surrender.

The French wasted no time in attempting to retrieve their fortress. However, one major fleet which slipped the British blockade was scattered by gales, while another was destroyed by Warren and Anson. A great naval victory by Hawke, off Rochelle in 1747, ended all French hopes of recapturing Louisburg by a feat of arms. But in the end it was returned to Louis XV at the Treaty of Aix-la-Chapelle, which ended the war; conquests by Maurice de Saxe in the Low Countries were useful bargaining counters. For once, the French land strategy had succeeded. Thus, the enterprise of the New Englanders had been largely in vain.

Opposite, the city of Savannah, the first settlement in Georgia, the year after its establishment in 1733; the colony was established as a buffer between the main British colonies and those of Spain in the south.

The final conflict

The great world conflict known as the Seven Years War actually began in America some years before the war was formally declared in Europe. In 1753, the advancing French built Fort Duquesne at the great river intersection where the Ohio River begins and where the city of Pittsburgh stands today. Upon learning of this the colony of Virginia, which also claimed the area, despatched a small force commanded by the young George Washington with orders to dispossess the French. Washington was surrounded and forced to capitulate to superior French forces, but the British government decided to support Viginia strongly. A year later, General Edward Braddock, with 3,000 British regulars under his command and with Washington as aide-de-camp, marched westwards to destroy Duquesne. But in the wilderness near the Monongahela River, Braddock led his forces to a signal defeat.

On 9 July a French force, much smaller than Braddock's advance group of 1,500 men, blundered into the British and its commander was killed. Jean Dumas, the French second-in-command, spectacularly reversed what should have been a French defeat. Splitting his men into two groups, and sending them into parallel ravines, he caught the British in a raking cross-fire. Braddock's van reeled back; his rear advanced; the main body of his men was

caught in a struggling melee into which the French continued to pour their fire. Braddock, as brave but less cunning than a bull, rode about the field shouting, had five horses killed beneath him and was finally shot down. Two-thirds of his men fell with him. Washington and the remainder hastily retreated into Virginia.

News from the north was not much better. Admiral Boscawen failed in an attempt to waylay a French fleet bringing reinforcements for Canada, and these fresh troops were soon joined by an exceptionally able commander, the Marquis de Montcalm. Then, in 1756, war broke out on a full scale in Europe, and the British government faced a major political crisis. At last, England's sick genius, William Pitt, was called in to take direction of the deteriorating situation.

Pitt's war strategy was simple and direct. He wished to weaken France's position as a great power as much as was possible. But England would generally avoid facing France's large continental armies; that area

Above, Louis Joseph de Montcalm (1712–59), the French general who recaptured Lake Ontario from the English in 1756 and took Fort William Henry the following year. He was killed during the British capture of Quebec in 1759.

Left, the struggle for control of North America in the mid-eighteenth century. Britain's eventual success was mainly a result of superiority of numbers.

Opposite top, the capture of the French fortress of Louisburg, on Cape Breton Island, in Canada, by a force of New Englanders in 1745. Rivalry between France and England spilled over into North America, but events there were seen as of minor importance, and Louisburg was soon restored to France in exchange for Madras. National Maritime Museum, London.

Opposite bottom, the capture of the French citadel of Quebec by the English led by James Wolfe in 1759. The daring attack, made by scaling a cliff known as the Heights of Abraham, led to the collapse of French power in North America. National Army Museum, London.

Map legend:
- English colonies
- Territory surrendered by the French in 1714
- Territory surrendered by the French in 1763

of action would be left to Britain's powerful ally, Frederick the Great of Prussia, whose military machine would be primed with British money. Instead, Britain would concentrate on using her advantages at sea to the utmost. France's colonial empire was to be destroyed and her overseas commerce ruined. According to Pitt's grand strategy, the French navy would be blockaded in its home ports while British armies would be transported across the ocean to conquer North America. To achieve these ends, Pitt sketched out the campaigns himself. He also chose good men to execute them, removing senior but incompetent officers and promoting promising juniors. Men like Wolfe, Saunders and Amherst performed magnificently in the field, but the arm that reached across the ocean was unquestionably Pitt's.

Yet it took another year for matters to begin to improve. In 1756, Montcalm in a daring raid, seized the British fort of Oswego on Lake Ontario; in 1757, he ranged deep into New York, taking Fort William Henry,

where many of the British garrison were subsequently massacred by the Indians.

In 1758, however, came Pitt's great three-pronged attack. One British wing moved west towards Fort Duquesne, another north-east to besiege Louisburg, while the centre advanced up the Lake Champlain-Richelieu River route to attack the very heart of New France. The plan was only partially success-ful. The dying General Forbes cut his way across the mountains and occupied Du-quesne, while Louisburg eventually capitu-lated to Amherst and Wolfe after a long siege, but Abercromby's vital push in the centre was a failure. At Fort Ticonderoga, Montcalm, commanding in person, had built a huge redoubt of fallen trees. Aber-cromby, with a foolishness which ap-proached criminal negligence, sent his Scottish Highlanders to their deaths in direct frontal assaults. After losing 1,500 men, the British withdrew.

Not until 1759, therefore, did the great assault against Quebec take place. In June of that year a huge fleet commanded by Admiral Charles Saunders and conveying 8,500 troops, led by the thirty-two-year-old James Wolfe, moved up the St Lawrence. The British pilots, among whom was James Cook—later to be known as the greatest navigator of the age—plotted the course with scrupulous care, and at the end of the month, Saunders had reached Quebec with-out losing a single ship. But Montcalm proved resourceful in defending his great fastness, and Wolfe spent the summer deliberating on the best way to come to

grips with him. Finally, as the campaign season was drawing towards its close in September, he selected one of the least likely tactical plans on his list. Sailing down river at night, the British troops secretly landed and scaled the forbidding cliffs by a narrow path which was providentially almost un-guarded. Thus, at 6 a.m. on the morning of 13 September, both armies faced each other outside the walls of Quebec on the Plains of Abraham, and Wolfe and Montcalm pre-pared to meet a destiny that would be both historical and personal. The steady fire of the British regulars won the day over Montcalm's raw militia. Both commanders were killed. Quebec was quickly besieged and fell a few days later.

The great citadel had fallen, but the war was not yet over. Montcalm's second-in-command, the courageous Chevalier de Lévis, gathered together the still significant French forces in the area and retreated to Montreal. Saunder's fleet and many of the English were forced to depart before the St Lawrence froze over. Then, in April of 1760, Lévis, with a mixed force of 7,000 men, reappeared on the Plains of Abraham, challenged and defeated General James Murray's weakened garrison of 3,000. The British retreated inside Quebec and were in their turn besieged by the French. A month later, when the ice melted, a British squadron sailed up the St Lawrence to the relief of the fortress.

Lévis was forced to retreat again to Montreal but was determined to stay in the field. Perhaps the British, in spite of their

overshelming force, would make some terrible blunder. Even with Quebec lost, a French army still on its feet and fighting would make a great difference in a peace treaty if the war ended in the meantime. But Amherst, who had captured Niagara and Ticonderoga when Wolfe was taking Quebec, made no blunders. Up the Richelieu River, up the St Lawrence, down river from Lake Ontario—the British forces moved on Montreal from three directions. On 6 September 1759 Governor Vaudreuil ordered capitulation. Lévis burned his battalion flags in a last gesture of defiance. French dominion in North America had ended.

With the fighting in continental North America over, and with the command of the sea firmly in their hands, the British now turned with a vengeance to the West Indies. In that area opportunities for conquest had been suddenly increased, for Spain had foolishly and precipitously entered the war on the side of France. In 1759 Guadeloupe was taken, as well as some French slave-trading settlements in West Africa. Mar-tinique, however, successfully resisted a major British attack. But in 1762, two huge amphibious operations were aimed at both Martinique and Cuba. The former fell to Rodney and Monckton in February, the latter to Pocock and Albemarle in August. Finally, after France and Spain had hastily signed a treaty of peace, news came that a British expedition had captured Manila in the faraway Pacific as well.

Thus, the war saw most of Pitt's dreams

THE EUROPEANS IN AMERICA

Date	Latin America	North America	Europe
1500			Charles of Spain becomes Emperor Charles V (1519)
	The Conquest of Mexico (1521)	Giovanni de Verrazano reaches the coast of New York (1523)	
	Creation of Royal and Supreme Council of the Indies (1524)		
	The Conquest of Peru (1531)	Jacques Cartier begins exploration of the St Lawrence (1534)	
	Mendoza's administration in Mexico begins (1535)		
			Ignatius Loyola first president of Jesuit order (1541)
	Las Casas achieves new laws for the Indians (1542)		
	Discovery of silver mountain at Potosí (1545)		Council of Trent (1545) Disputation on the rights of the Indians at Valladolid (1550)
	Toledo's administration in Peru begins (1569)		
	University of Lima founded (1572)	Sir Humphrey Gilbert claims Newfoundland for England (1583)	Portugal absorbed by Spain (1580)
			Death of Philip II of Spain (1598)
1600			English East India Company founded (1600) Death of Elizabeth I of England. Accession of James I (1603)
	Spanish Jesuits at La Plata (1605)		Gunpowder Plot (1605)
		Jamestown founded by Christopher Newport (1607) Champlain founds Quebec, reaches Great Lakes (1608) The Dutch on the Hudson River (1609)	
		John Rolph starts tobacco cultivation in Virginia (1612)	Assassination of Henry IV (1610)
	Raleigh in Guiana (1616)		Richelieu becomes Secretary of state (1616)
	The Dutch in Guiana (1620)	Pilgrim Fathers arrive at Cape Cod (1620)	
	The French in Guiana (1625)		Death of James I. Accession of Charles I (1625) Richelieu organizes Company of New France (1627)

Date	Latin America	North America	Europe
1630	The Dutch in Brazil (1630)	Founding of Maryland by Cecil Calvert (1632)	
	The Dutch leave Brazil (1640)		Portugal regains independence (1640) Execution of Charles I (1649)
		Capture of Jamaica by the British (1655)	
	University of Mexico founded (1663)	Carolina Charter (1663)	Restoration of Charles II (1660)
	Hudson Bay Company awarded royal charter (1670)		Treaty of Madrid (1670)
		Marquette and Joliet reach the Mississippi (1673) La Salle follows Mississippi to its mouth (1682) Hostilities between England and France (1689)	War of the League of Augsburg (1689) Treaty of Ryswick (1697)
1700		Sack of Deerfield by Indians (1707) Nicholson secures Nova Scotia for England (1710) Loss of Hill's fleet in the St Lawrence (1711)	Bourbon dynasty in Spain, Philip V (1700)
	Creation of Spanish Ministry of Marine and the Indies (1714)		Treaty of Utrecht (1713)
	Creation of new vice-royalties of New Granada and La Plata (1717)	Founding of New Orleans by Bienville (1718) Founding of Georgia by Oglethorpe (1733)	
			War of Jenkins' Ear (1739) Treaty of Aix-la-Chapelle (1748)
		Montcalm seizes Oswego (1756) British take Louisbourg (1758) Wolfe captures Quebec and Montreal surrenders (1759)	Accession of Charles III of Spain (1759) Peace of Paris (1763)
	Expulsion of the Jesuits from Paraguay (1767) Rebellion of Tupac Amaru in Peru (1780) Rebellion of Tiradentes in Brazil (1792)		

realized. The same could not be said for the Peace of Paris, signed in February of 1763. By then Pitt had been driven from power, and negotiations had been carried on by the less imperially minded Earl of Bute. Britain's gains were great, but France's world power had only been weakened and she could still hope for yet another war of revenge. Nevertheless, Britain kept the huge areas of Canada and the eastern Mississippi valley as well as several small West Indian islands. Spain ceded Florida to the English, in order to get Cuba back, and was granted Louisiana as compensation by her French ally. After nearly a century of conflict, Britain was at last supreme in continental North America.

But Europe's disposition of North America, drafted in 1763, would last but for a season. The house that Pitt had built fell apart within twenty years through the spirit of colonial rebels. The great empires of Spain and Portugal similarly crumbled soon afterwards. Nevertheless, the long period of colonial conflict established some enduring realities. The vast areas where Spain, Portugal, France and England planted their progeny have kept, with modifications, the indelible stamp of their parent nations.

The collapse of the colonial empires did not alter these basic factors. However important the American Revolution may have been, more important still was the fact that the largest part of the rich North American continent was going to be inhabited by English-speaking peoples carrying with the their English cultural, political and economic heritage.

The impact on world history created by the development of the American hemisphere has been inestimable. This epic story, still unfinished, began with the European mastery of the oceans, the discovery and settlement of the New World. Conquest, colonization, slave-trading and imperial rivalry—all called into being new nations and new peoples ready to take their part in the succeeding age of national, industrial and ideological revolutions that has shaped our modern world.

Opposite, The Death of General Wolfe, *painted by Benjamin West. Despite personal illness, James Wolfe led the daring British assault on Quebec which took the city in 1759. Royal Collection.*

Chapter 23

The Far East

In the seventeenth century the Manchu conquerors of China created the largest and most powerful realm that had existed since the time of Mongol supremacy. Japan, under the Tokugawa shoguns, achieved internal peace and enjoyed a century of economic and intellectual development. In southeast Asia the kingdom of Siam grew in power and resources, while its neighbours and rivals, Burma, Cambodia and Vietnam, suffered from internal strife.

The rulers of these countries were strong enough to dictate the terms of such intercourse as they permitted with Europe. Visitors from the West recorded with admiration the magnificence of their capitals and the myriads of their armies. Nevertheless the foundations of Western domination were established over northern Asia and in the Indian Ocean at this time.

The Russian conquest of Siberia

In 1581 a Cossack adventurer, Yermak, crossed the Ural mountains and captured the town of Sibir, the capital of a local Tartar chieftain, and from this time the whole vast region between the Urals and the Pacific was called Siberia. Although Yermak himself subsequently met his death, by 1600 the Russians were firmly established in western Siberia, where they founded a settlement at Tobolsk. From here the Russians, few in numbers but equipped with firearms, pushed rapidly eastwards, subduing the scattered native tribes whom they encountered. They overcame the difficulties of travel by making use of the great rivers, much as did the contemporary French voyageurs in Canada. By 1649 they had reached the Pacific and founded the settlement of Okhotsk. They then turned southwards and by 1651 had explored Lake Baikal and established the town of Irkutsk. Thence they pushed eastward to found Nerchinsk in 1654 and to sail down the Amur River. Here, however, they came into collision with the Manchus and were for the time being checked.

The Cossacks were brave and hardy adventurers but fierce and ruthless in their treatment of the natives. These were held down by building a chain of *ostrogs*—

stockaded trading posts something like the frontier posts of the American West. The lure of Siberia lay in its wealth of fur-bearing animals, and the conquered tribes had to pay a tribute of furs to the Russian government. The illegal exactions of the Russian settlers were much heavier, and they inflicted the most savage penalties upon those who failed to satisfy their demands. In 1637 the tsar established a department of Siberian affairs at Tobolsk in an attempt to enforce order and justice, but many of the local officials were among the worst offenders.

Behind the soldiers and fur traders came peasants, who were mostly exiles seeking to escape from serfdom or political disorder in European Russia. Settlement grew slowly, but by 1700 there were some 250,000 Russians in Siberia and the vast region was becoming an increasingly valuable part of the expanding Muscovite Empire.

The contest for the spice trade

In the seventeenth century the maritime supremacy of the Portuguese in the Indian Ocean was destroyed by the Dutch and the English. The Dutch began direct ventures to the East Indies because they were excluded from the spice trade at Lisbon by Philip II. In 1602 the government of the Netherlands consolidated a number of concerns into a single Dutch East India Company. This company waged war against the Portuguese in Indonesia where they had previously monopolized the spice trade. In 1622 the Dutch founded Batavia (Jakarta) which became their headquarters. Malacca, the chief Portuguese settlement in Malaya, was captured by them in 1641, and they drove the Spaniards from the Moluccas, although they failed to expel them from the Philippines. In China the Dutch were defeated in an attempt to take Macao, though from 1623 to 1662 they held part of Formosa.

The English East India Company, which was organized in 1600, tried to secure a share of the spice trade, but although England and Holland had been allies against the Spaniards the Dutch would not tolerate English competition in the East Indies. In 1623 they seized the English trading post at Amboina and put to death most of the Englishmen there. The English East India Company could not match the resources of the Dutch one and eventually gave up the contest. By the end of the century the Dutch had reduced the native sultans to vassalage and had firmly established their empire in the East Indies.

In India the English company, despite opposition from the Portuguese and the Dutch, secured trading rights from the Mogul emperor Jahangir. But so long as they had no secure base of their own their position was precarious. In 1639 they secured a grant of land on the Coromandel coast from the local ruler and there founded Fort St George (Madras). On the west coast the Portuguese held Goa and also the island

of Bombay. In 1661, when King Charles II married the Portuguese princess, Catherine of Braganza, Bombay was part of her dowry. In 1667 Charles gave it to the East India Company and, under the capable administration of its first governor, Gerald Aungier, it grew from a neglected village into a thriving city, since it was secure from both Mahratta raids and the exactions of Mogul governors. Calcutta, which became the third centre of British trade and influence, was also a place of no importance until Job Charnock established himself there in 1686. After a period of hostilities with the Mogul governor of Bengal, East India Company control was finally recognized by Aurangzeb in 1691. Meanwhile the Dutch drove the Portuguese from Ceylon and wrested trading posts from them in southern India.

After the Dutch and the English came the French. In 1674 they secured a settlement at Pondicherry and another at Chandernagore in 1688. The French were active in missionary work and French missionaries went to Burma, Siam, Cambodia and Vietnam. For a time, during the reign of Louis XIV, the French seemed likely to secure political and commercial ascendancy in southeast Asia, especially in Siam, but their activities provoked a reaction which, together with the wars of Louis in Europe, checked the French expansion.

The Spaniards in the Philippines

The conquest of Manila by Legaspi in 1571 established Spanish power in the Philippine islands, but their hold upon the archipelago as a whole remained very limited. Much of the mountainous interior regions remained

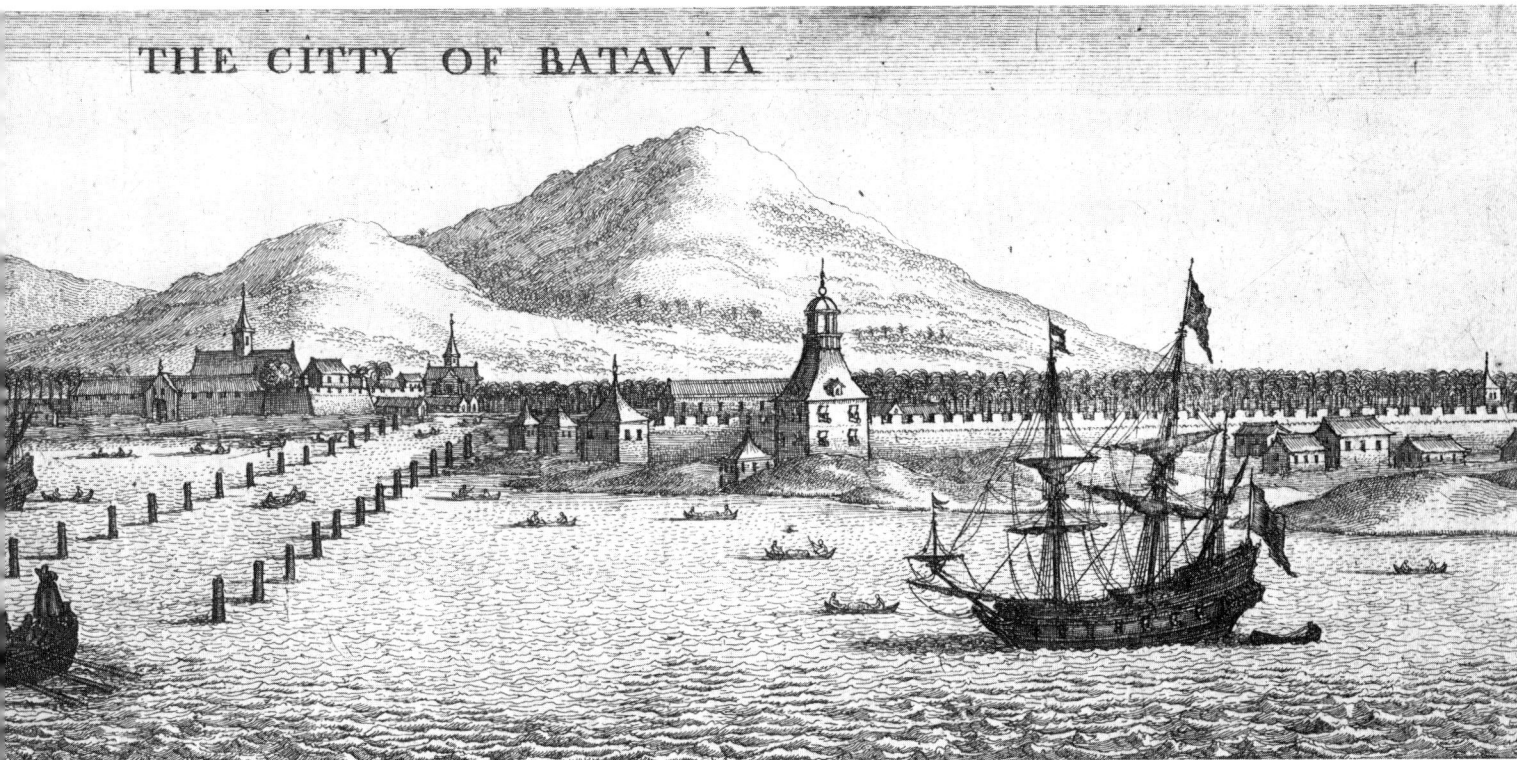

virtually untouched by them, while in Mindanao and Sulu they were held at bay by the fanatical converts to Islam whom they called Moros. The Philippines were governed by a captain-general, or governor, with subordinate officials. He was responsible to the viceroy of Mexico, since the Spaniards regarded the Philippines as an offshoot of their colonies in Latin America, which in many ways it came to resemble. As in Latin America, Spanish officers who had taken part in the conquest were given large estates, *encomiendas*, which they ruled as feudal fiefs. The Church also became a large land-owner, and the clergy, especially the friars, exercised great authority.

Chinese junks brought silks and porcelains to Manila which the Spaniards purchased with silver dollars brought from Mexico in the galleons from Acapulco, so that the Mexican dollar became a standard currency in the Far East. The Spaniards were nervous of the large Chinese settlement in Manila and they even massacred some of the Chinese on suspicion of revolt.

The Manchus

The country northeast of the Great Wall which was to become known as Manchuria consisted first of all of a southern part which had long been settled by Chinese, although it was still rather a colonial area. The plateau and steppe region to the northwest was the home of nomad Mongol tribes, while the mountain and forest region in the northeast was inhabited by Tungus tribes, of whom the Manchus were one group. Their chiefs were given high-sounding titles by the Ming and so encouraged to remain faithful tributaries. One such was Nurhachi, who was born in or about 1559. He proved to be

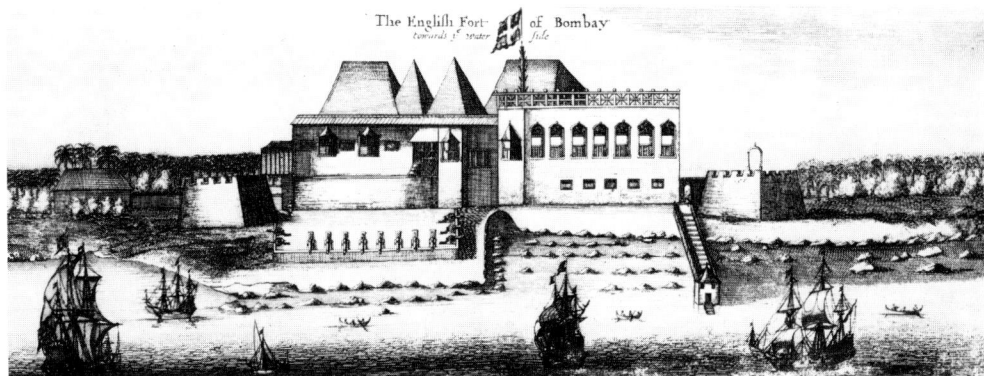

a leader of genius, who built up his power in a long series of successful campaigns until he had gained control over many of the tribes and in 1616 assumed the royal style. The Ming court, alarmed at the growth of his power, sent aid to his enemies. Nurhachi in reply invaded the Chinese-settled area of Manchuria. His army, divided into divisions or banners, defeated the Ming forces, took Mukden and overran most of Manchuria. Many of the Chinese there, sickened by Ming misrule, readily joined them. These were also organized in banners, there being ultimately eight Manchu and eight Chinese banners.

The Ming forces, aided by cannon made under the supervision of the Jesuits, managed to check the Manchu advance upon Peking by way of the Shanhaikuan pass. Nurhachi died in 1626 and his son endeavoured to outflank the Chinese defences by overrunning western Manchuria and Inner Mongolia. Some of the Mongol tribes were defeated while others allied themselves with the Manchu ruler, and in 1635 they gave him the state seal of the former Mongul emperors, thus recognizing him as the rightful inheritor of the empire

Above, the English fort at Bombay; the town was a Dutch possession from 1534 until 1661, when it was handed over to England. The English made it their foothold in the west of India, and also the headquarters of their East India Company until 1858.

Top, the town of Batavia on the island of Java, the headquarters of the Dutch East India Company from the early seventeenth century and the main base from which the Dutch kept their fierce hold over the profitable spice islands.

of Genghis Khan. The Manchu ruler now assumed the dynastic title of Ch'ing or Pure, which signified his intention to overthrow the Ming in China itself.

To meet the cost of the war against the Manchus the government greatly increased the land tax and other levies. This deepened the disaffection among the landowning class, while the peasantry were afflicted by drought and famine especially in north China. Among the consequent leaders of rebellion a Shensi peasant, Li Tzu-cheng, became pre-eminent. The imperial forces sent against him were defeated or else went over to him, and in 1643 he took Sian, the capital of Shensi. In 1644 he advanced on Peking which he captured and sacked. The Ming emperor committed suicide and Li proclaimed himself emperor. But the best forces the Ming still possessed were under the command of General Wu San-kuei, who was guarding the Great Wall. He elected to side with the Manchus rather than with the ex-brigand Li and made an agreement with the Manchu Prince Dorgun who was acting as regent for the infant grandson of Nurhachi. Consequently, Li was defeated and the Manchus entered Peking.

After the fall of the capital a relative of the deceased Ming emperor was set up in Nanking, but he was soon defeated and killed by the Manchus and their Chinese allies. Another prince of the Ming house held out, first at Canton and later in the extreme west of China. He was aided by the pirate leader, Cheng Cheng-kung, who for a while held much of the south coast. The Ming claimant to the throne in gratitude gave him a title of honour, which Europeans rendered as Koxinga. After he could no longer hold out on the mainland, Koxinga in 1661 established himself in Formosa, from which he expelled the Dutch. He and his son continued to wage war against the Manchus at sea. The conquest of southern and western China was accomplished by Wu San-kuei and other Chinese generals who had joined the Manchus. After years of fighting the last Ming forces were driven

into Burma; but for a while much of the south and west of China was under the almost independent rule of Wu San-kuei.

The Manchu dynasty gave China good government, internal peace and increase of empire. Under the dynamic K'ang Hsi (1662–1722) and his successors, Yung Chang (1723–35) and the extremely able Ch'ien Lung (1736–96), the Chinese Empire reached the greatest extent in its long history. The lands adjoining China proper were brought firmly under control, the Mongols were crushed; the area northwest of China was organized as Sinkiang ('the new dominion'); the Tibetan Dalai Lama became a Chinese nominee; and the borders of Manchuria were stabilized by treaty with the Russians at the northernmost reaches of the Amur River. Formosa was conquered and integrated into the empire; Korea, Annam, Burma and Nepal acknowledged the suzerainty of the Celestial Emperor.

Internal peace ensured prosperity, for China was a rich, self-sufficient land. The area under cultivation was notably increased, and population rose steeply, reaching some three hundred million by 1800. No significant changes were introduced—which was, to the Chinese, entirely proper. Reverence for ancestors, for the past, for long-established practices, was a prime feature of the Confucian ethic, reinforced by the remarkable continuity of Chinese history.

Chinese conservatism was in fact becoming still more deeply ingrained. One of many fields in which this became apparent was literary activity, a great deal of which consisted in encyclopedic compilations of literary classics and an increasingly sophisticated apparatus of critical scholarship. The same tendency, already perceptible under the previous Ming dynasty, appeared in all the arts, with the partial exception of porcelain. (Though, significantly, the new decorations the Chinese discovered were mainly applied on export ware.) The skills of the past were employed to produce fine works of craftsmanship, often superbly executed in the great styles of the past; but creativity was absent.

Change is not, so to speak, compulsory; and attachment to the past has been the rule rather than the exception in history. Chinese indifference to new ideas was to prove disastrous in the nineteenth century, not because China was in some absolute sense 'in decline', but because her society was forced open by the aggressive, technologically advanced culture of Europe.

Much the same can be said of nineteenth-century Chinese political history. In his later years Ch'ien Lung leaned upon a favourite minister, Ho Shen, who seems to have carried financial corruption to the most extravagant lengths. The tangle of injustice and extortion produced by a corrupt civil service provoked the first revolts for almost a hundred years. Henceforward they were to be frequent until the end of the dynasty— and the empire—in 1912. The incapacity of

Ch'ien Lung's successors indicates that the Manchus were following the pattern of previous dynasties: vigorous early emperors were succeeded by increasingly effete sovereigns, until an energetic usurper created a new dynasty—which followed the same pattern. Again, it was not so much a question of Chinese decline as of a period of weakness coinciding with the irruption of a dynamic society—the West—into the closed world of China.

The Jesuits in China

The one source from which the Chinese might have acquired new knowledge without loss of face was the Christian missionary. The overwhelming majority of missionaries were Catholics, of whom the most distinguished were the Jesuits. A Jesuit, Matteo Ricci, had been the first European Christian missionary in China since the Tang period (AD 618–907) and had commended himself to the Ming emperors as an astronomer and mathematician. Jesuits continued to act as scientific advisers under K'ang Hsi, who appreciated their reform of the Chinese calendar (a most important feature of Chinese religious life) and in 1692 issued what was in effect an edict of toleration.

The Jesuits proved equally adaptable in their attempts to convert the Chinese, whose eclectic approach to religion made them impatient of claims to their exclusive devotion and who were besides deeply attached to the rites honouring ancestors. To attack these was to attack the fundament of Chinese civilization, and Ricci and other Jesuits achieved some success by desisting, arguing that the Confucian ethic and filial piety were not incompatible with Christianity.

The question of 'the rites' was hotly debated within the Church, at least some of the opposition to Jesuit practice deriving from jealousy of the order within the Church. In 1715 the pope condemned the rites, later reinforcing his condemnation with the Bull *Ex Illa Die* (1742). The hitherto benevolent K'ang Hsi, who had backed the Jesuits, was deeply offended by this insult to Chinese culture. New Chinese decrees effectively prevented the spread of Christianity (1717), and Chinese Christianity went into a decline that was hastened by the papal dissolution of the Jesuit order (1773).

All questions of religion aside, it was a misfortune for the Chinese too. Contact with the Jesuits enabled the Chinese court to become familiar with the inventions of the Western barbarians without publicity and therefore without loss of face. Not that the conditions existed in China for an industrial revolution of the sort about to begin in the West; but the Chinese might at least have come to understand the extent of Western power and the workings of the Western mind. Since Europeans were no better informed, mutual incomprehension was responsible for much of the violence

MAKOU

Above, Matteo Ricci, a Jesuit priest, and Ly Paulus, a Chinese convert, who introduced Christianity to China between 1580 and 1610. Ricci encouraged intellectual contact between China and the West, and, although he was not able to win many converts to Christianity, he was held in great respect by the Chinese.

Above centre, Lord Macartney, who led the first British mission to China in 1793, in an attempt to win trading concessions. The emperor, however, had no interest in trade or any other contact with the 'barbarians'. National Portrait Gallery, London.

Above left, the Amboina massacre of 1623, in which the Dutch killed an English trading settlement on one of the islands of the East Indies, suspecting a conspiracy against their trading monopolies. This incident provoked the first break between the two Protestant countries, which had previously been united in their opposition to Spain and the Spanish Empire.

Left, Dutch ships in the Chinese port of Macao in the 1660s; in the previous century Macao had been the centre of the Portuguese monopoly of trade with China.

Opposite, Nurhachi (1559–1626), the Manchu leader who united the tribesmen of Manchuria and began an all-out attack on the Ming dynasty of China in 1618. The Manchus eventually won control of the whole of China in 1644.

with which East and West met in the nineteenth century.

The Chinese conception of the world made other forms of contact impossible. Insulated for millennia by seas, deserts and mountains from states of comparable power and civilization, the Chinese had known only cultural inferiors—like the steppe nomads, who had sometimes overrun China, only to adopt Chinese speech and customs—and imitators like the Japanese.

Understandably, therefore, they had come to believe that their state was 'the state' and that Chinese culture was 'culture'. The emperor was the only ruler below heaven, though not all barbarians had yet submitted to him or mastered the ways of civilization. Of diplomacy, which presupposes the existence of more than one state, the Chinese had no conception.

When Britain sent embassies, they were greeted as tribute-bearing missions. The arrival of Lord Macartney (1793) and Lord Amherst (1816) was met with impressive ceremony and great politeness, though the question of whether the ambassadors would kowtow to the emperor (thus acknowledging Britain's tributary status) caused dignified wrangles. But there was no question of a permanent embassy: tributaries delivered gifts, heard the emperor's commands and took themselves off.

The China trade

Inability to establish diplomatic relations became increasingly irritating with the growth of trade with China, particularly to the British, who outstripped their commercial rivals in the eighteenth century. The China trade was extremely profitable but subject to strict limitations. The Portuguese in Macao, the British and other Europeans in Canton, existed in waterfront 'factories' sealed off from China. They dealt solely with a guild of Chinese merchants, the Hong, who were able to fix prices arbitrarily; official China ignored their existence. European representations failed to make any impression on the Chinese.

From their own point of view, the Chinese had good reasons. If diplomatic agreements were unthinkable, diplomatic regulation of trade was a still more absurd notion: merchants (even Chinese merchants) were a despised class, and the emperor could not participate in their activities. Furthermore, there was no place for foreign merchants within the structure of Chinese society: their presence on the waterfront was 'overlooked', and if they misbehaved the Hong merchants were punished. An imperial officer taxed the Hong, of course, so that the emperor was able to profit by the arrangement without being contaminated.

This attitude was reinforced by China's self-sufficiency. Europeans wanted Chinese silks, porcelain, tea; China wanted nothing from Europe. There was an important economic aspect to this situation: China had to be paid in bullion, which had been intermittently drained from the West since Roman times. The imbalance of trade between East and West led Europeans to wink at illegal traffic in the one commodity Chinese wanted: opium. From 1773 the East India Company had a monopoly of its manufacture and sold it to all comers: what they did with it was their business. By 1800 large quantities of the drug were being sold over the sides of the European ships in the Canton River.

The nineteenth century witnessed a tremendous development in the opium trade and increasingly direct participation in it by Europeans. Diplomatic redress was impossible without diplomatic relations; mutual incomprehension excluded moderation. Chinese notions of collective responsibility made it natural for them to blame all Europeans for the behaviour of a few; and an unfortified coast and a non-existent navy made threats or reprisals directed against the European merchant community the natural response to European self-assertion. The pattern of nineteenth-century conflict was already predictable.

Japan

Japan was closed to the West even more firmly than China. The Europeans who

arrived from 1542–43 taught the Japanese to use firearms and build fortifications on the European model. They also brought Christianity, which enjoyed considerable popularity in the sixteenth century but became increasingly identified with political subversion and external aggression. The Japanese reaction was ferocious and extreme: by 1638 Christianity had been uprooted by force and Japanese ports shut to Europeans: even Japanese abroad were forbidden to return. Previously a roving people with a reputation as fearless soldiers and pirates, the Japanese became introverted and let a sizeable fleet and an expanding trade run down.

The only exception was trade with China and with the Dutch, who were allowed to operate from the islet of Deshima. They lived in cramped conditions and under close supervision of a sort that made the lot of Europeans in Canton enviable; and once a year they were brought to grovel at the imperial court. Through the Dutch, the Japanese acquired some knowledge of Western science, especially medicine, though by the early eighteenth century only two Dutch ships were arriving each year. Until the Industrial Revolution, Japan knew enough of the West to be certain that she remained secure against interference; and she wanted to know no more.

Ming China
Territories subject to the Ming

NOMAD CENTRAL ASIA

MANCHURIA
Mukden
Peking
Yellow River
Grand Canal
Nanking
Yangtse Kiang
KOREA
JAPAN
BURMA
Canton
Macao
HAINAN
VIETNAM
LAOS
SIAM
Mekong
CAMBODIA
Saigon
Malacca
SUMATRA

Temple of the Earth
Temple of Confucius
Temple of the Moon
Imperial Palace
Temple of the Sun
Temple of Agriculture
Temple of Heaven

Left, a male costume for the Nō theatre, dating from the Edo period, of around 1600; by this date the forms of the Nō theatre had become highly stylized.

Below, a Dutch trading post at Nagasaki in Japan; the Dutch began to trade there in 1567, but after 1640 they were confined to a small island in the harbour – the only Europeans allowed to enter Japan.

Opposite, China in the early seventeenth century, shortly before the Ming dynasty was taken over by the Manchus. The inset shows the Inner City of Peking, built by the Mongols in the thirteenth century.

The Tokugawa regime

Isolation was not unfamiliar to the Japanese. The mountainous archipelago of Japan was most densely populated on the east coast, away from the Asian continent; even China was far away. Once in every few centuries the Japanese took some part in Asian wars, and their early history had been deeply influenced by the superior civilization of China; but extended contact was impossible, and Japanese society absorbed Chinese influences without losing its distinctive character.

Isolation, an agrarian economy and a regionalism created by the irregular topography of Japan had led to the development of a military feudal society in which central authority was hard to maintain for any length of time. Since the twelfth century, the real head of the Japanese government had usually been a shogun ('generalissimo'). The emperor was a ceremonial figure, deeply revered but powerless. However, the shogun might in turn be the puppet of a powerful noble house with a 'clan' of relatives and military retainers (the famous *samurai*). Japan easily became the battlefield

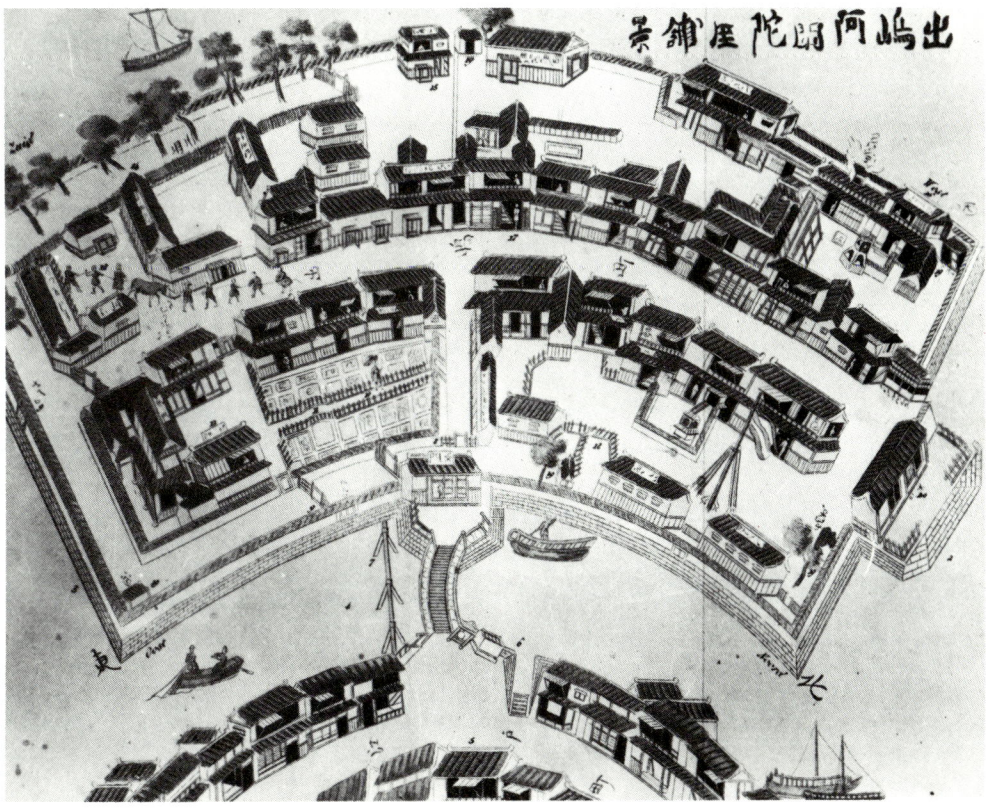

of rival clans, as was once more the case during most of the fourteenth and fifteenth centuries.

From 1603 to 1867 the shogunate was in the hands of the Tokugawa family, who greatly strengthened it. But, although Japan enjoyed a long period of peace under the Tokugawas, the price was high. Unity and stability—and Tokugawa power—could be maintained only by ceaseless vigilance. Access to the imperial court at Kyoto was rigidly controlled by the shogun. The great nobles were compelled to build villas at the effective capital, Yedo (later Tokyo), where their families resided permanently, as permanent hostages; noble fiefs were changed so that suspects were always neighbours of powerful loyal vassals; the nobility was coerced or encouraged to spend lavishly so that they should not become too powerful; travel was viewed with suspicion; and the country was filled with spies and spies on spies. The Tokugawa regime was as near a police state as pre-industrial technology allowed.

Extended peace aided the growth of a prosperous merchant class and a money economy, and these were accompanied, from the late seventeenth century, by the development of a sophisticated urban society. Yedo, with almost a million inhabitants, was in the forefront, swollen with officials, noble families and their servants, merchants looking for a good time, and an army of entertainers both reputable and disreputable, hawkers, beggars and hangers-on. A new kind of audience stimulated the production of a vigorous and realistic popular art, including the puppet and *kabuki* theatres for which Japan's greatest dramatist, Chikamatsu Monzae-

mon (1653–1725), wrote his works, and the great woodblock artists, of whom the most famous were Hokusai (1760–1849) and Utamaro (1754–1806).

Tokugawa decay

The contradictions inherent in the Tokugawas' policies became apparent in the eighteenth century. Without external enemies (for the outside world had been abolished), a military aristocracy could not exist unchanged during a long period of peace. The shoguns, on whom the whole system rested, were not always fit for their post; and, lacking military occupation, many *samurai* and some of the great nobles fell into dissipation and debt. Masterless *samurai* became something of a social menace, a privileged caste of unemployed who were disbarred from useful work and made quarrelsome by pride and poverty.

Though the population remained at about 30 million throughout the eighteenth and well into the nineteenth century, agrarian disorders became frequent from the 1780s. The peasant's lot was always difficult in mountainous Japan, where more than half the land was uncultivable and the work of years was liable to destruction by earthquake, flood or typhoon, but things seem to have become appreciably worse in the eighteenth century, probably because landlords attempted to solve their own difficulties by evictions and increased demands on the peasantry.

The last shogun to make serious efforts to restore stability was Yoshimune (1717–44), and his programme amounted to little more than a revival of regimentation. He also issued the first of many decrees favouring debtors—for it was no part of the Tokugawas' intentions that merchants should become more powerful than their social superiors. Indeed, rigid maintenance of social distinctions had been one of the formulas of Tokugawa stability.

Other developments threatened the position of the Tokugawas themselves. They had encouraged Confucianism because it inculcated reverence for law and civil authority; but the Confucian cult of the emperor was less welcome to a military dictatorship. Revival of interest in Shinto, the indigenous religion of Japan, also fostered imperial sentiment, since it proclaimed the emperor's descent from the sun-goddess. From about the mid-eighteenth century a spirit that was at once deeply nationalistic and hostile to the shogunate became manifest. Other disquieting events, including the restiveness of the great feudatories in outlying areas (never effectively controlled by the Tokugawas), indicated that the 200-year-old police state could not endure much longer.

What would have replaced it remains a matter of speculation. The merchants—bankers and money-lenders rather than a mercantile or industrial middle class—would almost certainly not have done so. It is more likely that another cycle of feudal in-fighting would have commenced. In fact, Japan was to be wrenched out of her seclusion by the intrusion of Western ideas and technology, announced by the arrival of the American, Commodore Perry, in 1853. Unlike China, she proved capable of integrating them into her existing society, just as she had integrated Chinese culture a thousand years before. Post-Tokugawa Japan re-entered world history, but as a curious hybrid of old and new.

Siam

In the late sixteenth century Siam was conquered by the Burmese ruler Bayinnaung. But after his death in 1581 revolt in Burma against his son gave the Siamese prince, Pra Naret, the opportunity to reassert Siamese independence. In 1587 he defeated a Burmese attempt to take Ayuthia, the Siamese capital, and he also repelled a Cambodian invasion. In 1590 he became King Narasuen and inflicted further defeats upon the Burmese and Cambodians. The latter were for the time being crushed, and the former lost the provinces of Tavoy and Tennasserim. Narasuen, who is one of the great heroes of Siamese history, died in 1605. His immediate successors were less warlike and the Burmese were able to regain some of the territory they had lost.

The Siamese kings were ready to welcome foreign traders. They had already established relations with the Portuguese and the Spaniards and at the beginning of the century they admitted Japanese traders. A number of Japanese, some of them exiled Christian converts, were enlisted as mercenaries in the royal guard and for a time, under their leader, Yamada Nagamasa, played an important part in Siamese politics. The Dutch were allowed to establish trading posts at Patani in 1602 and Ayuthia in 1608. In 1609 the first Siamese embassy to visit Europe was received at The Hague. The English East India Company was given trading rights in Ayuthia in 1612 but found it difficult to compete with the Dutch and in 1622 withdrew from Siam for some years. During the reign of King Prasat T'ong, from 1630 to 1656, the Japanese, who had conspired against him, were driven out. These events left the Dutch in a position to monopolize the foreign trade, and this the Siamese naturally resented.

In 1657 King Narai came to the throne. As a curb to the aggressive Dutch, he welcomed the resumption of trade by the English in 1661, and he also showed favour to French Catholic missionaries, who in consequence mistakenly believed that he might be converted; in fact his real object was political. In 1675 a Greek called Constantine Phaulkon, who had entered Siam in the service of the English East India Company, rose to be superintendent of foreign trade and became very influential with the king. As the result of a quarrel with the agents of the English Company Phaulkon used his influence to promote French interests. A French embassy arrived in Ayuthia in 1685 and the Siamese sent representatives to Versailles in 1686. Meanwhile, Phaulkon had been converted by the Jesuits and he promoted an arrangement whereby French troops were to be stationed in Mergui and Bangkok, ostensibly for protection against the Dutch. The troops arrived in 1687, but a section of the Siamese nobility, headed by a general called Pra P'etraja, saw in this a menace to Siamese independence. In 1688 King Narai was taken ill and Pra P'etraja became regent. He immediately seized and executed Phaulkon. Then King Narai died and the regent succeeded him. Pra P'etraja then turned on the French; a number of them were killed and others had to leave the country. The result of this episode was that the Siamese attitude towards foreigners became less liberal. The trade privileges of the Dutch were curtailed and the English once again withdrew from Siam.

Burma

Upper and Lower Burma were reunited by King Anaukpetlun, but after his death in 1629 his successor Thalum, who removed the capital from Pegu to Ava, was faced with fresh revolts by the Mon people of the Irrawaddy delta region. He was a capable administrator, but his son Pindale, who ruled from 1648 to 1661, was incompetent. In addition to more trouble with the Mons and the Siamese, Pindale became involved

Opposite top left, an 18th-century print of ladies of the Japanese court.

Opposite top centre, a woodcut of ladders built to celebrate a festival by Katsushika Hokusai (1760–1849).

Opposite top right, a Japanese religious scroll of one of the holy texts of Shintoism, dating from the Tokugawa period.

Opposite bottom, a print by Utamaro of two women talking.

in difficulties with China. In 1658 Yung Li, the last Ming emperor, was driven out of Yunnan into Burma. He was imprisoned and his followers then pillaged parts of Upper Burma. Pindale was deposed in 1661 and his brother, Pye, who succeeded him, had to placate the Manchus by surrendering Yung Li to them. His defeated soldiers then dispersed. For the remainder of the century Burma was at peace, but its rulers were weaklings dominated by their ministers.

Annam

The kingdom of Annam—the modern Vietnam—still remained under the nominal rule of the descendants of Le Loi, the national hero who in the fifteenth century had freed his country from Chinese rule. But in fact power had fallen into the hands of feudal noble families, among whom the chief contenders were the Trinh and the Nguyen. The Trinh held Hanoi and the Red River valley, the Nguyen dominated southern Annam. From 1620 to 1674 civil war raged between the two families. The Nguyen, who received some help from the Portuguese at Macao, were able to hold their own and in 1674 a peace was made which left the Nguyen as rulers of southern Annam. For the sake of trade the Nguyen tolerated Catholic missionaries, although there were occasional severe persecutions. It was the missionaries who invented a romanization of the written Vietnamese language, which is still in use.

The Nguyen rulers, especially after they had made peace with the Trinh, expanded their territory southwards at the expense of the Cambonian kingdom, weakened by wars with the Siamese and by internal strife. Consequently by the end of the century it had lost most of the country around Saigon to the Vietnamese.

Laos

The remote and mountainous region of Laos, which had fallen under Burmese control in the sixteenth century, regained its independence in 1591. From 1637 until 1694 it was ruled by King Souligna-Vongsa, with his capital at Vientiane. In 1641 the first European made his appearance, a Dutchman named van Wuysthof. He came on a trading mission, but because of the difficulties of communication nothing came of it. In 1642 Father Leria, an Italian Jesuit, came to Vientiane and remained for five years, but the opposition of the Buddhists prevented him from opening a mission. After his departure Laos remained untouched by European influence until the nineteenth century. After the death of Souligna-Vongsa succession disputes broke out and at the beginning of the eighteenth century Laos became divided into the kingdoms of Vientiane and Luang Prabang.

ASIA IN THE SEVENTEENTH CENTURY

Date	India	China	Japan	South-east Asia	The Russians in Asia	Date	India	China	Japan	South-east Asia	The Russians in Asia
1500				Conquest of Manila by Spaniards (1571)				Li Tzu-cheng sacks Peking. Last Ming emperor commits suicide (1644)	Christian revolt. Shimabara (1638)		
					Cossacks cross the Urals (1581)		Kandahar abandoned to Persians (1648)				
				Accession of Narasuen of Siam (1590)							Russians reach the Pacific (1649)
1600			Battle of Sekigahara. Ieyasu master of Japan (1600)		Russians established in western Siberia (1600)					King Narai of Siam. New contacts with Europe (1657)	Nerchinsk founded (1654)
		Matteo Ricci in Peking (1601)	Tokugawa Shogunate (1602)	Establishment of Dutch East India Company (1602)			Aurangzeb seizes throne (1660)	K'ang Hsi becomes emperor (1661)			
	Death of Akbar Accession of Jahangir (1605)			Siamese embassy to Holland, the first in Europe (1609)						Constant Phaulkon becomes superintendent of Siam's foreign trade (1675)	
	Persian victory at Kandahar (1622)	Nurhachi in control of Manchuria (1616)		Founding of Batavia (1622)			Mahratta wars (1681)			Execution of Phaulkon. Siamese self-isolation (1688)	
	Death of Jahangir Accession of Shah Jahan (1627)	Death of Nurhachi (1626)									Frontier between China and Russia defined (1689)
	Famine in India (1630) Building of Taj Mahal begins (1631)			New Burmese capital at Ava (1629)				Treaty of Nerchinsk with Russia (1689) Catholic missionaries given permission to preach by K'ang Hsi (1692)			
		Manchus assume dynastic title of Ch'ing (1635)				1700	Death of Aurangzeb (1707)				
	Kandahar regained from Persians (1637)			Establishment of department of Siberian affairs (1637)							

Chapter 24

The Mogul Empire and the Rise of British India

Upon the death of the Emperor Akbar in 1605 his son, Salim, succeeded. He took the title of Jahangir, which means Lord of the World. In 1611 he married a Persian lady, on whom he bestowed the title of Nur Mahal, or Light of the Palace. She was an ambitious woman who, with her brother, Asaf Khan, exercised great influence over the emperor. Jahangir was a competent ruler who continued the policy of toleration towards his non-Muslim subjects which Akbar had begun. His somewhat erratic character was well described by Sir Thomas Roe, who was in India from 1616 to 1619 as the ambassador of King James I. The emperor could be just and generous, but he could also be fiendishly cruel. This uncertainty of temper came partly from his nightly drinking bouts. He was a patron of the arts and was himself something of a painter.

While Jahangir won victories in Bengal and Rajputana, he suffered defeat at the hands of the capable Shah Abbas of Persia, who took Kandahar in 1622. Jahangir attempted to extend the conquests which Akbar had made in the Deccan, but the city of Ahmadnagar, ruled by a capable Abyssinian minister, Malik Ambar, long held out against him. His son, Prince Khurram, won a victory in the Deccan in 1616 and was given the title of Shah Jahan, King of the World, by his grateful father. Later, however, the prince became estranged from his father and from 1623 to 1625 was in actual revolt against him. This was because Shah Jahan had insisted upon marrying the lady of his choice and not the one selected for him by Nur Mahal. The revolt ended in an outward reconciliation between father and son, but in 1626 Mahabat Khan, a prominent general, rebelled against the dominance of Nur Mahal and her brother, and Jahangir was taken prisoner. The empress succeeded in freeing him, but in 1627 the humiliated emperor died.

Shah Jahan

Shah Jahan defeated and executed pretenders to the throne and in 1628 proclaimed himself emperor in Agra. He kept Nur Mahal in strict confinement until her death. Once he had secured his position he maintained the policy of general toleration and was anxious to act justly towards all his subjects. But his reform edicts had little effect in checking the avarice of the provincial governors and lesser officials. Shah Jahan, like his predecessors, tried to prevent civil and military appointments from becoming hereditary and in this way to preserve imperial control over the nobles. But in a huge and loosely knit realm it was difficult to stop them from exercising a large degree of local authority, especially as the emperor, in times of foreign war or succession disputes, was dependent upon their loyalty. Moreover, the conquests and building projects in which Shah Jahan indulged had to be paid for by heavy taxation, so that the splendours of Agra and of New Delhi contrasted with the squalor and misery of the peasantry. From 1630 to 1632 a great famine, in which thousands died, afflicted Gujerat and parts of the Deccan.

Above, the Mogul Emperor Jahangir (reigned 1605–27) holding a portrait of his father Akbar. Jahangir encouraged both the Portuguese and the English to trade within his empire. Musée Guimet, Paris.

Shah Jahan was devoted to his empress, Mumtaz Mahal, the mother of all his children. When she died in 1631 he commissioned Persian and Indian architects and craftsmen to build the magnificent mausoleum at Agra known as the Taj Mahal, or Jewel of the Palace. Another architectural wonder, constructed in Agra, is the Pearl Mosque. While he thus beautified Agra, Shah Jahan set to work to build a new capital near the old town of Delhi. This he achieved during the ten years from 1638 to 1648, and he called the new city Shahjahanabad, the city of Shah Jahan. The French traveller Bernier, who saw it in 1663, described New Delhi, as it was to become known, as built in the form of a crescent on the right bank of the Jumna River, with walls extending for six or seven miles and a population as great as that of Paris. The main streets, crowded with shops of all kinds, led to the royal square, beyond which was the fortified palace, a building which Bernier considered to be twice as large as any palace in Europe. Here was the great Hall of Audience, where the emperor appeared daily before his nobles and courtiers, all grouped in strict precedence. The emperor, seated on the Peacock Throne, so called from the golden peacock with outspread tail made of precious stones which crowned it, heard petitions from his subjects.

In Afghanistan, Shah Jahan fought with the Persian Shah Abbas II and managed to recapture Kandahar from him in 1637. But in 1648 the Persians surprised and again seized the town, and in the face of the superior Persian artillery the army of Shah Jahan was obliged to retire. Kandahar was abandoned and left in Persian hands. The emperor was equally unfortunate in his attempts to conquer part of Turkestan. He led an army across the Hindu Kush mountains but was soon in difficulties in the rugged terrain and harassed by the Uzbek tribesmen. Shah Jahan returned and sent Prince Aurangzeb to continue the struggle. But the prince and his military advisers saw that the country could not be held; they succeeded in getting the army back over the mountains into India, but at the price of heavy losses in men and equipment.

Shah Jahan was more successful in the Deccan. Malik Ambar died in 1626 and his unworthy son betrayed Ahmednagar to the Mogul armies. The city fell in 1633 and was annexed to the Mogul dominions in 1636. Aurangzeb, who was appointed viceroy of the imperial territories in the Deccan, waged war against the sultans of Bijapur and Golconda and would probably have conquered both kingdoms but for the jealousy of his brother Dara, who prevailed upon Shah Jahan to accept their offers of submission and payment of tribute in 1656.

The Succession War

Shah Jahan had four sons—Dara, Shuja, Aurangzeb and Murad. In 1657 the emperor was taken ill and could no longer attend the court audiences. At the time Dara, his eldest and favourite son, whom he wished to be his successor, was in Agra. The other three all held governorships away from the capital. When Shuja and Murad heard that their father was no longer seen in public they declared, and perhaps sincerely believed, that he was dead but that Dara was concealing this. Each proclaimed himself to be emperor and began to advance upon Agra. Aurangzeb, masking his own ambitions, joined forces with Murad. In May 1658 Dara was defeated at the battle of Samugarh, near Agra. Aurangzeb took the capital and proclaimed himself emperor in July 1658. He had his brother Murad condemned on a charge of breaking Islamic law by his drunken habits, and after three years of captivity Murad was executed. In 1659 the fugitive Dara was betrayed into the hands of Aurangzeb, who had him put to death. Shuja defeated near Allahabad, fled into Bengal and thence to Arakan, where he was murdered. By 1660 Aurangzeb, who styled himself Alamgir, Conqueror of the World, had crushed all opposition to his rule. He kept his father, Shah Jahan, a prisoner until the unfortunate emperor died in 1666.

Aurangzeb was an able general and a skilful diplomat. He was cold and reserved in manner and gained the admiration, rather than the affection, of those who came into contact with him. He was a devout orthodox Muslim who, as far as a Mogul emperor was able, followed the teachings of the Koran and lived a simple and indeed ascetic life. He knew the Koran by heart and made copies of it which he sent to Mecca and Medina, since his responsibilities as a ruler forbade his making the pilgrimage himself. Had he contented himself with ordering his private life in this fashion, the change from the profligacy of Jahangir and Shah Jahan might have been beneficial. But he allowed his religious beliefs to shape his policy towards his subjects. He appointed Muslims to office in preference to Hindus and he revived the *jizya*, or poll-tax, upon all who were not Muslims. Since these amounted to some three-quarters of the population of the empire, this policy caused widespread disaffection and revolt. It involved Aurangzeb in a long and ultimately unsuccessful war in Rajputana. The fierce warriors of this region, once reconciled to Mogul rule by the conciliatory policy of Akbar, had formed a most valuable part of the imperial army; now many of the Rajput forces became hostile to the Mogul Empire and their defection was a grave source of weakness.

Aurangzeb at war

During the first part of his reign Aurangzeb was mainly concerned with re-establishing the authority of the Mogul Empire in the north of India. In 1662 his army, under the leadership of an able general called Mir Jumla, defeated the Ahoms, who had taken advantage of the civil war in the Mogul Empire to invade Bengal. They were driven out again and Assam itself invaded, but the unhealthy climate proved fatal to many of the imperial soldiers including Mir Jumla himself. There were also wars with the Afghan tribesmen, especially the afridis, who in 1674 inflicted a defeat upon the Mogul forces. These Afghan frontier struggles absorbed many of the best troops of the empire at a time when they were needed elsewhere.

It was the great ambition of Aurangzeb to conquer the Deccan and to bring the whole of India under his sway. He was determined to extinguish the kingdoms of Bijapur and Golconda, both for political reasons and because their rulers belonged to the Shia sect among the Muslims, which he, as a Sunnite, regarded as heretical. But by the time he was able to turn his full attention to the south, a new enemy had arisen. The Mahrattas were a Hindu people who lived in rugged plateau country overlooking the southwestern coast. Here there were many natural hill fortresses from which the Mahratta horsemen could sally out to raid the lowlands and in which they could offer a desperate resistance to an attacker. The Mahrattas were united under a leader called Sivaji who became the terror of much of the Deccan and raided the Mogul territory there. In 1664 he sacked Surat, although he was repulsed from the foreign settlement there by English and Dutch resistance. By the time of his death in 1680 the Mahrattas had become a formidable fighting force.

In 1681 the emperor left his capital to take command in the Deccan, where he was to wage war for the next twenty-five years. He took Bijapur in 1686 and Golconda in the next year. But against the guerrilla tactics of the Mahrattas he could gain no decisive success. The huge Mogul army, which was swollen by hosts of camp-followers, especially when the emperor was present, could win pitched battles, but could not cope with a swiftly moving enemy who raided its lines of communication and constantly harassed it. In 1689 Aurangzeb succeeded in capturing Sambhaji, the son of Sivaji, and put him to death. But the Mahrattas continued the struggle and the Mogul army suffered heavily in attempts to invade their country and storm their hill fortresses. The aged but indomitable emperor fought on, but his troops became more and more discouraged. Aurangzeb was compelled to admit failure and to retreat to Ahmadnagar, where in March 1707 he died at the age of eighty-nine.

It was in Aurangzeb's long reign that the seeds of ultimate collapse began to appear. Aurangzeb was more intolerantly Muslim than his predecessors, and his policies produced a reaction in many sections of the Hindu community. Territorial expansion in itself merely made the empire more cumbersome. Moreover, there was a certain hardening of the arteries of the Mogul bureaucracy —lack of resolution and disregard for the importance of office. And once the empire began to deteriorate, it was unlikely that it would be regenerated by the Indian community. For all the years it had ruled the country, the Mogul dynasty was still an alien institution of Turkish origin. It had often commanded respect, rarely affection; if it were to be reformed, then reformation would have to come from the top or not at all.

On Aurangzeb's death authority at the summit became divided and vacillating. After a shaky period of palace revolutions, Muhammad Shah emerged as emperor in 1719. The new ruler was shrewd and crafty but unable to provide the leadership. During his twenty-nine years reign, he constantly mortgaged the future to keep possession of the present. Large areas began to break away from centralized control, giving only nominal allegiance to the fading Moguls. Nevertheless, in Muhammad Shah's reign, the rot proceeded behind a facade that was still impressive. But when he died in 1748 the facade peeled away, exposing the wreck within. Titular and puppet emperors would succeed one another for a further century, but after 1750 the real question about Mogul power was what would replace it.

Persians, Afghans and Mahrattas

That the withering Mogul Empire might be replaced by a European one seemed anything but likely at the time, and indeed the idea was not even considered. Instead, eyes turned to India's menacing neighbours, Persia and Afghanistan, and also to the formidable Hindu power of the Mahratta Confederacy.

The Persians were the first in the field. In 1710 the old Safavid dynasty of Persia was ended by an Afghan invasion, and it seemed that the Persian Empire would fall to rapacious neighbours; Afghans, Russians, Turkomans and Turks all seized a share. But in 1730 a new Persian military leader appeared on the scene in the form of Nadir Shah, who first posed as a champion of the Safavids and then claimed the imperial throne for himself. Rapidly defeating the Afghans and the Turks. Nadir then succeeded in driving out the Russians, and a campaign which began with the securing of his eastern frontiers led to the invasion of India. In 1739 he defeated the Moguls and sacked Delhi. Somewhat unaccountably, however, he then replaced Muhammad Shah on the throne and withdrew. Perhaps he expected to return, but after more wars in central Asia Nadir was assassinated in 1747. Persia disintegrated once more.

The Afghans now regained their independence and found their own military genius in Ahmad Shah. After consolidating his own mountain kingdom, Ahmad rode through the passes and sacked Delhi in 1756. Meanwhile, in India itself, the Hindu

Above, the Mogul Emperor Aurangzeb (reigned 1658–1707); his devotion to Islam undermined the basis of Mogul authority in India, which was founded on religious toleration and the employment of officials of all races and religions. Musée Guimet, Paris.

Opposite, the Mogul Emperor Jahangir on an elephant. The emperor was more concerned with the arts than with politics, but he granted important trading concessions to the Portuguese and to the recently founded English East India Company.

British and French

About two decades before the Battle of Panipat, it was becoming clear that a new relationship was developing between the Indian political powers and the Europeans who traded in the subcontinent. Previously, the Europeans had shown no interest in occupying Indian territory but had remained in their little trading factories and enclaves—the British in Madras, Bombay and Calcutta, the French in Pondicherry, the Portuguese in Goa and Diu—rather like frogs around the side of a pool. But what changed this situation was the increasing rivalry between the British and the French.

The English had arrived in India to find themselves competing with the Dutch and Portuguese; even the Danes and Germans had shown some interest in the area. But England had bested the Portuguese, while the efficient Dutch had devoted most of their trading activities to the Indonesian archipelago. The activities of the other nations had not amounted to much. The Moguls were in fact friendly to the English, and in the seventeenth century the East India Company's ships had often acted as the Mogul Empire's navy.

It was not until Colbert founded the French East India Company in 1664, and gained Pondicherry ten years later that England had a really serious competitor. The new company made slow headway at first, and by the beginning of the eighteenth century French interest in India seemed on the wane. But in the reorganization of colonial enterprises that took place after John Law's great débâcle, the French East India Company was put on a better footing. By 1740 it was quite a profitable concern, and besides Pondicherry and two other small posts on the mainland also controlled the very important islands of Mauritius and Réunion in the Indian Ocean. Mauritius, especially, with its good harbour and its strategic position astride the main trade route from Europe, provided an excellent base from which France could protect her own shipping and menace that of Britain in time of war.

However, it was not until 1744 that conflict actually came. Previously, even when their respective nations had been at war in Europe, the British and French settlements in India had remained at peace—partly because the Moguls wished it that way and partly because it was more profitable to do so. But when the War of the Austrian Succession broke out the British governor rebuffed the overtures of the French to maintain the peace. What the Moguls wished no longer counted, and the British, who had a small squadron in Indian waters, thought they might quickly destroy the factories of their rivals. This move was almost a disaster. The French governor of Mauritius, Mahé de la Bourdonnais, quickly improvised a little fighting

Mahrattas had begun throwing off the shackles of Mogul dominion as soon as Aurangzeb had died. Forming a confederacy and developing highly mobile military techniques, they spread right across central India to Orissa. Then, when the Afghans invaded, the Moguls called upon the Mahrattas for help. For a time, the Mahratta Peshwa drove back Ahmad Shah's forces, but this only made the Peshwa increasingly overbearing towards the Moguls. Soon the only thing that seemed in doubt was whether it would be an Afghan or a Mahratta emperor that replaced the great Mogul. But, in 1761, both of these competitors for the imperial throne unexpectedly eliminated each other. In the decisive battle of Panipat, fought in January of that year, the Mahrattas were thoroughly crushed by the Afghans. Then, at the height of their power, the Afghan soldiers mutinied over back pay and Ahmad Shah's forces withdrew from India when it seemed that the country was theirs for the taking.

fleet of armed merchant vessels, drove the British squadron away from the coast and attacked and captured Madras. This, however, was the extent of the French success. The arrival of a British fleet under Admiral Boscawen precluded any further French offensives, and although Boscawen failed to take Pondicherry Madras was returned to Britain in the Treaty of Aix-la-Chapelle that ended the war.

There now seemed to be no reason at all why commercial affairs in India should not return to their normal course, but in fact Joseph Dupleix, the French governor of Pondicherry, was about to upset the balance for ever.

Joseph Dupleix

During the war, Dupleix had fallen foul not only of the British but also of the local Indian ruler, the Nawab of the Carnatic. When the latter sent a large army against him, Dupleix easily defeated it with a small European-trained force. This significant event made Dupleix realize that it was now possible for Europeans to interfere far more in Indian political affairs than had been possible in the days of Mogul strength. If

by intrigue, diplomacy and small military campaigns the French could set up Indian puppet rulers who would support them, or if they could even control territory for themselves, then it would be possible for them to eject the English and monopolize the whole trade of the subcontinent. At first this conclusion seemed dubious. The expense of wars, subsidies and territorial administration would surely outweigh all the profits that might be made from eliminating the English. Such an idea would scarcely appeal to the commercially minded directors of the French East India Company. But Dupleix had an answer for that as well. Parts of India were very rich in agricultural produce, textiles and many other items. If the French could control such areas to the extent of levying and collecting taxes from the inhabitants, it would be possible to build a wealthy empire that would cost the company and the French government nothing.

In 1748 the deaths of the two most important Indian potentates in the south and the resultant succession disputes gave Dupleix the opportunity of putting his plans into operation. The French backed their own candidates and actively supported

Above, the Mogul emperor, now controlling little real power, granting to Robert Clive, the representative of the English East India Company, sovereign rights over Bengal in 1765. India Office Library and Records, London.

Opposite, the Mogul Emperor Shah Jahan (reigned 1628–58) with one of his sons. Shah Jahan spent most of his energy on his building programme at Agra and Delhi. Victoria and Albert Museum, London.

243

them. When the Nizam of Hyderabad attempted to interfere, Dupleix's intrigues resulted in the Nizam's murder and a great extension of French influence. When the new Nizam visited Pondicherry, Dupleix, in Muslim robes, was seated beside him on the throne and created personal governor of an area not much smaller than France.

The British company's officials, although disturbed by this train of events, could at first think of no riposte. But Thomas Saunders, a tough governor who took over command in Madras in 1750, began replying in kind. Chanda Sahib, the French candidate for Nawab of the Carnatic, soon found the British supporting his rival, Muhammad Ali. Shortly afterwards, opposing Indian armies, stiffened by British or French troops, were on the move and there was fighting throughout the Carnatic. This complicated pattern of warfare continued for three years and was made famous by the exploits of Robert Clive and Stringer Lawrence for the English and of the Marquis de Bussy for the French.

Dupleix himself was hopeless as a military leader, and when Bussy was forced to go north to Hyderabad to restore a position there that was becoming shaky the English gained the ascendancy in the south. It was now that Clive really came to the fore. Muhammad Ali had long been urging a diversion against Arcot, one of Chanda Sahib's principal possessions. The British were dubious, but when the young Captain Clive offered to make an immediate attack Saunders gave him his head. To everyone's astonishment, Clive's force of less than 300 easily occupied the city when the Indian garrison of 3,000 withdrew without fighting. Chanda Sahib quickly sent forces to besiege the place, but Clive held out for two months until relieved, so gaining the British their first considerable success. It was rapidly followed by others. Stringer Lawrence and Clive quickly cleared the whole of Arcot and then attacked Chanda Sahib, who was besieging a British force in Trichinopoly. In the ensuing engagement, several hundred French were captured, while Chanda Sahib was seized and put to death by an Indian rival.

Further north, however, the French were doing better. In Hyderabad, Bussy was quite successful in getting his candidate, Salabat Jang, installed as Nizam and in defending him against several rebellions. In return, Salabat made many concessions to the French, granting them the right to levy taxes and raise revenue in the Carnatic, which was nominally under his overlordship. This, in theory, was the fulfilment of Dupleix's policies, and the latter wrote an excited letter to the directors of the French East India Company stating: 'This affair, of the highest importance to the Nation deserves the closest attention, for it will dispense with the need of sending funds to India for your investment.'

Yet this was a triumph in theory only.

For the Carnatic, so freely given to the French by Salabat, was actually falling into the hands of the British candidate, Muhammad Ali, after the death of Chanda Sahib. Dupleix did his best to retrieve the situation. He now had difficulty in finding Indian candidates to support and even thought at one point of getting himself declared Nawab of the Carnatic. In the meantime his Indian allies besieged Trichinopoly again. Dupleix sent French reinforcements, but Stringer Lawrence, defending the city, held out through most of 1753. Dupleix then resorted to the desperate gamble of an assault with scaling ladders during the night. It came close to being a suprise success but in the end was a heavy defeat for the French, Dupleix losing about 400 of his regular troops.

Such events proved too much for the directors of the French East India Company. Dupleix's plans had been unorthodox in the first place and his dealings with his superiors cavalier in manner. His failure to fulfil his plans could have but one end. In 1754 he was recalled in disgrace. But he had set forces in motion that would not be stopped easily.

The Black Hole of Calcutta

For the moment an effort was made to turn back the clock. The English and French companies entered into negotiations and produced a treaty in 1754 that delimited spheres of influence. Fighting was to end and once again it was to be business as usual.

It was an Indian ruler who upset the new balance. In the northeast, Alivardi Khan, the Nawab of Bengal, had been increasingly disturbed by the European intrigues and fighting to the south. However, he had wisely remained neutral and contented himself with forcing the English and French in his own area to keep the peace. But when

Alivardi died in 1756, his successor, Sirajud-Dawlah, decided on more direct action. Europeans in Bengal were ordered to limit the military defences of their forts. The British in Calcutta refused, and Siraj attacked them. Decrepit old Fort William was easily overwhelmed, and 146 of the captured British defenders were then locked up in a tiny unventilated room where all but twenty-three stifled to death in one night. This incident—the Black Hole of Calcutta—was really a case of criminal negligence rather than of premeditated murder, but it provided the British with an emotional rallying cry and a cause to be avenged. In October Clive was ordered to retake Calcutta and given command of a force of 1,800 Europeans and sepoys, as Indians trained by Europeans were called. Calcutta was easily retaken in the following year, and Siraj was defeated and forced to sign a treaty confirming the rights of the company. It was at this point that the outbreak of the Seven Years War again transformed the situation.

The Seven Years War

As soon as news of the war arrived, Clive demanded permission from Siraj-ud-Dawlah to attack the French trading factories in Bengal. Siraj, however, now seriously worried at the growth of British power, began intriguing with Bussy in Hyderabad. Clive then determined that Siraj would have to be overthrown and in June 1757, with 3,000 British and sepoy troops, marched to Plassey where Siraj lay encamped with 50,000 men. Clive, brilliant, moody, reckless, spent the night before the battle in deep depression. So did Siraj. But in the morning they both determined to fight and in the ensuing curious encounter Clive suffered less than thirty casualties and Siraj only five hundred. Yet Plassey had the same result as a crushing and decisive victory.

Siraj's army fled precipitously, he himself was hunted down and killed, while Mir Jafar, a British candidate, became regent in his place. The British were masters of Bengal; if they could deal with the French, they might be masters of all India.

In the south, the French moved first. By early 1758, troop reinforcements had arrived at Pondicherry under the command of the Comte de Lally. In the late spring, Lally took the offensive and won several small victories over weaker English forces, capturing Arcot, Cuddalore and Fort St David. At sea, however, Admiral Pocock defeated a French fleet, and Lally's advance then bogged down. Bussy was now recalled against his will from the north, and he and Lally together laid siege to Madras. In Fort St George, however, Stringer Lawrence held out for three months until a squadron arrived from Bombay and broke the siege. The tide now turned, and following Bussy's enforced departure the French situation to the north began to deteriorate. Revolts broke out in Hyderabad, and even Salabat Jang, a French puppet for eight years, began negotiating with the British. He ultimately signed a treaty ceding some of his dominions to the East India Company. At the same time, the arrival of a large French squadron failed to shake Pocock's control of the sea, and in January of 1760 Eyre Coote heavily defeated the French forces in the Battle of Wandiwash. From then on the French were in retreat. At last, after a long siege, Pondicherry capitulated in January 1761. At the Peace of Paris in 1763, it was returned to France along with other minor settlements she had established in India before 1750. But French influence was now strictly limited to these enclaves; Dupleix's dreams of empire had perished for ever.

Clive

The war over and the French defeated, Clive, rich with gifts and bribes he had accepted from the Indian enemies of Siraj, departed for England. But he left behind him a Bengal where chaos, far from ending, was getting worse.

Clive's successor was Henry Vansittart, who at twenty-eight had already seen fifteen years in the company's service. Not nearly so weak a man as contemporaries claimed, Vansittart wished mainly to establish honest methods of trading. It was the actions of his subordinates that allowed matters to get out of hand. He took a rapid dislike to the incompetent Mir Jafar, deposed him and put Mir Kasim in his place. With the latter Vansittart concluded an agreement freeing external trade from duty but taxing all internal traders, English and Indian alike, at a rate of nine percent. Vansittart's own council repudiated this, however, and the English would neither pay the duty nor allow Mir Kasim to abolish it for Indians as well. Mir Kasim in a rage massacred 150 British merchants at Patna. The company then launched a military offensive and destroyed Mir Kasim's armies in the battle of Buxar.

This victory in a sense opened the road to Delhi, where a Mogul emperor still maintained a shadowy existence, and it brought to the surface divided counsels among the company's servants. Some became inflamed with grandiose ideas of empire; others, like Vansittart, wished to return to the old trading pattern; most of them simply wished to become rich. For the latter occupation, the times were propitious. The company's officers now wielded great power and accepted little responsibility. Huge sums were extorted or wheedled from the Indian potentates who in turn ground the peasantry with heavier taxes. Individuals became fabulously wealthy almost overnight. The East India Company, however, did not; indeed its profits fell as its servants ignored it and traded for their own interest. Soon Bengal was reduced to a state of misrule and anarchy as to make even Clive blanch when he returned.

Clive returned in 1765 with full powers to end the corruption. He opposed the abuses and the anarchy resolutely enough but had by no means solved the confusion when he departed again in 1767. More important for the future was the political system he left behind him. By a treaty with the nominal emperor Clive set up a dual system of government which left the Nawab of Bengal with only formal power. The crucial *diwani*, or right to collect the revenue, was granted to the East India Company in the rich territories of Bengal, Bihar and Orissa. The taxes in these areas could more than pay for the company's administration expenses there. Thus was the logic of Dupleix's system ultimately vindicated — but to the benefit of the British and not to that of the French.

Above, Joseph François Dupleix (1696–1763), the French East India Company official who built up a vast sphere of influence in the years around 1750, and whose independence and ambitions caused the French to call him home.

Top, Warren Hastings (1732–1818), his wife and servant, painted by Johan Zoffany. Hastings became governor of the British possessions in India in 1774 but was tried for corruption in the late 1780s. Victoria Memorial, Calcutta.

Opposite, Delhi in the eighteenth century; although it was now the main residence of the Mogul emperors, it was no longer the capital of India in any sense.

Area under the effective rule of the Mogul emperors

Area controlled by the Mahrattas

AFGHANISTAN

TIBET

SIKH STATES

Indus

Panipat

Delhi

RAJPUTANA

Himalayas

NEPAL

Brahmaputra

Buxar

BIHAR

Patna

Ganges

Plassey

MARATHA CONFEDERACY

Chandernagore

Calcutta

Hooghli

Fort William

GUJARAT

DIU

BERAR

ORISSA

Bombay

BAY OF BENGAL

Satara

TERRITORY OF THE NIZAM

ARABIAN SEA

Goa

MYSORE

Arcot

Madras
Fort St George

Wandiwash

Pondicherry

Fort St David

Cuddalore

Trichinopoly

THE CARNATIC

TRAVANCORE

CEYLON

INDIAN OCEAN

Warren Hastings

The man who became governor of Bengal in 1772, and who was destined to mould the state from the territory that Clive had secured, was little known outside company circles. Small, steely and self-contained, Warren Hastings was to construct the framework of British India. Arrogant and opinionated, he could also show inexhaustible patience. He could stain his record by executing an inveterate Indian opponent for forgery, when forgery was a capital offence in England but not in India. Yet he thought more highly of Indians than many of the men who would follow him. 'Among the natives of India', he wrote, 'there are men of as strong intellect, and sound integrity and as honourable feelings as any of this kingdom.' It was Hastings' belief that British government should benefit the people of India culturally and materially in addition to filling the coffers of the East India Company.

He arrived in a province racked by famine, extortion and military troubles, with the Marathas on the borders. He attempted to tackle everything. The idea of dual government was abandoned. If the Company were to receive the revenue of Bengal, it must also take over the responsibilities of the internal administration. But Hastings' task was made inordinately difficult at the outset by an action of the British government.

Lord North's Regulating Act of 1773 was prompted by the misrule in Bengal and represented an attempt to bring Indian policy in the broadest sense under the control of parliament, although the East India Company would be left to work out details of administration. The Regulating Act promoted Hastings from governor of Bengal to governor-general in India and gave him powers over the presidencies of Bombay and Madras. Yet it also circumscribed him, giving real executive power to a council which could outvote him. In fact, the council was to obstruct Hastings consistently, especially when the opposition was led by Philip Francis, who wished to return to the system of combined rule. The Hastings-Francis rivalry was a long and enervating struggle lasting over six years, but in the end the governor's opponents 'sickened and died and fled'.

Once Hastings had thus outlasted his adversaries, he was able to get on with his work. Of great importance both to Bengal and to the East India Company were his successful commercial reforms, particularly the long-overdue ending of the private trade of the company's servants. Administratively, he began the arduous overhaul of the all-important revenue-raising system, although this task was not to be completed until long after he had departed from the scene.

Yet it was in the preservation of the state he was building that Hastings was to play his greatest role, for soon the British were encompassed on all sides. From the beginning Hastings was confronted with the problem of uneasy borders around Bengal and felt the necessity of making alliances with friendly Indian princes and of supporting his allies in their disputes. This was the policy that would point in future to the slow march of British territorial dominion across the whole of the subcontinent. The securing of borders would involve the conquering of fresh territory, but this in turn would mean new borders, new troubles, new conquests.

Nevertheless, Hastings was able to restrain this policy of reluctant empire-building for the moment so far as Bengal was concerned, though his unruly subordinate presidencies of Bombay and Madras involved him in grave trouble. Rash actions at Bombay provoked war with the Marathas, now finally recovered after Panipat, and led to the annihilation of a small British army. The situation at Madras was even worse; there, the policy of the presidency

Above, a British factory in Calcutta in the 1790s;
the British used the great wealth that they won
from India both to enrich themselves and to
introduce European values and styles of art to
their empire. British Museum, London.

Above left, a European officer being entertained by
Mahadaji Sindhia, an Indian soldier who won
control of much of the area ruled by the Mogul
Empire in the 1760s and 1770s; the European
powers were able to exploit the political vacuum
that permitted such adventurers to rise to power.

Left, an Indian nabob or local ruler being carried
in a litter; the Indians were used to a rigid social
hierarchy, and the arrival of European overlords
made little difference to their way of life.

Below left, the reception in 1792 of Tipu Sahib,
the Prince of Mysore, by Lord Cornwallis; Tipu
Sahib had attacked British territory three years
before and was defeated by Cornwallis. He
rebelled again in 1798–99, and his kingdom was
shared between the British and the Nazim of
Hyderabad on his death. National Army Museum,
London.

Opposite, India in the late seventeenth and early
eighteenth centuries; as Mogul power declined,
the Mahrattas and others created virtually
independent kingdoms, and the Europeans were
able to exploit their rivalries.

Date	Europeans in India	India	Neighbouring states	Date	Europeans in India	India	Neighbouring states
1600	English East India Company trading post at Fort St George, Madras (1639)			1740			French take possession of Réunion and Mauritius (1740)
		Accession of Aurangzeb (1658)			Dupleix captures Madras from British (1746)		
	Founding of French East India Company (1664)		First Russian mission to Persia (1664)				Assassination of Nadir Shah. Ahmad Shah assumes power in Afghanistan (1747)
		Chittagong annexed by Aurangzeb (1666)			Madras returned to British. Treaty of Aix-la-Chapelle (1748)		
	Charles II grants Bombay to the East India Company (1668)				Clive seizes Arot. Dupleix recalled to France (1755)		
	French established at Pondicherry (1674)				Black Hole of Calcutta (1756)	Sack of Delhi by Ahmad (1756)	
	Establishment of English factory at Calcutta (1689)				Battle of Plassey (1757)		
						Battle between Mahrattas and Afghans at Panipat (1761)	
1700		Death of Aurangzeb. Accession of Muhammad Shah (1707)	Kandahar proclaims independence from Persia (1706)				The English establish trading post at Bushire on the Persian Gulf (1763)
		War between Sikhs and Moguls (1708)			Battle of Buxa. English in control of Bengal and Bihar (1764)	Massacre at Patna. Indian armies defeated at Buxar (1764)	
	English East India Company secures exemption from customs duties (1717)	Rise of the Mahrattas (1717)	Afghans secure independence from Persia (1706)		Clive leaves India (1767)		
					Dissolution of French East Company (1769)		The English at Basra (1770)
		Hyderabad proclaims independence from Moguls (1724)	Afghans invade Persia (1722) Shah Mahmud's reign of terror in Isphahan (1724)		Warren Hastings governor of Bengal (1772)		
			End of Safavid dynasty in Persia. Nadir Shah seizes throne (1736)		Lord North's Regulating Act (1773)		Afghan power at its zenith Death of Ahmad Shah (1773)
		Sack of Delhi by Nadir Shah (1738)		1785	Warren Hastings leaves India (1785)		

provoked a really colossal confederation against the British of all important powers in the area—the Marathas, the Nizam of Hyderabad and Haidar Ali, the formidable ruler of Mysore—and led to the defeat of two British armies.

It was at this juncture that the outbreak of the American Revolution allowed the French to begin intriguing again and ultimately enabled them to take direct military action. Yet Hastings overcame all difficulties. The governor of Madras was suspended, and proper military dispositions were made. Then superb diplomacy neutralized the Nizam and also the more important Maratha leaders. Haidar Ali went on fighting but died in 1782. By the time French arms actually arrived on the scene, there was little they could do. The fleet of the brilliant French admiral, Suffren, was fended off by the workmanlike British commander, Sir Edward Hughes. The famous Bussy arrived with an army only to find that the war had ended before he could launch an offensive. At the peace, the French were again returned their trading settlements which Hastings had overrun but again received nothing more. British dominion in India was more firmly established than ever when, in 1785, Hastings was replaced as governor-general by Lord Cornwallis.

The brilliant careers of Clive and Hastings ended in tragedy. Clive found no scope in England for his restless, unstable genius. His great years in India were investigated by parliament at the instigation of his enemies, who accused him of peculation. He was eventually acquitted but became morose and committed suicide in 1774. Hastings, expecting to be received as a hero on his return, found himself instead impeached by the House of Commons. The intrigues of Philip Francis had persuaded Edmund Burke to this course; Burke was sincerely but mistakenly convinced that Hastings was the author of many of the abuses he had been trying to suppress. The trial dragged on for eight years, during which Hastings was obliged to justify his achievements. He did this with tenacious dignity and in the end was acquitted—but his ordeal, which began in his vigorous middle age, left him an old man.

For Cornwallis, his successor in India, this course of events was to be reversed. He went to India from the humiliation of the surrender at Yorktown in the War of American Independence—and stayed to build a great career. Under him the state which Clive had conquered and Hastings had formed was to be fashioned into a practical administrative reality.

Chapter 25

Africa in the Eighteenth Century

European colonial and commercial rivalries were important in eighteenth-century Africa, but there the European presence was largely confined to the coast. This was partly because the interior of the continent held few obvious attractions and partly because penetration inland was precluded from large areas by the prevalence of malaria, sleeping sickness and yellow fever. On the coasts, however, the presence of the Europeans was becoming increasingly important. In the north, the rather disorganized Arab and Berber principalities were drawn into closer commercial relationship with Europe. In the extreme south, the Dutch were inadvertently laying the foundations of the one African state which would eventually have really significant numbers of white settlers. On the west coast, and increasingly on the east, the slave trade was of prime importance, but whereas the former area saw the heyday of European traffic in human beings in the latter region a weak European power was replaced by a strong Arab one.

The Mediterranean north

In those parts of Africa which bordered on the Mediterranean, the most notable characteristic of the period was the continuing decline of the Turkish Empire which was nominal ruler over much of the area. This created an effective political fragmentation, and the local scene in most regions oscillated between bouts of outright anarchy and periods of stern dictatorship. In Egypt, real power remained with the Mamelukes—former slaves from Georgia and Turkestan —but within their ranks individuals rose and fell with bewildering rapidity. Sometimes a strong ruler emerged, such as 'Ali Bey, who between 1757 and 1772 secured full control of Egypt and also occupied parts of Arabia and Syria, but too often the scene was one of chaos and decrepitude. Yet for all this, and for all its grave commercial decline, Egypt managed to retain a precarious independence both of Europeans and its nominal Turkish overlords.

In Tunisia and Algeria, conditions resembled those in Egypt, although with important local variations. The pashas, representing the Sultan of Turkey, were forced to delegate most of their powers to local beys and deys. These often fought among themselves, and the two states also warred against each other; but the European commercial presence was much stronger than in Egypt. Some rulers were violently xenophobic and turned the foreigners out; others, however, made important commercial concessions and signed treaties with the Europeans, especially with the French. More and more the once formidable fleets of pirates and corsairs that these areas had formerly supported gave way to normal shipping connections. This was also true of the huge and independent kingdom of Morocco. Despite its unwieldy size and a period of anarchy in mid-century, Morocco, especially during the reigns of Mulay Ismail (1672–1727) and Mulay Muhammad (1757–90), saw long periods of peace and order. Moreover, despite an inveterate dislike of the Portuguese, who controlled some of their coastal cities, the Moroccans were willing to come to terms with other Europeans. The Danes were given a monopoly of trade on the Atlantic coast, while the Dutch and French were very active on the Mediterranean.

East Africa

During the fifteenth and sixteenth centuries, the ancient, Islamized city-states of the east African coast, such as Kilwa and Mombasa, had been subdued by Portugal as part of the latter's strategy for dominating the entire maritime commerce of the Indian Ocean. During the seventeenth century, however, Portugal fell into decline, and many of the outposts of her eastern empire were commandeered by the English and the Dutch.

Above, Mulay Ismail, ruler of Morocco (reigned 1672–1727); Morocco was a virtually independent state which relied on capturing slaves by piracy for its wealth.

Top, Algerian pirates landing their slaves at Algiers in about 1700; the Europeans did not manage to assert their control over the southern coast of the Mediterranean until the nineteenth century.

Opposite, British officers watching a cockfight at Lucknow, in India, in 1786.

NAMAQUA HOTTENTOTS from Ireland

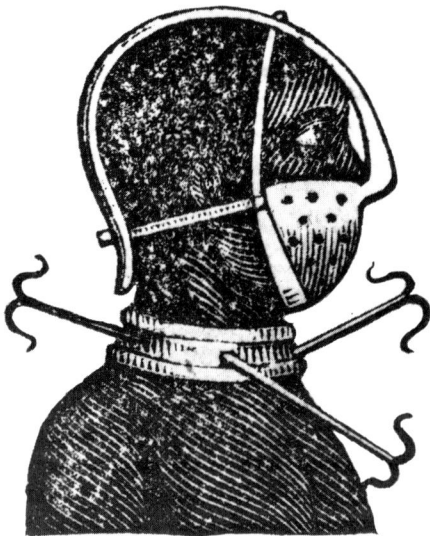

But neither of these powers was much interested in East Africa, and here the failing hand of the Portuguese was gradually displaced by Arabs from Oman, the principality that had claimed the trading cities before the Europeans arrived. Finally, in 1698, the chief bastion of Portuguese power, Fort Jesus in Mombasa, fell to the Imam of Oman after a two-year siege. In the early eighteenth century the Portuguese made some attempts to recover their lost supremacy but only met with further defeats. By 1730, their power had ceased to exist north of Mozambique.

Despite their victory over the Portuguese, troubles in Arabia itself kept successive imams occupied, and it was not for another century that Oman was able to occupy Zanzibar effectively and establish a firm hegemony over the coast. During the eighteenth century, therefore, each city-state was usually governed by a local Arab dynasty, although the predominance of the Mazrui family brought some measure of political cohesion. It was during this period

that the East African slave trade became a major factor, and great Arab caravans bought slaves inland to be sold eventually in the markets of Turkey, Arabia, India and Persia or to the French colonies of Mauritius and Réunion. Thus began the period when pipes sounded on Zanzibar truly made men dance in the region of the inland lakes.

The Dutch in the south

The most important European incursion in the history of Africa began on 6 April 1652, in the southern part of the continent. On that day Jan van Riebeeck dropped anchor in Table Bay with three ships and a small group of settlers. The Dutch East India Company had decided to make the Cape of Good Hope its chief provisioning station between Holland and the Indonesian archipelago. In the ensuing years more settlers came, including a few French Protestants. But thoughout the whole period of Dutch rule the progress of the colony was slow, tortuous and trammelled by restrictions. The Cape was truly a company settlement, and the colonists were continually hedged in by the instructions given by the directors of the East India Company in Holland.

Nevertheless, the Dutch settlers were fortunate in their temperate climate, spectacular scenery and in the lack of competitors for the land. The only African peoples in the immediate vicinity, the bushmen and the Hottentots, were few in number. The tiny, Stone Age bushmen proved to be sly enemies and the Dutch did not hesitate to exterminate them or drive them back. Relations with the Hottentots were better. Despite some conflicts, a reasonably cordial understanding was established with many of these more sophisticated, cattle-raising and copper- and iron-working

people. Some of the Hottentots were willing to work on the Dutch farms; other labour was provided by negro slaves brought to the colony from West Africa. This latter factor was to increase in importance especially when the Dutch East India Company took the momentous decision in 1717 that slave labour rather than free was to be the basic rule for the settlement. The eastern part of the colony was expanding rapidly, and in 1776 Dutch frontiersmen met with westward-moving Bantu tribesmen in the region of the Great Fish River. First contacts were friendly, but by this time years of slave-owning experience had indelibly fixed in the minds of the settlers some very definite ideas about the place of the negro in the Dutch God's scheme of creation. The implications for the future were tremendous.

West Africa and the slave trade

There had been a slave trade in West Africa for centuries before the coming of the Europeans. South of the Sahara, in the vast grasslands area known as the Sudan, great civilized negro empires had grown up in medieval times. These states had long raided the forest areas for slaves, who were then transported across the desert for sale in the markets of Morocco. But the Sudan had been falling into increasing chaos and decline since 1590, and soon the flow of slaves was moving south to the ocean rather than north to the desert.

Throughout the eighteenth century, the harbours of the West African coastline, reaching from Senegal to Angola, was annually infested with European ships seeking to purchase slaves. The great and increasing demand for sugar in Europe had in turn created an insatiable demand for slave labour in Brazil and the West Indies, where the sugar was grown. So, to sweeten the beverages of Europeans, millions of Africans were kidnapped, branded, shipped across the ocean and worked to death on the plantations of the New World. Exactly how many were taken we shall never know. Perhaps 8,000,000 slaves arrived in America in the course of this century alone; perhaps 2,000,000 more died on the way.

The trade was very well organized, and the Europeans did not capture slaves themselves as a rule. Rather, the latter were captured far inland, in great slave-raiding wars, then sold through a series of African middlemen down to the coast, where Europeans acquired them from local chiefs in exchange for goods in demand in Africa, such as guns, copper and iron ware, rum and textiles. Trading methods varied widely from one part of the coast to another, and certain areas were generally considered the preserves of particular European nations. The English, for example, dominated the trade in the Gambia and Sierra Leone, the French in Senegal and Gabon, the Portuguese in Angola. But in other places, like the Niger delta and Dahomey, ships of several nations traded together. On the Gold Coast, where the competition was most keen, the British, Dutch and Danes had about twenty forts and large castles interspersed one with another.

Most of the European nations originally found it expedient to grant a monopoly of their share of the slave trade to large chartered companies with great resources of capital. The prototype of these was the Dutch West Indies Company, formed in 1621, which quickly asserted its power and drove the Portuguese from most of West Africa by mid-century. Other peoples— English, French, Danes, Swedes and even Germans from Brandenburg—all formed national trading companies in imitation of the Dutch. Few survived the intense competition. In the long run the British did better by abandoning the chartered Royal African Company, formed in 1672, which was losing much trade to 'interlopers'— English individuals or firms who illegally ignored the company's monopoly and got away with it. In 1750, the corporation was dissolved and replaced by a new association called the Company of Merchants. This body did no business on its own account but existed to facilitate the slave trade for all English merchants who wished to participate in it. Anyone could become a member of the company by paying a small annual subscription, and this abolition of monopoly proved advantageous. The English share of the trade steadily increased during the century, and by 1785 Britain was buying and selling more slaves than all other European nations combined.

Among the side effects of the slave trade was the influence it had on African political development. The tiny city-states of the Niger delta adapted traditional tribal institutions to the demand for slaves and created quite astonishing and complex commercial organizations. In other areas the introduction of firearms encouraged African tribes to expand their territories. In the interior of the Gold Coast, the Confederation of Ashanti steadily grew throughout the century, defeated its rivals and by 1800 was threatening the European position on the coast. Further east, under a series of strong and implacable kings, Dahomey began empire-building in the same fashion. Thus, the inhuman trade had created powerful vested interests in Africa and America as well as in Europe. The fight to abolish 'the abominable traffic' was bound, in these circumstances, to be both protracted and arduous.

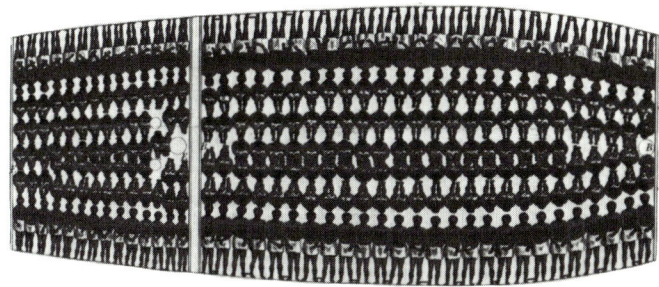

Above, British naval officers making a treaty with Africans in 1815. After the English outlawed the slave trade in 1807, they were to take a greater interest in the internal affairs of Africa. Bibliothèque Nationale, Paris.

Top, a diagram of the way in which slaves were packed into the ships that took them across the Atlantic in the 1780s. The slaves were rarely allowed on deck, for fear that they would mutiny, or jump overboard.

Opposite top left, the Hottentots or Khoikhoi people of southern Africa, who at first accepted the Dutch settlers in their sparsely populated land but later suffered enslavement and extermination.

Opposite right, a chain of slaves taken from the interior of Africa to the coast for shipment to the New World. The Europeans themselves did not round up the slaves – this job was left to the Arab traders and to the King of Dahomey, whose power was greatly increased by this trade with the Europeans.

Opposite bottom, an iron mask, and collar, shackles and spurs, all used by Europeans to restrain Africans taken for slaves in the New World. In addition to the human suffering it caused, the slave trade brought social instability to vast areas of central and western Africa in the eighteenth century.

Chapter 26

The Pacific World

At the beginning of the eighteenth century there were still vast areas of the globe of which Europeans knew nothing: the African interior, most of the Americas, the Pacific. The great exploratory achievement of the century was to chart the largest of these areas—the Pacific: an islanded expanse of water which covers about a third of the world's surface, framed by eastern Asia, the Americas and both polar regions and comprising a great diversity of climatic conditions, flora and fauna which—before the European came—supported widely different societies.

In the sixteenth century, Europeans established themselves in the East Indies (modern Indonesia) and the Philippines. The first European crossing of the Pacific was made by three Spanish ships commanded by Magellan, which went on to complete the first circumnavigation of the earth (1519–22). After this, Spanish voyages in the Pacific became frequent, and a regular trade began between Manila and Spanish America; but, though the Pacific was used as a waterway, little progress was made in charting or exploring it.

There were several reasons for this—the frequency with which great naval powers became involved in European wars, the secrecy with which any seemingly lucrative discovery was guarded—but the fundamental reason was navigational. A less than perfect ability to determine longitude did not prevent a ship from locating a sizeable land-mass; but it made it impossible to chart and rediscover the position of a Pacific archipelago. Hence the early Spanish explorers kept discovering islands and losing them again; Mendana discovered the Solomons on his first voyage (1567), only to miss them at a second try (1595) and end up in the Marquesas. The islands sighted by Quiros on his voyage in search of a southern continent (1606) were also 'lost'. And though Quiros's deputy, Torres, discovered a passage through the reefs and shoals separating Australia from New Guinea, the fact was not widely known for generations. It continued to be believed that Australia and New Guinea were part of the same land-mass, and even in 1768 Bougainville was not sufficiently convinced to make an attempt on the passage.

Terra Australis

Lack of progress in exploring the innumerable islands of Oceania is understandable; lack of interest in the island continent of Australia, close at hand, is at first sight inexplicable, especially in view of the European obsession with 'Terra Australis', the great southern continent that was believed to exist somewhere between the Cape of Good Hope and Cape Horn. Marco Polo had described its enormous wealth; Biblical interpretation supported Marco; and symmetry and sense required the existence of a land mass to balance those of the northern hemisphere and stop the earth toppling over.

There were, however, practical difficulties in pursuing the quest for the southern continent. Spanish ships came from Peru, Mexico or round the Horn—when the southeast trade winds lifted them steadily towards the Equator, so that they missed most of the actual Polynesian islands as well as the mythical Terra Australis—or sailed north from the Philippines to catch the westerlies that took them to Spanish America.

Nor were the Dutch better placed in New Guinea, though they were inhibited by more mercenary considerations. In 1605 William Jansz discovered New Holland (Australia), and the north and west coasts were soon fairly well known; but as they happen to be the least attractive areas of Australia and were inhabited by aborigines who seemed dirty, utterly primitive and poverty-stricken, there was no great incentive to explore further. This could not be the fabled Terra Australis.

The Dutch were right in this respect, as they discovered when a serious voyage of exploration was at last undertaken. In 1642, by sailing eastward from Mauritius so that the winds enabled him to stay in a high latitude (i.e. far south), Tasman proved that there was no Terra Australis in the Indian Ocean. He reached what is now Tasmania and went on to New Zealand, Tonga and the Fiji Islands. It thus became clear that Australia was an island (though New Guinea and Tasmania were still believed to be parts of it), and it was the *known* southern land (Terra Australis *Cognita*). Belief in the southern continent (Terra Australis *Incognita*) remained unshaken, though its projected area was diminished; Tasman himself thought that New Zealand might be its northern promontory.

And there matters remained for more than a century. The Dutch East India Company, like the Spanish Council of State before it, decided that it had better things to do with men, ships and money than to search for the southern continent. Europeans became preoccupied with their wars, and when the British, the seafaring people *par excellence* in the eighteenth century, appeared in Pacific waters, it was as buccaneers (like Dampier) or predators on enemy shipping (like Anson). Only after the Seven Years War was Europe to begin its decisive irruption into the Pacific.

Cook

Credit for this achievement is rightly given to Captain James Cook. The Englishmen Wallis and Carteret discovered—or rather rediscovered—Tahiti and Pitcairn Island in 1767; and in 1768 a French ship under the command of Bougainville also visited Tahiti; but it was Cook's three great voyages from 1768 that literally put the Pacific islands on the map.

Cook (1728–78) was the son of a Yorkshire farmworker. He had run away to sea in his teens, worked on colliers on the east coast and then joined the service. His record was distinguished and of the most valuable kind for his future activities—charting the shoals of the St Lawrence during the Seven Years War and surveying the coasts of Nova Scotia; but his rise was slow, perhaps because of his humble birth. He was thirty-nine, and newly made a lieutenant, when he was given the command that made him famous.

He had all the requisite qualities. He was completely professional, popular, brave and audacious—though his courage and audacity were expressed in such a matter-of-fact executive thoroughness that they are easily overlooked. Like other eighteenth-century commanders, he kept order among his men—the disreputable haul of the press-gangs—by harsh discipline; but his scrubbing-brush-and-vegetables regime almost banished the seaman's worst enemy, scurvy.

The public (and genuine) objective of Cook's first voyage (1768–71) was to observe from a mid-Pacific station the transit of Venus across the face of the sun—in itself an important task, undertaken at the instance of the Royal Society. But when Cook left England in August 1768 it was with secret and quite explicit instructions to search for the unknown southern continent, to bring back specimens of Pacific flora and fauna, to cultivate the friendship of any natives he met and to take possession, in the king's name, of such territories as he discovered.

Cook's ship, the *Endeavour*, was an adapted collier: a slow but sturdy vessel whose shallow draught made her ideal for surveying in coastal waters. With him Cook had the most up-to-date navigational aids: the sextant, which made it possible to take astronomical readings despite the ship's motion, and accurate lunar tables with which to interpret the readings. On his second voyage Cook was to secure even better results by taking an improved chronometer that measured distances at sea. Thus it had at last become possible to navigate and chart the Pacific accurately.

The *Endeavour* also carried the naturalist Joseph Banks, an astronomer and an artist; and Cook's later expeditions were similarly accompanied. His were therefore the first scientific expeditions activated by an unprejudiced curiosity, which extended to the human fauna, towards whose customs Cook and the scientists displayed a sympathy and tolerance worthy of the Age of Reason.

First voyage: the south Pacific

The *Endeavour* reached Tahiti via Cape Horn in April 1769 and stayed for three months—the first protracted contact between Europeans and Polynesians. The easy conditions of Polynesian life—and the absence of Western sexual taboos, of which the sailors took full advantage—made the island seem a paradise. The accounts given by Cook and others on their return lent credence to the myth of 'the noble savage'. In Tahiti itself, one of the effects of European contact soon appeared: half of Cook's men contracted the venereal diseases presumably brought by Bougainville's or Wallis's sailors. Nevertheless, apart from the Tahitian propensity to steal anything they could lay their hands on, relations between Europeans and natives were excellent.

After observing the transit of Venus—an activity almost prevented by the theft of the quadrant—Cook followed his secret instructions, sailing south and then west to New Zealand. He spent six months methodically charting the 2,400 miles of the coastline. The warlike Maoris, who had scared off Tasman, were handled with tact and remained friendly. By establishing that New Zealand consisted of two islands, Cook further diminished the possible extent of the legendary southern continent.

From New Zealand he sailed to Australia, making landfall at what was christened Botany Bay, in a part of the island continent that was far more inviting than the barren shores hitherto known: Cook called it New South Wales. Within a few years it was to be the home of English convicts and their keepers. The expedition explored the 2,000 miles of the eastern coastline, narrowly escaping disaster on the Great Barrier Reef, and observed the seemingly primeval landscape of Australia—the 'blackfellows' who seemed like the first men, the hopping kangaroo and flying fox (opossum). The final achievement of the voyage was a passage through the Torres Strait, virtually rediscovered after 160 years, which confirmed that Australia was a separate island from New Guinea. The *Endeavour* now returned via the Cape to England (1771), having circumnavigated the world.

The explorers' reception was a compound of scientific and literary enthusiasm. They had revealed the existence of an innocent world which had never known the Fall, mapped it and brought back a vast quantity of botanical, zoological and geological specimens and drawings, as well as native tools and clothing. The papers on which the naturalists Banks and Solander dried their specimens were, ironically, proof sheets for a commentary on Milton's *Paradise Lost*.

Second voyage: Terra Australis vanishes

Cook did not stay long to enjoy his fame. In July 1772 he set out on his second voyage with the *Resolution* and the *Adventurer*, both adapted colliers like the *Endeavour*. This time he followed Tasman's example and entered the Pacific from the west, determined to hold a course as far south as possible. And during the three summers (1772–4) of this second voyage, the *Resolution* ventured into the South Polar Sea, three times crossing the Antarctic Circle and once reaching as far south as latitude 71 degrees. By the end of the third summer it had effectively circumnavigated the Antarctic.

Above, the fruit of the plant Myrmecodia beccarii, *better known as ant house, found in Australia by Cook on his first voyage; the exploration of Australasia revealed many species of animals and plants previously unknown, and naturalists such as Joseph Banks were important members of the expedition. British Museum, London.*

Top, a tattooed Maori warrior, according to a member of Cook's first voyage. The Maoris had been established in New Zealand since the thirteenth century and had built up a series of strong and warlike kingdoms. British Museum, London.

Opposite, a sketch made by Captain Cook of Tolaga Bay in New Zealand. British Museum, London.

expedition's artist, Hodges, painted a picture which effectively conveys their remote, unreal presence. The exploration of the Oceanic islands alone would have justified Cook's second voyage; the circumnavigation of the Antarctic made it an epic. His return to England in 1775, again loaded with drawings and specimens, sealed his fame.

Third voyage: the Northwest Passage

Again he scarcely paused to enjoy it—which indicates that, for all his matter-of-factness, Cook suffered from the compulsive wanderlust attributed to the explorer in folklore. In 1776 he sailed to lay another myth: the Northwest Passage. Two centuries before Cook, Englishmen had tried to find a northwest passage from Hudson's Bay into the Pacific; now he was to seek it from the Pacific. There was also a political motive for the voyage: Cook was instructed to discover how much of the Pacific coast of North America was in Spanish and Russian hands.

On this, his last voyage, Cook sailed into every sizeable inlet along the Alaskan coast without finding the Northwest Passage, passed through the Bering Strait across the Arctic Circle and explored the Arctic coast of America, discovering and naming Cape North. Further south, he discovered Christmas Island (1777) and the Hawaiian Islands (1778); and it was to Kealakekua Bay in the Hawaiian Islands that he returned from the Arctic (1779) and met his death.

As in the previous year, he was welcomed as a god. His ships, the *Resolution* and the *Discovery*, left Kealakekua Bay for home, but were forced to turn back by two days of storm. The homage due to a god was repeated, despite the tiresome impropriety of

The fabulously wealthy southern continent had once and for all been proved a myth; below the southern oceans there were only walls of ice, numbing cold, gales and fogs. Cook thought that there probably was a land-mass centred on the South Pole; but the question of its existence seemed of little interest and incapable of solution. The hazards encountered by the *Resolution* understandably led Cook to believe that no explorer would be able to penetrate further. He wrote, the Southern Hemisphere has been sufficiently explored, and a final end put to the searching after a Southern Continent, which has at times engrossed the attention of some of the maritime powers for near two centuries past, and the geographers of all ages.

The wealth hoped for in Terra Australis

Incognita did exist, though not in the form envisaged by readers of Marco Polo and Quiros. Cook's exploration of Tierra del Fuego, South Georgia and the Sandwich Islands revealed that the polar regions supported an abundance of wild life, including whales, seals and sea-lions. The existence of such prey was to bring large numbers of Europeans into the South Pacific within a few years of Cook's voyages.

Cook and his men recuperated from the rigours of Antarctica by spending the winters roaming the Pacific, discovering or rediscovering the Marquesas, the Society Islands, the New Hebrides, New Caledonia, Norfolk Island and many other islands. Perhaps the most fascinating rediscovery was Easter Island, on which great crumbling figures gazed mysteriously into the distance. The

the god's reappearance; but trouble blew up when some Hawaiians stole one of *Discovery's* boats. Cook had faced this situation before and made his standard response by taking hostages to compel the return of the boat. But this time something went wrong: Cook's men fired at some canoes and killed a chief. The Hawaiians attacked Cook's party on the shore. The explorer was stabbed in the back and fell face down in the water, and the incensed Hawaiians surrounded his body and cut it to pieces. A friendly native later brought some of his remains out to the ships, and they were buried at sea.

Pacific cultures

Cook and his men, like other Europeans, found it difficult to distinguish between the various peoples they encountered: 'Indians' were either happy, like the Tahitians, or miserable, like the natives of Tierra del Fuego, whom Cook described as 'perhaps as miserable a set of people as are this day on earth'. In the course of his three voyages, Cook became aware that Oceania contained a diversity of races and cultures; and the realization that the Tahitians took part in savage intertribal wars, practised infanticide and indulged in occasional human sacrifices disabused him of any idea that Pacific peoples were 'innocent'.

In fact, Pacific societies were the product of a long evolution, and even the least advanced had made a complex adaptation to their surroundings. They had elaborately regulated codes of social behaviour, extensive mythologies and highly developed skills. Among other things they produced striking drawings, paintings and objects for magic and ritual purposes. They were, however, inferior to Europeans in certain essential respects: they did not use metal, they

had not developed a system of writing, and they had no draught animals. They also took for granted many rites that were repulsive to the European moral sensibility; though it may be questioned whether the self-mutilation of the aborigine or the cannibalism of the islanders was crueller than what actually went on in European slave ships and prisons.

The Tasmanians and Australian aborigines were the most backward peoples in the Pacific: they were hunters and food-gatherers, like men of the Paleolithic (Old Stone Age) period. The Tasmanians, now extinct—or, rather, extinguished by the white man in the nineteenth century—were a dark-skinned, woolly-haired people, possibly of Papuan origin. Where they came from and how they reached Tasmania is unknown. As toolmakers they lagged behind the aborigines, since they had neither spears nor boomerangs. They probably numbered only 5,000.

Australia, too, was sparsely populated, with only a few hundred thousand aboriginal inhabitants, who had come to Australia from Asia before the two land-masses had separated. Australia lacked cereals and herding animals, which limited the possible development of the aborigine. But though his existence was a hand-to-mouth one, his few skills—making weapons, hunting, fishing, gathering berries and grubs—were developed to an extraordinary degree and ensured survival even in periods of draught. A complex kinship system linked the various clans within a tribe, and every tribe had its totem—a common ancestor, plant or animal —which was celebrated in ceremonies. All aborigines practised some form of initiation of the young at puberty (usually circumcision) which entailed the infliction of great pain. Aboriginal painting and drawing—on

Above, HMS Resolution, *one of the two ships taken by Cook on his second voyage. Mitchell Library, Sydney.*

Top, the inhabitants of Tierra del Fuego, as found by Cook in 1769. British Museum, London.

Top left, a bearded pensuin, recorded on Cook's second voyage. British Museum, London.

Opposite top left, the Resolution *and the* Adventure, *the ships that Cook took on his second trip to the south Pacific, in 1772–75, anchored off Tahiti. National Maritime Museum, London.*

Opposite right, Otoo, or Tu, the King of Tahiti, whom Cook met on his second voyage and for whom he had great friendship and respect. National Library of Australia, Canberra.

Opposite bottom, the island of Tahiti, depicted by a member of Cook's second voyage. British Museum, London.

bark, on the ground, in caves—ranged from extreme stylization to a vivid naturalism.

Melanesia

The peoples of Oceania were at the Neolithic (New Stone Age) level of development; that is they lived in permanent settlements, cultivated the land and had domesticated animals. All subsisted on 'garden' and tree products such as yams, coconuts and breadfruit.

But the differences between them were as important as their similarities. Oceania was inhabited by three distinct races, though there was inevitably a good deal of crossbreeding and cultural interchange. The Melanesians ('black islanders') were the least advanced, dark-skinned, woolly-haired peoples who had spread from New Guinea to the neighbouring islands (the Solomons, the New Hebrides, New Caledonia, part of the Fijis). The dense vegetation in most parts of Melanesia led to the development of isolated, widely different communities with separate languages.

The Micronesians ('people of the small islands') were predominantly Mongoloid, relatives of the peoples of eastern Asia. They had yellow-brown skins and straight black hair and were small and slight. Both racially and culturally they were more hybrid than the other Oceanic peoples, Polynesian influence being particularly strong. They occupied the Marianas, the Carolines, the Marshalls and the Gilbert Islands.

The Polynesians ('people of the many islands') were the latest arrivals in the Pacific. Where they came from remains in dispute: most scholars believe it was Asia, but Thor Heyerdahl has put forward a strong argument in favour of South America, proving by his famous Kon-Tiki expedition (1947) that it was possible to make a journey by raft from Peru to the Society Islands. Whatever their origin, the Polynesians were undoubtedly a remarkable seafaring people. According to the orthodox account, between the ninth and thirteenth centuries AD they spread out from the Society Islands over a vast area of the Pacific, reaching the Hawaiian Islands, the Ellice Islands, New Zealand and Easter Island.

They were a Caucasian people, with good physiques, light-brown skins and straight or wavy hair, and occupied the most favoured areas of the Pacific (free from malaria, supporting the sweet potato, etc.). These facts largely account for the European prejudice which even now leads people to identify 'Polynesians' and 'South Sea Islanders'. However, it is true that they were most advanced of the Pacific races. Apart from their seafaring exploits (less in evidence by the eighteenth century), they made a sophisticated study of oratory, were skilled musicians and possessed an appealingly dignified code of manners. On his second voyage, Cook brought a Tahitian called Omai back to England, where he became a society lion with no difficulty at all, meeting George III and sitting for two romanticized portraits by Sir Joshua Reynolds. The less attractive side of Polynesian life included diseases (yaws, hookworm), cannibalism and a variety of murderous burial and sacrificial rites.

Easter Island deserves to be mentioned separately, since it has been the subject of much speculation. It is a thousand miles from the nearest Polynesian island (Pitcairn) and two thousand from South America; so that, whichever direction they came from, the Polynesians must have accomplished a great feat of navigation in reaching it. The island has two features of intense interest: the gigantic statues carved from soft volcanic rock, which in the eighteenth century were still crowned with hats carved from a different red stone; and wooden tablets carrying undeciphered writing or hieroglyphs—the only example in the whole of the Pacific. Both are now attributed to the Polynesians rather than to a 'lost' race, but the almost complete destruction of the island's population during the nineteenth century effectively terminated any oral tradition that might have provided more information on the subject.

The European invasion

Australia had few inhabitants, whereas the Pacific islands were densely populated, perhaps even overpopulated. Europeans were soon to reverse this situation by colonizing Australia and visiting a whole series of misfortunes on the islanders.

The explorers behaved well, exemplifying rational curiosity and a humanitarian enthusiasm which extended to providing friendly natives with seed, iron tools and domestic animals—the introduction of the pig greatly improved the islanders' diet. Cook set a high standard of conduct that was generally followed by his sucessors, of whom the best-known are the French commanders La Pérouse (1785–8), Freycinet (1818–19) and D'Urville (1826–9 and 1837–40).

All the same, the explorers were indirectly to blame for the coming disaster: they made the Pacific accessible to the European. Cook himself repeatedly expressed doubts as to the benefits of European influence on the natives, though he mainly thought in terms of a fall from grace on their part. Up to a point he was right: the islanders quickly became dependent on European tools and began to lose some of their old skills; and European firearms made tribal wars much more deadly.

The civilized attitudes of the eighteenth-century gentleman-officer-scientist were not shared by sailors and most other Europeans. The famous mutiny on the *Bounty* (1789) provided a clear warning: the mutineers, who have become heroes of romance for setting the tyrannical Captain Bligh adrift in an open boat, mistreated the natives and fought among themselves wherever they went (Tahiti, Tubai, Pitcairn).

The depredations of the European were to be on a much larger scale than this. The Pacific became the stamping ground of the escaped criminal, the deserter and the ne'er-do-well. Traders invaded the area, greedy for sandalwood, copra, pearls and *bêche-de-mer* (an edible sea-slug very acceptable to the Chinese palate). 'Blackbirders' kidnapped or

hoodwinked thousands of islanders to work in the sugar-cane fields of Queensland and the mines of Mexico and Peru. Whalers and sealers disrupted native society with alcohol, violence and disease, as well as destroying the wild life of the Antarctic. Missionaries resisted these intrusions but suppressed the island cultures, forbade singing and dancing and (regardless of climate) thrust the men of the islands into singlets and shorts and the women into 'Mother Hubbard' shifts. If the demoralized natives escaped kidnappers, press-gangs, alcoholism and venereal disease, they succumbed to European ailments against which they had built up no immunities.

Most of these developments were in full swing by the end of the eighteenth century. The most striking result was a catastrophic decline in population, visible by the mid-nineteenth century, when the European powers began to annex the island groups. Generally speaking, annexation improved the native's lot by giving him some sort of legal protection; but the damage had already been done. The booming trade in copra brought Chinese, Indian, Japanese and other immigrants into the Pacific in the nineteenth century. But the islanders themselves made a partial demographic recovery only in the present century, and the cultural adjustment is still not complete.

The fierce Maoris of New Zealand, in origin a Polynesian race, were slightly more fortunate. They were given to fighting among themselves and eating each other but proved capable of resisting the white man with remarkable success. The arrival of European traders enabled them to acquire firearms, which increased inter-tribal bloodshed but also put them on an equal footing with the European. When annexation inevitably took place (1840), the Maori race was still intact and able to secure relatively favourable terms.

The birth of white Australia

European governments were slow in annexing and settling the Pacific lands, partly because of preoccupation with European events, partly because of a growing conviction that political control was unnecessary and burdensome. The single exception, Australia, was made only because Britain had lost her American colonies, and with them a dumping-ground for convicts. In 1788 eleven ships under Captain Arthur Phillip arrived at Port Jackson (later Sydney), just above Botany Bay, with a cargo of 717 male and female convicts and a New South Wales Corps raised in Britain to guard them. The eastern half of Australia was formally claimed by Great Britain.

Guarded chain-gangs of convicts continued to work in the new continent as before: the rigours of the British penal system were simply transferred unchanged to a new setting, except that uncertain supplies, rum and the unreliability of the New South Wales Corps made for greater confusion and hardship. For two decades Australia was governed despotically by naval commanders, who spent much of their time trying to suppress the traffic in rum and curtail the power of the

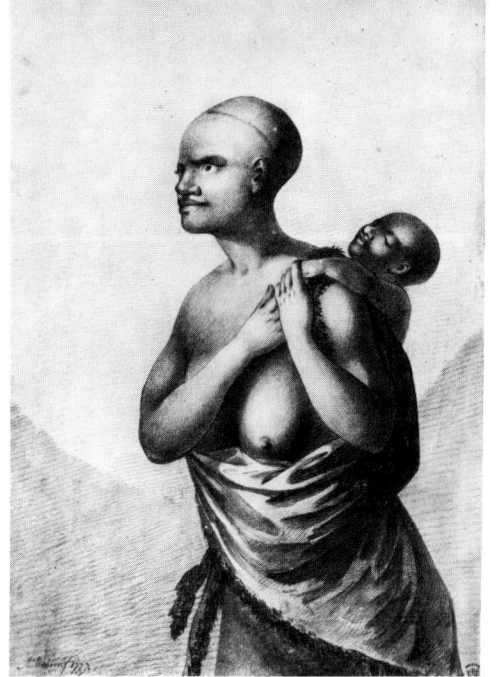

Above, a woman of New Holland, later known as Van Diemen's Land, or Tasmania, as recorded on Cook's third voyage. British Museum, London.

Top, the interior of a winter house found by Cook in one of the Aleutian islands, off the coast of Alaska; the roof was covered with turf. Peabody Museum, Harvard University, Cambridge Massachusetts.

Top left, HMS Resolution at anchor off Vancouver Island, Canada, on Cook's third voyage, on which he tried to find the western end of the north-west passage. British Museum, London.

Above left, an eskimo of Alaska, depicted by a member of Cook's crew. He is wearing a visor against the glare of the snow. Peabody Museum, Harvard University, Cambridge, Massachusetts.

Opposite left, the ceremonial presentation of a pig to Captain Cook in Hawaii in 1778; he was treated as an incarnation of the god of peace and happiness. Bernice P Bishop Museum, Honolulu.

Opposite right, a sketch of Hawaiian men dancing; Bernice P Bishop Museum, Honolulu.

EUROPEANS IN THE PACIFIC

Date	The Pacific	Europe
1500	Balboa sights Pacific (1513)	Luther's 95 theses (1517)
	Magellan crosses Pacific (1520)	
	Mendana: first voyage (1567)	
	Sir Francis Drake in Pacific (1578)	
	Mendana: second voyage (1595)	
1600	Janszoon: 'New Holland' (1605)	Gunpowder plot (1605)
	Voyages of Quiros and Torres (1605)	
	Hartog explores western Australia (1616)	
	Tasman's voyage (1642–4)	English Civil War (1642–6)
	Dampier on north coast of Australia (1699)	
1700	Roggeeven discovers Easter Island and Samoa (1721)	
		Seven Years War (1756–63)
	Wallis and Carteret (1766–7)	
	Bougainville (1767–9)	
	Cook: first voyage (1768–71)	
	Cook: second voyage (1772–5)	
		American War of Independence (1775–83)
	Cook: third voyage (1776–9)	
	Voyage of La Pérouse (1785–8)	
	Australia: convicts at Botany Bay (1788)	
		Storming of the Bastille (1789)
	Bounty mutineers on Pitcairn (1790)	
	Australia: first free settlers (1793)	
	First mission on Tahiti (1798)	
1800		Battle of Waterloo (1815)
	Voyage of Freycinet (1818–19)	
	D'Urville: first voyage (1826–9)	
	Australia annexed (1829)	Great Reform Bill (1832)
	D'Urville: second voyage (1837–40)	Victoria becomes Queen (1837)
	New Zealand annexed (1840)	
1850	French begin island annexations	

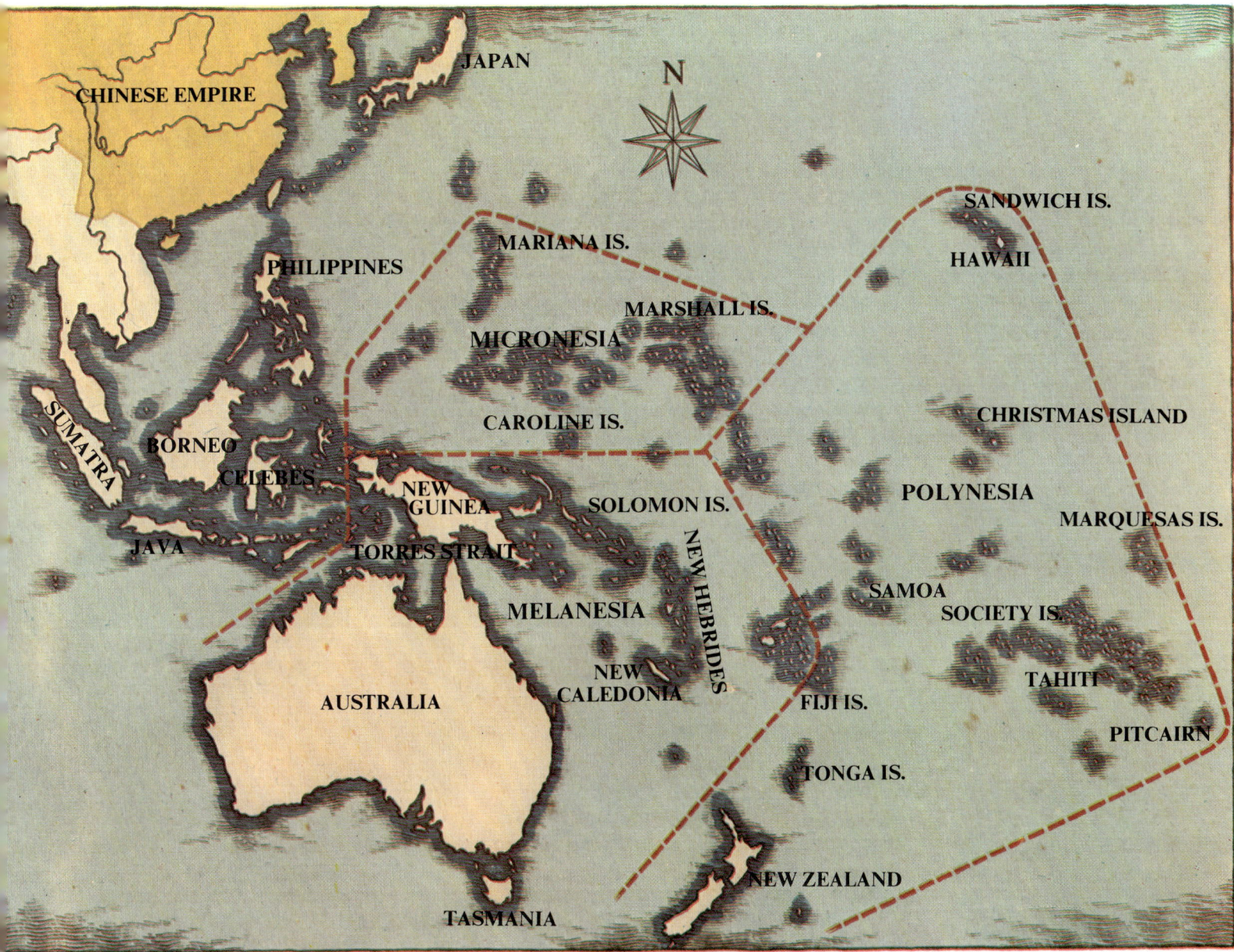

CHINESE EMPIRE
JAPAN
N
MARIANA IS.
PHILIPPINES
MARSHALL IS.
SANDWICH IS.
HAWAII
MICRONESIA
SUMATRA
BORNEO
CELEBES
CAROLINE IS.
CHRISTMAS ISLAND
NEW
GUINEA
SOLOMON IS.
POLYNESIA
MARQUESAS IS.
JAVA
TORRES STRAIT
NEW HEBRIDES
MELANESIA
SAMOA
SOCIETY IS.
AUSTRALIA
NEW
CALEDONIA
FIJI IS.
TAHITI
PITCAIRN
TONGA IS.
TASMANIA
NEW ZEALAND

officers of the Corps, who had become great landed proprietors. The aborigines were driven from their hunting-grounds and became pitiful hangers-on or retired further inland, where they killed and were killed by any white man they came across. The settlement of Tasmania began the process by which the white man rapidly destroyed the native population. There was an insurrection of Irish convicts (mainly political prisoners from the Irish rebellion of 1798) in 1804 and a 'rum rebellion' in 1808 against one of the governors, the unlucky Bligh of the *Bounty*. It was in many respects an unpromising beginning.

More constructive efforts were also being made. The first free settlers arrived in 1793, provided by the British government with tools and grants of land. The convicts too were given land when their sentences expired. Sheep-raising began in the 1790s. In 1798 George Bass discovered the strait separating Tasmania from the continent, and in 1802–3 Matthew Flinders completed the exploration of the south coast and circumnavigated Australia. The continent had

become a British preserve, and it was only a matter of time before it was annexed (1829).

The nineteenth century was to be one of continued hardship, dissension and exploitation (convicts were transported to Australia until 1867) but also one of settlement, exploration and eventual self-government. For better or worse, a new nation came into being in the South Pacific.

Above, convicts breaking stones in the English penal colony of New South Wales, established in 1788. Private Collection.

Top, Australasia in the eighteenth century.

Opposite left, a native of Tahiti wearing full mourning outfit, painted by one of Captain Cook's crew in 1770. British Museum, London.

Opposite right, Sydney Harbour in about 1810; the original colony of Botany Bay was soon overtaken by Sydney.

Part V

THE AGE OF REVOLUTIONS

Introduction

The second half of the eighteenth century is the classic Age of Revolution. There is more in revolution than transition of a particularly rapid and violent kind, and the revolutions in the western world—the Puritan revolution in England, the Russian Revolution, and the American and French Revolutions—have all had a constructive purpose and outcome. Indeed, it has been wisely said that a revolution is an unlawful change in the conditions of lawfulness. Revolution is always illegal, but its aim is not lawless. It begins by defying an older authority and ends by creating a new one, and so the American revolution concluded with the establishment of the new government of the United States, the French with Napoleon's organization of modern France.

There is good reason to treat the American and the French Revolutions together. It is true that France and the Thirteen Colonies were in many respects very different. France was ten times as populous, more urbanized and more civilized and much more troubled by the problems of wealth, poverty and privilege with which an old and complex society is often afflicted.

Yet events in the two countries formed part of a larger whole. It was French support that enabled the Americans to win a clear decision in their war of independence. That war was, in fact, one of the series of Anglo-French conflicts that ran intermittently from the time of Louis XIV to that of Napoleon. But in thus helping to dismember the British Empire, the French monarchy was only briefly to enjoy its moment of revenge. The expense of the American war turned its chronic deficits into financial paralysis and brought about a breakdown of the social order. The example of rebellion in America had a direct consequence in the French Revolution.

While educated Americans such as John Adams and Thomas Jefferson read mostly English books, they also shared in that European enlightenment for which French writers were the principal spokesmen. On the other hand, various of the French who became revolutionaries in 1789—Lafayette, Mirabeau, Condorcet, Brissot and Mounier—had long talked, thought or written about the American Revolution and the new American ideas.

The ideas shared in France and America were to inspire all the liberal and democratic movements of modern times. Some had been anticipated in England in the seventeenth century. Some were again expressed in demand for reform in England, Scotland and Ireland, which became audible at about the time of the American Revolution and made itself increasingly heard until the days of Gladstone.

Similar ideas existed in most other parts of Europe also. It thus happened that when, during the French Revolutionary and Napoleonic wars, the French occupied Italy or Germany, Holland or Poland, they found men in those countries who were willing to work with them. The Revolution 'expanded'. The French empire under Napoleon may have resembled the German control of Europe under Hitler in some ways, but certainly not in spirit. Napoleon appealed to the enlightened and progressive forces in Europe; Hitler loathed them. Hitler annihilated the Jews; Napoleon, while caring nothing for Judaism, insisted that the Jews receive equal rights.

The common fund of revolutionary ideas was mixed, various and internally conflicting. Some ideas fared better than others at different times and in different places, but it is easy to establish a general list. There was the principle of the sovereignty of the people, which sometimes meant national self-determination or independence and sometimes meant that ultimate authority must lie with the governed and not with the government, a governing class, or a ruling elite or family.

This principle passed into either republicanism or constitutional monarchy. It involved ideas of representation and limited government, which had existed in Europe since the Middle Ages but now took a more modern form. An equality among citizens, rather than a hierarchy of ranks and orders, was to be the base of representation. Liberty, an old ideal, now carried the ring of individual freedom.

There must be freedom of thought and expression, subject to the needs of public order, which at times, as under Robespierre or Napoleon, were construed to mean the silencing of political opposition. There must be freedom of religion. In the modern state people of any religion or of no religion should enjoy the same civic rights and have the same duties. There should be a written constitution, a document deliberately and rationally contrived and agreed upon, not a mere inheritance of familiar customs and practices.

Closely related was the idea of separation of executive, legislative and judical powers. All magistrates, from the king (if any) downwards, were to possess only a delegated function, and law courts were to be more rational, expeditious and humane. Men had rights, by nature and as citizens, to be specifically declared and secured against arbitrary power. The Americans and the

French issued many such pronouncements, and the French Declaration of 1789 was the most memorable document of the era.

But if the French and American Revolutions were alike in some of their ideas, they were also very different. The American was much milder and much less of a revolution. The ruling groups in America before the Revolution were less entrenched, less ostentatiously rich, less obstinate and less detested than in France. British rule was not really oppressive, and before 1776 the British governors and regiments in America were not considered as foreigners. They made themselves very objectionable, but there is a whole school of thought that has seen the American Revolution as a civil war within the British Empire, with discontented persons on both sides of the Atlantic opposing crown and parliament as they then existed. The ultimate cause of the rupture must be found in the fact that England and its colonies had developed in contrary directions in the four or five generations since the first settlement. Relatively speaking, the colonies were already 'democratic', whereas England was in the heyday of its landed aristocracy and the oddities of the unreformed parliament.

The American Revolution is remembered, in part, as the first successful case of colonial independence. It initiated the break-up of the first European overseas empires and was followed later by the Latin-American revolutions and by increasing autonomy for Canada and the British dominions.

It is sometimes seen also as a precedent for the twentieth-century, anti-colonialist revolutions of Asia and Africa. There are indeed parallels, and the Americans did reject a distant authority that was increasingly felt to be alien. However, the racial feelings and the deeper cultural differences that have animated the recent movements of decolonization had no part in the American Revolution, especially since at that time it was only the white Americans—then mostly of English or Scottish origin—who counted.

The French Revolution was vaster and more widely significant and became the prototype of revolution itself. It passed through a series of increasingly radical phases and was opposed by organized counter-revolutionary attempts. It developed a psychology of world liberation matched by the Austro-Prussian intervention to uphold the French king's authority in 1792. The result was the fall of the French monarchy, more civil struggle, more radicalization of the Revolution, the Terror and French military victories that went on interruptedly for twenty years.

In France, unlike America, the whole social structure was transformed. Old forms of income disappeared, such as the right to receive feudal dues and tithes, and also class privileges in taxation which were, in effect, a form of income. Much more real property changed hands, when lands and buildings, both in the towns and in the country,

Above, George Washington's reception on his way to Philadelphia in April 1779 to be inaugurated as the first President of the United States of America.

Above left, the execution of Louis XVI of France in January 1793. The execution represented the failure to achieve any constitutional solution to France's problems and paved the way for a series of radical experiments.

On page 260, a crowd gathering outside the Palais Royal in Paris early in July 1789, a few days before the fall of the Bastille.

belonging to the Church or to nobles who had fled abroad were bought up by peasants and the middle classes.

Changes in local government, including a new plan of municipal organization, altered the social relationships of gentry and common people, and proved more lasting than constitutional reforms at a higher level. The Church was revolutionized from top to bottom. Roman Catholics, Protestants, Jews and the non-religious received the same rights. So did free negroes. Slavery itself was abolished in the colonies in 1794, although soon restored. Marriage, the family, the schools and the selection and training of an educated elite were put on a new basis.

The economy was opened up by the abolition of guilds, regional tariffs and older forms of commercial law. It benefited from new technical schools, public museums, the awarding of prizes to inventors, decimal currency and the metric system. War itself was transformed. The army of the citizen soldier, resting on popular enthusiasm and promotion to the highest ranks according to merit (a phenomenon already seen in America but unknown in Europe), was now made more systematic in France, as befitted a country of 25,000,000 inhabitants at war with the powers of Europe.

All such developments heightened the national consciousness, or sense of membership, commitment, unity and common advantage, within the state. But the main immediate beneficiaries of the French Revolution were undoubtedly the middle classes, people in town or country who had, or could obtain, some property, education and social position. Many of the former aristocracy remained disaffected. The wage-earning and artisan classes received no lasting or tangible satisfaction.

The Revolution was marked by acute class conflict. The beginnings of a working-class movement in 1793 were soon put down. It is true to say that there was in the French Revolution no socialism of any developed kind, but when a revolutionary socialism appeared in the next generation it looked back to the French Revolution for precedent and encouragement. Since the end of the eighteenth century the idea of revolution, either belief in it or fear of it has been a permanent feature of our world.

Chapter 27

The American Revolution

The British colonies in North America in 1763 were not limited to the Atlantic seaboard. They stretched from the Hudson Bay Territory, Newfoundland, Nova Scotia and Quebec in the north down to the Florida keys in the south and across to the islands of the Caribbean, from Bermuda to Jamaica and from Dominica and St Vincent to Grenada. Britain also controlled Belize and the Mosquito Coast in Central America. France held the Caribbean sugar islands of Guadeloupe, St Domingue (Santo Domingo), Martinique and St Lucia (which some contemporary observers thought more valuable than empty Canada) and Cayenne in Guiana. Louisiana, Cuba and Hispaniola were Spanish possessions.

Nevertheless, it was Britain which dominated both the mainland and the Caribbean with 8,000 ships at sea and 70,000 sailors. Britain saw its American empire as maritime and its purposes as mercantile. America's raw materials—sugar and rice, tobacco and timber, furs and fish—precisely because they could not be produced easily (or at all) at home were the justification for the colonies' existence.

In exchange for all these things the colonies were given military and naval protection and trading bounties and were sold the manufactures, the cambrics, the necessities and the luxuries which they needed. The British Empire, like all empires, was founded for the profit of the mother country, not its glory. Without this motive, the Empire would not have existed.

The mainland colonies extended for 1,600 miles along the coast of North America and in 1763 hardly reached more than 100 miles inland. At each end there was a military or naval outpost: Newfoundland was a tiny settlement of 6,000, but its numbers were doubled in the summer as the Grand Banks were swept for cod and mackerel. Florida, won from Spain in 1763, was seen as a frontier against the Spanish-controlled west and against Spain's Indian allies—the Creeks, the Choctaws and the Cherokees. To the acquisitions of 1713—the Hudson Bay Territory, Newfoundland and Nova Scotia—there was added in 1763 the vast province of Quebec. Nova Scotia had been given a representative assembly in 1758 and by 1775 its population had reached a total of

20,000. Quebec, however, was French in character, unready yet for any form of representative government, with only nineteen Protestant families living outside Quebec and Montreal.

The British colonies, from Massachusetts to Georgia, varied greatly in character, government and economies. By 1763 the majority were under the direct rule of the Crown, except for Pennsylvania, Delaware and Maryland (owned by private families) and the self-governing provinces of Connecticut and Rhode Island, both of which had elective governors and legislatures. The governors, whether appointed or elected, had considerable vice-regal powers, even though they were in almost all cases now dependent for money on the grants made by the colonial assemblies. Whatever their powers and whatever their dependence on Britain for protection and trade, the colonial assembles were well-established and had all too frequently discussed the issues of taxation and representation along lines familiar in English history.

The social structure of the mainland colonies was aristocratic. Power in Virginia, in South Carolina and in the Hudson Valley lay with the long established families, and it was rooted in the land. The land owned by the Fairfax family in Virginia ran from the coast to the headwaters of the Potomac. Maine was all but a private holding of Sir William Pepperrell, the conqueror of Louisburg. Much of Georgia was owned by Sir James Wright. Even in Congregationalist New England, seating in church, like the lists of students at Harvard and Yale, went according to property and social class: it was 'property, virtue and intelligence' in that order. From these men of property the colonial councils were recruited. These were 'the friends of government'.

Yet colonial society was not a rigid one. The ease with which property was acquired weakened the sense of class division. George

Washington, a protégé of the Fairfaxes, was ill-educated and largely self-made. So were John Macpherson, an enterprising shipowner of Philadelphia, Benjamin Franklin, who owed everything to his pen and his printing press, John Hancock, the merchant-smuggler, and J. S. Copley, the artist. There was abundant opportunity to make one's way into the gentry.

Below these people were the 'middling sort' of clergy and shopkeepers, teachers and craftsmen, and beneath them, in turn, the large working class, many of whom made their way to North America by serving under contract for a term of years. Among the last group were numerous Germans in Pennsylvania and, particularly in the west and on the frontier, Scots-Irish.

The working class, too, included men of enterprise: Matthew Thornton of New Hampshire, who signed the Declaration of Independence; William Buckland, who built Gunston Hall; and Charles Thomson, Secretary of the Continental Congress. 'You may depend upon it', said William Allen, an American clergyman and author, 'that this is one of the best poor men's Country's in the World.'

It was, moreover, a growing country. If it moved west slowly before 1763, it pushed more rapidly in the direction once the French threat was removed. It was increasing fast in numbers: high birth rates and large families were the rule. The average number of children a family was 7·5 and the population doubled each generation. 'An old maid or an old bachelor are as scarce among us and reckoned as ominous as a blazing star', wrote William Byrd. The population in 1763 was almost 2,000,000 of whom approximately one quarter were German and Scots-Irish and approximately one-fifth negro. By 1775 it was 2,500,000. Fifteen years later, in 1790, when the first census was carried out, it was 3,929,214, of whom 757,208 were negroes.

The problem of the west

Very few contemporaries in 1763 foresaw or predicted independence for the British colonies. Some French observers did, of course, hope for trouble. 'Colonies are like fruits which cling to the tree only until they ripen', was the view of Turgot, the French statesman and economist. Benjamin Franklin, the most balanced and shrewd of observers, foresaw a world in which the weight of population and of economic power would lie on the American side of the Atlantic, although he did not want it to be a future of separate states. In the 1760s Franklin was an 'Old England man'. So were the vast majority of Americans.

There was no reason why in 1763 independence should have been contemplated. The colonies of mainland North America were English foundations, reflecting Old World values and institutions. The sea was their line of communication and their trade was linked profitably to Britain by the mercantile system. Their own land boundaries were moving very slowly inland and were menaced by fierce and unpredictable Indian tribes against whom Britain gave protection. The Iroquois of New York might be friendly but the Creeks, Choctaws and Cherokees were not, and there was an ugly war with the Cherokees between 1759 and 1761. In 1763, angered by the prospect of British rule and still more by the prospect of land grabbing by white settlers, the Ottawas rose under their chief, Pontiac. They were defeated in 1761 by Colonel Henry Bouquet, but not before they had captured every western post except Detroit and Fort Pitt and had killed about 200 settlers and traders. Moreover, they were defeated once again at the hands of British regular soldiers, obligingly paid for by the home government, and not by any colonial army. North America still seemed a vulnerable, sharply divided and dependent world.

To meet the Indian threat to the frontier communities and to placate the Indians, in 1763 the British government proclaimed that the land west of the Appalachians was an Indian reserve. In the reserve white settlement was forbidden and Indian traders were to be licensed. This liberal measure was largely the achievement of the Earl of Shelburne as president of the Board of Trade and was designed not only to reassure the Indians but to guarantee the fur trade. It had the further effect of confining the settlers to the coastal and inland areas, and it was hoped thus to discourage not only the westward movement but also the growth of population and thus of colonial manufacturing industry.

What was welcome to the Indians was repugnant to the colonists. Land settlers and frontiersmen saw in the proclamation a barrier to be overturned or to be ignored. It was an obstacle in their path to the good bottom land of the western river valleys and hence to profit. It was, they said, an infringement also of the 'sea to sea' clauses of colonial charters, which permitted steady expansion westward.

Many prominent colonists, like George Washington at Mount Vernon or Franklin in London seeking a charter for his land project in the Ohio Valley, resented interference with their plans. (Washington in fact ignored the restrictions altogether.) Moreover, the machinery for regulating Indian trade and the military posts established in the west to check further Indian rebellions imposed a heavy financial burden on Britain. The national debt stood at £133,000,000 in 1763, an increase of £60,000,000 in eight years. The extra cost of colonial defence would be crippling. The time had therefore come for a new policy. It was thorough and thoughtful as would have been expected from George Grenville, the first lord of the Treasury. Ironically, it was also the first stage on the road to revolution.

The Stamp Act

Grenville planned to station a standing army in America to guard the settlements not only against the Indians but against any resumption of French attack and considered it fair that the colonists should meet one-third of its cost. He sought also to enforce more strictly the Navigation Acts of 1651 and 1660, which had confined colonial manufactures to British or colonial shipping, and in 1764 passed the Sugar Act, by which the duty on sugar and molasses was reduced in order to make it easier to collect. The laws were to be enforced. To raise revenue to meet part of the costs of defence a Stamp Act was to be passed, imposing a duty on newspapers and pamphlets, cards and dice and legal documents. The Stamp Act was a device used in England since 1694. The taxes to be raised by it were much less severe than those in Britain. Colonial opinion was fully canvassed in advance and the colonial agents (appointees stationed in London) fully consulted, but no alternative plan was put up by them. Indeed, the speed with which some distinguished colonial figures, such as George Mercer of Virginia and Jared Ingersoll of Connecticut, accepted the posts of stamp distributors gave no indication of an approaching crisis.

In fact, colonial opposition was instant and all but uniform. In the Virginia House of Burgesses, Patrick Henry presented a series of resolutions, attacking the act and the king. 'If this be treason', he said, 'make the most of it.' In Boston Sam Adams organized a group which took the name 'Sons of Liberty' with the intention of preventing the sale of stamps by threats of direct action against those using them.

Eastern merchants boycotted British goods, and delegates from nine colonies met in City Hall, New York, in the so-called Stamp Act Congress, demanding repeal of the act and issuing a 'Declaration of Rights'. This claimed that since the colonists were not represented in Parliament they could not be taxed by it without their consent.

The fact that the British government expected no resistance to its proposals but met a massive protest is an indication of the gap dividing the Old World from the New. It was partly a matter of the geographical distance: 'Seas roll and months pass between the order and the execution,' said Edmund Burke. It was partly—and more fundamentally—a matter of national psychology. The New World was now peopled by many who had no ties of affection or concern with England and who, if they were English, were Dissenters and Nonconformists by religion and by situation. A distinct attitude was emerging—sombre, evangelical and hostile to the Church of England in religion, close to nature, self-dependent and socially fluid—that was utterly alien to the status-bound ways of England. Some 3,000 miles of isolation from Europe made real representation impossible. The same 3,000 miles made it not only impossible but increasingly unsought.

Many colonies were coming to be in practice independent states, as some perceptive governors like Sir Francis Bernard of Massachusetts and Robert Dinwiddie of Virginia recognized. One of the strands that was gradually being severed was the religious one: there was a mounting fear in the colonies of Anglicanism and of the imposition of religious control from London. As in seventeenth-century England, it was to be

but one step from 'no bishop' to 'no king'. Dissenting academics and the small schools which acquired the name of log colleges kept the memories of the Puritan Levellers of 1649 alive.

When Grenville passed his Stamp Act he had little notion of the mettle of the colonies. The saddest fact of all was that there were few in Britain who were aware of the extent of the differences between them and the colonists or who sensed that there was in the thirteen rival colonies a nation in process of birth. Those who did know were unconsulted and powerless.

Not for the first or the last time parliament bent before the storm. It did not accept the principle of 'no taxation without representation', since more than ninety percent of the home population was as much disfranchised as the Americans. Moreover, without any abrogation of sovereignty— indeed a Declaratory Act was passed asserting that parliament had complete authority to make laws binding the colonist 'in all cases whatsoever'—the government, now headed by the Marquis of Rockingham, repealed the Stamp Act in February 1766. This was partly a result of Franklin's skilful pleading at the bar of the House of Commons, still more because of the economic consequences of the boycott. However, the colonists felt that they had won round one of the struggle and celebrated with bonfires and the erection in New York of statues to King George III and William Pitt. Neither the mood nor the statues lasted long.

The challenge to authority

The colonists' choice of heroes—Rockingham, John Wilkes and William Pitt—was

significant. Grenville, with a lawyer's logic, had thought it both lawful and expedient to tax the colonies. Rockingham, one of the earliest of British party leaders, thought it lawful but not expedient. The Earl of Chatham, as Pitt became in 1766, thought it neither lawful nor expedient. He was, however, a frequent absentee from the government he headed in 1766–8, as a result of gout and temperament in equal proportions.

In 1767 his chancellor of the exchequer, Charles Townshend, sought to honour a rashly-given pledge to reduce the land tax at home by raising an American revenue, not from taxes but from duties on certain imports—tea, glass, paper and paints. He believed it was legitimate for parliament to impose such trade levies. With the revenue he would pay the salaries of colonial governors and judges and free them thereby from colonial control. To stop smuggling, vice-admiralty courts would be strengthened in power and increased in number.

These measures proved to be as unwelcome as the Stamp Act. In his *Letters of a Pennsylvania Farmer* John Dickinson distinguished between acts intended to raise revenue, which he saw as illegal, and those intended to regulate trade, which he accepted as valid. By this standard Townshend's duties on imports were plainly unconstitutional. At this point, indeed, the colonists began to abandon the distinction between internal and external taxes altogether and to take the primitive but very popular line that all taxes, however imposed, were bad and that government was best which governed least. The Massachusetts General Court issued a circular letter—the work of Sam Adams, James Otis and Joseph Hawley—appealing to the other colonies for common action and asserting that only Americans should be permitted to tax Americans. Governor Francis Bernard of Massachusetts branded it as seditious, but seven colonies endorsed it.

When John Hancock's sloop *Liberty* was seized for smuggling, a riot followed in which the over-efficient customs officials were mobbed and had to take refuge in Castle William on an island in Boston harbour. The Boston garrison was strengthened by two regiments of infantry, the 14th and 29th, in an atmosphere that Thomas Hutchinson, Bernard's successor, described as frankly revolutionary. Reports to parliament on the Boston situation in 1769 led both houses to resolve that 'wicked and designing men' were responsible and should be suitably punished.

To Sam Adams in Boston the situation was certainly explosive. By 1770 the movement was no longer led by the merchants of Philadelphia or New York, who were now cautious and not a little frightened of the forces they had unleashed. Effective leadership was now in the hands of the 'Sons of Liberty' in New York and the group organized by Adams and operating from 'The Green Dragon' tavern in Boston. To them the presence of British redcoats—'the lobsterbacks'—was both inflammation and pretext. In New York in January 1770 soldiers and civilians clashed round a liberty pole. There was bloodshed, but no fatalities, in this episode known as 'The Battle of Golden Hill'. In March in Boston the taunting and snowballing of soldiers, first by schoolboys and then by citizens, led to shots being fired, and five Bostonians, one of them a negro, Crispus Attucks, were killed. The soldiers were acquitted after a skilful and courageous defence by their counsel, John Adams. However, their presence was proving to be not a safeguard but an irritant and they were more often the victims than the masters of the local situation.

After 1770 the soldiers were carefully confined in Castle William, and the British government repealed the Townshend duties except for the penny a pound on tea, retained, like the Declaratory Act, to assert a principle that was increasingly being seen to be only a form of words. Ironically even this decision was taken in cabinet by the casting vote of the new prime minister, Lord North. Had it not been taken there might well have been no need in 1773 to aid the East India Company's tea trade and the history of the world might have been different. However, the colonists had also won the second round of the contest. Once again, under whatever guise, the government had retreated. Now the cause had martyrs too. For revolutions these are more necessary than issues and easier to identify.

Between the second and third rounds of the contest there came an interlude, a return of prosperity and a reaction against the radicals. The merchants abandoned their boycott, and Sam Adams lost control of the Massachusetts Assembly. Yet this was the period when he worked hardest to keep the cause alive, by writing pamphlets under a host of pseudonyms and by the organization of the 'Committees of Correspondence'. Governor Thomas Hutchinson described

Above, the people of Boston tarring and feathering an exciseman, while in the background cases of tea are thrown into the sea; Britain's determination to tax the colonies was the main immediate grievance of the colonists.

Top, the Boston massacre in March 1770, when British troops opened fire on a crowd protesting against new taxes; they killed three men and wounded two others. It was the first violence between the colonists and the British troops.

Above left, George III of England (reigned 1760–1820), whose determination to oppose any reforms in the American colonies contributed to the tension that led to the outbreak of hostilities in 1775.

Opposite, the trustees of the state of Georgia presenting the Indians who sold him land to the colony's trustees in London in 1734.

the Boston Committee as composed of 'deacons', 'atheists', and 'blackhearted fellows whom one would not wish to meet in the dark'. However, they began to emerge in each colony and to constitute an unelected but nevertheless representative body of those with grievances, providing a basis for intercolonial action, should the crisis ever come. Although there is no evidence that the colonists had serious grievances, Adams' great achievement was to maintain a feeling of unrest and to produce a machine for action. In 1773 the opportunity came.

The British government, alarmed at the near bankruptcy of the East India Company, allowed it to send tea to America without paying the duty of one shilling a pound, thus making it cheaper than smuggled tea. This certainly would have hit hard at smuggling and at the profits of those who, like John Hancock, traded in smuggled tea. Thus, the third round of the contest began, oddly enough, with a mass protest against cheaper tea.

In December 1773, three ships carrying cargoes of tea reached Boston. Sam Adams addressed a large crowd, estimated at 7,000, on the evils of drinking cheap and legal tea, and from this meeting a group moved to the docks disguised as Indians. They dropped 342 tea chests to the bottom of the harbour, stoving them in as they did so.

This action was difficult to justify and it was indeed condemned by all responsible colonial opinion, including John Adams and Franklin, and by many merchants. Moreover this time parliament was not prepared to yield. Since 1769 it had been considering an inquiry into Massachusetts. The rendezvous of the navy had already been moved from Halifax to Boston. Half-measures would no longer suffice.

In the spring of 1774 further measures were passed. The port of Boston was closed until the tea was paid for. The Massachusetts charter was annulled, and the governor's council was henceforth appointed by the king. Arrangements were made to quarter troops in occupied as well as empty dwellings. Officers or soldiers accused of crimes were to be sent to Britain for trial.

The Quebec Act was also passed. This was planned beforehand and was not intended as a punitive measure, but it was seen as such in the colonies. It killed all hopes of new colonies in the northwest by transferring to the province of Quebec the lands (and the fur trade) between Ohio and the Mississippi, in which Virginia, Pennsylvania, Connecticut and Massachusetts held interests. Moreover, and even more ominously as the colonists saw it, it gave to this region French civil law and the Roman Catholic religion. The regime provided was centralized, in keeping with customs of the province, and there was to be no jury trial. This was a liberal and intelligent measure, drafts for which had existed since 1763. However, Chatham, Burke, Barré and Fox attacked it as pro-French, autocratic and wicked, and the vehemence of their

attacks confirmed colonial suspicions. The timing, as distinct from the merits, of the measure was unfortunate. The colonists now feared the use of arbitrary power and the influence of the Roman Catholic and Anglican Churches.

There were now two firm positions. 'The die is cast', said King George III. 'The colonists must either triumph or submit.' Joseph Reed put it differently in a letter from the first Continental Congress to Lord Dartmouth. 'The people are generally ripe for the execution of any plan the Congress advises, should it be war itself.'

The First Continental Congress

The measures passed in 1774 marked the end of the period of economic and commercial grievance. The issues now were clearly political and were seen as such in the colonies. Resolutions of sympathy and supplies of food reached Boston. When royal governors dissolved assemblies that were loud in their expression of support for Massachusetts, the members promptly formed themselves into illegal provincial congresses. Indeed, in Virginia the call to the first Continental Congress went out from Hays' Tavern, just across the street from the Williamsburg capitol.

This congress, which met in Carpenter's Hall, Philadelphia, in September 1774, was a gathering of fifty-five diplomats from twelve colonies. Each colony except Georgia was represented. John Adams was greatly stirred by it: 'There is in this Congress a collection of the greatest men upon this Continent in point of abilities, virtues and fortunes. The magnanimity and public spirit which I see here make me blush for the sordid venal herd which I have seen in my own Province.'

Adams was especially impressed by the Virginians and not least by Washington— 'six feet two, and straight as an Indian'. Though not gifted either in speech or with the pen, Washington looked like a soldier and had experience of the west shared by few. He was still loyal to the king but was a critic of parliament. He never forgave being refused a colonelcy in the French and Indian War. An alliance of north and south—of radicals and merchants plus planters and 'sultans'—began to emerge.

The First Continental Congress was nevertheless evenly divided between radicals and moderates—'one-third Tories, another, Whigs and the rest Mongrels', said Adams. Joseph Galloway's plan for a Grand Council to be chosen by the colonial assemblies headed by a president-general and acting as a kind of third House of Parliament was rejected, although only by a single vote. John Dickinson wanted to move slowly: action should be taken 'peaceably—prudently—firmly—jointly', or, as he said later, 'procrastination is preservation'. There were,

however, other voices. The Declaration of Rights and Grievances demanded 'the rights of Englishmen', the repeal of the measures of 1774 and the dismissal of the king's 'designing and dangerous' ministers. And the 'Resolves' forwarded by Suffolk County, Massachusetts, denied all obligation to obey recent acts of Parliament, described George III as a sovereign 'agreeable to compact' and threatened armed resistance. The Continental Association was formed to bring pressure by boycott on British merchants.

In 1774 British authority in Massachusetts all but collapsed. County conventions and a provincial congress took over the functions of the legally constituted government. Minutemen were formed and in all colonies militia forces came into being. When Washington returned home after the Congress, he was offered the command of seven of the militia companies in Virginia. He put on the buff and the blue of Fairfax County and made it the colours of liberty on two continents. Newspapers now openly discussed independence and, as a contemporary put it: 'Sedition flowed openly from the pulpits.' Colonial governors stored arms, not always discreetly.

When a new parliament assembled at Westminster in November, it was fortified by an improved trade with Europe and prepared to be—at last—tough. 'The New England governments are in a state of rebellion,' said the king. 'Blows must decide.' In February Parliament recognized the fact of rebellion in Massachusetts, and in August acknowledged that this was equally true of all the other colonies. In April, General Thomas Gage, the military governor of Massachusetts, tried to capture Sam Adams and John Hancock and to seize the stores being assembled at Concord. Paul Revere, by trade an engraver and silversmith, by calling a patriot, gave the alarm to a whole countryside. At Lexington, while on the retreat, the redcoats were sniped at with deadly result from every hedgerow. They lost two hundred men and the Americans ninety-three. This was no war.

The Second Continental Congress

It was against this background that the Second Continental Congress met in May 1775. Sixty-five delegates were there, to be joined by five from Georgia in September. John Dickinson's petition, known as the 'Olive Branch' petition, was adopted, only to be scorned in London. In June, Washington was appointed commander-in-chief and set off to take command of the assembling New England militia outside Cambridge, Massachusetts. Before his departure he heard of the second open battle of the war. at Bunker Hill, where the British lost 1,150 out of 2,500 engaged. Nevertheless, Washington was appalled at the state of his

army and made slow progress in training it and forcing on it a genuine acceptance of rank and discipline.

With Washington in command of an army that was in name opposing not the king but his parliament, there were now, in a sense, two centres of resistance. Although quite devoid of legality, the Congress acted as the central government, raised troops, established a treasury, issued paper money and negotiated alliances with Indian tribes and European allies. It did so by means of about eighty committees with John Adams on a great many of them. However, it hesitated about independence. The majority of the population were still opposed to independence. They were still content to claim the rights enjoyed—or deemed to be enjoyed —by British subjects. But, with an army in being, the momentum of events now moved firmly towards separation. John Adams declared that every day and every post, independence rolled in on Congress like a torrent. Unless Congress acted swiftly, Hawley wrote to Sam Adams, a 'Great Mobb' would march on Philadelphia, purge Congress and set up a dictator.

Britain had declared the colonists to be rebels and proclaimed a blockade. Governor John Dunmore of Virginia called on the slaves to rise in rebellion. British attacks were made or planned against coastal towns like Norfolk and Charleston. Britain was seeking to raise mercenary troops—Germans certainly and Russians, too, it was rumoured. By May 1776 North Carolina, Virginia and Massachusetts had instructed their delegates in Congress to vote for independence. On 7 June, Richard Henry had introduced his resolution that 'these United Colonies are, and of right ought to be, free and independent States.' Because of the hesitation of Pennsylvania, New Jersey, South Carolina and New York a vote was postponed for three weeks.

It was however the existence of an army that was to prove decisive. The dashing and utterly unreliable Ethan Allen, at the head of his so-called Green Mountain Boys, seized Ticonderoga from a sleepy and incredulous British commander. An expedition to liberate Canada was planned, although it

proved a failure. In March 1776, with Washington in control of Dorchester Heights above Boston, the British decided to evacuate the city. When they sailed away they took some 200 loyalist merchants with them. The war was now a civil war also. Behind the formal battles it was a struggle not only between the Old World and the New but over who should rule at home.

The army in the field was the arm of the civil Congress. In July 1775 the Congress had issued its 'Declaration of Causes of Taking Up Arms'. Americans it said, would die rather than be enslaved, but the declaration also stated that independence was not the goal. By July 1776 the hesitations were gone. Washington was partly won over in January 1776 by reading Tom Paine's pamphlet *Common Sense*. To Paine, who urged an immediate declaration of independence, the king was no God above the battle but 'the royal brute'. The pamphlet sold well. The note of republicanism was struck late, but it became the dominant theme. In the eyes of the colonists it was no longer parliament that was the tyrant but the king.

Independence

The aims now were separation and republicanism. Congress no longer claimed 'the rights of Englishmen' but 'natural rights'. When Thomas Jefferson, at the behest of Congress, drafted the Declaration of Independence, he claimed that thus far the American people had voluntarily associated themselves with Britain and had voluntarily acknowledged the same king. This king, by his despotic acts (twenty-seven specific charges were listed), had forfeited this allegiance. There was no reference at all to acts of trade or to parliament. This statement was prefaced by one of the noblest testaments of faith in liberty and in man's capacity for it which has ever been written:

We hold these truths to be self-evident, that all men are created equal; that they are endowed by their creator with certain unalienable rights; that among these are life, liberty and the pursuit of happiness. That,

Above, Thomas Jefferson (1743–1826), the chief drafter of the American Declaration of Independence and a protagonist of the rights of the small farmer against the aristocracy. His followers later developed into the Democratic Party of America.

Top, the second Continental Congress of 1775–76, at which the representatives of the colonies voted to accept the Declaration of Independence and which set itself up as the temporary government of the rebels.

Above left, George Washington (1732–99) taking command of the American army at Cambridge, Massachusetts, in 1775; despite the disorganization and indiscipline of the army, he was able to begin to attack the British positions by early 1777.

to secure these rights, governments are instituted among men, deriving their just powers from the consent of the governed; that, whenever any form of government becomes destructive of these ends, it is the right of the people to alter or to abolish it, to institute new government, laying its foundations on such principles, organizing its powers in such form, as to them shall seem most likely to effect their safety and happiness.

The same sentiments, without the same eloquence but with greater vivacity were expressed by an old soldier to whom John Adams talked many years later:

'Captain Preston, why did you go to the Concord fight, the nineteenth of April 1775?' The old man, bowed beneath the weight of years, raised himself, and turning to me, said: 'Why did I go?' 'Yes', I replied. 'My histories tell me that you men of the Revolution took up arms against "intolerable oppressions".' 'What were they?' 'Oppression. I didn't feel them.' 'What, were you not oppressed by the Stamp Act?' 'I never saw one of those stamps, and always understood that Governor Bernard put them all in Castle William. I am certain I never paid a penny for one of them.' 'Well, what about the tea tax?' 'Tea tax! I never drank a drop of the stuff—the boys threw it all overboard.' 'Then I suppose you had been reading Harrington or Sydney or Locke about the eternal principles of liberty.' 'Never heard of 'em. We read only the Bible, the Catechism, Wells' Psalms and Hymns and the Almanack.' 'Well, then, what was the matter, and what did you mean in going to the fight?' 'Young man, what we meant in going for those redcoats was this: we always had governed ourselves, and we always meant to. They didn't mean we should.'

These two views have, in their different ways, become the spirit of the Revolution. The American Revolution was the first successful act of rebellion by a new nation in modern history. The shots fired at Lexington Green and Concord bridge have echoed round the world. Almost all the independent states of Africa and Asia today, and many of the new nations in Europe, as part of the legend of their own independence find links with 1776. The statues that are grouped outside the White House in Washington are a reminder of those from other nations who then saw in the struggle for American independence a symbol and a portent of the struggle of other nations to be free. It is indeed impossible to calculate the consequences for the world that have followed from the events that took place on the narrow Atlantic seaboard in the years from 1763 to 1776.

The War of Independence

The Declaration of Independence was proclaimed on 4 July 1776. The day before, Sir William Howe seized Staten Island and led a British army ashore from the largest armada which had ever assembled in North American waters. New York was a loyalist centre, and it seemed possible to move up the Hudson Valley from New York to cut off rebellious New England from the other, less resolute colonies and to command the overland route to Canada.

The task of suppressing the rebellion, however distasteful, did not appear to be too difficult. The British had overwhelmingly superior numbers, outmatching the colonies by four to one in manpower and in ships of war by a hundred to one. Command of the sea—until the entry of the French—allowed them to strike at points of their own choosing. At times, trying to anticipate where the

blow would fall, Washington found himself 'compelled to wander about the country like the Arabs in search of corn'. Britain had superior credit, could hire foreign mercenaries and had a professional army and navy—even if a few of its senior officers like Lord Amherst and Admiral Keppel refused to serve against Americans. Against them were untrained, ill-clad, undisciplined and usually unpaid militia, led by officers who, with the exception of Charles Lee, Horatio Gates and Washington, had as little experience of war as themselves and little taste for it.

However, from the first it was for Britain a story of tactical successes left unexploited, of basic strategic errors and of some irredeemable disasters. Sir William Howe put his men ashore on Long Island with ease, defeated Washington's army and forced it to retreat across the Sound to Manhattan. He drove up the island with the same unhurried effortlessness and Washington made another hasty retreat over the Hudson and through New Jersey. The Americans lacked flour, clothing and money to pay their soldiers. Paine wrote in *The Crisis*: 'These are the times that try men's souls. The summer soldier and the sunshine patriot will, in this crisis, shrink from the service of their country; but he that stands it *now* deserves the love and thanks of man and woman.' Washington's view of events was more laconic: 'I think the game is pretty near up.'

At any of these points Howe could, it seemed, have destroyed the enemy army completely and captured its leader. That he failed to do so was overwhelmingly because he saw himself as an arbitrator and diplomat rather than as a soldier. If he pressed them a little more, they would surrender. The diplomat's role did not harmonize with the soldier's. After each tactical triumph he expected that negotiations would now begin. On the other hand, British morale was being steadily eroded by the procrastination and delays.

On Christmas night 1776, Washington carried through one of his cleverest manoeuvres of the war, and certainly the most psychologically effective. He crossed the Delaware with 2,400 men, surprised Colonel Rall and his still festive German troops at Trenton and took 1,000 prisoners. Colonel Rall paid for his card game with his life. Leaving his campfires burning to deceive the hurriedly summoned British reserves, Washington outflanked them and appeared at Princeton to strike again.

By the time both armies went into winter quarters—war was still a game played according to a gentlemanly, and seasonal, calendar—Howe's troops were no longer safe beyond the Hudson, and Washington had regained the advantage. If he failed to stop the transfer of Howe's forces in 1777 to Philadelphia, he at least managed to hold his own small force together.

Left, the Battle of Bunker Hill (June 1775) was one of the first engagements of the American War of Independence. Despite the eventual British victory, it proved a great boost to the morale of the Americans, whose defeat was primarily caused by a shortage of ammunition.

Opposite, a satire on the explosive impact of the Boston Tea Party of 1773; although unplanned, the incident brought the anti-British feeling in the American colonies to the surface and made militant resistance acceptable.

Left, the Declaration of Independence, formally adopted on 4 July 1776. The declaration combined an attack on the abuses of recent British rule with a statement of the rights of man and the principles of government; in these ideas Jefferson, who was mainly responsible for the document, was influenced by the ideas of the Enlightenment. Yale University Art Gallery, New Haven, Connecticut.

Left, an incident during the naval war in August 1776, when the British aimed for control of Lake Champlain and the Hudson River, to isolate New England from the other colonies.

271

The road to Saratoga

The winter of 1777–8 was the real testing time—one that tried not only men's souls but their stomachs. Valley Forge, where the American troops were quartered, was, said Washington, 'a dreary kind of place and uncomfortably provided'. 'Poor food—hard lodging—cold weather—fatigue—nasty clothes—nasty cookery—vomit half my time—smoked out of my senses—the devil's in't—I can't endure it,' wrote Surgeon Albigence Waldo. But the Americans did endure. They were now better drilled than ever before thanks to Friedrich Von Steuben, the Prussian soldier who had offered his services to Washington. Washington's greatest achievement was to keep an army in being at Valley Forge. He said afterwards that Howe could still have won the war had he attacked at that point. By October 1777, however, it was beginning to look too late for a British victory.

While Howe was taking Philadelphia and relaxing in its comfort, General John Burgoyne, with 7,000 men and a vast baggage train, was seeking to cut a path south from Canada via Lake Champlain and the Hudson Valley. The intention was to bring reinforcements to Howe (who, Burgoyne had expected, would come north to meet him), to cut off New England permanently and to divert Washington's attention.

However, Burgoyne's transport was inadequate. One of his raiding columns hunting for food in Vermont was destroyed by the Green Mountain Boys. A parallel force, which was to move down the Mohawk River to join him, gave up the attempt and went back to Canada. Meanwhile, the American force under Horatio Gates that blocked his path increased in numbers and in spirit day by day. By the end of September Burgoyne was outnumbered four to one. On 14 October he surrendered at Saratoga, abandoning arms and supplies and undertaking that his men would not serve any further against the Americans. This was not only a British disaster, it was a humiliation

and it proved to be the turning-point in the war.

Until the news of Saratoga the French had hesitated about giving open support to the Revolution. The French monarchy had no taste for governments that were overthrowing kings. However, any dissension in Britain's colonies was worth cultivating. On the outbreak of war, Congress sent to Paris a three-man team to act as negotiators for money, supplies and for an open, they hoped, alliance with France. The quest for foreign aid had been active from the start. The new nation wanted the commercial contracts with Europe which the colonial mercantile system had banned. And it not only sought them for themselves. Without foreign aid it could not long survive.

The three men who served as emissaries were the irascible and self-important Arthur Lee from Virginia, the wily merchant-politician Silas Deane from Connecticut (who proved to be in Britain's pay and passed everything on to the British government) and Benjamin Franklin, who became the principal agent and ambassador. During his years in Paris (1776–85), when he was already over 70, Franklin emerged not only as the architect of the alliance but as the favourite of the salons of Paris, admired and worshipped as both scientist and diplomat, man of affairs (both business and amatory) and, indeed, as Jean-Jacques Rousseau's 'natural man' made visible. There were Franklin rings, Franklin snuff boxes and even Franklin chamber pots. His wig, worn to hide his eczema, became a symbol of liberty. The old man was amused, and he not only enjoyed the experience but exploited it to his own benefit.

From the first the French were prompt with aid, 1,000,000 livres being given through the fictitious company, Rodrigue Hortalez et Compagnie. Spain proved equally generous. However, aid could not be openly avowed without inducing a declaration of war by Britain. The surrender of Saratoga led to the planning of a peace mission by Britain, and Franklin craftily allowed it to be known in Paris that

he favoured its prospects. France moved towards open intervention and in February 1778 the Treaty of Alliance was signed—the United States' first entangling alliance. France recognized the United States as independent and each country undertook not to make a separate peace. Each also undertook to treat the other commercially as a 'most favoured nation'.

Spain entered the war a year later not as an ally of the United States but as an ally of France. Its motive was the reconquering of Gibraltar, which the Spanish besieged for four long years. By 1780 Britain was also at war with Holland and with the League of Armed Neutrality (Denmark, Sweden, Portugal and Russia). The war was now a world war. It was fought in places as far apart as India and the Caribbean. The American naval commander, John Paul Jones, provisioned from Brest, raided the Scottish and Yorkshire coasts, and a French landing in Ireland was planned. The American theatre of war now became in British eyes little more than a side-show.

This dramatic transformation of the situation was a great relief for the Americans. French aid was in any event substantial. French gifts and loans amounted in the end to $8,000,000, a large sum for an eighteenth-century war. The entry of France also helped to guarantee the Dutch loans to the United States. With money there also came men and ships. After 1778 French fleets prowled the Atlantic coast, and Britain lost its naval preponderance. The operations of the French naval commander, the Comte d' Estaing, diverted British troops to the West Indies and speeded the evacuation of Philadelphia in 1778 and Newport in 1779. It was the appearance of a French fleet off the Virginian coast that sealed the fate of a British army under Lord Cornwallis at Yorktown in 1781. The siege of Yorktown itself was made possible by the presence alongside Washington's army of 9,000 regular French troops commanded by the Comte de Rochambeau, with the Marquis de Lafayette, one of the earliest and most fanatical of French volunteers, leading a

brigade. When General O'Hara, deputizing for Cornwallis—who feigned illness—surrendered his sword, he sought to surrender it to Rochambeau. Rochambeau refused and indicated Washington. Lafayette, for his part, never forgot his American experience and at the beginning of the French Revolution saw himself as playing a Washington. If his role in French history never in fact matched his own hopes for it, the French Revolution certainly owed much to the enthusiasm of those who had helped the American cause.

The Treaty of Paris

With the surrender of Cornwallis at Yorktown, the war was virtually over. King George III was with difficulty dissuaded from abdicating. Lord North resigned as prime minister in March 1782, Shelburne becoming first secretary of state and, on Rockingham's death, prime minister. At first Shelburne opposed the idea of independence but not for long.

With the merchant Richard Oswald acting as his emissary in Paris, negotiations were opened with Franklin in April 1782 and concluded in November of that year. Franklin broke his word in concluding a separate peace, but in the thick air of spying and counter-spying in Paris it was hardly possible for the French foreign minister, Vergennes, to be unaware of what was happening.

By the terms of the treaty Britain recognized the independence of the United States and accepted its western boundary as the Mississippi River. Britain conceded the right of navigation on the Mississippi and fishing rights off Newfoundland. Congress agreed to recommend to the individual states that they indemnify the loyalists and pay their debts to Britain. This was easy to say but hard to implement.

The United States won more by diplomacy than its victories entitled. If Saratoga and Yorktown were disasters for the British, this was in large measure because of their own folly. By 1783, however, Britain had

averted direct invasion, and Admiral Rodney's victory in 1782 off Dominica in the West Indies gave Britain additional bargaining power. Spain and France had not done particularly well out of the war. Spain regained the Floridas but not Gibraltar. France won some West Indian islands and a huge debt, the full interest on which would be six years in falling due. For the Americans it was a total triumph.

Yet by 1783 the evidence of triumph was hard to see. The new nation had not acquired a written constitution until 1781, the 'Articles of Confederation', drafted by John Dickinson. These provided for a single-chamber government in which each state had one vote. There was no president and no supreme court. The government was in form and in fact a federal union of unwilling members. Congress had no power to levy taxes, regulate commerce, raise an army or enforce the laws. In the last years of the war Congress had even been driven from Philadelphia when unpaid regiments rebelled.

Above, the capture of Yorktown and final surrender of the British forces under General Cornwallis in October 1781. The English were unable to fight against the combination of French and American soldiers and French blockade.

Top, the British embarking German troops to send to the American colonies in 1783.

Top left, Benjamin Franklin (1706–90), the American scientist, at the court of France, where he had been sent in 1776 to win recognition for the new republic. The French sent a fleet to support the Americans in 1778.

Opposite left, George Washington capturing almost 1,000 German troops under British command in December 1776 at Trenton, New Jersey. This was the first real American success of the war.

Opposite right, the surrender of General Burgoyne at Saratoga in October 1777, after the British had lost the support of their Indian allies and had been surrounded. After this defeat, the British had little real hope of winning the war.

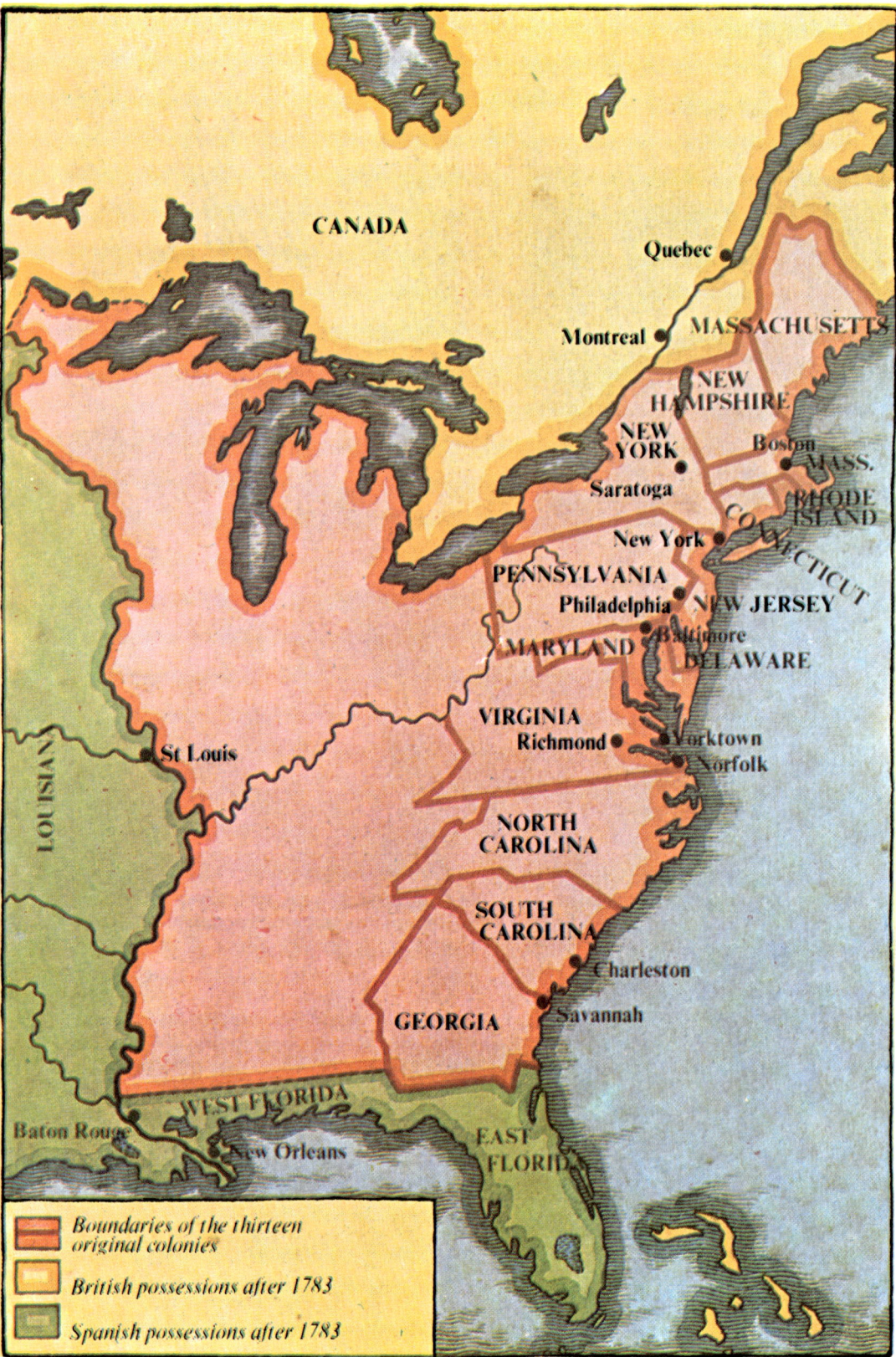

CANADA

Quebec

Montreal • **MASSACHUSETTS**

NEW HAMPSHIRE

NEW YORK

Boston

Saratoga

MASS.

RHODE ISLAND

CONNECTICUT

New York

PENNSYLVANIA

Philadelphia • **NEW JERSEY**

MARYLAND • Baltimore

DELAWARE

VIRGINIA

St Louis • Richmond • Yorktown

Norfolk

NORTH CAROLINA

LOUISIANA

SOUTH CAROLINA

Charleston

GEORGIA • Savannah

WEST FLORIDA

Baton Rouge

New Orleans

EAST FLORIDA

Boundaries of the thirteen original colonies

British possessions after 1783

Spanish possessions after 1783

This period, from 1781 to 1787, was given the name of 'The Critical Period' by the American historian, John Fiske, in 1888, and he attributed the difficulties to the lack of real sovereignty in the existing government, that is, the government under the Articles of Confederation, agreed on by 1781. The commercial crisis, however, was not only a result of the Articles but the end of the wartime boom and of the dislocation of American trade that followed it. Congress could have done little to affect this. Moreover, no direction by it to the states to honour their debt or to treat the loyalists sympathetically would have had much influence, when there was no general wish to do either.

However, the diplomatic achievements of the period were considerable. The Treaty of Paris and the Northwest Ordinances of 1785 and 1787 were remarkable by any standards. The first of the Ordinances provided for a system of land surveys based on townships six miles square and subdivided into thirty-six sections. The latter set out the stages whereby a territory (5,000 inhabitants) and finally a state (60,000 inhabitants) would be established. Out of the entire territory of the old northwest five states were in the end formed: Ohio, Indiana, Illinois, Michigan and Wisconsin. In them freedom of religion, trial by jury and due process of law were guaranteed, slavery was forbidden and the newly-created states were seen and treated as equal in importance to the original thirteen. The west was peopled fast. This generous and far sighted provision, essentially the handiwork of Thomas Jefferson, was to prove almost as significant as the constitution itself. It was its federal character as much as its republican constitution that made the United States in the nineteenth century the 'last best hope of man'.

The constitution

Nevertheless the political weaknesses of the Articles pointed to a need for revision. James Madison of Virginia persuaded his state to discuss with Maryland their common interest in the navigation of Chesapeake Bay and the Potomac. The Mount Vernon Conference in 1785 established the need for a wider agreement and all the states were invited to Annapolis in 1786 to discuss interstate commercial regulations. Five states sent representatives—New York, New Jersey, Virginia, Pennsylvania and Delaware.

Alexander Hamilton, the brilliant young West Indian-born lawyer who had served as Washington's aide-de-camp, moved a resolution to invite all the states to meet the following year to revise the Articles. Fifty-five men, representing all the states except Rhode Island, met in the Philadelphia State House in May 1787. They decided on a totally new document and they hammered

There was no power to enforce even the Treaty of Peace. Moreover, Congress could not enforce uniform import duties against foreign countries or prevent the customs and boundary wars of state versus state. For money it relied on issues of paper, which depreciated fast—'not worth a Continental' is still a phrase in use in the United States. Some states printed their own paper money and other states refused to honour it. When in Massachusetts creditors foreclosed on the properties of the debt-ridden farmers,

about 1,500 of them, led by Daniel Shays, seized the arsenal at Springfield and closed the courts.

The economic situation was worsened by the exclusion of the new state from the British Empire and the loss of trade with the West Indies. British markets, bounties and guarantees were also lost. Britain retained the fur posts, claiming that loyalists had not been indemnified or debts to British merchants repaid. There was no matching power of retaliation available to Congress.

COMMANDER OF THE AMERICAN ARMY, 1775. PRESIDENT OF THE UNITED STATES, 1789.
INITIATED, NOVEMBER 4TH 1752, IN FREDERICKSBURG, LODGE No 4, VIRGINIA. PASSED, MARCH 3RD 1753 RAISED, AUGUST 4TH 1753.

Above, Alexander Hamilton (1755–1804), the New York lawyer who supported a strong federal authority, both in the debates on the Constitution and during the 1790s when he served as Secretary to the Treasury and as a supporter of Thomas Jefferson.

Left, George Washington in his masonic regalia; his future political power was based primarily on his great success as a military leader. Henry Francis du Pont Winterthur Museum, Delaware.

Opposite, the North American Atlantic seaboard after the independence of the United States.

out agreement on its through the long, hot summer. They ended by drawing up a constitution, 4,000 words in length, for a farmer's republic of 3,500,000 people. The same document, amended only occasionally and mainly in inessentials, is still the binding form of government for a vast cosmopolitan society of more than 200,000,000 people living across and beyond a continent. The Founding Fathers were remarkable men. Thomas Jefferson called them an assembly of demi-gods.

There was much on which the delegates agreed: a written constitution, the separation of powers, the need for the federal government to be strong and to have the power to declare war and make peace and to tax and regulate commerce. There was much on which agreement was reached only slowly by careful compromise. Perhaps the most serious basic political disagreement was on the issue of representation. The large states, whose case was presented by Edmund Randolph of Virginia, favoured a bicameral legislature, with representation in each based on size of population. There was also to be a single executive and judiciary, both chosen by the legislature. This caused bitter feeling, for the disparity of the states in size was striking. Delaware had 60,000 people and Rhode Island 68,000. On the other hand, Virginia, which then included Kentucky, had 750,000, of whom 300,000 were slaves. Massachusetts, excluding Maine, had 380,000, very few of whom were slaves.

New Jersey countered the Virginia plan with its own, presented by William Paterson: a legislature of one house, elected by the states regardless of population and with an executive consisting of more than one man elected by Congress. After a month's debate agreement was reached on a compromise— the 'Connecticut compromise'—providing for equal representation of each state in the Senate, while maintaining the principle of representation by population in the House of Representatives.

This system is still in force, although, until the 17th Amendment of 1913, the Senate was elected indirectly by the state document was not submitted directly to the people and contained no bill of rights. Indeed, to meet this criticism a bill of rights was added to it, in the shape of the first ten amendments, ratified in 1791. In other words, the constitution was not perfect, like any other product of the hand of men, and a bitter civil war was to be fought in 1861 over the interpretation of it. Yet it was a remarkable document. Its ambiguity, as James Madison, the fourth president of the United States, said, was the price of unanimity. The Founding Fathers knew that paper constitutions would only survive if they were brought to life and made workable by men and women. The American nation has been built up in 1787 and since not by federal or judical enactments but by the common life lived and chosen by its members.

Much of the anxiety that the convention might have aroused was removed by the general awareness that, whatever the form of election, George Washington was likely to be the universal choice for president. With John Adams as his vice-president, Washington took his oath of office on the balcony of Federal Hall, New York, in April 1789. He chose Jefferson (who had succeeded Franklin as ambassador in Paris) as his secretary of state, Hamilton as secretary of the treasury and Henry Knox (a Massachusetts bookseller turned general) as his secretary of war.

Washington's contribution to the presidency was immense, since all the decisions he took set precedents. He brought dignity and decorum to the office: a coach and four, weekly levees and an address to Congress similar to the British sovereign's speech from the throne. Both the Senate and Supreme Court, he discovered, refused to grant advice before negotiation of treaties or legal cases, so presidential initiative was increased and presidential authority heightened. The judiciary was organized, with a chief justice and five associate justices. Washington's administration was also distinguished by the work of his two brilliant secretaries, Hamilton and Jefferson.

Hamilton believed that the new federal government would be strong only if its credit was thoroughly established. Nations—like individuals—must pay their debts. He therefore recommended to Congress that the national debt, both foreign ($12,000,000) and domestic ($24,000,000), should be paid at face value and that the federal government should accept and meet the debts contracted by the states. He proposed to do this by funding the debt, that is, by offering a new loan. There was no opposition to the payment of the foreign debt but much to the payment of the domestic one, since speculators (mainly northerners) had been buying up government bonds at cut rates and thus stood to gain appreciably. Moreover, those states like Virginia, which had already begun to meet their obligations, objected to the indirect aid being given to their less generous or less wealthy rivals. However, Hamilton

legislatures and not directly by the people. Yet fears of rivalry between great and small states proved largely illusory. Maryland, a small state, and Virginia, a large one, shared on the Chesapeake a common economy of tobacco plantations and slave labour. Connecticut and Massachusetts had similar commercial interests. The rivalry of state against state has never been as important in American history as the clash of sectional interests.

The second major compromise appeared at this time to be less important but was to have far-reaching consequences: how were slaves to be counted both for representation and for taxation? The northern states, with businessmen's logic, wanted slaves excluded from representation, since they were neither citizens nor voters, but included for tax purposes, since they were property. In other words, they themselves had few slaves, and they wanted it both ways. The south disagreed: it did not want to be taxed without some matching representation. In the end the 'three-fifths' compromise was reached. A slave was counted as three-fifths of a person for purposes of both taxation and representation. It was also agreed that there would be no interference with the importation of slaves until 1808. Slavery was not yet the emotional issue it was to become. Even the revolutionary fires of the French Revolution that led to Toussaint l'Ouverture's rebellion in Santo Domingo sparked few fires in the United States. The most bitter attack at the constitutional convention came in fact from Virginia. As masters on their deathbeds often freed their slaves, as did Washington, slavery was expected gradually to die out.

There was one other basic compromise: on the election of the executive. There were many among the Founding Fathers who distrusted 'the people' and opposed direct election. It was therefore agreed, in the

closing stages of the convention, that the president and vice-president should be chosen by an electoral college, equal in number to the number of senators and representatives, meeting in each of the states and forwarding the names of its choice to the federal government. The college still survives, weakened by the growth of political parties, as a curious relic of eighteenth-century political mechanics. It makes it possible for a president to be elected who (as in 1888) has fewer popular votes than his opponent. Furthermore, since a president must have an absolute majority of electoral college votes and not merely be head of the list, it is possible for the choice of president to be thrown to the House of Representatives, voting by states, as was done in 1824. The system is a reminder that, although the three branches of government were nicely balanced by the compromises of 1787, only one half of one branch, the legislature, was directly elected. The president chose the judges, and he himself was indirectly elected.

In all the states there was also a property qualification for the suffrage. As a result it has sometimes been said that the Founding Fathers feared democracy rather than favoured it. Certainly, there were those among them, like Alexander Hamilton and Gouverneur Morris, who thought the constitution a 'weak and worthless' document. Nevertheless, Hamilton himself rendered immense service by the campaign he waged in New York to secure the ratification of the constitution in the New York state convention and also by writing, with John Jay and James Madison, the series of masterly articles in its support known collectively as *The Federalist Papers*.

It is true that the majority of the delegates at Philadelphia were beneficiaries of the Constitution—investors, land speculators, merchants and slave owners. Moreover, the had his way, in part by agreeing to placate the south by locating the planned national capital (then spoken of as the 'federal city') on the banks of the Potomac and near Mount Vernon. This device by Hamilton won the support of the moneyed class for the constitution and the federal government.

Hamilton also set up a national bank, although Jefferson and Madison opposed what they saw as a monopoly and a threat to the state banks. He also proposed an excise tax and a higher tariff to encourage manufacturers, and again he had his way.

Hamilton and Jefferson

Policy-making was one thing; implementation was another. Hamilton's excise tax ran into difficulties. He had urged an excise tax on distilled liquors in part to impress upon the western frontiersmen the powers of the federal government. These men had for a long time been accustomed to convert their corn and rye into whisky, since in this form it was easier to transport over the mountains and more readily saleable. They resented the tax bitterly and in 1794 in Western Pennsylvannia they offered resistance to the federal collectors, in what was known as the 'Whisky Rebellion'. Hamilton called out the militia and, at the display of force, opposition melted away. Hamilton never lost the reputation of having engineered this deliberately and he showed a disposition throughout his career to be over-assertive in government.

Gradually a division on both political and personal matters appeared between Jefferson and Hamilton. The latter was a supporter of strong federal government, of manufacturers, of 'the rich, the well-born and the able' and of the British connection; the former was an advocate of states' rights, freedom for the farmer and support for France. Jefferson began his period in office as an admirer of France and as a sympathizer with the French Revolution. He cooled in these views, partly because of the undiplomatic exuberance shown by the French ambassador, Edmond Genêt.

In 1793, misreading the American scene and invoking the alliance of 1778, he assumed US support for revolutionary France, equipped 'revolutionary' ships to raid British shipping and planned 'liberating' armies that were to march into the Spanish-owned west. In April 1793 Washington issued his neutrality proclamation. In August the cabinet voted to ask the French government to recall Genêt.

Robespierre retorted by asking in return for the recall of Gouverneur Morris, the arch-Tory minister of the United States to France. In the end Genêt persuaded the US government not to send him back and wisely settled in the Hudson Valley.

Foreign policy divided the two emerging parties as much as economic issues. Broadly, Jefferson and the Republicans were pro-French and the Hamiltonians pro-British. Paradoxically, however, New England and the seaboard towns, normally anti-British because of their trading rivalry, were now pro-British, fearing revolution, French privateering and 'popery'. The Virginian planters, usually pro-British, were now pro-French, because of their taste for Parisian ways and a dislike of Yankee capitalism and Hamilton's excise taxes. From now on the rivalry of parties covered a more fundamental division between sectional interests.

When war between France and Britian began in 1793, American neutrality was inevitably threatened. Britain was still in occupation of the fur posts and proposed to continue to occupy them until the debts left unpaid in 1783 were settled. Britain began to seize US shipping engaged in trade with the French West Indies and to impress US sailors into British service. Although pro-French feeling in the United States declined after Genêt's excesses were revealed (Jefferson himself resigned office in December 1793), nevertheless, Washington was alarmed at the prospect of war with Britain in alliance with a terrorist revolutionary regime in Paris. He was still more worried at the rising tide of war feeling: militia were drilling on village greens and harbours were being fortified.

Accordingly, in 1794 Washington sent Chief Justice John Jay to London to try to settle his disputes with Britain. Jay succeeded in averting war but only at the expense of American national pride. The Jay treaty secured a British promise to evacuate the northwest posts and to submit the boundary and debts question to commissions. However, the United States had to surrender its position on neutral rights. It was given a few concessions in the British West Indies and agreed to open its own ports without restrictions to British shipping. The treaty was as a result extremely unpopular. Jay was burned in effigy, Hamilton stoned in the streets and Washington began now to feel biting public criticism for the first time.

The treaty was in the long run a step towards the use of arbitration in the settlement of disputes. It stimulated the settling of disagreements with Spain, and the 1795 Treaty of San Lorenzo allowed Americans the right of navigation of the Mississippi and of depositing and transferring foodstuffs at New Orleans. These were major commercial concessions. However, it also widened the breach between Federalists and Republicans and Washington signed it only with reluctance. Hamilton himself resigned office in 1795.

Despite these tensions and despite the emergence of two distinct parties in Washington's second term, Washington's presidency was to be as significant in foreign policy as in domestic. This policy, developed further by the Monroe Doctrine of 1823, left the United States neutral towards Europe after 1793 and thus able to profit from the twenty-five years of war into which

Above, John Adams (1735–1826), a lawyer from Boston who was a leader of the American cause. He is shown here in his role as ambassador to Britain in 1785–88, and later he became the second President of the United States (1797–1801), adopting a conservative policy. Fogg Art Museum, Harvard University, Cambridge, Massachusetts.

Opposite, the Constitution of the United States, signed in Philadelphia in September 1787; based on the principle of the sovereignty of the people, it aimed to balance the power of the executive, legislature and judiciary, and to compromise on the question of state independence versus federal authority.

Europe was plunged by the French Revolution and Napoleon. By the time that struggle was over the United States was a strong and distinct society, which could afford to be indifferent to Europe.

Nevertheless, Washington's second term was far from happy. He was distressed by the feud between his two lieutenants and by the rising spirit of party (the contemporary word was 'faction'). He was bitterly attacked in the popular press despite forty-five years of public service and found it distasteful. He made it plain in 1796 that he did not want a third term of office and this too became a precedent. Washington's farewell address was a comment and a confession. He deplored the 'baneful spirit of party', though to no avail. He stressed the need for union as 'the main prop' of American liberty, and he urged his fellow countrymen to shun foreign connections and permanent alliances. He was happy to retire at last to 'his own vine and fig tree' at Mount Vernon, where he died suddenly in 1799 from a chill caught while riding round his farms in the rain.

John Adams

The advice of the farewell address was ignored in the bitter partisanship of the four years of John Adams' presidency (1797–1801). Since his opponent, Jefferson, had the second highest vote in the 1796 election, the latter became vice-president and thus the two leading figures in the administration were in opposite parties. What was worse, Hamilton, the leading federalist thinker and planner, conspired against Adams and had great influence over Adam's chief cabinet officers. Adams, though honest and high-minded, was vain and prickly. He, with some justice, disliked Hamilton as much as

Hamilton with less justice, disliked them. It was a miserable four years.

Adams had one achievement to his credit. Despite the tensions between the United States and revolutionary France as a result of French interference with US commerce, and despite the obvious attempt by Talleyrand and his agents to solicit bribes from the US negotiators in 1797, Adams ignored public opinion and succeeded in keeping the peace with France. However, he was unable to prevent Congress, under Federalist control, from exploiting anti-French feeling and passing in 1798 four acts that were obviously intolerant and which in the end strengthened the Republicans rather than the Federalists.

The Naturalization Act extended the residence period of aliens seeking citizenship from five to fourteen years, thus hitting at the Republican party to which foreigners tended to flock. The Alien Act authorized the president to deport any aliens whom he considered dangerous. The Alien Enemies Act empowered him to deport the aliens of any country with which the United States was at war. Finally, the Sedition Act made it possible to punish by fine or imprisonment anyone publishing any 'false, scandalous and malicious writing'. Under this Act ten republican editors were convicted or punished.

The intent was clearly to silence all opposition, and this gave Jefferson and Madison their chance. In the Kentucky and Virginia Resolutions, they set forth the Republican or states' rights view—that the federal government was created by the states and might be criticized by the states if it exceeded its powers. They claimed, in fact, that, as the constitution stated, power remained with the states or with the people. In the presidential election of 1800, Jefferson and Aaron Burr, each with 73 votes in the Electoral College, defeated Adams and

Charles C. Pinckney. The final choice of president was made by the House of Representatives, which, after thirty-six acrimonious ballots, chose Jefferson.

To prevent a recurrence of such a tie in the future, the twelfth amendment was passed in 1804 to allow for the election of president and vice-president on separate ballots. Jefferson, highly cultivated, idealistic and liberal, moved into a still uncompleted presidential mansion (not yet the White House), in a far from completed federal city (not yet Washington), to preside over a tenuously united United States. Nevertheless, the year 1800 marked, in mood, in direction and in consequences a real revolution.

THE FORMATION OF THE UNITED STATES

Date	North America	Great Britain	France	Date	North America	Great Britain	France
1765		Rockingham becomes prime minister (1765)		1785			Affair of the queen's necklace (1785)
	Repeal of Stamp Act (1766)	Earl of Chatham forms government (1766)	Corsica ceded to France (1768)		Philadelphia Convention: Establishment of federal government (1787)		Dissolution of Assembly of the Notables (1787)
			Birth of Napoleon Bonaparte (1769)		Franco-US alliance (1788)	Impeachment of Warren Hastings (1788)	Recall of Necker (1788)
1770	Boston 'Massacre' (1770)	Lord North prime minister (1770)				Regency crisis (1788)	
		Royal Marriages Act (1772)	Accession of Louis XVI (1774)		George Washington first president (1789)		Summoning of the Estates-General: outbreak of the Revolution (1789)
	Boston Tea Party (1773)						
	Quebec Act (1774)	Warren Hastings governor-general of India (1774)	Turgot controller-general of finance (1774)	1790	Creation of a national bank		Civil Constitution of the Clergy (1790)
	First Continental Congress (1774)				Jefferson founds the Democratic Republican party (1791)	Canada Act (1791)	
1775	Outbreak of war (1775)						Abolition of the monarchy (1792)
	Battle of Bunker's Hill (1775)					Britain and France at war (1793)	
	Battle of Trenton (1776)	James Cook's third voyage to the Pacific (1776)	Fall of Turgot (1776)				Fall of Robespierre (1794)
	Declaration of Independence (1776)						Formation of the Directory (1795)
	Lafayette in America (1777)		Necker director-general of finance (1777)				
	Surrender of Burgoyne at Saratoga (1777)	Death of Earl of Chatham (1778)	Abolition of serfdom in the royal domains		John Adams president (1797)	Naval mutinies (1797)	
1780		'No Popery' riots in London (1780)			Death of George Washington (1799)		Establishment of the Consulate (1799)
	Surrender of Cornwallis at Yorktown (1781)		Dismissal of Necker (1781)	1800	Washington becomes the capital of the United States	Act of Union with Ireland (1800)	
	Treaty of Versailles: Britain recognizes independence of American colonies (1783)	Pitt the younger prime minister (1783)	Calonne controller-general of finance (1783)				
		Government of Indian Act (1784)					

Chapter 28

The French Revolution

The French Revolution was neither the only nor the first of the disturbances that shook the old order in Europe in the late eighteenth century, but it was the most spectacular and the most important. It broke out in one of the largest, most populous and powerful of European countries and one which was for many the very centre of culture and civilization. In its principles and its practice it went much further than the American Revolution both politically and socially. Moreover, unlike the American Revolution, the French Revolution was propagandist and aggressive, challenging the old order outside its boundaries with armies as well as ideas.

In twenty years of war it carried revolutionary ideas throughout the length and breadth of Europe, and no place it touched was quite the same thereafter. Its influence extended even to places where its armies never set foot and persisted long after the event, and it found an echo in those movements of nationalism and democracy—liberal, radical and even socialist—which dominated so much of the politics of the following century. For generations it provided the very image or idea of revolution, for those who dreaded it as well as for those who desired it.

There is no single, simple explanation of this great episode, if only because the Revolution itself was not a single, static event. It was a dynamic series of events, whose development depended upon the interaction of a variety of forces and circumstances. Undoubtedly the most important of these factors was the middle class bourgeoisie), and it is possible to see the Revolution simply as a major episode in the onward march of the conquering middle classes. They represented the new forces in society, growing in numbers, importance and ambition and increasingly out of sympathy with the existing values and institutions (political, social and economic), which were still geared to the conditions and needs of a bygone age. They provided most of the leaders of the Revolution, the men who dominated its assemblies and committees. They compiled the indictments against the old regime, and in the 'Declaration of the Rights of Man' they proclaimed the principles of the new order. It was they who shaped the new institutions and it was they who

emerged in the end as the major beneficiaries of the subsequent regime.

Even so, the Revolution was not purely a battle of the middle classes against aristocracy and absolutism. Without the activity of humbler elements of society, the peasantry and the urban lower classes, the Revolution would not have followed the course it did. The fate of middle-class revolutionaries often depended on, and their policies were often conditioned by, the role of these other groups, which were driven on by discontents and aspirations which did not always coincide with those of the middle classes.

The situation, for example, which led to the summoning of the Estates-General, and which was to give the middle-class spokesmen their opportunity was not primarily the doing of the bourgeoisie or its popular

Above, Marie Antoinette (1755–93), with her children; she opposed Necker and Turgot in their attempts to reform the finances of the monarchy, and her lack of sympathy with the French people aggravated the unpopularity of the crown. National museum, Stockholm.

allies. It was the product of the difficulties of the monarchy and the ambitions of the aristocracy. By 1973 'royalists' and 'aristocrats' might appear to the popular mind as the two great enemies of the revolutionary ideals of liberty and equality, but in the 1780s the most obvious conflict in France was between the crown and the aristocracy. And it is this which explains the outbreak of revolution, even if thereafter there was a realignment of the forces involved.

The old order

The absolute monarchy of eighteenth-century France marked the peak of the crown's ascent to authority. Internal rivals to its political power had been reduced to submission in the seventeenth century. Nobles who had once challenged the crown in battle now waited on its pleasure. The palace of Versailles, the splendours of the court it housed and the royal power it symbolized—all these served as models to other continental rulers to be admired and imitated. Theories of divine right and absolutism reflected the crown's triumph. According to the absolutist theory, all the powers of the state—legislative, executive and judicial—rested with the king himself. 'It is in my person alone', said Louis XV, 'that sovereign power resides . . . it is from me alone that my courts derive their authority . . . it is to me alone that legislative power belongs completely and exclusively.'

There was no constitutional check on the king's powers, no body of elected, representative people with which he must work or to which his servants needed to answer. Hereafter, no doubt, the king would have to answer to God, but on earth he was God's agent and wielded his powers by divine right. 'The royal throne', the seventeenth-century theologian Bossuet had claimed, 'is not the throne of a man but of God himself.'

By the 1770s, however, the practical weaknesses of the crown were as important as its vast theoretical claims. This was partly a matter of character. Louis XIV's successors were weaker individuals, and the administration lacked the effective direction and coordination which only a dedicated monarch, or a chief minister with his steadfast backing, could provide. There was, moreover, a real decline in the profession of kingship ('le métier du roi'). But the main weakness was the chronic inadequacy of the monarchy's finances. Its money troubles were not the result of extravagant favours and pensions lavished on idle courtiers, though these were an extra burden. They were mainly the price paid for the long series of increasingly expensive wars that France had fought over the last 100 years. The annual interest due on the debts incurred in these was now swallowing about half the royal revenue. Current military costs, also an increasingly heavy item, took another quarter. It was only in peacetime, and then

with luck, that the monarchy could stumble along just on the right side of bankruptcy.

Financial difficulties were a symptom as well as a cause of weakness. They did not reflect any dwindling in the resources of the country but rather the crown's inability to draw on these resources more fully, to increase them or to reorganize the tax system so as to make it more productive. Important groups and regions enjoyed privileges, exemptions in taxation, and some of the more recently acquired provinces, the so-called *pays d'états*, had successfully claimed the right to negotiate their own contributions to taxation. Many towns, or groups within the towns, were either exempt from the *taille* (the most important direct tax) or arranged to pay it on easier terms. A previous royal device for raising money—the creation and sale of offices—had by now resulted in a horde of hereditary, irremovable office-holders, exempt from certain taxes.

Indirect taxation was contracted out to private companies, the farmers-general, and the country itself was divided by a network of natural barriers where these customs dues and tolls were levied. The Church owned about ten percent of the land of France and its revenues were large; but its contribution to royal revenue was limited to its own occasional 'voluntary grant'. The nobility, owning about twenty-five percent of the land, was exempt from the *taille* and, although not exempt from other direct taxes—the *capitation* and the *vingtième*—it often secured a favourable assessment for these. The taxes were collected efficiently enough but the drawbacks of this undergrowth of vested interest were not only that they represented a loss in revenue but also that the tax burden bore all the more heavily on the poor, increasing their hardship and discontent. Moreover, internal customs hindered the growth of domestic commerce and the expansion of the nation's resources. In fact, the chief beneficiaries of the system of tax collection were the farmers-general themselves.

By the middle of the eighteenth century there were signs that royal ministers were fully aware of this deplorable state of affairs. There were schemes for reforming the fiscal system, for persuading the privileged classes to give up some of their tax immunities and for cutting away some of the tangle of local barriers and particular interests which restricted the growth of the nation's wealth.

However, every attempt to introduce such reform met fierce protests from the beneficiaries of privilege, especially the nobility. Tax exemptions had a monetary value which was important to many impoverished country nobles. They were a valuable mark of social status, which mattered to them all. Nor were the nobles keen to sacrifice their cherished rights to please an absolute monarchy, which had excluded them from what many considered their historic right to a share in political power. Indeed, in the eighteenth century

there was an aristocratic resurgence as the nobles moved to the counter-offensive against royal absolutism. By the 1780s the crown's financial plight had become the aristocracy's opportunity.

The main spokesmen of the resistance to reforms and of the attack on absolutism were the *parlements*, especially the *parlement* of Paris, the most important of a dozen in the kingdom. They were essentially courts of law and the special preserve of the judicial aristocracy, the *noblesse de robe*. In one important respect their powers were more than judicial: all royal decrees had to be registered with them and they could present protests before registration took place. Although the king could then override their protests, these were nevertheless an important weapon of resistance, one used to great effect. Any scheme which affected privilege called forth the protests of the *parlements*.

With the cooperation of the local estates in Brittany and Languedoc and the assembly of the clergy, they thwarted moves for more fiscal equality in the early 1750s and again in 1763. During the 1760s they backed the estates of Brittany in a long resistance to the royal representative. In the course of this conflict they asserted that only the Estates-General, the old assembly which had not met since 1614, could ratify new taxes. Louis XV, in a burst of energy during his last years, had overriden the *parlements* and then suppressed them so that his ministers could get on with reform programmes. However, Louis XVI, in one of the first and most misguided acts of his reign, restored the *parlements*. They then resumed their campaign of obstruction up until 1788.

The effect of this conduct on the part of the *parlements* was not only to thwart useful reforms and to prop up the system of privilege but also to bring absolutism into growing disrepute. Although their resistance was inspired by petty self-interest, they presented it as the defence of liberty, constitutionalism and law against the onslaught of a despotic crown. When the king set their objections on one side, and still more when he suspended the *parlements*, it merely seemed further evidence of the tyranny in action.

The terms in which they framed their protests helped to make familiar notions of limited monarchy, representative institutions, fundamental laws and the rights of the nation. Their own interpretation of these was, in fact, narrow: liberty meant their privileges and representative institutions a body dominated by the nobility. Yet they were liked by the common people. This was partly because of skilful publicity and well-organized demonstrations, but it was also because the attack on despotism struck a popular note. Liberty and representative institutions, although in a wider sense than the *parlements* contemplated, had attractions for many who found themselves outside the privileged orders.

The social order

In this political conflict the aristocracy might feel that popular opinion was with them against despotism. Social discontent, on the other hand, made for a different alignment of forces.

Society under the old regime was still essentially aristocratic: prestige and pre-eminence in the social hierarchy were accorded to those of noble birth or possessing titled rank and landed estates. These distinctions enjoyed official legal recognition in the traditional concept of society as consisting of three estates: the clergy, the nobility and the rest, the first two orders being entitled to special privileges.

Some of the nobility's privileges were honorific, like the right to carry a sword. More materially, they were exempt from paying the *taille* and favoured in other aspects of direct taxation. A noble land-owner was entitled as *seigneur* to exercise jurisdiction in manorial courts and to retain the fines imposed. He was also allowed to hold certain monopolies in his manor, such as the winepress, whose users had to pay him a fee. Finally, he was entitled to a variety of feudal dues, in the shape of money payments —some annual and some occasional—as well as services from the peasantry.

Within the nobility there were differences and distinctions, such as those between the few thousand great ones who frequented the royal court at Versailles and the lesser, often hard-pressed, provincial nobles. There was a further distinction between the older nobility 'of the sword' and the office-holding, judicial nobility 'of the robe'. But by contrast with all non-nobles, the small group of perhaps 400,000 had this distinction in common: all held by law a superior, privileged position in society.

There were signs, especially from the mid-eighteenth century, that they were maintaining this position more exclusively and exploiting it more thoroughly. The *parlements* tried to restrict entry into their ranks to those who were already of noble descent. From 1781 most commissions in the army were open only to those who could prove that they stemmed from generations of nobility. They appropriated more and more of the better posts which had before been open to non-nobles, especially those with money. By the 1780s all the bishops, all the intendants (provincial administrators) and almost every one of the royal ministers were nobles. In the countryside, perhaps under the pressure of rising costs of living, they began to exploit their seigneurial rights more strongly, even to the extent of resurrecting old, unenforced ones and claiming payment of arrears.

The Third Estate, the non-privileged order, comprised more than ninety-five percent of the French population. They were not nobles and they were not clergy but they might be anything else. The Third Estate was a legal category and not a social or economic class. The wealthiest and most progressive element covered a wide and ill-defined range of comfortably-off townsmen. They flourished especially in such activities as finance, commerce and industry, administration and the liberal professions. They were the chief beneficiaries of the remarkable commercial expansion of France during the eighteenth century.

Between the 1720s and 1780s foreign trade had trebled, colonial trade multiplied five times, industrial output doubled, prices rose and profit margins increased. The great ports of Marseilles, Nantes and Bordeaux enjoyed an unprecedented prosperity. In towns and cities a rush of building projects —elegant town houses, public squares and gardens, promenades and parks—bore witness to the new wealth. Only big financiers, organizing the loans for central and local authorities, or the great tax farmers could outdo in fortune the merchant-princes of the foreign and colonial trade.

Industry, like domestic trade, suffered from the hindrances that impeded economic activity under the old regime—the internal tariff barriers, government regulations and guild restrictions. Even so, large-scale enterprises based mainly on a domestic system were appearing.

The administrative and professional groups, the holders of small offices in the courts and the bureaucracies, and the lawyers, doctors and writers could not match the wealth of the businessman, but they were far more numerous and included a mass of talent—educated, articulate, enlightened and ambitious. From this section more than any other came the leadership in the Revolution, the men who dominated its assemblies and committees, shaped its legislation and conducted its policies.

These middle classes, growing in size and wealth and conscious of their importance

LES QUATRE VERITEZ DU SIECLE DAPRESENT

Above, a cartoon of the ancien régime: *the priest who prays for all, the soldier who fights for all, the peasant who works for all and the lawyer who feeds off all. Nevertheless, lawyers played a large part in the Revolution.*

to the country, were not likely to tolerate indefinitely old systems, institutions and values which barred them from a share in power, hindered their freedom of industry, restricted economic enterprise and relegated them to an inferior social status. Yet they were slow to act in independent opposition to the privileged orders. Many of them not only aspired to reach these social heights themselves but for a long time had enjoyed opportunities to do so. The crown had often drawn its servants from these sections of society rather than from the feudal nobility. Wealthy bourgeois had benefited from the royal practice of creating offices for sale, for these could confer noble status. They might marry their children into the families of needy nobles or use their wealth to get their son a promising position in the judiciary or the administration. They might buy land together with seigneurial rights and to that extent live like lords.

From the mid-eighteenth century the growing exclusiveness of the nobility hindered advance through these traditional channels and probably increased social resentment. Everywhere, according to the politician Antoine Barnave, privilege barred the path to all but trivial careers. Georges Danton complained of a system which gave educated men no opportunity to show their talents. Even so, the injured self-esteem and frustrated ambition of the middle classes were slow to transform themselves into weapons of revolution. Only when it became apparent that the aims of the aristocracy did not include any abandoning of their privileged position did the middle classes break away and strike out on their own.

Below the minority of comfortable bourgeoisie came the vast majority of townsfolk. In Paris they accounted for well over 400,000 of the city's population of half a million. They ranged from small trades-men and shopkeepers, workshop masters, craftsmen and journeymen down to labour-ers and domestic servants, paupers and

vagrants. These were the common people, a collection of small-income groups including wage-earners. There was little development as yet of a distinct wage-earning proletariat and virtually no organization of workers.

Most workshops were on a very small scale. Masters, themselves craftsmen, worked alongside their few employees, and journeymen often lodged with their masters. Masters and men together resisted the attacks of big employers on the guild regulations which protected the crafts. As small earners, whatever their activity they easily felt the pinch of rising prices, especially of bread, and their normal collective response to this was not strikes and wage demands, but food riots, calls for price controls and action to improve the town's supplies of grain. In this respect they lived in a different world from the bourgeoisie, who were strangers to this kind of economic distress.

Most Frenchmen, however, were not townsmen at all. More than eighty percent of the population were rural; and the great majority of them were peasants. They were free individuals—there was very little serf-dom left in France—and in this respect they were better off than the peasantry of many other countries. Many of them, perhaps a quarter, had come to own their land. Others were tenant-farmers on a rent or share-cropping basis. Many (in Normandy per-haps thirty percent) were little more than landless labourers. Except in the case of a fortunate minority their conditions, even if better than at earlier times, were oppressive. Even those who held land had so little that they needed to supplement their earnings. Most got little benefit from the rising prices of foodstuffs, since few had much surplus for sale. The population rose by about 6,000,000 (or thirty percent) during the eighteenth century, and this increased the competition for land, encouraged the subdivison of holdings, swelled the ranks of the landless and checked advances in wages. In addition, the peasants bore the full weight of royal taxes—the *taille* and the salt tax. They paid tithes to the Church and dues to the lord of the manor. They also faced increasingly heavy pressure from those with a more com-mercial approach to agriculture. Progressive landlords threatened to depress the poorer peasantry still further by enclosing common land and by depriving them of traditional rights, however desirable this might be for agrarian advance. Finally, their *seigneurs* squeezed harder for feudal dues—the most detested burden of all, as the complaints and conduct of the peasants in 1789 were to show.

These discontents acquired an additional significance with the growth of public discussion of critical ideas about man, government and country. The *philosophes*, whose writings provided much of the material for discussion in salons, literary clubs and philosophical societies, were concerned with far more than politics, and their political notions did not always agree.

Not revolutionaries in the normal sense, they nevertheless encouraged a revolution of rising expectations and helped to under-mine confidence in the existing order. Inspired by the triumph of physical science in discovering the grand, simple laws of nature, they favoured a similar rational approach, questioning all traditional beliefs, customs and institutions. Their writings encouraged this critical attitude.

Their chief target was the Church as the stronghold of irrational belief and super-stition, insisting on blind, unquestioning obedience to apparently absurd dogmas and preventing by censorship and perse-cution the spread or even the holding of other opinions. The powerful attacks by the *philosophes* on this bulwark of tradition helped to weaken the hold of traditionalism in general. Above all they were concerned with freedom, the essential condition of the better society they hoped for: freedom to question, to hold opinions and to com-municate them by speech and writing. In conditions of freedom rational man, as they understood him, seemed capable of great achievements.

Louis XVI

The reform of institutions from above would not have been impossible, but it would have been extremely difficult. The crown would have had to prove itself a despot equipped with a vigour and ruthlessness of which it had as yet given no evidence, in order to rouse feelings against it. Moreover, the 'despot' would need to be magnanimous enough to admit limitations on his own authority.

All this called for a mixture of authority and finesse, in which the new king, who came to the throne in 1774, was sadly lacking. Louis XVI was a well-meaning young man who wanted to be liked. He had simple tastes and was not very fond of the glittering round of court life. Rather shy and awk-ward, fat and not very lively, he preferred the harmless pleasures of eating, hunting or tinkering at his work bench. He would have done well, Madame Roland thought, in some obscure position in life. The business of government and administration bored him. He lacked the strength of character to stand by a subordinate against the untiring pressures, intrigues and influences around him. He showed no personal initiative of his own at all.

His queen, Marie Antoinette, was shallow and fickle and did nothing to offset his weaknesses. She had many enemies, through no fault of her own, but her indiscreet behaviour gave them opportunities for campaigns against her which lowered still further the reputation and popularity of the monarchy.

Louis XVI's earliest actions, designed to show his goodwill, were misguided. He brought back the *parlements* and dismissed the ministers who had got rid of them. This was a popular move but it proved disastrous for the prospects of reform. It cancelled out the otherwise promising appointment of Turgot as controller-general of finance. Turgot was a devoted servant of the crown, an experienced administrator who had achieved impressive results as *intendant* of Limoges and a disciple of progressive economic thought. He believed that the way to increase national wealth was to abolish the internal barriers which limited the circulation of goods and the restrictions which hampered industrial enterprise. He also believed that the way to improve royal finances was to make all landed proprietors pay taxes. His measures embodied this: he freed the internal market in grain, abolished the privileges of the guilds and substituted a general tax on land for the peasants' obligation to do road work. He transformed an annual deficit of 21,000,000 livres into a surplus of 11,000,000.

The opposition to these reforms was fierce. The *parlements* protested, declaring that Turgot's attack on privilege threatened the whole existing social structure. Louis ignored them, but the vested interests persisted in their opposition. The queen's circle murmured against Turgot; other ministers undermined his position. Despite Turgot's pleas to Louis to hold firm, to stand by him and to ride out the storm, Louis dismissed him in 1776. In doing so he sacrificed his best, if not his last, opportunity. Turgot was quick of tongue and temper, but he had ability and integrity, and these were qualities in short supply in 1776.

In the next confrontation with the privileged opposition, the crown's needs were once more desperate and its position more precarious than ever. Within ten years the monarchy was bankrupt, and its weakness was the aristocracy's opportunity to force its demands for a share in power.

The crucial development was the French intervention in the American Revolution. The French government obtained what it had sought since 1763—revenge for its defeat by Britain in the Seven Years War. It was, however, to prove the most expensive act of vengeance in French history. This was partly because association with the American cause stimulated the fashionable notions of liberty and representative government. Much more important was its shattering effect on the weak royal finances.

Turgot's successor as director of the Treasury was Jacques Necker, a Swiss banker. Since he was a Protestant he was not made controller-general of finance or a member of the royal council. Necker financed the war from loans, raised often at eight or ten percent interest. This not only sent the total debt soaring but required an even greater share of the annual revenue for paying the interest due on the debts. The charges had more than doubled since 1774 and were swallowing more than half the state income. An annual budget deficit had never been unusual, but it was now more

than double the deficit which Turgot had faced.

Retrenchment would make little impression on this, nor could borrowing go on at such a rate. Moreover, existing taxes could not be fruitfully increased, especially since the economy had slumped since the late 1770s and those whose tax burden was

Above, Louis XVI (reigned 1774–92), who attempted to institute long-overdue reforms; his dull personality was not adequate to deal with the mounting crisis that faced him.

Opposite, a French peasant woman, weighed down with the burden of supporting the Church and the nobility, both of which were exempt from taxation.

already heavy were suffering a decline in real wages. The only solution was to recast the tax system so that all paid, regardless of status. The sole fiscal reform which would meet the crown's need inevitably involved an attack on the existing social system of privileged orders.

This was the essence of the programme proposed by Calonne, who was controller-general from 1783 to 1787. The ending of the American War hid the real position for a time, as did an excellent harvest and a trade treaty with Britain. For a time Calonne lived in a false boom, built roads and harbours and raised big loans. In 1786, however, he reverted to Turgot's policy. He proposed to replace the *vingtième*, in which the nobility were favoured, with a new tax on all land regardless of the status of its owner. To stimulate productivity internal barriers were to be abolished. There were to be new local assemblies to help to advise in taxation, which would be based on land-owning not social status: wealth, not birth and rank, would be the measure. Moreover, they were to be controlled by the royal agent, the *intendant*.

The new tax would ease the crown's finances, by providing a permanent broad-based tax on all land. The composition of the new assemblies would check the social exclusiveness and political pretensions of the privileged nobility. They would also give greater opportunities to wealthy, local middle-class men to play a role. They would increase the efficiency and uniformity of administration and they would, under the *intendants*, be acting as agencies of the crown. At the same time the removal of economic barriers would at once promote a greater unity within the kingdom and provide more incentives to economic enterprise.

The retreat from absolutism

For these same reasons the policies could expect opposition from both the defenders of the existing system and the critics of royal despotism. Calonne hoped to avoid this by summoning a handpicked assembly of notables drawn from the high nobility, the men of the *parlements* and the leading clergy. If careful explanation and persuasion could win their approval beforehand, subsequent opposition from the *parlements* might be less automatic and less effective.

The notables disappointed these hopes. Some were ready to give up their tax privileges, but even they were not convinced of the need for new taxes, nor were they keen on assemblies which ignored distinctions between the three estates and looked like institutions to strengthen the ministerial authority. When Calonne tried to appeal to a wider public, he lost whatever influence he had had with these notables, and Louis was persuaded to dismiss him.

Calonne's successor, Loménie de Brienne, an ambitious cleric and one of Calonne's leading critics in the Assembly of Notables,

had no more success. For all his criticism of Calonne, Brienne's own proposals were only a slightly modified version of his predecessor's. Despite Brienne's standing with the notables, the Church and the queen, his proposals were rejected. The notables had done nothing to relieve the financial position. By defending privilege and the status quo they had angered the Third Estate. Real reform could come only from some higher body, preferably the Estates-General, which had last met in 1614.

Thwarted in his first approach, Brienne turned next to the traditional method: he brought forward his decrees to be registered by the *parlement* of Paris. The result of this was the appearance in full force of the revolt of the nobility. The two driving forces in the *parlement*, the one concerned to preserve privilege and the other aspiring to a check on despotism by constitutional means, had both been encouraged by the rebuffs already delivered to the monarchy by the notables. They refused to register the tax proposals and demanded the summoning of the Estates-General as the one body competent to agree to a tax on land. Months of conflict came to a head in May 1788. The *parlement* issued a manifesto denouncing arbitrary government, arrest and taxation and asserting the rights of the Estates-General in matters of taxation. Brienne sent troops, arrested leaders, had all the *parlements* suspended and proposed to transfer their powers of legislation and appeal to a new set of tribunals.

Far from settling matters, this act provoked the biggest demonstrations witnessed so far. The *parlements* were seen—far from accurately—as a barrier against tyranny. In Paris and the provinces the despotism of ministers was denounced. The Assembly of the Clergy protested, as did the leading nobles. Hundreds of pamphlets appeared championing the Paris *parlement*. Riots broke out in provincial cities. In Brittany, where provincial feeling was always strong and the local Estates were flourishing, the machinery of resistance was highly organized. Elsewhere, as in Dauphiné, where the local Estates had long since died out, campaigns were begun to restore them. At Grenoble popular riots prevented troops from removing the local *parlement*, and a hastily summoned provincial Estates refused to pay the new taxes until these were sanctioned by the Estates-General.

Faced with this widespread protest the government gave in. The notion of new tribunals, along with other projected reforms, was abandoned. Brienne resigned and was replaced by Necker; his last act was, in fact, to declare the nation bankrupt. The crown agreed to summon, in May 1789, the Estates-General. In September 1788 the *parlement* of Paris was restored amid popular acclaim. The privileged classes, with wide popular support from members of the Third Estate, had forced absolutism to retreat. To accept the Estates-General was

to admit the right of a representative body to a share in power and thus to a permanent limitation in the authority of the crown. However, the successful aristocratic revolt to end the autocratic power of the crown had merely opened the way to a revolution that was to end the power of the privileged aristocracy. As the French writer, François de Chateaubriand, later said: 'the patricians began the Revolution and the plebeians completed it.'

The common front of nobility and commoners against absolutism had hardly won its victory in the summer of 1788 when it began to disintegrate. The reason for this was the Third Estate's discovery that the nobility's intentions were very different from its own. Once it became apparent that the nobility's idea of a constitution was one which ensured its own predominance and perpetuated the existing system of inequality of status, the Third Estate denounced its former allies and struck out on its own. 'Despotism and constitution', wrote an observer, 'are now minor questions. The war is between the Third Estate and the other two orders.'

There had already been signs of this division of interests, notably in Brittany, even at the height of the common resistance to Brienne. But the great revelation of how narrow the aristocracy's aspirations were came with the announcement by the *parlement* of Paris, just after its restoration, that the Estates-General should meet in its ancient form. Each Estate was to return the same number of representatives, each was to meet separately and each was to vote separately.

This would condemn the Third Estate to permanent inferiority and impotence. Since two of the three orders were privileged, vote by order would mean that the Third Estate could always be outvoted by two to one and certainly would be on anything which touched the privileged status of the other two Estates. Royal absolutism would be exchanged for a constitution dominated by privileged orders. In seconding the nobility's demands for a constitution, the middle classes had not meant to revive a medieval relic which would perpetuate the concept of stratified estates and enshrine their own inferiority. They added to the protest against absolutism their own clamour against privileged status. The Revolution was to be about equality as well as liberty.

The indignation at the Paris *parlement*'s announcement was immediate and widespread. The *parlements* lost their traditional popularity, and the privileged orders in general became the major target of denunciation. In a great outpouring of pamphlets and petitions the Third Estate proclaimed its own ideas and demands. These were that the Third Estate should have as many representatives as the clergy and nobility together (the 'doubling of the Third'), that all the orders should meet in a single assembly and that voting should be by individuals, with the decision going by majorities. In such a mixed assembly the Third Estate would be powerful, since its representatives could expect support from the more liberal nobles and from the poorer clergy.

The general mood is well illustrated in the best-known of these pamphlets, *What Is the Third Estate* by the Abbé Siéyès. It was useless, he said, for the Third to be represented under the ancient forms: 'Its presence would only consecrate the oppression of which it must be the eternal victim.' It would prolong the 'odious injustice' whereby, whatever a man's talent, industry and public service, the path to honours and high position would stay closed to him and be open only to the privileged orders. He went further when he dismissed the aristocracy as a tiny (and useless) minority. The Third Estate represented the nation: 24,000,000 commoners mattered more than 400,000 of the privileged. The Third Estate was 'everything'. So far it had been treated in practice as if it were 'nothing'. It demanded in future to count for something.

There were the beginnings also of organization to promote the Third Estate's views. Liberal aristocrats like Lafayette enlightened *parlement*. Men like Adrien Duport and Hérault de Séchelles, clerics like Talleyrand and Siéyès, and even princes of the blood like the Duke of Orléans associated with the 'patriotic' party.

One request, for the doubling of the Third Estate's representation, was conceded by the king in December 1788. He did not say whether the orders should sit and vote together, but it seemed as if the crown were coming down on the side of the Third Estate's demands.

The Estates-General

The preparations for the coming assembly of the Estates-General added to the air of excitement and expectation. In thousands of meetings throughout France men assembled to elect the representatives of their order for their district and to discuss and draft the lists of grievances (*cahiers*) they would take with them to Versailles. The nobility, like the clergy, chose their representatives directly, but the deputies for the Third Estate were chosen indirectly. Most Frenchmen over the age of twenty-five could vote in a local assembly, but they usually picked electors who proceeded to a higher meeting of electors which actually chose the deputies.

This process favoured the men of some eloquence, education and local standing, especially as these same meetings had to discuss and draft the list of grievances. It favoured the urban, professional middle class: men like Maximilien Robespierre in Artois and Antoine Barnave and Jean Mounier in Dauphiné. Of the 610 deputies, about two-thirds were lesser office-holders

J.'somm' du Tier-État.

or lawyers, and another five percent came from other professions. About thirteen percent were from commerce, manufacture or finance and about ten percent were farmers.

The general list of grievances of the Third Estate was mainly the work of this middle-class group. Some of the demands of the peasantry and poorer people were neglected or glossed over. But they do reveal the line of divergence between the middle classes and the privileged orders. The grievances submitted by all the orders usually denounced arbitrary government, demanded a constitution, a representative body to control taxation, freedom of the individual and the press and the abolition of internal customs barriers. But the nobility, though sometimes ready to give up its tax exemptions, still insisted on its honorific privileges and on its special status—the retention of the system of separate orders. For its part the Third Estate demanded complete civil equality: the nobility was to lose all its privileges and its special status.

There was in all this another opportunity for the king. The alliance of people and nobility had broken down. The groups which had so often sabotaged ministerial plans for reform were unpopular with the spokesmen of the Third Estate. By his agreement to meet a representative body in order to discuss reform and by his concession which enabled the representation of the Third Estate to be doubled, Louis had won popularity and trust. An alliance of crown and people on a basis of moderate reform was feasible. But it was expecting a great deal of a monarch whose whole upbringing and outlook were cast in a traditional mould

Above, Jacques Necker (1732–1804), the French financier who introduced reforms of government finances in the 1770s and 1780s but who was shackled by opposition within the court. His dismissal in July 1789 prompted the storming of the Bastille.

Top, a craftsman and a washerwoman drinking the health of the Tiers État, *whose voice was to be heard for the first time in 175 years when Louis XVI summoned the States-General in 1789. The* Tiers État *included all those who were neither noble nor clergy.*

to throw over the nobility and join with a collection of provincial lawyers and bureaucrats. It was too much for a monarch as indecisive as Louis XVI, who was surrounded by influences favouring the established system.

As the Estates-General assembled in May 1789, the hopeful deputies of the Third Estate were soon disillusioned. The traditional ceremonies underlined their inferior status: they had to wear black, enter by a side door and go bareheaded, while the other orders wore hats. They were received in a different room. When Necker announced that the Estates should meet separately, not in a common assembly, disillusion was complete. On this vital point the king had agreed with the privileged orders.

Recognizing that to accept this was to accept the defeat of their hopes, the deputies of the Third Estate determined to ignore it. They embarked on a tactic of passive resistance and began a war of nerves. They refused to take any step, however small, until the other orders should join them. For weeks no business at all was transacted. On 17 June they went further and took a clearly revolutionary step: they proclaimed themselves to be, not the mere representatives of the Third Estate, but the National Assembly. On 20 June, finding their normal meeting

hall locked, they adjourned to a nearby tennis court and took an oath not to disperse till a constitution had been finally established.

On 23 June they carried their defiance still further. Louis, addressing all the orders in a special session, outlined important reforms but said that the ancient distinction of the three orders would be preserved in its entirety and ordered the estates to assemble in their separate halls the next day. The deputies of the Third Estate sat firm. 'The nation when assembled', declared Jean Bailly, the president of the Third Estate, 'cannot be given orders.' 'We will not leave our places', said Mirabeau, 'except at the point of a bayonet.' Many of the clergy including the Archbishop of Paris (from fear) and Talleyrand, Bishop of Autun (from calculated enthusiasm), had already responded to the Third Estate's exhortations to join them. So did about forty of the nobles, including the Duke of Orléans. Louis, perhaps alarmed at the growth of unrest in Paris, yielded. On 27 June he instructed the First and Second Estates to merge with the National Assembly.

The Third Estate had won its war of nerves with the king and the nobility. Henceforth, there were no representatives of the Estates of France, only representatives of the French nation.

Despite their impressive defiance the position of the middle-class deputies remained precarious. The royal orders of 27 June did not mark the conversion of Louis to their ideas but merely a temporary expedient. Recalcitrant nobles and court circles were urging him to use force. He began to summon regiments to Paris and Versailles. He dismissed Necker and replaced him with a court favourite, the Baron de Breteuil. It looked as if the last argument of kings was to be used against the upstart deputies. What saved the day for the National Assembly was the appearance of new forces in this complex movement. And these forces had their own interests and aspirations which made them invaluable but disturbing and uncertain supporters of the middle class in the Assembly.

The beginning of the Revolution

It was the intervention of the people of Paris that thwarted any royal plan for using force. This was not merely a gesture of solidarity. Economic distress caused by high prices and shortage of food was particularly acute. The price of bread in Paris was acute. The price of bread in Paris was double

the normal rate. Wide popular unrest over this had shown itself in demonstrations, so that when the political crisis of July arose the Parisian people were already in the streets in an angry mood. Feelings about politics might not have brought them out in such strength or worked on them with such effect had it not been for these economic grievances. Time and again during the Revolution food shortages and rising prices would appear as the great driving force behind popular discontent. Yet, although high prices could provoke riots, these would have had no more significance than they had had in the past but for the political situation.

The Parisians were kept in touch with the latest developments as news and rumours came through from Versailles. The great distributing centre was the Palais Royal, a favourite public resort, where every night orators and agitators, in particular Camille Desmoulins, addressed the crowds. They warned the people of aristocratic schemes to launch troops against Paris and urged them to take up arms. Excited and alarmed, the crowds surged through the streets seeking weapons, which they found in the Hôtel de Ville and the Hôtel des Invalides.

On 14 July they converged on the Bastille in the Faubourg Saint-Antoine. It was thought to contain weapons. Also it was suspect as the stronghold from which the royal troops would attack, and its guns were trained on the streets. In panic the small garrison opened fire. The angry crowd, supported by rebellious soldiers with artillery, forced the governor De Launay to surrender and killed him. 'This is a revolt', said the king. 'Sire', replied a courtier, 'it is not a revolt, it is a revolution.'

The fall of the Bastille had important consequences. The king had lost control of Paris. At the same time, the body of electors who had chosen the deputies for Paris and who had continued to meet thereafter threw out the old city authorities and set up themselves as the municipal council—the Commune. They established a militia, the National Guard, both to resist any aristocratic plots and to check excessive popular disturbances. Its commander was Lafayette; its badge the tricolour.

Throughout the towns of France similar new bodies took over from the old authorities and set up similar national guards. Meanwhile, on 17 July the king had recalled Necker and had visited Paris where at the Town Hall he accepted the national cockade: the red and blue of Paris with the white of the Bourbons in between. The most intransigent nobles began to flee from France.

The same month another popular force made its weight felt in the Revolution. In the years before 1789 the position of the masses of the peasantry had worsened, with the growing pressure of population and the more rigorous exaction by *seigneurs* of their dues. In the economic recession and the bad harvests of 1788 the peasantry suffered badly, and the surviving lists of grievances of rural assemblies indicate the nature of their many complaints: enclosing landlords, tithes, heavy taxes and, above all, the seigneurial dues.

From early in 1789 there was widespread unrest, and attacks on grain stores and convoys took place. The peasants had expected good news from Versailles and when none came rumours spread: the aristocrats were not only conspiring to prevent improvements but they were planning to launch armed vengeance against the peasants, and the instruments of the aristocrats were to be the brigands. This legend was strengthened by the movement of unemployed labourers and vagabonds. Such rumours spread like wildfire creating panic armong the peasantry over large areas. The 'great fear' resulted in a wave of peasant

uprisings, in which they attacked châteaux, destroyed the manorial records of the detested seigneurial dues and overturned enclosures. Many believed, or pretended to believe, that they were acting in the king's name.

The middle classes in the Assembly were alarmed. Such widespread disorders and attacks on property were not to their taste. Yet they had no forces which could put down disorders on such a scale. The only way to restore peace to the countryside was to make swift concessions. This was the underlying reason for the destruction of the feudal regime by the Assembly on 4 August. One deputy proposed the surrender of feudal rights and an orgy of sacrifice followed, as one after another tax privileges, tithes, seigneurial rights and the privileges of provinces and cities, guilds and corporations were offered up. It was an impressive occasion, but essentially it was the recognition of an accomplished fact. Indeed, the Assembly later stipulated that the peasants should redeem the seigneurial dues. But this could never be enforced. Just as the action of townspeople throughout France had thrust aside the municipal authorities of the

old regime, so the action of the peasantry had destroyed some of the traditional structure in the countryside.

Yet another popular movement in Paris during October set the seal on the revolutionary triumphs of 1789. Once again it was brought about by a combination of economic distress and political excitement. The latter sprang from revived suspicions of the king's intentions. Louis had stubbornly refused to give his assent to the decrees in which the Assembly had embodied their abolition of feudalism on 4 August. Some deputies felt he needed another push. Their impatience was reinforced by alarm early in October, when a regiment was called to Versailles and at a welcoming banquet drank royal toasts and trampled on the tricolour cockade. The orators of the Palais Royal were quick to pass on this ominous news to their excitable audiences and to suggest thwarting such aristocratic plots by removing Louis from the poisonous atmosphere of Versailles to the pure patriotic air of Paris.

The food shortages had not been eased. There were riots and angry denunciations of the authorities, especially by the housewives of Paris. It was during a demonstration by the women at the Hôtel de Ville that someone suggested that they march to Versailles to petition the king and the Assembly for bread. Several thousand women made the twelve-mile journey. The Assembly arranged that their petition for bread should reach the king and suggested that political demands—his assent to their decrees—be added. Further persuasion appeared in the shape of 20,000 Parisian National Guards under Lafayette, presenting the demand of the Paris Commune that Louis should return to Paris. On 6 October, accompanied by cheering crowds, Louis made the journey from Versailles, to be followed in a few days by the National Assembly.

'It is finished', wrote Desmoulins. 'The aristos are at their last gasp, the patriots have triumphed.' It was not finished and Desmoulins would not live to see the end. The alliance of the middle-class Assembly and the common people of Paris was to prove uneasy and unstable. Indeed, the Assembly in Paris soon took severe measures, including the imposition of martial law, to check the excessive energies of the people.

Nevertheless, Desmoulin's optimism was understandable. The aristocracy's plans for the future of the constitution and of society had been defeated; their attempts to bring in armed force had been thwarted; and many of them had fled the country. The Assembly, backed, however fortuitously, by the people, had triumphed. The king was in Paris under their eyes. The people were calm, partly because of sterner disciplinary measures but also because the Assembly improved the flow of food to Paris and because the next harvest was good. They could proceed to reshape the institutions of France along the lines of middle-class aspirations.

The National Assembly

Between 1789 and 1791 the National Constituent Assembly carried through a great reconstruction of French institutions. Not all its measures were permanent or satisfactory: some worked poorly; some were quickly abandoned. The decision-makers were essentially men of the middle classes, who dominated the Assembly, together with some 'patriotic' nobles and clergy. For this reason their vision was often limited to the boundaries of a comfortable middle-class liberalism. Nevertheless, much of what ultimately survived from the Revolution was the work of these years, and it represented a radical change in every aspect of life in France.

In its 'Declaration of the Rights of Man and Citizen' (August 1789), the Assembly proclaimed the principles on which the new order should be based and rejected those of the old Regime. Liberty and Equality—'men are born and remain free and equal in rights'—was the negation of arbitrary government and aristocratic privilege. Social

Above, the women of Paris marching to Versailles in October 1789.

Left, the nobles in the Estates-General renouncing their privileges on 4 August 1789; this concession to popular feeling came too late to affect the course of the Revolution.

Opposite top left, the fall of the Bastille, drawn by an eyewitness; the Parisians were supported by rebel detachments from the army, who brought artillery.

Opposite top right, the Parisian mob carrying the head of the governor of the Bastille in a demonstration outside the Hôtel de Ville on 14 July 1789; the capture of the Bastille involved the loss of royal authority in Paris.

Opposite bottom left, the mob in the salon of the Tuileries palace in Paris in August 1789.

Opposite bottom right, the lynching of Joseph François Foullon, the French intendant of finances whose severity was hated by the people. He was killed on 22 July 1789, one of the first victims of the Revolution.

distinctions were to be based on public usefulness only, not on inherited status. Public offices were to be open to all on a basis of talent, not reserved for a privileged few on a basis of rank. There was to be freedom of opinion, of speech and of writing and freedom from arbitrary arrest and imprisonment. Popular sovereignty—'the source of all sovereignty resides in the nation'—was a total reversal of the previous theory of royal sovereignty.

These principles, though fatal to the old order, were not meant to imply extreme measures of democracy in the new era. Equality meant equality before the law and a career open to talents, not a levelling out of economic inequalities. The fact that men had a natural right to property did not foreshadow some great redistribution: it meant

that the individual property owner had a right not to be deprived of it. When the Assembly did contravene this 'sound and inviolable right', it was always with excuses and usually resulted in compensation for the affected person. Nor did popular sovereignty mean universal suffrage. The Assembly wanted to keep power in responsible, educated, middle-class hands. Hence, while all citizens enjoyed civil rights, only those paying a certain sum in taxation were classed as 'active citizens' and given the right to vote in national or local elections. Even most of the 'active' citizens could vote only in primary assemblies, the election of deputies coming at a later stage and being

confined to voters with a higher tax qualification. Some deputies, notably Robespierre, protested at this creation of a new aristocracy of wealth and managed to obtain some modifications, but the main distinctions remained.

In a variety of measures the Assembly carried through the destruction of the old regime which was implied in their declaration. Decrees like those of August 1789 swept away large numbers of the old privileges in shoals. The National Assembly was to a certain extent merely recognizing facts already accomplished by the peasantry. They defined some seigneurial rights as legitimate property rights which the peasants

should purchase from the lord. However, since the peasantry never recognized this fine distinction, in practice a great host of feudal and seigneurial dues and obligations and payments were abolished. Serfdom was also abolished where it still lingered on. All tax privileges and exemptions of provinces, towns and corporations as well as privileged groups were suppressed, as were tithes. Hereditary nobility and titles were abolished: all men were now citizens. The old venal offices were swept away (a generous gesture from an Assembly nearly half of whose members held such offices), although all holders were to be compensated for their loss. The old *parlements* were abolished and the judges compensated for the loss of proprietary rights in their seats.

Among the most radical and enduring of the institutional changes was the reform of local government. The Assembly struck at the most disagreeable characteristics of its old structure. Local government was a confused patchwork of complicated divisions, overlapping authorities, differing institutions and areas of special jurisdictions and particular immunities, in which *seigneurs*, priests, village notables and royal officers all had a hand. The confusion was itself the result of the system of unequal privilege and fostered barriers and divisions by its stress on provincialism. Moreover, the royal authorities were imposed from above and controlled from the central government.

The Assembly aimed to replace this by a more uniform and rational system, embodying equality of treatment and the elective principle. France was divided into eighty-three departments, subdivided into 374 cantons, which were in turn divided into communes. All the 44,000 communes had equal status, similar powers and similar authorities, elected in each commune by the active citizens. This was also the case with cantons and departments, although in these larger units the governing council was elected indirectly in stages.

The reform was not an immediate success. All the authorities were too short of money to carry out effectively their administrative responsibilities. Moreover, there were conflicts between the departmental authorities

and those of the communes: in the former, indirect elections produced councils of more wealthy and cautious citizens, whereas in the communes direct election in a small area produced more radical, lower-middle-class councillors. In their desire to avoid the objectionable centralization of earlier days, the Assembly established no clear links between the local authorities and the central government. In time, however, under pressure of emergency, strong links were forged, and the leaders of France then had an administrative machine which could carry their commands through France with an efficiency no absolute monarch had ever known.

In their judicial reforms the Assembly achieved a notable success. The old system had been chaotic and confused, with a variety of courts ranging from the seigneurial courts and special ones like the ecclesiastical courts to the sovereign courts—the *parlements*. All, including the *parlements*, were swept aside. A simpler, uniform system of courts, geared to the new local government units, replaced them. The new judges and justices of the peace were to be elected. Again privilege suffered, for many of these courts had been the embodiment of privilege. Venal judicial offices were abolished, although compensation was to be paid.

Judicial procedure was reformed in enlightened and humane ways. Arbitrary imprisonment was forbidden. The accused was innocent till proved guilty, trials were to be public and juries were introduced in criminal cases. Barbarous practices and punishments such as torture, branding and breaking on the wheel were abandoned. The death penalty was retained, though some like Robespierre argued for its abolition. Even here privilege was abolished. Previously aristocrats had enjoyed the distinction of being beheaded whereas commoners were hanged. In future all would be beheaded. The deputy, Dr Guillotin, recommended, although he did not invent, the new machine for this purpose, which was named after him.

In their economic legislation the Assembly mainly favoured the progressive, individualist approach and dismantled many of the controls and restrictions of the old regime. They introduced a uniform system of weights and measures. They abolished the system of local tolls and internal customs barriers, although these free trade notions stopped at the national frontier. The guilds and corporations, obstacles to individual enterprise, were suppressed. New types of association, the trade unions, were as unacceptable as the old ones. The le Chapelier law prohibited associations of workmen.

Reform and the Church

Whatever such measures might do eventually to increase the national wealth, they were of little help with the immediate financial problems. The Assembly had to devise a new tax system to replace the inadequate, unequal one of the old regime. They proposed to do this with three taxes, the main one falling on all landed property. These taxes were not very productive in the still disordered condition of France, nor would they clear the great debt inherited from former days. There was no question of repudiating this debt. The deputies were financially orthodox, and the middle classes from which they were drawn included many bondholders. Indeed, they had considerably increased the national debt by paying compensation to those whose offices had been abolished.

The solution was to confiscate the vast property of the Church, which the Assembly argued could be seized, since it was not private property and since it was supposed to promote purposes like education which the state would henceforth discharge. The sale of Church property would replenish the Treasury and, pending its sale, the property provided backing for the issue of a paper currency, the *assignats*. As Church land was sold, *assignats* to this value would be called

Above, a dance held on the site of the now-demolished Bastille, on the anniversary of its fall, 14 July, 1790. Musée Carnavalet, Paris.

Top, the wholesale attack on privilege and rank inspired by the events of 4 August 1789, when the nobility and clergy voted to abandon the feudal rights traditionally due to their rank.

Above left, the abolition of tolls paid on goods moving into and out of Paris in May 1791; the high price of bread and other basic foodstuffs had contributed to the frustration that had been voiced in 1789.

Opposite left, the march of the women of Paris to Versailles in October 1789; they captured the king and queen and took them to the Tuileries to prevent a counter-revolution.

Opposite right, the first victims of the French Revolution – de Launay, the governor of the Bastille and Foullon, the intendant of finances.

in and destroyed, so that inflation would be avoided.

The move had important consequences. It worked well at first, but in time the temptation to print *assignats* in excess of the resources backing them was too great. The resulting inflation contributed to that economic distress which underlay so much of the popular unrest throughout the revolutionary years. The main purchasers of Church lands seem to have come from the middle classes and the wealthier peasantry. These great beneficiaries became hardened in their resistance to any attempts to put the clock back to 1789 and equally determined to oppose any radical attempts to put it too far forward.

The move also played a part in one of the most fateful acts of the Assembly, its reorganization of the Church. As the state had commandeered its wealth, the money for the upkeep of the Church would have to come from state funds. Most deputies were soaked in the anti-clericalism of the philosophers and believed that the Church needed a thorough overhaul, the more so if it were to be supported from public money. In the Civil Constitution of the Clergy in July 1790, the Assembly redrew diocesan and parish boundaries, made bishops and parish priests subject to election and dissolved many of the religious orders. They demanded that all clergy take an oath of loyalty to the constitution including these last arrangements. Even the clerics in the Assembly, good 'patriots' till now, hesitated to do this before some religious authority—the papacy—had approved of this secular scheme. After nine months' delay, the papacy condemned the Civil Constitution in March 1791. Nearly all the bishops and most of the French clergy had already refused the Assembly's command to take the oath, and the papal pronouncement confirmed their resistance. The 'non-jurors' were deprived of their posts, which were given to compliant, 'constitutional' clergy, but in many districts, especially in northern and eastern France, parishioners stuck by their clergy and ignored the 'constitutional' ones. In addition, the 'non-jurors' became identified as counter-revolutionaries, with a potential support among devout parishioners, so an extra bitterness and alarm was injected into the whole revolutionary situation, which was increasingly precarious.

The threat to the monarchy

Meanwhile, in their major task, the framing of a new constitution, the deputies experienced their fiercest divisions. The reactionary right, consisting of sullen nobility, had gone by August 1789. All the members of the Assembly hereafter could call themselves patriots. Moreover, they all agreed that France should have a constitutional monarchy, with a loyal executive directed by a popular legislative assembly. But on the precise powers of that executive and its relations with the assembly there were differences. Some wanted a strong executive, feeling that a weak one would lead to the spread of disorder. In particular, they felt that the crown should have the right to veto legislation and that royal ministers should sit in the Assembly to ensure coordination of both branches of government. The majority, however, were too distrustful of the executive to invest it with large powers. They believe that a powerful executive was the main danger to the individual liberties they prized. They feared, too, that a royal veto would be used to destroy revolutionary legislation and suspected that ministers in the assembly would become the means whereby a crafty king would dominate it.

On every issue, the opponents of a strong executive—with Barnave and Robespierre their most cogent spokesmen—carried the day. Jean Mounier and Pierre Malouet, the leaders of the 'strong' monarchy men, had given up in October 1789, in protest at the way in which popular intervention had been allowed (or used) to sway the decision on the veto. Only Mirabeau, the *déclassé* noble, forceful, clever, ugly and dissipated, remained as a powerful voice for a strong royal executive. Mirabeau's ability and vigour, together with his leading role in the events of 1789, gave him great personal influence in the Assembly. Even Mirabeau's weight, however, could not overcome the Assembly's distrust of a strong monarchy, nor indeed was the king willing to act on advice from so prominent a revolutionary.

When the constitution was finally agreed in September 1791, Louis XVI, now King of the French by the grace of God and the will of the nation, was chief executive, but with very limited powers. He could choose his own ministers but they were not to be drawn from, nor could they sit in, the Assembly. He could not initiate legislation. He could not veto the Assembly's legislation completely but merely delay it for a time. He could not dissolve the Assembly. The latter, as the elected representatives, embodied the sovereignty of the people and the general will of the nation.

Even before the constitution was completed there were ominous developments for the future of constitutional monarchy. Louis XVI was never reconciled to his position from the summer of 1789, and his dislike of it increased after the Civil Constitution of the Clergy. Mirabeau's death in April 1791 removed the one influence which might have countered the more hot-headed schemes of Marie Antoinette. She argued that the royal family should escape from Paris to the northeast frontier near Metz, where the army commander was sympathetic to the royal cause. From there Louis could issue an appeal which would be answered by the *émigré* nobility congregated across the frontier and, it was hoped, by the queen's brother, the Emperor Leopold, with Austrian forces. On the night of 20 June 1791, the Queen's admirer, Count Fersen, smuggled the royal family out of Paris. But Louis was recognized at Saint-Ménéhould, caught at Varennes and brought back under heavy armed escort to Paris.

Within the capital there had for some time been signs of anti-monarchical feeling. This was not apparent in the Assembly (where all were monarchists whatever their differences over its powers) nor in the favourite club of the deputies, the Jacobins. But other less reputable clubs, with small subscriptions and a lower-class clientele, especially the Cordeliers, had fostered more radical notions among the Parisian populace. Many of these were discontented with decisions

like the restrictions on suffrage. In these circles the flight to Varennes confirmed their worst suspicions of the king and provoked open demands for a republic. The Cordeliers Club demanded that France be no longer a monarchy.

The Assembly, while angered at Louis' move, was uncomfortable at this surge of popular republicanism. To depose Louis might bring foreign armies down upon them. Nor did they care for the social implications of republicanism, championed as it was by demagogues and the town populace. Barnave argued for an end to the Revolution before it degenerated into a general attack on property. Hence the members of the Assembly clung to the monarchical constitution, saving their faces with the fiction that Louis had been abducted on 25 June, so that his 'flight' was not evidence of any ill-will on his part.

The effect was to reveal only more clearly the deep rift within the ranks of the Third Estate. The popular Parisian demand for Louis' removal was not stifled. On 17 July great crowds assembled in the Champs de Mars to sign a petition against a monarchy. The municipal authorities, who shared the outlook of the Assembly, sent in the National Guard who opened fire, killing about fifty people. This was followed by a fierce repression. Ringleaders were arrested and popular papers suppressed. The Champs de Mars marked the end of the notion of a solid Third Estate in Paris. It was the opening conflict between the comfortable rulers and the *sans-culottes*, as the Parisian lower-class republicans were called.

The Assembly hastily finished drafting their constitution, obtained the king's agreement on 16 September and dissolved. A new Legislative Assembly would be elected to work the institutions they had devised.

The bulk of the members of the Assembly,

as they broke up in September 1791, might well feel that, with all the changes they had made since 1789, the work of Revolution was accomplished. The evils so loudly denounced in 1789—despotism and legal privilege—had been overthrown. France could now proceed to a more normal and much more satisfactory regime with its new institutions and new social order. Yet within about twelve months their main work, the constitution, was overthrown. Many of those who had shaped it, revolutionary heroes in 1790, were regarded as renegades, and the Revolution had moved into a new stage, which was repugnant to them.

Such optimistic expectations had been unrealistic even in 1791. The constitution itself had weaknesses which only goodwill and cooperation could overcome. These were unlikely to be forthcoming from a monarch who had shown such dislike for his role and persisted in hoping for foreign assistance to restore him to his true position. The flight to Varennes had added to the popular suspicion of the constitution and stimulated the hankerings after republicanism which increased the difficulties of working it. Moreover, the constitution had laid down that none of the members of the present Assembly should be eligible for the new body. Thus the new deputies lacked colleagues with any experience.

The Legislative Assembly

The main forces impelling the Revolution further forward emerged clearly only in the course of the new Legislative Assembly from October 1791 onwards. These forces were: first, the struggle for power within the ranks of the middle-class revolutionary politicians; second, the mounting pressure of the common people of Paris, intensified by

Above, the Marquis de Mirabeau (1749–91), the early leader of the Tiers État *in the Estates-General; he sought to establish a constitutional monarchy on the English model but never won the support of Louis or Marie Antoinette.*

Top, Louis XVI's speech to the nation of 4 February 1790; he had little interest in establishing a workable compromise with the revolutionaries.

Top left, a caricature of the funeral of the Church, in recognition of the decision of November 1789, according to which ecclesiastical property was expropriated by the nation.

Opposite left, looting the houses of the nobility in Paris in November 1790; by this time a large proportion of the nobility had already gone into exile.

Opposite right, a magic lantern show of the abuses of the Church, for the entertainment of the Parisians.

economic distress and political discontent with their middle-class rulers; and third, the advent of war in 1792. The effect of these forces was heightened by the interaction between them. Thus politicians in their conflicts were ready to exploit the fears and hopes of the Parisian people.

War transformed the situation. It stimulated the hopes of those who disliked all that the Revolution had done and intensified the fear and determination of the revolutionaries. It contributed to the inflation and shortages which fostered Parisian grievances and made more tense the atmosphere in which rumours of conspiracies and treacheries flourished. It presented politicians with massive new problems, in meeting which they had to make moves and sanction measures that took them far beyond the intentions of 1789 to 1791. And the monarchy, discredited and disliked, might have managed to survive in peace, but in the desperate days of war it was among the first casualties.

The war itself, however, was not a thunderbolt hurled by a malevolent providence against innocent, unsuspecting revolutionaries. It was in fact provoked by revolutionary politicians in pursuit of power. The Legislative Assembly, like its predecessor, was not divided into organized parties with coherent policies. There were no divisions of social or economic class, since the vast majority were, as before, from the same comfortable middle classes. Politically, most were connected to no special group, though they all wanted to maintain the gains so far made by the Revolution and would support those who seemed most likely to ensure this. Of those who were committed, the majority group were constitutional monarchists, supporters of the 1791 constitution, and the ministers were at first their associates.

In the National Constituent Assembly these had formed the more 'popular' element, members of the Jacobin club and advocates of a weak executive against the right-wing spokesmen for a strong monarchy. But in the new Assembly the constitutional monarchists appeared as the 'right' wing. Significantly, they had seceded from the Jacobins and set up their own club, 'The Feuillants'. The other main political group, a minority at first, continued to frequent the Jacobins (or the Cordeliers) and to attack the Feuillant ministers from a more popular and vaguely republican standpoint.

The leading spokesmen of the left were the Brissotins (later known as Girondists), the circle grouped around J. P. Brissot. His main activities before 1789 had taken place in the twilight world of popular agitation and inflammatory journalism. He had been a frequenter of the Palais Royal, had run an extremist journal since 1789 and had played a part in organizing the demonstration on the Champs de Mars. A fluent, rhetorical speaker, he was ambitious and an intriguer, though not without a naive idealism. His

FORCE

FRATERNITÉ

SÉCURITÉ

GÉNIE DE LA GUERRE   LIBERTÉ DES CULTES   ÉGALITÉ DE DEVOIRS

PROSPÉRITÉ

PUDEUR

JUSTICE

GÉNIE DE LA PAIX   LIBERTÉ DE MARIAGE   ÉGALITÉ DE DROITS

GOUT

LUMIÈRE

PUISSANCE

GÉNIE DES ARTS   LIBERTÉ DE LA PRESSE   ÉGALITÉ DE RANGS

RICHESSE

INDUSTRIE

COURAGE

GÉNIE DU COMMERCE   LIBERTÉ DES PROFESSIONS   ÉGALITÉ DE COULEURS

associates included some of the most eloquent orators of the Revolution, Pierre Vergniaud, Armand Gensonné and Gaudet, all deputies from the Gironde. In his struggle for power and the limelight, Brissot was ready to work recklessly on popular fears and passions.

From the beginning the Brissotins preached a violently militant line, demanding ruthless action against internal enemies of the Revolution, such as refractory priests, and against external dangers. By 1792 the numbers of *émigrés* massing on the frontier, especially at Koblenz, was a source of alarm in Paris. Austria and Prussia had both expressed sympathy with the French king. This was in fact a substitute for action, not a prelude to it, but the revolutionaries did not appreciate this. Consequently Brissot's urging—'if you wish with one blow to destroy the aristocracy, the refractory priests, the malcontents, then destroy Koblenz'—struck a sympathetic note. So did Vergniaud's argument that they should attack first, not wait to be attacked. They saw such a conflict as 'a war of peoples against kings', a triumphant crusade in

which the forces of liberty would brush aside the effete, mercenary armies of Europe and be welcomed by the oppressed peoples. Moreover, war would consolidate the Revolution internally. Opponents would be seen and dealt with as the traitors they were and the people would be roused to new revolutionary ardour. 'We need war', declared Brissot, 'to consolidate freedom, to purge

Above, an attack on the Tuileries palace, the residence of the king and queen, in February 1791; republicanism had not been strong in 1789, but the intransigence of the monarchy made it soon appear to be the only solution.

Top and above left, the arrest of Louis XVI at Varennes in June 1791, after he had tried to flee abroad to organize support against the revolutionaries. This failure meant the imminent downfall of the monarchy.

Left, Jacques Pierre Brissot (1754–93), a journalist who led the Girondist faction, arguing for the need for a revolutionary war to liberate the rest of Europe from monarchy. He was executed by the Jacobins.

Opposite, playing cards depicting the various benefits that the Revolution would confer: prosperity, might, wealth, good taste, industry, enlightenment, modesty, religious understanding, security, justice, power and courage.

grievance. The *assignat* began to depreciate rapidly. By June 1792 it was down to about half its face value. Bread prices rose and provision merchants were suspected of hoarding supplies till prices rose still higher. The Brissotins diverted this popular wrath from themselves by accusing the court of treachery, all the more vehemently when Louis dismissed their friends from the government. Their behaviour encouraged a new wave of popular intervention which in its first stage took the form of a demonstration at the Tuileries and forced Louis to restore the Brissotin ministers.

Now, however, the Brissotins had helped to summon up a force they could not control. Alarm and excitement rose higher as the enemy invaders advanced, as rumours spread of counter-revolutionary plots and as Brunswick threatened a 'memorable vengeance' on Paris if the royal family were harmed. Demands for the deposition of the king mounted. The Brissotins, who were fonder of the people as an emotive phrase in debate than as a reaility in the streets exerting its own rough pressures, hesitated. Agitation—now that it had served their purposes—ought to stop. Hoping that provincial forces might offset the Parisian ones, they summoned national guardsmen from other towns to Paris. But these men, the so-called *fédérés*, merely swelled the ranks of the Parisians, providing them with extra forces and a rousing new march, the 'Marseillaise'.

Other politicians were now bypassing the Brissotins. Robespierre in the Jacobin Club supported the popular cause by demanding a National Convention elected by universal suffrage to frame a new constitution. Popular feeling in Paris had by now an organizational basis of its own in the meetings in the forty-eight sections, the electoral divisions of Paris. In July these went into permanent session, so that meetings could be held any time. They began admitting 'passive' (that is, voteless) as well as 'active' citizens. Thus the lesser shopkeepers and tradesmen, the master-craftsmen and artisans and the small people of Paris in general could congregate to frame their own demands and provide local leaders. By August, forty-seven of the forty-eight demanded that the Assembly depose the king.

On 9 August they made their own move. Representatives from almost thirty of the sections moved into the Hôtel de Ville, where the municipal authorities of Paris sat, and proclaimed themselves the new 'revolutionary commune'. Under their direction, on the following day crowds from the sections and contingents of *fédérés* moved on the Tuileries.

After a savage conflict, which cost the attackers 400 lives and the defenders, mainly Swiss Guards, about 800, the Tuileries was taken. The royal family had fled to the Assembly building which offered Louis personal protection. But the intervention of the

away the vice of despotism.' War would also bring triumph to the war party, the Brissotins.

The policy paid handsome dividends. The Brissotins carried the Assembly to a man. They held the majority in the Jacobins Club against the criticism of a small group which included Robespierre, who feared that war might strengthen the position of the crown and make more enemies than friends abroad. The king, too, was confident that war would work to his advantage, and so he was prepared to agree to a war policy. The Feuillants ministers were dismissed, being replaced by sympathizers of the Brissotins, and in April 1792 war was declared on Austria.

The Revolution gathers momentum

The immediate effects showed how misleading had been the easy optimism of the Brissotins. The French forces were desperately short of officers, more than sixty percent of whom had abandoned their commissions, and of trained men, equipment and supplies. They broke and ran at the first contact with the Prussian and Austrian forces. Only the excessive caution of the aged Prussian commander, the Duke of Brunswick, hindered a swift advance to Paris by the Prussians and Austrians.

Popular fear and anger over the military danger was exacerbated by an economic

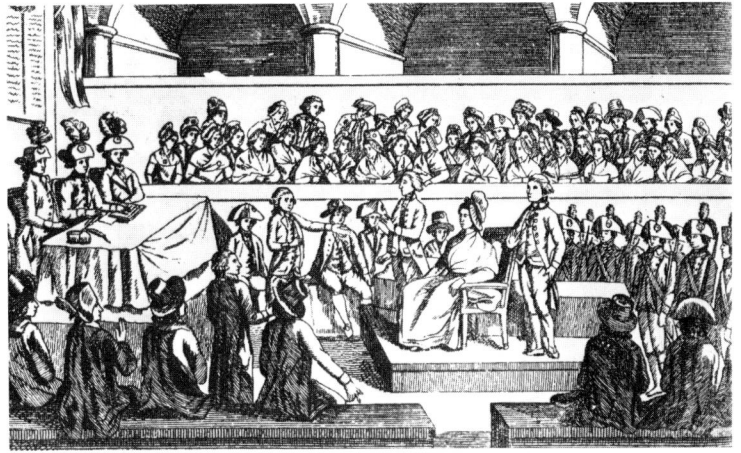

Above, the execution of Marie Antoinette on 16 October 1793.

Top, Marie Antoinette facing her accusers in October 1793. Found guilty of treason for secretly encouraging the Austrian invasion, she was executed the following day, 16 October.

Top left, a 400 livres note of 1792, decorated with the name of the Republic and its symbol, the Jacobin cap.

Centre left, the massacre of the nobility in Paris in September 1792 and of other people arrested on suspicion of sympathy with the Austrian invaders.

Left and far left, royalist prisoners and women killed during the days of early September 1792, when a great wave of fear swept France that the revolution was being betrayed, by an alliance of royalists and Austrians.

Opposite top, the idyllic and pastoral ancien régime contrasted with the violent and militaristic revolutionary age, in two counter-revolutionary satirical prints.

Opposite bottom, the fatherland in danger in July 1792; the readiness of the Austrians to interfere on behalf of the king encouraged the revolutionaries to execute him after the Austrian defeat in September.

people had killed constitutional monarchy and the Brissotins were compelled to recognize this. They suspended Louis, set up a provisional executive council including the non-Brissotin but highly popular Danton and arranged elections for a National Convention to draft a new constitution.

All this took place against a background of crisis abroad and at home. Longwy (22 August) and Verdun (2 September) fell to the Duke of Brunswick; Lafayette went over to the enemy. The road to the capital was open. On 2 September the Commune issued a panic-stricken call: 'To arms! The enemy is at the gate!' Between 2 and 10 September some 1,400 priests and prisoners were killed.

It was no time for political reflection. Indeed, there were few voters in the election for the Convention. Many were excluded by law, and some excluded themselves out of fear. It is probable that this Convention represented the will of only some seven out of a hundred of the population as a whole.

The Convention

The first months of the new assembly were marked by a fierce struggle for power among the revolutionary politicians. Two small active factions fought to command the support of the majority of deputies, the 'Plain', who were concerned to hold the ground gained by the Revolution but were

not committed to any particular political group. The first of the active factions were the Brissotins, more generally known at this stage as the Girondins. They were at first the dominant group, controlling the executive committee and holding the majority in the Convention. Their old 'right-wing' antagonists of the Legislative Assembly, the constitutional monarchists, had gone from the scene, but they were themselves attacked by the small radical group known, from the high seats which they occupied in the Convention, as the 'Mountain'. Their main spokesmen were Robespierre, Marat, Billaud-Varennes and, later, Danton.

It is not easy to see sharp contrasts of political or social principle between these two contending groups. Socially, both were the same kind of substantial middle-class deputy who bulked as large in the Convention as in its predecessors: lawyers and office-holders, doctors, businessmen and merchants. Both were strong believers in the rights of private property and subscribed to enlightened notions of economic liberalism and laissez-faire. Politically they were republican and agreed, as the first act of the Convention, to the abolition of the monarchy, the declaration of a Republic and the

dating of a new era from this, 'Year I'. Both were also determined to save the Revolution and carry out the war energetically. Their leaders belonged to the Jacobin Society, though the Mountain retained the name, while Brissot's group became known as the Girondins. The main differences lay in their attitudes towards the popular movement in Paris and the suspicions that they had of one another.

The *Sans-Culottes*

The Parisian movement was an important element in the power balance at this stage. It had actually shown its strength in the summer and remained influential in the Commune and active in the sections. The *sans-culottes*, the backbone of the popular movement, were not the dregs of Paris; they comprised the small masters and their journeymen, small shopkeepers and tradesmen and clerks and wage-earners. They were not a proletariat, indeed they were not a well-defined social or economic group at all. They consisted mainly of poor people who suffered when prices rose and food was in short supply. As a result, they demanded economic controls of prices and supplies

and the punishment of hoarders and profiteers. They were credulous and excitable, susceptible to rumours of plots and treason and were informed by popular journals like Marat's *Ami du peuple* or Hébert's *Père Duchesne*. They were exploited, but they were not a passive instrument. Above all, the *sans-culottes* were zealous patriots, republicans and revolutionaries, although they had a rough and ready common man's attitude to democracy compared with the more sophisticated approach of the better educated but often just as zealous middle-class representative. They showed a positive pride in *sans culottisme* as against the knee-breeches of the more refined classes and also favoured the more democratic usages like 'citizen'. They were suspicious of wealth, elegance and fine gentlemen and even maintained that the Convention only contained 'fine talkers who eat well'. The poor people practised a kind of direct democracy in their sectional assemblies and felt strongly about their rights as the 'sovereign people' to control their representatives, to make their wishes known in a forceful way and to 'insurrect' if need be. They had oversimplified views, looked for traitors when things went wrong and demanded quick solutions.

Left, Jean Paul Marat (1743–93), the scientist and revolutionary who helped to arouse revolutionary feeling in the summer of 1792, and who supported the Jacobin cause against the Girondists until he was killed by a Girondist supporter, Charlotte Corday.

Opposite, the execution of Louis XVI by guillotine on 21 January 1793; earlier there had been hopes that the Revolution would preserve a constitutional monarchy, and this execution was widely regarded as the triumph of fanaticism over reason.

There was much in this of which no group in the Convention could really approve: their crude manner, the disrespect which they often showed for the dignity of the nation's elected representatives, their un-enlightened demands for economic controls, their indiscipline and disorder. But the Jacobins were realistic enough to appreciate that this was a power to be reckoned with, a force which could aid the revolution as well as promote the Jacobin cause. Some, like Robespierre and Marat, may have had a genuine sympathy with many of their notions, but all were ready, in an emergency, to submit to the demands of the *sans-culottes* for some of the time, whatever their reluctance and reservations. And as the leading Jacobins were deputies for Paris, they were readier to excuse the conduct of their constituents and able to maintain contacts with the movement.

The Gironde on the other hand were more hostile and less flexible in their attitude since they were alarmed at these popular manifestations, which were already out of control by the summer. Their distaste was enhanced since the Jacobins, their rivals for power, were associated with them. Their electoral background reinforced this for, as deputies from the moderate provinces, they obviously had an interest in resisting the pretensions of Paris to dominate the revo-lution and in opposing a movement which posed a threat to order and property.

The struggle between the two factions was bitter. Charges and counter-charges over the activities of the previous summer, the behaviour of the Commune and the September massacres served the purposes of each group which strove, by every possible method, to discredit the other side. The Girondins denounced the Jacobins for trying to establish a dictatorship of Paris over the rest of France. The Jacobins interpreted Girondin references to the rights of the other eighty-two departments as a federalist scheme to disrupt the unity of the republic and their attacks on the popular movement as evidence of their desire to save the benefits of the revolution for the wealthy.

On the question of the fate of the deposed king, the Jacobins took the popular line, insisting on his death; the Gironde, on the other hand, clung to more moderate elements and delayed and evaded. This merely incensed popular suspicions, especially when the discovery of Louis' correspondence with the Austrians left no doubt of his treason. Indecisive and divided the Girondins lost, the Convention voted for death, and on 21 January 1793 Louis XVI went to the guillotine.

The enemy at the gates

The perpetual wrangling produced disorder and confusion in the assembly, but there was one consolation: the war was going well. It was because of this success, especially after halting the enemy advance at Valmy in September, that the Gironde managed to maintain a majority in the Convention. In the same month, French armies occupied Savoy and Nice, and in October French forces crossed the Rhine and took Frankfurt. In the following month, Dumouriez, the Girondins' favourite general, defeated the Austrians at Jemappes and entered Brussels.

In November and December the exultant Convention issued a provocative challenge to the established order in Europe. They offered assistance to all people wishing to regain their freedom; order the abolition, in all territories occupied by the French, of tithes and feudal dues; stated that existing authorities were to be replaced by elective bodies and that royal properties should be confiscated. French officials were to work with them to arrange the support and supplies for the French forces.

In January 1793 Danton proclaimed the doctrine of natural frontiers: France should extend to the Alps, the Pyrenees and the Rhine and international agreements, scraps of paper signed by unrepresentative monarchies, should not stand in the way of the rights of the nation. In February the Convention welcomed Brissot's move to declare war on Britain and Holland and, in March, on Spain. Soon France was at war with almost all the powers of Europe—'all the tyrants of Europe' as Brissot put it, except Switzerland and Scandinavia.

From early 1793, however, the situation rapidly deteriorated and a new crisis even more alarming than that of the previous summer developed. Dumouriez, far from pressing on to invade Holland, was defeated at Neerwinden. Worse still, blaming the politicians for his defeat, he tried to march his armies against Paris and, unsuccessful in this, deserted to the enemy along with most of his staff. The Austrian forces pushed over the border on to French territory and behind them came the *émigrés*. Further south, other French armies were forced back from the Rhine. At the same time civil war broke out in France itself. A move by the Convention to raise a levy of 300,000 men met stubborn resistance in some regions, especially in the Vendée. Here the religious measures of 1791 had already created unrest and an attempt to conscript the peasantry brought on an open revolt which local nobles were quick to exploit. Not surprisingly the rebel armies, having employed to advantage the difficult terrain they knew so well, soon established control of this region.

News of defeat, treason, invasion and counter-revolution poured in on Paris where agitation exacerbated economic distress. Financing the war effort had promoted inflation; the *assignat* had fallen to about one third of its face value, and food prices had risen sharply from early in the year. Extremist agitators, like the radical priest Jacques Roux, gathered a large following as they voiced popular demands for controls on prices and currency, for requisitioning food supplies and for tough measures against hoarders and speculators. Jacobins as well as the Girondins disapproved of the activity of these *enragés* or wild men. They distrusted their influence over the *sans-culottes* and disliked their unenlightened

programme of economic controls, as well as their petitions, their deputations and demonstrations to put pressure on the assembly and the violence of their language, which showed little respect for politicians of any kind. But it was the Gironde, still the dominating element in the assembly, and the most outspoken in denouncing both the notion of economic controls and the activities of the *sans-culottes*, who were most blamed for the Assembly's indifference to the people's demands.

The Girondins became the target of more determined onslaughts as military setbacks added alarm to discontent. They were especially damaged by the defection of Dumouriez since he had been so closely associated with them. They seemed as reluctant to respond to popular demands for drastic measures in this emergency as to those for economic controls. True the Assembly did take steps in March which were to be of great importance. They strengthened the executive by establishing a Committee of Public Safety, set up a Revolutionary Tribunal and began to reassert central direction by sending deputies out on mission to the localities.

In all this it was the Jacobins who took the initiative, especially Danton. The Girondins aired dislike of a strong executive, the more so since it was being pressed by popular demands and advocated by the Jacobins. The latter openly aligned themselves with the *sans-culottes* and not only intensified their longstanding criticism of the Girondins but also declared that the Revolution could only be saved with the help of the people. In May, they championed the popular economic demands about which they had been silent before. At the same time the sections denounced the Girondins as hindrances to the determined action needed to save the Revolution and demanded that the Assembly should purge these guilty men. By May, three-quarters of the sections had submitted such demands and threatened to act themselves if the Convention refused. Another popular revolution was in the making.

Revolution and insurrection

The revolution took place between the 31 May and the 2 June. The Girondins, desperate because of constant criticism, took action which only confirmed popular distrust and hurried on the insurrection. They tried unsuccessfully to have Marat condemned by the Revolutionary Tribunal, set up a Commission to enquire into the recent conduct of the section and arrested popular agitators like Hébert, whom they were later forced to release. The Girondins also talked of dissolving the Commune and summoning a new Assembly in the provinces. In short they appealed to their constituencies against Paris, threatening to annihilate the capital if the insurrections continued so that men would 'search the banks of the Seine for signs of the city'.

The effect of all this heightened popular fury and hurried on popular insurrection. At the end of May, delegates from the sections set up a central revolutionary committee which directed operations from 3 May. On 2 June, the Assembly was surrounded by *sans-culottes* and national guards: 'We have come to demand, for the last time, justice on the guilty.' The deputies, prevented even from leaving the Assembly, had to submit to this force and accept a Jacobin motion to expel about thirty of the leading members of the Girondins.

The expulsion of the Gironde, followed as it was by the departure of many alarmed deputies, gave the Jacobins control of the Convention. However, they were in a desperate situation, for the threat of foreign invasion was mounting. The Austrians from the north and the Prussians from the Rhine continued their advances and took three major fortresses in Italy. In the south, Spanish forces crossed the Pyrenean frontier and in the southeast the Piedmontese pushed back in Savoy.

Within France the rebellion of the Vendée was still dominant in the west and seemed likely to move against Paris. To this was now added a widespread outburst of protest from the provinces against the events of 2 June. Over sixty of the eighty-three departments denounced the highhandedness of the Parisians who presumed to interfere with the elected representatives of the nation.

Important cities like Bordeaux, Lyons, Marseilles and Toulouse went beyond protest, turning out local Jacobins and encouraging armed resistance. This stimulated forces elsewhere hostile to the revolution to emerge. In Toulon a royalist faction secured control and handed over the port, along with a large part of the French fleet, to the British. In Paris, the popular hero Marat was assassinated in July by the Girondin sympathizer Charlotte Corday. In these circumstances moderates no less than Jacobins felt that only resolute and ruthless action would serve.

At the same time the Jacobins were under constant pressure from below, from the *sans-culottes* who had put them in power. The Jacobins had promptly drafted a democratic constitution in June which along with universal suffrage, direct elections and the referendum recognized society's obligation to provide work for the able-bodied, relief for the needy and education for all. But this, though promising, was not to be implemented immediately.

With the news of defeats and betrayals, mounting inflation and disrupted food supplies popular tension grew. Throughout July and August, the assembly was bombarded with requests from the sections for effective legislation on prices, for stiffer laws against aristocrats and hoarders and for severe punishments against offenders.

The clamour reached a peak early in September with large-scale demonstrations and a mass march on the Assembly. The Jacobins, apart from any special sympathy for a more 'popular' revolution, recognized their crucial importance. These demonstrations represented a danger in that they might, in an excess of furious impatience, sweep away the whole Convention, Jacobins and all; but they also represented, despite their drawbacks, the most zealous forces which the revolution possessed at this desperate time. It was only in order to keep their support that the Convention introduced price controls on food and a wide range of consumer goods, levied a forced loan on the rich and sanctioned the establishment of 'revolutionary armies' to forage for food. The demonstrators also wanted strict laws against suspects and hoarders of food and revolutionary justice meted out against offenders. Now, under the twin pressures of

Above, the murder of Marat in his bath by the aristocratically-born Charlotte Corday in July 1793. She was later guillotined.

Top, the massacre of some 6,000 citizens of Lyons in December 1793 after a brief counter-revolutionary rising, which had required a two-month siege to break. The city was then deprived of its name, being known as Ville-sans-nom.

Opposite, Georges Jacques Danton (1759–94), an early advocate of the French Revolutionary Wars and radical opponent of the monarchy; he later criticized Robespierre for his dictatorship, was tried for conspiracy and executed. Musée Carnavalet, Paris.

A View in Perspective.

The Zenith of French Glory; — The Pinnacle of Liberty.

which, month after month, returned the same twelve Jacobins to the Committee, and debate dwindled.

In earlier regimes the assemblies had been the centres of activity, where the main struggles had been fought out in long verbal battles. Ministers had been shadows. Now that the executive committee was the centre of the real work, the Assembly had to listen to the Convention's explanations and pass the decrees they required. The committee wielded enormous powers over the whole field of domestic and foreign policy, though police matters were left to another body, the Committee of General Security. Earlier ideals of decentralization likewise were abandoned as the Committee steadily strengthened the central government's grip over all local institutions.

In December the respresentatives on mission, hitherto vested with wide powers to eliminate trouble makers, were brought directly under the Committee, their authority limited to carrying out the Committee's policies. The local institutions and departments were bypassed, the smaller cantons and communes made the big units. In each of them the central government appointed national agents who were supposed to report to the government every ten days. The Paris commune had its powers restricted. The 'revolutionary' armies of sans-culottes, invaluable in the summer, were disbanded, the committees of the sections put under central government and their leading officials paid or transformed from popular spokesmen to government agents. And along with executive power went ruthlessness. In September 'Terror' became the rule as the processes of revolutionary justice were made more swift and summary and the instruments—revolutionary tribunals and committees—used more fiercely.

The Committee of Public Safety

The direction and the driving force of revolutionary government came from the Committee of Public Safety, the twelve-man team which, with very few changes, ruled France for twelve crucial months. All deputies and Jacobins, they were mainly men of that provincial urban professional middle class which played the major role in all the revolutionary assemblies. Hérault de Sechelles, the chief architect of the Jacobin constitution of 1793, was an exception; he was a former aristocrat and parlementaire. Lazare Carnot, mainly responsible for the organization of the armies of the revolution, was a former captain of engineers; Claude Prieur de la Côte d'Or, another military engineer, worked closely with Carnot.

Robert Lindet, a lawyer from Normandy, had the special task of supervising supplies and provisions and was assisted by Pierre Louis Prieur de la Morne. Jeanbon Saint-André, a Protestant clergyman and once

a national emergency and popular clamour, a new kind of revolutionary government began to take shape and each successive stage was to bring about a new alignment of forces.

The climax of the Revolution

The twelve months from July 1793 to July 1794 saw the Revolution at its most dramatic. Under the rule of Robespierre and the Jacobins it reached its peak of effective government in the Committee of Public Safety, of ruthlessness in the Reign of Terror and of radicalism in the alliance of Jacobins and sans-culottes.

In these circumstances the Jacobin leaders recognized that only the most resolute and ruthless action would be effective. Besides, they had no intention of putting their new democratic constitution into operation; it was for show and for the future, not for immediate use. Its suspension was made official in early October when the Convention decided that the government was to be revolutionary, that is of an emergency character, until the coming of peace.

The main instruments of revolutionary government were already in existence from the spring; the executive committees of Public Safety and General Security and the Revolutionary Tribunals and Committees. What the Jacobins did was to wield them with a new determination and ability. The Convention remained legislative authority and appointed the main Executive Committee of Public Safety by monthly election. But previous notions of a weak executive and the separation of powers were dismissed, for the Jacobins dominated the Convention

a sea captain, now concerned himself primarily with reshaping the navy. Bertrand Barère from Toulouse, another lawyer, acted as a kind of public relations man for the Committee, expounding and defending its policies in the Convention. Billaud-Varennes, who had been many things in his time, including both a pamphleteer and a teacher, and Collot d'Herbois, actor and playwright, were both extremists with a strong influence in the Commune and the sections. Both were appointed after the extremist agitations of early September, probably to reassure the popular forces and to strengthen the Committee's connections in that important region.

Georges Couthon, a crippled lawyer from the Auvergne, and Antoine Saint-Just, a twenty-five-year-old law graduate, both spent much time on special missions. Couthon, a gentler man than some of his speeches suggested, and Saint-Just, cold and arrogant, were also the close associates and admirers of the dominant figure of the Committee, Maximilien Robespierre.

It was Robespierre, the lawyer from Arras, who came to seem the embodiment of the revolutionary government. He was in his early thirties, a small man, not much over five feet, with a thin, pale face and a harsh voice. He was always neatly dressed, fastidious in his tastes and reserved and withdrawn in manner. A bachelor, he lived in modest lodgings, indulged in little social life and had few friends. He was no demagogue and could hardly have looked less like a *sans-culotte*, but he inspired popular trust because of his incorruptibility.

By his adherence to principles and his constant praise of the common man, he had established a reputation as a zealous revolutionary, a formidable parliamentarian and a popular hero. Likewise his criticism of the constitution in 1791, his opposition to Brissot in the Jacobin Club in 1792, and his championship of the Mountain and the popular cause in the Convention had all kept him prominently in the public eye. Despite this, he had no official supremacy in the Committee, nor was he its dictator. The people in the Committee worked harmoniously as a body and met daily, from early morning till late at night. All those who were in Paris came along and took part in discussions, and if they agreed on the policies signed the documents. Dissenters abstained. They were determined men, set on saving the republic from counter-revolution at home and outside enemies, and all were ready and responsible for whatever measures were needed to achieve this end.

It was here, in the Committee and the Convention, that Robespierre had a stronger influence than any other politician. On the Committee he assumed no special 'department' and never went on any mission to visit the armies or the provinces. He was thus constantly on the spot, assiduous in Committee attendance and free to brood over general policies and to make speeches in which he discoursed on the principles and character of the true Republic. He was the Committee's most conspicuous spokesman in the Assembly and the Jacobin Club, and his integrity and dedication were never in doubt: 'He will go far', Mirabeau had prophesied, 'he believes what he says.'

The Terror

The new regime showed its resolution in its vigorous onslaughts against the counter-revolutionary forces within France. Its

Above, a revolutionary poster, proclaiming liberty, equality and fraternity and demonstrating the unity of interest between the people and the army. The Jacobins, whose symbol was the cockade cap, insisted on the need for radical reform and the efficacy of naked power.

Opposite, an English satire on the excesses of the French Revolution, suggesting that the fine rhetoric of the politicians meant little more than a violent attack on the Church. English support for the early days of the Revolution soon evaporated.

great weapon was terror, the use of fierce intimidation to destroy or deter the republic's foes and reassure its supporters. Hitherto terrorism had flared sporadically in the shape of lynch law, as in the prison massacres of 1792. From September 1793, when the Convention had decreed that 'terror was the order of the day', it became official government policy. There should be no restraint, said Saint-Just, for 'between the people and its enemies there is only the sword'. In the same month the Law of Suspects decreed the immediate arrest of all persons suspected of disloyalty, a crime it defined in broad and vague terms, and the Revolutionary Tribunal was reorganized to deal more effectively with the increasing number of those accused of treachery.

Under the terror about 40,000 people were executed and many times that number imprisoned. It was concerned with disloyalty wherever found, not with social class, and the victims came from all walks of life. About ten percent of them were nobles, six percent clergy, fifteen percent middle class and the great majority poorer classes and peasantry. Some were executed under the economic laws against hoarding and speculation, but the majority suffered for broadly political reasons, armed rebellions, voting against recruitment or advocating counter-revolutionary opinions.

The weight of the new regime also made itself felt in those districts which had risen in rebellion. Throughout the autumn Government armies steadily reduced the rebel centres. Marseilles surrendered in August, Bordeaux and Lyons in October, and Toulon was recaptured in December after an artillery bombardment from an 'officer of outstanding merit', the young Napoleon Bonaparte. In the Vendée, insurrection continued to smoulder for years, but

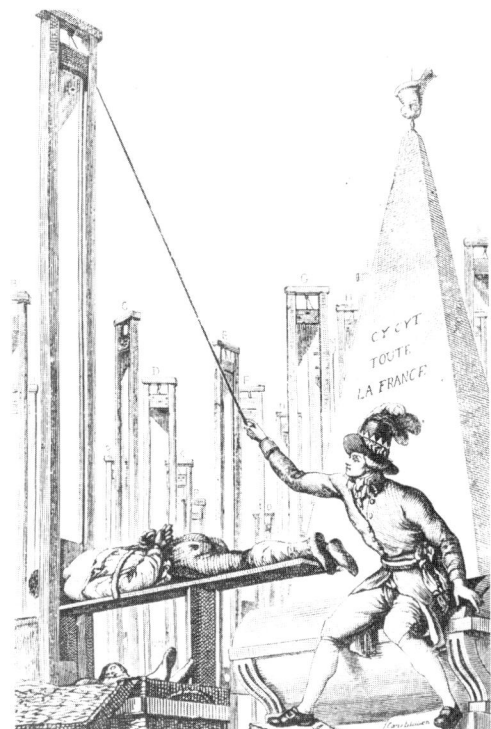

TRIBUN REVOLUTIONNA DELION

Above, a revolutionary tribunal, which was empowered to meet counter-revolutionary activity with a sentence of death in 1793 and 1794.

Top, one of the Revolutionary tribunals during the Reign of Terror.

Top left, Robespierre executing even the executioner; during the reign of terror of April 1793 to July 1794, more than 1,300 people were guillotined.

Left, the execution of Brissot and the other leading Girondists in October 1793, whose support of the interests of the provinces against those of Paris led to opposition from the mob and from the Jacobins.

Opposite top, Bonaparte attacking the royalist insurrectionaries at Quiberon in July 1795.

Opposite bottom, Maximilien Robespierre (1758–94), the autocratic ruler of France from July 1793 for about a year. Basing his actions on a rigorous radicalism and morality, he won the odium of the people for his ruthless use of the guillotine in putting down his opponents; he died the same way, in July 1794.

the main rebel armies were scattered in October and December by experienced republican troops. Behind the armies came the deputies on mission to punish the rebels. In Lyons the guillotine did not work fast enough for Collot d'Herbois; he called in firing squads to its aid, and then cannon. The victims were herded in batches, mowed down by cannon fire and shovelled into graves. The houses of the wealthy were destroyed and the name of Lyons struck off the map: 'Lyons made war on liberty, Lyons no longer exists.' At Toulon, Barras and Fréron used firing squads for mass executions: 'Every day since our entry, 200

Toulonnais have been shot.' In the Vendée, Carrier executed Republican vengeance by drowning 2,000 rebels in the Loire, and having another 3,000 shot. Jacobins on the local revolutionary committees throughout France acted as agents, unearthing and denouncing suspects.

Throughout these same months when they were suppressing the internal enemies of the Republic, the Jacobins also had to conduct the war against invading armies on several fronts. Their achievement was astonishing and novel, a great drive to mobilize the nation's manpower and re-sources for the war effort. 'The Republic',

declared the Convention in August, 'is a great city in a state of siege: France must become one vast camp.' It proclaimed a *levée en masse* (mass mobilization); young men would go to the front, married men see to weapons and food and women make clothing and do hospital work. In fact the first age groups recruited, eighteen to twenty-five, produced barely half a million recruits.

To feed and equip new forces on this scale, the government had to play a bigger role in directing the economy. Under Lindet, a central food commission saw to the supply and distribution of food according to the needs of the armies and the regions of the country. Under Claude Prieur the munitions industry was directly controlled by the government. State factories were established, buildings commandeered, labour and materials requisitioned. Carnot speedily fashioned a new army and each unit of raw

men was seasoned with a few veterans. New tactics were introduced to make the most of their advantages of great numbers and high zeal. New young generals were promoted, and celebrated names made their appearance—Jourdan, Hoche, Pichegru, Bonaparte. By early 1794 France had a million men under arms and a dozen armies in the field. The Austrian advance from the north had been checked at Wattignies, the Spaniards driven back over their frontier, the Piedmontese pushed out of Savoy and the Prussians thrown back across the Rhine.

By the spring of 1794 the national emergency was receding, but the regime became more dictatorial, not less. Terror, instituted as a weapon against the counterrevolutionary enemies of the republic, was now wielded against the revolutionary critics of the government. Prominent among these were the left-wing extremists, linked

with the popular agitator, Jacques Hébert, who ran a notorious journal, the *Père Duchesne* and was influential in the commune, sections and popular societies of Paris. For the Hébertistes the revolution was still not popular enough. They wanted more measures to ease the social and economic hardships of the *sans-culottes* and more ruthless repression of those who exploited them. Even though inflation had been checked, prices remained high, wages were never high enough and controls never a complete success. They championed more direct action by the people, more scope for popular bodies to terrorize their enemies and more power for the people's revolutionary armies.

The Committee's response to this was increasingly cold. The Jacobins were more radical than other middle-class politicians, had more sympathy with the popular movement and were ready to make concessions.

They had introduced economic controls, abolished without compensation the remnants of seigneurial rights, made land purchase easier and furthered schemes for free education. Robespierre and Saint-Just had sponsored a large scheme for distributing the property of suspects among needy patriots, but they would not champion the interests of the *sans-culottes* exclusively, still less allow the control of the revolution to pass into their hands.

The Jacobins

The Jacobins' economic ideals were basically different from the *sans-culottes*: they envisaged a free enterprise economy, not one which, like that of the old regime, was choked with controls and restrictions. They were ready to introduce some controls, but these were merely temporary measures to meet the exigencies of a siege economy and the exceptional demands of a wartime emergency. They did not represent, as the *sans-culottes* were reminded, a desire to champion the exclusive interests of a particular class, by the fact that wages and prices were to be contained and labour strictly disciplined. Again the extremist campaigns were alarming and alienating the middle classes, and Jacobism needed to hold the support of these as well as of the *sans-culottes*.

Jacobins preferred to stress the unifying aspects not the divisive ones of class. For them the touchstone was the quality of man's patriotism and republicanism rather than his occupation or income. They had a suspicion of great wealth and a preference for the modest property-owner, but they did not intend any large redistribution of property, since this to them, as to the men of 1789, was an inviolable right. The Jacobins' dislike was directed mostly at the bad Republican rather than at the prosperous property owner. Moreover, the Jacobins now saw the scene from the point of view of a government. Popular pressure against earlier regimes, which the Jacobins had denounced as incompetent, selfish and reactionary was praiseworthy; against their own regime which was effective, enlightened and looked with wisdom to the best interests of all Frenchmen, it was unnecessary and undesirable. Democracy, explained Robespierre, did not mean that all the people in a vast gathering could participate directly in decisions or that a myriad of small discontented groups could blithely pursue their own fancies regardless of the rest. It meant that they returned delegates to an assembly which made decisions on their behalf; and, in practice, the revolutionary government's advance towards ever more centralized control was running quite counter to that more direct democracy in which the *sans-culottes* indulged. The independent activities of the sections, of 'revolutionary armies' and of unofficial terrorism, became objects of disapproval to an authoritarian regime which desired prompt obedience and no rivals. It was ironic; no one had clamoured more loudly for, or done more to help to install, an effective government than the *sans-culottes*, but effective government meant a curb on *sans-culotte* freedom.

The Hébertiste movement was all the more unwelcome for adding to its usual activities a new campaign for dechristianization. The Jacobins generally, it is true, had little regard for traditional religion; they were enlightened rationalists and staunch anti-clericals. The Convention had readily adopted in October 1793 a new Republican calendar, with natural names for the months and a ten-day week: this broke the religious pattern of the year, obliterating Sundays, Saints' days and religious holidays. But unofficially the movement went further. In Paris, promoted by Hébert and the Commune, it spread into attacks on the clergy, compelling them to resign. Churches were plundered, ceremonies prohibited and statues destroyed. Mock processions aped those of the despised religion. The Commune closed down the churches or used them for secular celebrations, and busts of Voltaire and Rousseau were set up in place of statues of the saints.

The government feared this 'religious terror' would only upset much of their support and give counter-revolutionaries further arguments for discarding the revolution. In November 1793 the Feast of Reason was celebrated in Notre Dame with Reason represented by a woman of the streets, wearing a cap of liberty.

Robespierre in particular disliked it since he believed in God and insisted that there was an important place in the revolution for religion. He deplored impiety with the strongest epithet a revolutionary could use:

Above, the adoration of the goddess of Reason, in the form of an actress, in the nave of the cathedral of Notre Dame; this atheistic religion was opposed by Robespierre, who had its founder, Jacques Hébert, executed.

Opposite top, the siege of Toulon in 1793, after the royalists had given the city up to the English. The siege was notable for the part played by the young Napoleon Bonaparte in recapturing the city.

Opposite bottom left, the bombardment of Lyon by the Republicans in October 1793; at this stage royalist groups had won control of large areas of south and west France, and severe repression was needed to restore republican authority to these regions.

Opposite bottom right, the festival of the regeneration of nature, in August 1793. After the abolition of Christianity by the Revolution, several alternative religions were established, including the cult of Reason, set up by Hébert, and the cult of the Supreme Being, instituted by Robespierre.

'Atheism is aristocratic!' This proved to be an additional source of confusion at a time when the enemy was moving steadily nearer.

The downfall of Robespierre

To halt the drift towards atheism and social disruption a deistic religion was devised—the cult of the Supreme Being. But there were other dangers, for the Hébertistes by their speculation had emptied the Treasury and weakened the state. Desmoulins in *Le Vieux Cordelier* mounted a counter-attack on them not only for their atheism but also for their treachery. Moreover, the Committee of Public Safety was now afraid that it would lose power to the Commune and to the Cordeliers Club which the Hébertistes dominated. Danton for his part wanted the machine of Terror dismantled, the end of controls and a negotiated peace. When in March, therefore, the Hébertistes threatened an insurrection on the model of that of June or September 1793, Robespierre and Danton arranged for their arrest and execution. Six days later Danton, Desmoulins and Hérault went to the guillotine (April 1794) on a charge of conspiracy with foreign financiers. It was an easy action to perform, but it was also significant, for this was the Terror at its height, the summit of Robespierre's dominance. It was to last for just three and a half months.

The Thermidorians

On 22 Prairial (10 June 1794) Robespierre persuaded the Convention to pass a law which deprived prisoners of the aid of defending counsel and made death the sole punishment. He also sought to control wages in a desperate effort to control the economy. Yet the need for such terror and discipline began to seem more and more unnecessary as foreign armies retreated and France's frontiers seemed secure. In May Pichegru beat the Austrians, in June Jourdan routed Coburg at Fleurus, the British fell back into Holland and the Austrians to the Rhine. There was a growing fear of Robespierre and a bitter hatred of his parade of civic virtue and his pride in his own incorruptibility. The cult of the Supreme Being was as unpopular as the cult of Reason, and the great procession in his honour from the Tuileries to the Champ de Mars, organized by the painter David on 8 June, alienated many.

The climax approached when Robespierre recalled many representatives on mission who now began to fear for their lives. However, the real break occurred on 8th Thermidor (26 July 1794) when he rashly spoke in the Convention of defending himself by one last act, namely the removal of a group of enemies whom he did not specify by name. The next day he was shouted down and arrested. He went to the guillotine on 10 Thermidor (28 July); eighty-seven members of the Commune soon followed him.

It is wrong to describe the Thermidorian reaction as the end of the Revolution, but it was certainly its climax. Barère and Barras assumed that the government would continue intact, for 10 Thermidor was for them but a 'partial commotion'. Within a month, however, the apparatus of the Terror was abandoned; the law of 22 Prairial was repealed; within six months the regulation of wages and prices was scrapped; within nine months the surviving Girondins returned; within a year Barère himself and his colleagues were on their way to Devil's Island. The Thermidorians when joined by the released Girondins and a few royalists emerged as a 'republic of proprietors', led by Barras and Fréron, Cambon and Siéyès. They said that they sought a return to 'the principles of 1789' but swept along by the tide, the Jacobins were hunted down and the Jacobin Club closed. A new terror, but of a different political complexion, had been unleashed. However, press and theatre were free again; and in the salons the style was set by Thérésa Tallien and the widow Josephine Beauharnais. However, as prices rose, so did unemployment, and in March and May 1795 popular insurrections erupted, with demands for the re-enactment of the Law of the Maximum and the 1793 Constitution—'Bread and the Constitution of 1793'. For a moment the

Above, the army of the Prince of Condé (1736–1818), made up of French counter-revolutionary activists; the army fought for the Austrians until 1797 when Condé joined the Russians. It was dissolved in 1801.

Top, the closing of the Jacobin club in July 1794, as a result of hostility to the severity of the Reign of Terror.

Opposite top, the Battle of Fleurus in southern Belgium, where the Austrians were decisively defeated by the revolutionary armies. It was the first battle in which balloons were used for reconnaissance. Musée de l'Armée, Paris.

Opposite bottom, the arrest of Robespierre in July 1794 by members of the Committee of General Safety; in the struggle he tried to shoot himself and was wounded in the jaw. He was guillotined shortly afterwards.

Date	Internal history	Foreign policy	Events in Europe	Date	Internal history	Foreign policy	Events in Europe
1789	Meeting of the Estates-General (5 May) Oath of the Tennis Court (20 June) Storming of the Bastille (14 July) Abolition of privileges (3–4 August) Declaration of the Rights of Man (26 August)		Act of Union in Sweden Revolt of Austrian Netherlands Establishment of Belgian Republic	1792	Storming of the Tuileries (10 August) September Massacres (2–5 September) First session of the Convention (20 September) Abolition of the monarchy (21 September) Trial of the king (11 December)	War with Austria (20 April) The Brunswick Manifesto (25 July) Battle of Valmy (20 September) Battle of Jémappes (6 November) Conquest of Belgium	Treaty of Berlin between Austria and Prussia Accession of Francis II of Austria Assassination of Gustavus II of Sweden End of Russo-Turkish War
1790	Civil Constitution of the Clergy Priests required to swear allegiance to the Civil Constitution	Repudiation of the Family Compact	Austrian forces overthrow Belgian Republic Pope condemns Civil Constitution of Clergy End of Russo-Swedish War Accession of Leopold II of Austria	1793	Execution of the King (21 January) Rising in La Vendée Committee of Public Safety Constitution of the Year I	Annexation of Nice (31 January) War with Britain (1 February) Battle of Wattignies (16 October) Bonaparte recaptures Toulon from British (19 December)	Formation of First Coalition against France Meeting of Polish Diet Second Partition of Poland
1791	Flight of the king Constitution approved by Constituent Assembly and ratified by the king Legislative Assembly meets	Ultimatum to the Elector of Trier Avignon annexed to France	Austria and Turkey sign treaty of peace Declaration of Pillnitz Turkey defeated by Russia				

'Furies of the Guillotine' reappeared. These were ruthlessly suppressed, and in June 1795 the Parisian *sans-culottes* finally ceased to be a major factor in Revolutionary politics. What Generals Pichegru, in April, and Menou, in May, did to the mob in the *faubourgs* of Paris, General Napoleon Bonaparte with a 'whiff of grapeshot' did to the Parisian Royalists when they rose in October. Significantly the *sans-culottes* did not rise with them, for they were finished politically and the Revolution now became safe for the men of property.

Dominated by the Thermidorians, the Convention completed a new Constitution, the Constitution of the Year III, in August 1795. It was designed for the propertied classes and was largely the work of Boissy D'Anglas. A single-chamber assembly was now seen to be dangerous so the Legislature was now to consist of two houses—a Council of Five Hundred aged thirty or over which was to initiate legislation and a Council of Ancients numbering 250 who had to be over forty and married, presumably because this made them more responsible, which had the right to veto. Executive authority was vested in five Directors elected by the legislative councils—each holding office for five years. They could neither sit in the Councils nor initiate laws, but they controlled the army and the police, the civil service and foreign affairs. The departments were left as they were, but each was controlled by a commissioner appointed by the Directory—a forerunner of Napoleon's prefect. The deputies were chosen by an elaborate system of indirect election, and property qualifications were needed for the primary and secondary assemblies. And though liberty of speech and of worship were spoken of as sacrosanct, the press was tightly curbed, and political clubs and the right of insurrection were forbidden. The attempt was clear: to create a balanced government in order to prevent the dictatorship of an assembly, a committee or of a single man. Its very rigidity proved to be its undoing.

Chapter 29

From Revolution to Empire

In retrospect, the Directory is inevitably seen as an interlude between the Revolution and the inevitable dictatorship. And the post-1799 Bonapartist press destroyed what little was left of its reputation. It saw itself, of course, quite differently, as the end of an ugly road. Although Barras was unscrupulous, immoral and lazy, the rest were men of some worth. Fearing dictatorship, of one man or of a mob, they set up a mixed government. Also, to guarantee continuity and stability and to prevent new waves of unrest from left to right, they stipulated that 500 of the 700 legislators must come from the Convention itself. Those who were re-elected were known as 'perpetuals' who saw themselves carrying on the Revolution against royalism, continuing the war and enforcing the October 1795 decrees against clergy and *émigrés*. Because they feared dictatorship, annual elections were prescribed, but these only served to guarantee unrest, dissension and disorder.

The new members were moderates who wanted an end to the war and a constitutional government. A few of them were monarchists; many more would have settled for limited constitutional government. Generals Menou and Pichegru made no secret of their royalism.

The Directory could perhaps have survived this political division. It could not survive economic chaos and corruption. There was wild inflation because the *mandats*, issued in April 1796 to replace the *assignats*, had soon fallen to one percent of their face value. The state was internally bankrupt by September 1797, and all classes suffered. The Directory was in part induced to continue the war not for frontier defence, but in order to draw the treasures of foreign countries into France. Thus Napoleon took 750,000 francs and part of his portrait gallery from the Duke of Modena, 21,000,000 francs from the kingdom of Naples and 20,000,000 francs and the promise of more from the pope. Had the war stopped, the French army of a quarter of a million men would have had to be paid from State funds, and these were totally inadequate. It lived on foreign grain and foreign gold.

To financial chaos was added corruption. Many of the supplies Paris required from

the provinces never arrived because of smuggling and inefficient administration. Bridges and roads fell into disrepair and the Paris mobs lived on doles. Bids for peace from Britain met a request from Barras for £500,000 before negotiations began; Talleyrand made a similar request in the XYZ affair when John Adams made overtures in 1798.

In this context, the Babeuf conspiracy is understandable. Ever since 1798 'Gracchus' Babeuf had advocated an agrarian law for the common sharing of goods. He was the first and perhaps the sole French Revolutionary socialist. In the winter of 1795–6 he planned to overthrow the Directory by force in a conspiracy joined by ex-Jacobins; his plan was based on a series of radiating groups and depended on the rising of the sans-culottes. Again, as in 1795, they failed

Above, the Battle of Aboukir, or the Battle of the Nile (August 1798), an important English victory in which Nelson destroyed the French fleet and virtually ended Napoleon's attempt to win control of the Middle East and to cut Britain off from India.

Top, Napoleon dismissing the Council of Five Hundred on 18 Brumaire (9 November 1799); by this act he overthrew the government of the Directory and set up the Consulate instead.

Opposite top, a meeting of the Directory in 1796, which was soon accused both of inactivity and of corruption.

Opposite bottom, the festival of the foundation of the republic celebrated on 22 September 1797; this re-enactment of Roman chariot races emphasizes how much the revolutionaries modelled themselves on the example of the Roman republicans.

311

to respond. A police spy reported the plot in May 1796 to Carnot and, as a result, Babeuf and some forty of his associates were either shot or guillotined. The same fate overtook the conspiracy of the royalist Abbé Brottier in January 1797. But Babouvisme was to live on in the writings of his friend, the Tuscan Philippe Buonarroti.

In the 1797 elections there came an influx of royalists into the Assembly and the great mass of 'perpetuals' was eliminated. Pichegru was elected President of the Five Hundred and Barbe-Marbois, another royalist, President of the Ancients. Measures were passed favouring priests and the relatives of *emigrés*, but in the Directory the two pro-royalists, Carnot and Barthélemy, were still outnumbered, and the Triumvirate, fearing a royalist coup, appealed to the generals to save the Revolution. Napoleon, who had swept through northern Italy in 1796 and was forcing its treasure back into France, had by the spring of 1797 driven the Austrians north from the Piave and Isonzo, when he responded to the call; so did Hoche at the head of the Army of the Sambre-et-Meuse. Augereau, Napoleon's lieutenant, marched on Paris; Barthélemy and Pichegru were arrested; the Councils were purged of over 200 deputies, and sixty-five were exiled to the 'dry guillotine' of Guiana. Carnot, the only lucky one, escaped to Switzerland. The date was 18 Fructidor (7 September). It was the first of the coups, and the beginning of the heavy indebtedness to Napoleon.

The rise of Napoleon

From now on, the Directory dominated over the Legislature and severe measures were taken against priests and returned *emigrés*. In the coup d'état of 22 Floreal (11 May 1798) the Directors annulled the elections of their opponents and nominated their own deputies. Blessed by good harvests, the price of grain fell for the first time in a decade. But in fact the Directory, despite a powerless legislature, faced a rising tide of unpopularity, because of religious persecution, the Law of Hostages which provided that relatives of *emigrés* might be seized as hostages and because of the maritime war with Britain which had forced up prices and kept tariffs high. The law of Conscription of September 1798 made all unmarried Frenchmen between twenty and twenty-five liable for service, but it was bitterly unwelcome and evaded. Added to this the French armies in 1799 met defeat at Stockach, Magnano and Novi.

Meanwhile, fortune favoured Napoleon. In 1797 he had formed the Ligurian Republic (Genoa) and the Cisalpine (Lombardy). At Campo Formio he obtained a guarantee from Austria of the Rhine as the boundary of France, thus securing Belgium and acquired a bridgehead at Mainz. Venice was given to Austria and in June 1797 a Venetian fleet in French service seized the Ionian

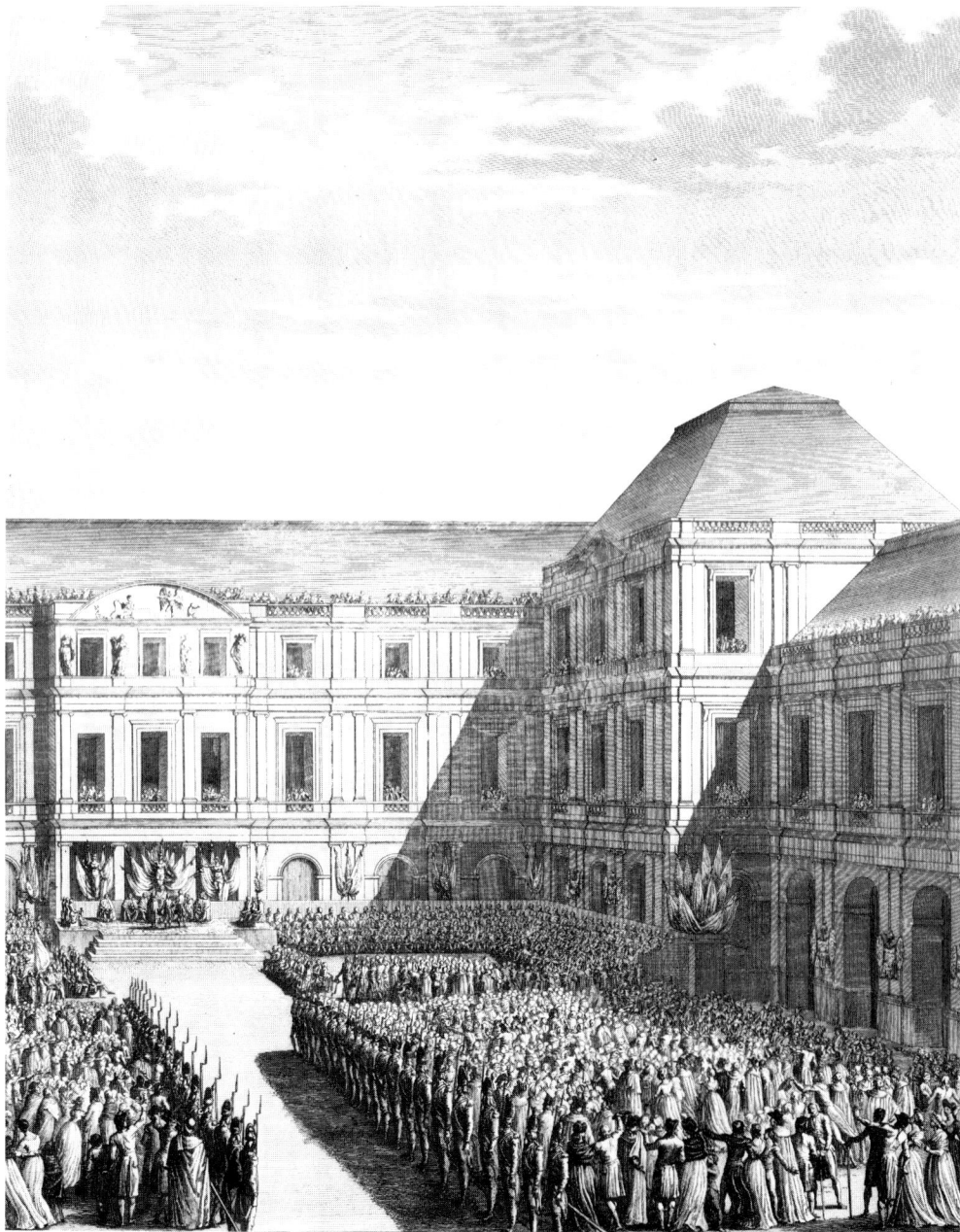

Islands and aroused Napoleon's eastern ambitions. With an invasion of Britain a very risky enterprise, and with his power rising dangerously, the Directory resolved to attack Britain through the east and saw the Ionian Islands as a base against Egypt. In May 1798 Bonaparte sailed from Toulon with 35,000 men, took Malta in June and landed at Alexandria in July.

This only further alarmed the Directory and to make matters worse the Belgian Provinces suddenly revolted. In the April 1799 elections, two-thirds of the government candidates were defeated and Siéyès replaced the senior director, Reubell. Siéyès wanted a new constitution and, with the support of Barras, he carried through a parliamentary coup, offering as justification the defeats on the frontiers and the rallying cry of *la patrie en danger*. The other three directors were persuaded to resign, and the new Director, Ducos, joined Siéyès and gave him the majority he sought. Siéyès was backed by a group who were to prove themselves in a distinct way perpetuals—Murat, Talleyrand and Fouché. Siéyès then looked for a general sympathetic to the cause of the Republic in danger. He approached Joubert, but was killed at Novi. As for Moreau and Bernadotte, they refused. At this juncture—when in fact the tide was turning on the French frontier, since in September Masséna had defeated Suvorov in Italy and the Duke of York was defeated in Holland—Napoleon landed at Fréjus. His campaign in the east had not been a success: he had been blocked by Sir Sidney Smith at Acre, and he had abandoned his troops on the Nile, who now saw him as a deserter. But his landing and his timing were providential, and he had about him the glamour of victory and a Jacobin past. He was, he liked to say, the

child of the Revolution. He was also to be its destroyer.

The Consulate

Napoleon's plans almost went awry. The Legislature was persuaded to meet at Saint-Cloud on the grounds that the Paris mob was unreliable. However, when Napoleon appeared in person, with his grenadiers massed outside, there were many protests about military dictatorship, and such was the poor impression that he made that he was shouted down. It was only his brother Lucien, presiding over the Five Hundred, who saved the day by summoning the troops to drive the legislators from the hall. A remnant of

Above, the return of Napoleon from Egypt in 1798; despite the defeat at the Battle of the Nile, the expedition had captured the imagination of the French in its bold strategic intentions.

Top, Napoleon's fleet capturing Malta in 1798 from the Knights Hospitallers, as a first step to establishing French superiority in the eastern Mediterranean.

Opposite top, the French armies taking works of art from Venice to Paris in 1797, before handing the city over to Austria.

Opposite bottom, the celebrations in Paris after the signing of the Treaty of Campo Formio in October 1797; its terms gave the Austrian Netherlands to France and conceded the French conquests in north Italy to Austria.

313

this body declared the Directory abolished and a provisional consulate of Ducos, Siéyès and Napoleon established, until such time as a new Constitution could be drawn up. It was the 18 Brumaire of the Year VIII (9 November 1799).

But Siéyès had made a mistake. He had expected Napoleon to select his senior officials along Washington's lines and to play the role of a president above politics. In fact Bonaparte made himself the First Consul and the power-house of the state. In December 1799 yet another Constitution appeared, the Constitution of the Year VIII. Siéyès and Ducos were persuaded to resign and were replaced by silent allies in Lebrun and Cambacérès. All three were to hold office for ten years and be re-eligible, but only the First Consul could appoint and dismiss officials and promulgate laws; the second and third had only a 'consultative voice'.

The Council of State was the key to the system. This constituted the group of experts and officials who prepared the laws and ran the government. It was the same with Napoleon as it had been with an earlier grand monarque: the Council was the inner bureaucracy, appointed, dependent, ultra-conscientious, loyal and efficient. It appointed prefects and mayors and through them Paris governed France; local government was bereft of its powers and died. In and around the Council were the lieutenants of the Master: Talleyrand, foreign minister (1799–1807), Berthier, war minister (1800–07) and Fouché, police minister (1799–1802 and 1804–10). No other institution matched the Council. The tribuneship could not initiate measures and was abolished in 1807 and the Legislative Body of 300 members had no powers of debate. It was true that the Senate of eighty members, all over forty and appointed for life, had powers to annul laws, but this power waned, and in the Year XII the Senate was nominated by Napoleon and no longer limited in number. In theory there was universal suffrage, but in fact the Senate nominated the members of the assemblies from a 'national list', itself chosen from 'departmental lists' and from communal lists in an elaborate system of indirect election.

The Press was tightly controlled, and education became a department of state. Even the salons were disciplined and Madame de Stael was banished from Paris. This was absolutism as naked, centralized and thorough as Louis XIV could have wished. He would have found it familiar and acceptable. The prefects were his *intendants* but more powerful, and they are still there. Napoleon was not only the child of the Revolution but also the heir to the best in the government of the Bourbons.

The *condottiere*

There is a curious anomaly about intense nationalism; it is apt to be felt most sharply on the perimeter of the nation. Thus Hitler, the great pan-German, was born across the frontier in Austria; Stalin, who was an autocrat of all the Russias in the line of the Tsars, was born in Georgia; and Napoleon, perhaps the greatest of all Frenchmen, was born French only by accident and raised on the fringes of France.

Perhaps the truest description of him was that he was neither truly a nationalist nor a revolutionary but that he was at heart a *condottiere* of genius, a leader of men. His methods were always more Italian than French, the leanings always Machiavellian. The advice he gave Eugene he followed himself: base your statecraft on dissimulation and strive only to be feared.

Napoleon Bonaparte was thirty on 18 Brumaire. He was born in 1769 in Ajaccio, Corsica, a year after Genoa had sold its stormy island to France. Only a few months before his birth, French troops had crushed the Corsican rebellion led by Pasquale Paoli. Bonaparte was the second son in a large family of the lesser nobility, and there were four brothers and three sisters, all dominated by their formidable mother, *née* Litizia Ramolino, Madame Mère. His father saw him from the outset as a man of genius: he was lean and pinched in appearance but with a piercing hawk-like gaze, great will-power and intensity. He went with a scholarship to the military school at Brienne and the École Militaire in Paris, and he went with a purpose: to free Corsica. He studied hard with this intent and was utterly out of tune with the rich sons of the nobility around him who had come there by easy roads and with no such design. He was commissioned a second lieutenant of artillery in 1785; and he read assiduously, not least Rousseau and the *philosophes*.

Like Caesar before him and like Hitler after him, the army was his ladder, his tool and his passion. He wrote a tract or two, but his weapon was the sword, not the pen. He exploited the Revolution and saw it as his cause and made it at once Corsican and French. In 1792 and 1793 he tried to seize Ajaccio for the Revolution, only to be defeated by Paoli fighting for Corsican independence and prepared to call on monarchists and anglophiles as allies. In 1793 the Bonaparte family was expelled from Corsica, and the France of the Revolution now became his own cause—apart, that is, than himself. His batteries helped to expel the British from Toulon in 1793, and his commander, du Teil, gave him most of the credit. By the age of twenty-four he was a brigadier. On Robespierre's death, he lost his mentor, so he attached himself to Barras, the least reputable of the Directory. Vendémiaire and the 'whiff of grapeshot' brought him the command of the Army of the Interior, the rank of major-general and the hand of Josephine de Beauharnais, one of Barras' discarded mistresses. He may well have loved her for a while, if he had room for any other passions than war. She may have grown in her fashion to love him, for there was an incandescent quality here and immense physical magnetism. However, four days after the marriage, Napoleon was on his way to Italy. The victories of 1796—Lodi, Castiglione and Arcole—and of 1797 —Rivoli—to name only the most important of the twenty-six battles won in twelve months made him a revolutionary hero at a time of economic discontent and political frustration and, in a military sense, were his greatest achievements. He dominated northern Italy as far as Rimini, occupied Florence and Leghorn, compelled the British to evacuate Corsica and merged Milan, Modena and Bologna into the Cisalpine Republic. At Campo Formio the Machiavellian emerged: he gave much of the Venetian Republic to Austria, in return for the Ionian Islands, an advance base for a campaign in the East. To the Corsican, the Venetians, like everyone else, were expendable. And there followed the Egyptian campaign.

Napoleon rendered immense service to France. But the Napoleonic legend, which via Louis and Napoleon became a legacy and via Boulanger, Pétain and de Gaulle a heavy liability, is bound up with the autocrat and the adventurer and battles won on foreign soil. The idea of *La gloire* in French history goes back, of course, long before Brumair, but the first, overwhelming image of Napoleon is of the conqueror.

Originally this was not his intention, for, on becoming First Consul, he had offered terms of peace to Britain and to Austria, the surviving members of the Second Coalition, only to have them scorned, for the Austrians were now dominant in North Italy except for Genoa, which they were besieging. Napoleon dispatched Moreau across the Rhine and he drove the army commanded by Kray back to Ulm. He himself crossed the St Bernard Pass, entered Milan and struck at Melas's army in the rear. Genoa had already surrendered, its streets piled with corpses from disease and famine. But at Marengo (June 1800) the tide had turned. Helped by Desaix's corps—and by Desaix's own death in action—Napoleon won back North Italy in a single day and the Austrians again abandoned Genoa, Piedmont and Milan. By July, Moreau occupied Minden and in December had won the Battle of Hohenlinden, Brune and Macdonald's joint army then moving on Vienna. The emperor was forced to make peace at Lunéville on 9 February 1801. Lunéville destroyed all that was left of the Holy Roman Empire, which Voltaire had said was neither holy, roman nor an empire. Austria ceded to France all territory west of the Rhine, including Belgium, and also recognized the independence of the new republics, the Cisalpine and Ligurian in Italy, the Batavian (Holland) and the Helvetic (Swiss), all of which were formed in the image of France. The Adige became the frontier between France and Austria in North Italy, and Austria accepted the right of France to

Left, the entry of Napoleon into Milan in May 1796; during this year Napoleon won a series of brilliant victories in his lightning campaign through northern Italy.

Below left, Napoleon's army crossing the Alps in 1800, surprising the Austrians and defeating them at the Battle of Marengo.

Bottom, the Battle of Marengo, fought in June 1800, was an important victory for Napoleon, destroying the Austrian threat to France from north Italy and beginning an attack on Habsburg power that led to the abolition of the Holy Roman Empire in 1806. Château de Versailles.

315

intervene in Germany in the affairs of the princes. The minor states of Germany were now as much at the mercy of Napoleon as they had been the puppets of Richelieu 160 years before. To save herself, Vienna abandoned Germany; and this too was to be a bitter legacy. The Tsar Paul became the friend of France and revived the Armed Neutrality of Russia, Sweden and Denmark against Britain. In March 1801 Spain ceded Louisiana to France and plans were made for a great empire in the Caribbean. But the assassination of Paul in March allowed Alexander I to make peace with Britain; and Nelson's victory at Copenhagen destroyed Napoleon's attempt to wreck Britain's trade with the Baltic and the North.

By 1802 Britain had lost almost all her allies. If she had averted a direct French invasion and thwarted Napoleon in Egypt, the National Debt had doubled and there was starvation. She controlled the sea but seemed powerless to stop France on land: it was a war of whale versus elephant. And so a truce was made at Amiens in March 1802. France had withdrawn from Egypt in 1801; she agreed to restore Malta to the Knights and to evacuate Naples. All of these were but a recognition of facts. Britain surrendered all her own conquests except Trinidad, which had been Spain's, and Sri Lanka, which had been Holland's. 'A peace which all men are glad of', said Sheridan, 'but no man can be proud of.' It was a triumph as well as a truce for Napoleon, and even if it was short-lived, it was the first time that France had been at peace in a decade. It was the high point of Bonapartism, In August he made himself a Consul for life, in a plebiscite that gave him 3,500,000 votes, against only 8,300 who had the courage to say 'No!' The new constitution gave him the right to choose his successor and to amend the constitution, to make

treaties and to dissolve the Assemblies.

Thus fortified he looked west. A French army was sent to Santo Domingo and the negro revolutionary Toussaint l'Ouverture was seized and sent to France and execution. But his followers fought a bloody war against the new Imperialism, and what they failed to do yellow fever abetted for there were over 20,000 French deaths within a year. These facts, and the fear of a revival of war with Britain, led to the abandonment of the dream and the sale of Louisiana to Jefferson's emissaries. Thwarted in the west, Napoleon turned back to Europe. He became, in his own person, president of the Cisalpine Republic and master of Lombardy, which was renamed the Italian Republic. He annexed Piedmont, Elba and Parma and strengthened his French forces in Holland and Italy—all in denial of the terms of Lunéville. In April, he sought to close to British commerce all the ports which he controlled. He published reports that indicated a resumption of the war in the east. Britain protested, and in May 1803 the war was resumed—the War of the Third Coalition. More than ever it was the land giant versus the mistress of the seas.

War brought with it the threat of internal sabotage, treason and plot. Napoleon claimed that the Count of Artois alone was maintaining sixty assassins in Paris. In February 1804, the plot of Georges Cadoudal and General Pichegru to murder Napoleon and restore Artois (the later Charles X) was discovered. A month later, the young Duke of Enghien was kidnapped by French troops on the neutral territory of Baden, brought to Paris and executed on the false charge of having been involved in the Cadoudal-Pichegru plot. And so, in May 1804, and in the interests of the state, Napoleon became emperor. This time 3,500,000 were for and only 2,500 against. On 2 December 1804, the

Above, the Battle of Copenhagen in April 1801, in which the British fleet of Hyde Parker and Horatio Nelson destroyed the Danish fleet, shortly after Denmark had joined the League of Armed Neutrality. According to this its members – Prussia, Russia, Sweden and Denmark – refused to allow the British to search neutral vessels.

Opposite, Napoleon Bonaparte at the Battle of Arcole in 1796, in a painting by Antoine Jean Gros. The battle represented an important victory over the Austrians in Italy. Musée du Louvre, Paris.

Corsican heir of all the Bourbons took the crown of Charlemagne from the hands of Pope Pius VII and put it on his own head. And as David's canvas portrays, a stiff and high ceremonial settled on the parvenu court. The Legion of Honour had been established in May 1802. There were grandiloquent titles, and all the Bonapartes were honoured: Joseph was Grand Elector and Louis Grand Constable—and these were but preludes to even greater honours, for all of Napoleon's brothers, except Lucien, later became kings. Sixteen generals became Marshals of France, and Murat, the ally of Vendémiaire, became Grand Admiral. Napoleon was to create, honour and endow princes and senators: 31 dukes, 388 counts, 1,090 barons and 1,500 knights were created in a great hierarchy designed to make even chivalry and pomp instruments of his statecraft. The Court was to cut Napoleon off in some measure from the nation, but around this particular throne were men of outstanding ability and of outstanding loyalty and devotion.

The First Consul

But behind the general and the pomp and pageantry of empire lay the achievement: in law, the Church and education.

These were the 'blocks of granite' on which he believed his power rested. In the three years from 1800 to 1803, the Paris years, he carried through most of his reforms. It was as if Louis XIV had been reincarnated with a team of outstanding talent—Talleyrand, Cambacérès, Lebrun Gaudin, Portalis and Thibaudeau.

In the codes of law drawn up by his Committees between 1804 and 1810, Napoleon drew heavily on the legislation of the Constituent and Legislative Assemblies. A uniform Civil Code had been a dream since Louis XIV, for there were no less than 360 local codes in existence, but until Napoleon all efforts to introduce one had failed. Napoleon himself participated directly in the discussions and his influence and vigour were vital. Indeed, he took greater pride in the Civil Code than in all his forty battles. The Code Napoleon was promulgated in March 1804 and it expressed in law the first principles of the Revolution: equality before the law, including the equal distribution of property among sons and daughters, though it was possible to leave a little more to one child if the family contained several children; freedom to work and to worship; freedom of conscience and the secular character of the state. It defined a modern property law freed of all manorial or seigneurial features, and it aimed to make the law uniform, understandable, rational and lucid, in contrast with the customary laws of France and England. In some ways it was strongly conservative for it put marriage and the family (not merely divorce) on a civil basis of the Old Regime. It encouraged firm

parental authority both in family and state, for the cohesion of the family group was itself the basis of the cohesion of the state. The father's control in the family was made absolute; a wife was seen as subject to her husband and could not acquire or sell property without his consent. The principle of divorce was admitted—for adultery, cruelty and for grave criminal offences—but once only.

The Civil Code proved the most durable part of Napoleon's handiwork and it was carried throughout Europe by his armies. In France and beyond, it stood the test of time. It was reinforced by a Code of Civil Procedure, a Commercial Code, which was the least durable of the enactments, and by Criminal and Penal Codes. Yet valuable as they were, the Codes were essentially comprises between the Old Regime and the Revolution, between the authoritarianism of Rome and the liberalism of customary law. Though equality was proclaimed, most of the provisions of the Civil Code were devoted to the protection of property. In the Criminal Code, though penalties were carefully prescribed, they were far from liberal: capital punishment, imprisonment or deportation for life, branding and slavery in the colonies were firmly established: the jury system was tightly curbed and used for judgement but not for accusation, and the juries themselves were chosen by prefects. While accused persons were tried in public and allowed to speak and to use counsel, they were not allowed to hear the case against themselves as it was being assembled in the preliminary investigation; there was no system of habeas corpus; the Codes were authoritarian in temper and far removed from the spirit of the *philosophes*. They were well designed to detect crime and to ensure fast and speedy trial; but there was no attempt to see the law as a barrier against arbitrary executive power. And in economic terms the Codes said little about wages and conditions of work: it was property, not labour, that was sacrosanct. Employers were given freedom so that the economy should boom, and in wage disputes the master's word was taken against the worker's: in the Penal Code, the le Chapelier Law of 1791 was reintroduced and associations, whether of masters or of workers, were forbidden.

Yet, however illiberal they were, the Codes were immensely valuable. In them the permanent shape of the Revolution became clear: the objective was a secular state based firmly on a peasant proprietor class: the protection of private property mattered as much as did equality: but, since all men had equal rights, there was a genuine chance for the 'men of talent' to find their own way to property, fame and fortune.

Napoleon's own taste also emerged clearly: the taste for order and for 'men of talent' not for the common man. Here again he was in the tradition of the Old Regime. Like Louis XIV, Napoleon chose his servants from diverse backgrounds and,

Above, Napoleon, as First Consul, dictating to a secretary in the early years of the nineteenth century. Administrative work, for the upkeep of the army, and for the institution of his many reforms in French government and law, occupied much of Napoleon's time.

Left, a French tribune in 1803, a member of the body which discussed legislation under the Consulate, but had little power.

Opposite, Napoleon Bonaparte (1769–1821), painted by Gerard; Napoleon's genius was to take the chaos of France during the 1790s and turn its energy entirely to his own will.

as Louis had been frightened by the *fronde*, so Napoleon had seen enough of the *sans-culottes* and of the extravagances of the Directory to judge them harshly. Also, much in the same way as Jefferson, the democracy he sought was that in which able men would rise rapidly to the top. It was to be equality to allow the flourishing of unequal talents of unequal men. And what the Codes did in law, Fouché did in practice at the Ministry of Police: it was a regime that offered a widening of opportunity and also an extension of censorship and repression. By 1810 each department had a single newspaper, tightly controlled by the prefects, and by 1811 all the Paris newspapers had been confiscated.

The same spirit permeated the educational system. Primary education remained in local hands and was seriously handicapped by lack of funds. The secondary schools of the Directory were replaced by *lycées*, advanced secondary schools in which military drill and style were curiously married to a classical curriculum. By 1814 this had become and was to remain one of his great achievements. But it was, of course, masculine. As he wrote in 1807, 'what we ask of education is not that girls should think, but that they should believe.'

In 1808 an Imperial University was set up, the Grand Master of which was the educational autocrat of the whole system. A degree from the Imperial University became a prerequisite for teaching. There was even

for a time an Imperial Catechism, to teach loyalty to the emperor. Napoleon also gave new life to those creations of the Convention which were its most valuable legacy: the École Polytechnique, set up in 1795 to train engineers, the École Normale Supérieure, to train teachers, and the Institut de France. Much was done to encourage industry and applied science with technical schools, rewards for invention and industrial exhibitions. But again the intention was clear—education was a department of state, and its watchwords were training, discipline and centralization. Some of its discipline lasted a very long time.

Central to the Napoleonic strategy were good relations with the Church. If he could secure this he would, at one blow, weaken both royalists and revolutionaries and gain the support of the great number of faithful Catholics. The clergy, he said, would join the police in generating contentment. To him, the arch-secularist, religion was necessary not for its own sake but for his, as a further buttress to loyalty and sentiment. 'In religion', he said, 'I do not see the mystery of the Incarnation, but the mystery of the social order.' 'If I were governing the Jews, I would restore the Temple of Solomon.'

The Concordat concluded with the pope in 1801 and sanctioned in 1802 was, again, primarily his own handiwork. All bishops were required to resign their Sees and the bishoprics were regrouped so that there were now ten archbishoprics and fifty bishoprics. Napoleon nominated them and they were consecrated by the pope. The clergy took an oath of obedience to the government and got in return, as good servants of emperor as well as God, a fixed salary. The bishops were given absolute authority over them but ecclesiastical property, confiscated in the heyday of the Revolution and bought by the *bourgeoisie* and the peasants, still remained in the hands of its purchasers. Roman Catholicism was recognized as the 'religion of the great majority of Frenchmen, but equal rights were granted to other faiths—a basic principle of the secular state which was unknown anywhere before the Revolution.

In other words, the spirit like the mind was disciplined in Napoleon's service, and the Church, like the schools, became a Department of State. The *Journal des Curés*, the only clerical newspaper to appear after 1806, carried his imprimatur, sermons were strictly censored and there were to be no papal bulls, papal legates or investigations from Rome. But if it was to gain little for Pius VII, at least most of the religious orders returned, as did the Sabbath and the Gregorian calendar. Also the Concordat ended Gallicanism.

Yet when the quarrel with Rome came it was not over these issues. The strongly Gallican spirit in France long pre-dated Napoleon: his attempts to exploit it for his own purposes had the effect of driving his clerical opponents into ultramontanism: that is, they recognized the pope as the supreme head of the Church. Pius VII disliked the extension of the Code Napoleon to Italy, since it authorized divorce; Napoleon despoiled Rome of the Legations of Bologna and Ferrara, which he added to the kingdom of Italy, and he handed over Ponte Corvo and Benevento to Bernadotte and Talleyrand respectively. Pius objected to Joseph Bonaparte's accession to the throne of Naples, and in 1806 he refused to expel the enemies of France from the Papal states. In May 1809 Rome was annexed by France; in June Pius excommunicated Napoleon and the pope was arrested in the following month and imprisoned in Fontainebleau.

In the end the pope returned to Rome as a result of the allies' triumph at Leipzig, and his steady resistance undermined all Napoleon's efforts. Napoleon found that it was his own unbridled ambition and not the Concordat which succeeded in alienating

many Catholics, for he tied Church and state so closely together that their alliance has been a continuous source of tension and danger to France. However, the Concordat survived the quarrel and remained in force until 1905.

Law, Church and education were, then, the instruments of this enlightened despot and far more successful and durable than those of his eighteenth-century precursors, mainly because of his own abilities and his organizing and technical efficiency. However it is only fair to add that the success of Napoleon's reforms was a result not only to his own talents but because the Revolution had swept away all the interests, privileges, habits and established groups whose opposition had blocked similar changes since the time of Louis XIV. Absolutism ensured order and it came close to guaranteeing prosperity.

In 1800 the Bank of France was established with the sole right of issuing banknotes. There was active state interference in industry, laws to regulate the supply of food and for the registration of workers with the police. The wars with Britain were calamitous to trade but a stimulus to industry. The wool and silk trades prospered; the government paid its bills promptly, helped by foreign treasure brought in by the nation's armies; the French peasant who in 1789 kept only nineteen out of every one hundred francs he earned kept seventy-nine after 1800.

Indeed, Napoleon's regime was based on the support of two classes, the workmen, whom Napoleon feared and who gave him an illogical devotion, and the peasantry. The last were the great beneficiaries of the Revolution who, having profited from it, rejoiced now to see its excesses curbed. By 1810 there were seven million rural proprietors in France, which was all but self-sufficient as its agriculture flourished. It was of course, after Russia, the most populous state in Europe: some 26,000,000 aginst divided Italy's 17,000,000, Britain's 15,000,000 and Spain's 11,000,000. France's armies had battle experience and, at least until the disastrous Russian campaign of 1812, almost unlimited numbers. The army poised to cross the Channel in 1805 had 200,000 men, of whom more than half had war experience. This was a strong, cohesive and disciplined state. In the years of the Consulate, Napoleon gave it the stamp of his own authority and energy, his realism and detail, his respect for order and his scorn for abstract rights. The student of Rousseau had progressed a long way in a decade. So also had the Revolution.

Above, Napoleon giving the insignia of the imperial eagles to his armies, according to an engraving after a painting by Jacques Louis David. Napoleon's success was always based on the enthusiasm he could summon up from the army.

Opposite, the coronation of Napoleon in December 1804 as Emperor of the French. Although the pope was present to perform the coronation, Napoleon snatched the crown from his hands and placed it on his own head to symbolize his independence from the Church. Musée du Louvre, Paris.

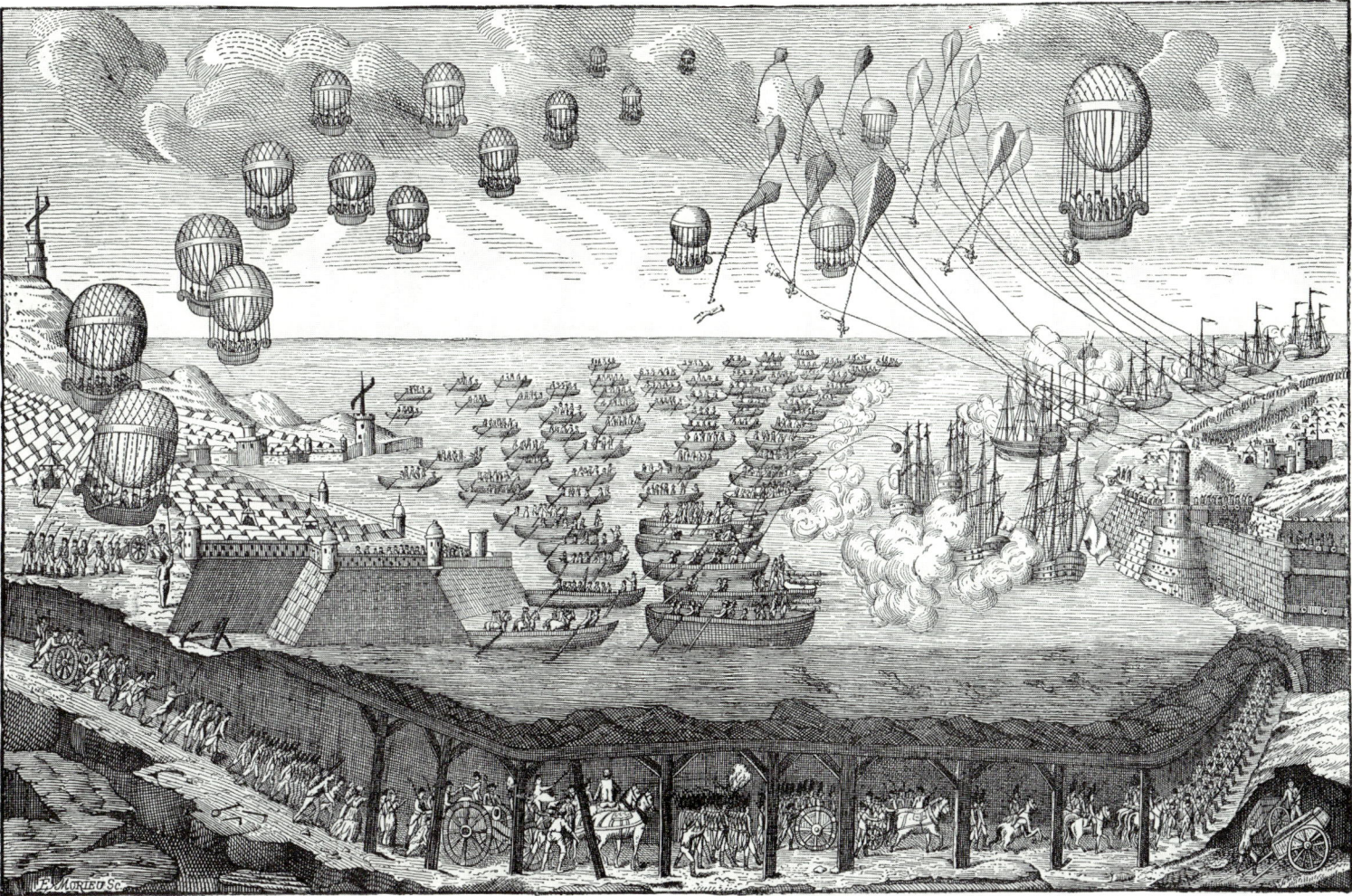

Above, Napoleon accepting the surrender of the city of Ulm in September 1805. This victory was a triumph for Napoleon's tactic of quickly encircling the enemy. Château de Versailles.

Top, an engraving of Napoleon's invasion plans of England before the Treaty of Amiens in 1802; Napoleon actually began building a tunnel under the Channel, but his invasion plans required superiority at sea, which he never fully won.

Left, the Battle of Trafalgar in 1805, a decisive victory for the British over the French navy; British control of the Atlantic and Channel proved a crippling blow to Napoleon's strategies. Musée de la Marine, Paris.

Opposite, Napoleon, seen as the child of the Devil; his aggression against the whole of Europe, his demonic energy, his ruthlessness in turning France into a military machine and his ambition in setting his family on the vacant thrones of Europe made him feared everywhere.

The Empire to Tilsit

The years of the Consulate revealed a ruler of outstanding ability who had turned from war to peace. However, after the collapse of the Treaty of Amiens, the old image was restored, Napoleon as Attila the destroyer. The state he commanded was so strong and the cause he was thought to champion so explosive and popular that for a decade he swept through Europe as the Goths had done twelve centuries earlier. As a result, the war of the Third Coalition was total war of a kind unknown before.

It began with the attempt to invade Britain. Nelson's blockade of Villeneuve's fleet at Toulon and Collingwood's blockade of Ganteaume's fleet at Brest prevented the assembling of the transports: Villeneuve escaped to the West Indies and returned to be checked at Finisterre. He put in to Cadiz to refit and Nelson, prowling the Atlantic in baffled pursuit, was able to overtake him at Trafalgar in October 1805, and by his victory end the risk of invasion and give Britain supremacy at sea which was to last for a century. It was only these ships which stood between Napoleon and possible world

dominion. In the meantime Pitt had created a Third Coalition of Britain, Alexander of Russia, Austria, Sweden, Sicily and Naples, while Prussia equivocated.

To meet the Austrian danger Napoleon broke up the armed camp and the 200,000 veterans of the Army of England were dispatched east in seven divisions under the ablest commanders in modern history: Ney, Marmont, Davoust, Augereau, Soult, Lannes and Bernadotte. With them went Murat with the cavalry and Bessières with the Imperial Guard of 10,000 men. They covered 200 miles in a fortnight, faster than Austria or Russia believed possible and before either of them had time to plan their defence. As a result Mack was surrounded, overwhelmed and surrendered with 25,000 men at Ulm in October. The following month Napoleon entered Vienna.

Napoleon now found that his lines of communication were extended, and therefore the Allies, not least an impetuous Tsar, resolved to attack. The result of this was that Napoleon won what was his greatest victory—Austerlitz, north of Vienna, on the anniversary of his coronation. His losses were 9,000 out of 70,000; the

Austrians and Russians lost 30,000 out of 80,000. Partly it was speed of movement: partly great tactical skill: most of all brilliant leadership with plans communicated frankly to all his men in advance. 'It is by speaking to the soul that men are electrified.' Austria made peace and Russia hurriedly withdrew into its own territory. Ferdinand pulled back to Sicily, safety sheltered by the British fleet and in January 1806 Pitt died, broken by thirteen years of war. By the Treaty of Pressburg Austria surrendered all her Italian possessions— some of them the ancestral estates of the Habsburgs. The Holy Roman Empire was formally abolished.

Napoleon now organized an array of satellite states: his brother Joseph was made King of Naples and Louis King of Holland. The Confederation of the Rhine was set up as a pro-French barrier in Europe and it made a defensive alliance with France: 63,000 Rhinelanders fought in French armies.

Prussia at last decided to move, only to be destroyed at Jena and Auerstedt in October 1806. Napoleon then marched through Berlin, from which city he issued the Berlin

Above, the Battle of Jena in October 1806, at which Napoleon defeated the Prussian armies; Napoleon occupied Berlin, the Prussian capital, shortly after the battle.

Opposite top, Napoleon's entry into Vienna, the Austrian capital, in November 1805. Less than a month later he destroyed the Austrian and Russian armies at Austerlitz and Austria was forced to make peace with France.

Opposite bottom, the Battle of Austerlitz in Moravia, in December 1805, at which Napoleon won his greatest victory, sweeping aside the combined armies of the Austrians and the Russians. Château de Versailles.

Decrees enforcing the Continental System and a blockade of Britain by the whole of Europe. He demanded the surrender of all Prussian territory, first west of the Elbe, then west of the Vistula. Frederick William III fell back into East Prussia hoping for Russian help. By December 1806, Napoleon was in Warsaw.

At last Russia moved again. Eylau (February 1807) was a drawn battle with heavy losses on both sides. And though each member of the Coalition talked of action, no common action was taken. At Friedland in June the Russians were overwhelmed and driven across the River Nieman. The two rulers, the emperor and the tsar, met in July 1807 on a raft moored in the river and signed the Treaty of Tilsit.

Tilsit was the climax in the Napoleonic story: the high point of empire. The two emperors divided Europe between them. Napoleon dominated the West, from the Nieman to the Channel. Prussia was heavily despoiled when her Polish acquisitions became a grand duchy of Warsaw which Napoleon gave to the King of Saxony; her lands west of the Elbe went to form a new kingdom of Westphalia, given to Napoleon's brother Jerome; her army was to be limited in size and she was to close her ports to British trade. Alexander for his part recognized France's acquisitions and ceded the Ionian Islands; he was urged to take Moldavia Walachia from the Ottoman

Map legend:
- Offensive against the Prussians
- Offensive against the Russians
- Prussian movements
- Russian movements

Map labels: Lübeck, Hamburg, Bremen, Stettin, Prenzlau, Berlin, Auerstedt, Jena, Kronach, Danzig, Czarnow, Warsaw, Eylau, Friedland

Left, Napoleon's spectacular campaign of 1806–67, in the course of which he subjugated Prussia and forced Russia to make a treaty favourable to France.

Opposite top, the Battle of Eylau in February 1807, at which the French were unable to defeat the combined forces of the Russians and Prussians; but Napoleon was only delayed six months in asserting his authority over the Prussians, in the Treaty of Tilsit signed in July 1807.

Opposite centre, the meeting of Napoleon and Alexander I, Tsar of Russia, on a raft in the River Niemen at Tilsit, in June 1807; at the meeting they agreed peace between their empires and Russia promised Napoleon help in the event of further war between France and Britain.

Opposite bottom, the Emperor of Russia introducing Frederick William III of Prussia to Napoleon at Tilsit following Napoleon's victory over Prussia at Friedland; Napoleon drastically reduced the size of Prussia's lands and armies and made Frederick William virtually a puppet prince.

Empire and was promised French help in the attempt. After the destruction of the Holy Roman Empire, the Ottoman was to suffer in a similar manner. Thus both rulers agreed to fasten the shackles of the Continental System on Europe, to keep British and neutral shipping from trading with Europe and to isolate, blockade and finally to destroy Britain.

FRANCE FROM ROBESPIERRE TO THE EMPIRE

Date	Internal history	Foreign policy	Events in Europe
1794	Fall of the Dantonists Cult of the Supreme Being Fall of Robespierre	Invasion of Catalonia Capture of Antwerp and Cologne Invasion of Holland	Habeas Corpus Act suspended in Britain Polish revolt crushed British capture Corsica
1795	Attempted insurrection of Prairial White Terror Formation of the Directory	Treaties with Prussia, Holland and Spain Batavian Republic formed under French protection	Acquittal of Warren Hastings Failure of Quiberon Bay expedition
1796	Suppression of *assignats* Babeuf conspiracy	Bonaparte's Italian campaign Moreau's campaign in Germany	Failure of attempted French invasion of Ireland Corsica returned to France
1797	Royalists triumph in elections *Coup d'état* of 18 Fructidor	Battles of Rivoli and Mantua Establishment of Cisalpine Republic Treaty of Campo Formio	Accession of Frederick William III of Prussia Mutinies in the British Navy
1798	Electoral success of the Jacobins *Coup d'état* of 22 Floréal	Campaign in Egypt	Rebellion in Ireland suppressed Nelson's victory at Aboukir Bay
1799	Return of Bonaparte *Coup d'état* of 18 Brumaire The Consulate and the Constitution of the Year VIII	French repulsed in Syria Overthrow of Cisalpine, Roman and Helvetic Republics	Combination laws prohibit trade unionism in Britain Second Coalition against France
1800	Constitution approved by Plebiscite Attempted assassination of Bonaparte	Austrians defeated at Marengo and Hohenlinden	Act of Union between Britain and Ireland

Date	Internal history	Foreign Policy	Events in Europe
1801	Measures against the Jacobins Concordat re-establishes Roman Catholic Church in France	Peace of Lunéville Treaty with Russia	British naval victory at Copenhagen Paul I of Russia murdered
1802	Amnesty for the *émigrés* Bonaparte consul for life Constitution of the Year X	Peace of Amiens Peace with Turkey Annexation of Piedmont	
1803	Laws restricting workers' freedom Cadoudal and Pichegru conspiracy	Intervention in civil war in Switzerland Army encamped at Boulogne for invasion of England	Britain at war with France
1804	Execution of the Duke of Enghien Napoleon crowned Emperor	France and Russia break off diplomatic relations	William Pitt British prime-minister
1805	Napoleon becomes King of Italy	Russians and Austrians defeated at Austerlitz	British victory over French and Spanish fleets at Trafalgar
1806	Napoleon's breach with the pope	End of the Holy Roman Empire Prussians defeated at Jena and Auerstedt Berlin Decrees	Death of William Pitt
1807	Disgrace of Talleyrand	Battles of Eylau and Friedland Treaty of Tilsit	British fleet bombards Copenhagen

Chapter 30

The Fall of Napoleon

At the close of 1807 the weaknesses of the Continental System were still not apparent. Napoleon reigned supreme. Europe was at his feet, and no one could have prophesied that within seven years his great empire would lie in ruins, his attempts to bring about the collapse of Great Britain's financial and commercial prosperity having alienated influential opinion within the areas he already ruled and helped to bring about his downfall.

In spite of three defeats at the hands of the French in little over ten years and the great expansion of Napoleonic power, by 1808 the Austrians were again ready to attempt to defeat the ruler of Europe. Their natural desire for revenge and their hatred of Napoleon were stimulated by the events in the Iberian peninsula. In November 1807 French troops conquered Portugal, causing the Portuguese royal family to flee to Brazil, and in March 1808, when a French force marched on Madrid, an internal revolt forced the Bourbon king, Charles IV, to abdicate. Napoleon soon gave the Spanish throne to his brother Joseph. The Habsburgs had good reason to fear a ruler who could deal so summarily with the royal families of the Iberian peninsula. Moreover, the Spanish people were demonstrating that resistance to the French was possible. In May 1808 the population of Madrid rose against the new French rulers, and the French found themselves drawn into extensive guerrilla warfare.

If Austria could wage war successfully her previous losses could be restored, and there was a growing belief in the country that the Austrian army was now much stronger and might well be capable of defeating Napoleon. Since the disasters of 1805 the leadership in reforming the Austrian army had been taken by Archduke Charles, brother of Emperor Francis, and by the new chancellor, Count Johann Philip von Stadion. The reforms had produced a marked improvement in the regular army, which was augmented by the creation of an enthusiastic reserve army by 1808. Stirred by the events in Spain, the Austrians were again becoming ready to risk combat with the French.

Napoleon was quickly discovering that it was easier to create a great empire than to maintain it. In the summer of 1808 he condemned the Austrian rearmament and once again arranged to meet Tsar Alexander in an effort to cement Franco-Russian friendship before embarking on an expedition which he hoped and expected would crush Spanish resistance. His meeting with the tsar at Erfurt was unproductive. Alexander avoided making any major promises to Napoleon, showing far less admiration for him than he had at Tilsit in 1807: he gained an ally in the French statesman Talleyrand, who now showed himself willing to work secretly against Napoleon. Both Alexander and Napoleon were accustomed to daily flattery and found it difficult to compromise their dignity by yielding supremacy.

Although Napoleon took personal command in Spain late in 1808, his efforts produced no conclusive result, and early in 1809 he returned to Paris to prepare for a campaign against the Austrians.

In the early months of 1809 Napoleon waited for Francis I to make the first move. In Austria troops were flocking to the colours with considerable enthusiasm, but the Austrians could expect little aid from outside. The other German states either remained neutral or indeed actually fought on the side of the French, and Great Britain could offer no direct aid. She did promise a diversionary movement in the north, but the

disastrous Walcheren expedition came too late to be of any use even in diverting French attention from the main scene of operations.

The campaign began early in April 1809 when Archduke Charles advanced into Bavaria. Napoleon reacted with speed and confidence. By mid-April he had arrived in the vicinity and at the battles of Abensberg and Eckmühl drove the Austrians back. On 12 May the French entered Vienna and a week later crossed to the north bank of the Danube to attack the Austrian army. In the two-day battle of Aspern and Essling the Austrians succeeded in repulsing the French forces; they withdrew to the island of Lobau. Losses had been severe on both sides; the French suffered nearly 20,000 casualties and the Austrians themselves several thousand more.

After this bloody engagement there was a pause in the campaign while both sides attempted to strengthen their armies. Early in July, after being reinforced by Eugène Beauharnais, Napoleon once again crossed to the north bank of the Danube. He had with him an army of approximately 170,000 men to meet an Austrian army of more than 30,000 fewer. The French attack at Wagram was launched on 6 July, and although Napoleon carried the day it was no Austerlitz. The Austrians put up a stubborn resistance, and both armies suffered severely. On 12 July the two sides concluded an armistice and prepared to make peace. Instead of gaining revenge, Austria was now in danger of additional losses.

While the main armies clashed near Vienna, the people of the Tyrol took up arms against the Bavarians, who had gained that area at the Peace of Pressburg in 1805. Under Andreas Hofer the Tyroleans waged a brave struggle. Innsbruck was taken in the spring, and even after the Austrian defeat at Wagram the uprising continued until the end of the year. Hofer was eventually captured, tried by the French and executed.

Other signs that Napoleon faced increasing disgust at his attempt to control the whole of Europe came from Germany. The Duke of Brunswick raised volunteers to fight the French, took Dresden and after the Austrian defeat at Wagram managed to escape with his army northwards across Germany, to be taken off in British ships. This force, whose death's head insignia became famous, later served in the Peninsula. In Prussia Major Friedrich von Schill attempted to organize a military uprising against the French. He took Stralsund in May but was killed when the town was stormed by the French and the Danes. It was becoming all too clear that many in Europe regarded Napoleon as a tyrant to be overthrown.

Yet, for all the heroics, and in spite of the greater Austrian enthusiasm, Napoleon had won, and in October 1809 he forced the Austrians to sign the Treaty of Schönbrunn.

Below, Napoleon crossing the River Danube before the Battle of Wagram in July 1809; his artillery proved too strong for the Austrians, who were forced to sign another armistice shortly afterwards. Wellington Museum, Apsley House, London.

Opposite, Napoleon entering Madrid in December 1808, after a year of confusion in that country following the accession of Joseph Bonaparte to the Spanish throne. But Napoleon was unable to expel the British forces supporting the Spaniards.

It was a harsh peace. Napoleon never learned the value of moderation in victory. Francis I was shocked by the loss of more than three-and-a-half million subjects. Salzburg was given to Bavaria, west Galicia to the Grand Duchy of Warsaw, and Austrian possessions between the Save River and the Adriatic were taken by France and made part of the Illyrian Provinces. Austria would clearly not rest content until some of this territory had been regained, and this humiliating settlement planted the seeds of future wars. It was obvious that Metternich, the new Austrian chancellor, would wait for an opportunity to weaken France and restore Austria's fortunes, although to help Austria he was prepared to work with Napoleon until the right moment for revenge.

Having again preserved his power by military victory, Napoleon now turned to marriage in an attempt both to secure the future of his dynasty and to ensure future Austrian cooperation. It now appeared that his first wife Joséphine was too old to bear him a son, and Napoleon craved not only immediate power but also the creation of a legitimate dynasty. Napoleon gave consideration to both a Russian or an Austrian marriage, and on returning from his victory over Austria he made the definite decision to divorce Joséphine. Joséphine had no choice; in December 1809 she had to consent to Napoleon's wishes, and the French Senate

was necessarily obliged to follow suit.

With Napoleon casting around for a future empress, Metternich seized upon the opportunity to ensure Austria's temporary safety; available as an offering was Marie Louise, daughter of Austrian emperor Francis I. The possible religious objections were overcome by Napoleon's pressure on the hierarchy of the French Catholic Church; it was agreed that the marriage to Joséphine could be annulled. The marriage to Marie Louise took place by proxy in Vienna in March, and civil and religious ceremonies took place in France at the beginning of April. In an effort to create a legitimate dynasty Napoleon was prepared to use every possible illegitimate device, and it soon appeared that the abandonment of Joséphine had proved a success; within a few months Marie Louise was pregnant. The birth of a son, the King of Rome, in March 1811 for a time gave purpose to the whole hurried divorce and remarriage, but the joy was short-lived.

Prussia

While Austria yet again attempted to overcome Napoleon, Prussia seethed under the humiliation of her 1806 defeat. The French troops who occupied Prussia after the victory of Jena left only after the Prussians agreed to pay a huge cash indemnity and to

maintain their army at no more than 42,000 men. Napoleon's unwillingness to deal more leniently with his defeated opponents in this case, even more than his harshness towards Austria, helped to produce internal changes which contributed to his eventual downfall. Prussians who had little faith in reform were eventually persuaded to accept it as the only means by which a national revival could be engendered and the hated Napoleon be defeated.

The key figures in the Prussian revival were the king, Frederick William III, and his ministers Hardenberg and Stein. After the events of 1806 the king had to acknowledge that the great army and system created by Frederick the Great were not enough to cope with a revivified France under the leadership of a military genius. Inspired by Hardenberg and Stein the king was prepared to force reform measures on often reluctant aristocrats.

The most practical and tangible reform here, as in Austria, was in the army, and this improvement depended on the leadership of two soldiers—Scharnhorst and Gneisenau. An attempt was made to modify a system which had depended for its discipline on the imposition of frequent punishments; aristocratic birth was no longer to be the sole attribute for promotion, and an attempt was made to induce a Prussian national pride in the army. Also, by training and then discharging bodies of men it proved possible to avoid the absolute limits on the size of the army established by Napoleon.

A far-reaching internal reform was set in motion by the edict abolishing serfdom in October 1807. The ensuing land reform gave the Prussian peasants a much firmer stake in

the land. Without the crisis brought about by Napoleon's overwhelming victories, this could hardly have occurred at so early a date. Much less far-reaching as a reform, but of significance, was the establishment of a degree of municipal independence by allowing the local election of town officials.

A distinctive feature of the Prussian revival after 1807 was the burst of intellectual and cultural nationalism. Ultimately, this was probably more important for future German history than for the age of Napoleon. The most important figure in this nationalistic revival was Johann Gottlieb Fichte, who in his famous lectures at Berlin in these years preached the necessity of a Germanic revival; a revival which would be based on patriotic virtue and a sense of a mystical German past. This was hardly the theme to fire the peasants, but it did create a ferment among the Prussian intellectuals. This group were also influenced by the activities of the *Tugendbund* ('League of Virtue') formed among professors at Königsberg. These men hoped to achieve a moral regeneration of the nation.

More practical in its results was the reform of the Prussian educational system inaugurated by Wilhelm von Humboldt. At the core of the reforms was the intention to create a national system of education, and a structure was established which culminated in the new foundation of the University of Berlin.

Although the German states of this age were fragmented and subject to the political and military whims of Napoleon, they had a remarkably fruitful intellectual and cultural life. In Prussia a strong emphasis was placed on moral regeneration and the creation of a

vague sense of a Prussian and German soul, but elsewhere the flourishing cultural life was less tied to nationalistic reform. At Weimar Duke Charles Augustus had gathered around him the most distinguished philosophers and writers in Germany, and Goethe made the city famous throughout Europe. To the south Beethoven thrilled Vienna. To many Napoleon's first victories in Germany had seemed a deliverance, a blow by which feudal privilege and archaic law were to be swept away. As the years passed, however, the development of tyranny and the constant demands for men and money alienated even those who had been his friends.

Europe under Napoleon

Although Austria and Prussia retained their identity and even found a new burst of national enthusiasm under the crushing defeats inflicted by the French, much of Europe either quite happily accepted French rule or had neither the power nor the allies to make resistance possible. Those areas closest to France were under the greatest domination by the French system.

Holland had been given to Napoleon's brother Louis Bonaparte in 1806, and French administration had not been particularly onerous for the Dutch; indeed the French law and government had been an

Opposite and above, Napoleon and Marie Louise, whom he married and made empress in 1810. She was made duchess of Parma, Piacenza and Guastalla by the Congress of Vienna in 1816.

Centre, the marriage between Napoleon and Marie Louise, the daughter of the Emperor of Austria, in Paris in 1810. Napoleon's intention in this marriage was more to gain acceptance for his rule than to establish a permanent peace with Austria.

improvement over the old Dutch system and had helped to unify the country. The chief possibility for real conflict, as in so many areas of the French empire, was the attempt to exclude British trade by the introduction of the Continental System. As a major commercial people, the Dutch found the attempts to restrict their trade intolerable. Louis showed himself willing to compromise and allow loopholes in the Continental System to placate his people, but in 1810 Napoleon deposed him and annexed Holland. He also annexed the Duchy of Oldenburg and the Hanseatic towns of Bremen, Hamburg and Lübeck to extend his control along the German coastline. Denmark was not annexed, but it obeyed the Continental System.

Sweden was going through turmoil in the period following the French-Russian agreement at Tilsit. After that settlement the Russians had occupied Finland, and following further difficulties the Swedish king Gustavus IV was deposed, and his elderly uncle replaced him as Charles XIII. As he had no heirs, a group of Swedish officers suggested that the throne should be offered to Napoleon's Marshal Bernadotte. After obtaining Napoleon's permission, Bernadotte accepted in 1810. He quickly espoused the cause of Sweden, and the French emperor was soon to discover that the elevation of his marshal had made Sweden anything but a satellite.

Napoleon was more fortunate with his intervention in the affairs of Switzerland. By the 1803 Act of Mediation he had moved to unify Switzerland and to guarantee the reforms brought about in that country by the French Revolution. Napoleon took for himself the position of Mediator of the Swiss Confederation. The Swiss were to maintain their neutrality throughout the decline of Napoleon's power, although their territory was violated when an Austrian army marched across their borders in order to obtain a convenient route for the invasion of France.

Napoleon's dreams of reconstituting the whole map of Europe were clearly revealed by his attitude towards the Poles. His position was complicated by his attempted friendship with Russia after Tilsit. The Russians were extremely reluctant to accept any measures which might revive Polish nationalism. Yet, in spite of Russian fears, Napoleon in 1807 established the Grand Duchy of Warsaw out of Prussian Poland. The King of Saxony was made Grand Duke of Warsaw, and in 1809 it was enlarged with Austrian territory. Napoleon had taken on an impossible task if he hoped both to encourage Polish national aspirations and at the same time retain the friendship of Tsar Alexander.

In 1810 Napoleon still ruled a great empire and had satellites throughout Europe, but weak spots were becoming apparent. The was in the Iberian peninsula continued, costing French lives and giving the British a foothold on the continent. Throughout Europe, and even in France, there was discontent both at the enforcement of the Continental System and at Napoleonic exactions. The French emperor himself was becoming more tyrannical. He was less willing to accept advice, made more arbitrary decisions and showed little willingness to appease any groups within his empire. If Napoleon hoped to establish a dynasty and to create a Europe under French leadership, then the time had come for consolidation and accommodation, not fresh adventures, more requisitions, more fighting and more deaths. Yet Napoleon could not be satisfied, and the cracks in the empire that appeared in Spain and in the enforcement of the Continental System were soon to broaden and undermine the foundations of the precarious and ramshackle structure that he had built from military victory.

Russia

In the five years after Tilsit the French and the Russians maintained an uneasy peace that could hardly be called friendship. The meeting of Alexander and Napoleon at Erfurt in the autumn of 1808 did nothing to cement a firm alliance between the two nations. The tsar had hoped by his agreement with Napoleon at Tilsit both to hurt Great Britain and to advance Russian ambitions in eastern Europe, but he quickly developed resentment against the overbearing power of the French emperor.

A continual source of irritation was Napoleon's promotion of the grand duchy of Warsaw. Alexander was particularly disturbed when Austrian Galicia was added to the duchy after the defeat of Austria in 1809. Although Napoleon maintained that he had no intention of creating an independent Poland, Russia had ample reason to distrust French assertions. Napoleon himself showed little concern to placate the Russian tsar. In December 1810 he annexed the duchy of Oldenburg, although the heir-apparent was married to Alexander's sister Catherine. Napoleon's affront to her husband ensured that there would be an influential advocate of an anti-French policy with immediate access to Alexander.

Tsar Alexander had also become increasingly irritated by Napoleon's arrogance and found it difficult to accept him as the arbiter of Europe. Alexander's own ego was such that he would view with satisfaction any diminution of the Napoleonic glory.

In practical terms, however, Russia's reluctance to enforce the Napoleonic Continental System became the major point of contention between France and Russia. Throughout 1810 Napoleon continued to hope that his restrictions on British trade would bring Great Britain to disaster, but Alexander showed great reluctance to make Russia an economic satellite of the French. In December 1810 he issued a *ukase* (order) which restricted the importation of French luxury goods and opened Russian ports to other shipping. It was clear that Alexander was ready to separate himself from the French connection as soon as the chance arose, and in 1811 the two powers began to prepare for war.

Napoleon well knew the difficulties and dangers of a campaign into the depths of Russia, and he was determined that his army for this enterprise would be the greatest he had ever assembled. By the spring of 1812 he had gathered in Poland more than half a million men for his campaign. Less than half of these troops were French, for Napoleon's armies were bolstered by troops from allies, satellites and conquered countries all over Europe; even Austria and Prussia had no choice but to provide troops for the campaign. Fired by the prospect of a great military victory, Napoleon, as the months passed, showed less and less willingness to allow for all the dangers which would beset any army plunging into the interior of Russia. Rational thoughts of enforcing the Continental System or ensuring that Russia would not join the British were submerged in grandiose dreams of glory and empire.

At the beginning of the conflict, Alexander could place in the field nothing like the force assembled by Napoleon: the Russian tsar had not many more than 150,000 men to meet the initial French advance. He had, however, achieved two diplomatic successes before the war began; in April Napoleon's old subordinate Bernadotte, now heir to the Swedish throne, had reached an agreement with Russia, and in May the Turks had concluded a peace.

On the night of 23 June Napoleon's army began to cross the Niemen river into Russia. He was in high hopes that he could quickly bring the Russians to battle, defeat them and force Alexander to sue for peace. Apart from Napoleon's main army, separate wings of the attack were sent towards Riga and St Petersburg, and in the south the Austrians advanced under Prince Karl von Schwarzenberg.

Napoleon's hopes of bringing the Russians to battle were frustrated in the early days of the campaign. The French advance stirred unexpected depths of resistance in the Russians. The ruling classes, fearing the wholesale changes and reforms instituted by Napoleon elsewhere, naturally had no desire to accept any quick French victory. Moreover, even the Russian people, who logically might have been expected to welcome the possibilities of general changes in their condition, responded to the threat to their tsar and to mother Russia. With a primitive religious fervour they, like their rulers, were prepared to suffer great hardship to resist the desires of the French emperor.

The difficulties of maintaining discipline and of supplying Napoleon's motley army proved impossible to overcome. There was no great victory to maintain morale, and throughout the campaign the desertion

Opposite, Napoleon in camp, shown here in typical pose.

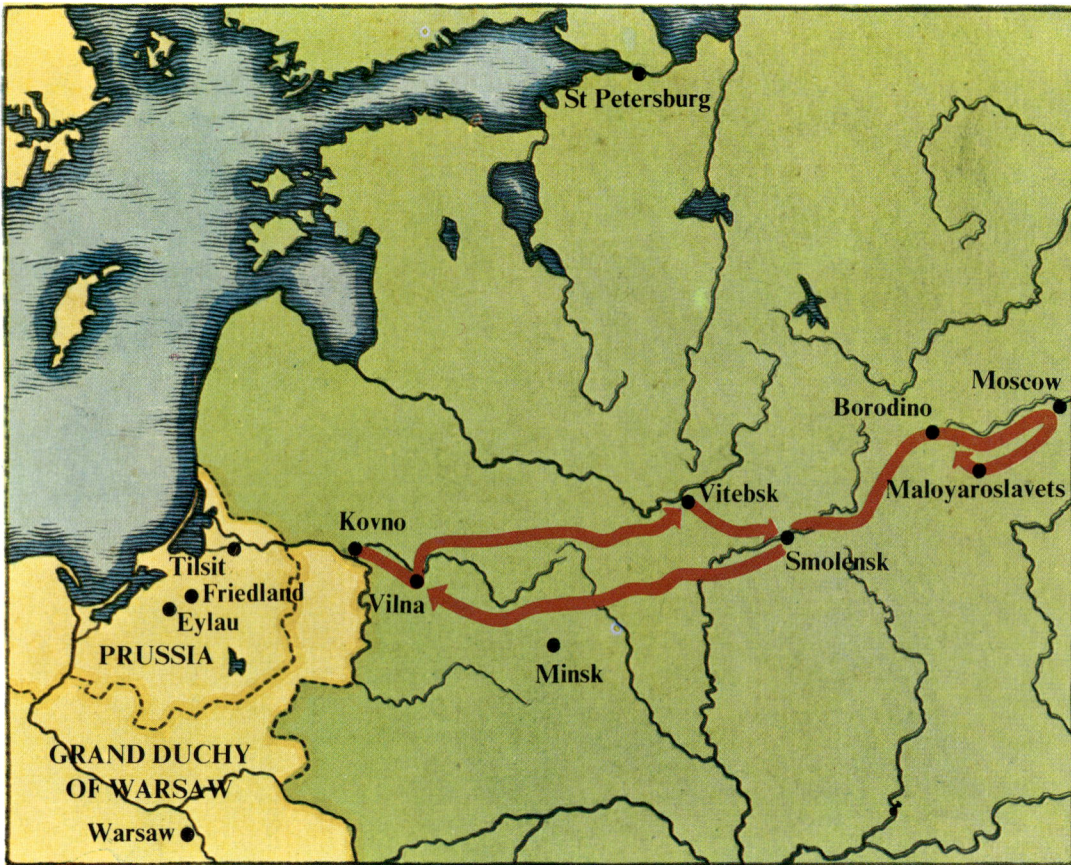

rate exceeded all expectations. Within a
week the French were in Vilna, but already
there had been difficulties in maintaining the
flow of supplies. After more than two weeks'
delay, the French pressed on, reaching
Vitebsk by the end of July. Still there had
been no major battles, although the French
had encountered severe resistance from the
Russian rearguard. Again Napoleon delayed for two weeks.

The Russian retreat, and their destruction of all that might aid the French, was
producing great consternation among the
French generals. As the French army advanced further and further from its base,
an increasingly large number of troops had
to be detached to protect the lines of communication, and the task of supplying the
main army became extremely complicated.
Already Napoleon's generals were advising
retreat, and Napoleon himself seemed unable to decide on the best course to pursue.
Although he ignored his generals and continued to advance, his thrust into Russia
lacked the inspiration of his earlier campaigns. His very anxiety to ensure that he
had a large enough army to preclude defeat
had given him a force incapable of rapid
action.

Napoleon's main hope now was that he
would be able to meet the defeat the
Russians at Smolensk. He hoped and expected that there the Russians would make
a stand and that by defeating them he could
force Alexander to sue for peace. For two
days his artillery bombarded the city, but
on the night of 17 August the Russian
general Barclay de Tolly withdrew along the

road to Moscow with his army. Junot, who
had been sent around Smolensk to prevent
the retreat, failed to arrive in time. Yet again
the Russians escaped.

The Russians simply did not have the
army to make a stand at Smolensk, but in
spite of this weakness it was becoming increasingly difficult for Barclay to defend his
constant withdrawal. Although Napoleon
feared more than anything else that he would
be unable to bring the Russians to battle,
Russian politicians were urging a battle to
save Moscow. Alexander was persuaded to
remove Barclay and replace him with Kutuzov, who had made his reputation against
the Turks. It was understood that Kutuzov

would fight to stop the French advance.

A week after entering Smolensk Napoleon's army again pressed on towards Moscow. Kutuzov had determined to make his
stand at the Moskva River, and his army
entrenched itself near the village of Borodino. On 5 September the French encountered the Russians. Believing that he
did not have the resources to risk dividing
his army to flank the Russian position,
Napoleon decided that it would have to be
taken by a direct frontal attack. The attack
was launched on the 7th.

In spite of all Napoleon's hopes of a huge
army in Russia, his actual force for the
attack amounted only to some 120,000 men:

Above, the Battle of Borodino, outside Moscow, in September 1812; the battle opened the way for Napoleon's occupation of the Russian capital but did not give Napoleon the decisive victory for him to subdue Russia.

Left, the ruins of Moscow after the fire of September 1812.

Opposite top, Napoleon's invasion of Russia and his retreat, in 1812; the enormous distances involved in this invasion proved too much even for his well-organized supply system.

Opposite bottom, Moscow in flames in September 1812; it is probable that after the city had been occupied by Napoleon, Russian patriots set fire to it to force the French out.

the Russians had slightly more in the field. All day the French surged into attack against the Russian positions. This was no brilliant strategic victory on the part of Napoleon but a struggle of bloody attrition. By the end of the day the French were in possession of the field, but they had suffered some 30,000 casualties; Russian casualties were over 50,000. All the talk of French glory, and of justice and unity for Europe, were revealed in their true light in the reality of tens of thousands of dead and dying, sacrificed to the vanity and ego of a brilliant Corsican soldier of boundless ambition. Borodino was not the victory he needed. Although the Russians had lost practically half their men as casualties, they had not been routed or annihilated. There was still a Russian army.

Moscow, however, was now open to the French, and Napoleon still hoped for Russian emissaries to announce that Alexander was suing for peace. But nothing happened. Kutuzov retired beyond Moscow, and Napoleon entered the city on 14 September. It was a strange sight. Many civilians had followed the Russian army, and the French troops marched in through deserted streets. On the same night fire broke out— it was never certain whether by accident or design. In the following days fire gutted the city, and the French troops wandered

through the deserted houses seizing valuables soon to be destroyed or discarded. Napoleon desperately needed a Russian request for peace. He had driven deep into the heart of Russia, but it was now September. Winter was near. Soon the snow would come.

The retreat from Moscow

For over a month Napoleon waited for the tsar to seek peace, but there was no news. There were no letters seeking terms, there were no emissaries. There was to be no peace with the French despoilers. When Napoleon finally decided in the middle of October that he would have to retreat, it was too late. He still had more than 100,000 men, but he had to find food and shelter before winter set in. Even before he began the retreat the task seemed practically hopeless. Morale was low, there was a shortage of food, there was far too little warm clothing for an army retreating at the beginning of a Russian winter, and the Russians were ready to fall on the hated French.

An immediate problem that faced Napoleon was that the road he had travelled from Smolensk to Moscow had been pillaged by the passage of the armies; there was no food and little shelter. The French army would have had far more chance of survival along the road further to the south which ran towards Kaluga, but Kutuzov's army was blocking that alternative route. Napoleon decided to try to force his way along that road, and on 19 October the French army of some 100,000 moved southwards out of Moscow. Napoleon had left men to blow up the Kremlin, but their inefficiency saved all the important buildings. The retreating army moved slowly, burdened not with essential supplies but with loot from the Russian capital. When the Russians checked the French at Yaroslavetz on 24 October, Napoleon decided that he dare not risk attacking the whole Russian army and turned north to return by the route along which his army had advanced.

The first test of the French army was the long march along the devastated road to Smolensk. It was already obvious that the French faced complete disaster. Although it was not yet bitterly cold and there was little snow on this section of the march, the French troops were already exhausted and hungry. They entered Smolensk on 8 November. There was little food, not nearly enough for the whole French army, which was rapidly becoming more an undisciplined mob than an organized force. They marched on from Smolensk after several days' rest. The French rearguard under Ney was separated from the main army. In desperate fighting it rejoined Napoleon, but Ney lost over 7,000 out of a total force of 8,000 men.

It now seemed possible that the whole campaign would end at the Beresina River. Three Russian armies amounting to over

120,000 men were converging on the crossing. The only bridge had been destroyed, but the French engineers moved to the north and succeeded in building two temporary bridges across the icy water. Even yet it seemed that the whole French army might well be annihilated. On 26 and 27 November the army began to cross, but on the 28th troops on both banks and those crossing the river were under heavy fire from the Russians. Amid scenes of horror hundreds were thrown into the water, and on the next day the French destroyed the bridges, leaving thousands of stragglers on the east bank. Yet 60,000 troops had crossed the Beresina: this had seemed impossible a few days before.

In the following two weeks many thought they would have been better off drowning in the Beresina. The temperature fell to well below zero, and the French troops, already exhausted by the marching, the fighting and the lack of food and warm clothing, collapsed on every side along the way. Desperately the survivors struggled on to Vilna, hoping that there they would find food and shelter. They found some, but not nearly enough, and by this time the army was a rabble. In the middle of December Marshal Ney crossed the River Niemen with the last of the rearguard. Over 500,000 men had

been used on the Russian campaign: fewer than 50,000 could be reassembled in Polish territory.

Napoleon was no longer with the remnant of his army when it crossed the Niemen out of Russia. On 5 December, after previously dictating a bulletin announcing his defeat, he set out with all possible speed for Paris. The reason for his haste was to re-establish his position in France and to demonstrate that he had not died on the Russian campaign. He had heard of the conspiracy of General Claude François de Malet, who for a brief time had remarkable success in Paris by the simple expedient of announcing that Napoleon was dead. Although Malet was soon taken and shot, Napoleon was shocked to discover that no one had rallied around Marie Louise and his son, the King of Rome. He travelled rapidly to Paris to establish his own position and that of his dynasty, arriving at the French capital on 18 December.

In 1808, when Napoleon had been at the height of his achievements, it had seemed that the only blemishes on the whole fabric of French European power had been the uprising in the Iberian peninsula and the discontent caused by Napoleon's determination to crush the British through the use of the Continental System. By 1812 these minor

Above, the French army retreating from Moscow in the winter of 1812–13; it suffered equally from hunger, cold and the enemy's guerrilla tactics, and the campaign cost Napoleon almost 500,000 casualties.

Opposite top, Prince Golenischev Kutusov (1745–1813), the Russian commander in 1812, who held the Russian army together after the defeat at Borodino and successfully harassed Napoleon on his retreat from Russia.

Opposite bottom, Napoleon's armies crossing the River Beresina, in central European Russia, in November 1812. The French lost 20,000 men and only narrowly escaped total annihilation or capture by the Russians. Musée de l'Armée, Paris.

blemishes had become gaping holes. Enforcement of the Continental System had caused resentment through much of Europe and in France itself and had helped to send Napoleon on his disastrous expedition into Russia. The little regarded uprising of the Spaniards had in four years been transformed into a major conflict, which was constantly draining French troops and resources.

In 1812, while Napoleon pushed into Russia, Wellington had defeated the French at Salamanca in July and for a time occupied Madrid. The French had found it impossible to suppress the Spanish uprising and throw the British from the peninsula. With the loss of a huge army in Russia, Napoleon was now at bay.

It is difficult to summon sympathy for the French emperor in 1812. The thousands upon thousands of men who had died or had been maimed on the battlefields of Europe had perished largely because of Napoleon's overwhelming ambition and his refusal to set reasonable limits to his power. In Russia there had been too large and unwieldy a French army, it had been inadequately supplied, and no proper precautions had been taken against the dangers of campaigning in a Russian winter. The emperor returned neither frost-bitten nor hungry, but men from all over Europe were left frozen in the snows of Russia.

The turn of the tide

Such had been the effect of Napoleon's crushing victories since 1805 that even after the disasters of 1812 those European powers who had suffered from his military genius were reluctant to send their armies into the field against him. Many did, however, take the opportunity to sever the French alliances into which they had been forced.

The Prussians, who had been engaged on the northern wing of the advance into Russia, hated the French for earlier humiliations, and on 30 December General Yorck, who had commanded the Prussian contingent on the Russian invasion, signed the Convention of Tauroggen with the Russians. Frederick William of Prussia was still undecided whether to throw his country fully into the conflict against Napoleon, but once he was sure that the Russians intended to press on into Germany against the French he was willing to sign an agreement with Alexander; this was accomplished by the Treaty of Kalish on 27 February. In the middle of March Frederick William formally declared war against France.

While a variety of European powers were trying to decide what to do, the Russians in the first months of 1813 were advancing to the Elbe. The French under Eugène Beauharnais left garrisons in key Prussian defence points, but the main body of troops had no choice other than to retreat while the Russians moved into Germany.

This steady advance of the Russians helped to bring another country on to the side of Napoleon's opponents. Since assuming the control of Sweden, Bernadotte had shown no inclination to act as a satellite of Napoleon. In spite of Napoleon's desires, the Swedes had not taken part in the invasion of Russia in 1812. At the beginning of March 1813 Bernadotte agreed to join the allies, and his troops soon entered Germany to swell the number of France's enemies. With the Russians and Prussians facing the French in Germany, the Swedes soon to join them and the British firmly established in the Iberian peninsula, Napoleon had both to raise men as quickly as possible and attempt to placate his allies and the neutrals.

Through the early months of 1813 Napoleon set about the task of raising another army. In response to the emergency he used extreme measures to raise men, including calling up the conscripts for 1814. Inevitably, the constant demands for men caused resentment in France and ensured that it would be difficult to create the enthusiasm of the early Revolutionary days in an effort to preserve the Napoleonic empire.

In the middle of April 1813 Napoleon left Paris to join Eugène in Germany. He still had hope, and he still had allies. Although Russia and England had been joined by Prussia and Sweden, Austria was still in doubt. It was not that Napoleon's father-in-law had any love for him but rather that Metternich did not intend to risk defeat and

that he feared the Russians as well as the French. In spite of British and Russian hopes, Austria bided her time. The various states of the Confederation of the Rhine also feared to desert Napoleon until they were quite sure that his fangs had been drawn, and Denmark threw in her lot with the French emperor. As there were also Italian and Polish troops in the French army, the struggles of 1813 cannot be explained simply in terms of patriotic nationalists intent on throwing off the French yoke. In reality, the rulers of the various European states, big and small, were still pursuing their own personal and political ambitions. There were expressions of nationalistic sentiment, particularly in Prussia among the intellectuals, but most important for Napoleon was to convince the traditional rulers of Europe of his power. If Napoleon could demonstrate that he had the military skill and resources to win battles in his old decisive manner, then the European rulers would again have to reach an accommodation with him.

When Napoleon took command at Erfurt late in April he had available some 200,000 men; this was more than the Russian and Prussian forces combined. However, the more time that passed without the French winning a decisive victory, the more this advantage would diminish. The first engagement took place at Lützen (Gross Görschen) near Leipzig at the beginning of May when the Russian General Wittgenstein's force met Ney. Both sides suffered heavy losses and the allies were forced to retreat, but the French had not won a decisive victory.

The French again attempted to transform the situation at Bautzen on 20 May, this time with Napoleon in direct command; once more the fighting was fierce, again the French won, but still no army had been annihilated. On 4 June Napoleon agreed to an armistice, presumably hoping that this would be to his advantage, allowing him time to bring up additional troops and in taking away the enthusiasm of the allies for continuing the advance. It was a miscalculation. Although Napoleon used the armistice (which lasted into August) to increase his force in Germany to over 400,000 men and strengthened his cavalry in the hope of taking better advantage of his victories, the allies profited greatly from the pause.

The main blow to Napoleon during the armistice was the commitment of the Austrians to the allied cause. In June at Reichenbach Great Britain agreed to supply Prussia and Russia with subsidies, and Austria, Prussia and Russia signed an agreement by which it was decided that the three powers would present a list of demands to Napoleon: the duchy of Warsaw was to be broken up, Prussia was to regain her 1806 boundaries, the Illyrian provinces were to be restored to Austrian control and the Hanseatic towns were to be given their independence. Metternich was the guiding spirit behind these proposals. Even if Napoleon would not accept these terms, and their rejection

Above, the Battle of Salamanca in Spain in July 1812, at which the British under Wellington defeated the French army; by the following year he had driven the French out of Spain altogether. National Army Museum, London.

Opposite top, Napoleon crossing the Rhine in 1812, pursued by the allies.

Opposite bottom, the Battle of Badajoz, in southern Spain, in 1812, when Wellington drove out the French armies, which had occupied the town since the previous year. Badajoz was a centre of Spanish nationalist opposition to the French, and it had withstood a French siege in 1808–09.

seemed extremely likely, Metternich could well hope that their rejection would help to unite opinion against the French emperor.

Metternich met Napoleon in Dresden, and although Napoleon promised no concessions it was agreed that a conference would be held in Prague. The conference lasted from the middle of July until near the middle of August, but there never seemed any real chance of success. Napoleon would not yield to the ultimatum of the Reichenbach allies, and on 12 August Austria, who had received promises of British money, declared war on France. Two days later Napoleon accepted in substance the Metternich proposals, but it is doubtful whether he would ultimately have abided by them, and in any event the allies were now ready to move in for the kill.

For Napoleon to maintain his power it was essential that he should move swiftly to defeat the separate allied armies before they could act in coordination to move westwards across Germany. There were three main allied armies on the German front: the Prussian Marshal Blücher commanded just over 100,000 Prussians and Russians in Silesia, Bernadotte commanded over 120,000 Swedes, Prussians and Russians in the north, advancing from Prussia, and in the south

the Austrian Marshal Schwarzenberg had nearly 250,000 men under his command. When the campaign began Napoleon centred his forces in the region of Dresden: he hoped he could beat the allies separately, but appeared undecided whether or not to commit the mass of his army in the hope of achieving decisive victory. The Russian disaster had left him uncertain of the quality of his troops and also perhaps unwilling to take the risks that once would have seemed natural.

Instead of moving decisively, Napoleon detached smaller forces against the allied armies, and the French suffered defeats: at Grossbeeren by Bernadotte's army and at Katzbach by Blücher's. When Schwarzenberg attacked Dresden late in August Napoleon won a victory on the 26th and 27th but suffered exceedingly heavy losses, and lost all advantage from it when three days later Vandamme's army of 10,000 men was forced to capitulate at Kulm.

By September 1813 Napoleon was in dire trouble. He had won no decisive victory, he had lost a great many men, the allies were receiving reinforcements, and the French now faced encirclement as the increased allied armies combined against them. Under this pressure Napoleon retreated to Leipzig.

He decided that here he would make his stand. As the ring tightened the allies were hardening in their war aims. By the Treaty of Teplitz on 9 September Prussia, Russia, and Austria agreed to fight for the restoration of the 1805 boundaries of Prussia and Austria and for independence for the states of southern and western Germany. A month later Bavaria agreed to join the allies.

When the Battle of Leipzig begain on 16 October Napoleon had 160,000 men: the allies had twice that number. It was a three-day struggle. On the first day Napoleon attempted, unsuccessfully, to rout Schwarzenberg's forces. On the 17th both sides desperately attempted to reorganize and reform, and the allied army was stiffened in the course of the day by the arrival of numerous reinforcements. On the 18th the battle was decided. The Saxon troops left Napoleon to join the allies, and Bernadotte's troops arrived. That night the French flight into and through Leipzig began, and it continued on the next day. It was a scene of chaos. Napoleon and many of his troops crossed the Elster River by the bridge, but this was blown up too soon, and many French troops were left in the town. The French had been routed, and they fled westwards across Germany.

The collapse of Napoleon's empire

After Leipzig Napoleon's empire was in ruins. At the end of October some 60,000 French troops fought their way through the Bavarians at Hanau to cross the Rhine. All over Europe there was a rush to join the allies. The German states deserted Napoleon, by mid-November Holland was in revolt, and the Italians were up in arms. In the Iberian peninsula Wellington's victory at Vittoria on 21 June had forced the French to retreat into France. By the end of the year Wellington was invading from the south.

Even yet the allies presented peace terms rather than advancing across the Rhine into France. Again Metternich was the instigator of the proposals, and as in the case of the earlier offer at Prague there were ambiguities clouding the suggested terms. It appeared from the Declaration of Frankfurt, which was agreed on by the allies in November, that they were prepared to offer the French their 'natural frontiers' of the Alps and the Rhine and to leave Belgium to France, but this was not specified in so many words.

Metternich, as earlier in the summer, had mixed motives. Undoubtedly he was hoping that whatever settlement was eventually decided upon would not so crush France as to upset completely the balance of power in Europe; Austria feared Russia almost as much as Napoleon. Yet if Napoleon accepted negotiations on Metternich's terms he had good reason for believing that he would have difficulty obtaining all he wanted in actual treaties; England was in no mood for generous concessions. If Napoleon turned down the offer of negotiations, then it could be argued that his overweening ambition had prevented France from accepting peace on the basis of her early Revolutionary victories.

Napoleon, as so often in 1813, appeared not quite sure how to proceed. In December he replied agreeing to negotiations on the basis of the allied offer, but by then this was no longer enough. The British government had made it quite clear that it was not prepared to accept a peace which gave France a firm stake in the Low Countries. Moreover, Alexander had the ambition of leading his armies in an invasion of France.

The invasion of France

Late in December 1813 the allies began to cross the Rhine to invade France. Napoleon was desperately trying to raise an army to meet them, conscripting any men who had avoided the army in previous years and calling on those who should have been conscripted in 1815. He had lost hundreds of thousands of men in eighteen months, and many of those veterans who were still under arms were cut off in fortresses scattered all the way across Germany. It seemed that all that could save Napoleon now was a mass

uprising and a burst of nationalistic fervour of the kind that had been seen at the start of the Revolutionary wars. But the French people had suffered too much in the previous five years to defend with passion a ruler who had become increasingly arbitrary from the time that his empire had reached its greatest extent. In January 1814, all his efforts not withstanding, Napoleon could put into the field only some 60,000 men to meet the invaders.

The allied invasion was made in overwhelming force. First across the Rhine were the Prussians under Blücher, who invaded northeastern France; in addition the second army, led by Schwarzenberg, violated the neutrality of Switzerland to invade France further to the south, Bernadotte's force was advancing into the Netherlands, and in the south Wellington's army was continuing its steady penetration.

Napoleon first concentrated his efforts against Blücher's army and then turned against Schwarzenberg. Of necessity Napoleon led an army of manoeuvrable size, and at this moment of disaster his military genius was at its greatest. On 29 January he met Blücher's Prussians at Brienne and routed them, but he suffered a reverse at La Rothière three days later on 1 February

and lost many men. At La Rothière the allies simply had too many troops, as Blücher's Prussians had linked up with a force from the south.

After La Rothière Blücher advanced rapidly into France, making the mistake of scattering his army along the valley of the Marne. Napoleon took full advantage of this, and in a series of engagements in the first two weeks of February inflicted repeated defeats on Blücher's forces. He then quickly moved against Schwarzenberg and forced that army to retreat in engagements culminating on 18 February. In less than three weeks, with a much inferior force, Napoleon had hit again and again at the allied armies. Schwarzenberg was ready to order a full retreat, but the British and Russians were not dissuaded by the military reverses.

While the armies were clashing on French soil in February, a series of negotiations were carried on between France and the allies at Châtillon. There never seemed any real chance of success in these negotiations. At first Napoleon had empowered his emissary Caulaincourt to make any possible peace, but his victories early in February then made him reluctant to accept even the best terms the allies were now likely to offer him. With their armies actually in France

the allies were prepared to offer few concessions to the French emperor: they now intended that France should return to her pre-Revolutionary boundaries. The leadership in bolstering the allied determination was taken by the British Foreign Minister Lord Castlereagh.

On 1 March 1814, the allies signed the Treaty of Chaumont. Great Britain, Austria, Russia and Prussia agreed to fight to enforce France's pre-Revolutionary limits and to make no separate peace while Napoleon refused to accept this settlement. Great Britain agreed to subsidize the other powers while the war continued. Apart from sharing the burden of the military operations she promised to add an additional five million pounds a year to be divided among the other three powers. The allies also made a number of other agreements regarding the postwar territorial settlement: Holland and Belgium were to be combined under one monarchy, Italy was to be divided, and Swiss independence and neutrality were to be guaranteed as well.

After Chaumont it was clear that there was to be no turning back. On 7 and 9 March the relentless Blücher, who had never had Schwarzenberg's doubts about the necessity of crushing Napoleon in France, met Napoleon's army in bitterly fought battles at

Craonne and Laon. Although Blücher could claim no clear victories, Napoleon was by now so badly outnumbered that there was little he could do. He did take Reims, but at the battle of Arcis-sur-Aube on 20 and 21 March he was outnumbered by over three to one. Still he thought of attack, and planned to move against the allied lines of communication. The allies captured a letter telling of this and determined to march to attack Paris and ignore what was left of Napoleon's army. On 17 March Napoleon had made a last effort to secure a negotiated peace when he sent new instructions to Caulaincourt, but though he was now much nearer to accepting the allies' demands, the allies were in a position to impose any peace they desired. They no longer felt any need to conciliate Napoleon. His gesture was ignored.

As the allies closed rapidly on Paris, the Empress Marie Louise and Napoleon's son left the capital. On the 30th there was fighting outside Paris, Marchals Marmont and Mortier trying to defend the capital with fewer than 30,000 men against some 200,000 on the side of the allies. Although Napoleon was rapidly approaching the city, nothing could be done to save it. On 31 March Tsar Alexander and King Frederick William of Prussia were able to enter the city.

Napoleon's abdication and exile

Napoleon would have been willing to see still more deaths and destruction in an effort to save his position, but more reasonable men prevailed. Talleyrand wanted to protect France, not Napoleon, and he persuaded Alexander that the soundest course would be the restoration of the Bourbons. The French Senate met at the beginning of April, quickly established a provisional government and announced the deposition of the emperor. On 6 April, at the urging of several of his marshals, Napoleon signed his act of abdication. His efforts to have his son recognized as emperor failed.

The fate of Napoleon was settled formally by the Treaty of Fontainebleau on 11 April. By this treaty Napoleon renounced the throne of France. He would now be emperor only of the island of Elba and would be granted two million francs a year. The Empress Marie Louise was given Parma and Piacenza in Italy, and Joséphine was given an annuity of one million francs. For a man whose ambitions had brought death and suffering to millions it was hardly a harsh settlement, but for Napoleon the fall was great. On the 12th he attempted unsuccessfully to commit suicide by taking poison.

On the 20th the ruler of Elba had an emotional parting from the Guard and set off for his island. His journey was an ignominious one and for a time the fearful emperor was disguised in Austrian uniform. He was taken to Elba on a British frigate. He arrived on 4 May, the day after Louis XVIII had arrived in Paris.

Louis XVIII

The new king now had the immediate tasks of signing a peace treaty with the allies and establishing a new government with himself as king. The Treaty of Paris was signed on 30 May 1814. France was given her 1792 boundaries, and most of her colonies were returned to her. On her part she recognized the independence of the German and Italian states, of the Netherlands and of Switzerland. Although other general principles were agreed on by the allies, it was resolved that the precise settlement would be decided upon at a congress in Vienna.

In an effort to establish a government that would be acceptable to a country which had passed through both the Revolution and the rule of Napoleon, Louis XVIII incorporated liberal features into his royal regime. The charter which he issued in June in principle promised representative government

Above, a cartoon of the Russian armies, which included Cossack peasants, entering Paris in 1814, only two years after the French had marched into Moscow.

Opposite, the entrance of the allied forces into Paris in March 1814, after what appeared to be the final collapse of Napoleon's ambitions. The emperor was exiled to Elba but returned to France less than a year later to stage one final bid for glory, an attempt that ended at Waterloo in June 1815.

Fac Simile of the abdication of Napoleon in 1814.

6. avril 1814.

Les puissances alliées ayant proclamé que l'empereur Napoléon était le seul obstacle au rétablissement de la paix en Europe, l'empereur,
fidèle à son serment, déclare qu'il renonce pour lui et ses enfants, aux trônes de France et d'Italie, et qu'il n'est aucun sacrifice, même
celui de la vie, qu'il ne soit prêt à faire aux intérêts de la France.

For the translation of the above see page 250.

(through two chambers—one hereditary, one elected), freedom of the press and permanence for the land reforms of the Revolution. But in practice many found that Louis XVIII had learned too little from the Revolution and from the death of his brother, Louis XVI. The French people feared that the liberties granted to them would gradually be eroded. More important for Louis' immediate power, he also alienated the army by showing more favours to old courtiers than to the Napoleonic veterans. A France which had seen the world-shaking reforms of the Revolution and the imperial glory of Napoleon could hardly be expected to greet the mediocre government of Louis XVIII with any enthusiasm.

The Congress of Vienna

While France attempted to accustom herself to her reduced state, the victorious allies met in Vienna to decide the future of Europe.

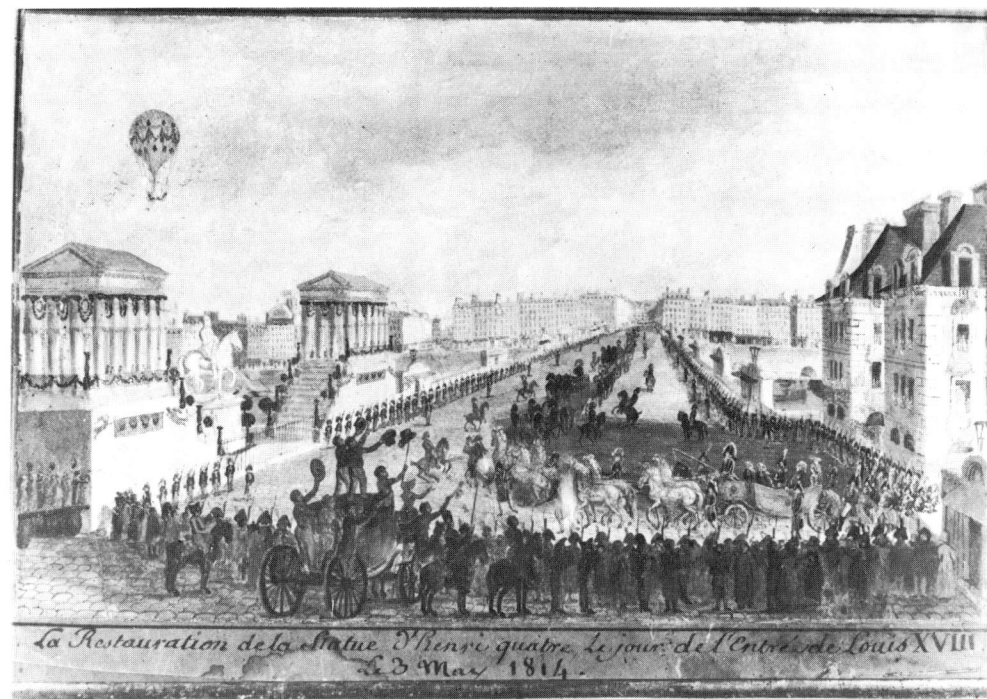

La Restauration de la Statue d'Henri quatre le jour de l'Entrée de Louis XVIII le 3 May 1814.

Above, Louis XVIII, King of France (reigned 1814–24), the brother of Louis XVI; he was restored to the French throne by the allies in 1814 but had to abdicate briefly in 1815 when Napoleon returned from exile in Elba. Victoria and Albert Museum, London.

Above left, the return of Louis XVIII to Paris, in May 1814; his restoration of some of the abuses of the ancien régime, and his disavowal of the glory that France had won under Napoleon, quickly lost him the support of most of his people.

Left, The Congress of Vienna of September 1814, at which princes from all over Europe met to re-establish the status quo. Kungl Bibliothek, Stockholm.

Opposite top, the Battle of Arcis-sur-Aube, in March 1814; the last battle fought by Napoleon before the allies took Paris. Residenz, Munich.

Opposite bottom, Napoleon's note announcing his decision to abdicate, for himself and his heirs, all claims to the French throne, in April 1814; in exchange he was granted a pension, and a relatively comfortable exile in Elba.

This famous gathering which lasted from the autumn of 1814 to June 1815 had representatives from all over Europe; the real power, however, lay in the hands of Great Britain, Russia, Austria and Prussia. The negotiators were distinguished: Alexander came in person to represent Russia, Castlereagh acted for Great Britain, Hardenberg and Wilhelm von Humboldt for Prussia and Metternich for Austria. In view of the reason for the Congress it was remarkable that Talleyrand, who came to Vienna on behalf of France, should also have exercised such influence on the proceedings of the Congress; that he did stemmed in large part from the jealousies and dissensions which beset the victorious powers.

The eventual territorial settlement arranged by June 1815 followed the lines already established in the agreements made by the powers when advancing against Napoleon. The settlement was reached, however, only after major quarrels between the powers; these quarrels were to help to inspire Napoleon to a new effort.

Prussia gained massively by the settlement, obtaining a large part of Saxony together with territories on the Rhine. That Saxony survived at all was because of the vigorous efforts of Great Britain, Austria and Talleyrand. Germany, apart from Austria and Prussia, was organized into the Germanic Confederation of thirty-nine states and cities; they controlled their own internal affairs but ceded some powers in external affairs to the Confederation. Although Alexander did not obtain all he wanted, much of Poland came under Russian control. Holland and Belgium were united as the Kingdom of The Netherlands under

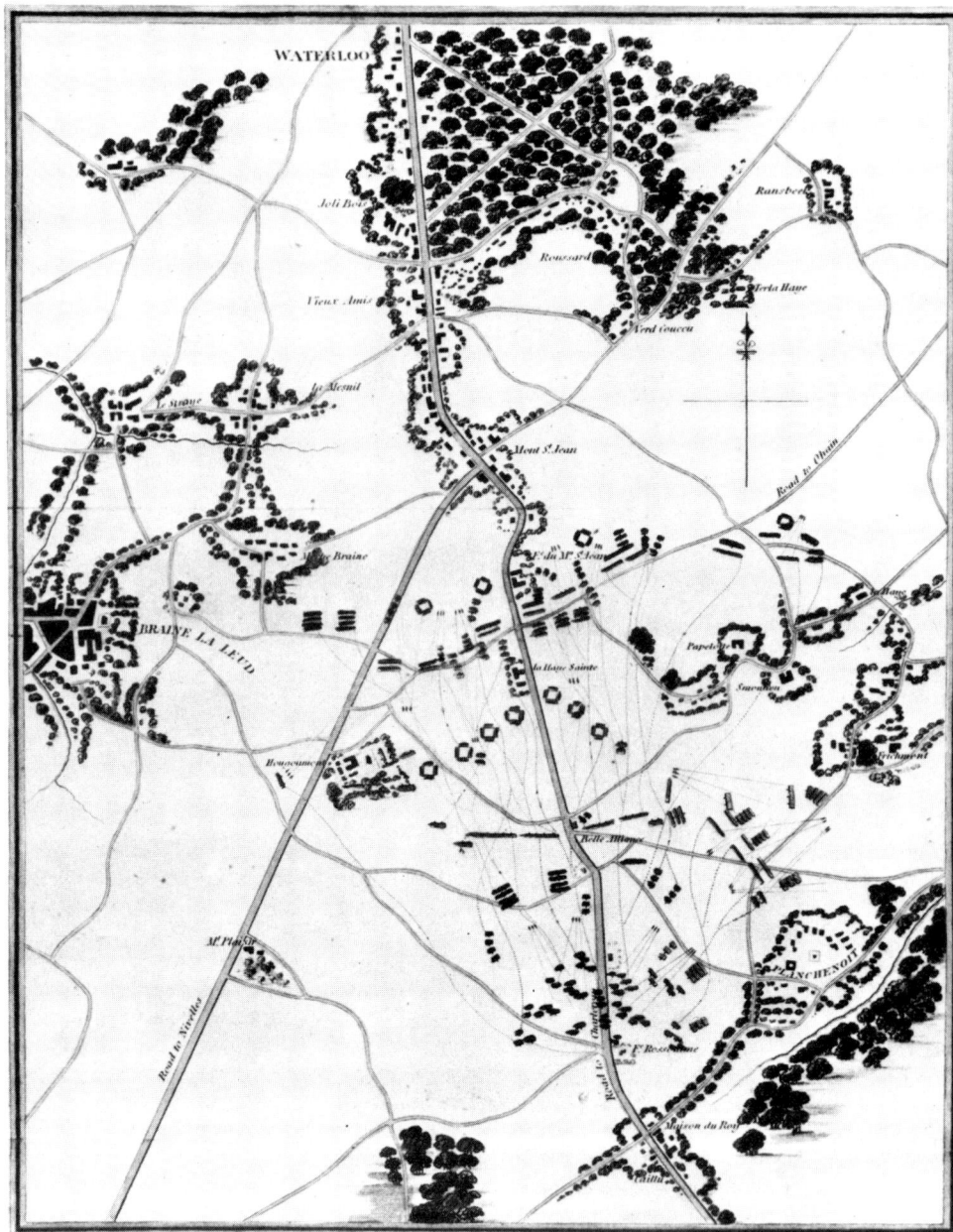

the House of Orange, and Switzerland was established as a confederation of cantons. Italy remained a collection of independent states, and Venetia and Lombardy were given to Austria. Napoleon had been defeated, but his reshaping of Europe left its mark on the peace settlement in 1815.

In late 1814 and early 1815 the situation in France and in Europe proved particularly favourable to the exiled Napoleon. In France Louis XVIII had done little to endear himself to the French people, and many looked back longingly to earlier days. In Vienna the allies showed signs not only of dissension but even of resorting to war. The greatest argument had been over Saxony, but Poland had also helped to drive a deep rift between the victorious powers. Prussia hoped at Vienna to annex the whole of Saxony, while Russia hoped for Poland. Their efforts to force their territorial demands on the Congress had by the end of 1814 pushed Great Britain and Austria together and had persuaded them both to enter a closer relationship with the defeated French. Early in January 1815 Great Britain, Austria and France signed a secret treaty pledging themselves to resist Prussian and Russian demands. The signs of discontent in France and of tension in Europe were keenly watched by Napoleon from the island of Elba.

The Hundred Days

Since arriving at Elba Napoleon had shown little inclination to sink into a pleasant retirement. He ran the little island like an empire in miniature, although he had no empress. Marie Louise would not join him with their son, and she was able to find consolation elsewhere. At Elba Napoleon was supplied with information from the mainland of Europe and knew of the difficulties in France and at Vienna. He also had reason to complain that Louis XVIII had not paid the annuity agreed on. Yet, of course, it was not for the sake of an annuity that he was prepared to make another dramatic throw. It was power and glory that drove him; an insatiable hunger that could not be assuaged on the little island of Elba.

On 26 February 1815, Napoleon set sail for the mainland. He had fewer than a thousand men with him, but he had all the confidence of a man who had ruled Europe. On 1 March, after good fortune had helped

him to avoid the British navy, he landed on the mainland. The whole episode was in the balance until he reached Grenoble, where he was welcomed with enthusiasm. From there support flocked to him, and Napoleon was again willing to encounter the combined powers of Europe. On 20 March he entered and took command of Paris. The king had fled.

In Vienna the news of Napoleon's landing had arrived by 7 March. The allies acted promptly. Napoleon was declared an outlaw, and on 25 March the four main powers signed an alliance by which they promised to fight until their old enemy had been completely defeated. With foreign powers quickly combining against him, Napoleon felt that his main hope was to appear as the liberator of the French people. To rally the French nation behind him he attempted to create a liberal façade such as he had never felt to be necessary when he had dominated Europe.

Late in April he issued the so-called Additional Act, which tried to embody liberal

reforms, including two chambers, freedom of the press and promises of a reign of liberty for French citizens. The whole plan was so clearly dictated by necessity that it aroused no enthusiasm. In general, Napoleon's attempts to arouse the French people during the Hundred Days achieved little success. The reality was not the promised liberties but rather the certainty of more war and more deaths. Napoleon's advantage was that his veterans were now in France rather than scattered in garrisons throughout Europe, and in essence it was on these veterans that Napoleon depended. He soon had assembled an army of nearly 250,000 men, and when he moved to attack the allies he used half of these as a striking force.

A major problem confronting Napoleon in the spring of 1815 was a lack of allies. One possibility was Murat, King of Naples, who had earlier deserted Napoleon. But Murat made his move too early, in March, when he attempted to arouse Italy against the Austrians. As a result, by the time Napoleon was ready to move he had already been defeated and had fled from Italy. Napoleon would have to depend on the army he could raise in France, and he was certain to be greatly outnumbered.

At Vienna the allies planned for three armies to invade France. More than 250,000 Austrians, Bavarians and Russians under Schwarzenberg were to cross the upper Rhine; more than 150,000 Prussians under Blücher were to attack across the lower Rhine; and Wellington was to command more than 100,000 British, Hanoverians, Dutch and Belgians in the Low Countries. Wellington, who had driven the French out

of Spain, had earlier in the year replaced Castlereagh as the British representative in Vienna. He was now to fill a more active role.

The Battle of Waterloo

Before the general plan of attack on France could unfold, the actual course of events was precipitated by Napoleon. He was determined to strike before the allies could assemble and drive into France. He wanted to take the offensive, defeat Wellington and Blücher and then engage the largest army under Schwarzenberg. To achieve maximum effect he would have to attack before Wellington and Blücher had combined their forces.

Napoleon left Paris on 12 June. He commanded some 125,000 men and knew quite well that he would have to strike quickly. Wellington had under his command approximately 90,000 troops, consisting of British, Germans and Dutch-Belgian forces. Blücher commanded about 125,000 Prussians; they were strung out along the Sambre and Meuse rivers, resting their right on Charleroi. Wellington's force was to the right of the Prussians, although troops were assembling as far north as Brussels. They hoped to combine for an attack into France, but the French forestalled them. The allies were not in prepared defensive lines and indeed were vulnerable as they were attempting to assemble for their own advance.

The French crossed the frontier on 15 June. Napoleon's first hope was to split the allies, rout them, and drive on to Brussels. Quickly the French drove the Prussians from Charleroi and occupied the town.

Above, the Battle of Waterloo in June 1815; despite France's exhaustion after twenty years of virtually continual warfare, it was a remarkable measure of Napoleon's popularity that he could raise an army of 75,000 even though he had been in exile for a year.

Opposite top left, a cartoon by George Cruickshank of the vital part played by the Russians in the defeat of Napoleon, and the sudden growth of Russian authority in the years after 1812. Victoria and Albert Museum, London.

Opposite bottom left, the entry of the allied armies into Paris in 1814; by this time France was drained of resources, both of money and of manpower, by twenty years of war throughout Europe. Korrermuseum, Dresden.

Opposite right, the plan of the Battle of Waterloo. Wellington took up position south of the village of Quatre Bras, and Napoleon launched a series of attacks against the centre of the allied position.

347

Napoleon now pushed on with the main part of his army in order to engage the Prussians, while Ney was ordered to advance towards Wellington's force. Wellington moved slowly and was able to assemble only part of his army at Quatre Bras. Napoleon did not achieve the complete victory that he needed. The Prussians were concentrated at Ligny, and Napoleon drove them from the field on the afternoon of the 16th after bitter fighting. Ney was also able to force the allied army to retreat at Quatre Bras, but neither there nor at Ligny were the allies pursued and annihilated. The Prussians retreated in good enough order to keep in contact with Wellington's force and were ready to support him if necessary.

Wellington's army retreated towards Brussels, and Napoleon, believing that he had effectively knocked out the Prussians, detached Grouchy with 33,000 men to follow their retreat, while he prepared to attack Wellington with 74,000 men. He had divided his army on the false assumption that the Prussians were retreating away from the British.

Napoleon came up to Wellington's troops on the evening of 17 June; they were drawn up near the village of Waterloo at Mont Saint-Jean. Wellington had the assurance of Blücher that if necessary the Prussians would come to his aid. Napoleon was confident of success. He had 74,000 French veterans against Wellington's polyglot army, which was slightly inferior in numbers but markedly inferior both in cavalry and artillery, and Napoleon believed that the Prussians were incapable of taking part in the battle. Indeed, he expected that Grouchy's force of over 30,000 would be able to detach itself from the defeated Prussians and come to his aid. His only immediate problem was that the heavy rains had left the ground wet and heavy, but he hoped to solve this difficulty by delaying his attack on the morning of 18 June. The delay was far more important than Napoleon realized.

Napoleon believed that he could defeat Wellington with a direct frontal attack, and he finally sent his troops into action at 11.00 a.m. For the next five hours his infantry threw themselves with great bravery against the allied lines, but with equal bravery the allied troops held their ground. At 4.00 p.m. Napoleon decided to use his cavalry, and the British troops faced the awesome sight of massed French horsemen thundering down upon them. The squares held, and Ney re-formed his men, threw in more cavalry, but was again unable to break the British squares.

From 4.00 to 6.00 p.m. charge after charge failed; 15,000 horsemen were unable to sweep the infantry aside. By 6.00 p.m. Napoleon was very near failure, for the Prussians were now arriving on the field (Grouchy never arrived). In a desperate attempt to break through Wellington's army, Napoleon at last threw in the Guard. All their tradition and bravery was not enough, they

too failed, and with Wellington's troops now moving forward and increasing numbers of Prussians throwing themselves into the battle the French began to crack and finally fled in panic. Now the allied cavalry were flung into action and pursued the fleeing Frenchmen. It was a complete rout. The losses were great. Wellington suffered nearly 15,000 casualties, the Prussians 7,000. The French never formed to assess their losses, but their casualties certainly exceeded those of the allies.

The last act

Napoleon fled from the battlefield, arriving in Paris on the 21st. After so many deaths, so much tragedy, he still talked of raising another army, of madly continuing the fight, as if the French desired nothing more than to pour out their blood in a desperate attempt to maintain Napoleon and his relatives in grandeur. Led by Fouché, the minister of police, the Chambers held firm for their own rights against Napoleon's suggestion that only a dictatorship would save the country. On 22 June Napoleon again abdicated and proclaimed his son as French emperor. It was no use. The Prussians entered Paris on 7 July, and Louis XVIII followed them on the next day.

Napoleon now hoped that he would be able to seek sanctuary in America or even find asylum in England, but the British government decided to place him on St Helena, far away in the South Atlantic. He died there on 5 May 1821. His complete reversal of fortune helped to build his legend, and in his own writings and conversation he attempted to give reasonable explanations for the many vagaries of his career.

Europe had been profoundly changed because Napoleon lived. Some of the changes had been clearly desirable, but the transformations had taken place at an incredible cost in human suffering. The Corsican adventurer had gloried in war. He had been a military genius, but part of his strength had been his very callousness, in the manner in

THE COLLAPSE OF THE FRENCH EMPIRE

Date	French Internal Politics	External Politics	Battles	Date	French Internal Politics	External Politics	Battles
1808		Franco-Russian conference at Erfurt Invasion of Spain	French defeated at Vimeiro	1812	Annulment of the Concordat The pope at Fontainebleau Second conspiracy of Malet	Russian campaign Retreat from Russia	Smolensk, Borodino Burning of Moscow Crossing of the Beresina
1809	Imprisonment of Pope Pius VII Napoleon excommunicated	Treaty of Schönbrunn	Battles of Corunna and Talavera Austrians defeated at Wagram	1813	Concordat of Fontainebleau	General coalition against France Joseph Bonaparte driven from Spain	Lützen and Bautzen Rout of the French at Leipzig
1810	Measures strengthening the emperor's dictatorship Napoleon's marriage to Marie-Louise Disgrace of Fouché Publication of the Penal Code	Peace with Sweden Annexation of Holland Decree of Trianon		1814	Fall and abdication of Napoleon Recall of Louis XVIII Declaration of Saint-Ouen	Campaign in France Congress of Chatillon Treaty of Chaumont Congress of Vienna	Brienne, la Rothière, Monterau, Laon, Arcis Surrender of Paris
1811	Birth of the king of Rome	Annexation of the German coast lands of the North Sea	Defeat of Marshal Masséna at Torres Vedras in Portugal	1815	Napoleon returns to France Louis XVIII flees and returns after Napoleon's abdication and banishment to St Helena	Napoleon escapes from Elba Allied troops defeat French army	French victories at Ligny and Quatre Bras Napoleon finally defeated at Waterloo

which he was not repelled by the killing. Europe had been shaken out of her complacency. Many reforms in law and government had been brought by the French armies; many others had been induced by the desire of European states to reform to resist Napoleon. In 1815 Europe tried to recover its stability and rebuild forms of government that were doomed, but they were doomed more because of the French Revolution than because of Napoleon.

Across the Atlantic, in the New World, the return to stability attempted in Europe was never possible, for there the changes of the Napoleonic years and of the previous generation were irreversible. In North America the success of the experiment in republican government had been in doubt since independence from Great Britain had been obtained in 1783; after 1815 it was in doubt no more. In South America the European wars had given the possessions of Spain the opportunity to emulate the British colonists to the north and break away from Europe. Their attempt at independence still seemed in some doubt in 1815, but in reality they had begun a move for separation which could not be stopped.

Left, Napoleon on board HMS Bellerophon, *the ship to which he surrendered after Waterloo in June 1815. Despite his hope for asylum in England, he was taken to exile in St Helena, a south Atlantic island*

Chapter 31

Independence Movements in Latin America

In the age of Napoleon the Spanish and Portuguese possessions on the American continent were divided into five huge areas of rule: the Viceroyalty of New Spain, which extended through modern Mexico and central America, the Viceroyalty of New Granada in the north of South America, the Viceroyalty of Peru on the west, the Viceroyalty of La Plata on the southeast and the Portuguese possession of Brazil. These great administrative divisions were, however, only lightly superimposed on settlements isolated from each other by immense distances, towering mountains, impassable jungles and interminable plains. The population was less homogenous than that of North America. At the very top was a small ruling elite sent from Europe. The local ruling class was the creoles, the colonial-born Spaniards or Portuguese, but there was also a large downtrodden Indian population, as well as the *mestizos*, who were half-European, half-Indian and a large population of negro slaves, particularly in Brazil, where there were also many mulattoes.

The creoles were the leaders in the movement for independence. Although they lorded it over the majority of the population, they also had a variety of grievances against colonial rule. One obvious grievance was that the highest positions of political and social power were denied to them by the *peninsulares*, the native-born Spaniards, who looked down upon the creoles as inferior.

More practically, the creoles began to look longingly at the prospects of trade outside the Spanish imperial system. The United States had waxed rich economically since breaking out of the British imperial system in the Revolution, and the creoles also thought of the prospects of trade expansion. Moreover, the creoles complained of taxation and the general economic subservience of the colonies.

In spite of underlying grievances it took a series of developments outside Latin America to produce widespread uprisings. The intellectual base for revolution had been laid in the eighteenth century. The ideas of the European Enlightenment had been influential throughout the New World; the emphasis on political and religious freedom and on the natural rights of man held a

particular fascination for Latin American intellectuals. The American Revolution also had a profound effect in stimulating ideas of independence and reform in Latin America. Not only had the North American colonies achieved their independence from Great Britain, they also had succeeded in forming a political union.

Of more direct impact on the Latin American colonies was the French Revolution and the turmoil which ensued in Europe. At first the Revolution appealed to many intellectuals, but as in North America the excesses and violence which followed the earlier constitutional phase brought fear to many creoles; they had no desire to see a social revolution which would produce an uprising of *mestizos*, Indians or perhaps even slaves. Many wanted more control of the political and economic policies for their own regions and a higher social position, but they were not asking for complete equality for the rest of the population.

Perhaps more important in Latin America than the egalitarian ideas of the late eighteenth century was the manner in which the wars of the French Revolution and Empire

revealed the extent of the decline of Spain. Buffeted by France and Great Britain, Spain revealed only too plainly how far she had declined from the great power that had established a world-wide empire.

After 1796, and the conclusion of an alliance with France, the Spanish had great difficulty in maintaining connections with Latin America. It was painfully apparent to the creoles that Spain could do little against British naval power. Also, direct British influence was made possible by their occupation of the island of Trinidad in 1797; the British now traded extensively with the Latin American colonies. Spanish naval power reached a low point in 1805 when most of their navy was destroyed by the British at Trafalgar; it now seemed that the Spanish had little or no ability to defend or control their Latin American colonies.

In June 1806 a British expedition captured Buenos Aires without Spanish interference. By August, however, the inhabitants themselves had defeated the invaders. In the following year another British force occupied Montevideo, but in the early summer the British were repulsed when they attempted

to take Buenos Aires and withdrew from the whole region. These episodes gave the local inhabitants confidence in their ability to defeat a European expeditionary force and revealed yet again that the Spanish had no real means to defend their colonies in the New World.

The catalyst for revolution in Latin America was Napoleon's intervention in the Iberian peninsula in 1807 and 1808. In late 1807 French troops invaded Portugal with the object of closing her ports to British ships and British goods. The royal family, with thousands of Portuguese aristocrats, sailed to Brazil before they could be taken by the French. They arrived in the New World in January 1808.

Next Napoleon intervened decisively in Spanish affairs. In May 1808 he deposed the Bourbons and gave the Spanish throne to his brother Joseph. This intervention was to bring Napoleon a bloody war against Spanish insurgents, but even before the Spanish uprising could affect the Latin American colonies the colonists had reacted to the deposition of the Spanish monarchy.

The French emissaries who were despatched to Latin America to bring news of the takeover were rejected by the colonists. Indeed, the first assertion of independent action was in favour of the Bourbons against the French usurpers. Once, however, this

degree of independent action had been taken it was only a short time before the possibilities of struggling for full independence became apparent. There was to be no unified, coordinated action, but circumstances had simply left much of Latin America to its own devices.

Simón Bolívar

There had been a number of revolts in Latin America in the second half of the nineteenth century, but the possibilities of creole demands for independence had been revealed most clearly in the career of Francisco de Miranda, who was born in Caracas in 1750. As a young man he travelled extensively in Europe and the United States and eventually settled in England. He dreamed of the liberation of Latin America and in 1806 led an abortive expedition from the United States against Venezuela; when this early attempt at revolution failed he returned to England but was soon involved again in the early efforts to free Venezuela.

With the development of Spanish resistance to the French, Latin American creoles in a number of cities formed local juntas, emulating the Spaniards fighting against Napoleon who had formulated these local committees to organize the struggle against the French. The juntas in Latin America

Above, the proclamation of the independence of Venezuela in July 1811, with Francisco de Miranda as head of the new republic. He was unable to maintain his authority, especially after the chaos caused by a severe earthquake the following year, and it was left to Simón Bolívar to complete the work of making Venezuela independent.

Opposite, Franciso de Miranda (1750–1816), the Venezuelan revolutionary who learned his radical ideas during the American and French Revolutions. Despite leading the revolution in Venezuela in 1810–12, he surrendered to the Spanish and was eventually deported to Spain.

became more interested in independence than in supporting the Bourbons against France. These local revolutionary movements began in widely scattered areas in Latin America in 1810 and they inaugurated the first phase of the struggle for Latin American independence. For the most part these first uprisings were unsuccessful, although they were to persist in some regions until 1816.

In northern South America the independence movements in Venezuela and in New Granada (Colombia) were entwined in the years from 1810 to 1816. In Venezuela the local inhabitants had refused to recognize French rule in Spain in 1808, and in the following year some argued for separation from Spain. In 1810 a local junta was formed in Caracas, and though some argued that this was to protect the rights of Bourbon Ferdinand VII the movement quickly became more extreme. In July 1811 a congress declared the independence of Venezuela from Spain.

The leadership of this early Venezuelan movement was taken by the most important of the revolutionaries, Simón Bolívar. Bolívar was born in Caracas in 1783 and like his compatriot Miranda had travelled extensively in Europe. In 1810 he was sent to England in an attempt to obtain aid for the Venezuelan revolution. This effort failed,

but at the end of 1810 Bolívar returned accompanied by Miranda (who had been living in England). Miranda became commander-in-chief of the insurgent forces. He had a difficult task. There was internal opposition to the revolution, and the Spanish General Juan Domingo Monteverde had successfully reconquered large areas of the country.

Another blow to the patriot cause was the great earthquake of March 1812, which was felt far more severely in the rebel than the loyalist areas of Venezuela and caused great damage and many deaths. Looked upon by many as a judgement of God, it reduced support for the rebellion. In July 1812 Miranda capitulated to the Spanish and was then seized by Bolívar and his supporters who argued that he had betrayed the cause. He was turned over to the Spanish and died in prison in Spain in 1816.

Bolívar now led the revolution in the north, and, with the uprising in Venezuela for the time being crushed, he went to Cartagena in New Granada to aid the revolutionaries in that region. Cartagena had risen in revolt, and a junta had been formed there in the spring of 1810. A few months later there was a revolt in Santa Fé de Bogotá. After fighting briefly in New Granada, where there was considerable internal turmoil in the next few years, in

1813 Bolívar crossed the Andes with a few hundred men to attempt to revive the revolution in Venezuela. For a time he was remarkably successful, and in August 1813 he entered Caracas.

The renewed success in Venezuela was only temporary. Loyalist forces soon recovered lost ground, retook Caracas and Bolívar fled to New Granada. Again he succeeded in temporarily improving the position for the revolutionaries in New Granada, but the whole northern revolution was now in jeopardy, as in April 1815 General Pablo Murillo arrived from Spain with 10,000 troops. For a time Bolívar had to exile himself to Jamaica and Haiti, and his attempt to re-establish himself in Venezuela in 1816 was a failure. In 1815 and 1816 Murillo crushed the revolution in New Granada.

In Chile as in New Granada there had been considerable internal dissension. The creoles had taken the initiative in forming a junta in 1810, but any feeling of unity was soon dispelled by the development of a more radical movement under José Miguel Carrera. Many of the creoles placed more faith in their leader Bernardo O'Higgins, and the split between Carrera and the O'Higgins forces severely hampered the revolutionary movement in Chile. The victory of the loyalists at the battle of Rancagua in October

1814 temporarily quelled the Chilean revolution, and many patriots fled to Argentina.

In the viceroyalty of New Spain the movement for independence took a somewhat different form from that in other areas, in that at first it deeply involved the Indian inhabitants of Mexico. The creoles of Mexico were planning what appears to have been a more typical rebellion in the autumn of 1810 but were forestalled when their plans were discovered by the authorities. One of the planners, Father Miguel Hidalgo y Costilla, decided to go ahead immediately, and on 16 September 1810 in Dolores he urged the inhabitants of the region to rise in rebellion and invoked the name of the Virgin of Guadalupe in support of his cause.

Hidalgo's revolt met with initial success, won extensive support from the most downtrodden classes in Mexico but soon began to alienate the creoles. His decision to restore lands to the Indians and to abolish slavery was hardly likely to appeal to prosperous Mexican landowners. In January 1811 Hidalgo and his unruly followers were defeated by loyalist troops. Hidalgo was soon captured and was shot in July 1811.

After Hidalgo's death the leadership of the Mexican revolution was assumed by another priest, José María Morelos. Like Hidalgo, Morelos urged the abolition of slavery and the end of social and racial injustice. Mexican independence was declared in November 1813, and a constitution was drafted a year later, but in 1815 Morelos was captured and shot. The struggle continued, but soon only isolated bands fought for independence while most of Mexico was again under Spanish control. Efforts at resistance in the rest of New Spain, in central America, were mainly under the leadership of José Matías Delgado, but by 1814 there was little overt resistance, and the area needed a more general collapse of Spanish rule if it were to win its independence.

The only area of Spanish rule which was able to proceed reasonably steadily towards separation without major setbacks was the viceroyalty of La Plata. At Buenos Aires the inhabitants had demonstrated their strength in victories over the British in 1806 and 1807, and in May 1810 a junta of creoles was formed there. Although this junta was to have more success in maintaining itself than those in most of the other Latin American colonies, it encountered difficulties when it tried to unite the distant regions of the huge Viceroyalty.

Attempts were made to win control of what became the modern countries of Bolivia, Paraguay and Uruguay, but in each area the Argentinians were unsuccessful. Montevideo was for a time taken by an Argentinian army, but the people of

Uruguay showed a marked reluctance to place themselves under the rule either of Argentina or of their other large neighbour, Brazil.

In spite of its failure to unify the outlying regions of the viceroyalty of La Plata, the Buenos Aires junta did manage to maintain itself as an independent body. Mariano Moreno was its first important leader, but he was forced out and from 1811 the government was in the hands of a triumvirate. In spite of many quarrels, a declaration of independence was finally agreed on in March 1816 at Tucumán. Yet, in spite of the success, the influence of Argentina on the uprisings in the rest of Latin America was less by example than by the fighting qualities of José de San Martín. With Bolívar he was the key figure in the final success of the Latin American independence movement.

San Martín

San Martín was a creole, born in 1778 in what is now northern Argentina. He had travelled to Spain as a boy and had served in the Spanish army for some twenty years. In 1812 he returned to Buenos Aires, and offered his services to the revolutionary government. By 1814 he was the military leader of Argentina, and he revealed that he had ambitious plans not only for the independence of Argentina but also for the freeing of South America from Spanish rule. His strategy was based on the assumption that the vital stronghold of the Spanish position in South America was in Peru, and that the Spanish would have to be beaten there, where they were strongest. To achieve this he decided that it would be necessary to invade Chile from Argentina, conquer it for the patriots and then launch the attack on Peru. In 1814 he obtained an appointment as governor of the province of Cuyo in western Argentina.

From 1814 to the end of 1816 San Martín organized and trained his invasion army. It consisted of Argentinians, refugee Chileans and adventurers from as far away as Europe. He was supported by Bernardo O'Higgins, who had already fought the loyalists in the earlier phase of the Chilean revolution. When at last he was ready to move in January 1817, San Martín had an army of some 5,000 men. In two detachments they made a remarkable march over the Andes into Chile, losing a great many horses and mules but few men.

On 12 February San Martín's force completely defeated the Spanish at the battle of Chacabuco and entered Santiago. San Martín could have been ruler of Chile, but he stood aside in favour of O'Higgins. Southern Chile was still controlled by the loyalists, and in March 1818 the patriots suffered a severe defeat, but as the royalists advanced northwards San Martín defeated them at Maipù on 5 April 1818. San Martín now turned his attention to Peru.

Efforts at a revolutionary movement within Peru itself had achieved little success in the years after 1808. Creole attempts at uprising had been quelled by the Spanish troops, and in 1814 and 1815 an Indian uprising was crushed. If the Spaniards were to be thrown out of Peru, it needed an outside force, and after his success in Chile San Martín immediately began organizing for invasion.

San Martín's immediate needs were financial support and a navy. He succeeded in obtaining some financial support by journeying to Buenos Aires, and to command his navy he was lucky enough to secure the services of Admiral Lord Cochrane, who had been dismissed from the British navy, though his dismissal was not directly related to his qualities as a sailor. The navy consisted of ships bought or seized by San Martín or O'Higgins; with Cochrane in command it was powerful enough to carry and protect San Martín's force on its invasion of Peru.

In September 1820 San Martín landed with over 4,000 troops in southern Peru. He did not wish to risk his force in a direct attack on the coast near Lima, and after recruiting more men and attempting to raise the country to arms he moved north beyond Lima along the coast. All the time he was attempting to win over more of the Peruvian population to the rebel cause, and he also began negotiations with the Spanish authorities in an attempt to arrive at a satisfactory settlement. Although these negotiations were unsuccessful, the growing resistance in Peru caused the Spanish to withdraw from Lima into the mountains in July 1821.

Left, the Battle of Chacabuco of 1817, at which San Martín surprised and routed the Spanish army in Chile, following a dramatic march through the Andes. The victory ensured the independence of Chile.

Below, the Chilian navy in action against a Spanish frigate at Callao in 1821; the Chilean admiral was Thomas Cochrane, Earl of Dundonald, a former British commander who later assisted the Greek navy against the Turks.

San Martín entered Lima a few days after the Spanish withdrew, and on 28 July he proclaimed Peruvian independence. San Martín became 'Protector' of Peru, although the Spanish still held much of the country. As in 1820–21 impatient supporters urged him to attack immediately, but San Martín preferred to wait and to use the time to win more inhabitants from their allegiance to the Spanish. The chance for more decisive action came in 1822 with a meeting between the two great liberators—San Martín and Bolívar.

Bolívar's triumph and disappointments

The low point in Bolívar's efforts to liberate northern South America had been reached in 1815 and 1816. In March 1816 Bolívar had again journeyed to Haiti after making little impression on the Spanish in Venezuela. In 1817 he determined to try again and this time to attempt a different strategy with new allies. He decided to ignore Caracas and to concentrate on the valley of the Orinoco. There he allied himself with José Antonio Páez, leader of the *llaneros*, the wild horsemen who inhabited the plains of the Orinoco region.

Bolívar also gained assistance at this time

from the British. Several thousand recruits arrived from Great Britain in the years after 1817, and as many of them were veterans of the European wars they were a great aid to his army. Bolívar established a base at Angostura (Ciudad Bolívar) on the Orinoco and there carried out the detailed planning necessary for his new strategy: he had resolved to attack up the Orinoco, across the Andes and strike against Bogotá in New Granada.

In spring 1819 Bolívar began an epic march with several thousand men. It involved trekking for hundreds of miles in rain and heat, and then up 13,000 feet into the Andes in icy cold. The horses did not survive the journey, many men died, but Bolívar reached New Granada with an army. On 7 August 1819, Bolívar met and defeated the loyalist army at the Battle of Boyaca, and on the 10th he entered Bogotá. Bolívar was now anxious for union in Latin America, and later in the year Gran Colombia came into being; it combined Venezuela with New Granada and the Presidency of Quito (modern Ecuador), although Quito was still under the control of Spain. Bolívar was appointed president of the new country.

Bolívar still had to win control of Venezuela. This was mainly accomplished by his victory over royalist forces at Carabobo in

June 1821. Later that month Bolívar entered Caracas, and, although the last Spanish forces in Venezuela were not defeated until 1823, Colombia and Venezuela were now effectively freed. In August 1821 a constitution for the combined Colombia–Venezuela was drafted—Bolívar became president and Francisco de Paula Santander vice-president. Bolívar had no intention of stopping at his successes of 1819 to 1821; he now wanted to carry the revolution farther south and to expand his concept of South American union.

In the Presidency of Quito (Ecuador) there had been unsuccessful uprisings in the immediate aftermath of Napoleon's intervention in the Iberian peninsula; an attempt to establish a creole junta in 1809 had failed, and efforts at achieving independence in the next few years were similarly unsuccessful. In 1821 General Antonio José de Sucre was sent by Bolívar to lead an uprising in Ecuador. He landed at Guayaquil, marched towards Quito and in May 1822 won the Battle of Pichincha and with it the revolution in Ecuador. Bolívar reached Quito in the next month, and Ecuador became a part of Gran Colombia, along with Venezuela and New Granada.

In July 1822 the two great South American liberators, Bolívar and San Martín, met at Guayaquil. The actual details of their

Above, the Battle of Ayacucho, in December 1842, at which the Peruvian nationalists under Sucre defeated the Spaniards and secured Peruvian independence. The battle also represented the final success of the Latin American revolution against European rule.

conversation are unknown, but after the meeting San Martín determined to retire from the area to avoid any basic divisions between himself and Bolívar. His active role in the independence movement had ended, and he went to Europe, where he died in 1850.

Bolívar now had the task of ending Spanish control of large areas of Peru. He did this with the major aid of General Sucre. The main battles were fought in 1824; in August, at Junín, Bolívar and Sucre won the first major victory, and in December at Ayacucho Sucre won the battle that ended any effective Spanish control of major areas of Peru: the few remaining Spanish troops could easily be defeated.

Upper Peru (Bolivia) also achieved its independence as a result of the 1824 victories. There had been uprisings there in the years after 1808, and Argentina had taken an active interest in attempts to free the area from Spanish control, but Bolivian independence did not come until 1825. Sucre became the first president.

Mexican independence

After the executions of Hidalgo and Morelos a sporadic struggle continued in Mexico, the Spanish administration attempting a policy of conciliation after 1816. The major effort at revolution in the following years was made by Francisco Xavier Mina. Mina was born in Spain in 1789, had fought first against the French and later against the Spanish regime of Ferdinand and after going to England had decided to attempt an expedition to Mexico. He obtained some support in the United States and eventually landed in Mexico in April 1817. He won some success but in the autumn was defeated, captured and shot.

After this renewed failure, the turning point in the Mexican Revolution did not come until after 1820. Decisive here was the change of affairs in Spain. Napoleon's intervention in 1808 and the temporary deposition of the Bourbons had created the opportunity for liberalization in Spain. The organization of patriotic juntas to combat the French led to the calling of a representative body, the *Cortes*. In 1812 a constitution was adopted which tried to provide for more popular government through an elected *Cortes*, with the king as a constitutional monarch.

The Bourbon restoration which brought Ferdinand back to the Spanish throne in 1814 also produced an attack on the acts of liberalization. Ferdinand abandoned the constitution of 1812 and crushed liberal ideas. In 1820 there was a revolution in Spain, in which the king as a result of pressure, restored the constitution of 1812. Ferdinand later disavowed the measures of liberalization and called in other European powers to restore his power in 1823. By that time, however, the developments in Spain had inspired action in Mexico.

The 1820 Spanish revolution convinced the conservative Mexican creoles that the time had come to press for independence as a means of preserving their own power. As their military leader they settled on Agustín de Iturbide. Iturbide was a prominent creole and had fought against the revolutions of Hidalgo and Morelos. He had proved himself to be a ruthless, conservative figure, and the creoles had good reason to believe that with Iturbide leading the struggle for independence there was no danger of any radical reforms.

At the beginning of 1821 Iturbide joined with the rebels in southern Mexico, who had maintained the struggle against the Spanish government. Iturbide and the rebel leader, Vicente Guerrero, reached an agreement at Iguala on 24 February 1821. The 'Plan of Iguala' called for an independent Mexico in which there would be a monarchy, with a European ruler, in which the position of the Roman Catholic Church would be maintained and in which there would be equality between creoles and native-born Spanish. Iturbide and Guerrero amalgamated their forces, and for the time being the divergent groups in Mexico united behind the movement for independence.

On 24 August 1821, the Spanish viceroy signed the Treaty of Córdoba by which Mexico was declared independent; the 'Plan of Iguala' was to be followed in forming the new government. The Spanish government, however, refused to honour the agreement of its viceroy, and, instead of a Spanish Bourbon prince, Iturbide was elected as Emperor Agustín by a national congress in May 1822. Agustín I had a short reign. In the following year he was forced to flee the country. He returned in 1824 but was captured and shot.

Central America

Central America did not suffer the intense fighting that characterized the independence movement in much of the rest of Latin America. There had been some agitation under Delgado after 1808, but after 1814 there was little activity in the movement for separation until an impetus was given to revolutionary ideas by the Mexican reaction to the Spanish revolution of 1820. In September 1821 a declaration of independence was issued in Guatemala City.

In the first years of Central American independence from Spain, the main issue was whether or not the whole area should be part of Mexico under Iturbide. With the fall of Iturbide, a firm decision was taken for separation. On 1 July 1823 a constitutional assembly from the five provinces of Central America declared that the region was independent as the 'United Provinces of Central America'. In 1825 Manuel José Arce became the first president of the United Provinces. He was soon to discover the enormous difficulties and problems of maintaining a unified government.

Brazil

The independence of the huge Portuguese colony of Brazil was achieved in a manner very different from that of the Spanish colonies. This was as much because of force of circumstance as any inherent difference between the Spanish and the Portuguese possessions.

The first decisive step in Brazilian independence was the invasion of Portugal by the French late in 1807 and the flight of the Portuguese royal family and many of the nobility to America. The convoy carrying the royal family and its supporters arrived in Brazil late in January 1808. Regent John, acting in place of his mother, the mad Queen Maria, became ruler of Brazil, and in March 1808 he established his court at Rio de Janeiro.

John quickly moved to inaugurate reforms in the colony he was now to rule directly. Of greatest importance for Brazilian prosperity was his decision to throw the colony open for the ships and goods of all nations, though he also tried to stimulate local industry. His reforms extended into the cultural and social sphere: he established a national library, museums and medical schools and made a variety of attempts to create a less provincial atmosphere in his capital.

On the death of Queen Maria in March 1816 the regent became King John VI and seemed quite willing to remain in Brazil. However, his rule was meeting with increasing opposition. Some resented the power of the Portuguese nobles, others voiced republican sentiments, and nearly all objected to increased taxation. In 1817 a revolt broke out in Pernambuco, but it was suppressed within the year, and it took another basic change in European events for Brazil to alter its government.

While the Braganzas lived in Brazil, power in Portugal was exercised by a regency. In 1820, in the aftermath of the Spanish Revolution, the government of the regency was overthrown, and the Spanish constitution of 1812 became the rallying-point of the Portuguese revolutionaries. They now wanted John to come back to Portugal and rule as a constitutional monarch on the basis of the 1812 constitution.

In Brazil the Portuguese developments produced a new demand for liberalization and forced John to accept the Spanish constitution of 1812 for Brazil as well as Portugal. At first John intended to send his son Pedro to Portugal, but fearful of the new demands in Brazil he sailed for Portugal himself in April 1821, leaving Pedro to rule in Brazil. It soon became clear, however, that the Portuguese liberals who had forced the changes in 1820 were not liberal in their attitude towards Brazil. They showed no inclination to respect Brazil's desire for greater independence and also ordered Pedro to return to Portugal.

Many Brazilians now sought to achieve independent status under Pedro, and the leadership in this movement was taken by José Bonifácio de Andrada e Silva, a scientist of marked abilities in government. Dom Pedro announced in January 1822 that he would stay in Brazil, and Bonifácio became his most important minister. On 7 September 1822 Dom Pedro declared Brazilian

independence, and in the following month he became emperor.

As there were still Portuguese garrisons in Brazil, it was now necessary to expel them, and for this Dom Pedro called on the aid of Admiral Lord Cochrane, who had done so much for the success of San Martín's expedition against Peru. By the end of 1823 the Portuguese had been driven from Brazil, and the country had achieved its independence with the aid of the Portuguese royal family.

Foreign recognition

By 1824 the Latin American colonies of Spain and Portugal had effectively separated themselves from Europe. There were still some fears that there might be attempts to renew European control, but these were effectively ended by the attitude of the United States and of Great Britain.

The United States could really do little in these years to keep European forces out of Latin America, but she did use her influence to encourage Latin American independence. Many in the United States were delighted to see their neighbours to the south follow their example in throwing off European rule, and others were delighted at the prospect of additional trade opportunities. The United States delayed recognition while the issue in Latin America still seemed in doubt and while the United States was still anxious to secure Spanish agreement to the cession of the Floridas, but after this was accomplished in 1821 the United States government in 1822 accepted the principle of recognition for the new countries of Latin America. In December 1823, in the Monroe Doctrine, the United States indicated her own special interest in maintaining a Latin America free from European interference. The lack of American power to enforce this idea was made somewhat irrelevant by the attitude of Great Britain.

Since Great Britain was anxious to develop and expand her trade connections with Latin America and had no desire to see a renewed expansion of European influence in the area, her interests in this matter coincided with those of the United States. When it seemed possible in 1823 that the European powers in the Holy Alliance would help Spain to regain her lost colonies, England at first hoped to act in concert with the United States to prevent this. But the United States preferred to make an independent statement. With the British navy in command of the Atlantic, the Latin American powers were safe from any new attempts by the European powers to recapture the area.

By 1825 the huge provinces of the Spanish Empire in Latin America had already been shattered by separatist movements from within as well as by uprisings against Spain. Some still had high hopes of general unity, but within fifteen years the modern states had been created in their general outlines.

Left, Agustin de Iturbide, the Mexican revolutionary, receiving the keys of the city of Mexico in September 1821; after winning control of the country suddenly in the previous year, he became emperor (1822–23) but his conservative policies led to a further revolt against his rule.

Opposite, José de San Martín (1778–1850), the liberator of Chile and Peru from Spanish control. He served as protector of Peru from 1821 to 1822, when Bolívar persuaded him to give up the country. San Martín then retired to exile in Europe.

On page 362, a slave market in Rio de Janiero in the 1820s; slavery continued in Brazil until the 1880s, when its abolition led the plantation owners to overthrow the emperor.

On page 363, Pedro I, Emperor of Brazil (reigned 1822–31) at his coronation. Pedro was the son of the exiled King of Portugal, who declared Brazil's independence from the mother country. National Library of Australia.

The most imaginative effort to achieve unity in Latin America was that of Bolívar, who in his years of victory over Spain had formed Gran Colombia (consisting of the modern states of Venezuela, Colombia and Ecuador) and had dreamt that he would be able to include Peru and Bolivia in one mighty nation. In a few years after his victory over the Spanish he saw his dreams crumble. The distances were vast, the terrain formidable, there were entrenched local interests, and a general gulf existed between creoles, *mestizos*, Indians and slaves. The Congress of Panama in 1826, in which Bolívar placed so much hope, was an abject failure, and by the time of his death in 1830 Gran Colombia was breaking apart.

The Mexican Empire under Iturbide met a fate similar to that of Bolívar's, although it had never promised as much. On Iturbide's fall in 1823 Central America broke away and for a time remained united as the 'United Provinces of Central America'. But by 1839 this had collapsed into its constituent parts of Guatemala, Honduras, E. Salvador, Nicaragua and Costa Rica. Panama was a part of Colombia until 1903. Other attempts at unity were equally disappointing; an attempt to link Peru and Bolivia after 1835 soon failed, and although Argentina and Brazil at times had hopes of annexing Uruguay these ambitions had failed completely by 1828.

The problems of independence

The problems of nineteenth-century Latin America were immense. Unity had proved impossible, and now a variety of different countries was attempting to establish stable relations with each other and the outside world and at the same time to achieve political stability and economic prosperity. Whether their aims also included racial and social equality depended on the outlook of particular individuals. Although some of the revolutionaries had hoped for equality as well as independence, many of the creoles had merely fought for the right to control their own affairs not to change the whole political, social and economic structure of their countries.

Democratic constitutions were numerous in nineteenth-century Latin America, but there was little democracy in practice. There had been little tradition of self-government in the colonial period, and too often an autocratic system was readily transferred to the independent countries, the creoles used their political power to enhance their position within a still aristocratic society. Many remained poverty-stricken and oppressed. The turmoil and warfare in and between these newly independent nations soon allowed the *caudillos*—the opportunistic, military dictators—to take over many governments.

The economic dislocation of the struggle for independence severely hindered the development of prosperity, and in many areas it was the middle of the century before steady economic advance began. Yet, even with the coming of greater Latin American prosperity, wealth was heavily concentrated in a few hands. Huge landowners dominated the countryside, aristocratic creoles the urban centres. Although the Roman Catholic Church at first suffered from the revolutions, it maintained its dominant position, and in many areas there were bitter struggles with the clergy. For many the fine hopes of independence vanished in suffering and despair. Revolution after revolution, and constitution after constitution, still left the mass of the people illiterate, impoverished and subject to the vagaries of innumerable petty dictators.

The Brazilian Empire

By far the largest of the independent Latin American states was Brazil. It was also unusual because it was Portuguese in origin, the revolution having produced a splintering of the colonial area of government, and independence having evolved gradually through the cooperation of the Portuguese royal family after their flight from Europe; in addition the country was governed as a monarchy until 1889.

The Brazilian Empire lasted from 1822 to 1889. There were three distinct periods: the rule of Pedro I from 1822 to 1831, the Regency from 1831 to 1840, and the long reign of Pedro II from 1840 to 1889. The reign of Pedro I was a tumultuous one of internal revolt and foreign war. In spite of the effectiveness of his first chief minister, José Bonifácio, Pedro became unpopular. He was more autocratic than those who had helped to place him in power expected, was extravagant, and his reputation was hurt when he was obliged to recognize the independence of Uruguay in 1828. The main political achievement of this period was the constitution of 1824 which served, with modifications, as the basis of government until 1889.

Although the constitution of 1824 gave extensive power to the emperor, including the right to appoint the presidents of the various provinces, it did allow popular participation in government and attempted to protect individual liberties. Ultimately, however, the nature of the government depended upon the emperor, and it seemed for a time that the system established in 1824 would be short-lived.

The pressures on Pedro I increased throughout his reign. He exceeded the ample powers given to him by the constitution, and his immorality became so notorious

that it offended even his tolerant subjects. Clearly, he had been more successful than most of his contemporary South American rulers in maintaining the unity of his nation and in promoting its advance, but his unpopularity was such that in 1831 he was forced to abdicate in favour of his son, the future Pedro II, who was only five years old.

The Brazilian regency lasted from 1831 to 1840, and during this period Brazil was in danger of breaking up as the country was disrupted by civil war. Partially because of good fortune, partially because of the dedication of individual men in the government, Brazil survived and in 1840 Pedro was declared of age. In July 1841 he was crowned.

Brazil was remarkably fortunate to have Pedro II as its ruler from 1840 to 1889. Not the least of Brazil's debts to José Bonifácio was the two years he spent as the first tutor of Pedro II. He set a standard that was continued throughout the regency, and by the time he assumed the throne Pedro II was extremely well-educated. As he had the intelligence to make use of his education, he became a tolerant ruler, modest and moral in his life, and capable of appreciating the changes that were occurring in nineteenth-century Europe. He encouraged innovation and scientific endeavour as well as acting as a patron of cultural activities.

The initial problem confronting the new

emperor was a continuation of the internal dissension which had plagued the regency. A number of revolts were crushed in the early years of his reign, and by 1845 there was peace in Rio Grande do Sul, an area which had long been in a state of disruption. After the failure of an uprising in Pernambuco, Brazil settled into a period of calm which again accentuated the difference between this former Portuguese colony and many of its Spanish-speaking neighbours.

The ending of major internal uprisings did not bring complete peace to Brazil, for in the 1850s and 60s the country engaged in two foreign wars. In 1851 and 1852 the Brazilians combined with Uruguay and Argentinian revolutionaries in overthrowing the Argentinian dictator, Manuel Rosas, and between 1864 and 1870 Brazil combined her forces with those of Argentina and Uruguay in fighting Paraguay. Although the sufferings of Brazil were slight compared with those of Paraguay, she lost many dead. As in earlier Brazilian struggles a key factor in bringing about the conflict was the argument over possible external control of Uruguay. The country survived these foreign entanglements without severe injury.

The huge country of Brazil was relatively sparsely populated in the nineteenth century, but from little more than five million inhabitants in 1830 Brazil had grown to some

eighteen million by the end of the century. The Brazilian population at the beginning of this period was composed of those of Portuguese ancestry, negroes, Indians and those of mixed race. Immigration was only slight in the first half of the century, but after 1850 increasing numbers crossed the Atlantic.

Another immigration that continued until the middle of the century was that of negro slaves. An act to end the foreign slave trade had been passed as early as 1831 but it was not effectively enforced until the early 1850s. After the middle of the century there was growing sentiment among liberals for the ending of slavery itself. They were helped by the support of the emperor, who had freed his own slaves, and who was strongly in favour of abolition. At last in 1871 the Rio Branco law provided that all children born of slave mothers would now be free. Pressure for total abolition continued, and in 1885 all slaves over sixty were freed. The final act came in May 1888 with the abolition of all slavery. There was no compensation for the owners.

As the internal disorders died down by the end of the 1840s, the economy of the country began to advance rapidly. Brazil had great natural resources, and although they were not properly tapped the country advanced spectacularly compared with most South American nations. Coffee became increasingly important in the second half of the century, sugar and tobacco were also grown extensively, and there was a very large cattle industry. The southern area of Brazil was particularly stimulated by this economic advance, and the province of São Paulo became of major importance in the Brazilian economy.

There was also a marked increase in industry and general commercial activity in the second half of the century. Financial stability was promoted by the foundation of the Bank of Brazil in 1853. Manufacturing increased at this time, and there was considerable expansion of transport and communications facilities. These were stimulated by foreign capital which was attracted by the comparative stability of this Latin American nation. The most important of the Brazilian speculators was Ireneu Evangelista Mauá, who established a banking fortune and invested in all aspects of Brazil's expanding economy.

The construction of railroads began in the 1850s, and by the end of the empire in 1889 there were over 6,000 miles of track. Steamship lines and a telegraph service were also developed. Most of Brazil was still undeveloped and there were still incredible problems of communication, but against the background of most other Latin American nations the advances appear remarkable.

Despite all these advances, Brazil remained a country of large landowners, rich aristocrats and numerous poor people. Although Pedro II was greatly interested in education, most of his people were still illiterate at the end of his reign. For the future of the empire, however, it was more important that Pedro began to lose the support of influential groups and that a republican party began to gain strength.

In the 1870s the government alienated many Catholics by siding with the Freemasons in a dispute with the Church. The government had already lost the support of many of the great landowners because of the partial abolition of slavery in 1871, and lost others because of total abolition in 1888. A third area of vital support was lost by the emperor's attitude towards the army. Pedro II was no militarist, and many officers had begun to feel that the military would receive greater recognition under a different type of government. With many of the military, the Church and the great landowners alienated and liberals demanding a republic, the empire came to an end in 1889. A bloodless army revolt forced Pedro II to abdicate. He died in Europe in 1891.

The republic established in Brazil in 1889 at first provided little stability. In 1891 a constitution based on that of the United States was put into effect, but until near the

Above, the port of Buenos Aires in 1858; disputes over the authority that the city wielded over the rest of the country led Buenos Aires to secede from the rest of Argentina between 1853 and 1862.

Opposite, the city of Buenos Aires, the capital of Argentina, in 1847.

end of the century Brazil was again beset by internal revolts; whatever the constitution the country was for a time ruled by the military. It was not until 1898 that it was again possible to restore something approaching normal conditions and to begin to rebuild the economy. In the early years of the new century the country again began a steady economic advance.

Spanish Latin America

Any discussion of the ex-Spanish colonies in Latin America in the nineteenth century is complicated by their lack of uniformity and the internal chaos that existed for so many years in these countries. Although it is possible to group them for convenience into certain divisions—the Rio Plata countries of Argentina, Uruguay and Paraguay the two Andean groups of Chile, Bolivia and Peru and Venezuela, Colombia and Ecuador, and the former New Spain area of Mexico and Central America—the countries within any one group frequently had little in common with adjacent states and pursued their own ambitions. For many of these years, the history of these Latin American countries is a sorry tale of internal turmoil, bloodshed and despotism and frequently costly and senseless external conflicts. Bolívar's dream all too often became a nightmare in nineteenth-century Latin America.

Argentina

From the beginning of the independence movement in 1810 to the end of the 1820s it proved impossible to establish a unified Argentina. Some hoped that Uruguay and Paraguay would form part of a great nation, but even the unity of Argentina itself was not possible. Buenos Aires attempted to make itself the centre of a unified nation, but the outlying provinces, led by their *caudillos*, refused to recognize its leadership, and by the 1820s had effectively separated themselves, after a series of wars, from the control of the Buenos Aires region.

The development of the power of Buenos Aires came with the rise to prominence of Juan Manuel de Rosas. Rosas was born in Buenos Aires in 1793 but had spent years ranching, an experience that helped him greatly in winning the respect and support of the *gauchos*, the hard-riding horsemen of the Argentinian plains. In 1829 Rosas became governor of the province of Buenos Aires, and soon became one of the most powerful *caudillos* in Latin America. He served three years as governor but then left Buenos Aires to fight the Indians in the south. In 1835, when Buenos Aires politicians persuaded him to take power again, he inaugurated a dictatorship. Although he was still officially governor only of Buenos Aires, he also dominated the rest of the Argentinian provinces.

Rosas' rule lasted from 1835 to 1852. These were years of tyranny, brutality and

murder. Rosas exterminated his rivals and ruled by terror. He discouraged immigration, showed a total lack of imagination in his economic policies and engaged in a variety of foreign quarrels. He was finally brought down by a combined army of Argentinian opponents, Brazilians and Uruguayans in 1852. He fled to England and died there in 1877.

The main Argentinian opponent of Rosas, Justo José de Urquiza, became President of

Argentina in 1853 under a new constitution based on that of the United States. The confederation united all the provinces except for the most important one of Buenos Aires, which remained independent. When Buenos Aires finally joined the other provinces, after Urquiza had retreated from the forces of General Bartolomé Mitre in 1861, it was essentially on her own terms. In 1862 General Mitre became president of the now united Argentina, and he rapidly began to develop a more prosperous nation, encouraging immigration and stimulating the economy. Progress slowed in 1865 when Argentina joined in the war against Paraguay, but when Mitre's term ended in 1868 he had done much to establish a unified and prosperous country.

The 1870s brought rapid advance economically in the newly unified Argentina. At last Argentina was free from internal and external struggles, and under the presidencies of Domingo Faustino Sarmiento (1868–74), Nicolás Avellaneda (1874–80) and Julio A. Roca (1880–86) seemed to be achieving prosperity. Sarmiento reflected his own background as a teacher and writer encouraging education. He was a forward-looking politician, encouraging immigration and promoting the national economy, particularly in improved communications.

Sarmiento's successor, Nicolás Avellaneda, having first put down a revolt by Mitre, who objected to the manner in which Sarmiento had helped to defeat Mitre's own candidacy, continued the economic advances. Cattle ranching, long of vital importance, was expanding rapidly, and wheat was becoming of increasing importance. Moreover, in the last years of his administration, Avallaneda's minister of war, Julio A. Roca, extended the area that could be farmed in the south by waging a war against the Indians in that region. These campaigns helped to create Roca's political career.

One of the last and most important acts of Avellaneda's government was the federalization of the city of Buenos Aires. This was done against the will of the province of Buenos Aires and was a major issue in the 1880 campaign for president, in which Roca was supported by the existing administration. When Roca won, Buenos Aires attempted to resist the desires of the other provinces but soon capitulated. The last stage in political unity had been achieved.

The prosperity of the 1870s continued into the 80s, but there were now more signs of weakness in the economy, as first President Roca and then President Miguel Juárez Celmán allowed, or even connived at, public corruption. The inflated economy of the 1880s brought great profits to many, as the long-established foreign trade in hides had now, with the development of refrigeration, expanded into trade in meat. By the 1880s Argentina, with its extensive foreign trade in beef, mutton and wheat had changed remarkably from the pre-1850 country of Rosas. This boom period came to an end in 1889 with a major economic crisis.

In 1890 a rebellion against the government was crushed, but with opinion firmly against him President Celmán soon resigned, and Vice-President Carlos Pellegrini took over. His policy was caution and honesty. In spite of his avowals, the election of Luis Sáenz Peña in 1892 inaugurated a period of political turmoil and internal dissent. In 1895 Peña resigned, and his vice-president, José Uriburu, took over. Not until 1898, when Julio A. Roca was elected to serve once again as president, did order return and the nation regain its prosperity. Those who wanted political reform were not satisfied, however, and in the new century the Radical party grew rapidly in strength. In 1916 it ousted the long-established ruling elite.

Uruguay

The small country of Uruguay, which was created from the region known until 1828 as the Banda Oriental, was a region of almost constant turmoil in the nineteenth century. Logically, Uruguay seemed destined to become part of one of its large neighbours, Argentina or Brazil, but in reality their rivalry allowed Uruguay to achieve a precarious independence, which in the twentieth century developed into a more prosperous stability.

The struggle for Uruguayan independence began in 1811 under the leadership of José Gervasio Artigas, a gaucho who had gained military experience in the Spanish army. His struggle for independence was complicated by the necessity of winning freedom not only from the old Spanish rulers but also from Argentinian revolutionaries, who hoped to make the region and its main city, Montevideo, dependent upon Buenos Aires. Another difficulty was the Portuguese royal family, who after they came to America hoped to add the region to their domains. The precarious independence won by Artigas collapsed, and he fled to Paraguay where he died in 1850.

From 1821 Uruguay was controlled by Brazil, but in 1825 the Uruguayan Juan Antonio Lavalleja entered the country with a tiny group of compatriots—the 'immortal thirty-three'—to wage war for independence

Above, Justo José de Urquiza (1801–70), the Argentinian politician who opposed the rule of Rosas and became president of the confederation of Argentina in 1854; nevertheless he was unable to prevent the temporary autonomy of Buenos Aires province.

Above left, Juan Manuel de Rosas (1793–1877), the Argentinian dictator who, as governor of the province of Buenos Aires between 1829 and 1832, and again between 1835 and 1852, was able to rule the entire country. He suppressed all opposition ruthlessly and planned to extend his rule over Paraguay and Uruguay.

Opposite, Latin America in the early nineteenth century, showing the dates in which each region won its independence.

against the Brazilians. He was supported from Argentina, and a Brazil–Argentina war ensued which was finally settled, with the aid of British pressure, in 1828. The peace treaty which was signed in August 1828 gave a Brazilian and Argentinian guarantee of the independence of Uruguay. Although her powerful neighbours were still to interfere in the country, never again was Uruguay in such danger of being annexed.

From this time until the first decade of the twentieth century Uruguay was the scene of constant tumult, revolution and internal division. The initial struggle (in the 1830s) was between the partisans of the first president, Fructuoso Rivera of the Colorado party, and Manuel Oribe of the Blanco party, who became president in 1835. The Colorado party, which claimed progressive ideas, and the Blanco group, which was more conservative, were rallying-points for rival factions in the following years, although any true liberal–conservative division was completely obscured by the continual struggles of a variety of *caudillos*. It was the twentieth century before a president could take office without the constant fear of being violently overthrown.

In spite of the political turmoil, Uruguay began to make some economic and social advance, particularly from the 1870s. The population, which had been only 70,000 in 1830, had reached nearly 1,000,000 by 1900, aided by the immigration of thousands of Europeans. Stock raising was by far the most important economic occupation of the country, although political turmoil prevented development of the refrigeration facilities essential for a successful export trade until long after Argentina had acquired them. Similarly, it was not until the 1870s that definite progress began to be made in education. Few observers in nineteenth-century Uruguay would have dared prophesy the degree of success achieved in the twentieth century.

Paraguay

Paraguay had a disastrous nineteenth-century history and has remained one of the most backward and isolated of the Latin American nations. Its population, largely Indian mingled with Spanish, suffered incredibly in the nineteenth century.

The first efforts at Paraguayan independence came in 1811, when the Spanish were overthrown and a junta established. The Spanish had previously resisted the efforts of the Argentinian revolutionaries to absorb the area. By 1814 the country was in the control of José Rodríguez de Francia, a lawyer of mixed Portuguese and Spanish creole parentage. By 1816 he was established as dictator for life.

The Francia regime was a strange one. Francia was dedicated and frugal but also cruel and ruthless. He totally crushed oppo-

sition in Paraguay and then isolated the country from foreign influences, preventing immigration and allowing only limited trade. His country suffered none of the chaos prevalent in much of Latin America at this period and its agricultural development was promoted, but there was no freedom, no education and no refreshing outside influences.

Francia, a man of whom little is known, created his own little island in the middle of South America and kept all the power in his own hands. His death in 1840 brought turmoil for a short time, but by 1844 Carlos Antonio López was installed as president for a ten-year term. López and his son were to dominate the nation until 1870. López, like Francia, ruled as a dictator, but the nature of his rule was similar to that of other Latin American rulers. He opened the country to foreign contacts and pursued an ambitious foreign policy, in 1852 helping to bring down the Argentinian dictator Rosas.

On the death of López in September 1862 control of Paraguay was taken by his son, Francisco Solano López. He soon made the Paraguayans realize how fortunate they had been under the moderate dictatorship of his father. The young López was a cruel, ambitious incompetent who inflicted suffering on his country to an extent that has rarely been experienced in any nation. He sought foreign glory and as a result of his ambitions led Paraguay into a war against Brazil, Argentina and Uruguay simultaneously. The Paraguayan war lasted from 1865 to 1870, and more than half of the Paraguayan population of 500,000 was dead at the end of the conflict. Fewer than 30,000 men were still alive and López had been killed. Paraguay was defeated and was forced to pay an indemnity.

After 1870 the main political change was

that the dictators succeeded each other with great rapidity. No political stability was achieved, and Paraguay entered the twentieth century as a sorry example of man's ineptness and cruelty. Economic and social progress had been slight, communications were atrocious, most of the population lived in primitive conditions, and there was general illiteracy. Wealth was confined to a very small minority.

Chile

The elongated nation of Chile, stretching along much of the Pacific coastline of South America, achieved a notable degree of stability in the nineteenth century. In the colonial period Chile had been overshadowed by Peru, but in the nineteenth century the area was to achieve more success than its neighbours.

The internal struggle for power in Chile began as early as 1810, but it was not until 1817 and 1818, when San Martín invaded the region, that independence was won from Spain. The first leader was Bernardo O'Higgins, whose Irish father had risen to be Viceroy of Peru. Bernardo was illegitimate—his mother a Spanish creole. He governed as a progressive dictator, but was forced out in 1823. In the years to 1830 Chile appeared to be drifting into total disorder. General Ramón Freire held power until 1827, but for the next few years there was a rapid change of rulers.

An advance towards stability in Chile came in 1830 with the victory of the conservative group known as the *Pelucones*. This group had been contending for power with the liberals, the *Pipiolos*. The most important architect of the new regime was Diego Portales, who set up a conservative

Above, one of the main streets of Santiago, capital of Chile, in the mid-nineteenth century, showing the customs house and the Jesuits' Church. British Museum, London.

Above left, the sinking of a Brazilian gunboat by Paraguayan boats using torpedoes, during the War of the Triple Alliance, in 1865.

Left, Bernardo O'Higgins (1778–1842), the Chilean revolutionary whose father was Irish and who was supreme director of the country from its independence in 1818 until 1823.

Opposite, fighting in Uruguay during the War of the Triple Alliance of 1865–70, when Paraguay's aggression was opposed by Brazil, Argentina and Uruguay. By 1870 Paraguay was devastated.

ruling clique of landowners and clergy, and effectively stifled both military and liberal opposition.

The constitution of 1833 was a conservative document, placing considerable power in the hands of the president and establishing Roman Catholicism as the official religion. Although this was not what South American liberals had hoped for, Chile did not have the tyrannical, brutal rule inflicted on so many other areas in these years. Under the presidencies of Joaquín Prieto, Manuel Bulnes and Manuel Montt from 1831 to 1861, Chile advanced steadily economically, and there was some progress in education.

In 1861 the liberals were at last able to take over in Chile, the government having alienated some of its supporters by a quarrel with the Church and the abolition of primogeniture (inheritance solely by the eldest son). Liberal rule from 1861 to 1891 wrought no radical changes, but the conservative system created by Portales was slowly modified, even though the presidents were still in a position of great power. The prosperity of the nation continued to increase, and its boundaries were enlarged by the War of the Pacific with Peru and Bolivia between 1879 and 1883.

The liberal regime ended in 1891 when President José Manuel Balmaceda, who had come to power in 1886 and had carried out an extensive programme of public works, was opposed when he went further than most Chilean presidents in attempting to rule outside the constitution. Balmaceda was overthrown, and from 1891 the Chilean Congress was better able to control the power of the presidents as parliamentary rule came to Chile. There were still many poor, many who played no part in government, but compared with much of Latin America Chile had achieved a reasonable measure of success as an independent country by the beginning of the twentieth century.

Peru

Peru had been a centre of Spanish power in Latin America. The Spanish had exercised a tight control over the largely Indian and *mestizo* population, and not until San Martín's invasion in 1820 and 1821 and the victories of Bolívar and Sucre in 1824 were Spanish hopes in Peru crushed.

Bolívar had been invited into Peru in 1823 to unite the revolutionaries and drive out the Spanish, and he ruled as a virtual dictator until he left the country in 1826. The government he had placed in power was overthrown in the following year, and the period from 1827 to 1844 was filled with conflict and struggles for power among warring factions. Between 1835 and 1839 a Bolivian, Andrés Santa Cruz, united Peru and Bolivia in a confederation, but this collapsed. No stability was achieved until

Ramón Castilla came to power in 1845.

Castilla was a *mestizo* of Indian, Spanish and Italian forbears. He was the main force in Peruvian politics from 1845 to 1862, serving as president from 1845 to 1851 and from 1855 to 1862. Between his terms in office the country was ruled by José Rufino Echenique, a far less able leader, who was overthrown by Castilla in 1855. Castilla brought far more political stability than had been known earlier, and the country also advanced economically and socially during his rule. Guano exports increased greatly, communications were improved and slavery was abolished. Constitutional revision took place, culminating in the conservative constitution of 1860 which was to be the basic document until 1920. The president was given considerable power, and Roman Catholicism was made the official religion of the country.

After Castilla Peru again had difficulty achieving any real political stability, and few presidents were able to serve out their terms in peace. Only President Manuel Pardo between 1872 and 1876 achieved moderate success, but his administration foundered financially. The 1860s and 70s were also marred by foreign entanglements. A brief war with Spain produced no major disasters, but the War of the Pacific (1879–83) against Chile was a crushing blow. Although allied with Bolivia, Peru was unable to protect even her own territory. Lima was occupied and the economy suffered a major setback.

In the aftermath of the war, military leaders struggled for control of the country, and it was not until 1895, when Nicolás de Piérola came to power, that a modicum of stability was achieved. Even then the majority of the Peruvian people were not represented in the government.

Peru had been the heart of the Spanish empire in South America, but its progress in the nineteenth century was extremely limited. The country was unable to achieve a progressive and responsible government, and there was no great economic advance. Guano was of importance, but Peru had

lost its nitrate assets in the war against Chile. There had been some advance in the development of railroads, but the profits helped the British, who owned them, more than the Peruvians. All in all, the Peruvian experiment in independence had been a major disappointment.

Venezuela

Bolívar's hope that Venezuela would become part of his great confederation had been shattered at a very early date. The key figure in the early history of Venezuela was José Antonio Páez, a general under Bolívar, who was left in command in Venezuela when Bolívar went south to conquer new lands. Páez was a llanero, a cattleman from the great Venezuelan plains. He exercised a peculiar fascination over Venezuela's large *mestizo* population, although his rule in effect benefited the white minority.

Venezuela withdrew from Bolívar's confederation in 1829 and in 1830 drafted a constitution and made Páez the first president. He was to dominate the politics of the country until 1846, and even returned as late as 1861 to rule until 1863. Although Páez was basically an autocrat, he allowed a certain degree of freedom, restored the prosperity of a country badly hurt by the wars of liberation and attempted to encourage Venezuelan trade. It was not a democratic regime, but for the most part it was a reasonable one.

The collapse of Páez's power in the mid-1840s was brought about by the Liberals, but in reality power still rested with a narrow group of Venezuelans, and from 1846 to 1858 control of the country was in the hands of José Tadeo Monagas and his brother José Gregorio Monagas. Apart from the abolition of slavery in 1854, this was no liberal regime, and little was accomplished for the mass of the population.

The fall of the Monagas regime in 1858 precipitated some twelve years of turmoil in Venezuela, although Páez did come back and attempt to restore order in the early

Left, Francisco de Paula Santander (1792–1840), the Colombian leader who served as assistant to Bolívar from 1821 to 1828, when he was banished. After the collapse of Greater Colombia he served as president of New Granada from 1832 to 1836.

Opposite, fighting between government troops and insurgents during a rebellion in Chile in the main square in Valparaiso in 1852.

1860s. For the most part these were years in which *caudillos* struggled for power, ignoring the interests of the great mass of the population. The turmoil ended with the rise to power of Antonio Guzmán Blanco in 1870. He controlled the country until 1888.

Guzmán Blanco put himself forward to the people as a man sympathetic to their aims and ideals. In reality, he ruled ruthlessly, spent a great deal of money and indulged his remarkable vanity in extravagant living. Yet, for all this, he was an able ruler who made a definite attempt to develop his country. He was able to create economic prosperity by encouraging exports (particularly coffee), improving communications, attracting foreign capital and generally providing the stability necessary for economic advance.

The rule of Guzmán Blanco did little, however, to break down the great gulf in Venezuela between the privileged few and the mass of the poor and deprived. Indeed, his rebuilding in Caracas served to emphasize the physical distinction between the prosperous few and the poverty-stricken masses in their rural hovels.

After the fall of Guzmán Blanco stability was again lacking in Venezuela. It was won back, but at a terrible price in cruelty and oppression, under Cipriano Castro from 1899 to 1908 and under Juan Vicente Gómez from 1908 to 1935. For most in Venezuela, Bolívar's dreams of liberty and freedom proved illusory.

Colombia

Bolívar's attempt to include what is now Colombia in his unified state of Gran Colombia had failed by 1830. As in Venezuela, settlers of European origin were in a minority; the majority of the population was *mestizo*.

In the 1820s the dominant political figure in the region was Francisco de Paula Santander. He was forced to flee the country in 1828, and the secession of Venezuela and Ecuador brought an end to Gran Colombia. In 1832 a constitution was adopted at Bogotá for the state of New Granada. Santander, who returned in 1832, became the first president. In his years of rule to 1837 he provided an orderly and honest government and promoted the economic and educational well-being of his population.

In spite of Santander's efforts to establish a firm basis of government, the next fifty years brought internal turmoil and constant struggles for power. The country (which became the 'United States of Colombia' in 1863) was racked by interminable arguments between liberals and conservatives. There was some advance—slavery was abolished in 1851—but the failure to agree on basic policies prevented the country from achieving any steady progress economically, socially or politically. In the 1860s and 70s the liberals controlled the country, and by the constitution of 1863 they allowed considerable local autonomy, though they alienated many by their attack on the Catholic Church.

A conservative regime returned to power when Rafael Núñez was elected president in 1880. He had received liberal support, but once in power he created a new party—the Nationalist party—which became a major conservative force. He was president until 1894 (except between 1882 and 1884) and codified the principles of his regime in the constitution of 1886. This ended local autonomy, and created a highly centralized system and also gave back to the Church the position it had lost under the liberals. A concordat with the pope in 1887 completed the re-establishment of the position and power of the Church. Núñez built so carefully that the conservatives were to hold power in Colombia until well into the twentieth century.

Economically and socially Colombia made little progress in the nineteenth century. In 1900 communications were still poor, agriculture was primitive, and even coffee had not yet achieved a position of great importance as an export. These difficulties were compounded by a civil war from 1899 to 1902 in which the liberals attempted to overthrow the conservatives and were defeated only after a major struggle which brought great destruction and many deaths. To add to Colombia's troubles, in 1903 Panama became independent as a result of the intervention of the United States. In view of its nineteenth-century record, Colombia was to make surprising progress in the twentieth century.

Ecuador

Early attempts to establish the independence of Ecuador had failed in the years after 1809, and the region did not establish its independence from Spain until 1822. The union of Gran Colombia existed for a few years, but in 1830 Ecuador became independent. Juan José Flores, a Venezuelan who had served under Bolívar, became the first president of the independent state, ruling until 1835 and again from 1839 to 1845.

The constitution of 1830 gave considerable powers to the president, and Flores used them to establish an autocratic regime. His main opponent was the liberal Vicente Rocafuerte. In 1834, to avoid being overthrown, Flores agreed that Rocafuerte would be the next president. In his term, which ran from 1835 to 1839, Rocafuerte liberalized the government and attempted some progressive reforms. Flores returned to power in 1839 and in 1843 changed the constitution to extend his term, but was overthrown in 1845. There followed a time of chaos.

Order returned in 1861 when the conservative Gabriel García Moreno, an aristocrat of Spanish ancestry, came to power. He was in control of the country either in person or through his unfluence until his assassination in 1875. García Moreno's rule was remarkable because of the extent of the power he was prepared to give the Catholic Church. He gave it a monopoly of religion in the constitution of 1861 and then allowed it to control all education. Although García Moreno ran the country as a dictator, he was honest and made a determined effort to stimulate the economic development of the country. On his assassination in 1875 Ecuador sank into twenty years of turmoil.

When the Liberals came to power in 1895 their dominant figure was Eloy Alfaro, who was president from 1895 to 1901 and from 1906 to 1911. Alfaro attempted to limit the power of the Church, practised religious toleration and removed clerical privileges. He did not achieve any massive changes in the country, but he did improve communications and attempt to bring Ecuador a little more into the modern world. At the beginning of the twentieth century the mass of the Ecuadorian people, who totalled some one-and-a-half million, still lived as their ancestors had lived. Power and wealth were held by a tiny white minority.

Mexico

Mexico was the most heavily populated of the newly independent Latin American nations, and only Brazil was larger in area. The difficulties in achieving a stable government were numerous. Many of the creoles who wanted to separate from Spain wanted even more to prevent the *mestizos* and Indians creating a social revolution. Even among the ruling elite there were sharp differences—some were enthusiastic for a loose federalism, others for a centralized state. These conflicting views plunged Mexico into a turmoil from which the country

scarcely emerged until the dictatorship of Díaz more than fifty years after the achievement of independence.

The collapse of Iturbide's hopes of establishing an empire in Mexico came in 1823, and in the following year a constitution was adopted which embodied the ideas of the federalists, who opposed a highly centralized system. Within little over ten years, however, this constitution was replaced by a centralized dictatorship under the leadership of Antonio López de Santa Anna.

Santa Anna was the most important political leader of the first thirty years of Mexican independence. He was a creole who had gained military experience in the Spanish army, and he assumed power in 1834. Santa Anna was a ruthless, unscrupulous power seeker, and until 1855 he had a decisive role in Mexican politics, even when he was not serving as president.

The immediate effect of the abolition of the federal state system was the secession of Texas from Mexico in 1836. The Americans who had settled in that area since 1820 now decided to fight to separate themselves from Mexico; many hoped that they would then become a part of the United States. Santa Anna was completely defeated in Texas in 1836, Texas achieved de facto independence and after much effort was finally accepted into the United States in 1845.

In May 1846, after a clash between Mexican and United States troops, the United States declared war on Mexico. The basis of the difficulty was ownership of the northern Mexican possessions. Although the United States had grievances against Mexico for non-payment of claims, the basic reason for the war was United States pressure on the northern regions of Mexico. The Mexicans defended their country fiercely, but the war was a disaster for them. The United States won a complete victory. At the Treaty of Guadalupe Hidalgo in February 1848 Mexico had to agree to almost the modern boundary between the two countries. The size of Mexico had been nearly halved.

Santa Anna had ruled as a dictator, raiding the national treasury and bringing misery to the mass of the Mexican population. Even after the disasters of the Mexican war, he regained power once again in 1853 and ruled the country until forced to flee in 1855.

The fall of Santa Anna inaugurated a twenty-year effort at liberal reform, which brought more turmoil to this troubled nation. In this period the Indian, Benito Juàrez, dominated the government. First serving under President Juan Alvarez, Juàrez himself ruled the country for much of this time. The liberals took firm measures against the Church, expelling the Jesuits and reducing the size of Church land holdings. The constitution of 1857 provided for freedom of speech and of the press, restored the federal system and limited the powers of the president. The liberal reforms led to civil war, and although Juàrez was victorious (bringing far stricter measures against the Church) he found himself with a major problem in foreign policy.

In 1861 Great Britain, France and Spain agreed to intervene in Mexico to secure the payment of debts owed to their citizens. It soon became clear that France wanted more than the payment of debts. Napoleon III, beset with dreams of grandeur, had decided to establish an empire in Mexico. England and Spain withdrew, but the French troops entered Mexico City in 1863. The United States could do nothing as she was torn by the Civil War. In the same year a hereditary monarchy under the Habsburg archduke,

Ferdinand Maximilian Josef, brother of the Austrian emperor, was established. He arrived in Mexico in 1864. Juàrez continued the fight, and Maximilian was deserted when, under American pressure France withdrew her troops. Without French support Maximilian could not maintain his government. In 1867 he was captured and shot.

Juàrez now ruled the country until his death in 1872, and even then his policies were continued until 1876. The end of the Juàrez era was brought about by the mestizo Porfirio Díaz, who had led Mexican armies in the war against France and Maximilian. In 1876 he led a military revolution against the government and assumed the presidency. With the exception of the years from 1880 to 1884, when he continued to rule behind the scenes, Díaz held office until 1911.

Díaz brought order and peace to Mexico, although he ruled ruthlessly. He restored the position of the Church and attempted to achieve Mexican prosperity by stimulating economic activity. This involved improving communications, encouraging foreign capital, developing mining and manufacturing and establishing a stable financial system. Yet, though Mexico was now more prosperous and stable, only a small minority within the country and the many foreign investors obtained the benefits of this prosperity. The great mass of the people were

untouched by the improvements. The rural areas were poverty-stricken, had few schools and no say in how they were governed. Mexico achieved greater stability and prosperity under Díaz, but most of the Mexican people did not share in the improvements.

The Central American states

For a time after the achievement of independence, it seemed possible that the five modern countries of Guatemala, El Salvador, Honduras, Nicaragua and Costa Rica would achieve some unity, but these hopes nursed by the revolutionary generation such a short time before.

The collapse of the 'United Provinces of Central America' was not surprising. Its five parts thought of themselves as distinct units, there were massive problems of communication and local leaders were desirous of enhancing their own political careers. The total population of the region was something between one and one and a half million. Most of these were Indians, many were *mestizos* and there was a small minority of creoles. After the collapse of the United Provinces in 1839, there were other attempts at unity, but none of them was successful. Separate, impoverished, the countries of Central America were the scene of constant turmoil in the nineteenth century.

The dominant political figure for over twenty-five years after the break-up of the confederation was Rafael Carrera, a *mestizo* who controlled Guatemala from 1840 to 1865. He was a dedicated conservative who allied himself with the Church and exerted great political influence on Honduras, El Salvador and Nicaragua as well as on his own country. In 1840 and 1855 he helped to turn out the liberals in Honduras, and in the 1840s and 50s he also intervened in El Salvador to support the conservative faction.

The first change to a liberal regime in Guatemala came in 1871 under Justo Rufino Barrios. His ideas were more liberal than those of Carrera, but his rule was still autocratic. He controlled the country tightly until his death in 1885. Little progress had been made in Guatemala by the turn of the century. Economic development was slight, and most of the population was poor and illiterate.

Honduras, Nicaragua, and El Salvador had similarly unfortunate experiences in the nineteenth century. Honduras was poorer than Guatemala, and developed little. Nicaragua was beset with liberal–conservative quarrels, and in the 1850s an American adventurer, William Walker, was even able to take over the country for a time after being invited in by the liberals. In the latter part of the century the clash continued, but

374

Nicaragua made great progress in agriculture, bananas and coffee becoming of increasing importance.

Tiny El Salvador, only some 13,000 square miles, experienced the same turmoil as the rest of Central America and sank into obscurity for much of the nineteenth century.

Costa Rica was unlike the rest of Central America in that the majority of its population was of European origin. Its history for much of the nineteenth century was also less tragic than its neighbours, and it suffered less from dictators and adventurers than did the other Central American countries. All in all, however, Central America could hope for little while so many of the people of the area were impoverished and illiterate and political fragmentation prevented the desired economic cooperation.

The history of Latin America in the nineteenth century demonstrated quite clearly that independence from European control did not in itself create enlightened, democratic and prosperous regimes. A colonial heritage of autocracy, racial and social gulfs, a lack of economic development, the failure to achieve unity, a problem of terrain and climate and the intolerance and cupidity of individuals combined to produce a Latin America which fell far short of the high hopes nursed by the revolutionary generation such a short time before.

Above, the Battle of Rivas in the war between Costa Rica and Nicaragua in 1856. An American adventurer, William Walker, had made himself President of Nicaragua earlier in the year, but this defeat at the hands of his neighbours led to his surrender to the US fleet the following year.

Opposite, a Mexican delegation at the court of the Archduke Maximilian of Austria in 1863, offering the crown of Mexico. He found little sympathy with his new lands, relied entirely on French support for his authority and was expelled from the throne and killed in 1867.

Further reading

Among the most distinguished texts dealing with the period covered in this volume are those published by Fontana in paperback; each contains a useful bibliography: J. H. Elliott, *Europe Divided 1559–1598* (Fontana/Collins, London, 1968); John Stoye, *Europe Unfolding 1648–1688* (Fontana/Collins, London, 1969; Harper and Row, New York, 1970); David Ogg, *Europe of the Ancien Régime 1715–1783* (Fontana/Collins, London, 1967); George Rudé, *Revolutionary Europe 1783–1815* (Fontana/Collins, London, 1964; Harper and Row, New York, 1966).

The best national histories include: Robin Briggs, *Early Modern France 1560–1715* (Oxford University Press, London and New York, 1977); Alfred Cobban, *A History of Modern France*, vols. I and II (Penguin Books, Harmondsworth, 1963, 1965; Penguin, New York, 1966); J. H. Elliott, *Imperial Spain 1469–1716* (Penguin Books, Harmondsworth, 1970); H. V. Livermore, *A New History of Portugal* (Cambridge University Press, 1966); G. M. Trevelyan, *England under the Stuarts* (Methuen, London, 1965); R. K. Webb, *Modern England from the Eighteenth Century to the Present* (Allen & Unwin, London, 1969; Harper and Row, New York, 1968); Pieter Geyl, *The Netherlands in the Seventeenth Century* (Benn, London, 1963); Ivo Schöffer, *A Short History of the Netherlands* (Allert de Lange bv, Amsterdam, 1973); Richard Pipes, *Russia under the Old Regime* (Penguin Books, Harmondsworth, 1977; Scribner, New York, 1975); Eda Sagarra, *A Social History of Germany 1648–1914* (Methuen, London, 1977).

For fascinating and wide-ranging social history see: Fernand Braudel, *Capitalism and Material Life 1400–1800* (Harper and Row, London and New York, 1974); Philippe Ariés, *Centuries of Childhood* (Penguin Books, Harmondsworth, 1973; Random House, New York, 1965); Henry Kamen, *The Iron Century: Social Change in Europe, 1550–1660* (Weidenfeld and Nicolson, London, 1971); J. H. Elliott, *The Old World and the New 1492–1650* (Cambridge University Press, 1970; New Rochelle, New York, 1970); G. Pagès, *The Thirty Years War 1618–48* (Adam & Charles Black, London, 1970); Michael Roberts, *Gustavus Adolphus and the Rise of Sweden* (English Universities Press, London, 1973; Lawrence Verry, Mystic, Connecticut, 1973); Pierre Goubert, *The Ancien Régime: French Society, 1600–1750* (Weidenfeld and Nicolson, London, 1973; Harper and Row, New York, 1974); Ragnhild Marie Hatton, *Louis XIV and his World* (Thames and Hudson, London, 1972).

A fine general introduction to seventeenth-century English constitutional issues can be found in: G. E. Aylmer, *The Struggle for the Constitution* (Blandford Press, London, 1963; Humanities Press, Atlantic Highlands, New Jersey, 1968); Lawrence Stone, *The Causes of the English Revolution 1529–1642* (Routledge and Kegan Paul, London, 1972; Harper and Row, New York, 1972); Christopher Hill, *God's Englishman: Oliver Cromwell and the English Revolution* (Penguin Books, Harmondsworth, 1972; Harper and Row, New York, 1972). Still useful is the brilliant little book by G. M. Trevelyan, *The English Revolution 1688–1689* (Oxford University Press, Oxford, 1938; Oxford University Press, New York, 1965). The following will also be found useful:

M. S. Anderson, *Peter the Great* (Thames and Hudson, London, 1978); Robin Briggs, *The Scientific Revolution of the Seventeenth Century* (Longman, London, 1969); Thomas Kuhn, *The Copernican Revolution* (Harvard University Press, Cambridge, Massachusetts, 1972); Paul Hazard, *The European Mind 1680–1715* (Penguin Books, Harmondsworth, England, 1973); Peter Gay, *The Enlightenment*, vol. I, *The Rise of Modern Paganism*, vol. II, *The Science of Freedom* (Weidenfeld and Nicolson, London, 1967, 1970; Norton, New York, 1977); Walther Hubatsch, *Frederick the Great: Absolutism and Administration* (Thames and Hudson, London, 1973; Thames and Hudson, New York, 1977); Ernst Wangermann, *The Austrian Achievement, 1700–1800* (Thames and Hudson, London, 1973; Harcourt Brace Jovanovich, New York, 1973); T. C. W. Blanning, *Joseph II and Enlightened Despotism* (Longman, London, 1970).

A classic of urban history is: M. Dorothy George, *London Life in the Eighteenth Century* (Penguin Books, Harmondsworth, 1966; Putnam's, New York, 1965). Controversial and stimulating is: E. P. Thompson, *The Making of the English Working Class* (Penguin Books, Harmondsworth, 1968); John King Fairbank, *East Asia: Tradition and Transformation* (Allen and Unwin, London, 1973; Houghton Mifflin, Boston, 1977); Percival Spear, *A History of India* (Penguin Books, Harmondsworth, 1965; Penguin Books, New York, 1966); J. D. Fage, *A History of Africa* (Hutchinson, London, 1978); C. Duncan Rice, *The Rise and Fall of Black Slavery* (Macmillan Press, London, 1975; Harper and Row, New York, 1975).

Indispensable for a study of the American revolution is: Bernard Bailyn, *The Ideological Origins of the American Revolution* (Harvard University Press, Cambridge, Massachusetts, 1967); Esmond Wright, *Washington and the American Revolution* (Penguin Books, Harmondsworth, 1973).

The most recent introduction to the French Revolution is J. M. Roberts, *The French Revolution* (Oxford University Press, London and New York, 1978).

For a study of the French Revolution in a worldwide context see R. R. Palmer, *The Age of the Democratic Revolution*, 2 vols. (Princeton University Press, 1959, 1964); Norman Hampson, *The Life and Opinions of Maximilian Robespierre* (Duckworth, London, 1974); Vincent Cronin, *Napoleon* (Penguin Books, Harmondsworth, 1973).

On what various French historians have said about Napoleon since Waterloo see Pieter Geyl, *Napoleon: For and Against* (Penguin Books, Harmondsworth, 1965).

A good survey of Latin American history is George Pendle, *History of Latin America* (Penguin Books, Harmondsworth, 1969).

Acknowledgments

The illustrations on pages 75, 76, 178 right and 228 are reproduced by gracious permission of Her Majesty the Queen.

Photographs

Alinari, Florence 11 centre, 23, 191; Archives Photographiques, Paris 11 bottom, 12 left, 22 right, 48, 187 top left; Ashmolean Museum, Oxford 82 bottom left; Biblioteca Marucelliana, Florence 123; Bibliothèque Nationale, Paris 57 bottom, 251 bottom, 305 bottom right, 332; Bildarchiv Preussischer Kulturbesitz, Berlin 139, 140, 141, 142, 143 top left, 155, 158 left, 162 left, 163 top, 168 right, 170 top, 172, 223; Bernice P. Bishop Museum, Honolulu 256 left, 256 right; J. Bottin, Paris 35 top; British Museum, London 26 bottom, 35 bottom, 65, 67 bottom, 81 top, 91 bottom, 94, 104 top, 121 top, 149 right, 163 bottom, 165 centre right, 183, 194–195, 199, 202 bottom, 206 bottom, 216 right, 252, 254 bottom, 255 top right, 257 top left, 257 bottom right, 258 bottom, 260, 288 bottom left, 295 centre left, 297 top left, 301 top, 305 bottom left, 308 bottom, 311 top, 321, 330–331, 334 bottom, 337, 344 bottom, 348 top; J. E. Bulloz, Paris 110 bottom, 187 bottom; Chicago Historical Society, Illinois 210; P. & D. Colnaghi & Co., London 192 top; Cooper-Bridgeman Library, London 81 bottom, 118 top; Cooper-Bridgeman Library—Christie Manson and Woods 71; Country Life, London 132; Courtauld Institute of Art, London 136; Crown copyright reproduced with permission of the Controller of Her Majesty's Stationery Office 97; Deutsche Fotothek, Dresden 37 bottom left, 50, 58 bottom right, 130, 137, 143 bottom right, 153, 157, 159 top, 167, 346 bottom left; Henry Francis Du Pont Winterthur Museum, Delaware 266; Mary Evans Picture Library, London 83, 87 top right, 108, 128 bottom, 169, 233 top left, 249 bottom, 263 left, 283, 285 bottom, 287 top left, 287 bottom left, 288 top left, 288 top right, 288 bottom right, 289, 291 left, 292 right, 293 left, 294, 295 centre right, 295 bottom, 298, 301 bottom, 302, 306 top, 310 bottom, 312 top, 313 top, 315 centre, 323 top, 326 top, 343, 348 bottom, 352, 367 left, 367 right, 368, 369 top left, 370, 371, 372, 373 left, 374; Franshalsmuseum, Haarlem 91 top; Photographie Giraudon, Paris 8, 14, 17 left, 17 right, 18 left, 20 right, 22 left, 24 bottom, 25, 27, 30, 31 bottom, 36 right, 38, 39, 60, 62 bottom right, 66, 68, 102, 103, 104 left, 104 right, 106, 107 bottom, 109, 112, 124 left, 131, 146, 147 top, 188, 189 top left, 189 top right, 190, 243 bottom, 285 top, 287 right, 316, 320, 323 bottom right, 324 bottom, 325, 345 top left; Guildhall Art Gallery, London 181 left; Hamlyn Group Picture Library 28, 31 top, 33 bottom, 40, 42, 46 left, 46 right, 47, 49, 54 top, 62 bottom left, 84, 90, 99, 121 bottom, 127 top left, 144, 159 bottom, 165 top, 179 top right, 182, 216 right, 219 left, 226 top, 235, 241, 242, 247 top right, 251 top, 253 top, 253 bottom, 254 top left, 255 top left, 255 bottom, 281, 286 left, 297 centre right, 304 top, 307, 313 bottom, 319 right, 355, 360, 362, 369 bottom, 369 top right; Hispanic Society of America, New York 44 bottom left; Historisches Museum, Frankfurt am Main 340; India Office Library, London 243 top, 247 top left; Kongelige Bibliotek, Copenhagen 166; Kungl. Armémuseum, Stockholm 54 bottom; Kungliga Biblioteket, Stockholm 116 bottom, 117, 168 left, 345 bottom left; Kungl. Husgeradskammaren, Stockholm 53 bottom; Kungl. Livrustkammaren, Stockholm 57 top; Larousse, Paris 19, 29 left, 34, 113 top, 200 left, 217 top, 240, 291 bottom right, 292 left, 296 bottom, 305 top right, 315 top, 324 top, 328; Library of Congress, Washington, D.C. 200–201, 201 right, 202 top, 204, 205 top left, 205 bottom, 206 top, 209 top, 211, 216 left, 218 left, 221 left, 221 right, 222, 250 bottom, 251 top, 353, 354, 357 top, 361, 364, 373 right, 375; MacClancy Press, London 267 left, 267 top right, 267 bottom right, 269 left, 269 top right, 271 top, 271 bottom, 272 left, 273 top left, 275 right, 282, 290 right, 293 top right, 295 top, 296 top left, 296 top right, 297 centre left, 297 bottom left, 297 bottom right, 305 top left, 306 bottom left, 306 bottom right, 309 bottom, 311 bottom, 322, 330 left, 331 right, 338 top, 338 bottom, 342, 346 right, 347, 350–351; Mansell Collection, London 11 top, 12 right, 16 left, 16 right, 18 top right, 18 bottom right, 20 left, 21, 24 top, 29 right, 35 centre, 36 left, 37 top left, 37 bottom right, 43, 51, 52, 58 left, 58 top right, 63, 126 right, 127 right, 129 top, 177 top, 195 bottom, 208, 230–231, 233 top right, 233 bottom, 290 left, 291 top right, 293 bottom right, 299, 303, 309 top, 310 top, 312 bottom, 319 left, 327 bottom; Mansell-Alinari 32; Mansell-Bulloz 300; Mansell-Giraudon 286 right; Bildarchiv Foto Marburg 100, 162 right, 236 top left, 236 top centre, 236 top right, 236 bottom right, 324–325 top; Mas, Barcelona 33 top, 44 top, 195 top, 218 right, 358–359; Musée de la Marine, Marseilles 323 bottom left; Musée de L'Armée, Paris 308 top, 336 bottom; Musée Guimet, Paris 239; Musées Nationaux, Paris 26 top, 61 top, 93 bottom, 95 right, 173, 315 bottom; Museo del Prado, Madrid 44 bottom right; Museum Plantin-Moretus en Prentenkabinet, Antwerp 67 top; Muzeum Wojska Polskiego, Warsaw 93 top; National Army Museum, London 134, 174, 177, 226 bottom, 247 bottom, 339; National Gallery, London 41 top, 41 bottom, 56; National Library of Australia, Canberra 254 top right, 258 bottom, 363; National Maritime Museum, London 82 top left, 85 right, 87 bottom left, 87 bottom right, 88 top, 96, 113 bottom, 114 top right, 116 top, 249 top, 251, 317, 356–357; Nationalmuseum, Stockholm 118 bottom, 279; National Portrait Gallery, London 72, 73, 74, 79, 82 top right, 82 bottom right, 98 left, 98 right, 124 centre, 127 bottom, 128 top, 148 left, 179 top left, 179 bottom right, 180, 184, 186, 203, 233 top centre; Nederlandsch Historisch Scheepvaart Museum, Amsterdam 44–45, 235 bottom; New York Historical Society 212 left, 212 right, 213, 214 bottom, 224; Novosti Press Agency, London 114 left, 115, 143 bottom left, 165 centre left, 165 bottom left, 170 bottom; Orbis Publishing, London 263 right, 275 left; Orbis—J. Banfield Art Galleries 264; Orbis—Bibliothèque Nationale 269 bottom right; Orbis—John Carter Brown Library 270; Orbis—Bulloz 304 bottom; Orbis—Colonial Williamsburg 265 left; Orbis—Fogg Art Museum 277; Orbis—Giraudon 318; Orbis—Library of Congress 265 right; Österreichische Nationalbibliothek, Vienna 156, 161 top, 161 bottom, 162 centre; Peabody Museum, Harvard University, Cambridge, Massachusetts 257 top right; 257 bottom left; Pennsylvania Academy of Fine Arts, Philadelphia 214 top; Enoch Pratt Free Library of Baltimore, Maryland 209 bottom; Radio Times Hulton Picture Library, London 80, 85 left, 88 bottom, 101 top, 101 bottom, 119 left, 119 right, 124 right, 125 top, 125 bottom, 126 left, 151 top left, 151 top right, 178 left, 192 bottom, 219 top right, 219 bottom right, 232, 244, 250 left, 250 right, 276; Rijksmuseum, Amsterdam 87 top left; Ann Ronan Picture Library, Loughton 122, 129 bottom; Jean Roubier, Paris 100 top; Royal Geographical Society, London 231 bottom right; Sammlung Handke, Berlin 273 top right; Scala, Antella 194; Staatliche Schlösser, Gärten und Seen, Museumabteilung, Munich 344 top; Statens Museum for Kunst, Copenhagen 55; Svenska Porträt Arkivet, Nationalmuseum, Stockholm 53 top, 143 top right; Tate Gallery, London 151 bottom; Thomas Gilcrease Institute, Tulsa, Oklahoma 196; Victoria and Albert Museum, London 64, 175, 181 top right, 329, 345 right, 346 left; Victoria Memorial, Calcutta 245; H. Roger-Viollet, Paris 114 bottom, 147 bottom, 148 right, 149 left, 152, 158 right, 164, 185, 247 centre, 326 centre, 326 bottom, 335 bottom, 336 top, 349; Wallace Collection, London 61 bottom, 187 top right; Western Americana Picture Library, Brentwood 227; Yale University Art Gallery, New Haven, Connecticut 271 centre, 272 right, 273 bottom; Z.E.F.A. (UK), London 62 top.

Index